THE DARK SIDE OF REASON
Fictionality and Power

THE DARK SIDE OF REASON

FICTIONALITY AND POWER

Luiz Costa Lima

Translated by Paulo Henriques Britto

Stanford University Press
Stanford, California
1992

Stanford University Press
Stanford, California
© 1992 by the Board of Trustees
of the Leland Stanford Junior University
Printed in the United States of America

Chapters 1, 3, 4 (in part), and 7 are translated from *Sociedade e Discurso Ficcional* (Rio de Janeiro: Editora Guanabara, 1986); chapters 2, 4 (in part), 5, and 6 from *O Fingidor e o Censor* (Rio de Janeiro: Forense-Universitária, 1988). The Foreword by Hans Ulrich Gumbrecht and Chapter 8 are published here for the first time.

CIP data appear at the end of the book

Contents

Foreword
 Passion for the Unnameable: History and
 the Aesthetic Dimension in the Work of Luiz
 Costa Lima, by Hans Ulrich Gumbrecht   vii

ONE   History of a Ban   1

TWO   The Religious Control of Imagination   12

THREE   The Joys and Sorrows of the Self   65

FOUR   Literature and Society in Hispanic America:
 Nineteenth and Early Twentieth Centuries   110

FIVE   Diderot: Philosopher and Art Critic   189

SIX   An Approach to Jorge Luis Borges   236

SEVEN   A Proscribed Concept: Mimesis and Avant-Garde
 Theory   270

EIGHT   Oblique Fiction and *The Tempest*   310

References Cited   331

Foreword

Passion for the Unnameable: History and the Aesthetic
Dimension in the Work of Luiz Costa Lima

HANS ULRICH GUMBRECHT

Over the centuries of Western history, what we used to call "Reason" (with a capital "R") has been repressing and controlling the streams of the imaginary. Indeed it was this very function that brought Reason into being. Such is the basic argument of three books published by Luiz Costa Lima in Brazil during the 1980s. But it is not only his particular view on the origins of Reason that makes him refer, in the title of this American publication, to the imaginary as "the *dark* side of Reason." While language is often presented as so intimately associated with the principles of Reason that we tend to see the sheer possibility of speech and discourse as depending on them, Costa Lima treats the imaginary as the Unnameable—at one point he even refers to it (quoting Freud, not Heidegger) as "das Unheimliche," that which is "strangely familiar." Renouncing, then, any conceptualization of the imaginary, Costa Lima is far from intending his project to be a theory of the imaginary—so far indeed that he does not even explicitly mention this negation.

Different from the imaginary, what we can observe, analyze, and write about are the devices by which works of art appeal to the human faculty of imagination. Costa Lima subsumes such techniques under the notion of *mimesis*. But instead of an introductory chapter providing a definition of this notion as a basis for the arguments to follow, we find in his book a reiteration of passages that amounts to a complex and tentative convergence of aspects of the concept of mimesis. If they have a common denominator at all, it is the well-known paradox displayed in Aristotle's *Poetics*, according to which mimesis allows us to enjoy things that terrify us if encountered in real life. Mimesis, Costa Lima insists, instead of being an imitation of reality, always establishes such a difference—and this difference finds different materializations under varying historical and social circumstances. In Cervantes's *Quixote*, for example, where Costa Lima (among others) has the literary imagination of Western modernity begin, mimesis articulates itself in a double negation: the negation of pure fantasy (as it was displayed, e.g., in the contemporary pastoral novels) and the negation of, as he writes, an "untouchable reality" (or rather the negation of the law that marks a certain social knowledge about Reality as untouchable). If mimesis then changes the world without simply proposing an "other" world of fantasy, this is achieved by what Costa Lima labels the author's "critical difference." Attitudes of irony and distancing, through which the reality represented appears in a different frame, are for him the key to an understanding of modern literary mimesis. By relating such strategies of critical difference closely to the imaginary, he also very strictly sets them apart from those politically motivated perspectives that are normally hailed as "critical," and, at the same time, from any effort to generate specifically "literary" languages by means of linguistic estrangement or complexification. Not the least reason for which Jorge Luis Borges's texts stand as one of the great contemporary paradigms of literary imagination in Costa Lima's book seems to be the simple fact that they are written "in normal Spanish." Finally, if there is any passage at all where the critic's own passion, the driving force behind his project, shines through, it is again his reading of Borges. As Borges's specific mode of mimesis abandons the dimensions of time and space, he catches a glimpse of redemption from the "fate of our physical being."

But it is not exclusively through the techniques of mimesis that we can become aware of the power of the imaginary. The historian and the critic at least may search for the institutions and discursive rules by which socially constructed realities have protected themselves against the threat of destabilization that the imaginary implies. And although the traces of such taming of the imaginary can obviously not stimulate our imagination, it is mainly through their history—as a negative history—that Costa Lima tries to prove the power of the imaginary. Read as cultural historiography, his book gives indeed more emphasis to the varieties of that control than to the positive side of a possible history of mimetic strategies. Whereas it does not come as a surprise that, within this negative history, he interprets the Renaissance principle of *imitatio naturae* as a strategy for exercising such control, Costa Lima proves himself to be much more radical than many of his predecessors by integrating into this perspective the interest of early modern painting in the anatomy of the human body. While we may find immediately plausible his view that the importance of the dimension of *vraisemblance* for such playwrights as Corneille and Racine is connected to the emergence of a new reality under the protection of the absolutist state, we are not used to seeing Rousseau's ferocious attack on theater in *La lettre à d'Alembert sur les spectacles* and Diderot's contemporary plea for a liberation of the stage from the classical "rules" grouped together as forms of the domestication of the imaginary. Even the vanishing of control's materializations in the present age is—somehow paradoxically—identified as a symptom of control's continuing existence, when Costa Lima points to "the diffuse and invisible" power that the technical media of communication impose on contemporary societies.

Here, of course, lies the blind spot in his project—and I know that he would not be reluctant to admit it. What if someone proposed—as does, for example, René Girard—to interpret mimesis *not* as the creation of a difference that is different from and tamed by *imitatio*, but as a desire for imitation that launches a chain of violent consequences whenever it is fulfilled? The only possible answer to this question comes strikingly close to the only possible apology for Foucault's *Histoire de la sexualité* in the face of those who, perhaps understandably enough, are not ready to decipher the discourses of "sexual emancipation" as a *dispositif* of sexual repression. Both Foucault's and Costa Lima's projects seem motivated by a passion for elementary human faculties—as opposed as their respective *teloi* may be—and a narrative of repression (allowing for the paradox of emancipation's appearing as the ultimate device of repression) is the form in which they both choose to stage their passions. In addition to this plot, Costa Lima and Foucault share—despite the antagonism of their respective passions—an austerity in their views of Western history. There is hardly a text or an author who is not ultimately convicted of being contaminated by the law, rules, and devices controlling the imaginary. Even Horkheimer and Adorno's *Dialektik der Aufklärung*, which those who continue believing in Enlightenment as an eternal intellectual principle, have eliminated from the canon of critical theory for overemphasizing the ambiguity of this tradition, is dismissed by Costa Lima for its failure to criticize Enlightened Reason. At the same time, he refuses to take deconstruction seriously for self-indulgently staging itself as the overcoming of Enlightenment. Finally, because he is so often associated with deconstruction, Costa Lima even hesitates to exempt Borges's work from the series of texts that control the imaginary by pretending to emancipate it.

Typically enough, in Costa Lima's austere vision of Western culture, only two authors—whose austerity is proverbial—seem not to become the objects of similar suspicions: the seventeenth-century French moralist La Rochefoucauld and the Mexican novelist Juan Rulfo. In his reading of La Rochefoucauld, it becomes apparent that Costa Lima does not see the relation between the imaginary and the destabilization of the *doxa* as a one-way movement: it is La Rochefoucauld's refusal to accept the ethical orthodoxy of his contemporary society that, according to Costa Lima, enables him to invent a form of discourse that appeals to the aesthetic experience. Costa Lima's appreciation of Rulfo sets the critic apart from the mainstream of Latin American studies, with its notorious preference for "politically correct" authors. Whereas many Latin Americanists—if not the majority—have been concentrating on the so-called "testimonial literature" for its value as documentation of political repression and injustice, Costa Lima highlights the impossibility of identifying the "critical difference" of Rulfo's texts through this reading. But he goes much further in his deviation from such well-intentioned expectations as one might project onto a South American critic and theorist. On the one side, Costa Lima's analysis of the political, economic, and intellectual history on the subcontinent since the conquest is characterized by a stunning density of information and a perhaps unique insistence on national differences. On the other side, however, he never gives in to the temptation to romanticize South America as a victim and its culture as a paradise of freedom or a source of subversion. If Costa Lima pays much attention to the specific regional conditions under which European culture entered and came to dominate the subcontinent, he insists that all the strategies that had been used to control the imaginary in early modern Europe continued to exert their impact on the New World. They were even strengthened by its dependence on the shallow didacticism of the Spanish Enlightenment, and they finally led, owing to the incapacity of the urban elites to assume intellectual leadership, to the dead end of "testimonial literature," with its confusion between mimesis and empirical sociology.

This is an astonishingly cold version of a history we are used to having staged with exuberant emotional undertones. For unlike the historiographic plot structure through which Costa Lima narrates the antagonism between the imaginary and its control, his history does not allow for a polarization of oppressors and victims. If anything, European literature is as much affected as South American literature by the control of the imaginary—and perhaps one must say by the *necessity* of this control. For, although Costa Lima's passion for the imaginary seems closely related to his belief in its potential to destabilize institutionalized realities, he never propels his discourse into hymns of revolution and liberation. The fight between the imaginary and its control, the antagonism between establishing and destabilizing realities, it appears, might be one of those tensions to which human life has been doomed since it crossed the threshold of *social* life. This reading of Costa Lima's project could explain why he renounces not only a definition of the imaginary, but even a theorization (or a typification) of the circumstances in which the imaginary can escape control. If, by generalizing the historical conditions in which they were written, he suspended the character of texts like La Rochefoucauld's, Rulfo's, or Borges's *as events*, such a generalization would inevitably encumber them with the status of ethical *exempla* to be imitated, repeated, reproduced.

Instead of arguing for morality (and repetition), Costa Lima seeks the rare *events of the imaginary* in the concrete dimensions of their historical occurrence. At a moment when the divergence of literary history and literary aesthetics seemed complete, his writing combines these discourses in an unexpected—and perhaps unique—way.

THE DARK SIDE OF REASON
Fictionality and Power

CHAPTER ONE

History of a Ban

> Dirán que siempre salgo de orden al mejor tiempo para contar cosas viejas. (They will say I always abandon the [chronological] order at the best time to tell of old things.)
> —Díaz del Castillo, *Historia verdadera de la conquista de la Nueva España*

THE DISCUSSION REOPENED

In recent works, Howard Bloch, Jacqueline Cerquiglini, Hans Ulrich Gumbrecht, Jacques Le Goff, and Paul Zumthor, in different ways, have all pointed out that the crisis of Christian cosmology, particularly beginning in the fourteenth and fifteenth centuries, discredited the notion that truth was inscribed upon things and phenomena, and was therefore readily manifested in the appearance of the world; correlate to this notion was the idea that the divine will revealed itself to its creatures through clear, unmistakable signs.

These authors have also shown that, with this crisis, subjectivity came to be increasingly valued as a means of investigating truth. As God gradually withdrew from the Earth, as it were, subjectivity became ever more important as an instrument for the revelation of truth.*

The rise of subjectivity can be seen on several planes: Le Goff shows its effect on celestial geography, with the late-twelfth-century introduction of a new territory, purgatory, where souls were to suffer punishment *for a variable period, according to the value of the prayers of the de-*

---

*For further details, see Costa Lima 1988, esp. pp. 3–15.

ceased one's relatives and friends (Le Goff 1981). This must surely be seen as the Church's acknowledgment of the subjectivity of the faithful as a force capable of appealing to and even exerting indirect pressure on divine justice. And Howard Bloch shows how, at about the same time, judicial procedure in criminal cases began to change, as greater emphasis came to be laid on collecting and interpreting evidence for or against the defendant (Bloch 1977).

In the case of poetic expression, the signs of this upheaval appeared later. According to Zumthor, the tendency to use *je* in poetry to refer to the author's personality, rather than as a mere grammatical figure to be temporarily assumed by the subject who pronounced it, became more widespread and generalized in the fourteenth century (Zumthor 1975). This was a break with a traditional practice that Georg Misch traces back to the ancient East:

As a rule, . . . the use of the first person in royal inscriptions was no more than a traditional literary form. . . . The situation was similar in the case of Egyptian funeral biographies, although for a different reason: here the use of the first person was suggested by the religious purpose of exerting influence on the destiny of the deceased. (Misch 1950, 1: 46)

Zumthor's insight is taken up by his student J. Cerquiglini, who, writing on Guillaume de Machaut, shows that the presence of the subjective *je* results from the fourteenth-century perception of the impotence of allegorical readings (Cerquiglini 1980). There is no longer an immediate movement from the specific text to its figurative interpretation, a movement upon which the sufficiency of allegorical reading depended; thus the authorial *je* must bear witness to the truthfulness of what is said, certify it by his or her experience of the world, saturate it with personality.

This approach is more than just a new path for academic research. On the contrary, it implies consequences that clash with time-honored traditions that are rooted in all the tendencies of the scholarly world. The first of these consequences is a head-on attack on the view of history as a continuum. Implicitly or explicitly, this view holds that subjectivity, if not everything we subsume as "human," has existed ever since Logos came to be taken as both the instrument and the proof of reason. Thus subjectivity was a "Greek discovery," part of the "Greek miracle," and once achieved it was henceforth forever to be present in human—that is, Western—history. Curiously and paradoxically, the continuum view of history begins by dehistoricizing its own object, since from the outset it disregards the specific contents assumed by the categories and values historians deal with. Greece is supposed to have reached the very heart of the human—a heart so stable that from classical antiquity to the present day it has never beaten with a different pulse. Thus all that we—the elect descendants of Greece—need do is follow the constant course of the themes first raised by the Greeks.

At the price of dehistoricizing history, the task of the humanities is made secure and self-confident. Thus, for example, there is no reason why one should torment oneself with all this annoying literary theory when we can identify literature directly in the Homeric epic. Given sensibility and erudition enough, the argument runs, one can recognize the *well-written*, the literary, from Homer on. Sensibility is conceived as an inborn gift, a sign of aristocracy of the spirit, something that cannot be taught.

The approach outlined above has been extensively criticized, beginning with Nietzsche, and in our day most notably by Michel Foucault. History can no longer be envisaged as a sort of Olympic race in which each generation hands down to the next the torch it received from the previous one; or as a continent crossed by a shining path, it being the case that among natural instincts, most of them selfish and evil, there is one that points in the opposite direction: an infallible thirst for truth. This smug, optimistic conception envelops the world in a reassuring certainty and sees the role of the thinker in unproblematic terms: the athlete who bears the torch of truth.

If, however, we abandon the reassuring myth, we see that history is made up of leaps and standstills. There is no such thing as an unquenchable thirst for truth, nor is there any torch to be borne and handed down. There is nothing a priori that stabilizes and justifies human productions. History is discontinuity, a place where values are constantly changing. Logos is not sound and sense, but rather sound and fury. Or rather, it is sound and sense only if we realize that its sense is simply what conforms to a historicized fury. Thus Logos is no longer seen as a timeless cell, which could be tracked down in its different manifestations in sets called "texts." Logos becomes a dated inscription, which we must now learn to analyze, understand, and, after we understand it, analyze once again in its discursive configurations. The term "discourse" is not simply a French fashion sold in the boutiques of the Western world to consumers grown weary of texts. "Text" is a neutral term, an indicator of material properties—a set of signs that narrate or describe something, aiming at completeness and having temporal references. "Discourse" is a concept implying that signs have the quality of forming distinct territories. Were I writing in Spanish, I would use the same words that Borges might choose; this, however, would not place my text in the region of Borgian *ficciones*—unless I saw my activity as a branch of fantastic literature, as Borges sees metaphysics. Critical discourse is not a literary genre, not because it is necessarily less inventive, but simply because it is not one of the forms of fiction.

Let me then set forth the theme of this essay. Beginning with the discovery of subjectivity in the late Middle Ages—a discovery that could also be considered a rediscovery, since there had been subjectivity in earlier times, though liable to other indicators—I will attempt to show that it caused the appearance of a *discursive dispersion*, something unknown in the early Middle Ages. I will also try to demonstrate that this dispersion implied the emergence of the problem of fiction;* and that this problem, born in the European context, stowed away aboard the ships bound for the New World, where it took on new strength.

CERVANTES: THE SEPARATION BETWEEN THE FICTITIOUS AND THE FICTIONAL

When the first part of *Don Quixote* was published in 1605, the romance of chivalry was already moribund. Henry Thomas shows that between 1508—the year in which *Amadis* was probably published for the first time—and 1550, almost one romance of chivalry appeared every year on the average; between 1550 and 1587, however, no more than nineteen new titles were published; and in the eighteen-year period before *Quixote* only three new books appeared (Thomas 1920: 147–48). Thus Cervantes seems to be flogging a dying horse; his ridiculing of a genre that was losing its old prestige, his biting irony directed at knights-errant, it would seem, could count on the indulgent smile of the better-informed public.

But, this said, we seem to be accusing Cervantes of opportunism. This is plausible enough: Spanish booksellers, who had to bribe the functionaries of the Crown and the Inquisition so that they would shut their eyes to suspect works, could argue that the avowed purpose of *Don Quixote* was to mock the heroes of chivalry, which by now were ludicrous anyway. The Church's harsh censors could rejoice in the fact that the conduct of the clergymen in the story was always impeccable—all were upright, charitable defenders of proper doctrine. Nor could Crown officials object to anything, for nowhere in the book does anyone criticize the king's jus-

---

*When I speak of the emergence of the problem of fiction I do not necessarily mean that this problem did not exist in the ancient world. All I mean is that the parameters were then different. For Eric Havelock, for instance, Plato's attack on poets was related to the conflict between the masters of the spoken word, the "poets," and the masters of written culture, the philosophers—for all Plato's own denouncements of the deleterious effects of written culture (see Havelock 1963). Moreover, since modern fictional discourse implies a given conception of the self and of its role in the discovery of truth, the modern conception of fiction could only be in agreement with the Greek conception if our notion of the individual were already known to the Greeks. (Against this view, see below, Chapter 3.)

tice—not even the convicts freed by Don Quixote. Clearly Cervantes was shrewd enough to avoid offending all the zealous authorities of his day. He had suffered too much poverty and misery to risk his neck any further. But it would be inexcusable shortsightedness to let the matter rest with this observation. We must proceed to a rereading of *Don Quixote* in terms of the problem we have been considering.

Anyone who has read *Don Quixote* will surely remember that the hero is mad only where cavalry is concerned. There are countless passages underscoring this fact, as if Cervantes wished to make sure that it would not go unnoticed. In one of them, the curate, invested with the twofold authority of priest and friend, observes that "apart from the silly things which this worthy gentleman says in connection with his craze, when other subjects are dealt with, he can discuss them in a perfectly rational manner, showing that his mind is quite clear and composed; so that, provided his chivalry is not touched upon, no one would take him to be anything but a man of thoroughly sound understanding" (Cervantes 1952: 112–13). Elsewhere, after Quixote has dwelt on the respective advantages and drawbacks of arms and letters, those who had heard him were sorry "to see a man of apparently sound sense, and with rational views on every subject he discussed, so hopelessly wanting in all, when his wretched unlucky chivalry was in question" (p. 147). Even before the action starts, at the very opening of the book, the chronicler about to tell the story observes: "His fancy grew full of what he used to read about in his books, enchantments, quarrels, battles, challenges, wounds, wooings, loves, agonies, and all sorts of impossible nonsense; and it so possessed his mind that the whole fabric of invention and fancy he read of was true, that to him no history in the world had more reality in it" (p. 2).

What is the precise nature of Don Quixote's madness? Clearly it consists in his inability to make a distinction between the world of the feats of his favorite heroes and that of quotidian existence. More precisely, Quixote's madness lies in the fact that he cannot separate the thematization of sense perception from the world of imagination, that he cannot draw a boundary separating one from the other. This is where Sancho comes in as a foil of fundamental importance to Cervantes's purpose. In the episode in the Sierra Morena, for instance, Don Quixote, torn between the models of Roland, the renowned warrior, and Amadis, no less renowned as a lovelorn sufferer, decides for the moment to emulate the latter. He tells his squire that, before delivering his letter to Dulcinea, he must witness the insanities he is about to perform for her. The madman is to assume the role of madman. But Sancho will have none of it; one madness is, to him, quite enough; and he reminds his master that Amadis's beloved had given him reason for going mad, whereas the chaste Dulcinea had done no such thing: " 'It seems to me,' said Sancho, 'that the knights who behaved in this way had provocation and cause for those follies and penances; but what cause has your worship for going mad? What lady has rejected you, or what evidence have you found to prove that the lady Dulcinea del Toboso has been trifling with Moor or Christian?' " (p. 83) Faithful to his good perceptual reason, Sancho tries to avoid the danger of madness-within-madness, trying to talk his master into conforming to the principles of verisimilitude. But this would mean persuading him to act according to a certain logic—in other words, to act within his madness according to the dictates of causality and common sense—whereas for Quixote "the thing is to turn crazy without any provocation" (p. 83).

Could it be that Cervantes, in his own fiction, is giving support to the arguments of Antonio de Guevara and Pedro Mexía, using humor to demonstrate the noxiousness of such literature? At first this might seem to be the case. But a closer reading will show that an answer cannot be given in terms of black or white, yes or no. In this connection, E. C. Riley's observation is pertinent: "One of the most disconcerting things about the romances is indeed their authors' inability either to treat them as pure fiction or to sustain the illusion that they were fact" (Riley 1962: 22). Cervantes establishes the difference between his work and the romance of chivalry both by resorting to irony and by repeatedly emphasizing the method in Quixote's madness and its limits. Quixote is mad in that he imposes on quotidian reality a kind of thematization that disturbs it. But this disturbance does not yet characterize the *fictional*, only the *fictitious*.

Other passages tell us that this disturbance, this inability to find the proper thematization, was not peculiar to the Knight of the Rueful Countenance. Let us recall the exchange with the landlord concerning romances of chivalry. Whereas the good curate is ready to do away with his books in an auto-da-fé just like the one he has performed earlier with the Don's library, the landlord expresses so forcefully his pleasure in hearing those stories and his conviction that the feats they tell of are true, that Cardenio says, in an aside: "As he shows, he accepts it as a certainty that everything those books relate took place exactly as it is written down; and the barefooted friars themselves would not persuade him to the contrary" (p. 119). Thus Quixote's illusion was no idiosyncrasy of his: simple folk, like the landlord, fell prey to the same error. But in the landlord's case there was a difference, for he made a distinction that the absolute believer in the fictitious was unable to make: "I shall not be so mad as to make a knight-errant of myself; for I see well enough that things are not now as they used to be in those days, when they say those famous knights roamed about the world" (p. 119). Although the landlord justified his belief in the truthfulness of such books by pointing to the fact that they were "printed by the license of the Lords of the Royal Council" (p. 119), he protects himself from Quixote's madness by means of a temporal distinction: times have changed, and today such practices would no longer be conceivable. Note that the temporal argument is also used by Quixote himself, but with opposite intent, naturally. Finding himself caged by the curate and the barber, supposing himself to have been enchanted, Don Quixote finds it strange that he is being hoisted by slow-moving oxen. Perhaps, he tells Sancho, it is just because times and customs have changed: "But perhaps the chivalry and enchantments of our day take a different course from that of those in days gone by" (p. 181).

By now we can see how Cervantes conceives the problem of fiction. According to moralists, the fictional can be justified only when the ancient Horatian principle *prodesse et delectare* applies. As the canon says to the mad gentleman:

And if, still led away by your natural bent, you desire to read books of achievements and of chivalry, read the Book of Judges in the Holy Scriptures. . . . Here, Señor Don Quixote, will be reading worthy of your sound understanding; from which you will rise learned in history, in love with virtue, strengthened in goodness, improved in manners, brave without rashness, prudent without cowardice; and all to the honor of God, your own advantage and the glory of La Mancha.
(P. 289)

This, however, is not Cervantes's own position. To support my contention, I will now turn to the second decisive observation, which is in fact connected with the first and is a development of it.

The space of fictionality in Cervantes assumes a critical stance in the very act of creation. For this he must resort to distancing, the author's ability to place himself outside of his narrative. As Riley correctly observes: "Don Quixote the reader of popular romances is the grandfather of Emma Bovary and Joyce's Gertie McDowell. What distinguishes him from them is an obsession with the most impossibly fabulous form of fiction that could be imagined" (Riley 1962: 36). Thus it is important to emphasize that when modern fiction appears, critical activity is seen not as a mere supplement to creation, but rather as an activating part of its makeup. *Against the naïveté presupposed by pre-Cervantine fictitiousness, based on the illusion that its own territory is not to be distinguished from that of truth, modern fictionality is based on irony, on distancing, on the creation of a complexity that, without alienating the common reader, does not present itself to him as a form of illusionism.* Cervantes prizes his readers, knows that he depends on them, and, as his characters observe, likes to know that *Don Quixote* circulates among readers of all kinds. In other words, he is aware that the problem of literature of "entertainment" cannot be solved by the moralist's formula, let alone by the application of the classical aesthetic principles he has learned in Italy.

At this point, however, I take issue with the illustrious Cervantes scholar E. C. Riley. Riley believes that the author sets forth his own views on the role of romance and poetry in the curate's and the canon's speeches. Thus Cervantes objected to romances of chivalry because, contrary to the Renaissance reading of Aristotle, they presented "purposeless *desatinos* or *disparates*" (Riley 1962: 23). But I feel that things are not as simple as that.

In order to justify my position, I will now turn to the prevalence of *imitatio* and the function of decorum and verisimilitude in relation to the role of distancing. The force of these elements, which are decisive for classical poetics, is evident in the curate's and the canon's discussions of literature. Owing to considerations of space, we will examine no more than two passages in the canon's speech. In both of them we notice that the canon is not presenting a purely theological argument, but attempting to harmonize religion and aesthetics. In the first passage, the canon justifies his disapproval of books of chivalry:

> Plots in fiction should be wedded to the understanding of the reader, and be constructed in such a way that, reconciling impossibilities, smoothing over difficulties, keeping the mind on the alert, they may surprise, interest, divert, and entertain, so that wonder and delight joined may keep pace one with the other; all which he will fail to effect who shuns verisimilitude and truth to nature [*imitación*], wherein lies the perfection of writing. (P. 184)

What is explicitly condemned here is the avoidance of imitation and verisimilitude. The principle of decorum appears shortly after, in the same speech: "And besides all this they are harsh in their style, incredible in their achievements, licentious in their amours, uncouth in their courtly speeches," and so on (p. 184).

In both passages, the influence of the Italian preceptists is evident, particularly where the ethical-religious argument becomes aesthetic. The presence of a literary viewpoint is even more obvious when the curate explains why he will refrain from burning some of Quixote's books. The *Amadis* is preserved because it has begotten a large progeny, though an evil one; Ariosto would also be spared if it were in the original Italian; the *Palmerin* is saved because it is said to have been written by a Portuguese king; *Tirante el Blanco*, because unlike most romances it is not overly fanciful. Though liberal, however, the curate's doctrine is the same as the canon's. They agree as to the reasons why, for all their absurdity, such books are still written and read. Having heard the opinion of learned and intelligent men as well as of ignorant people, says the canon, from all he obtained "flattering approval." And, even though such works clash with the principles (aesthetic ones, we would say nowadays) they ought to follow, still people write them because authors and actors care more for the bread they gain from the admiration of the many than for the criticism they hear from the few (see Cervantes 1952: 185–88).

Could this be Cervantes's actual position? If we believe that the most advanced poetics of his time amounted to construing religious reasons as pseudo-Aristotelian justifications, then we will tend to agree with Riley, and answer the question in the affirmative. But this answer seems to disagree with what *Don Quixote* itself shows. Let us consider the most important argument: the question of *imitatio*. In support of his argument, Riley comments that such a famous preceptist as A. S. Piccolomini had already anticipated and defended imitation within imitation: "And in truth, when imitating an imitator, one also in a certain fashion imitates what is true, since it is true that that imitated imitator imitates" (quoted in Riley 1962: 47). But let us see what happens in *Don Quixote*.

The adventures of the mad gentleman are at first said to have been based on the writings of several chroniclers of La Mancha. However, their chronicles break off at an early point, and the author could not have finished his work had he not discovered a manuscript in Arabic, which he bought for a trifle and had translated by a Morisco. The real author, then, was Cid Hamet Benengeli, an "Arab historian." Cervantes's device was, and is, a very familiar one: by means of it, the real author washes his hands of his creation, so to speak, and attributes it to someone else. But what is Cervantes's purpose in this? To begin with, the device gives him ampler possibilities for irony and for breaking with the illusionism of the fictitious. Thus Cervantes can mention himself in passing, as the author of *La Galatea*, or as a poet with "more experience in reverses than in verses" (Cervantes 1952: 16), or yet as one Saavedra, whom a Christian freedman remembers having seen among the Spaniards imprisoned by the Moors. In addition, the Morisco translator allows himself certain liberties, now questioning the truthfulness of the tale, now shortening a chapter. Let us skip these well-known details and concentrate on the characterization of the alleged author of the story as an Arab. Immediately after he tells us about the discovery and the translation of Cid Hamet's manuscript, the narrator warns us: "If against the present [history] any objection be raised on the score of its truth, it can only be that its author was an Arab, as lying is a very common propensity with those of that nation" (p. 23). But this epithet is not attributed to the Arab historian with any consistency. Rather, Cervantes has much fun presenting Cid Hamet in the most contradictory ways: from unfaithful chronicler to "a historian of great research and accuracy in all things" (p. 44).

Thus, to conclude that Cervantes follows the precepts of classical poetics would seem to be naive, at the very least. On the contrary, he adopts them as a sort of legitimating disguise, which at the same time concedes him some protection against the rigor of humanists and religious authorities and allows him to free the space of fictionality from the requirements of normative truth. Indeed, the distance between Cervantes's fictional practice and the liberal rules proposed by Piccolomini, the future Pope Pius II, is very large. If *imitatio* presupposes truth as the center and model, what is the truth that *Don Quixote* imitates? The conclusion seems far from trivial. It shows that Cervantes is aware, in his work, that classical poetics tames writers, and also that fictionality—unlike fictitiousness—must challenge the common truths.

Finally, it should be stressed that this critical potential, exercised simultaneously with artistic creativity, would not be possible except in a given context. Whereas fictitiousness presupposes oral speech, which implies the general principle of truthfulness, fictionality places truth in brackets, so to speak, and presupposes written language. As Nick Spadaccini observes, Cervantes's interludes were intended for private consumption so that demystifying and subversive material could be included.

In *Don Quixote* fictional discourse bears the marks of written language, of private reading, of demystification. They are manifest not as a distancing from quotidian reality—which would be subject to the control of the moralists—but precisely in the suggestion of a new relation to it. *Don Quixote* relates the fictitious to the quotidian, but not just to make fun of the latter and reinforce the wholesome common sense of the latter. If such were the case, it would be merely sanctioning the ban on fiction. But neither does it follow the lead of the romances of chivalry, where the fanciful and the would-be verisimilar are hopelessly confused. With Cervantes, modern fictionality is born from a double negation: the negation of undiscriminating fantasy and the negation of the ineffability of the quotidian. Cervantes demystifies precisely because he denies the exclusiveness of both the world of knights-errant and the world of the squire Sancho.

If we see *Don Quixote* as the first manifestation of literary fiction—that is, of the discursive category that begins to reflect and theorize about itself only in the late eighteenth century—we must add that it also works a peculiar sort of *Aufhebung*. The original sense of this German word, as is well known, implies something that at once conserves and transcends its initial terms. The *Aufhebung* of *Don Quixote* is peculiar because it relies on the negation of its own terms: both the belief in the adventures of Amadis and his imitators, and the belief in the exclusiveness of quotidian space—that is, of a space that could only be covered with the perceptual appetite of Sancho Panza. Peculiar, too, because the initial terms are not contradicted so that, as in Hegel, a higher synthesis could be reached.

In the peculiar *Aufhebung* of fiction, the fictitious (fantasy) and the quotidian (supposedly unquestionable reality) are retained, but also seen with some distancing—subject to irony, to questioning, to relativization. *Don Quixote* is not, as some have suggested, the allegory of another world or simply a put-down of *fingidas y disparatadas historias*. If we see it as either, we fail to understand that Cervantes gave *the alternative answer* to a problem that had been given its first solution by Fernão Lopes.* If we listen only to the answer given by the Portuguese chronicler—and we can hear it even without reading him—we will understand why History has come to assume its intellectual role in the West. If we fail to listen to Cervantes's answer, we will go on unconsciously domesticating imagination and banning fiction.

*On Fernão Lopes, see Costa Lima 1986: 21–34.

CHAPTER TWO

The Religious Control of Imagination

IN THE BEGINNING WAS THE QUESTION

If we ask a layman or a specialist in other areas what the object of history is, we are likely to get the following answer: the reconstruction of what actually happened. So complete has been the success of factualistic history over rival conceptions since the nineteenth century that this answer has been assimilated into common sense and become almost inevitable. But in the realm of knowledge, too, there is a history of the defeated.

Against factualistic history, already dominant in his time, Gustav Droysen emphasized, from the first version of his *Historik*, that the question asked of the historical material was the real point of departure for research: "The point of departure for investigation is the historical question. Heuristic furnishes us with the materials for historical work. It is the craft of the miner, that of finding and bringing to light, 'underground work' (Niebuhr)" (Droysen 1971: 332).

The implications of his position are further clarified when we articulate the passage quoted above with two others. In the first, Droysen writes that "the historical question determines which remains, monuments, and sources are to be tapped in order to answer it" (p. 335). The second contrasts his view with the one that has prevailed since then. According to the latter, the historian's major instruments are his sources and the critique of these sources, by means of which he attempts to reconstruct the "true historical fact." Based on a naturalistic conception of science, the historian envisages his task as that of a painstaking craftsman who replaces each piece exactly where it had been before. Thus his "facts" could be seen as true. To Droysen, this entire conception is misguided: "The result of critique is not 'the true historical fact,' but rather the preparation of the material that will make it possible to arrive at a reasonably reliable and correct interpretation" (pp. 338–39).

Rather than a basically descriptive and reconstructive activity, which presupposes that the past is right there where it was left, lying still and ready to be unearthed, historiography changes according to the place occupied by its agent—that is, his political, philosophical, and ideological position, his sensibility, his background of expectations and knowledge, and not just his competence and discipline. All these multiple variables come together in the formulation of the *question* that points to its object and changes the position of the past as it variously organizes the "remains, monuments, and sources."

Starting with my volume *Control of the Imaginary*, my investigation has been guided by a basic question. If we accept the conventional label "modernity" for the period beginning after the Middle Ages, my basic question can be stated as follows: in this period, haven't the products specifically derived from the activation of imagination been subjected to a *particularized* control? By "particularized control" I mean one that is not to be explained merely in terms of a general political or economic control. Although, to be sure, particularized controls are eventually integrated into general controls, and the character of the latter influences the former, each particularized control, such as the one I am investigating, is a specific manifestation of power, and as such is included in what Michel Foucault calls the "microphysics of power." As Foucault writes: "It seemed to me that economic history and theory provided a good instrument for studying relations of production, and that linguistics and semiotics offered instruments for studying relations of signification; but for power relations we had no tools of study" (Foucault 1982: 778).

Literary fiction deals with the problem of power as a differentiated discursive form—that is, to the extent that its expressive potential conflicts or is liable to conflict with what is allowed by the discourse in power, the so-called discourse of truth. It may well be that one of the most serious problems that has weakened the sociology of literature is its inability to configure the mediations between its object and socially instituted power. If so, it is to be expected that such a research will help to establish a distinct sociological approach to literature. However, this expectation may be frustrated by a prior problem: from the outset our question must deal with an excessively long period of time. It would be extremely naive to suppose I have overcome this difficulty in my previous book, or that I will be close to doing so at the end of this volume. The question, as I see it, far outstrips the individual competence and the productive lifetime of a single investigator. I am aware that I have done no more than open a line of research, and that the most I can hope for will be to find that it has turned out to be a fruitful one.

From the beginning, I have assumed—although without anticipating to what degree this has taken place—that throughout modernity the control of imagination has taken different guises; further, we know that this control was not strong enough to block the rise, in late-eighteenth-century Germany, of a line of thought that led to the view of literature as the verbal mode of fictionality. This case is particularly relevant because it brings into sharp focus the first consequence of our question: as a specific discourse (let us avoid the term "autonomous"), as a privileged way of exploring imagination, literature can only arise in the struggle against the agent that controls imagination: the discourse of truth. To those who are used to the happy endings fabricated by the media, it may come as a surprise to learn that the rise of literature did not bring about the end of control, not even in the short run. If literature then began to present itself as Cervantes had conceived it—that is, as a space distinct from that of the fictitious but encompassing it (see Chapter 1)—and to exploit the unfoldings of the self that resulted from the collapse of the ethical code and lent such importance to the function of masks, as La Rochefoucauld understood so well (see below, the third section of this chapter)—this possibility was soon covered up and postponed. "Normal" romanticism—that is, the patriotic and sentimental form of romanticism that prevailed in the early decades of the nineteenth century—became the literary practice acceptable to the system of power. *Literature became institutionalized to the extent that it disguised or softened its fictional force.* With a few exceptions, such as the work of Leopardi and some of Hugo's, fictionality was usually reduced to an emotional expression of the self or adjusted to the interests of nationality, and saw itself as a branch of historical investigation. Thus, although born of the struggle against control, literature has never been an autonomous discourse; it has secured a beachhead, but has only found its way into histories of literature—the label is ironical here—to the extent that it has neglected its link with the imaginary and with its only form of creative negation: fictionality.* (The only exception has been Auerbach's *Mimesis.*) In any case, it would be pointless to develop the consequence of a question that has not yet finished justifying itself.

If something—whether a form of production, of expression, or of behavior—is subjected to control, it must be because it contradicts estab-

---

*On the relation between fictionality and the imaginary as a concretization that denies the diffuse negativity of imagination, see Iser 1983: 121–51.

lished practice. Why should fictional productions be controlled? As I have been explaining control, there are two reasons for its existence. The more comprehensive one is the following: at the end of the Middle Ages, the general schemes of interpretation of the world were no longer able to offer convincing explanations of the facts (see Costa Lima 1988, chap. 1). To use Timothy Reiss's terminology, the conjunctive mode operative in the Middle Ages suffered a crisis, and the analytico-referential mode was only beginning to assert itself (see Reiss 1982, esp. chap. 2). At the same time, from various areas there came signs of the growing importance of the individual and individual interpretation.

The most remote form of control, as exerted in the fifteenth century, was the attempt of the officially recognized intellectual subsystem to tame the risk posed by individual interpretation.* In the Middle Ages intellectual power had been exerted by the Church, which "had inherited from its origins in the Roman Empire a principle of universality and a centralized, hierarchical government" (Ferguson 1968: 65), so it was not to be expected that, with the changes of a new epoch, its members would try to change drastically either the functioning of the ecclesiastical institution or the solid dogmatic tradition that supported it. Since here I am doing no more than recalling the part of this research that has already been published, it will not be necessary to repeat demonstrations presented before. Suffice it to say that this surveillance of individualized thought aimed at keeping it from contradicting the official norms of interpretation and behavior. However, it would be a mistake to suppose that only official representatives of the Church were interested in restricting individual expression, at a moment when such expression might stimulate expansions of the imagination against the chains of truth. Fernão Lopes, arguably the

---

*Note particularly that this attack on individual judgment and interpretation would not have had such impact if orthodox thought did not rely on intellectual instruments that had been forged long before. Among these, I would underscore the struggle of monotheistic theology against both mythical interferences and the sects that were multiplying in the early Christian era. This consolidation of Logos against myth was to have a sensible impact on the language considered proper for expounding the divine message. H. Blumenberg observes the different status that separates Satan from other divine beings: "Contrary to theological requisites of reliability and commitment to men, . . . the devil's nature is precisely his lack of nature [hat seine Natur als Naturlosigkeit], the omnipotent ability to metamorphose and assume animal attributes. . . . In all his traits, he is the figure that opposes the substantial realism of dogma. In the figure of Satan, the myth was converted into the subversion of the dogmatically disciplined world of faith" (Blumenberg 1985: 141). Thus the effort to achieve conceptual purification of theology implied hostility to the changeable language of mythical metamorphoses. This is probably the oldest root of the force that, at the appropriate moment, came to the support of a Logos inimical to fictionality. However, since my investigation of control is limited to a narrower temporal range, I have decided to postpone the exploration of this much more complex field until our research is more consolidated.

first to legitimate history's right of expression as a science, asserted the superiority of history in opposition to those who, striving for song and beauty, scorned truthful accounts. Thus a new discursive form appeared outside the Church: the writing of history, attempting to establish its autonomy by grounding itself on the contrast with the "metamorphoses" of poets.

This first reason for control is historically close to the second one, which is to be found in the poetics of the Renaissance. Indeed, while Zumthor takes the fourteenth century as the period when the use of the first-person pronoun in poetry became more widely used in its referential function— that is, when *je* was no longer a mere grammatical figure to be assumed by whomever read or recited the poem—it was also in the fourteenth century, between 1350 and 1375, that Boccaccio wrote the first "modern" defense of poetry—Books XIV and XV of *De genealogia deorum gentilium*. What does this nearness in time mean? On the plane of actual poetical practice, the French poets of the late Middle Ages were no longer content to invest their poems and fables with allegorical meaning, and used their empirical selves as witnesses to what they said (see Costa Lima 1988, chap. 1). On the theoretical plane, in the early Italian Renaissance, Boccaccio felt it necessary to defend poetry against accusations old and new. For instance, the charge that poets are fools because they are not seen to flaunt their property and riches cannot possibly be medieval, given the Church's zeal to discourage the ambition for wealth. Besides, it should be seen that in his defense Boccaccio is careful to harmonize the voice of the poet with Christian teachings: "I do not concede that [poets] are fools because they pursue the study of poetry, and indeed hold them to be the wisest of men, for as good Catholics they acknowledge the true God" (Boccaccio 1930: 23).

Poetry, then, is a worthy endeavor because "as it dwells in the firmament and is added to divine counsel, it moves the minds of some heavenwards, to long for eternity" (p. 24). Thus arguing, the author replies to another charge: that poetic language is obscure. In a contemporary treatise, his friend Petrarch, instead of denying this obscurity, associates it with another kind of wisdom: "Thus, certainly, in poetic fictions a truth is inserted, to be uncovered by the subtlest of spirals" (Petrarch 1968b: 505). Poetic obscurity disturbs and repels the vulgar, that its treasure may be reserved solely for those who are able to recognize it. Like a sacred text, poetry selects its own officiants. But such a sacred text might hurt the truth by direct exposure. That is why poetry "veils truth as a beautiful, worthy garb of fiction" (Boccaccio 1930: 39). Fiction is an ornament that conceals and increases the value of the poetic. Although we are still relatively far from the praise of sight and the visible, of the world of sensible forms, new values are already surfacing in the attacks Boccaccio is defending poetry against—namely, that the poet does not grow rich and does not speak clearly.

To what extent does the new element predominate in Boccaccio's thought? The question has to do with what is said about the role of fiction. Could it be that seeing it as a veil that conceals and increases the value of truth was the continuation of the medieval practice of allegory, which according to Cerquiglini was rejected by contemporary poets? I am inclined to answer this question in the negative. The tendency to accept this continuity results from the tendency to think that the single aim of medieval allegory was to disguise the legacy of paganism with Christian trappings. But Erwin Panofsky and Fritz Saxl have shown that this notion, though not entirely unfounded, reflects lack of knowledge of the medieval context. Independently of ecclesiastical pressures, medieval allegorical transformation was a consequence of the fact that contemporary man no longer knew how to correlate classical themes with classical form, that classical culture had lost its original meaning:

> Knowledge of classical subject matter and appreciation of classical form were not lacking during the Middle Ages, but, because of the failure to relate them in practice, classical subject matter, especially in mythological stories, completely lost its original form, and classical form so lost its original subject matter that a Phaedra could be used as a Virgin Mary and a Venus as an Eve.
>
> (Panofsky and Saxl 1933: 264)

Though we must not underestimate the Church's efforts to neutralize the pagan tradition—which resulted in the transformation of the *Metamorphoses* into *Ovide moralisé*—Panofsky and Saxl suggest that the frequency of the use of allegory also derived from a social cause: medieval man's need to express his own categories through visual representations whose meanings he no longer understood. The changes that then took place were therefore not entirely conscious. Now, in Boccaccio we find a different justification for the use of allegory. In his books dedicated to the defense of poetry as well as in the whole of his treatise *De genealogia deorum gentilium*, his effort has a clear intention: his point is to argue that, through their gods and their myths, the ancients prefigured Christian truth. In this way, the allegory of these texts was, so to speak, the proof that antiquity had not been damned by God from the outset.

I am not denying that the passage in question by Boccaccio implies the medieval practice of interpretation *on four levels*—literal, metaphorical, allegorical, and anagogic; what I object to is the confusion between its allegorical and its purely medieval reading. This contention can be verified in a different way: shouldn't one expect the author, in stressing poetry's conformity to religious truth, to express only his own opinion as a believer? This would be admissible if we were unaware of the distance between the pious sublimity of Boccaccio's treatise and the comic licentiousness of his *Decamerone*. Perhaps because he did not feel that these stories could immortalize his name, in them he exploited ambiguity and lechery, spoke ill of respectable people, lay and religious. On the other hand, the sober *Genealogia* presents us with the problem of the Renaissance: in order to publicize or defend poetry one had to negotiate with the doctors of the Church. In short, the allegorical practice present in the affirmation of poetic fiction as a guise is no longer to be confused with the practice of medieval allegory. It now anticipates another situation, one in which poetry needs *less a different meaning than a strictly intellectual defense.*

The startled reader may well ask: is it even conceivable that there could have been control of the imagination in the Renaissance? How can anyone suggest that religious reason controlled artistic expression when we are aware of such an explosion of life, enthusiasm, and sensuality in the paintings of the period?

Though this question cannot be answered in a few words, I will try to find a reply that is both synthetic and comprehensive. Let us return to our starting point. The idea that the imaginary has been subject to control since the beginning of modern times must necessarily find its first concrete evidence in the Renaissance. Elsewhere (Costa Lima 1988) I have tried to demonstrate, through analysis of the various poetics of the cinquecento, that the basic instruments of control were *imitatio*, decorum, and verisimilitude. This argument, which still stands, had nevertheless two flaws, which perhaps weakened it.

First, I did not take the trouble to address the shock the reader must have felt to see his cherished image of the Renaissance contradicted. Second, I did not try to relate my results to the most fascinating field of expression of the period: the visual arts. Let me try to make up these lacunae and, at the same time, to advance my argument.

It will hardly be necessary to stress the importance of Jakob Burckhardt's *Die Kultur der Renaissance* (1860) for the recognition of the distinctive character of the Italian quattrocento and cinquecento. For the Swiss historian, these centuries represented a radical turning away from medieval darkness. The individual arose out of gray anonymity, of subjection to the yoke of authority; and the world cast off the suspicion that Christian thought had imposed on it. The Renaissance, the cradle of modern man, brought about the rediscovery of the world and of man himself. Instead of remaining attached to the land, tilled for the feudal lord's gain, instead of seeking the protection of the castles, where the moats and the battlements, the drawbridges and the thick walls betrayed a warrior's ethos, Renaissance man found that the doors were now open for his ambition, so that he could set off on an adventure of material and spiritual growth.

The very enthusiasm aroused by Burckhardt's ideas, however, encouraged a number of investigations that little by little undermined the simplistic, spectacular tenor of his theses.* To begin with, the clear-cut opposition between the Renaissance and the centuries that immediately preceded it was abolished. The idea that the late Middle Ages had ignored the value of the individual and the notion that Renaissance man was characterized by irreligiousness were both denied. These objections went so far as to question the appropriateness of the very label attached to the historical period. The initial exaggeration—seeing the Renaissance as a period of enlightenment, a harbinger of nineteenth-century individualism—was followed by the opposite excess of seeing in this view of the Renaissance no more than a projection of the longings of its "creators." To avoid both extremes, it is important to stress the conclusion arrived at by J. Huizinga more than 60 years ago. He showed that it was impossible to hit upon a homogeneous definition of the period, because it was marked by distinct tempos or rhythms that sometimes sharply set it off from the earlier period and sometimes marked it as a continuation of the previous mentality.

> The Renaissance can be considered as neither the antithesis of medieval civilization nor even as an intermediate zone between the Middle Ages and the modern world. The boundary lines that separate ancient from modern culture among Western peoples sometimes are drawn between the Middle Ages and the Renaissance, sometimes between the Renaissance and the eighteenth century, sometimes right across the Renaissance, and more than one crosses the thirteenth century, or, much later, the eighteenth century. (Huizinga 1938–39: 612)

Does this mean the ideas of the Swiss historian are now relegated to the dust of libraries? Not at all. Man's self-confidence, the cult of antiquity and of intellectual life freed from the shackles of Church rulings, the self-assertion of the individual have continued to be taken, at least outside the closed circle of specialists, as the marks of a time gone too soon. And such notions still survive because these traits have been assimilated into "the liberal myth of the Renaissance, [which] appeared to all minds penetrated by French eighteenth-century ideas as the radiant awakening of these spiritual values" (Chastel 1945: 9). But to say that the first characterization of the Renaissance as formulated by Burckhardt, Michelet, and G. Voigt was the mythical mirage of nineteenth-century liberalism does not mean that,

---

*For an overall view of theses concerning the Renaissance, see Huizinga 1938–39; for an analysis of the directions taken by the Renaissance as a period, see Weisinger 1968: 74–94.

for the historian, it was all a trick with mirrors. In order to arrive at a nonmythical image, it is convenient to examine how the men of the period envisaged their own times.

Now, their testimony shows that they were indeed aware of an ongoing *rinascita*. Thus, toward the end of *Dell'arte della guerra*, written around 1520, Machiavelli wrote of Tuscany: "This province seems born to resurrect dead things, as has been seen in poetry, in painting, and in sculpture" (Machiavelli 1954: 531). More significantly, in the Proemio of his *Vite*, Giorgio Vasari reviewed the causes of the decay of the visual arts after the fall of Rome; among them he included "il fervente zelo della nuova religione cristiana" ("the fervent zeal of the new religion") (Vasari 1967: 19). And in a later passage the author manifests awareness of and even pride in the resumption of the interrupted tradition:

> Men of those times, unused to seeing any other quality or greater prefection in things than what they saw in those before their eyes, marveled and, although barbarians, learned from the best of them. It was only gradually that those who were born at a later time, aided in some places by the subtleness of the air, elevated themselves so much that, about 1250, the heavens, moved by the piety of the beautiful creations that appeared day by day on Tuscan soil, restored them in their primitive shape.   (Vasari 1967: 28)*

The above-quoted passages show how Machiavelli and Vasari were aware of the novelty of their times. The significance of this fact is sharpened when we examine the conditions then prevailing in Italy: contrary to what was happening in France, until the early fourteenth century Italian cultural activities were rather mediocre (see Kristeller 1944–45: 349), and their major spokesmen were the Humanists, whose main object of study was grammar and rhetoric. Thus the Humanists' "main charges are against the bad Latin style of the medieval authors, against their ignorance of ancient history and literature, and against their concern for supposedly useless questions" (p. 355).

The sort of attack undertaken by the Humanists is reflected in the Renaissance concern with belles lettres, identified with elegance in expression and refinement in language. Even before the term "Humanist" had been popularized, Humanists saw themselves as members of the class *de oratoribus*, and the ideal orator was "master of many arts and governor of his fellowmen, through the force of his eloquence forging a link between the intellectual and practical spheres of human experience" (Gray 1968: 206).

The Humanists' self-identification with rhetorical practice makes it clear why the concept of literature created by the Renaissance, which

---

*For further information, see Ferguson 1939–40: 1–28, and Weisinger 1944: 625–38.

remained unchanged until the middle of the eighteenth century, laid emphasis on eloquence. Literature was indeed a form of eloquence. What is the primary meaning of this fact?

I believe no one has put it more aptly then Pascal: "*Eloquence.* —It requires the pleasant and the real; but the pleasant must itself be drawn from the true" (B. Pascal 1952: 175). Thus, the conception of literature as a form of eloquence assumed that it should draw from truth—that is, be subordinate to it—even when it was pure invention. The cultivation of letters still implied submission to the ideal of truth. The Humanists, masters of grammar and rhetoric, advocated the ideal of a correct and refined language. Thus if we consider the status of eloquence in literature and the service of truth it implied we can already see the distance between the real project of the Humanists and the liberal myth of the Renaissance. We must, however, take care not to fall prey to another sort of unilateral interpretation. We may reasonably suppose that the original intent of the Humanists was significantly altered when it was propagated among those who cultivated the visual arts. Let us bear in mind the difference in status between men of letters and artists.* Whereas rhetoric and grammar were part of learning, forming—together with dialectic—the trivium, to be completed with study of the quadrivium (geometry, arithmetic, astronomy, and music), painting and sculpture were considered mechanical arts, and were thus relegated to the level of handicrafts. For visual artists, then, the rediscovery of antiquity provided a means to achieve social recognition.

Thus for artists the idea of imitation had a meaning different from what it had for the Humanists. In a neglected 1920 essay, Huizinga asked: "What is, for Vasari, the great innovation of Cimabue and Giotto?" His answer already points to the difference I have been stressing: "The direct imitation of Nature. The return to Nature and the return to the Ancients are, for him, almost identical terms. . . . He who follows the Ancients finds his way back to Nature" (Huizinga 1938–39: 168). Nature, and no longer polished language, was the standard according to which artists perceived the ancients. From their different social positions, the artist and the man of letters understood the postulate of *imitatio* in totally different ways.

This contextualized investigation is beginning to bring to light some differences that are blurred by the liberal myth of the Renaissance. To begin with, there are the differences between the basically philological character of the Humanists' interest and the "naturalistic" bent it acquired among artists. Further, if we consider the Humanists' zeal for verbal purity and the pragmatic intention of eloquence (see Gray 1968: 203), we understand why the period is less important from the viewpoint of philosophical re-

---

*See especially Blunt 1956, particularly chap. 4.

flection. Also, we find it less surprising that the authors of poetics should demonstrate such a stern love for the rules imposed on poetry: the poem, as language itself, was denied a multitudinous practice.

When we emphasize the differences that existed in the Renaissance, we should also keep in mind that, in some cases, they actually amounted to areas of tension. Such was the case, as we have seen, of the meaning of *imitatio*. For the poets, it meant a subject compatible with their good social standing, a way of showing oneself worthy of being part of a ducal or princely court; for painters, imitation of the ancients provided a possible means for social mobility. But aren't we perhaps subordinating this tension to an unnecessary attack against the liberal myth of the Renaissance? We don't think so, for "the earliest historical definition of the Renaissance— that which sees it as the expansion of secular life accomplished in classical art, thanks to the reconstruction of antiquity—remains inevitably present as the backdrop for all research into the Italian Renaissance" (Chastel 1945: 19).

But could it be that this alleged backdrop is no more than an ideological fantasy? This possibility is denied when we see how painters' different approach to imitation developed. More explicitly, the liberal interpretation of the Renaissance does not contain only "mythical" elements; these are combined with real components. Thus, if my central idea of control is to become more plausible, I must venture into an area in which I am no more than an amateur, that of painting. This is necessary because one of the obstacles to the notion of control is Renaissance painting. How can one argue that Renaissance imagination was tamed when the interiors of palaces, the apses, ceilings, and walls of churches were often covered with pagan gods and mythological figures? How can one believe that painters were submitted to any form of prior control after looking, if only in passing, at such a sophisticatedly sensual painting as Raphael's *Venus Beseeching Jupiter*? Such a view, it might be argued, could only be advanced by one who, having learned of the existence of Savonarola, jumped to the conclusion, totally unwarranted by history, that the friar's rigor had curbed the cardinals' lechery. As early as 1940, Jean Seznec showed, in his *La Survivance des dieux antiques*, how the figures of gods and mythological heroes were justified at the time: either it was argued that their representation no longer implied any risk because paganism had been defeated or the meaning of these figures was neutralized by allegorical interpretations. Besides, wrote Seznec, since artists, given their lower social status, were unable to read Greek and Latin texts on their own, the Humanists, some of whom were princes of the Church, wrote informative encyclopedias, which were evidently Christianized, and furnished "programs" for the composition of works of art.

Seznec's book marks an important stage in the reversal of the common view of contemporary observers. Nonetheless, before Botticelli's *Primavera*, painted late in 1470, how can anyone deny that it is the glorification of earthly love? Even a viewer unable to identify all the figures will surely recognize Venus, in the central position; the little Cupid hovering over her, the three Graces by her side, in a harmonious movement, perhaps a dance. Admittedly the viewer will not identify Mercury, nor understand why he points to the heavens, nor recognize the beautiful Simoneta, Marco Vespucci's young wife, let alone the masculine figures behind her. But the central feminine triangle—formed by the Graces, Venus, and *la bella Simonetta*, here representing the goddess Flora—will still seem a radiant, disseminating, fecundative group, a sort of pleasant dream.

Against this normal reading, in a 1945 study, revised and republished in 1972, E. H. Gombrich showed how mistaken this usual reception is. The historian mentioned a letter by the Neoplatonic philosopher Marsilio Ficino to Botticelli's patron. In it, Ficino speaks of Venus less as the goddess of desire and love than as the incarnation of "Humanitas," a word that was at the time invested with a wide-ranging meaning: "Venus stands for *Humanitas* which, in turn, embraces Love and Charity, Dignity and Magnanimity, Liberality and Magnificence, Comeliness and Modesty, Charm and Splendour" (Gombrich 1978: 42). Ultimately, Venus was transformed into the incarnation of the true love of virtue.

Gombrich added that Ficino's letter must have served as the basis for the program that Botticelli's painting was to follow. This is not the place to present his hypothesis in detail or to evaluate it. In any case, we agree with the author that "in the best cases, expression in pictorial art remains an ambiguous language. Its elements need a context to acquire a well-defined meaning" (p. 39). This contextual value lends Botticelli's painting a meaning quite different from its usual "pagan" reading.

It would be arbitrary to generalize from this example and conclude that Renaissance painting seems to us to be full of expressive freedom only because we are no longer aware of its actual meaning. But while recognizing that such a generalization would be unwarranted, I must stress that the artist's modest erudition subjected him to the restrictions of the Humanists, who Christianized paganism. Thus we can already see the shadow of growing control, at least in the field of visual art. Granted, this control was apparently mild, a form of compromise that could not possibly cause the artist to revolt. But this result is not yet satisfactory. It will not do to adopt easier solutions so that our position will gain in credibility. Let us look for a different, if more arduous, path.

Beginning with Boccaccio, the defense of poetry was concerned with reconciling its sensible production with Christian virtue and making a creator of the poet, on the basis of the very etymology of the original Greek word. Now, this glorification of the artist, taking the word in its widest meaning, was combined either with the Renaissance praise of individuality or with the painter's struggle to rise above the status of craftsman. These factors, propagating in Northern Europe, were to make it possible for Albrecht Dürer to depict himself, in a self-portrait of 1500, as Christ himself. "It is indeed unquestionable that Dürer deliberately styled himself into the likeness of the Saviour. He not only adopted the compositional scheme of His image, but idealized his own features so as to make them conform to those traditionally attributed to Christ" (Panofsky 1971: 43).

The painter's decision should not be interpreted as a gesture of pride, of rebelliousness or individual self-assertion against prescribed religious standards. As Panofsky notes, "for Dürer, the modern conception of art as a matter of genius had assumed a deeply religious significance which implied a mystical identification of the artist with God" (p. 43). However, one may well argue: if such a control indeed existed, and if its earliest efforts were directed against the affirmation of a self-sufficient individuality, isn't the fact that there are no known protests against Dürer's self-portrait the decisive proof that our fundamental question is misguided? Note, to begin with, that the idea of control does not imply that, for any one of a number of different reasons, a given artist (again, in the widest sense of the term) could not have enjoyed freedom for a certain period. The control, as we see it, assumes a commitment to established truth; the representatives of this truth can be strict or complacent according to the circumstances, which vary considerably. If this is the flexible aspect of control, its opposite side, hard and stable, is the fact that the artist cannot present his fiction as a rival of truth, placing it on the same level as truth or even on a higher plane. Evidence of this hard side is also furnished by the example of Dürer: we can see his identification with Christ's face, as does Panofsky, as a metaphor for a mystical union with the Savior. On the other hand, it would have been unthinkable to accept the metaphor theoretically—that is, to conceive of the individual as a creator in his own right, with no reference to the religious "sun."

If Dürer's gesture was feasible in painting, nothing of the kind is to be found in verbal discourse. To be sure, in his *Poetices libri septem* (1561) Julius Caesar Scaliger did write that the superiority of the poet came from the fact that "he does not imitate things as an actor, but creates them as a second God" (in Ferraro 1971: 82). But we soon find that his audacity was counterweighed by the markedly ethical function he assigned to poetry. What was possible in painting was not permissible in verbal language. Considering the painter's lowly status, this fact seems strange, even confusing. But we must bear in mind the effect of the difference between the approaches of poetry and painting. Both of them cultivated antiquity and imitation, but we have already seen the difference between them in this respect. As Vasari wrote, when the painter imitates the ancients, he rediscovers the path of nature.

For the visual artist, the ancients, to whom he had no direct access, were not as much an aesthetic model as a way of freeing himself from the craft guilds and the general schemes of religious interpretation. Thus, far from denying that painting was imitation, Leonardo stressed its status as a science:

> If you despise painting, which is the sole imitator of all the visible works of nature, it is certain that you will be despising a subtle invention which with philosophical and ingenious speculation takes as its theme all the various kinds of forms, airs and scenes, plants, animals, grasses and flowers, which are surrounded by light and shade. And this truly is a science and the true-born child of nature, since painting is the offspring of nature. (Leonardo 1954: 854)

A daring view, which leads him to attack the alleged superiority of theology. For although Leonardo does not name it explicitly, he is evidently thinking of theology when he writes, "e si tu dirai, che le scientie, che principiano e finischono nella mente habbiano verità," in the passage below:

> No human investigation can be called true science without passing through mathematical tests; and if you say that the sciences which begin and end in the mind contain truth, this cannot be conceded and must be denied for many reasons. First and foremost because in such mental discourses experience does not come in, without which nothing reveals itself with certainty. (Leonardo 1952: 8)

The painter imitates the ancients not because he takes them as models, but in order to master nature. The mathematization of matter is reflected, first of all, in the study of the movements of bodies and their representation in space through perspective. It is as a painter that Leonardo is interested in a wide range of subjects, including warfare, anatomy, botany, and so on. Nothing could be further from the prescriptions of the dozens of poetics composed in the cinquecento than Leonardo's words. These poetics assign a central position to *imitatio*, which is based on the requirements of verisimilitude and decorum even as it conditions them. When the preceptist disagrees with what he takes to be the authorized reading of Aristotle and denies that *imitatio* is the cornerstone, it is because he believes, as does Scaliger, that imitation falls short of the ultimate object of poetry: to teach and be useful. "Poetical art is a science, a habit, which is to say, it is derived from a system of laws that teaches us that symmetry of form we call Poetry. —Therefore it contains three elements: matter, form, and execution. In the highest critical form a fourth element appears: the end, which is imitation, or the further end: instruction" (in Ferraro 1971: 93). But Scaliger is not really an exception. As his commentator writes, even the most orthodox Aristotelians took imitation in a different sense from what the Greek philosopher had in mind: "Renaissance critics are closer to Horace than to Aristotle in their attitude towards imitation. All of them, even the staunchest Aristotelians, emphasize the notion of art as idealized imitation of nature. . . . The term 'ideal' loses its Aristotelian sense of rationally 'universal' and assumes that of ethically 'exemplary' " (Ferraro 1971: 39).

The above passages highlight the different meanings assigned to imitation by poets and painters. The latter imitated in order to learn about (and from) nature; the former, in order to idealize it, submitting it to ethical and religious norms. Hence the great discrepancy between the ways in which theoreticians of one area saw their relations with the other area. Scaliger, an advocate of poetry, writes: "Only poetry includes all other disciplines, surpassing other arts; whereas the others [history and philosophy] . . . represent things truly, almost as talking portraits, the poet instead brings about a second nature . . . in so doing, he ultimately transforms himself into a second God" (quoted in Ferraro 1971: 82). Leonardo, on the other hand, argues:

> Although the poet has as wide a choice of subjects as the painter, his creations fail to afford as much satisfaction to mankind as do paintings, for while poetry attempts to represent forms, actions and scenes with words, the painter employs the exact images of these forms in order to reproduce them. Consider, then, which is more fundamental to man, the name of man or his image? (Leonardo 1954: 852)

This absolute contrast, it seems, cannot be explained unless we relate it to the social situation of poets and painters and their respective pursuits. In an aristocratic society such as that of the Renaissance, one who was a craftsman and could not read the cultured languages was held to be an ignorant commoner. The Humanist, in contrast, benefited from educational institutions, and sometimes belonged to courtly circles; his elegant speech was indispensable for parlor games, and his rhymes were important for the glorification of noblemen in their capacity as politicians and warriors. That is why, in *Il cortegiano*, Baldassare Castiglione discusses which tongue the ideal courtier should speak and write, whether Tuscan or some other known dialect. The language the author proposes as a model should not disregard "the speech of other noble Italian cities," let alone those Spanish and French words that were already current. But Castiglione was not interested in promoting a language that could be understood by all. His exclusive concern is the court, the purity and grace that ought to characterize verbal tournaments. "That is why if today, among men of letters, of talent and good judgement, some strive to write in this tongue [i.e., as the author has described] things worthy of being read, soon we shall find it polished and full of terms and fine figures, and capable of being used in the written form, like any other language" (Castiglione 1983: 56).

In such a purified language, imitation is less a way of grasping the world than a discipline obeying specific standards. To be sure, the ideal of individuality also permeated the upper echelons of society, as Book I of Castiglione's work makes clear. But in the case of Humanists and their clients, it had to be a carefully crafted individuality, conscious of limits that were not to be overstepped. "Wild" individuality was restricted to men like Dürer, Benvenuto Cellini, and Leonardo—that is, the prince's employees, not his guests. For his part, the courtier was expected to know the strict rules of the game. If the aim of decorum was not to grate on delicate ears, *imitatio* ought to respect the norms of the idealized world— that is, the principles and precepts of good society and religion. Thus the social situation of Humanists explains why for them *imitatio* meant taming, strict observance of the rules. In the case of dramatic poetry—poetry that could be staged—the rules implied the unities of action, time, and place; ultimately they implied respect for reason and virtue, so that one must avoid not only the fantastic and the marvelous but also the plebeian; so they presupposed the control of imagination. Conversely, it was the artist's own sociocultural inferiority that to a certain extent protected him from control; not that he was exempt from it, but he was not continually exposed to it.

But control cannot be explained solely by the social position of poets and painters; this is no more than one cause among others, and one, it should be stressed, of a political nature, although formulated in terms of strict respect to the religious code. (If this subordination of religion to politics were not taken into account, it would be difficult to understand why the preceptists' treatises are so much more rigorous than the actual practice of the cardinals. Thus, for instance, it is said that Cardinal Pietro Bembo was such an enthusiast of pagan authors that he once advised his colleague Sardoleto not to read the epistles of St. Paul lest his style be corrupted; see Monroe 1908: 9). But if control was politically based, why should it be enforced most emphatically on poetry? A passage by Leonardo suggests the answer to this question: "Le lettere representano con piu verità le parole al senso che non fa la pittura" ("Letters represent the meanings of words more truthfully than painting") (Leonardo 1970: 35). Here Leonardo touches on the different extensions of the two languages. If painting, being visual, has more immediate impact, the verbal sign has more narrative power, is more adequate for developing arguments, and therefore is more likely to be taken as true.

To summarize, the most important differences between the pictorial heritage of the Renaissance and the poetics of the period are these: First, given the diversity of their social positions, painter and poet understood the precept of imitation in different ways. For the painter, it was a tool for visual and cognitive mastery of man and nature, and he expected this mastery to be acknowledged so that his social status might be enhanced; whereas the poet thought of *imitatio* as a standard to be internalized so that writing would be an activity worthy of and proper to those who were of superior status. Second, given the difference between the expressive range of the two languages, verbal and pictorial, writing was affected by direct control, which made it toe the straight line of reason and avoid the propagation of harmful or dangerous fables. Since painting was unable to compete with writing as an argumentative instrument, Humanists were content to know that painters were neutralized by the allegories contained in the programs they imposed on them. Therefore allegory, now no more than a means of rationalization, preserved its decisive role, based on the distinct role it had played in the Middle Ages. It is fitting, then, that a defender of the separation between religious and scientific expression like Galileo should be vehement in his criticism of allegory:

> In his opinion, allegorical poems (such as Tasso's *Gerusalemme liberata*), forcing the reader to interpret everything as a recondite reference to something else, resemble those perspective trick pictures, known as "anamorphoses," which, to use Galileo's own words, "show a human figure when looked at sideways and from a uniquely determined point of view but, when observed frontally, as we naturally and normally do with other pictures, display nothing but a welter of line and colors from which we can make out, if we try hard, semblances of rivers, bare branches, clouds, or strange chimerical shapes." (Panofsky 1954: 13)

So far I have not changed in any substantive way the overall picture presented in *Control of the Imaginary*, but simply attempted to spell out more explicitly the reason for control and the different way in which it applied to painting. In addition, by relating the area where it is central— that of verbal language—to pictorial space, where it is less visible and less crucial, we see more clearly why the Renaissance was not a uniform period.

Even with these qualifications, the central question of our investigation has not yet found enough support in the best literature on the Renaissance. The (apparent) novelty of my endeavor would be flattering if, on the other hand, it were not worrisome. In fact, in an unpretentious work, Vernon Hall's *Renaissance Literary Criticism*, we find passages that express a position similar to mine. Here, for instance, the author compares Renaissance and neoclassical critics: "Order was the desideratum in both sets of literary critics, and literature was looked upon as a means of promoting an ordered society where everything and everybody would have an assigned place. The ideal of order in the Renaissance is almost Byzantine in its desire for hierarchical rigidity" (Hall 1959: 13). By stressing the extreme need for order shared by Renaissance and neoclassical critics, the passage implicitly underscores a link that deserves investigation: that between Renaissance aspirations and the political program that culminated in Louis XIV's absolutism.

The fruitfulness of Hall's insight becomes even clearer in a later passage:

Conscious of chaos and searching for form, the Renaissance critics took an authoritarian position. Laws were necessary, and in Horace and Aristotle they believed they had found them. . . . The hierarchical society they idealized was transferred to literary criticism in the hierarchy of genres, and as the distinction in life was one of social position, so the differences between the genres were determined by the class of the characters and subject matter treated. (P. 15)

Unfortunately, however, throughout the rest of the book the author treats his subject along traditional lines: the historical background is dealt with in the introduction, while the subject proper is exploited in the rest of the book. The question of control of imagination is, so to speak, projected onto the historical conditions, as if they *determined* the control. Renaissance poetical theory is repressive because the historical conditions favored an authoritarian order. With no mediation, a form of political control determines the character of contemporary cultural production.

Though the expository advantages of this kind of treatment cannot be denied, its fault seems to lie in the fact that it does not investigate the mediation between the level of power in general and that of the power exerted over poetry by the compilers of treatises. Thus the author misses the opportunity not only to gain a more concrete insight into the problems that "literature" faced at the time but also to understand why the emphasis on eloquence was less a consequence of the force of tradition than of the fact that eloquence could serve as an antagonist for the criterion of fiction—or, ideally, could be developed directly from Aristotle's *Poetics*. In addition, Hall fails to consider the example of control that Renaissance critics gave to future generations. For it is not just the authoritarian or would-be authoritarian state that has felt the need to tame imagination. Nevertheless, Hall's scheme at least has the merit of countering the mythical-liberal tradition usually associated with the term "Renaissance." Instead of a plenteous, radiant world, albeit infested with despots and strongmen, in which the individual could fully enjoy his earthly existence and indulge his wanderlust, we have a world subject to tensions. To André Chastel, this tension was caused mostly by the opponents of the Humanists, who thought that the Humanist endeavor was useless for moral life and dangerous for faith; the same accusation was raised against those who, like Petrarch, Ficino, and Erasmus, attempted to reconcile knowledge of antiquity with the Christian moral order, as well as against those Humanists who were little inclined to commit themselves fully to a Christian life (see Chastel 1945: 49).

These tensions help us to understand the reason for control. Its proponents were trying, rather consciously, to resolve the contradiction experienced by those who intended to preserve their delight in the world and in art without allowing freedom of imagination. Abolition of this delight was the goal of only the absolutely orthodox; freedom of the imagination was a proposal to be found hardly anywhere except in the notebooks of Leonardo. As a form of thematization that sets out by bracketing off the world—that is, by a priori denying existence any validity—the imaginary is inevitably seen as a threat to any system based on the singleness of a given truth; it is not the principle of truth, not even truth understood as adequacy to things, which in itself is hostile to the imaginary's denying power, but specifically the postulate that there is only one truth.

If we accept this interpretation, it is easier to understand what happened with the emergence of Protestantism and the beginning of the wars of religion. The need for control became much more intense. Its signs can be seen even outside the scope of art theory. Hall mentions the case of Pietro Pomponazzi, who in 1516 proved that the soul and the intellect were material and therefore could not survive the body's destruction. However, Pomponazzi was careful to add that, as a Christian, he was not allowed to accept the theory he defended as a philosopher (see Hall 1950: 96). The example of Erasmus is also relevant here. Recognized, and sometimes reviled, for his attempt to reconcile Protestant reformers and the Roman Church, respected as a Humanist who tried to harmonize intellectual activity and a religious posture, Erasmus, after the definitive breach with Luther, became a vocal critic of what he felt to be the paganism of Humanists. The cult of Cicero, he wrote, made Humanists ridiculous, and also exposed them to a much more serious charge: that their libraries were full of pagan works, but contained no Christian images (see Erasmus 1908: 75). The seriousness of this accusation is obvious when one remembers that similar ones led to punishment at the hands of the Inquisition. Now, many Renaissance treatises of poetics were written or at least published after the religious crisis had intensified. Thus the need for a compromise between poetry and Church doctrine must have been imperative.

The case of Scaliger is instructive. For political reasons, he was early forced to emigrate to the southwest of France. Although as a doctor and Humanist he became one of the notables of the town of Agen, in 1538

Scaliger was denounced to the Inquisition. He came off almost entirely unharmed—R. M. Ferraro, his biographer, writes that there must have been acquaintances or friends of his among the judges; however, when he proposed to write a treatise of poetics, late in life, it seems likely that he found it necessary to be extremely prudent. If this is borne in mind, it seems almost courageous of him to state that poetry cannot be condemned for its language since ornaments and tropes can also be found in the Scriptures (see Hall 1950: 122; Ferraro 1971: 50). (In the following century, Sor Juana Inés de la Cruz would use a similar argument in defense of her right to write secular poetry.) The relevance of this incident is more than just biographical, for it helps us to distinguish between two categories often confused: control and censorship. If Scaliger preferred to risk his own safety rather than conceal a legitimate justification for poetry, we cannot take any of his statements on the subject as the views of a censor. Censorship is, above all, an act, wherever it may draw on for support. Control is, above all, a compromise with the dominant order and reason. Censorship hinders, prohibits, destroys. Control proposes a negotiation at first: fiction is permitted as long as it respects certain limits—as long as it does not show itself to be fictional. Scaliger is not a censor, but he is clearly a controller. When a controller's ideas coincide with those of the institution, control may change into outright censorship, and the postulation of a control may function at the same time as a prohibition. More often than not, however, control is better represented as the sword of Damocles, powerful because of what it threatens.

CONTROL UNDER ABSOLUTISM

In the second half of the sixteenth century, the political stability of European nations was affected primarily by two factors: first, inflation in commodity prices, a consequence of the increasing amounts of gold and silver as circulating media; and second, the wars of religion that erupted as a reaction to the Protestant Reformation.

The conjugation of these two factors called for strong, centralized states, governed by absolute power. Thus the precondition for absolutism is the existence of national political unity. The lack of such unity was the reason for Italian decline, which began in the late sixteenth century: at first Italy became associated with the political interests of Catholic reaction, headed by Spain, and largely subject to direct Spanish rule; then, in the latter half of the seventeenth century, Italy was relegated to a secondary position as a political power. Its fragmentation into viceroyalties, principalities, duchies, and republics made it not only vulnerable to the

Turkish threat and to Spanish and French expansionism but also unable to preserve the cultural leadership it had wielded since the quattrocento. Nations without political unity were no match for unified nations; with it, they could face their political woes with some hope. Thus the Netherlands, although subject to Spain and then to French expansionism under the Sun King, was able to recover to such an extent that before the seventeenth century was over it rivaled England as a maritime power.

Italian decline was accompanied by the gradual ascension of France. Under Louis XIII (1601–43), with Cardinal de Richelieu as prime minister, absolutism—which had begun earlier, during the reign of Francis I— grew stronger and crushed the prerogatives of the aristocracy, though not without meeting the spirited resistance of the nobles. The final act took place at the time of Louis XIV's minority, with the episode of the Fronde. Since political history interests us only to the extent that it helps us to understand the control of imagination, for the moment let us focus on the single factor that favored royal power.

The influx of bullion, most of it coming from Spanish America, had increased the amount of money in circulation, which in its turn had raised the value of movable wealth, of commodities. Since the fortune of the nobility was based on landed property and on the taxes paid by those who worked the land, inflation had an immediate impact on the old nobility. Although royal houses also derived income from their property, they were not affected by inflation. The reason was that, since internecine struggle among noble houses made it necessary for them to rely on an authority that would protect them against the ambition of rival houses and at the same time preserve their privileges, the economic crisis, aggravated by the religious struggle, stimulated the growth of royal prerogatives. This came in the form of higher taxes and more commerce in public offices and in concession rights. Thus the decrease in the value of land did not affect the income of royal houses. In addition, the prices fetched by products helped the development of trade and industry, which in turn required a bigger state apparatus: "The expansion of trade cannot be understood without the increased state protection of trade routes and increasing legal protection for merchants, and vice versa. Without sufficient troops kings could not expect a secure income from taxation, nor would they have the troops without the income" (Elias 1983: 155).

This state of affairs made the king's situation more and more favorable. Since the proclamation of his majority, in 1651, and particularly since Cardinal Mazarin's death, Louis XIV (1638–1715) had become, much more than a balancing factor for noble houses, a shrewd manipulator of social forces. Instead of saving the nobility, threatened by declining land revenues, a situation made even worse by bad harvests, Louis XIV adopted a policy of strengthening and enlarging the machinery of state. The immediate justification for this was, besides the fear of another Fronde, the need to contain Spain, France's rival. Although in 1643 French armies had defeated Spanish troops, until then said to be invincible, the conflict dragged on up to 1659, at the least, or to 1667, when France put an end to Spanish rule in the Netherlands. But the wars abroad were the effect rather than the cause of the king's policy against his nobles.

It was a part of this policy to increase administrative offices, carefully excluding aristocrats from them:

Everywhere outside France, the machine of the State was still rudimentary, and what machinery there was was often controlled by great noble families, more feudal than royal in character. By her example, France showed how the power of *les grands* could be curtailed, how the king could make himself independent of Estates and great families alike, how he could become absolute, basing his power on a bureaucracy and a standing army. (Carsten 1961: 11)

This policy had not begun with the Sun King. Norbert Elias notes that, toward the late sixteenth century, most posts in the judicial system, in administration, and in the ministries had been taken from the hands of the nobility and handed over to the bourgeoisie (see Elias 1983: 167). Nonetheless, it was under Louis XIV that the policy became explicit, even as many ancient noble manors fell into disrepair. With the authority of a contemporary observer, Jean de La Bruyère wrote: "If certain dead persons came back to life and saw their great names and their best land, with their castles and their old houses, in the possession of people whose fathers were perhaps their tenants [*métayers*], what opinion should they form of our century?" (La Bruyère 1962: 186).

The king's policy consisted in attracting the newly rich bourgeois to his service, encouraging them to purchase offices, so that the upper stratum of the class would become a *noblesse de robe*. But Louis XIV had no intention of being a "bourgeois king," or of reconciling—as it was later said of the English monarchy after the Glorious Revolution—the bourgeois *ratio* with an aristocratic order. Rather, absolutist policy was characterized by its intention to subject all classes to the power of a single ruler, one able to maintain political stability while making everyone dependent on his personal and undelegated decisions. For this, an extremely strong government was needed, with a powerful fiscal machinery and an army capable not only of crushing popular discontent—in Louis XIV's case, exemplified by the peasant revolts—but also of being feared abroad.

French absolutism had two consequences. First, unlike English and Dutch absolutism, it created no effectively bourgeois *ratio*: "The road to great wealth lay as yet not in trade and industry, but rather in the royal finances, while much of the capital acquired in trade and industry was drained off into the purchase of *rentes*, of official posts, of land and titles" (Lough 1961: 227). Since the king's policy was to attract the upper bourgeoisie to his service, an ambitious man with no money had as his highest goal to amass a fortune so that either he or a descendant of his could invest the capital in the acquisition of a profitable and prestigious office. Then all that was needed was a marriage to some member of a noble family, to wash the stain of plebeian blood. Wrote La Bruyère, maliciously: "If a financier fails in his coup, courtiers mutter: 'He is a bourgeois, a nobody, a vulgarian'; if he is successful, they ask them for his daughter's hand" (La Bruyère 1962: 181).

The status of nobleman—that is, one who lives off one's income and royal favor—was encouraged, as opposed to the bourgeois *ratio*. Although the social consequences of this factor are evident, from our viewpoint it is the second consequence of absolutist policy that deserves emphasis. It is that the nobility had to choose between two alternatives: either preserve their independence, remaining in their dominions, or give up their autonomy and put their luck and connections to work at Versailles. "Alternatives," though, is not quite the word, for it seems to suggest that the advantages of the two choices were equivalent. This was not quite the case. For a nobleman, preserving his independence carried the risk of impoverishment, for it was impossible to balance his budget on a declining income. Besides, this was not a risk run only by those who were totally improvident; on the contrary, it might well be called inevitable. Given the sumptuary ethos of the estate society, choosing not to flaunt one's wealth and not to entertain lavishly meant excluding oneself from good society, the only society in which much-needed extra income was to be found. Though not considering all these subtleties, La Bruyère wrote, under the heading "Des Biens de fortune": "The most immediate cause of the ruin and misery of persons of the two conditions, *noblesse de robe* and *noblesse d'épée*, is that only social standing, not wealth, regulates expenses" (p. 203).

Securing a position in the court, submitting to the complex etiquette of court life, being seen by the king—these were indispensable conditions for the nobleman who wished to live the right life, which was necessarily a life of leisure, for if he were nominated to public office, it would be a secondary post or else a position abroad. If we are to understand the appeal of the *cour* to noblemen, we must bear in mind that its *ratio*, based on status and prestige, was quite distinct from bourgeois calculation:

The competitive pressure for status, prestige and power in this society is no less strong than competition for capital and economic power in industrial societies. Apart from inheritances, rich marriages and favours from the king or other great courtiers, loans were the means most readily available to people in this position to maintain their accustomed status-consumption, in the short term when their income falls. (Elias 1983: 73)

Consequently, aristocrats quit their dominions and went to live in Paris, knowing that the best they could hope for was to live in a room in the royal palace. Only through personal contact with the sovereign or prestige among his favorites could a nobleman be in a position to compete with his peers and rivals, to acquire a prebend or a diplomatic or military post. The situation was the same for the upper clergy. Ever since the Concordat of 1516, the Crown reserved the privilege of appointing occupants of prominent ecclesiastical offices. Consequently, Church dignitaries were not exempted from the submission imposed on other members of the nobility:

Most of the archbishops and bishops were first and foremost great noblemen who spent as much of the year as they could, not in the dioceses, but in their Paris mansions and the antechambers of Versailles, enjoying the social life of the capital and keeping themselves in the king's eye, on the watch for preferment or fresh favours for themselves, and for other members of their families. (Lough 1961: 225)

In short, the court included all who, whether their origins were noble or bourgeois, might threaten or overshadow absolute power. The bigger the potential strength of the threat, the more it was necessary to impose submission; and the more complete the submission, the more secure one's status.

The court, then, softened the virulence of the old aristocracy and the new aggressiveness of the bourgeoisie. Organized in the disciplined, gossipy ranks of *noblesse d'épée* and *noblesse de robe*, noblemen and bourgeois now made up what Erich Auerbach called "an integrated unity."

What are the consequences of this social shaping for the question of control? Contrary to what we have seen in connection with the Renaissance, where the liberal myth makes it difficult to accept the idea that there was a control exerted on art, the meaning of absolutism is so unmistakable that it would be strange indeed if it had left no marks in the field of literary expression. True, none of it transpires in Voltaire's famous *Le Siècle de Louis XIV*, which instead emphasizes the solar image of the central character: "A good father, a good lord, always decent in public, hard-working at his office, scrupulous in business, fair in his judgments, fluent of speech and kindly with dignity" (Voltaire 1968: 950). But this personal myth had no effect on the authoritarian image of his reign. Given this fact, my expository strategy in this section must necessarily differ from the procedure adopted in the previous one: the task now is not to stress the presence of a control, which is evident, but rather to find the marks of the relative change it suffered, as well as to show the surprising manner in which absolutism made it possible for a reflection conducive to an understanding of fictionality to arise among the excluded sector of the nobility (see below, the third section of this chapter).

At first, it seems as if the approach to imagination in seventeenth-century France was no different from that of Italian preceptists. Like them, the French were concerned particularly with dramatic poetry, specifically with elegant language; the discipline imposed on language and the requisite refinement was to move it away from the freedom of expression and the plebeian vein cultivated by Rabelais; furthermore, the Italians were admittedly the masters of the French, who inherited from them the precepts relative to the unities of time, place, and action. Also like the Italians, the French authors knew the care they should take where religious subjects were concerned. To Vauquelin de La Fesnaye (1575–1605), the best solution would be for lay writers to avoid them outright:

> Car ce n'est pas notre intention
> De mêler la religion
> Dans le sujet des choses feintes;
> Aussi jamais les Lettres saintes
> Ne furent donnés de Dieu
> Pour en faire après quelque jeu.
> (Quoted in Arnaud 1888: 19)

> For it is not our intention
> To mix religion
> With the matter of feigned things;
> Nor were the Holy Scriptures
> Given to us by God
> To be used in any playful way.

But the poet's caution was not enough. Religious power wanted to be respected even where worldly subjects were involved. It was not only religion that must be preserved, it was not only its values that must be protected, but also the reason of the upper strata of society. So it was that Renaissance poetics was not content to treat imitation as the central category, but threw in verisimilitude and decorum for good measure. In other words: under the guise of the religious argument we find the rationalism of the courtier, the scholar, the refined man trying to protect himself from vulgar tastes. With extraordinary insight, Auerbach saw this when he wrote that the verisimilitude prescribed at this time "combined the arrogant rationalism that refuses to be fooled by imaginative illusion with contempt for the *indocte et stupide vulgaire*, which is peacefully willing to be taken in by it" (Auerbach 1984: 158). The relations of compromise between religious doctrine and upper-stratum rationalism will now be inverted, so that the latter will lose its dominant position. But this is not an overnight change.

The earliest document in which this change is reflected is George de Scudéry's *L'Apologie du théâtre*, published in 1639. This brief, 99-page treatise, most of it devoted to a description of theatrical practice in antiquity, presents no doctrinal innovations vis-à-vis its cinquecento counterparts. Its most interesting feature is that it underscores the continuing opposition to the use of poetry, particularly in drama. This gives Scudéry an opportunity to elaborate a set of variations on the Horatian theme of edification and delight.

Without a combination of these two elements, he writes in the preface, Plato would have been right to banish poets, for they would have no better occupation than that of jesters. However, those who are opposed to poetry fail to see that "of all manners of instruction, it is surely the most pleasant, and thus the most useful" (Scudéry 1639: 3). For just as patients would rather be cured with sweet medicine, people "want to be persuaded rather than ordered about" (p. 4). Therefore authorities should defend poetical practice and purge it of its vices, with all the more reason because poetry is composed of words, and "the ear is surely that sense which, among all others, is closest to the seat of the understanding and reason, which is the brain; although it is also the one that can corrupt the soul most easily, when what one receives through it is not good" (p. 6).

Although Scudéry's argument is restricted to the theater, his historical survey shows that he is not concerned solely with dramatic poetry: "I might also add that poetry has always been the language of laws, of oracles, of sibyls, and of prophets, and, according to some, of the gods.... If we go further back in time we shall find that a glorious attribute of Thales of Miletus, one of the seven whom Greece chose to call wise, was that of lyrical poet" (pp. 40–41).

The passages quoted make it clear that Scudéry was an absolute nullity as a theoretician, and, since he emphasizes his participation in the controversy over *Le Cid*, that he is quite mediocre as a critic. But none of this diminishes the interest of his *Apologie* as evidence that poetry was in need of defenders.

Another document is significant in this context: an official proclamation signed by the powerful Richelieu, a protector of the theater. The proclamation, of April 16, 1641, is decisive evidence not only of the contradictions that characterized theatrical practice but also of the care taken to control it. These two reasons justify a rather lengthy excerpt:

Our fear lest the comedies that are usefully staged for the entertainment of the public be sometimes accompanied by dishonest productions, which leave bad impressions in people's minds, has led us to issue such orders as will avoid these inconveniences. For these reasons . . . all comedians are forbidden to represent any dishonest actions, subject to the penalty of being declared infamous and other punishments applicable in such cases; . . . and should the aforementioned comedians transgress our present proclamation, we enjoin our aforementioned judges to interdict their theater and start against them such procedures as they deem necessary . . . and should the aforementioned comedians regulate their theatrical performances in such a way that they are wholly exempt from blemish, we will that their activities, which can provide our people with innocent diversion from unwholesome occupations, be free of censure, and cause no damage to their reputation in public commerce. (Quoted in Barras 1933: 63)

In his twofold role as religious and political authority, Louis XIII's prime minister was well aware that he could not indiscriminately denounce all plays and authors, as the medieval Church had done; he was also aware, however, that he must not tolerate the abuses of "réprésentations peu honnêtes." To protect the theater was, in fact, to control it, just as to defend the purity of the language—one of the goals of the Académie Française, founded in 1634—was to control it so as to avoid forms of popular speech. In the case of the theater, the cardinal's concern was not limited to this proclamation only, which was in fact part of a wider policy: to reform the theater. Richelieu, it seems, had intended to assign this task to a man he trusted: Abbé D'Aubignac, preceptor of one of his nephews. As a biographer of D'Aubignac wrote, "a cardinal who was also a writer of comedies would not hesitate to nominate a priest to the office of supervisor of public performances . . . thinking perhaps that a churchman would be in a better position than any other to submit the theater to the law, or at least to Church morality" (Arnaud 1888: 186). However, D'Aubignac was unlucky; his protector died before naming him for the office he desired. All that he could do then was to write *Dissertation sur la condemnation des théâtres* (1644) and *Pratique du théâtre* (1657). Although the *Pratique* was famous in its time, it is the *Dissertation* that is relevant here, not because it is an important work, but because of the light it sheds on its time.

Though there are no significant differences vis-à-vis the *Apologie*, the *Dissertation* has the advantage of submitting its argument to a more detailed examination. The abbé begins by asking whether the Church's condemnation of the theater should be maintained. Two reasons ought to be taken into account: first, in antiquity, all games and spectacles were part of the *religion payenne*; second, "everything there was mysterious and sacred"; that is, was subordinate to and consistent with paganism (D'Aubignac 1644: 3). In chapter 2, after examining the religious origin of comedy and tragedy, he reinforces the first reason: "Demosthenes wrote that to engage in musical or theatrical games is to worship the god Bacchus" (p. 42). Likewise, he argues, in justification of the second reason: "And this consideration has led a sage of our times to say that the pagans had three theologies: that of priests in their temples, that of philosophers in schools, and that of poets in theaters" (p. 53).

Then D'Aubignac begins to state his own position. The title of chapter 3 declares: "The ancient Fathers of the Church forbade Christians to be present at theatrical games because that would amount to taking part in idolatry." However, the author adds, what was right then is no longer the case now, for "what was once a sacrilege is now no more than a pleasant form of public entertainment, which is no crime in this respect" (p. 91). The same works, once sacrilegious, have become admirable and acceptable because in them one can find "the poet's inventions and the actors' beautiful declamation" (p. 95).

In chapter 4, D'Aubignac concludes his defense of the theater. In the following chapters he continues his historical investigation. The condemnation of the theater in antiquity was restricted to plays that contained "discours malhonnestes" ("lewd discourses") and shameless actors; though buffoons and mimes were held in bad repute, they were not confused with comedians and tragic actors. In chapter 9 he repeats that, among the Romans, "seulement les Histrions ou les Basteleurs" ("only buffoons and mountebanks") were considered infamous.

In short, D'Aubignac attempted not only to liberate theater but also to dignify the occupation of actor. If we recall the difficulties faced by Molière all the way to his burial, we tend to think that the author of *Pratique du théâtre* was more successful in the former intent than in the latter. But this is not relevant here. D'Aubignac's success, if any, was his contribution to the control of dramatic poetry, a control that was still based on a religious argument. However, we cannot grasp Scudéry's and D'Aubignac's position simply by reading their treatises. We must also consider their involvement in the debate concerning Pierre Corneille's *Le Cid*.

In 1637, the staging of *Le Cid* provoked an illuminating controversy. Scudéry and D'Aubignac were among Corneille's denouncers. Both presented detailed analyses; Scudéry studied the play and its language, while D'Aubignac concentrated on the latter. Since they agree with each other, I will limit myself to a few short observations on Scudéry's text. His basic strategy is to accuse the play of being improbable.

With a presumption that was to have followers, he pontificates: "The poet whose purpose is to stir the spectator's passions through those of the characters, however lively, strong, and well produced they may be, can never hope to achieve his intent, if judicious, when what he would impress upon the soul is improbable" (Scudéry 1862: 443). Apparently the author is resorting to the old Italian category of verisimilitude. In fact, there is a major difference here. For the Renaissance theoreticians, verisimilitude, although polished by decorum, was in service of *imitatio*. Here, instead, verisimilitude depends on decorum, *bienséance*, and this, in turn, is reinforced by respect to *bon sens* and good morals. Not that the author says as much explicitly. But this is clearly what he means when he points to what he considers the major flaw in Corneille's play:

Here a heartless daughter speaks only of her follies, when she ought to speak of her misfortune; complains of the loss of her lover, when she ought to think only of the loss of her father; loves still him whom she ought to hate; tolerates, at the same time and in the same house, this murderer and this poor body; and, to culminate her impiety, joins her hand to that which still drips with her father's blood. After such a horrifying crime, is not the spectator right to expect a bolt to appear out of heaven, actually represented onstage, to punish this Danaid? Or, if he is aware of another rule that forbids blood in the theater, is not he to believe that, as soon as she leaves, at the very least a messenger will come and inform him of such punishment? But neither one thing nor the other happens; on the contrary, a king caresses a hussy, so that her vice seems to be rewarded, and virtue seems banished from the denouement of the poem; it is a lesson in evil, an incitement for wickedness, and, with these astonishing and harmful faults, it is directly opposed to the principal dramatic rules. (P. 446)

One might argue that the enraged critic remains within the ethicoreligious frame of reference, and that his indignation is aroused by the playwright's violation of the moral code of society. However, note that Scudéry argues that Corneille's offense is against verisimilitude, understood as the idealized representation of human actions. True, we have already pointed out that in the Renaissance, *imitatio* was taken in a basically Horatian sense, in which moral idealization prevailed. But contemporary judgment showed that the basic categories had changed by then. Invited to join in the polemic, the Académie expresses its position in *Sentiments de l'Académie sur Le Cid*. Although not entirely in agreement with Scudéry, the Académie not only endorses his denouncement of the play for its lack of verisimilitude but also explains what verisimilitude should be taken to mean. This concept is no longer to be taken as derived from the idea of truthfulness; instead, good sense and decorum set a clear boundary. Verisimilitude is respected to the extent that it purifies truth, abandoning or correcting it when it would not be acceptable to propagate it. The Académie expresses its position first in a generic statement, then in its practical application:

As to the reason why verisimilitude rather than truthfulness should be taken as the goal of epic and dramatic verse, it is because this art, its purpose being useful pleasure, finds it easier to lead man hither by way of verisimilitude, which finds no resistance in them, than by way of truthfulness, which can be so strange and terrible that men might refuse to be persuaded or guided by it. . . . *We hold that not all truths are good for the theater, and that some are like these enormous crimes whose records the judges order to be burned, together with the criminals.* (*Sentiments* 1862: 468; emphasis added)

Thus, even before the heyday of absolutism, the court imposed a new limit on the theater in order to reform it. The official text determines: authors must realize that the verisimilitude required of them is to be found less in the imitation of nature than in compatibility with "good morals." Significantly, the text of the *Sentiments* contains the expression "bonnes moeurs" but not, unless I overlooked it, "bon sens." That is because its paradigm was still a court not much permeated with bourgeois values. But from the good morals recommended it is only a short step to good sense. Like good sense, good morals include clarity, whose absence in Corneille, according to D'Aubignac, gives rise to "ces obscurités vicieuses et ces embarras importuns" ("these faulty obscurities and annoying awkwardnesses") (D'Aubignac 1971: 513).

The dissociation of verisimilitude from truth and its subordination to decorum has to do with the very spirit of absolutism. In his memorable *Kritik und Krise*, R. Koselleck shows that absolutist centralism justified itself by offering to put an end to religious conflicts; thus its theoreticians could no longer justify the prince's actions based on a strict religious code. "Whereas religious parties drew their strength from sources outside of the prince's control, princes could not impose themselves on those who broke the primacy of religion" (Koselleck 1976: 13). But this made it necessary to violate the primacy of individual conscience, which provided justification for religious conflict, and instead postulate, with Hobbes, the separation between private and public man. If privately each man could follow his own principles, publicly, as citizens, all had to obey the prince's law. Consequently, "the neutralization of conscience by politics favors secularization of morals" (p. 31). This is what is involved in the change that religious control introduced in the debate over the theater.

In short, Scudéry's and D'Aubignac's participation in the debate clearly shows the sort of theater reform they favored. Plays should be written in clear, refined language, obeying the rules the Italians had "drawn from" Aristotle, of which verisimilitude and decorum now predominated—that is, those rules most adequate to absolutist reason. Once again: verisimilitude, no longer the actualization of the *beau naturel*, now had to adjust itself to decorum. In the words of a contemporary, "it is not repugnant to reasonable belief . . . , to common sense" (quoted in Corneille 1971: 700).

But how did playwrights themselves react? For today we know that their critics were mediocre figures, now of interest only to specialists. In order to see that the position of these mediocre critics was far from irrelevant, we need only consider the prefaces and critical texts written by Corneille, Racine, and Molière. (For reasons of space, I will concentrate on Corneille and leave Molière out.)

In 1660, already a renowned artist, the controversy over *Le Cid* far behind him, Corneille published his theoretical reflections on dramatic art. The prudent and moderate position he adopts would be unthinkable if the reason defended by his adversaries were not politically powerful. By and large, Corneille is not opposed either to the use of the rules or to the habitual reading of Aristotle and Horace, but only to their mechanical utilization, so to speak. This is the playwright's subtle way of manifesting his dissent. Thus, for instance, concerning the properties that characters' morals must present, he writes: "If I be allowed to set forth my conjectures on what Aristotle enjoins [concerning morals], I believe it is the brilliant and elevated character of virtuous or criminal morals, according to what is proper and adequate to the person introduced" (Corneille 1971: 22).

Here, I believe, the implicit tension between the author's position and that of the controllers is quite perceptible. Because they obeyed the norms of good society, fearing lest they should endorse plays that might come to provoke "public sorrows," as the *Sentiments de l'Académie* puts it, or offend the susceptibilities of the religious authorities, the controllers condemned any character or action that could serve as a bad example. Corneille, on the other hand, was closer to Aristotle's actual position, and was more concerned with the consistency of the play. Thus "brilliant and elevated character" and "a noble soul" are not incompatible with wicked or even criminal acts. What really counts is that everything onstage be functional, "so that we do not show in the theater anything that is vicious or criminal unless as is made necessary by the theme we are dealing with" (p. 24). If this was to be the proper reading of Aristotle, controllers would have to adopt a different patron saint. But Corneille realized that control was a fact, one that could not be demolished by solid arguments; so he knew that the best he could do was to find loopholes for the imaginary. Although the autonomy of art is still a distant thought, in Corneille the tension between "aesthetic" interests and the power of control is already quite visible. The very fact that absolutism had to fight religious power and defend reason—which, however, found its fullest expression only in privacy—made this tension all the more imminent (see below, the third section of this chapter).

Aware of the struggle he is engaged in and of his own powerlessness to defend his position, Corneille uses this same strategy of compromise in his *Discours des trois unités*, also published in 1660. He accepts the validity of the unity of time, disagreeing with those who find it "tyrannical"; such a judgment could not be true, since this unity is based on "Aristotle's authority" and, more importantly, on "natural reason." Having conceded as much, he raises a qualification, which clarifies his own position: "I would prefer to leave the duration to the audience's imagination and never determine the length of time implied, unless the theme makes this necessary" (Corneille 1971: 65). He employs the same tactic in relation to unity of space. If he rejects as "un peu licensieuse" the opinion of those who find no justification for it in Aristotle or Horace, he adds that it is necessary to interpret this rule with a certain amount of flexibility.

The same prudence marks Racine's prefaces—not to mention his polemic against the Jansenist Pierre Nicole's *Visionnaires* (1665). Racine is even more accommodating than Corneille. In his preface to *Andromaque*, his defense is based on nothing more solid than irony: "The public's reaction has been far too favorable for me to be upset by the irritation of two or three persons, who would reform all the heroes of antiquity in order to change them into perfect heroes" (Racine 1980). And in his preface to *Phèdre* not even irony is used. As if aware of the more serious risk he now faces, he does no more than stress his conformity to moral standards:

Here the slightest faults are severely punished; the very idea of crime is seen with as much horror as the crime itself; the frailties of love are shown as frailties indeed; the passions are presented to the eye only to show all the disorder they cause; and vice is everywhere portrayed in the colors that make all its deformity visible. This should be the goal of every man who works for the public, and it is what the early tragic poets had in mind above all. (Racine 1980: 578)

This concession—not to mention the ending of his version of the myth, rendered less "criminal"—was an attempt to make it easier to accept the play's delving into the abyss of incestuous love, complicated by the fact that, in Racine, Phaedra is also moved by the contradictory desire to help her own son in Theseus's succession. Indeed, as theater moved away from Corneille's exploitation of the tragic-heroic mode, deepening psychological analysis instead, the tension between writers and official controllers could only increase. And what would happen when Molière transformed psychological observation into mockery and satire of highly placed social types? But this is not the angle that concerns me here. The well-known changes reflected in the works of Corneille, Racine, and Molière emphasize the growing importance of family life. The representation of noble (in both senses of the word) themes is little by little superseded by the interest in staging private—and therefore bourgeois—situations. This process is relevant here because it helps us to understand the changes undergone by control. Beginning in the Renaissance, religious and ethical control had corresponded to the dominance of aristocratic values. With the advent of absolutism, the growing importance of courtly society, subordinate to the king's decisions, brought into relief reasons of state and a more secular morality, highlighting good morals and a reinterpretation of the role of verisimilitude. In the latter half of the seventeenth century, Louis XIV's policies, neutralizing the class spirit of both the aristocracy and the stronger sector of the bourgeoisie and agglutinating them in *la cour et la ville*, were the crystallization of the relative change in controlling legislation. Control was grounded no longer on religious ethics but rather on *bon sens*. I do not mean that the former disappeared altogether or was not manifested in the new, modified control; the point is that religious ethics was no longer the only manifestation, or even the decisive one.

Evidence of the existence of dual controls and, what is more, of an antagonism between the two, is furnished by two familiar texts: Nicolas Boileau's *L'Art poétique* and J.-B. Bossuet's *Maximes et reflexions sur la comédie*. Let us begin with the *Maximes*, which represents the older form of control.

In 1694, when the great voices of classical French theater were already dead or silent and the reign of Louis XIV was in decline, the issue of the theater again came to the fore. An obscure priest, Père Caffaro, in a preface to the plays of Boursault, defended drama against the accusations of Scholastics and churchmen. This aroused a storm of indignation. In May 1694, the Faculty of Theology condemned the preface, and Bossuet, bishop of Meaux and the dauphine's preceptor, in a personal letter insisted that Caffaro retract or disallow his publication. Otherwise, Bossuet himself would see to it that he was punished (for further details, see Barras 1933: 119ff.). Although Caffaro was quick to explain that he had not authorized publication of the text, and Boursault himself confirmed it and apologized for having printed it on his own initiative. Bossuet was not appeased: in August he published his diatribe.

Now the men of the theater had to face not only the opposition of the strict Jansenists but also the wrath of the dauphine's preceptor. Rejecting Scudéry's and D'Aubignac's labored attempts to reconcile faith and fiction, Bossuet affirms that the two are incompatible. The actor's attitude toward passion, he writes, is the opposite of the true believer's:

What does an actor do when he wishes to represent a passion in a natural way but strive to recall as well as he can the passions he has felt, and which, were he a Christian, he would have drowned so completely in his penitential tears that they would never return to his spirit or, if they did, would only arouse his horror? Instead, in order to express them, he must revive them with all their lure and all their deceptive charms. (Bossuet 1828: 313)

The opprobrium attached to the actor, who is even denied a Christian burial, is wholly justified. Let us stop tampering, the bishop seems to be saying, with the Latin texts of Aquinas and other Church authorities.

Their teachings were clear and unmistakable. And Bossuet resorts to one of these authorities to deal his most effective blow:

> We must, writes St. Augustine, distinguish, in the workings of our senses, the need, the use, the vividness of a sensation, and, finally, the delight in it. Of these four qualities of the senses, the first three are the work of the Creator . . . but it is in the midst of this work of God that the forced delight in sensible pleasure and its uncontrollable attraction, to wit, in the lust introduced by sin, establishes its seat.
> (Bossuet 1828: 324)

There can be no compromise between Christian virtue and an activity that necessarily heightens what is reprehensible in the senses. But not even the bishop of Meaux has any intention of promoting a total purge; instead of proposing that all theaters be banned outright, as his severity would lead one to expect, he says he would be satisfied if they were "very few" (p. 380). In any case, this attitude of religious intolerance was anachronistic. For all the anathemas and condemnations from Church dignitaries who were encouraged by Bossuet's attitude, "the clergy's constant attacks against the stage seem to have had little effect on the patrons of the theater" (Barras 1933: 131). For absolutism could not accept that government policy be dictated by any subordinate group. Even though the king did not have as much room for maneuvering as in earlier decades, the classical theory of compromise remained intact. That is, control was not transformed into censorship.

The *Maximes et reflexions sur la comédie* shows clearly what classical theory had tried to disguise. In this sense, it can be taken as expressing the polar opposite of the position first stated by Boccaccio in his *Genealogia*. More importantly, it is the swan song of religious control. This is not to say that its power died or that, where the Reformation triumphed, it became more tolerant. But another social force had appeared and proposed a different form of control. This is borne out by Boileau's influential *L'Art poétique*.

Like his contemporaries, Boileau also paid tribute to the Italian preceptists. Like them, he was also concerned about the purity of the language and horrified by vulgar speech. But the Italians are not the objects of his devotion. To "l'éclatante folie" of Tasso and Ariosto, Boileau counterposes the cult of reason: "aimez donc la raison." And reason here means above all *bon sens*. When good sense is neglected, language is invaded by the grating trivialities of marketplace speech:

> Au mépris du Bon Sens . . .
> On ne vit plus en vers que pointes triviales.
> Le Parnasse parla la language des Halles.
> (Boileau 1966: 159)

> In face of Good Sense . . .
> Only trivial points were to be found in verse.
> The Parnassus spoke the language of the marketplace.

L'Art poétique has another element in common with the Italians, and also another point of contention with them. Like the preceptists, Boileau respects the rules and praises François de Malherbe for this reason. But he diverges from the Italians in that he emphasizes clarity, the twin sister of good sense: "Ce que l'on conçoit bien s'énonce clairment" ("What is well conceived ought to be clearly stated"). Good sense and clarity now assume a predominant role in poetic art, being added to the rules to which drama must remain faithful.

> Mais nous, que la Raison à ses règles engage,
> Nous voulons qu'avec art l'Action se ménage:
> Qu'en un Lieu, qu'en un jour, un seul Fait accompli
> Tienne jusqu'à la fin le Theatre rempli.
> (P. 170)

> But we, whom Reason commits to her rules,
> We would have Action handled with art:
> That in a Place, in a day, a single Plot
> Will keep the Theater full to the end.

Even more important was imitation, the very cornerstone of the edifice. With Boileau, indeed, the concept is defined most clearly. Thus, combining the primacy of verisimilitude over truthfulness with the inevitable need to please the reader or spectator, Boileau writes:

> Jamais au Spectateur n'offrez rien d'incroyable.
> Le Vrai peut quelquefois n'estre pas vraisemblable.
> Une merveille absurde est pour moy sans appas.
> L'esprit n'est point emu de ce qu'il ne croit pas.
> (P. 170)

> Never offer the Spectator the unbelievable.
> Sometimes the True may not be plausible.
> To me, an absurd wonder has no appeal.
> The mind is never moved but by that which it believes.

The last line synthesizes the interpretation that had been given to imitation for centuries: imitation is seen in terms of similarity; our beliefs invest things with verisimilitude by making them similar to our expectations. In force since the Renaissance, this principle is evidence of the unity of the centuries we have been examining. Reason tames imagination; reason authorizes the imagination as long as it respects the boundaries set by reason. But in connection with unity of time, we should not forget a change for which *L'Art poétique* also provides evidence. Ethicoreligious precepts are no longer in the foreground. The care to be taken when dealing with religious matters is now basically a question of decorum. This decorum, it is true, must be obeyed strictly, or else one may end up on the scaffold. *Bienséance* is imperative, and not just because courtiers have delicate ears. It is no less true that, in Canto 3, Boileau forbids poets to use pagan figures in the treatment of a Christian theme. The rationale for this prohibition is that one must not make a puppet out of the true God—"Du Dieu de vérité, faire un Dieu de mensonge." But by now this is no more than the backdrop of control. The foreground has been taken over by secular principles, in response to secular needs: reason and good sense, and the clarity that brings them out. Provisionally neutralized in the unity of *la cour et la ville*, bourgeois rationalism, though it still sported an aristocratic peruke, had begun to take over the mechanisms of control. But before examining the changes undergone by control, which will be dealt with in the chapter on Diderot, let us look at an unexpected effect of absolutism.

THE OTHER SIDE OF THE QUESTION

An almost insurmountable obstacle must be faced by even the most experienced student: the more one becomes aware of the complexity of one's object, the more one is tempted to resort to an explanation that imitates simplicity—not to be confused with simplicity in exposition. This temptation, nowadays in any case, is related to market pressures that favor the production of texts for quick consumption, like so many disposable cigarette lighters.

A thing is said to be simple when its makeup is such that it can perform its functions with a minimum of operations. A diamond is the paramount example of simplicity: with no loss or effort, it will scratch and cut glass; with no delay, it will refract sunlight.

It is this kind of simplicity and its approximations that concern us here. In the case in point, the temptation of simplicity consists in the tendency to channel all the available data into a single device that would explain the control of imagination, explain how a given society, without renouncing the pleasures of the fictional or even of the merely fictitious, submits them to rules that allow them to interact with external reality.

Such an effort would be commendable but for the fact that ultimately what it offers us is a partial model, more rigid than the society we intended to describe in the first place. Could it be that something of the sort is occurring in our investigation? We have seen that, under absolutism, religious control of the fictional—indistinguishable from the fictitious, since in both of them verisimilitude was conceived as similarity—adapted to courtly reason and brought verisimilitude closer to decorum.

Thus, although religion remained as the ideological cement of society and control still invoked it, its principles were now predominantly secular: reason and good sense.

If I ended this discussion at this point, I would be presenting a parody of simplicity, proposing a model that counterfeits simplicity but lacks its effectiveness. To avoid this, let us recall Koselleck's thesis, mentioned above. His analysis stresses that the legitimation of absolutism was based on a precarious solution. By abolishing the privilege of religious motives, in order to put an end to the wars of religion and pacify Europe, and promoting the rights of reason, the logic of absolutism implied, however, a separation between the private individual and the citizen. Discussing Hobbes, the historian writes:

> In Hobbes, man is divided in two, a private and a public part; actions and acts are wholly submitted to the law of the State, but conviction is free, "in secret free." From now on it is possible for the individual to emigrate to conviction without being responsible for it. As it takes part in the world of politics, conscience is transformed into a controlling agent of the duty to obey. (Koselleck 1976: 29)

For our present purposes, this aspect is of the utmost importance because it highlights the ineffectiveness of the straitjacket into which reason forces itself, a narrowness that was to lead the Enlightenment, in the name of reason, to struggle for the reunification of the private and the public— that is, personal conviction and its political expression—in the individual. Now, even before we arrive at the eighteenth century, we can see that the shaky foundations of secularized reason could change into panic as experienced by groups that, for one reason or another, felt vulnerable or even excluded from relations with the world. That this is no whimsical hypothesis seems to be borne out by the experience of those who took part in the Fronde. On the other hand, if examination of this episode is to lead to the desired understanding, we must see it through the eyes of a group of authors who, though not all of them participated in this event, belong under the same heading. I refer to the so-called moralists: La Rochefoucauld (1613–80), La Bruyère (1645–96), and L. de C. Vauvenargues (1715–47). Examining their work, particularly that of La Rochefoucauld, a former Frondeur, we will arrive at a more complex view of the issue of control.

As to the chronological situation of the three, first of all we observe that, although La Rochefoucauld describes in his *Mémoires* (1662) the Fronde's struggle against absolutist absorption, all of them write from the vantage point of the defeated noble, now circumscribed within his dominions or reduced to the condition of an idle satellite at the court. Idle and melancholy, or idle and submissive, these men are, respectively, either excluded from government or eager to receive a sinecure or a small share of power. All of them frequent the salons and cultivate the art of conversation, the activities that have become the paramount ways of passing time and giving a meaning to their emptiness or their ambition. La Bruyère, the only one of the three who was not noble, a bourgeois who had a seat at court, left us in his *Caractères* (1688) an invaluable testimony to the importance of *causerie*. Conversation was not a mere skill. As we have seen in the case of Castiglione, it had to obey a sophisticated stylization, in which purity and appropriateness of speech functioned as emblems of adaptedness to the milieu. In the beginning of the chapter "De la societé et de la conversation," La Bruyère wrote:

Some people can be found who, in conversation or in what little commerce we may have with them, disgust us with their ridiculous expressions, the novelty and I daresay the unsuitableness of the terms they use, such as the combination of certain words that are not to be heard together except in their mouths, words that are made to signify what their original inventors never intended them to mean.

(La Bruyère 1962: 153)

The function of this stylization, required in the world of *la cour et la ville*, had to do with rhetoric rather than with normative grammar; and it would be a mistake to think that its purpose was to separate the elect from the *indocte et stupide multitude*. Refinement in speech was necessary because the way one spoke was thought to be a sure indicator of one's psychological makeup and, consequently, of one's morals: "It is a great misfortune not to have enough wit to speak well, nor enough judgment to be silent. Such is the source of all impertinence" (p. 159). What was involved was not "aesthetic" curiosity about one's neighbor's psychology, hidden secrets, or idiosyncrasies; nor was it a fathoming of other people's souls, motivated by the desire to find out what they would rather not confess. Note that La Bruyère is speaking of a privileged milieu, the world of those who observe each other in order to know more about their potential allies or rivals in politics or business. Sharp psychological observation was the indispensable defensive weapon for these men, forced into a situation of gilded parasitism. But of course observing others was not enough; one had to observe oneself as well, to know in detail one's own gestures and inflections, and not just one's articulate speech. In short, language and observation were converted into the art of dissimulation. Thus it was in these terms that La Bruyère defined the ideal *honnête homme*: "It is a well-known fact that every man of integrity is an *honnête homme*; but it is pleasant to think that not every *honnête homme* is a man of integrity" (p. 367).

On the other hand, introspection and psychological observation, in the world of the court, implied an inability to get along without the word of the king and his favorites. What, then, happened to those who were left out? Stretching the image somewhat, we can take Vauvenargues as a representative of this type, although he did nothing that might jeopardize his right to frequent courtly circles other than having been born too late and dying before his merits were recognized. But no stretching whatsoever is necessary to include in this category the former Frondeur, La Rochefoucauld.

Early on in his memoirs, his motivation to write is related to his political fall from grace. After the Fronde's ultimate defeat in 1652, La Rochefoucauld found it prudent to spend the following year abroad. He returned in 1654, and was allowed (a euphemism; in fact, he was enjoined) to retire to his estate in Poitou. It was only in 1659, two years before Mazarin's death, that he was permitted to return to Paris—though not, of course, to frequent the court. These are the years he refers to in his opening paragraph:

> I spent the last years of Cardinal Mazarin's ministry in the idleness that is the usual consequence of disgrace, and during this time I wrote about what I saw of the disturbances of the Regency. Although my fortune has changed since then, my idleness is none the less for it: I have decided to employ it in writing about the most remote events in which chance has often granted me a share.
> (La Rochefoucauld 1950: 35)

A member of one of the oldest families in the kingdom, La Rochefoucauld presents as his memoirs a record of his years in court. His great enemies are Cardinal de Richelieu and, after his death, Cardinal Mazarin. The choice of such formidable opponents was not at all a random one: La Rochefoucauld portrays himself as, from an early age, a would-be knight-errant, always ready to right wrongs and defend the weak (to be sure, only the weak among his peers).

Thus he will always side with those he thinks of as the victims of injustice and persecution. Under Richelieu, "in an age where there is such enthusiasm for extraordinary and impressive undertakings," he sides with the queen, accused of secretly conniving with Spain, France's rival. This same chivalrous strain had made him support the queen mother, Marie de Médicis. But he had done so with such ineptitude that, as he himself puts it in *Réflexions diverses*, Henry IV's widow later ended up "abandoned by the other kings, her sons, who did not dare as much as receive her in their States, and died destitute, almost starving, in Cologne, after ten years of persecution" (La Rochefoucauld 1950: 388). In the case of the queen, Louis XIII's wife, fortune was more favorable. But not for La Rochefoucauld. His zeal to defend the interests of his party turned into rejoicing over his enemies' defeat. Writing, in his *Mémoires*, of what he expected to achieve in his machinations in favor of the queen, he says his pleasure was all the greater because he was to "rid the queen, all at once, of the king her husband and Cardinal de Richelieu, who was jealous of her, and separate Mlle. de Hautefort from the king, who was in love with her" (p. 47). Not surprisingly, when the plot was discovered, the writer fell afoul of the king and his minister, and suffered his first exile.

The short passage transcribed above gives us a glimpse of the atmosphere at the court. Palace intrigue is the sole concern of the duke-to-be, and in this we are safe to assume that he was like all the others.

Thus, it is only natural that all courtiers should develop psychological ingenuity to the highest degree. Although in the *Mémoires* the author's interest lies elsewhere, in some passages we can see how the members of this world engaged wholeheartedly in the activity of deciphering others' intentions. For instance, referring to the queen at a moment when she was not suffering any misfortune and he could expect a reward for all the sacrifices that, however indirectly, she had imposed on him, La Rochefoucauld writes: "I should have suspected that she was not telling me the true reasons; but then, perhaps she herself did not know them well enough to tell me" (p. 65).

Probably unconsciously, the image he presents of himself is that of a fish that never grew used to its native waters, though it never knew any others; thus he is destined to describe passions, their mutability, the change of masks, rather than use them for his own purposes. Consistently with this involuntary choice, La Rochefoucauld describes the changes the queen undergoes when, with the death of her husband, the king, she becomes regent; and, in spite of his ill will toward Mazarin, he shows the cardinal's adroitness at manipulating passions so as to win in the end and make himself indispensable in the regent's eyes. Every time the astute cardinal scores a victory, the noble knight suffers a defeat; so that, little by little and without premeditation, he becomes involved with the opponents of the regent and her minister. He is now on a downward course that will necessarily make him side with the Frondeurs, whose opposition to the court's centralism implied the nobles' struggle against the loss of their old privileges. La Rochefoucauld is privy to all plots, and participates in all phases of the struggle. The plots are so intricate that it would be futile to attempt to summarize them. At first the Prince de Condé sides with the royalists and against his own family, but soon after his victory, as the plot thickens, he turns against the cardinal. Condé and Mazarin fight for control of the Regency. Once again the minister's skill has the upper hand; the prince and his followers are imprisoned. La Rochefoucauld, picking up speed on his downward course, enters the second stage of the civil war in 1650. Since neither party is strong enough to crush the other, maneuvers and negotiations multiply endlessly. Not one character involved is ever entirely trustworthy (except for the narrator himself, which seems an effect of the memoir form itself rather than of a conscious intention of self-aggrandizement).

The members of the Parlement try to free Condé and his allies, and to come to terms with Mazarin at the same time. But they cannot let this fact transpire, lest they should lose the trust of the people of Paris. La Rochefoucauld, for his part, is in a delicate situation, for as an active participant in the negotiations for the freeing of Condé he cannot afford to favor either the cardinal or the Parlement. What is his real interest? We will never know any more than what he himself chooses to reveal—that is, that he will not help the cardinal's cause. For probably he does not know himself. The only concrete force is that of the inclined plane he has placed himself on. Condé is freed; negotiations with the minister fail; in 1651 Condé takes up arms. Where else could we have found La Rochefoucauld if not on the side of the rebellious nobles? But however brilliant the Great Condé's feats of war, sooner or later he must negotiate. And for all the prince's strategic genius, the only kind of genius he has, his lot is always disaster on the political plane. In Mazarin's case, on the contrary, however great his misfortune, when the time comes to use words as weapons he is always the winner. This is the second enigma that the *Mémoires* pose without solving. The first has to do with the author's own personal motivation— as opposed to that which derives from his caste affiliation. The second concerns his great opponent. Having had several opportunities to deal directly with him, La Rochefoucauld finds the cardinal an irresolute man, slow to come to a decision. We are left with the impression that Mazarin's political genius is manifested precisely in the signs of weakness he seems to exhibit, as if his trump card were the fact that he kept to himself the meaning of a language unknown to his interlocutor. Be that as it may, in 1652 the rebellious nobles were defeated. Condé, once again failing at the negotiations, was forced to flee to Spain. The fate of the nobleman cum knight-errant was now sealed. Condé and La Rochefoucauld were the last incarnations of this type. However, outside the political arena, the defeat had unimaginable effects. In order to examine them, we must consider the *Réflexions ou sentences et maximes morales* (1664).

When he wrote his maxims, La Rochefoucauld had the example of the moralists before him. In their investigation of human conduct, they strove to extend Church doctrine and to show that, in spite of his flesh, man was able to tame his passions and choose the righteous path. Among them, it is true, there were pessimists like Pascal and the Jansenists, whose impact on La Rochefoucauld's major work has been emphasized by its interpreters.

As often occurs in the study of influences, the parallel is correct,* but fails to do full justice to the character of the work. La Rochefoucauld is to be distinguished from both "optimistic" moralists and Jansenists because their praise of grace has no practical effect on the human condition. What is the consequence of the fact that they are characterized as moralists? It takes two basic conditions to make a moralist: the awareness of the existence of evil in the world, of the thousand paths that await us and tempt us, and the conviction that there is a center or source able to redeem the poor reed bent by contradictory winds. For the Jansenists, the center of grace could save a few chosen ones out of a multitude of creatures. Mysterious and inscrutable though it might seem to be to merely human eyes, grace was nonetheless sufficient. But La Rochefoucauld pays only lip service to the concept, which makes a single appearance in a passage of the second preface (see preceding footnote); belief in its power has no effect on the sphere of passions.

Although the Jansenist principle of grace is congenial with the author's psychological makeup, one cannot fail to notice that his reflections do not assume the existence of any center capable of interfering in the world of human action. Where could redemption from the passions be found? In his gilded exile, the duke seems to smile wryly at both the royal road promised by orthodox moralists and the Jansenists' narrow door. The retired rebel knows that virtue never commands passion or is exempt from it:

The passions are the only orators that are ever convincing. They are like an art of nature, whose rules are inflexible.

The passions contain an injustice and a self-interest that make it dangerous to follow them and advisable to mistrust them even when they seem to be most reasonable.

There is in the human heart a perpetual generation of passions, so that when one is destroyed almost always another is born. (Maxims 8–10)

Our conscience is not a peaceful land, it does not even have that peacefulness that belongs to wintertime; instead, it is subject to the constant struggle of successive and contradictory passions. As J. Starobinski would say, the passions stage an incessant "allegorical psychomachy." Self-love, "the greatest flatterer of all," "more skillful than the most skillful man in

---

*Here is the author's principal justification for the appropriateness of his reflections: "He who made them considered men solely in this deplorable state in which their nature is corrupted by sin; and thus his discussion of this infinite number of faults to be found in their apparent virtues does not apply to those whom God has preserved from such faults by a particular grace" (La Rochefoucauld 1950: 399).

the world" (Maxims 2 and 4), is an insatiable conqueror of new dominions: "Whatever discoveries may have been made in the country of self-love, enough unknown lands still remain" (Maxim 3).

The connection between the passions and self-love not only abolishes any possibility of morality—Nietzsche criticizes La Rochefoucauld for not having taken the next step, which we might call the formulation of a reverse morality—but also abolishes the very notion of a center: "Self-love, rather than a center of activity, a prime mover, a unifying principle, is in fact precisely what uncenters us" (Starobinski 1966: 19). Rather than firm and stable, as essences should be, self-love is movable and unstable, fickle in its choices. This does not mean that, alienated from moralistic views, La Rochefoucauld proposed an ethos of despair, of the inevitability of loss, of the absurd vanity of all effort. This interpretation would place La Rochefoucauld at another center, for all centered thought, whatever its aim, postulates the univocity of meaning. In La Rochefoucauld no univocity exists. If we are passionate reeds, not thinking reeds, this does not imply that no countermovement is possible: "The constancy of sages is no more than the art of containing one's agitation in the heart" (Maxim 20). The wise man does not defeat passions, but merely finds a channel for them. The psychomachy does not end until death. While we live, though, we are not mere puppets of the hidden entities that move us, for we can always change their course and open a new channel for them—or, as an unlikely follower of La Rochefoucauld would put it, sublimate them.

Out of the clash of blind passions and the will to resist, a powerful dialectic is formed, which opens up a third path. Maxim 477 is a good example: "The same tenacity that serves to resist love also serves to make it violent and lasting, and in fact weak people, who are tossed about by passions, hardly ever know them." If resisting love does not lead to overcoming it but rather to making it "violent et durable," neither does the struggle end with the defeat of the will to resist; a third path is added to the other two: love, now constant, becomes the privilege of possessing a passion different from what is experienced by those who were unable to resist it. The conclusion of the maxim could not but have displeased the true moralists, who were about to begin their attacks against the author. Already his contemporaries accused him of making generic judgments about man based on himself. Soon after, Vauvenargues changed the key without changing the melody: "So presumptuous are we that we believe ourselves able to separate our personal interest from that of mankind and curse the human race without including ourselves" (Vauvenargues 1857, 1: 399–400).

Leaving aside such autos-da-fé, the fact remains that La Rochefoucauld proposed an ethos that I would not hesitate to call disenchanted; an ethos that, although restricted to an elite capable of thinking without false pieties and of devoting their time to the analysis of their own passions, was nonetheless secular and unsubmitted to rigid codes. A disenchanted and elitist ethos, to be sure, but still comprehensive—that is, controlling. A few examples will suffice:

Jealousy is, to a certain extent, fair and reasonable, for it tends to conserve something that belongs to us or that we believe belongs to us, whereas envy is a rage that does not admit that something should belong to someone else.

The evil we do does not elicit as much hate and persecution as do our good qualities.

We make promises according to our hopes, and keep them according to our fears.

The old love to give good advice as consolation for the fact that they can no longer set bad examples.

Hypocrisy is the tribute paid to virtue by vice.

Disputes would not last long if only one of the parties were in error.
(Maxims 28, 29, 38, 93, 218, 496)

This secular, comprehensive ethos cannot be crystallized into a moral code, since the variety of inner struggles we are subject to makes it impossible to formulate a law for them. Within these reflections there is no room for moralists, among other reasons because there is no room for cure. In contemporary terms: there is no foolproof therapy against our phantoms; the analysis we undertake is bound to be interminable. (The proximity to Freud is here so evident as to make it unnecessary to draw attention to it.) Here is La Rochefoucauld's point of contact with Nietzsche:

Interest speaks all kinds of tongues and represents all kinds of characters, even the disinterested.

Sincerity is an opening of the heart. It is found in only a few; what is usually seen is no more than a thin dissimulation, for the purpose of attracting the confidence of others.

Virtue would not go as far as it does if vanity did not keep it company.
(Maxims 39, 62, 200)

But, since this vein has often been exploited, let us examine another one.
 In a nutshell, it is the inevitable circle drawn by self-love and the passions that separates La Rochefoucauld from the moralists. He still employs the same basic terms: deception, appearance, disguise, mask, lie, and

change are words no less common in the moralists' work than in his. But whereas in the moralists these terms are negative values, to be defeated by the well-guided soul—that is, the soul that follows the center introjected in it—in La Rochefoucauld they become autonomous and gain the right to live a life of their own. What is the meaning of this right? To understand it better, we may once again look at a series of maxims:

> Aversion to mendacity is often an imperceptible ambition to make our statements worthy of consideration and attract for our words the sort of respect accorded to religion.
>
> We can find no consolation for the fact that we are deceived by our enemies and betrayed by our friends. But we are often pleased to be thus victimized by ourselves.
>
> We are so accustomed to disguising ourselves as other people that finally we disguise ourselves as ourselves.
>
> We are sometimes as different from ourselves as we are from others.
>
> In all occupations, each affects a face and a facade such that whatever is believed of him appears; thus one may say that the world is solely made up of faces.
>
> (Maxims 63, 114, 119, 135, 256)

And, the better to emphasize my ultimate end, I quote the last one in the series separately: "Imagination would not know how to invent as many contrarieties as naturally exist in each heart" (Maxim 478).

The key terms in the *Maximes* are common to the enterprise of the moralists and the field of analysis of aesthetic experience, which did not exist at the time. By taking them from the former, the author made it possible to illuminate the latter. Evidently the former Frondeur's fixation on these words, his obsession with psychological observation, has to do with his court experience. Learning to fathom the hidden intentions behind the subtlest gesture, an unexpected smile or blush, an involuntary tightening of the lips, a fixed stare, learning to suit the elaborate ritual of precedences and good manners to one's interests—all of this was necessary for the courtier, who had to become, in fact, a skillful psychological investigator. At court, though, all this training was put to the service of a political career. This knowledge was not employed for aesthetic purposes because aesthetics was already controlled by religious morality and official taste. However literarily inclined he might be, the courtier could not enter the world of belles lettres except as a dilettante; writing was not an activity worthy of those whose blood was noble; besides, a writer had to submit to the norms of the day, or he would have to face a number of unnecessary conflicts. Paradoxically, La Rochefoucauld's misfortunes freed him from these restrictions. In fact, he himself was not helped by the leisure he earned, and were he given the choice he would never trade his present "freedom" for the "slavery" of the past. In any case, his previous experience, exile, and forced leisure afterwards allowed him to transpose a forbidden boundary: the refusal to submit his key terms to moral regulation allowed him to illuminate the aesthetic experience.

Therefore J. G. Weber's conclusion seems rather meager: "the dramatization of moral principles in the form of personification is to La Rochefoucauld's *Maximes* what the animals are to La Fontaine's *Fables*" (Weber 1974: 254). Far too meager, although there is something to be said for the comparison. It should be added that this dramatization, akin to Starobinski's psychomachy, is not an end unto itself. As we have seen, the fictional, then symptomatically confused with the fictitious, was allowed to the extent that it subjected itself to norms that were forced on it in the name of truth, morality, and reason. La Rochefoucauld changes the course: fictionality is no longer seen from the outside—that is, as a product not subject to general and previous precepts—and can now be seen from the inside—as a mask that does not deceive because it calls itself a mask. Thus the frustration with the ineffectiveness of the virtues did not make of La Rochefoucauld an actual follower of the Jansenists, who were friends of his family, or a follower of Pascal and his *Pensées*. What it did was to enable him—unintentionally, we can be sure—to understand another area, which in his time was so controlled that it had no name and was confused with the realm of eloquence.

Was it really because his message was strikingly novel that he had no followers? My references to La Bruyère have made it clear that, though he had lived in the same court milieu and had the same psychological discernment, the author of *Caractères* did not follow La Rochefoucauld's footsteps. Faithful to the ethics that should be accepted by anyone who desired to succeed, La Bruyère writes as a subtle moralist and, on the basis of his principles, condemns Rabelais: "Rabelais, in particular, is incomprehensible: his book is an enigma, whatever one may wish to say, inexplicable; it is a chimera, the face of a beautiful woman with the feet and tail of a serpent or some other, more misshapen, animal; it is the monstrous putting together of a fine and ingenious moral and the crassest corruption" (La Bruyère 1962: 82).

Nor was the passage of time, in the short run, favorable to the flexibility of the *Maximes*. When we read Vauvenargues's *Réflexions et maximes*, we are sometime startled to realize the extent of the retreat. For Voltaire's friend and protégé, the intention is precisely to repudiate the undignified old duke. This is what he attempts to do in the *Introduction à la connaissance de l'esprit humain*, where he distinguishes the negatively valued *amour-propre* from the positive *amour de nous-mêmes*: "*Amour-propre* . . . subordinates all to its convenience and its well-being; it is its own object and end; so that, while those passions that spring from *amour de nous-mêmes* cause us to give ourselves to things, *amour-propre* would have things give themselves to us and make us the center of everything" (Vauvenargues 1857, 1: 30–31).

This taste for reestablishing the interrupted tradition, together with the bourgeois sentimentality of his phrases, lends his maxims a smoother, less astringent tone, and makes them sound somewhat like almanac recipes: "Reason and freedom are incompatible with weakness"; "war is not as burdensome as slavery"; "it is not given to reason to repair all the vices of nature"; "the foolish cannot understand the witty"; and so on (Maxims 20, 21, 24, and 52). And this is not because Vauvenargues was only a beginner who had no time to polish his talent. This charitable explanation is less believable than another: Vauvenargues is quite close to the new ethos of his day, that of the bourgeoisie. That is, he is not merely an epigone of the old moralists, but rather the harbinger of a new view. Against La Rochefoucauld's empire of the passions, Vauvenargues proposes the cult of sentiment. He offers the corrective for the coldness of reason: "Reason does not know the interests of the heart"; "sentiment cannot be suspected of falseness" (Maxims 124 and 367). Sentiment is still confused with nature: "We call sentiment, rather than reason, nature" (Vauvenargues 1857, 2: 25).

In La Rochefoucauld, the unlimited power of passion made self-analysis indispensable, and the hopelessness of any attempt to master it opened the way for the unprejudiced study of people as masks, and therefore indirectly suggests that fiction is the best medium for developing the knowledge of man. Vauvenargues trusts sentiment and equates it with nature, offering man a center and a certainty. The immediate consequence of this is to subordinate fiction to this new center, as Rousseau was to do later and more effectively. Thus Vauvenargues's sentiment is not at all equivalent to La Rochefoucauld's passion; it is, in fact, an element with precisely the opposite function: it points to a new standard of conduct. This said, one may well ask whether there is a connection between Vauvenargues's sentimentalized center and his almanac wisdom. I believe the link is his praise of good sense. The following maxim is clearly in the service of good sense: "If order prevails among mankind, this is proof that reason and virtue are strongest therein" (Maxim 193). (Evidently, the alleged proof only holds for common sense.) I am not saying that the Marquis de Vauvenargues actually sided with the bourgeoisie: several of his maxims show his zealous defense of his privileges against the new rising class. But the fact remains that his identification of nature with virtue—"true virtue, that which they prefer not to call by this name, because it is not in agreement with their definitions, that which is the work of nature" (Maxim 296)— and his praise of sentiment and good sense place him very close to the philosophes. Since this is not yet the right moment to examine the question of the control exerted by the philosophes, let us simply observe that in his maxims Vauvenargues not only fails to take up La Rochefoucauld's break with tradition but also prefigures the elaboration of a new kind of control.

Given the exceptional quality of La Rochefoucauld's isolation, it seems convenient to insist on it. From the way I emphasize his deviation from the moralistic tradition and his liberating valuation of fictionality, the reader who is unfamiliar with the literature on La Rochefoucauld may well imagine that my thesis is widely diffused. But this is not the case, although the thesis, to a certain extent, has been anticipated by Roland Barthes and Jean Starobinski. In order to understand their positions better, I will summarize their line of argument.

For Barthes, the maxim, the genre particularly cultivated by our author, is a closed form, by virtue of which it approaches both the sacred and the poetic, and distances itself from the *raisonneur* and disciplined character of classical society. The juxtaposition of the sacred and the poetic is made possible by the "true metrical economy" of the maxim, an economy that replaces "versified languages"; and its distinctness from the prose of classical society is a result of the fact that "its thought, derived from a rationalistic movement, remains secular" (Barthes 1961: lv). This much given, the question is to capture the formal structure of the maxim. Barthes says that La Rochefoucauld's maxim is made up of stressed beats, which include the *virtues*—which are *irrealia*, composed of "vain objects, appearances of what reality must find"—and *real objects*, *realia*, which make up the world of which the virtues are merely dreams" (p. lxv). These *realia*, in turn, come in three types: passions; contingencies, which depend on chance; and attenuated realities, actions, faults, effects. Between the first stressed beat—the unreality of virtues—and the second there is a demystifying relation, "a relationship of deceptive identity" (p. lvii). Hence "the paradoxical result of this dialectic: ultimately it is the real disorder of man (disordered passions, events, humors) that lends him his unity. One cannot establish a structure of virtues, for they are no more than parasite values" (pp. lxix–lxx). This is the origin of the *vertige du néant, vertige de l'irréel, cauchemar de la verité*, which obsesses the exiled duke. What concerns us the most is not Barthes's conclusion but this observation: "If virtues occupy the first term of the relationship; and passions, contingencies, and actions form the second; and if the second term is deceptive relative to the first, this means that the appearance (or mask) is the subject of discourse, and reality is only the predicate" (p. lxxv). In short, the illusion of virtues and the corrosion of ethics point to the mask as the true subject of discourse.

The change that took place could not be other than the replacement of ethics by the theater; since experience, being deceptive, lost its pre-eminence, there was an implicit thematization of what, being formed by shadows and mobilities, made deceit impossible: the experience of the fictional. Barthes suggests such a conclusion, but does not actually formulate it. Starobinski comes closer to doing so.

According to the Genevan essayist, La Rochefoucauld's resignation to Christian morals leads him not to indifference, but to an "ersatz morality," "in which the determining criterion is *intensity*" (Starobinski 1966: 27). This intensity promises no form of salvation whatsoever; the traps laid by the world are like mirrors that, their opacity being greater than that of our bodies, show in the outer world what already existed in the inner world. The world's abysses disseminate the soul's. However, to live intensely does not mean to indulge in the voracity of passions, so that each individual would be the image of Rimbaud's *bateau ivre*, much less to indulge in all of them. (Let us recall that, in the *Maximes*, sloth was one of the major passions.) Though man knows he is unable to defeat them, this does not mean he has to subordinate himself passively to their sway. His resistance and his ability to know them may influence their direction, as we have seen in connection with Maxim 477. From the dialectic we mentioned, then, it follows that both partners—that is, man and his passion—change their original directions slightly, man because his resistance does not cancel passion, and passion because its natural instability is converted into violent and lasting feeling. This example will do in place of Starobinski's explanation of his concept of intensity.

From the affirmation of ersatz morality, the essayist moves on to the study of its effect, which is twofold: formal and social. The formal effect has to do with the heightening of language. Concern with precision and intensity of language becomes the goal of the man who is exiled from transcendence. The social effect is the reverse of the formal: conversation becomes not only a pastime, but an art and an occupation. La Rochefoucauld, in short, gives up the attempt to "formulate an ethics of action" and moves on to an "aesthetics of expression" (Starobinski 1966: 213), and by so doing frees us from the burden of moral obligations and makes us devote ourselves to the purpose of an "aesthetic transmutation" of life. The "responsible subject to whom ethics addressed itself is replaced by the subject who discourses" (p. 214). The pursuit of this ideal takes place in a privileged medium, the milieu of the *bonne compagnie*, devoted to intellectual hedonism: "The *bonne compagnie* consumes works of the spirit; it hardly ever produces them, except for portraits or maxims, occasionally novels, solidified fragments of the best conversation" (p. 218). Thus, for Starobinski, the ethics of intensity is transformed into a form of entertainment restricted to exiled nobles. (Machado de Assis's Councillor Aires would be a Brazilian representative of this type.) Aesthetic experience is then transformed into a sort of compensating game. Is it accompanied by *mauvaise conscience*? No, but certainly by a deep melancholy.

For all its brilliance, Starobinski's interpretation, like Barthes's, does not seem to exhaust the possibilities of another form of understanding. Let us assume, a priori, that it is historically grounded—that is, that this was precisely the experience of the nobles whose exclusion from the court did not force them to join the hard struggle for survival. This assumption is not gratuitous, for it helps to explain not only the hostility of Vauvenargues, who was willing to formulate another connection with the life that was simmering, but also the fact that the connection between La Rochefoucauld's maxims and the exploration of the fictional experience has not been studied. At this point, the divergence between our interpretations must be pointed out. Whereas Starobinski sees ersatz morality basically as aesthetic consumption, I tend to see it rather as a generator of fictionality. The former is conscious or intentional on the author's part; the latter can be unearthed only if we read it against the backdrop of control and of the vicissitudes of religious and moral values and of those of reason. It is because traditional values are affected by a morality in the process of becoming secularized and by a rationality of only limited applicability— the division between citizen and private individual—that fictionality can be taken out of the bottom of the well and presented as an alternative in the world.

Thus, as we have seen, our reading is based on the specific dislocation brought about by the *Maximes*: the basic terms with which it operates are common to the ethical and the aesthetic experience; the refusal to thematize them ethically, a consequence of the deceptive nature of the virtues (Barthes), began to correspond to the possibility of an inner view of the aesthetic experience. In other words, the aesthetic experience was repressed as long as ethical deontology was imposed; this being discredited and reason fragmented, thematization of the aesthetic experience made it possible to understand an uncontrolled fictionality.

If we read the *Maximes* side by side with the *Réflexions diverses*, we can develop the argument further. The individual portraits presented in, say, "Des Evénements de ce siècle" show that fiction—which, to be sure, was rarely produced by noblemen—draws on no events other than those that are part of everyday existence, and that it appears only when someone is able to single out some events from the general chain that neutralized them. Fictionality has no need for the sophisticated pastoralism of *L'Astrée*

(1607–27), for it is neither this side of nor beyond everyday existence, but rather is detached from it by means of a discursive strategy. What does this strategy consist in? To begin with, its material must be separated, must be extracted from the other everyday events with which it was articulated, so that, isolated and depragmatized, it can be the focus of the receiver's concentrated attention. In this way, the receiver is able to identify critically the functioning of the chain of everyday events, to see critically what is taken to be the world. If this critical-pleasurable function is to be exerted, however, more is needed than the simple act of detaching a part of the original chain of everyday events. Maxim 478 is still necessary: imagination cannot invent contrarieties more numerous or varied than those that already exist in each person.

What is necessary, then, is to deepen this effort of imagination directed at a possible fragment of everyday existence, making the effort assume an inwardly justified development. But why couldn't this be known before the *Maximes*? Because, as we have seen in the development of our argument, thematization of fictionality is impossible without the exercise of criticism. Where the latter is only tolerated, fictionality may be actualized, but it is always tamed by the fictitious—that is, it is always made into a product whose verisimilitude lies in its relation to the prevailing truth. Thus, under full religious control, Cervantes was able to establish modern fiction only by devising the strategy of making Don Quixote a madman, one who had lost his reason because of the bad examples of the romances of chivalry. The existence of control does not abolish the pure existence of fictionality; it only happens that, as long as control is not weakened, *knowledge* of fictionality is postponed.

If we gave such emphasis to the critical spirit, shouldn't we conclude that control disappeared with the defense and propagation of criticism in the Enlightenment? If, as Koselleck wrote, the Enlightenment tried to fuse into a unity of reason what absolutism still separated into two spheres, private and public, isn't this reason, wholly free of religious dogma, the very basis for the acknowledgment of fictionality? Such a conclusion would be a mystification of our recent past. If the control of fictionality inevitably includes the control of the critical spirit, the fact that the latter did not disappear with the advent of modernity simply means that eighteenth-century criticism had well-defined boundaries. At the opening of modernity, with the philosophes, reason itself was in charge of setting up a new form of control. All of this will be seen in detail later; for the moment let us emphasize another point.

It is not enough to stress that the critical spirit is indispensable if knowledge of fictional production is to be attained. There is also a discursive constraint that either favors or harms fictionality. By itself, critical genius will generate Kant's fundamental work; but no one would seriously argue that his three *Critiques* are works of fiction.

Instead of engaging in an unnecessary theoretical discussion, let us simply recall the example of La Rochefoucauld. In his memoirs, his intention was to relate the court intrigues and the twists of chance that made Condé an ally of the Frondeurs, although he was as much their opponent as he was Mazarin's; and to show his own dedication to the future regent and then to Condé. But he cannot find the adequate discursive space to support his reasons. Some of them, to be sure, may be supplemented by the receiver: the cardinal's political qualities seemed to be absent in the prince, his adversary; and if Mazarin lacked the Great Condé's military talent, the cardinal had the good fortune of being able to rely on no less a general than Henri de Turenne. But why should the regent accept Mazarin's proposals rather than those made by one as devoted to her as La Rochefoucauld? And why did La Rochefoucauld, who was so keen on political maneuvering, stubbornly cling to conduct similar to that of the fictional knights-errant? The reader finds no answers for these questions, perhaps because the author did not see them as such or was unable to answer them. In either case, since these points could not be clarified immediately and no factual evidence could be brought to bear on them, they could not be raised in a historical investigation. For each discourse is a territoriality, with its own limits of expressive possibility. Since the territoriality of the fictional does not imply respect for the truth of the facts, if it is not to be confused with the fictitious it must go beyond the world of as-if and exploit the larger possibilities of imagination. That is why even if, contrary to fact, imagination were, historically, not controlled, this would not imply the presence of imagination in all kinds of discourse that had been used innovatively. Even the word "innovation" must be seen within the discursive parameters in which it is actualized. Furthermore, without the notion of discursive boundaries one might be led to think that this entire investigation of the control of imagination is in fact a reflection of the fond hope for a better world in which imagination would be the fundamental category in human production.

One final point: in the history of the control of imagination, at least as far as our material has allowed us to go, those moments when its thematization verges on its theorization—in *Don Quixote*, in the *Maximes*—or even when theorization is outright—in early German romanticism, in the tradition started by Baudelaire and leading to the poetry and essays of Mallarmé—have been discontinuous moments. Perhaps there is nothing unusual about this fact, which would then be the very proof of the urge and force with which modern reason has controlled imagination. But there is another, disturbing way of considering the issue. According to Starobinski's analysis, the historical function of ersatz morality was to create an area of compensation. But the same situation is repeated in the thought of F. Schlegel, Novalis, and Hölderlin. What does this parallel mean? Could it be that the criticism we associate with fictional production is a utopian goal? Or, more seriously even, not only utopian—which etymologically means "with no place," yet with still the possibility of reaching such a place—but in fact atopian, with no possible place? This is not the best way to end a chapter. But, if our intention is to think, the best *stylistic* solution is that which is not afraid to break a comfortable fluency.

CHAPTER THREE

The Joys and Sorrows of the Self

AUTOBIOGRAPHY AS AN ISSUE

Ever since individuality became a value in the Western world, the eagerness to live has implied the eagerness to tell. And the narrative—true or fanciful—of one's own life has become a kind of story, a more reliable one than the plot of a novel or novella. Each century, each country, each region, has produced its quota of names. It makes no difference what they did or what labels they earned; whether they were famous, ignored, or obscure, successful men or utter failures; whether they wished to recapture their past experiences or simply recount the circumstances in which they did whatever it was that made them well known; in this last category, which includes Vico, Gibbon, Freud, Croce, and Collingwood, the autobiographer is concerned with a single strand, and he can write, as Collingwood does at the beginning of his narrative: "The autobiography of a man whose business is thinking should be the story of his thought" (Collingwood 1982: vii).

But this is surely not the most common variant of the form. In most cases, the individual will settle for nothing less than a full-length self-portrait. For memoirs and autobiographies are indeed the equivalent of mirrors. If mirrors, metallic and merciless, reveal the worn features, the dulled eyes, the protruding belly, we can always turn away from their cruelty and try to recapture what we used to be like, as if by recalling a long-lost landscape we could explain our own selves to ourselves.

At times there is a single, determined purpose behind the impulse to tell the story of one's life, as in the case of Thomas Merton's autobiography.

His object is to depict himself as a young and ambitious student, perplexed by the crossroads and contradictory impulses that will place him on a quite unexpected road: that of freedom through ascetic monasticism. At other times, as in Rousseau, the author is not interested in recapturing any particular aspect or period of his life, but rather in reconstructing his existence in its entirety, so that the reader can be his judge. More often, there is no intention of driving home any particular point or laying the grounds for any sort of trial; the idea is simply to preserve in words what has been lost in time; here no particular theme is favored: life itself is the theme.

It is true that any existence can be summed up in a few lines. It is just as true, as Nabokov notes in *Speak, Memory*, that "the cradle rocks above an abyss, and common sense tells us that our existence is but a brief crack of light between two eternities of darkness" (Nabokov 1966: 19). But however brief this moment, the telling of it is always varied; what can be said in a few words can also be the subject of hundreds of pages. And the hunger of publishers for autobiographical works clearly indicates that this amplification is not seen as redundancy; that in our times there is public enough to consume all kinds of memoirs, for all kinds of reasons. For as a genre, memoirs—let us provisionally take "memoirs" and "autobiography" to be synonyms—are a specific form of communication, a genre with its own rules and requirements that set it apart from other genres.

But this is precisely what is problematic about it—or rather, this is the problem we are interested in: since the eighteenth century, if not before, the prestige of individuality has been such that it is taken for granted, and thus it seems unnecessary to reflect on what characterizes a genre defined as the story of an individual's life. It is a characteristic of socialized values that they are seen not as cultural—and hence historically variable—categories, but as self-evident and self-justifying substances. No wonder, then, that even though early in our century Weber pointed to the heterogeneity of the notions covered by the term "individualism," most scholars tend to treat it as a timeless notion, and therefore to think of memoirs as a genre as old as Western civilization itself. The alleged self-evidence of what is understood as individuality and individualism explains why so few are familiar with Richard Müller-Freienfels's essay of 1919. In it, the author, influenced by Hans Vaihinger's study of the relevance of "as if" in everyday life—that is, the role played by fictions accepted as truths—attempted to prove that behind the commonsense notion of individuality there lay a full-blown fiction: "In an absolute sense, there is no such thing as a constant identity in personality; however, we behave in our everyday lives as if there were such a constant identity in our personalities, and relate with our neighbors as if they, too, were constant, self-identical individualities" (Müller-Freienfels 1919: 298). To the author, this supposed constancy was not a deception or a comfortable lie; on the contrary, it was "a very useful fiction, which allows a global causality of psychical reality" (p. 299).

In spite of the objections raised by authors renowned or obscure, the category "individuality" has remained so prestigious that quite recently Niklas Luhmann felt it necessary to observe that there is no anthropological constant that can explain personalized individuality "and the possibility of stylizing oneself or others as unique," traits that depend on specific sociocultural conditions. Thus, adds the sociologist, even love as a passion is not to be defined primarily as a feeling, a manifestation of an inherently human trait, but rather as a kind of conduct, a differentiated communication code, which the seventeenth century was already perfectly aware of: "Love, so to speak, moves in a capricious way, guided only by a generalized pattern of search, which makes it easier to choose an object, but at the same time may also hinder an emotionally deeper satisfaction" (Luhmann 1983: 23–24).

Now, if the love passion is a code and, as such, a historically bound manifestation, how could the emphasis on the individual self be expected to be valid in a timeless way? The relation between the two categories is quite evident: passion presupposes an emphasis on the self's demands, and as a code it socially validates a specific form of conduct, which is based on the individual's ability to refuse other forms of behavior. This problem directly interests us because the characterization of autobiography as a genre depends on the fate of individuality. As long as this fate is taken for granted, definitions of autobiography tend to present it as a nearly universal type. Let us see, for instance, what a deservedly renowned authority has to say on the subject: "A definition of autobiography . . . involves the reconstruction of the movement of a life, or part of a life, in the actual circumstances in which it was lived. Its centre of interest is the self, not the outside world, though necessarily the outside world must appear so that, in give and take with it, the personality finds its peculiar shape" (R. Pascal 1960: 9). By rightly stressing the presentation of the self, the author would necessarily be restricted to the study of modern history, lest he present an anachronistic view of the subject. Roy Pascal, it is true, is sensible enough to take Augustine as his real point of departure. However, he immediately adds that "there are numerous autobiographical statements in classical Greek and Roman literature" (p. 21). Pascal does not see this liberal view of the genre as contradictory to the definition transcribed above because he takes the centrality of the self for granted, as a natural fact.

Just as the timelessness of the memoirs genre goes unquestioned, so also its classification as a literary genre is presupposed. This presupposition has been widespread since the triumph of romanticism. Since "normal" romanticism was based on the expression of individuality and poetry was seen as the sincere expression of an exceptional soul, it was only natural that the romantic heritage should consider both the individualized self and literature as timeless manifestations—or, more exactly, join the two and see the history of literature as a "long-term" history of individual expression. From this it follows that the use of the word "genre" may give rise to a misunderstanding, for the term is usually taken to refer only to literary forms. But here "genre" has a precise meaning, and a wider extension than "literature": it refers to a historically recognized form of communication, whether literary or nonliterary, written or oral, in well-defined or diffuse discourses (such as everyday speech). In this sense, the category "genre" must be associated with and subordinated to "discourse." If, as I have said, discourses are forms of territoriality, which establish discontinuities in the continuum of *parole* and thus make it possible for the same statement to convey different senses according to its discursive context, genres are smaller frames, the modalities of manifestation of discourse. Thus, for instance, articles on science written for a lay public form a genre of scientific discourse not to be confused, as to language and form of presentation, with papers written for a general symposium, which in turn are to be distinguished from papers produced for a scholarly publication. Likewise, we can say that the reviews and critical articles published in newspapers form a specific genre of critical discourse, different from what one expects to find in a theoretical essay. Every genre must conform to a set of basic rules, which are not exactly normative but rather point to a desirable form of communication. If genre, then, is a category of discourse, why is it often confused with the domain of literature?

A likely explanation is that the usual, more encompassing conception of literature combines two determinations, different in origin and direction. The first derives from the Renaissance, while the other comes from romanticism. The historically older view identifies literature with a noble form of eloquence, with a certain exploration of combinations of words, its goal being to delight the receiver. According to Georg Misch, this more archaic version of literature begins with Demosthenes, who "was the first, since the fifties of that fourth century B.C., to publish in the service of his policy writings that were orations only in form and were not bound to the actual conditions of the orations *coram populo*" (Misch 1950, 1: 157). No longer merely pragmatic in function, public speeches—like epistles, meditations, and dialogues—were meant to be appreciated for their sublimity and persuasiveness, and their delight in language.

The Renaissance, with its cult of the ancient world, revived this tradition, taking Cicero as the model. The writer adopts the orator's language in his texts, which nonetheless are meant to be privately consumed. But this privacy as yet does not detract from the justification of discourse as a form of eloquence. Poetry, though taking different models, is also a modality of eloquence, an eloquent form of knowledge.

The romantic strand has a different goal. Here the object is less to seduce by means of skillfully wrought sentences than to move the reader by means of the strength of the feelings confessed. History had become secularized, the models of collective representation had lost their appeal, and the individual was seen as the true subject of the world.

Since then, the dominant literary canon has combined the two strata and considered literature as the eloquent—that is, verbally accomplished—manifestation of a self, which engages in confession, either directly or through transposition. This commonsense conception, not least because it deals with two strata different in origin and direction, is forced to emphasize the idea of genre, for the division into these categories helps to reconcile incompatible conceptions. Thus both lyricism and epic, as well as genres of more recent origin, such as the novel and memoirs, can be taken as parts of a single corpus, which could only be that of literature since those forms could not possibly belong to any other.

To the extent that this commonsense conception managed to survive, despite the radical turns taken by Mallarmé, Valéry, the avant-gardists or authors like Joyce, Musil, and Nabokov, and that these writers were "incorporated" by the academic establishment into the traditional standards, and that for all the objections raised against the heterogeneous notion of "individualism" the use of the term was unaffected, autobiography was still automatically classified as literature. All that was (and is) required of it is that it be written in an "elegant" manner and contain "interesting" confessions. The status of autobiography becomes problematic and questionable only when we set aside commonsense notions of individuality and literature. Beginning with *Mimesis e modernidade*, I have been trying to develop a view of literature as a discursive modality. Elsewhere I have attempted to show the antagonism between this view and the conception of literature as a modality of document; so it was inevitable that sooner or later I would take on the question of autobiography. And when I said that this question could only be posed when individual and literature were no longer seen as natural facts, I was implictly announcing the form that this article must necessarily assume: an analysis of the close relationship between the two. Let us begin with the question of the individual.

Since individuality was believed to be a timeless value, attempts were made to write comprehensive histories of autobiography. The most detailed of these was conceived by Georg Misch. So vast was his task that, although he devoted his long life to it, he had gotten no further than Dante's era by the time he died. Let us concentrate on Misch's examination of autobiography in antiquity. From the outset, we must face the question: if his history implies a long-term conception of the individual, isn't Misch's work today only an outdated mass of erudition, an archaeological curiosity to which one pays lip service, aware that it stands for a stage we have left behind? When one reads the first few pages, this expectation seems to be justified. Even if one bears in mind the vastness of the subject he must encompass, Misch's definition of his object is much too loose: "As a manifestation of man's knowledge of himself, autobiography has its basis in the fundamental—and enigmatical—psychological phenomenon which we call consciousness of self or self-awareness" (Misch 1950, 1: 8). The definition simply begs the question: if the history of autobiography can be traced to such remote times, it must indeed be because man is characterized by self-consciousness. On the other hand, Misch also justifies the inclusion of autobiography in literary art: in autobiography the inner form "can be most revealing, because recollection, growing out of the vivid personal experience, and thus eliciting its meaning . . . performs its creative work in accord with the man's intentions as worked out in his life, and so gives the recollected material form from within" (p. 11).

From Misch down to Roy Pascal, or even to more recent authors, the analysts of autobiography have never strayed far from these premises. But as one reads on in Misch's book one realizes that the author was compelled, to a certain extent, to qualify his definition. Let us examine only the most important passages. Here is Misch on the Greco-Roman world:

> In our days, if a man writes of his own experiences we feel some reassurance, but the ancients did not, and personal experience was not regarded as sufficient ground for taking up the *stilus*. The reason lay not simply in the assumption that no one would write his autobiography without a practical end in mind, but in a depreciation of the actual facts of a career as the subject of a literary work, a depreciation that is found again in the attitude taken up toward historical persons in general. There seemed to be no clear dividing line between the actual and the invented, so long as the latter was kept within the limits of the possible. (P. 188)

This passage contains two crucial ideas: first, personal experience in itself was not felt to be a subject worth writing about; second, there was no sharp dividing line between the narration of real facts and that of imaginary ones, as long as these were verisimilar. These two observations suffice to show that, even if one recognizes the existence of something like autobiography in antiquity, this contained traits that have nothing in common with those that characterize the genre in modern times. The importance of the first observation is stressed when we articulate it with K. J. Weintraub's comment: "Man was taught by his polis to perceive his very essence and being as a *zoon politikon*, a polis creature, a public man. He had no freedom to choose between a life committed to the public good and a decent private life. The good private life was derived from the good life obtained as citizen only" (Weintraub 1978: 7). While Misch felt that his qualification did not affect the historical extension of his general definition, Weintraub is perfectly aware that it would be an arbitrary and absurd anachronism to suppose that the writers of antiquity shared our notion of individuality. A life gained meaning to the extent that it was shaped by a model prevalent in a community. A private existence as such was unworthy of public consideration. That is, the category "individuality" was not to be identified with individualism—and in fact had nothing to do with it. Individualism was simply out of the question, whereas individuality presupposed a direct link with a public role.

As to the second observation, its consequences are even clearer. As Collingwood writes, "an autobiography has no right to exist unless it is *un livre de bonne foi*" (Collingwood 1982: vii). This means that no reader who is not overly naive will take an autobiographical confession to be an unequivocal expression of the truth; over Rousseau's protests, this reader realizes that the confession is no more than a personalized version, subject to error, confusion, forgetfulness, distortion, conscious and unconscious selectiveness. However, he or she will not admit the possibility that the author is consciously lying or mixing reality with fiction. The narrator's "I" must be the same as the one that signs the book—unless this "I" appears as a character in a work belonging to another category of discourse. Thus, for instance, no one will accuse Borges of fraud because he writes a dialogue between himself as an old writer and young Borges, a student in Geneva. However—even though memoirs are a less personalized variant of the genre—if an author publishes the memoirs of someone else without his or her permission, the author is sure to be sued. For the same basic rule presides over both variants, memoirs and autobiography: the reader assumes that the narrative is made *in good faith*. For if, as Pascal justifiedly observes, autobiography can cover up the truth as easily as it can reveal it (see R. Pascal 1960: 63), this duplicity, which the analyst is well aware of, does not contradict the genre's basic premise. On the contrary, the very possibility of dissimulation meets a true need of the memoirist or autobiographer; it, too, stands witness to the author's true position in relation to what he writes. The fact that the narrator is identical with the author means that he can never present a forged self or a fictional creation. Within a process of communication—and, as we know, genres ultimately point to this—the freedom of participants is limited by the rules that govern the discourse they produce (more exactly, the discourse that *speaks* them). Thus the fact that memoirs and autobiographies cannot be wholly reliable as historical documents does not detract from their status as discourses produced in good faith. The author who violates this basic principle is liable to social sanctions—he or she may be sued, or called a liar, or accused of romancing his or her life.

Several other of Misch's observations point to the same conclusion. Writing of autobiography in Egypt, he observes, in connection with the "Tale of Ahuri": "Here, as there, the autobiographical form serves to make credible the tales of marvels with which the narrative is filled" (p. 53). This is so because first-person narrative had functions other than vouching for the authenticity of the experience of the narrator's empirical "I." The "I" in the narrative could be a resource of the artist's, used in order to give fiction an appearance of reality, or it could serve a religious purpose, a political purpose, or even—as Auerbach demonstrates in relation to Tacitus—a rhetorical purpose. Given the rhetorical model of antiquity, it is not only inadequate to speak of ancient autobiography but also clearly arbitrary to think of literature as a continuum. It is only for our horizon of expectations that Homer and Greek drama appear naturally as literary manifestations. As Misch wrote, discussing Isocrates,

> rhetoric takes no trouble to give a picture of the individual existence based on realistic observation: its abstract postulates are based on an ideal picture of the type of life it envisages, and these postulates are vindicated if we can find them fulfilled in an actual person. But by means of this abstract process, which simply ignores the very refractory material of the particular reality, it is able quickly to present an ideal (not an actual) literary character as soon as it is known what kind of ideal is sought. (P. 163)

Thus, if Misch's *History of Autobiography in Antiquity* is to be more than a mere museological curiosity for us, we must go beyond the conventional definition the author proposed for autobiography and realize that the value of his research lies precisely in the fact that it shows why the genre did not exist in the period in which he was looking for it. And, in so doing, we not only rescue Misch from the shades of purgatory but also come to see that his findings are invaluable for an interpretive undertaking quite different from—even the opposite of—what the German scholar had in mind. Autobiography in antiquity? If "the peculiarity of autobiography lies in the way it mirrors the *unique, mutual interaction of the world and the individual's development*," the answer to this question cannot be less than categoric: the genre was unknown in antiquity because "in the ancient world only education for social life and morality presented a problem, so much so that in the last analysis the two were almost synonymous" (Heller 1978: 232).

Let us return to our original contention: since autobiography presupposes acknowledgment of the value of the individual self, only an anachronistic conception of the latter could justify the belief in the existence of autobiography as a genre at a time when it was in fact unknown. Furthermore, since the conception of the individual is one of the basic components of the commonsense conception of literature, our first conclusion implies the following one: that, as fictional discourse, literature did not exist in antiquity either, since there were no sharp boundaries between fictional forms and forms of presentation of the self.

This conclusion is clearly relevant for our research, and we might well pose the same questions in connection with a later period: Did autobiography exist in the Middle Ages? The answer, again, is a resounding no. In the Middle Ages, personal experience, which for a while had come to the fore in Augustine's *Confessions*, was transformed into a mere backdrop for spiritually oriented experience: "In medieval 'autobiographies,' observation and description of the external world completely disappear behind the depiction of spiritual facts and experiences" (Heller 1978: 231).

Also, we must remember that the self is not the only indispensable material for autobiography—otherwise it would be indistinguishable from the journal: for its basic characteristic is the interchange between an empirical self and the world. Autobiography, so to speak, has two simultaneous foci: how the self reacts to the world and how the world experiences the self. But in the Middle Ages it is not only this commerce that is absent: the subject itself, even when there is reference to a self, has no psychological dimension. In Paul Zumthor's precise formulation, "whatever, in effect, the circumstances that prevailed in the transmission of the various parts of the medieval literary corpus, this corpus appears to us as an almost completely 'objectified' poetry: that is, one whose subject escapes us" (Zumthor 1975: 166). The self assumes a vicarious form: that is, it is incorporated into the speaker who reads the text, which becomes the possession of whoever reads it.

> The person of the author appears in order to confirm the objectivity of the text. . . . If the author (perhaps identical with one of a succession of reciters) has made an "I" the subject of the enunciation, this "I" functions as a virtual form whose actualization varies according to the circumstances: it is hardly likely that the medieval hearer could interpret it in an autobiographical sense. (Zumthor 1975: 168)

And he adds, in connection with "lives" such as Dante's *Vita nuova*, "sense matters more than history (*sensus* more than *littera*): autobiography is the immediate revelation, through the royal road of emblem and allegory, *of the sense of the self, not of the events he or she experienced*" (p. 178).

For even though medieval man had a much narrower choice of life orientations than the ancients, in both cases there is a basic obstruction to autobiographical writing. We can state the nature of this obstruction in a simplified way by saying that autobiography is impossible wherever a model or a set of models of life are affirmed in such a way that the individual choice consists of no more than selecting one of them. In itself, individual idiosyncrasy disappears in order to be integrated into a general model of conduct that is necessarily impersonal. As Weintraub puts it: "The more universal that reason is thought to be, the more each life, in accord with reason, shares its form with every other one" (Weintraub 1978: 11).

But how are we to explain the exception of the *Confessions*? Augustine's text is the prize exhibit of those who are opposed to what they think of as a relativistic view of man. Since it is not my intention to analyze the *Confessions*, I will do no more than quote an observation made by none other than Etienne Gilson: "Augustine's masterpiece was a sort of spiritual autobiography rather than the story of his own life" (Gilson 1964: 7). Or, even more explicitly: "Although [Augustine] certainly was conscious of idiosyncrasy, he did not see it as anything of value in itself or deserving of cultivation. Quite to the contrary, the indications are that he saw in the story of one Christian soul, the one he could know best, the typical story of all Christians" (Weintraub 1978: 45).

It is only in the Renaissance that we find the effective conditions that make it possible for autobiography to appear. It was only then that *"the self-realization and self-enjoyment of the personality became a goal"* (Heller 1978: 200). As the Hungarian sociologist observes, there was no literature of inner life before the sixteenth century. According to her interpretation, during the Renaissance the medieval experience of *communitas* was gradually dissolved and the individual had to face himself, forced to play a number of roles, some of them contradictory, none of them justifiable by the adoption of a collective model, politically or religiously based. Thus it was only when the conditions to be expected according to a previous model of conduct were clearly destroyed, by the sixteenth century, that the question of individuality came to the fore. And it did so accompanied by the importance of *role-playing*, by the use of simulation and sincerity, examples of which are abundant in Shakespeare's plays. The complexity of Renaissance life—that is, of work and power relations—by itself renders impossible the survival of an ideal conduct, unified and collectively oriented, which can be taught. Henceforward *"one man could identify himself with different manners, different sets of rights and obligations, and the different concrete norms, and yet 'he' would not become 'them'"* (Heller 1978: 206).

But taking the Renaissance as a point of rupture can be both a help and a source of mistakes. Besides, since we no longer believe in the clear-cut boundary between the Middle Ages and the Renaissance that Burckhardt postulated, we must enrich our investigation with a glance, however cursory, at a few figures. Both because it is worthy of attention in itself and in order to form a basis for later comparisons with similar Renaissance works, let us begin with a medieval "autobiography."

ABELARD'S *HISTORIA CALAMITATUM*

Those who know the story of Abelard and Héloïse's love affair are apt to feel disappointed when they read the letter in which the philosopher recounts his sorrows. The text is surely interesting, even fascinating, but it fails to enhance the romantic aura that surrounds the unhappy lovers.

Abelard begins his letter, written between 1132 and 1136, by telling of the circumstances of his birth and his father's military career. Since Abelard early proved to be a brilliant student, he soon gave up arms and set off in search of a better education. Having heard of the excellence of Guillaume de Champeaux as a logic teacher, he went to Paris. He was well received, but aroused the master's jealousy and that of his disciples because of his brilliant performance in discussions: "From this my troubles began and have plagued me to this day; and the more widespread my fame has become, the more has the jealousy of others been enkindled against me" (Abelard 1964: 13).

Mars and Minerva had disputed over young Abelard's future. Opting for the latter, he had chosen the path of glory as his model, although he never came to despise martial conduct. The military model underlay Abelard's scholarly career: in a later passage, describing a conflict with another master, he says he left Paris and "pitched camp for my school outside the city on Mount St. Genevieve that I might, so to speak, lay siege to" his opponent (p. 19). Thus, despite the hostility of other logicians and theologians, Abelard's fame continued to grow. His debut in the field of theology was equally tumultuous. Having heard of the renowned Anselm of Laon, Abelard decided to become his student. And though until then he had studied only "philosophical books," soon he came to criticize the way the sacred books were taught, and took up the challenge of lecturing on this new subject. Although his colleagues tried to make things difficult for him, choosing an obscure passage in Ezekiel, Abelard was so successful that, as in his earlier experience, his master was jealous and began to persecute him.

By now he had become so famous that he was invited to work as the tutor of the young niece of an important Parisian clergyman, Canon Fulbert. Now something new and serious occurred. Writes Abelard: "At a time when I considered that I was the one philosopher in the world and had nothing to fear from others, I, who up to that time had lived most chastely, began to relax the reins on my passions" (p. 25). With no psychological transition, Abelard plunges into the brief narrative of his conquest. And, a few sentences later, he describes his delight: "We opened our books but more words of love than of the lesson asserted themselves. There was more kissing than teaching; my hands found themselves at her breasts more often than on the book. Love brought us to gaze into each other's eyes more than reading kept them on the text" (p. 28).

But the girl became pregnant, and the lovers were alarmed. To appease her powerful, angry uncle, Abelard decided to marry her secretly. The reason for the secrecy had nothing to do with his condition as a religious man: as J. T. Muckle (the editor and translator of the edition I am using) observes, the words used by Abelard, "*clericus et canonicus*, indicate that he was not a priest at this time for the term cleric alone in the writings of the age usually means one who is only tonsured or at most has Minor Orders" (in Abelard 1964: 36n). Against Héloïse's opposition—she felt that marriage was inappropriate for a man who wanted to be a great philosopher and theologian—Abelard carried out his plan. It is important to note that Héloïse objected not to the secrecy but rather to the fact of marriage itself, widely regarded as unworthy of a man such as Abelard. That Héloïse was right is borne out by Abelard's own words: "And further to appease Fulbert, I made an offer beyond his fondest hopes to make satisfaction by marrying her whom I had defiled, provided this be done secretly *so that my reputation would not be damaged*" (p. 31; emphasis added).

The proposal was at first accepted by Fulbert. But soon he grew unsatisfied with the secrecy of the union. And after the child was born and sent off to stay with Abelard's sister, Fulbert made the marriage public. Fearing that Héloïse's relatives might seek revenge, Abelard sent her to a convent. Fulbert, however, thought that by so doing Abelard was getting rid of his wife, and decided to punish him; when Abelard was asleep and off guard, Fulbert had him castrated. When morning broke and word got around, "the clerics and especially my students" grieved loudly; Abelard comments: "I felt the embarrassment more than the wound and the shame was harder to bear than the pain" (p. 39).

Wasting no time on psychological meanderings, Abelard next decided that both he and his wife would take holy orders. Contrary to the postromantic reader's expectations, there are no cries of despair or revolt. There might have been thoughts of revenge against the man who had inflicted such cruel punishment on him, but the canon's power must have discouraged any such plan. Nor is Abelard concerned with justifying such a sudden "conversion." His words are straightforward, and they indicate, in support of Luhmann's thesis, that love as a passion is still far from being a communication code. The author's comment is quite simple, and although there is mention of regret, this has to do rather with the betrayal of the model of glory he had opted for: "Filled as I was with such remorse, it was, I confess, confusion springing from shame rather than devotion the result of conversion, which drove me to the refuge of monastic cloister" (p. 40).

Nor should one think that the former lovers, now shut up in their cells as friar and nun, mourn their sudden separation bitterly. They may indeed have been sorrowful, for their love clearly seems to have been more than a passing affair. But love of this kind could not be expressed in writing, not because there was an explicit prohibition against it, but simply because such a subject matter could not be encoded. Thus both of them applied their energy to their new circumstances, and both achieved success. Héloïse rose to the rank of abbess; she remained Abelard's friend and occasionally relied on his protection. As to Abelard, he became even more famous; nor did his life become any less eventful or risky. He became an abbot, and his life was threatened by dissolute friars, who tried to poison him. He was involved in further intellectual controversies, and suffered another great shame when rival theologians had his book condemned and burned. Here is the lament of the author-narrator:

> I could then feel but cannot now express the grief which welled up within me, the shame that confounded me, the despair that upset me. I compared what I was then enduring with what I had formerly suffered in my body and counted myself the most wretched of men. I considered my former betrayal of little moment when compared to this injustice and I bemoaned the damage to my reputation far more than that to my body. (P. 52)

The comparison is too explicit for any explanation to be necessary. The damage to his reputation as theologian and thinker is deemed more serious than the physical punishment he has suffered. So, although toward the end of the letter he writes that "I was incessantly buffeted by conflicts without and anxieties within" (p. 75), by now the reader is in a condition to understand that conflicts and anxieties had not yet been thematized as psychological material in Abelard's age. Abelard's sorrows have to do with the damage—seen as unfair—to his intellectual reputation. His amorous choice and his religious choice are valued not in themselves, but only as functions of an external model imposed on the agent. Thus Peter Abelard's "autobiography" is not what we think of as autobiography. And this is so because at that time the individual was only an empirical reality, which in itself had no value and could acquire value solely as a reflection of the chosen model. His sufferings are personal only to the extent that they represent blemishes and losses in regard to the model with which the individual has been incorporated.

Let us take an equally brief glance at some later examples. After all, we can say that the choice between arms and letters was typically medieval. How would Renaissance man react, given a much wider range of possibilities?

PETRARCH'S *SECRETUM*: CARDANO AND CELLINI

Two texts by Petrarch are usually taken to be autobiographical: the "Ascent of Mt. Ventoux" and *De secreto conflictu curarum mearum*. Let us consider the more complex of the two.

The *Secretum* was written between 1342 and 1343, and revised between 1353 and 1358, in a particularly turbulent period in the poet's life, when his natural daughter was born and his brother decided to become a monk. The work is a long dialogue between Augustine, introduced by Truth, and the author himself. Since it is long, I will not be able to present a substantial summary of it, but will simply point to some of its aspects that are fundamental for our discussion.

Brought by Truth, Augustine introduces himself to Francesco as the one most fit to lead him out of the confusion that torments him. His opening words express his purpose: "What are you doing, you little man? What dreams are yours? What hopes? Have you thus forgotten all your miseries? Or do you not remember you are mortal?" (Petrarch 1968b: 439).

Augustine's position as guide and counselor and his authority are reminiscent of Dante's Virgil. But in fact the only meaning of the meeting of Petrarch and Augustine lies precisely in what makes it different from the earlier one. As Oscar Giuliani observes, the Latin poet is sent as God's answer to a prayer, and hence his trip "*cannot fail to answer its set purpose*," whereas Augustine is sent by the secular agency of Truth to Francesco, upon whom "no grace or divine dispensation has been bestowed, and therefore his salvation is not a necessary condition for the progress of the work" (Giuliani 1977: 56–57). In other words, the course of the dialogue in the *Secretum* is not a *fatale andare*; it does not contain a single, preordained path. This fundamental difference not only points to a drastic change that had taken place from Dante's time to Petrarch's but also explains the movement of the dialogue.

Evidently, no attitude could be expected from Augustine other than one of religious commitment, particularly since he himself knew the vital matter that fed the tormented Humanist. And his function is soon made known. After the opening exchange, Augustine assumes a severe tone, and accuses Francesco of a basic mistake:

> In truth, I believed you to be of readier wit, nor did I imagine you were still in need of admonitions fit for children. And surely, had you trusted to your memory those true and wholesome sentences of philosophers, which you read of even with me, and—allow me to say so—had you made an effort for yourself rather than for others, applying the fruit of your study of so many volumes to the task of giving a purpose to your life instead of courting the decadent applause of the vulgar and cultivating a preposterous vanity, you would not say such things, so insipid and coarse. (P. 443)

Francesco's reply to this accusation and the following ones are curiously contrary to our expectations. He either allows that he is ashamed to be caught red-handed or presents an ineffectual defense, as if he were more inclined to submit to the prescribed standards than actually to defend himself. Thus, for instance, throughout Book I he stresses the Augustinian thesis that only spontaneously is one hurled into unhappiness. Although his interlocutor faces this challenge, presenting himself as a living proof of the opposite—"dell'oposto io faccio tristemente prova in me stesso" (p. 447)—his resistance breaks down before arguments that do not impress us as convincing.

The reader of Bakhtin will remember his observations concerning the dialogical, and will say that here we are far from it. But I believe this information does not contribute to an adequate interpretation. For to use it thus abruptly would be to ignore the expectations that actually inform the dialogue. This will become clear when we have a more comprehensive view of the book as a whole. For the pattern of Augustine's accusations followed by Francesco's embarrassed acknowledgment of his own faults is repeated throughout almost the entire work. Augustine tells him that he has not dwelt sufficiently on death and has instead basked in his worldly renown as a poet and writer; that he loves Laura for the splendor of her body; that he has not properly understood the books he has read, placing his own cultural advancement above the teachings of the philosophers. His interlocutor's reaction is always the same: at first, he loudly protests, indignant and surprised; then, immediately and with no transition, he recognizes his faults and promises to mend his ways.

Why not accept Bakhtin's argument here? Because Francesco's "meekness" seems to indicate merely that, to the prestige of the model voice that soberly accuses and admonishes him, Francesco cannot counterpose the practice of introspection. Since Petrarch's time, introspection has become so common that we take it for granted and, finding it missing, tend to suspect that some personal deficiency is involved. If, however, we set our expectations aside and observe Augustine's interlocutor closely, we can easily see that Francesco portrays himself not as a weak-minded man who is no match for the intelligence of the former bishop of Hippo, but as a typical Humanist. What seems to us to be lack of introspection is misunderstood unless we relate it to the cult of models, the need to adjust private existence to the path prescribed by model figures. And Augustine is the product of a careful choice: he is the consummate type of the man who, with the force of his conversion and his wisdom, gave knowledge its due—that is, legitimated commerce with the thinkers, poets, and writers of antiquity, proposing a Christian reading of them. There would be no reason for the *Secretum* to adopt a "monological" tone if not for this respect for model figures.

This interrelation between the lack of introspection and the importance of conformity to models is particularly evident in those passages where Augustine accuses Francesco of following the opinion of the man in the street. The argument is particularly effective because it arouses shame in the poet, who feels that his search for renown is compromised by such a mean, lowly connection. But is not this thesis contradicted by Giuliani's formulation? Discussing the opposition between the *Divina Commedia* and the *Secretum*, he writes: "Augustine's specific purpose is to lead Francesco not to salvation, but rather to truth and self-knowledge" (Giuliani 1977: 70). And once again temporal remoteness confuses us. Our habit of indulging in psychological rumination makes us see as absurd Francesco's quest for self-knowledge when he proves to be so naive throughout the dialogue. However, the difficulty disappears when we recall that the modern conception of the individual is just beginning to be born.

The relevance of the comparison between Dante's work and the *Secretum* lies in the discovery of a characteristic of the latter that was not present in the former: the path of secular knowledge, which will lead to the increasingly common practice of examining through introspection the motives behind personal action. Obviously, I am not saying that there was no introspection before the Renaissance, but that it was only after the expectations and goals of life were secularized—relatively, at least—that introspection could focus less on God and Being than on the self.

The *Secretum* itself is proof that this secularization was beginning. Although Francesco is a meek interlocutor in almost all the dialogues, his attitude changes toward the end of Book III. After the third day of conversation, Francesco feels he is better prepared for a righteous life. But there remains one question to settle. Before the dialogue ends, says the Humanist, he wishes to hear the saint's "opinione conclusiva" concerning "whether you would have me give up my studies and live without glory or you recommend a middle way" (p. 589). In reply, Augustine does not tell him to live without glory, but advises him not to prefer "l'amore della gloria all'amore della virtu" ("the love of glory to the love of virtue").

Now, even if we do not accept Giuliani's equation of glory with epic and love with lyricism, the *Secretum* clearly implies that, for Petrarch, the cult of glory meant proceeding with his intellectual work, particularly his long poem *Africa*. It is precisely because of this identification of glory with his way of life that Francesco does not accept Augustine's final advice with his usual submissiveness. Not that he departs from his guide with an expression of opposition; nor is his meekness replaced by an outright contradiction. But Francesco's response is unmistakable. He attempts a compromise solution: on the one hand, he tries to make sure that the "ottimo padre" will still watch over him, for without his protection "la vita sarebbe per me senza attrativa" ("life would have no attraction for me"); on the other hand, he argues that, since he is living in the earthly world, life loses its meaning without the quest for glory (p. 597). Francesco knows that, from the viewpoint of the prevailing religious model, it would be safer to devote all his efforts to preparations for death, and thus he ought to give up his intellectual work. But he tries to justify himself: "non so frenare il mio desiderio" ("I cannot check my desire") (p. 597).

Thus the *Secretum* presents and defends a way of life no longer entirely submitted to the prevailing model of religious orientation. The compromise reached by the two interlocutors is rather precarious. The idea that poetic and intellectual endeavor could be a worthy goal in its own right, even though it might divert one from the path of preparation for the afterlife, was still thought to be dangerous and potentially misleading. But the fact remains that it is proposed by one who, as we have seen, was very far from being a rebel. This could be used as an argument for my thesis, proposed in *Control of the Imaginary*, that the prohibition of the fictional was simultaneous with the rise of the individual. But this possibility seems quite obvious and would lead us far astray from our immediate purpose, so I think I may as well leave it aside. I am more concerned here with stressing a different point.

From the moment that the right to secularized intellectual experience—that is, experience not subordinated to the greater glory of God and the salvation of the soul—is defended, albeit timidly, it becomes possible to distinguish between two investigative activities. If we call the first of these meditation, we may be sure that its basic object was to find out the origins and motivations of evils (sins), and that therefore we are dealing with a religious model. The fact that this model was practically absolute in the Middle Ages clearly shows how the possibilities of orientation for life had narrowed down in relation to the possibilities available in antiquity, when the religious experience was expanded by public life or channeled into contemplation. In the early Renaissance—if Petrarch is taken as the first Humanist, or one of the first—the near exclusiveness of the religious model is compromised, and meditation, as we have defined it, is changed into something else. Let us call it self-examination. Its object is the search for the reasons behind individual conduct. So we are now dealing with a psychologically oriented endeavor. By thus defining it, we implicitly take psychological orientation to be a result of the beginning of the secularization of human life. In spite of its etymology, "psychological" has less to do with "soul" than with the body, the body of an individual beginning to tread the path of individualism. It would, however, be inexcusable to assume that the attitude of self-examination is immediately actualizable, that the Renaissance was simply a leap across the boundary that separated it from the Middle Ages. My examination of the autobiographies of Cardano and Cellini, to which I now turn, will show that the individual that appears in their works is very far from the Francesco of the *Secretum*.

Geronimo Cardano (1501–1576) and Benvenuto Cellini (1500–1571) were contemporaries who probably never met. Their occupations were not likely to have brought them together. Cardano, a Milanese, was a physician, mathematician, and astrologer, who was interested in applying mirror science, then popular, to the development of military art. (Baltrušaitis has recently shown that Cardano's speculations on "burning mirrors" were put to practical use beginning with Buffon, in 1747; see Baltrušaitis 1978, esp. chaps. 4 and 5.) Cellini was a goldsmith and sculptor, who remains famous to this day. However, what is relevant here is not the difference between the latter's fame and the former's relative obscurity today, but rather the difference between their lives; for this difference points to a common frame of reference of beliefs and values, which will allow me to outline the shape assumed by the individual in their day.

Although not published until 1643, Cardano's autobiography, *De vita propria liber*, was written in 1575, a year before his death. The author was mostly concerned with the story of his professional career. He mentions the hardships of his youth, the negotiations he had to undertake in order to marry, the intrigues that for years caused official recognition of his position as a physician to be suspended, the sorrows caused by his children; yet all of this is no more than a backdrop for the description of his intellectual accomplishments. The author's exalted self-image and his contemporaries' high regard for him lead him to devote a full chapter—chapter 48—to an exhaustive list of those who had referred to each of his works. But this is not what concerns me here. What makes *De vita propria* interesting is a number of passages that would have seemed of secondary importance or even irrelevant to the author.

The first of these is to be found in the opening pages. Cardano describes the conjunction of heavenly bodies that had presided over his birth. The pattern formed by the stars, writes Cardano, could have made a monster of him. This did not occur, but the heavenly conjunction produced something extraordinary nonetheless—his own survival is seen as a near miracle. In any case, although his body survives, something in him is out of order, and at the same time he acquires a remarkable power. That is, the celestial conjunction somehow marks all who are under its influence—in other words, all who are born under it. In his case, the stars were content to stigmatize his genitals, so that from his twenty-first to his thirty-first year Geronimo was unable to sleep with a woman. On the other hand, the stars conferred on him an immense capacity for foreknowledge. Many times he was able to escape accidents thanks to this gift. Chapter 30 describes one of the shortest of these incidents:

In the following year, 1540, if I am not mistaken, when I was passing through the Via Oriental, it suddenly occurred to me, for no reason whatsoever, to cross from the left side to the right; and when I was once over, a great mass of cement fell from a very high cornice on the opposite side, precisely such a distance ahead of me that certainly, unless I had changed my course, it would have ground me to bits; thanks to God, I escaped. (Cardano 1930: 102)

Such is this scientist's interest in omens that he devotes a whole chapter to the subject—chapter 37. While the conjunction of Venus, Mercury, and Jupiter did not kill him at birth, it granted him a power that he must needs discuss in his intellectual biography, given his devotion to the investigation of phenomena. So that the modern reader can become aware of the author's intellectual climate and realize that this is not a case of a reputable scholar falling prey to superstition—the sort of thing that amuses those who read biographies of Freud—I will transcribe a passage in which Cardano describes one of his most peculiar abilities:

I am conscious that some influence from without seems to bring a murmuring sound to my ear from precisely that direction or region where someone is discussing me. If this discussion be fair, the sound seems to come to rest on the right side; or if perchance it approaches from the left, it penetrates to the right and becomes a steady hum. If, however, the talk be contentious, strangely conflicting sounds are heard; when evil is spoken, the noise rests in the left ear, and comes from the quarter exactly whence the voices of my detractors are making disturbance, and, accordingly, may approach from any side of my head. (Pp. 163–64)

But our physician-astrologer is not interested solely in his supernatural powers. His body as a whole interests him. Not that he thinks of himself as particularly beautiful or attractive. His own anatomy fascinates him in an impartial way, if such a thing is conceivable. For everything merits description. The shape of his feet is such that he must wear custom-made shoes; in contrast, his left hand is quite shapely, and his fingers are tipped with shiny nails. His body interests him in its entirety. And clearly he does not gloss over its most unpleasant aspects; for this machine is fraught with defects. He is afflicted with hemorrhoids, an incurable skin irritation, and—anticipating the most famous of all autobiographers—constant urinary incontinence. But his intention is not at all to depict himself as a victim, doomed by his presiding stars, tormented by a body that refuses to serve him properly. Nor is he inclined to follow the example of the Stoics, to despise the world and apply himself to controlling the body. To be sure, Cardano treats his own body as a testing ground, but his purpose is to cause smaller pains that will strengthen his general well-being:

> I have discovered, by experience, that I cannot be long without bodily pain, for if once that circumstance arises, a certain mental anguish overcomes me, so grievous that nothing could be more distressing. Bodily pain, or the cause of bodily distress—in which there is no disgrace—is but a minor evil. Accordingly I have hit upon a plan of biting my lips, of twisting my fingers, of pinching the skin of the tender muscles of my left arm until the tears come. Under the protection of this self-chastisement I live without disgracing myself. (P. 25)

One might even suppose that here is an innocent inkling of the Marquis de Sade. But in fact Cardano's painstaking examination has a different meaning. His own body is just as important as the stars, because all things act as determinants that the researcher must know in order to master. Lévi-Strauss (1962) once wrote that magic is distinguished from science by its belief in the absolute universality of its modus operandi. Cardano is a scientist who is spurred on by a magician's motivation. To him, determinacy is an objective fact, so that it is possible and indeed necessary to aspire to a *mathesis universalis*. In this meticulous realism there is no place for medieval concerns—for the religious dimension. If there is an afterlife, a dream the author confesses he has been cherishing for years, it is no more than the afterlife of fame. The model of glory we have seen in Abelard and Petrarch is now independent from the spiritual-religious path. But this very secular man has something in common with his illustrious forebears.

Let us recall the way in which Cardano indirectly justifies the writing of his book: "Vowing to perpetuate my name, I made a plan for this purpose as soon as I was able to orient myself. For I understood, without any doubt, that life is twofold: the material existence common to the beasts and the plants, and that existence which is peculiar to a man eager for glory and high endeavor" (p. 32). Although he has no great esteem for what his own body, such as it is, can do for him, or illusions as to what life still holds out to him, Cardano is not about to complain or wallow in melancholy. This is clearly a personal characteristic of his, rather than one common to his age. (A few centuries earlier, Petrarch had been given to melancholy.) If his impersonal way of looking at himself was indeed a personal characteristic of Cardano's, one should not confuse it with another characteristic, which was typical of the period: the lack of taste for or interest in psychological examination. Lest my assertion seem arbitrary, I will present a brief example.

The author willingly confesses to a number of vices, including gambling. On one particularly unlucky occasion, Cardano loses his wife's jewels. In chapter 30 he tells of one such episode, in Venice. On the previous day he had already lost a considerable part of his money. Nevertheless, he returned on the following day, and this time lost everything. However, he was shrewd enough to find that the cards were marked: the man who had defeated him, a senator, was a cheater. Indignant, Cardano attacked the man with a dagger, slashed his face and ran away from his retainers. That night, as he attempted to escape the police, he managed to fall into a canal. A passing boat picked him up. But the adventure was not yet finished: "When I scrambled aboard the skiff, I discovered in it, to my surprise, the Senator with whom I had just gambled. He had the wounds in his face bound up with a dressing; yet he willingly enough brought me out a suit of garments such as sailors wear. Dressed in these clothes, I traveled with him as far as Padua" (p. 105). The contemporary reader will be intrigued both by the victim's gentlemanly behavior and by Cardano's matter-of-fact acceptance of the clothes his former adversary offers him, as well as by the fact that the rest of the trip was uneventful. But as soon as the incident is over, another begins in the next paragraph. Indeed, Cardano's anatomical realism—it is perhaps what Auerbach calls "creatural realism"—is the correlative of the lack of a psychological dimension, or at least of what we think of as such. But before I attempt to formulate a general characterization of the Renaissance, let us turn to Cellini's *Vita*.

Cellini was less a contemporary of the sober Cardano than of the Spanish picaros. Not that he was ever a beggar or a blind man's guide; but like the Iberians, he was a blabbermouth, a spendthrift, a lover of the pleasures of bed and dinnertable. Born in Florence in 1500, he was only thirteen when his libertarian and adventurous spirit made him run away from home, where his father had forced him to study music. Sometimes in flight, he moves from Siena to Pisa, to Rome, to Florence, to Paris, then back to his hometown, where he works for Duke Cosimo I, though intermittently. Among his employers—or patrons, if a euphemism is preferred—were some of the most powerful noblemen of the Italian cities, popes Clement VII and Paul III, and Emperor Francis I of France. Of each one of them except for Francis, Cellini was to complain bitterly later. He accused Cosimo of being mean-minded and failing to provide him with the money to accomplish his most ambitious works; one can imagine what he had to say of Pope Paul III, who, persuaded by his malicious natural son, Pier Luigi Farnese, and offended by the artist's abuse, locked him up in the dungeon of Castèlo Sant'Angelo. Thus Cellini can be seen as a successful picaro, as a cloak-and-dagger hero, or as an exploited genius, a victim of the powerful.

But for our purposes this sort of interpretation is disallowed; Cellini's autobiography interests us only to the extent that it is revealing of the Renaissance individual. In this connection, it is immediately evident that, for all the differences between him and Cardano, in both there is a blend of "magic" and creatural realism. As to magic, since Cellini is no physician-astrologer, we of course will not ask him to explain his astrological chart or provide an interpretation of it in Latin. That is why we place "magic" between quotation marks, so that the reader will understand that in Benvenuto's mind the science of astrology is replaced by something akin to superstitious belief.

Here is an illuminating example, taken from one of the opening chapters. Benvenuto's precocious success aroused the envy of other Florentine goldsmiths. Unafraid, Cellini walked into the workshop of one of his rivals. He was abused and physically attacked; and this he would not stand. Undaunted, he knocked down his opponent with a blow. The goldsmiths took offense and sued for indemnity; the judges ordered him to pay a certain sum. But Benvenuto felt this was unfair; his blood boiled, and he swore he would be avenged. Soon he found an opportunity. As soon as the judges had left the palace, he fled to his enemies' house. At least when he was writing his memoirs, Cellini felt this decision had been an imposition of the stars: "At this point one may observe how the stars do not so much sway as force our conduct" (Cellini 1946: 27). Such was his fortune—or was it bad luck?—that he immediately ran into his bitterest enemy. The passage, though lengthy, is worth transcribing:

And Gherardo, who had been the cause of the quarrel, flung himself upon me. I stabbed him in the breast, piercing the doublet and jerkin through and through to the shirt, without however grazing his flesh or doing him the least harm in the world. When I felt my hand go in, and heard the clothes tear, I thought that I had killed him; and seeing him fall terror-stricken to earth, I cried: "Traitors, this day is the day on which I mean to murder you all." Father, mother, and sisters, thinking the last day had come, threw themselves upon their knees, screaming out for mercy with all their might; but I perceiving that they offered no resistance and that he was stretched for dead upon the ground, thought it too base a thing to touch them. I ran storming down the staircase; and when I reached the street, I found all the rest of the household, more than twelve persons; one of them had seized an iron shovel, another a thick iron pipe, one had an anvil, some of them hammers, and some cudgels. When I got among them, raging like a mad bull, I flung four or five to the earth, and fell down with them myself, continually aiming my dagger now at one and now at another. Those who remained upright plied both hands with all their force, giving it me with hammers, cudgels, and anvil; but inasmuch as God does sometimes mercifully intervene, He so ordered that neither they nor I did any harm to one another. I only lost my cap, on which my adversaries seized, though they had run away from it before, and struck at it with all their weapons. Afterwards, they searched among their dead and wounded, and saw that not a single man was injured. (Pp. 27–28)

This "tale"—for it is very much like a narrative by Boccaccio—is interesting for two features it presents and one that is conspicuously absent. The former are the superstitious allusion to divine mercy and the creatural realism, lively and dynamic. The incident lasts no more than a second. One moment Benvenuto believes he has killed his enemy, in the next he is rushing past the terrified relatives, then scrambling downstairs and grappling with the others who were waiting for him out in the street. And what is the absent feature? Psychological observation. One might argue, of course, that the fast pace of the narrative itself makes it impossible for the protagonist to interrupt his impetuous course in order to dwell on any feelings of joy or guilt, of fear or worry over the consequences of his act. But there is no technical impediment to this. His allusion to the role of the stars, made shortly before the narrative, seems more relevant here. The stars determine an individual's act; thus one should waste no time in such pointless ruminations. That is why the incident in question is never recalled once it is over; nor will the several murders Cellini is to commit play any role other than a circumstantial one in his narrative.

For here the analyst has an advantage that was missing in Cardano's biography. Since Cellini, unlike Cardano, sees himself as a mere craftsman and not as an important figure, he wants to present his direct life experience, life in its concrete manifestations. If, as scholars have shown, Cellini's memoirs omit references to certain shameful incidents in his life, not one of the murders he committed is left out. The motives of these crimes are just as trivial as that of the incident we have transcribed. The hotheaded Florentine was never one to take offense lightly, nor to waste any time on psychologically coherent explanations. He was as swift to draw his dagger as he was to bed the women he desired. When serving under Francis I, for instance, he became the lover of one of his humble models. A jealous man, like most southerners of his time, he warned one of his apprentices to watch over his house and, in particular, his woman. The effect of this warning was to drive the apprentice straight into the arms of Benvenuto's lover. When the artist found out, his revenge was terrible: he forced the traitor to marry the woman and invited her to remain working for him as a model and serving him in bed. Again, the reader should not expect *il maestro* to reflect on his own acts and repent. Life for him must be lived here and now; and our acts are determined by the power of the stars and whatever attention God may be willing to concede us.

Nor is this psychological shallowness affected when Cellini suffers violence at the hand of the pope. At no time, however wretched and filthy the damp dungeon he was thrown in, did it occur to Benvenuto that there was anything odd about the fact that the man who wanted to kill him was the pope. Introspection does not enter the picture here. In his predicament, fearing that the guards might kill him, or that the food he was given might be poisoned, the prisoner strengthened himself by praying with increasing fervor—and asserting his lust for life. This eventually led to a daring plan to escape the prison; he climbed down the high palace walls until, having used all his garments as rope, he was forced to jump, and broke a leg in the fall. Unfortunately, the episode is much too long, too crowded with details, to transcribe here. Let us only note that in spite of all this Benvenuto went on serving Paul III. This is to be explained less by the need to survive than by the horizon of values, the makeup of the individual of that period. Evidently, Benvenuto no longer trusted His Holiness. But, although he had no obligation to do so, he went on taking commissions from the Vatican before he accepted Francis I's insistent invitations.

All of this might lead one to see Cellini as an enslaved genius. But though such an interpretation might be legitimate for us, it would surely surprise Cellini himself. And, if we imagine ourselves playing the role of Augustine in the *Secretum*, we can easily picture Benvenuto's surprise at, or his ready acceptance of, our contention that he has not learned to deal with the powerful, that he lets them get the better of him, and so on. The fact is, Cellini would not see himself as enslaved or humiliated, for the self-image of an individual—at least one who had the humble occupation of craftsman—would not justify such a view.

In order to give my interpretation further support, I must resort to other examples. Let us look for more evidence of the importance attached to external forces. We have seen that Cellini is not an educated man like Cardano—and the very fact that he dictates his memoirs in the vulgar tongue is proof of this. Thus his ideas will necessarily be a popular, rather than an intellectualized, version of the belief in the power of the supernatural.

As to the power of the stars, we have already seen a brief example. If the stars determine men's actions, dreams are a channel of communication for the supernatural. In an early passage in *La vita*, Benvenuto, then in Rome, is called along with other musicians to a party, in honor of Clement VII. The pope is so pleased with the musicians that he expresses the wish to have them at his service. This, as we know, would have greatly pleased old Giovanni di Andrea, from whose house Benvenuto had run away as a boy in order to escape his music lessons. Caught in this dilemma, Benvenuto has a dream:

JOYS AND SORROWS OF THE SELF 89

The following night my father appeared to me in a dream, and begged me with tears of tenderest affection, for God's love and his, to enter upon this engagement. Methought I answered that nothing would induce me to do so. In an instant he assumed so horrible an aspect as to frighten me out of my wits, and cried: "If you do not, you will have a father's curse; but if you do, may you ever be blessed by me!" When I woke, I ran, for very fright, to have myself inscribed. Then I wrote to my old father, telling him the news, which so affected him with extreme joy that a sudden fit of illness took him, and well-nigh brought him to death's door. In his answer to my letter, he told me that he too had dreamed nearly the same as I had.
(P. 37)

The autobiographer feels no further explanation is necessary. Dreams determine behavior, as do the stars.

Likewise, he believes in the determinism of oaths. An oath is a serious thing indeed, for one's pledged word is heard in heaven, and so must be kept. Let me summarize an illustrative example. Once Benvenuto was invited to a party, to which each guest was to come with a woman. He obligingly handed over his companion to a less fortunate friend, and took with him a very pretty boy, disguised and made up. At the party, they were received enthusiastically, for everyone was astonished at the beauty of Benvenuto's "girl." But the women touched and pinched the boy and eventually found out the truth. The men, amused, threatened to force Benvenuto to pay a fine; meanwhile, Pantassilea, the woman he had handed to his friend, swore to avenge herself. On another occasion, the same group of friends got together at Benvenuto's house. One of them was Luigi Pulci, a young man who had once been cured by his host of a severe malady. Thinking of Pantassilea's oath, Benvenuto made him swear he would not try to approach her. Pulci said he would break his neck if he failed to keep his word. But soon he forgot his promise, flirted with the woman, and began to see her often. Benvenuto was filled with hate; I will skip his attempts to avenge himself. In spite of his hate—not because he loved the woman, but because his honor had been affronted—he was unsuccessful. But, as it turned out, no revenge was necessary. Pulci's broken promise brought about the intervention of Providence:

One day, among others, after it had rained a little, and he was making his horse curvet just before Pantassilea's door, he slipped and fell, with the horse upon him. His right leg was broken short off in the thigh; and after a few days he died there in Pantassilea's lodgings, discharging thus the vow he registered so heartily to Heaven. Even so may it be that God keeps account of the good and the bad, and gives to each one what he merits. (P. 63)

To this tremendous network of supernatural powers Benvenuto adds necromancy, which he learns from a priest. But since the book is readily accessible, I will let the reader enjoy this delightful scene on his or her own.

I have now collected all the evidence I need to understand the phenomenon that concerns me. In Cellini's world, each individual is expected to fend for himself. There is no single law applicable to all. The protection of a powerful figure is enough to excuse even one's most serious crimes—the pope himself can absolve his protégés from murder and exempt them from legal punishment—or, conversely, to threaten the life of one's enemy. Personal relationships are all-powerful, and the general rule is well formulated in the words by means of which Cardinal de Medici protects his friend: "Search diligently after my friend Benvenuto; I want to help and defend him; and whoso acts against him acts against myself" (Cellini 1946: 136). (Benvenuto, I should add, was wanted for another murder.) In such a social order, a common citizen is at the mercy of potentates, their retainers, their relatives. What Burckhardt wrote in connection with the previous century was still true of Cellini's time: "Good and evil lie strangely mixed together in the Italian states of the fifteenth century. The personality of the ruler was so highly developed, often of such deep significance and so characteristic of the conditions and needs of the time, that to form an adequate moral judgment on it is no easy task" (Burckhardt 1960: 49).

To use in a rather arbitrary way David Reisman's concept, which refers to another epoch and has a quite different meaning, Renaissance man was other-directed—in relation both to earthly and to supernatural powers. It should be kept in mind that although astrology, necromancy, and the belief in the divine seem to be experienced by Cellini as forms of superstition or magic pure and simple, among the learned astrology was a respected science. As E. Cassirer showed long ago, Renaissance theory of knowledge was marked by a peculiar tension between astrological determinism and free will. Writes Cassirer, on Pomponazzi:

> Pompanazzi's work also opens up for us a panorama of the more general problems taken up by Renaissance philosophy and of the contradictions it had to resolve. A new concept of nature and a new concept of humanity are about to be born. But the two cannot be integrated, since they not only embody different tendencies of the mind but are opposed to each other. The more clearly and sharply they are defined, the more inexorable the conflict between them. From the point of view of "nature," the world of freedom always remains a mystery, a sort of miracle. This miracle cannot be recognized without destroying the specific meaning of the concept of nature such as the Renaissance conceives it. For this meaning lies precisely in the idea of the unity and uniqueness of the explanation of nature.
>
> (Cassirer 1963: 115)

This theoretical and methodological monism explains the fundamental agreement we have found between the beliefs of a scientist like Cardano and those of an unschooled man like Cellini; this agreement consists in seeing the world's general phenomena as the product of a universal and absolute determinism. That is why this monism began to falter before the possibility of interpreting astrological charts as not completely determining. (In this context, it is relevant to observe that Cardano, as a scholar, did not find it strange that the stars could have either caused his death at the moment of his birth, or simply marked him with positive and negative signs, whereas Cellini believed that "the stars . . . determine our conduct.") Writes Cassirer on Marsilio Ficino: "This polarity, which lies in the stars themselves, and which had just been acknowledged and found its clear expression in the astrological system, now leaves life open to man's free will" (p. 119). No wonder, then, that in Pico della Mirandola's thought the praise of the individual should be accompanied by the disparagement of the stars: "The power we must recognize and venerate in the work of the great thinkers, statesmen, and artists is not that of the stars, but that of humanity. What raised Aristotle and Alexander above all their contemporaries, what gave them strength and significance, was not their better star, but their better 'ingenium'" (quoted in Cassirer 1963: 126).

Therefore we can say that between the medieval prevalence of religion and full secularization of life there stands the "magical" science of the Renaissance—a science that sets no limits to the relations of determinacy it establishes—a good representative of which is astrology. As the stars are gradually seen less as absolute determinants and more as susceptible to polar effects, a new conception of man is made possible, one in which free will plays a part. When this possibility is actualized, the modern conception of the individual is born.

We may then end our investigation. Cardano and Cellini are sufficient as examples of the way in which thought and life experience were secularized in the Renaissance. As we have said, this secularization slowly transformed the ancient practice of meditation into self-examination, and this, in turn, expanded as the experience of introspection was intensified. However, the two autobiographies we have looked at clearly show that this final step had not yet been taken. For all their differences in erudition and practical knowledge, in their ability to form an "objective correlative" of their lives, Cardano and Cellini are both immune to introspection. Cellini, who adored his father, upon returning to Florence soon after the city was hit by the plague, knocked at his family's door in vain, until a neighbor, an ill-tempered woman, told him that everyone had died, except for one sister. And Benvenuto sums up his reaction in a bare sentence: "As I had partly guessed it might be so, my sorrow was not so great as it would otherwise have been" (p. 77).

Can one, then, speak of autobiography in the Renaissance? Yes, though not in earlier periods. For in the Renaissance secularization of knowledge made it possible for man to act as an individual in the choice of his form of conduct. However, man remained other-directed; theoretical and methodological monism did not allow the acknowledgment of free will; and the individual was totally dependent on the whims of the powerful. For this reason, there was no room for radical self-examination; and thus the Renaissance individual was not yet a modern individual. As Louis Dumont observes, "when there is no longer anything ontologically real other than the particular individual, when the notion of 'right' refers not to a natural or social order but to the particular human being, this particular human being becomes an individual in the modern sense of the term" (Dumont 1978: 23).

But my position should not be overly simplified. I am not fixing a precise date for the birth of the individual. Proof of this is contained in the very text I have just quoted from, specifically in a comment on the juridical writings of a thinker who lived long before Cardano and Cellini, Ockham (1285–1347). This shows that the boundary of modernity is not a well-defined line, but rather one that moves back or advances depending on the field we are considering. In any case, as far as autobiography is concerned, the modern individual is not yet to be found in the earlier two-thirds of the sixteenth century. But one need only be reminded of Montaigne to realize that the individual is not very far off. Since, however, it is not my intention to present even a sketch of the history of autobiography, I will now consider the period when the existence of the genre is already indisputable: the eighteenth century.

ROUSSEAU: PARADIGM OF AUTOBIOGRAPHY

> Tous les animaux se défient des hommes et n'ont pas tort.
> (All the animals are suspicious of man, and with good cause.)
> —Rousseau, *Ebauches des Confessions*

Few writers have been as influential as Rousseau. In philosophy, in politics, in education, in psychology, in literature, his readers, admirers, and detractors have developed his ideas to extremes he could never have foreseen. Even leaving aside the thousands of pages Rousseau himself wrote, a complete bibliography of all that has been written about him or under his impact would be a nearly unfeasible task. But I am undaunted by this fact: here I will be considering Rousseau from the same narrow perspective I have been adopting; the *Confessions* will be examined not for their intrinsic interest, but in order to proceed with our reflection on the status of autobiography.

Written between 1764 and 1770, the *Confessions* are radically different from the other works we have been examining. Their immediate and comprehensive purpose is clear: to unveil the self by means of an investigation of its motivations, however remote, obscure, or unpleasant: "I have not promised to offer the public a great personage; I have promised to depict myself such as I am, and in order to know me in my old age it will be necessary first to know me well as a young man" (Rousseau 1969: 174). Here Rousseau is resorting to a sort of psychological causality: in order to know a man beyond maturity, one must learn to see him in childhood. Childhood is no longer seen as the golden age of innocence, where the shadows and traps of the adult world are denied entrance. This form of causality will be incorporated into the autobiographical genre. And most readers will expect the autobiographer to present his own self as a strictly consistent progress, where even hesitation and contradictory motivations are traced back to causes in the remote years of childhood. This is one reason why autobiography will come to be seen as the *document* of a life, told by its most competent narrator. The paradigmatic status of the *Confessions* justifies the presentation of this argument from the outset. But before developing its consequences, it is important to enumerate the elements with which Rousseau proposes to bare his heart.

To begin with, there is the pleasure of narrating, of translating oneself into print. Writes Rousseau at the beginning of Book I: "Let the telling of my story be as long as possible, that my pleasure may be protracted" (p. 22). But, in an apparent contradiction, a few paragraphs later he challenges the reader to hear the terrible tragedy of his life without quaking in horror. From the outset Rousseau counts on the reader's emotions, and trusts his own ability to keep them on edge. But in order to bring this effect about, he must introduce himself properly. Who is this old man bent over the page, commiting his memories to paper? He is someone naturally shy and loving, moved only by passion: "If I have to act, I know not what to do; if I have to speak, I know not what to say; if I am looked at, I feel embarrassed. When I fall in love, I sometimes find the right words to say; but in everyday conversation I can find nothing, absolutely nothing; such conversation is unbearable for me, because I am forced to speak" (p. 36).

Since this is the single fire that can set him aflame, Jean-Jacques recognizes his own inability to engage in regular work. The absolute self, the radical individualist, can see the other only by investing him or her with the halo of his own all-consuming passion. With unconcealed pride, Jean-Jacques dwells on the difference between himself and the scholars: "I was expected to write as a trade, as do all other scholars, whereas I could never write except when moved by passion" (p. 513). But if he is immune to material greed, if fame and prestige are no more than flattery to him, how could anyone ever have thought him the equal of those lackeys of the pen? Rather than interpret such passages as evidence of a monstrous arrogance—which would be fair enough—I prefer to see them in the light of the history of the genre. In Renaissance autobiographies, we found the opposite ideal. Not that Cardano and Cellini were ready to accept any transaction that might give them a title, easy money, or distinction. But their self-evaluation depended on their identification with a model. Honor, the respect of the powerful, the admiration of good society—these were the rewards that certified that one had achieved success according to a given model. In Rousseau, instead, what counts the most is commerce with oneself, the right to see oneself and others unmasked, bare-hearted. Deep down inside, the Genevan thinker believes that all around him there is nothing but arrogance and vanity, glorified nonentities and refined vilification. To keep himself to himself, to be ever on the watch, was not only a pleasure but also a duty to his own accusatory soul. Though long, the following passage is worth translating:

> Although I myself never had any station, I have known them all: I have lived in all, from the lowest to the highest, save for the throne. The Great know none but the Great; the small, none but the small. The latter never see the former but with admiration for their condition, and are never seen but with unfair contempt. The distance in between being great, both miss what is common to both, man himself. I, careful to remove his mask, have recognized him everywhere. I have weighed and compared their respective tastes, their pleasures, their prejudices, their maxims. Accepted in all houses as an unpretentious and inconsequential man, I examined them at length; when they were not in disguise, I was able to compare man to man and state to state. Being nobody, desiring nothing, I embarrassed and disturbed nobody; I walked in everywhere and attached myself to nothing, at times dining in the morning with Princes and supping in the evening with peasants.
>
> (Rousseau 1969: 1150–51)

On what we might call its first layer, the *Confessions* is inspired by the observing self's muted hostility to the world observed. Whereas for the Renaissance observer the world was marked by *positions*, the occupiers of which were associated with certain forms of deference (or with utter lack of respect), to Jean-Jacques's individualism the world had become a mass of wild atoms, a masquerade in which those who were already established in their masks attempted to impose a mask on new arrivals. From an early age, Jean-Jacques felt the malignant pressure the others wished to subject him to. He made a distinction, which would have been impossible centuries before, between what properly belonged to his own self and what belonged to the role that the circumstances attached to him: "She judged me less for what I was than for what she had made of me, and since she saw in me no more than a servant, I could not appear to her as anything else" (Rousseau 1969: 82).

This much evidence is enough to indicate the deeper purpose of the *Confessions*. We can interpret the book in two ways: as Jean-Jacques's way of avenging the miseries, persecutions, and injustices he had suffered or felt he had suffered, or as a full-bodied self-presentation before the reader, that the latter might be his judge. In fact, there is no need to choose between them. Both are correct, each in its own way; but they remain partial views.

Let us read the first page of the book: "I want to show my fellowmen a man in all the truth of nature; and this man will be myself. —I alone. I feel my heart and I know men. I am not made like any other man I have seen; I believe I am not made like any other that exists. If I am worth no more than any, at least I am different" (p. 5). Since I cannot transcribe the whole text, I will highlight or comment on each of its stages: "Let the trumpet of Judgment Day sound when it will; I will come before the sovereign judge with this book in my hand" (p. 5). Jean-Jacques knows he can do something no man had ever done: plunge into the inferno of his own private being. His mold was broken after he was made. He is not an exceptional man, except for the courage of undertaking such a journey. That is why he is not afraid of Judgment Day. The book he is writing will be less his defense than the proof that he was no worse and no better than anyone else. But the allusion to the trumpet has only the effect of concealing what is really involved here. Judgment will not come at the end of time; it begins right now, when the book, being finished, is placed in the reader's hand. This thick sheaf of pages and words is not a present to the reader, but rather an awful burden laid on his shoulders: the reader will be the judge. But this is not really a fair trial: the judge must find the defendant not guilty or else be proved a coward, unable to cast off the mask behind which he hides himself: "Let each one of them bare his heart in turn before thy throne with the same sincerity: and let a single one tell thee, if he dare: *I was a better man than he*" (p. 5).

Rousseau is Augustine's polar opposite: he does not see himself as one led astray, to whom divine illumination has revealed his error, and who now is eager to confess it to serve as a guide and comfort to those who are also of goodwill. No; Rousseau does not see his errors as uncommon. What is uncommon about him is only this thirst for truth, this inquisitive passion. But when he has finished the descent into his own night, he exclaims that he is like all the others; that all are like him—save for this one thing. Thus the *Confessions* is an experience in democracy: all men are equal. Likewise, his judges form a democratic tribunal: whoever presents himself before this tribunal must bow to the majority's decision. But—here is the supreme irony—this "inventor" of modern democracy starts out by expressing a qualification that contradicts his invention: it is true for all, save for himself. Radical individuality can dream of democracy, as long as it keeps up its sleeve the qualification that exempts itself from it. Thus, the reader who fails to absolve him proves to be unworthy of the trust he has been given. The decision of the majority will be subject to doubt unless it a priori certifies the purity of the man who claims to be pure. Jean-Jacques flaunts the charisma of the just, and where charisma comes in the vaunted democratic sovereignty is annulled. The confession of the modern individual, then, is born under the sign of equivocality. Writes Stephen Spender:

> At the end of the reading . . . Rousseau imagines himself challenging all his fellow beings to assert whether any of them dare say that after all he was a better man than this Rousseau, with all his sins and vices. God, who plays a rather passive role in Rousseau's heaven, is expected to call anyone who claims to have been a better man than Rousseau a liar. (Spender 1980: 120)

It is important to keep this contradiction in mind if one wants to see the *Confessions* from a nonauthoritarian perspective. And this is necessary in order to place oneself in a better position to appreciate the status of autobiography as a genre.

Rousseau bases the radical novelty of his undertaking on his complete sincerity. For him, the point is to hide nothing, even those acts that seem the vilest. Let us examine some of these. Jean-Jacques was still a child when he committed his first grave misdeed. When the house where he worked was in a turmoil because of a death in the family, he stole an insignificant object and blamed it on the cook. This episode will never cease to haunt him; indeed, he says it is one of the reasons why he decided to write his autobiography. But Rousseau is not content to atone for his act by confessing it. His sincerity forces him to dwell on the probable fate of the cook, who was unlikely to have ever found another job. But this is still not enough for him. He must tell the reader why he committed his act. However, instead of simply recognizing his guilt, Rousseau tries to justify himself: "Never has evil been farther from me than at this cruel moment, and if I accused the poor girl—however odd this may sound—this was because of my friendship for her. . . . I accused her of having done what I myself wanted to do and of having given me the ribbon because it was my intention to give it to her" (Rousseau 1969: 86).

The same wavering between guilty description and exculpatory rationalization can be seen in a more dramatic memory. Urged by Jean-Jacques, his wife leaves their children at the door of a foundling home. Not one or two children: as part of his punishment, Rousseau stresses that there were five of them. Here the author feels the accusation is more serious, and he mingles description with justification. How could a man with such a tender soul, sensitive to all that is good and virtuous, "trample unscrupulously upon the sweetest of all duties"? As if he sees himself standing before a judge, the narrator explains: "No, I feel it and say it proudly: this cannot be. Never, in a single moment in his life, was J.-J. a man devoid of feelings, of entrails, an unnatural father" (p. 357). But how can he prove his innocence? First he justifies himself for having covered up this fact: he has done so out of respect for poor Thérèse. However, he had told the truth to those who were his close friends at the time—Diderot, Grimm, Madame d'Epinay, and later Madame de Luxembourg. Clearly, it was one of them who had circulated the story that Rousseau had deserted his children one by one, thus causing great pain to the sensitive father. Traitors, this race of scribblers! But from his reader-judge Rousseau hides nothing; or, in other words, to him he reserves the whole truth. For he handed his children over to a foundling home because he could not support them, and he would like them to become honest workingmen and peasants rather than adventurers and swindlers: "I believed I was acting as a Citizen and a father, and I envisaged myself as a member of Plato's Republic" (p. 357).

Such is the peculiarity of Rousseau's sincerity: his acts seem to be evil only before we view them in full, before their motivations are known. If we only let him explain himself, we will see that in fact he was moved by noble intentions. Thus, if he falls out with his friends and protectors, whose fault can it be? His original misfortune was to have to live among writers. The origin of all his troubles, then, was the moment when, seeing that the Dijon Academy was offering its annual prize for an essay on the question "Whether the reestablishment of sciences and arts has contributed to purify our morals," he followed Diderot's advice and decided to compete. "The rest of my life and all my misfortunes have been the inevitable consequence of this one moment of folly" (p. 351). From now on he had to live in a world for which he had no inclination or gift. Because of his initial mistake, he was forced to duplicate it, "and became cynical and caustic because of the shame I felt; I affected to despise the politeness I was unable to display" (p. 368). A fish out of water, Rousseau builds an aquarium to exhibit himself in. But men will not forgive those who will not conform. And men of letters are monsters of vanity, as susceptible as prima donnas, and they balk at anything that seems to leave them in the shadow. Diderot and Grimm had been his friends. But what friends were these, who connived with their aristocratic patrons in trying to convince Thérèse and her mother to leave poor Jean-Jacques? "For I had clearly shown that, being unable to do anything for them, I could not even, because of them, do anything for myself" (p. 418).

For the autobiographer, this episode could not be seen as anything else than a conspiracy of false friends to harm him. Not once does he wonder whether he himself, in his self-absorption, could have caused the failures and misfortunes that crushed him. He never asks himself why Paris both attracts and repels him. If, for instance, he needs Thérèse so badly, why do his plans aim solely at his own well-being or, at most, imply only minor sacrifices on his part? And why exactly does he need Thérèse, an ignorant woman whom he had never professed to love, only acknowledging her unswerving loyalty?

We need not touch upon the delicate subject of Rousseau and women to realize the limits of his self-knowledge. We need only observe that here, again, for all his "sincerity" he fails to see the beam in his own eye. After all, what does his famous sincerity see? For one, the author never realizes that he combines his self-pitying tendency to cast himself always as the most downtrodden of men with a consistent exhibitionistic streak. Examples are many; let us look at a few. As a young man, Jean-Jacques, though he can hardly read music at all, proposes to write music and conduct an orchestra in public. What does this imply? Contempt for the discernment of his provincial audience? A talent for the picaresque or the parodical? But Rousseau loves himself too much to assume the role of a picaro, and nothing could be more alien to his thought than parody. Impudence? Yes, a little. But, above all, he feels a double urge to affirm a huge talent and to bring about his own humiliation. A great musician of our times once said he never understood why a virtuoso should feel nervous before a concert. According to him, this could only mean that the musician does not master the piece about to be played and should have practiced harder. Rousseau's case is precisely the opposite. He is aware of his insufficient training as a musician, but nevertheless, or maybe for this very reason, takes up a challenge in which the ambition to show off is mingled with the pleasure of making a fool of himself.

Let us look at another situation of the same kind. In Paris, one of his musical works is performed and is very well received by the court. The author decides to attend a performance. "On that day, I was dressed as on any common day; my beard was long, my wig was unkempt. Seeing this lack of decency as an act of courage, I thus entered the same room where in a short while the king, the queen, the royal family and the whole court would soon be" (p. 377). In the place that has been reserved for him, near the king's box, he could be seen by everyone. Then the exhibitionist turns masochist: "When the theater lights went on, seeing myself in such garb among people who were excessively well attired, I began to feel unwell: I wondered whether I was in my proper place" (p. 377). Jean-Jacques feels both flattered and humiliated. His work is acclaimed by elegant society, but the composer endeavors to give a masochistic turn to his own triumph. Now he thinks: To be myself, I should never feel ashamed to present myself as I have chosen, in any place whatsoever; now he tells himself: I must be able to suffer ridicule and censure, as long as they are not merited (see p. 378).

Admittedly, I have little sympathy for this side of Rousseau. But this is not a personal antipathy toward a writer who anticipated the good and bad sides of the romantic tradition, and who provided much of the impetus for contemporary thought. If, from a literary point of view, Rousseau's tearful self-exaltation was to have such a lamentable progeny, how could one forget that without him a Proust could not have come to be? What I dislike about the *Confessions* is the fact that this work set the tone for later autobiographies. Should autobiography be seen as true or false? Is it a literary genre at all? An eminent Rousseau scholar, whose name I would rather not mention, gives the usual reply: how could the *Confessions* be taken as deceitful if it is a literary work? This is an attempt to solve the two questions by mixing the two in a single sentence. The shape of the vicious circle makes no difference; either question can be taken as the answer to the other. The logical inconsistency is irrelevant, as long as the academic cliché is confirmed. Taking autobiography as a confession of truth—or, if untrue, as a fraud—implies taking it as the *document* of a life, which in turn assumes that the narrating "I" sticks to a consistent position—that is, he sees events of the past precisely as he saw them when they occurred. But Rousseau was already aware of the falseness of this assumption. He makes this point quite clearly in Book III: "I believe I have already mentioned that there are occasions when I am so unlike myself that I could take myself to be a man of completely opposite character" (p. 128). And, in Book IX, he observes another of his metamorphoses:

Until then I had been good; henceforth I became virtuous, or, at least, drunk with virtue. This intoxication had begun in my head, but it had passed to my heart. The noblest of prides here sprouted over the remnants of uprooted vanity. I no longer gambled; I became indeed what I showed myself to be, and for at least the four years when this great effervescence endured in all its force, there was no greatness or beauty that can enter a man's heart but I was capable of it between myself and Heaven. (P. 416)

Here it becomes clear that my feelings against the book have to do less with the book itself than with the norms it helped to set up. (Thus it was necessary to write what I have written in order to bring this distinction into sharp focus.) Is an autobiography indeed a document—that is, the sufficient proof that one lived or witnessed such and such an experience? How could it be so if the autobiographer's self admits that he is in a state of constant change, constantly changing roles? How could it be so if Rousseau himself states that the documents he had saved to use when he should write his *Confessions* had been lost, so that "I have but a single faithful guide to rely on: the chain of feelings that have marked the succession of my being, and, through them, the chain of events that were its causes or effects" (p. 278)?

No, an autobiography cannot be seen as a historical document, for it is no more than one's record of how one saw oneself and formulated one's belief that one was the *other* who called himself "I"—an other who is clearly related to the "I" now writing, with similar reactions and the same history, but still an other, living with the illusion of unity. But should we deny autobiography literary status? Indeed, isn't its disqualification for historical status the very proof that it is literature? Once again, Rousseau provides the elements for a subtler answer. Nowhere in his long account does Rousseau consider the scenes in his novels as representations of his own living experience. Evidently, if we read his novels and his autobiographical writings, we are in a better position to understand how Rousseau was able to create his fictional narratives, the relation between them and his actual life. But if his autobiography is based not on documents but on the *chaîne des sentiments*, the author's literary works are related to a different source. The decisive passage in this connection is not among the more familiar ones:

> It is a curious fact that my imagination should be particularly agreeable only when my own state is the least agreeable, and, conversely, least pleasant when all smile around me. My wicked head will not submit to things. It would not know how to beautify; it wants to create. Real objects can at most be depicted as they are; it can embellish only imaginary objects. I can portray spring only in winter.
>
> (Pp. 171–72)

But I will leave this material uninterpreted for the moment. Right now, I am less concerned with the status of autobiography than with Rousseau's version of the genre.

There can be no doubt that with Rousseau we find the individual such as we know him. Jean-Jacques's inability to become as transparent as he would like to be is the common fate of modern individuals. For Rousseau, sincerity had to be the axiom, the point behind which nothing else could be placed or demonstrated. He would make the heart as irreducible as Descartes had made the *cogito*. Rousseau does not yet realize that the desire to be sincere may be motivated by something prior to it; that the will to destroy all masks may give rise to another mask—in short, that there is no stable, primary, irreducible point that can be conquered and rendered in words. This is already part of the problem of the modern individual. Let us imagine what would happen if a time machine landed Cellini on a psychoanalyst's couch: clearly, an enormous confusion would follow.

What common language could they possibly find? How could the model of honor and glory deal with transference? If, however, Jean-Jacques saw himself in the same circumstances, the situation would be quite different. A *malade imaginaire*, paranoid, exhibitionistic, unable to relate to a woman on an equal plane—either calling her *maman*, transforming his lover into an incestuous "mother," or treating her as a helpless creature that must be taken care of and that will give material comfort in exchange—Jean-Jacques would be a prize patient for the old Viennese doctor. For—to touch upon my antipathy toward the *Confessions* one last time—if the book makes us feel uncomfortable, it is because it is so close to us.

AUTOBIOGRAPHY AS A GENRE

Of the possible fates that await a medium-length or long piece of writing, two immediately come to mind: it may be ignored or it may be summarized in a short passage. Since it is inconceivable that a writer should believe, even as he writes, that the fruit of his effort will turn to dust, I will try to reduce the previous pages to their basic core. We set out from the assumption that, if we take autobiography as a genre, we make it dependent on two variables: the individual, whose life experience it expresses, and its independence in relation to fiction. As Elizabeth Bruss puts it synthetically: "Autobiography as we know it is dependent on distinctions between fiction and nonfiction, between rhetorical and empirical first-person narration" (Bruss 1976: 8).

In demonstrating the first point, I found it necessary to examine a few examples of "autobiographies" from different historical periods, in order to distinguish between (a) cases in which one cannot properly speak of autobiography (Abelard and Petrarch); (b) cases in which the term "autobiography" is used appropriately as long as one keeps in mind that the individual in question does not share the experience of individuality as we know it, not because he has not had such experience but because he follows different parameters (Cardano and Cellini); (c) a case in which no qualifications are in order (Rousseau).

To be sure, my sample can be criticized as either too restrictive or too comprehensive. Perhaps both criticisms are reasonable. I myself would subscribe to them if I had considered the task concluded. But, rather than think of the following pages as a coda, we ought to see them as a sort of chessboard that is only now ready for the game, which necessarily will be shorter than the preparation for it. The first move will sound like a questioning of our enterprise: what, after all, does it mean to establish the status of a genre? Is it perhaps one more attempt at taxonomy, the sort of thing that structuralism degenerated into, which can be accused both of seeking refuge in the neutral territory of pure description and of covertly postulating a normative orientation? Although no writer ever knows how he or she will be read, I must say this is not at all my intention. If every genre, literary or not, is a form of communication, with rules one has to learn in order to avoid mistakes in interaction, the attempt to define a genre is not a normative act but rather an explanatory one; and the idea is to explain what is involved in the process of reading. That is why this effort will be void, partial, or contradictory unless the reader's expectations are taken into account. That is: the effort to determine the status of autobiography as a genre takes for granted that the contemporary reader recognizes it in practice and, whether or not he or she can or cares to define it, knows its distinctive features. As Barret J. Mandel has written, "the point is that fiction is fiction for a *subject*. Autobiography is autobiography for a *subject*. No amount of logic brought to bear to prove that because autobiography is not life it is actually fiction will convince any reader that autobiographies can or should be read as fiction. It is a total denial of the reader's experience" (Mandel 1980: 55).

Thus, if we envisage the analytical enterprise in the field of language as—among other things—the reconstruction of the experiences in question, we must consider their prior horizon of expectations. However, if reconstruction is not to be confused with description—whether naive or sophisticated—of the data, I must add that if readers generally make a distinction between the autobiographical and the fictional, they usually lack the information that might lead them to circumscribe the genre to a given historical period. That is why I believe the sample I have examined is interesting. But it is not enough to make sure that such a restriction is made and go on speaking vaguely of the "contemporary reader." In order to provide a more solid grounding for our judgment, let us examine the autobiographical reflections of contemporary authors.

The most illuminating example is the case of Nabokov. In 1955, this Russian-American writer became universally known as the author of *Lolita*. This fame had much less to do with his talent as a writer than with the supposedly pornographic nature of the novel. In time, the misunderstanding was dispelled, Nabokov's vast earlier production was rediscovered, and critics were able to see *Lolita* in the proper light. Conceived as the autobiography of one Humbert Humbert, who had died shortly before he was to be tried for murder, and introduced by "John Ray, Jr., Ph.D.," *Lolita* is an omnivorous parody, where genres as diverse as autobiography, the confessional novel, and the detective story, as well as stock figures such as the double, are all thrown in, shuffled, and exploited; it is like a story told by an Alice who has read and appreciated Joyce. The novelist himself, in an afterword later incorporated to the American edition, begins to unravel the skein, in an ironical vein: "After doing my impersonation of suave John Ray, the character in *Lolita* who pens the Foreword, any comments coming straight from me may strike one—may strike me, in fact—as an impersonation of Vladimir Nabokov talking about his own book" (Nabokov 1973: 328).

As the reader realizes the interplay of mirrors, he or she begins to understand that the allusions and parodies go far beyond a limited target. To begin with, Humbert Humbert's confessional "sincerity" is clearly a parody of Rousseau's *Confessions*. Also easily identified are lines by Eliot, whose poetry Nabokov disliked, and allusions to Proustian technique, although the author considered Proust one of the masters of contemporary prose. Thus one might think that for Nabokov the major function of memoirs is to serve as a vehicle for parody. This, however, would be a mistake. Nabokov wrote not only one of the best autobiographies of the century but also one that gives us important glimpses into his awareness of the distinction between the genres. The fictionist not only feeds on his real world but also does violence to it:

I have often noticed that after I had bestowed on the characters of my novels some treasured item of my past, it would pine away in the artificial world where I had so abruptly placed it. Although it lingered on in my mind, its personal warmth, its retrospective appeal, had gone and, presently, it became more closely identified with my novel than with my former self, where it had seemed to be so safe from the intrusion of the artist. (Nabokov 1966: 95)

Thus, after the effort of recovering the world of his old Swiss governess, he wonders whether he has "really salvaged her from fiction" (p. 117).

Similarly, although in a more commonplace reflection, Claude Roy observes: "One does not write one's life as one should, it seems, write a novel: avoiding a godlike position, leaving one's *creatures* free, never interfering with their freedom. Towards what one has done, given one's destiny, one is God, the all-knowing" (Roy 1972: 129).

Elias Canetti also ponders the distinction between fiction and autobiography. In the first volume of his memoirs, he recalls the view he had from his apartment of the insane asylum he intended to use in a novel. In fact, this novel never materialized. But Canetti remembers his intention:

That was the utopian aspect of my enterprise, and even though I had the town of Steinhof before me in the flesh, as it were, this utopian aspect stayed utterly remote in time. The figures only just emerging and their lives were so manifold that anything was possible, any twist of destiny. However, I excluded an irrevocable end, and it was as if I had given the figure most urgent for me, the Enemy of Death, a power over the lives of the others. (Canetti 1982: 324)

Like memoirs, fiction—and perhaps all other work employing language—is an attempt to impose order on the chaos of life such as it is presented to us. But within this common ground, fiction can postulate a utopia; in order to maintain it, it may even—as in the case mentioned—refuse to actualize itself in a work. Memoirs cannot duplicate it except as a fraud, or, more probably, a proof of madness. Thus, assuming the proof to be necessary, we find that fictionists of all kinds are aware of the boundaries that separate fiction from autobiography. It is scarcely worth emphasizing that these boundaries are not absolute; that fiction often feeds on our idea of ourselves; that fictional images are actualized in our everyday experience and, conversely, everyday experiences are transformed into fiction. This flexibility, though, does not erase the line between fiction and autobiography. They differ as to the role that each assigns to the self. Whereas in the case of fiction the writer's empirical self provides the basis for invention, in autobiography it is the source of experiences that are to be conveyed. Where the historico-cultural frame of reference does not allow such a distinction, fiction and autobiography are different artifacts from what they are for us. Thus the self can only be a legitimized source if it coexists with a given historical frame of reference. For autobiography only exists as a genre—that is, as a discursive form that predetermines a differentiated sort of expectation—if "one's calling (and later one's craft or art) . . . became a necessary factor in one's appropriation of reality, in one's education; *it mediated between the individual and the world insofar as it contained, objectively, both a person's most characteristic individual aspirations and the kinds of values, ideology, and sociality which he chose*" (Heller 1978: 234).

Therefore, it was only when models of political or religious order were no longer the single, indispensable requisites for recognition of the individual that the self could see itself and be seen as an individualized individual. This does not mean that there was no individuality in antiquity or in the Middle Ages, but that the individual's defining pattern and expected conduct then and its modern counterparts are not sections of a smooth continuum. It is only after the Renaissance that one can legitimately say that "the author of an autobiography gives a sort of relief to his image by reference to the environment with its independent existence; he looks at himself and delights in being looked at—he calls himself as witness for himself" (Gusdorf 1980: 29). When the self attains this sort of emphasis, when it turns into a figure that contrasts with its environment, it becomes a *discursive position*, clearly distinguishable from that of the historian. As Georges Gusdorf observes, "the prerogative of autobiography consists in this: that it shows us not the objective stages of a career—to discern these is the task of the historian—but that it reveals instead the effort of a creator to give the meaning of his own mythic tale" (p. 48). This difference explains why autobiographical material could not be mistaken for a historical document. It is, then, neither history nor fiction. The autobiographer's account can be "his own mythical tale," but it should not be forgotten that the myth is not experienced as fiction, that it is something one believes. Now, if it is true that autobiography is autonomous in relation both to history and to fiction, what then is its status?

To begin with, let us conceive a neighborhood of discourses formed by these three modalities: historiography, fiction, autobiography. The first and the second are polar opposites. Historians, unless they are naive positivists, want to be (knowing that they are) *relatively* impartial in relation to what they describe and analyze. (Relatively impartial even if they belong to a party, since partiality would hinder or destroy historical discourse.) Although we know that historians' position in society and the theory they consciously or unconsciously accept directly interfere with the choice and interpretation they offer, historians always profess—as they well should—to be presenting the "truth" about the subject. (The quotation marks here indicate that the truth is not something that can be found, but rather that must be built—in other words, that it always depends on the investigator's position.) Against positivists of all shades, who still proclaim the factual objectivity of history, the following fragment by Novalis is an eloquent argument:

> The historian organizes the historical being [*historische Wesen*]. Historical evidence is the mass to which the historian gives shape, vivifying it. It thus follows that history also is subject to the principles of vivification [*Belebung*] and organization, and wherever these two principles are missing, there a respectable work of history is not to be found, but only occasional traces of life, appropriated by an unwitting genius. (Novalis 1978: 270)

We no longer have to say that the rules valid for historiographical discourse mean nothing to the fictionist. To use Novalis's terms, vivification and organization now have a different aim. The fictionist's limit is not truth or "truth," but the possibilities of conceiving existence, as it is acknowledged by his or her values and accessible to his or her imagination. These two are the only parameters that condition the fictionist (a category that includes the poet).

The memoirist is placed between the two. Vis-à-vis the historian, the memoirist may only claim to present a testimony in good faith—in other words, may only claim that this is how he or she feels he or she behaved in a given situation or witnessed a given event. Memoirs present a personalized view of history. Vis-à-vis the fictionist, the memoirist must claim to have different rights—more limited on the one hand, since he or she may not "invent" what did not happen; more personalized on the other hand, for what is being written about is what has been actually experienced. Between fiction and autobiography, the self steps in as a dividing wall. Between history and autobiography, the dividing wall is the difference between the two genres' claims to "truth." All these distinctions, to be sure, presuppose a common, indistinct zone, which Goethe already alluded to: "Man knows himself only in so far as he knows the world, and becomes aware of the world only in himself, and of himself only in it" (quoted in R. Pascal 1960: 467). That is, these neighboring territories assume the necessary interrelation between subject and object, the impossibility of defining either of these terms except by their contact with each other. If nevertheless the discursive areas remain distinct, it is because this common interrelation is ruled by differentiated requisites. The self and "truth" are the features that define these neighboring discourses, according to their presence, modality of presence, or absence.

The reader who has followed me this far may feel satisfied. As the author, however, I cannot say the same. I invite my remaining readers to take one last step. In order to achieve a more comprehensive view, I must articulate the variables I have been using here with the larger ones I have developed throughout my theoretical endeavor. As a time-saving device, I offer the accompanying diagram.

Although too schematic, the diagram merits a word or two. From *Mimesis e modernidade*, through the essay "Social Representation and Mimesis," to parts of *The Control of the Imaginary* and of the present book, I have been stressing that mimesis—as Aristotle's *Poetics* already affirmed—was not restricted to artistic (fictional) activity. In fact, we might call it the phenomenon underlying all productive (poietic) processes. For simplicity's sake, in the diagram I call its field of action "field of active learning." (This terminology, however, has the advantage of not considering the productive process as a prerogative of the adult.) As such, mimesis assumes that a subject sets out—unconsciously, in most cases—to identify itself with a standard. In actual fact, the subject's identification project is translated into an assimilating process—that is, the process of becoming similar to the standard. Depending on the agent's psychological productivity, this searched-for similarity may be actualized as a form of greater or lesser difference. (Only in pathological cases does the search for similarity take the opposite path, so that the agent is converted into a copy or double of the standard.) For this reason, we have been defining mimesis as the production of difference; now it must be added that this takes place within a horizon of similarity. Thus defined, mimesis is a universal human category.

Equally universal are the forms by means of which the agent of mimesis

	Forms of Thematization	Discursive Forms	
Mimesis (extension) { Field of active learning {	Thematization of perception	: Discourses : of reality	{ from the pragmatic to the scientific
	Thematization of the imaginary	: Discourses : of the imaginary	{ from the oneiric to the fictional

relates to the world, thematizing it in a perceptual or imaginary manner. The historical connotation is already present in the line that separates forms of thematization from discursive forms. What we generically call "reality discourses" are characterized by their basic rule of conduct: the submission to the "true/false" requirement. On the other hand, the discourses that derive from thematization of the imaginary are characterized by the fact that they do not contain any truth that is not relative to the desires and values of its agent. Thus fictional discourse is seen as the result of a production of difference, subject to thematization of the imaginary, a territoriality characterized as nondocumental, pleasurable, and critical of the socially established "truth." (Let us not forget that these traits, taken together, characterize only the experience of modernity.) If this scheme has the advantage of clarity, it also has the fault of all products that are *intentionally* clear: oversimplification. (To begin with, it does not provide the elements necessary to treat the phenomenon of keying, which in "Social Representation and Mimesis" is said to be typical of mimesis. Since I cannot develop it here, let me just add that the idea of transposition of frames discussed in that essay is coextensive with what I am here calling "process of active learning.") Since our scheme is admittedly limited, let us use it less as an end in itself than as a means to go deeper into the relationship between the fictional and the autobiographical. This will allow us to use Nabokov's reflections more profitably. Recalling a childhood scene, he writes: "As often as not, [my parents] used to be out at that time, and in the gathering dusk the place acted upon my young senses in a curiously teleological way, as if the accumulation of familiar things in the dark were doing its utmost to form the definite and permanent image that repeated exposure did finally leave in my mind" (Nabokov 1966: 89). If we understand this passage as representative of the type "formation of the lasting image," it can be related to analogous scenes found in Claude Roy and Elias Canetti:

[In his last self-portraits, my father] patiently described the life of a face from which life is receding, the flesh wasting away, the muscles slacking, the mouth tightly pressed, and the attentive bewilderment in the eyes watching the shape they illuminate disintegrate little by little, refusing to look away from this slow defeat.
(Roy 1972: 344)

I learned from [Isaac Babel] that one can gaze for a very long time without knowing something, that one can tell only much later whether one knows something about a person: only after losing sight of him.   (Canetti 1982: 312)

The image presupposes a slow depuration of what was once familiar; a depuration that takes place outside the sphere of perception, amid the shadows, in the slow defeat of the visible. The work of imagination is not to be thought of as a sort of replacement or compensation; it is rather a slow metamorphosis, never completed. What has been lived and experienced is distorted, lengthened or foreshortened, condensed or prolonged into different traits, but in the poem a gate still slams shut, real toads croak in the imaginary garden.* Fiction is not distinguished from autobiography because the latter is immune from the work of images. In fact, autobiography is filled with images; only, it cannot let them proliferate beyond control. Because it lives off images, their slow accumulation, autobiography cannot be a pure document, ready to be used by the historian. Because it cannot freely submit to the unrestricted chemistry of the fictional, the territory of fiction is outside its bounds. This, however, does not mean that parts of it cannot break free and then be read as if they belonged to a different discursive zone. This is the case, for instance, of the characterization of the young cripple in Vienna, reduced to an almost wormlike condition, with whom, however, Canetti had philosophical discussions. A narrative such as "The Provider," in the first volume of his memoirs, can be fully enjoyed as fiction, although we know that it is no such thing, that if we see it as such it cannot be seen as part of the memoirs. Given its discursive position, autobiography suffers from permanent instability, now tending toward historical discourse, now toward fictional discourse.

This structural instability derives from a feature analyzed by Louis Renza. His thesis can be summarized as follows: each modality of expression envisages the reader in a certain manner; that is, it puts him in a

---

*Here I am alluding to two poems: Carlos Drummond de Andrade's "Paisagem: Como se faz" (from *As impurezas do branco*) and, of course, the original version of Marianne Moore's "Poetry."

condition in which he is able to share in the textual universe offered to him. The informational universe transmitted by the media is shared because the reader or hearer presupposes that such a thing has happened and is being adequately described. The fictional universe is shared because the reader presupposes that he is not being given information on actual facts, but rather simulacra of situations, the object of which is to give him pleasure and food for thought. The autobiographical universe, however, does not enable the reader to share what is being offered to him or her. The autobiographical escapes the commerce of meaning because only the author can mean his life for himself. Thus, Renza concludes, "we might view [autobiography] instead as a unique, self-defining mode of self-referential expression, one that allows, then inhibits, its ostensible project of self-representation, of converting oneself into the present promised by language" (Renza 1980: 295). In other words, autobiography is attracted by the idiolect, is tempted by solipsism. And, as expected, we find the confirmation of this in the very paradigm of the genre. In his first letter to Malesherbes, Rousseau wrote: "Personne au monde ne me connaît que moi seul." ("No one in the world knows me but I myself.")

Rather than the "veto of imagination," as Renza puts it, what characterizes the autobiographical genre is the temptation to veto communication. Here the radicalization of the autobiographical, by implying the impossibility of sharing the meanings, contains a clear alternative: at its limit, the genre either assumes the authoritarian form we find on the first page of Rousseau's *Confessions* or it enacts a sort of suicide: one kills oneself in order to contain in oneself the meaning of what one has lived. Isn't it the impossibility of a stable contract with the reader that makes autobiography now lean toward history, now toward fiction?

CHAPTER FOUR

Literature and Society in Hispanic America: Nineteenth and Early Twentieth Centuries

THE QUESTION OF LITERARY DISCOURSE

In the last twenty years, the need for a different approach to literature has become increasingly evident. The historiographic model, which prevailed in the nineteenth century, came to a crisis early in the present century. It had been characterized by the diachronic ordering of literary facts, seen as *documents* of an era, a nation, or an individuality, to be treated according to the principles of a positivist philology. Stylistics and Slavic formalism tried to establish another model. The former, more academic, emphasized the emotional function of poetic language. The latter, associated with avant-garde practices, saw poetry as a device for clearing up everyday language. However, they shared common traits: the same contempt for descriptive temporal sequences and for the study of the *environment*, and the emphasis on detailed internal analysis of the poetic—that is, of the operations that constituted it.

This drastic change could not be attributed to a presumed exhaustion of historiography on national and positivist bases, for even though it progressively lost prestige, the historiographic-positivist model did not vanish from scholarly practice entirely. It lived on, if only in the work of diehard epigones of Hippolyte Taine and Gustave Lanson, unable to do more than list names, titles, and dates, invariably disciplined by criteria of taste assumed to be *natural*—that is, criteria the reason for which they never dared question.

Whatever our distaste or disdain, it will hardly suffice to say that this model is outdated. If such a statement is true, the reason is that literature has changed its function since the mid–nineteenth century. In the nineteenth century the study of literature derived its legitimacy from the idea that literature was the expression of nation-states. Hence the prestige of the notion of *classic*; a classic was a work that contained the essence of national uniqueness. Thus understood, literature was seen as a basic ingredient of culture, a necessary part of good education. But since Baudelaire a chasm had opened. Language was still musical, verse preserved its alexandrine meter, but it pointed to the existence of cripples and beggars, disguised eroticism behind death, and affirmed that not even death would restore our peace of mind. Right-minded readers reacted with hostility to such texts. Only by means of bowdlerization and distortive interpretation could they be considered as the expression of something noble.

What was the new function of literature? A negative, disturbing function; it no longer reinforced noble feelings. And it was negative in relation to values of all kinds—political, social, aesthetic. Naturalism attempted to lend it a different sort of positivity: the support for biological science, the discovery of everyday life. The former was soon abandoned. The latter came to harp on a single theme: Beauty, sacredness? Mere reflexes that soil the shoes of the modern Ulysses in a muddy city. Half a century after Baudelaire, his negative attitude was intensified and exacerbated in Dada and surrealism. While Dada concentrated on destruction, surrealism refused to conceive literature in aesthetic terms, seeing it instead as part of a revolution in life itself—an ambitious program, which was attacked from the center, the right, and the left.

Surrealism failed. But who did not fail in the attempt to reinvent life? And it was the failure of surrealism that made the question even more urgent: What is the function of literature today? Since we cannot answer it in a positive way, analysts are content to name functions that, although different, are all negative: to refuse the optimistic view that ours is the best of all possible worlds, that what language tells us is reality, that art organizes chaos and harmonizes man with the world, that art redeems suffering, and so on. This negativity has met with such wholesale acceptance that it has turned into a kind of mystification: one need not take a stand on such and such an issue because one is an artist, or an art scholar, or a philosopher of art. If this is the situation we are in, there must be some historical obstacle that will not let us move beyond it. In our contemporary world, art (and not just literature) contains a purely negative potential: that of revealing the limits of projects and systems, casting an ironical eye on good intentions (which nevertheless remain necessary), parodying the builders of the future, even when it accepts that a different future must be built. All of this is so because we no longer acknowledge a solution that is positive *en bloc*. For art itself has learned to recognize its own limits. It is no legislator of anything, as the English romantic proposed; it is only something that, in its commerce with concrete reality, poses doubts and questions, that makes it possible to find pleasure in doubt.

Because of this historical limit, theoretico-analytical reflections on literature must necessarily be various and discordant. Nevertheless, they are all based on the same assumption: there is an urgent need to renew literary theory, or else it will come to be seen as a useless body of knowledge. This much is common to all views; but here they part company: they range from the recently developed, extreme notion that literature is a mirage, about to be dissolved in postmodernity, to its polar opposite, the tendency to confuse literature with creativity, a vast poiesis that refreshes the routine of the most diverse codes. Unless one is content to be a mere bureaucrat, to sit on the fence until it becomes clear which trend is the wave of future, one must take a stand in this rather bewildering situation. And this will necessarily depend on an individual decision.

Among the various currents of literary investigation, I have sided with structuralism, in its incarnation as discourse analysis, and the aesthetics of effects. By structuralism we mean the line of investigation that, beginning with Lévi-Strauss, had its bases rectified and extended by the pioneering studies of Michel Foucault. Thus when I speak of structuralism I am not referring, nor have I ever referred, to structuralist critics, from the most renowned, Roland Barthes, to the humblest. As the readers of Lévi-Strauss and Foucault are well aware, the notion of discourse has never been among the concerns of the anthropologist, while it played a fundamental role in the work of the prematurely deceased philosopher-historian.

Lévi-Strauss's task was to discover the logic of the sensible, the logical net underlying only apparently chaotic "discourses," such as those of myths and kinship systems, or of such trifling acts as the naming of pets. Lévi-Strauss's greatness—his extreme fecundity goes far beyond the boundaries of anthropology—is, however, compromised by his conception of science and his choice of Saussurian linguistics as the guiding activity. On the basis of these two assumptions he postulated the existence of *models* that underlie the actualization of myths, kinship rules, and naming processes, models that remain unaffected by their use. Myths think one another, independently of men, he writes in one of the volumes of his *Mythologiques*. One may readily agree that they are independent of the consciousness of their agents. But to affirm their immunity is merely to adopt a position that is the polar opposite of the assumption of philosophies based on individuality and consciousness. Thus Lévi-Strauss postulated the existence of a hard core—structure—that could be reached through its model, and that acted in the face of its agents' intentions. Freud was incorporated into the matrix of exact sciences. The unconscious began to be seen as an entity in the physico-chemical world. Thus Lévi-Strauss not only exempted himself from thinking about *discursive boundaries*—for discourses had no boundaries, being seen instead as mere *paroles* of a single mental structure, which was identified with man himself—but also a priori raised almost insurmountable obstacles for a recognition of the active role of history. Therefore his laudable interest in the sensible, no longer seen as devoid of seriousness and dignity, came to be compromised by an excessively stable *mathesis*. And the welcome stimulus he brought to the criticism of historiography and its liberation from the factual-diachronic modality could not contribute to the new historiography unless it suffered a change of course. So Lévi-Strauss's implicit promise of renewal could only be actualized when his basic assumptions were questioned: his view of science, his reliance on the linguistics of *langue*.

This is where Michel Foucault's decisive contribution comes in. While accepting the validity and even the revolutionary character of the idea of a logic of the unconscious, one must determine whether its actualizations connect with another pole: that of communication. That is, one must see that communication does more than simply actualize a framework fully given before the act of communication. Communication brings into play another set of rules, which adapt the logic of the unconscious to the need to respond to differentiated fields. Thus it is not enough to consider, as Lévi-Strauss does, the framework underlying the exchange of messages, which are then seen as overdetermined by it. It is not enough to conceive human verbal action as endowed with motivations that are independent of conscious purpose. Now it must also be recognized that both framework and unconscious motivations are guided and reshaped by the *field* in which they are actualized. Every act of communication, therefore, actualizes two poles, that of the logical unconscious and that of the discursive field. When this second factor comes into play, the stability of structures is dissolved. It does not nullify structures, but invests them with a mobility that makes models useless. Thus there is no return to the idea of a rational, conscious individual, the master of his or her products; but the logical mechanism that reduces human beings to the role of secondary pieces is abandoned.

For a better understanding of the notion of discursive field—or, more simply, discourse—we can use the notion of territoriality. In the study of animal behavior, territoriality implies the placement of marks that set the limits of a community within an undivided spatial extension. Thus, by means of its urine, a wolf signals to other wolves the boundaries of its pack's territory; the bear does the same by scratching the bark of trees. In the case of discourses, rather than an undivided spatial extension we have the speech continuum. Within it, certain verbal indicators appear with the function of signaling to the hearer or reader the kind of discursive territoriality that is being presented. Every discourse—literary and fictional, religious, scientific, journalistic—contains its own marks, which require differentiated receptions. Any violation of these marks compromises the expected interaction.

Of course, it is quite possible for a given discourse to appropriate or incorporate marks of another, either consciously or unconsciously. For instance, the mark of belief, ideally a characteristic of religious discourse, is often incorporated into political discourse; and the media, institutionalized as conveyors of information and opinion, are used to reinforce belief. Discursive territorialities interact, absorbing one another's marks or even changing into something else, pretending to retain their autonomy, or are pressured to act according to properties compatible with others. For even among discourses power is exerted, and one of them will act as the imperialist in relation to its colonies. Such was the case of religious discourse in the past; more recently, in the nineteenth century, the discourse of diachronic and factual history dominated the fledgling social sciences and literature.

However, by breaking up the sound-meaning continuum of *parole* into territorialities, we run the risk of *petrifying* them once again into self-contained units. Here it is convenient to recall Jürgen Link's observation that discourses are "components of the cultural 'interdiscourse'" (Link 1984: 149). In other words: before they are separated, these territorialities share a common core, of a material, formal, and pragmatic nature, present in all of them (p. 150). This previous interdiscursive zone is what makes communication possible between interlocutors belonging to different territorialities (say, a physicist and a punk, a historian and an athlete, a poet and . . . well, a literature professor). Here is an example, a short narrative from Brecht's *Geschichten von Herrn Keuner*:

> When it comes to having my head bashed in, said Mr. K, I have no courage whatsoever. The really important thing is for me to survive violence.
> In order to make himself fully understood, Mr. K told the story of the man who was visited by an agent of the ruling power, who said to him: "Do you want to serve me?"
> The man said not a word. And for seven years he served the agent of violence, who grew so fat that he died.
> Then the man wrapped the body in an old shawl and threw it away. He washed the bedstead, whitewashed the walls and sighed in relief.
> And he finally answered: "No!"
>
> (Brecht 1967: 375)

The effectiveness of interdiscursiveness depends on such marks as the ability to understand the allegorical function of the story, recognition of the biblical allusion to the seven years of service and its parodic use here, the character's "delay" in answering the request for service. The specific territoriality of the fictional is immediately grasped by default. The story could not possibly be part of a religious discourse because we know of no religion that values the ability to save one's skin; it could not be part of a historiographic discourse unless K were a real figure and his story an example of his resourcefulness; and so on. Fictionality is affirmed by what is not explicitly said, and thus by the request that the reader actively intervene by supplying the crucial element of irony. So decisive is the mark of fictionality that a reader who believed he or she had grasped the author's political position through the story would most likely take the author for a mere rascal.

In addition to the discursive approach, I have profited from the use of the aesthetic of effects developed by Wolfgang Iser. This is not the place to discuss whether the term "aesthetics" is adequate here or only a polite abbreviation for a difficult discussion concerning the deep-rooted taboo that reserves the term "aesthetics" to the experience of and the reflection on art. Leaving this discussion in brackets, as it were, I have given preference to the aesthetics of effect because, while its close relative, the aesthetic of reception, tends to be no more than an enlightened version of sociology of the reader, Iser's version presents theoretical instruments that can stress both the potential inherent in the fictional text and the norms and values that govern the reader's view (see Iser 1980: 62).

None of this aims at informing the reader as to which theoretical instrument will be "applied" here. No idea is more preposterous (or more common in the field of literary studies) than the notion that theories are "applied." No theory, as such, can be applied, since between theory and object there is a whole net of methodological procedures without which no theory could be operationalized. Thus the explanations above have a different aim: to specify which theoretical instruments have given me food for thought, which I have been favoring.

In addition to the unfavorable conditions for the production and dissemination of works of literary criticism, in Latin America we are often fearful of the political undertones that may be read into our reflections. Let me explain this point: Both in Brazil and in Spanish America—foreign specialists included—there is a tendency to identify nondocumental literature with José Enrique Rodó's spiritualism or with a defense of "ivory-tower" art. Lest they be labeled as conservatives or "purists," or seen as disdainful of political discussions, although their actual political orientation is opposed to that of reactionaries and conservatives, Latin-American critics and analysts have often preferred not to dwell on the issue. And there is another problem faced by literary scholars: since in Latin America there are no effective alternative structures in the field of intellectual production, and consequently no effective university presses and no effective university public, scholars must court newspapermen and reviewers so that their books will not pass unnoticed. Since they realize that journalistic discourse is the only one that really counts, they will tend to favor works that can be summarized more promptly, or that are more in harmony with their publishers' positions.

These, then, seem to be some of the major problems that are responsible for the backwardness of our field in Latin America. As to the nonexistence of alternative circuits for production, discussion, and distribution, I have no suggestions to make; however, I can summarize in a few words my stand on the issue of the fear of political connotations: I believe the best political contribution we can make must come *from our specific lines of work*, even if this means we have to take some flak from the hornets.

For the above reasons, I have found it necessary to present, in the first part of this chapter, a few aspects of the social history of Latin America that are directly relevant to the conception of literature prevailing in the region. Also, I will extend to Spanish America some of the points I have raised about Brazil elsewhere (see Costa Lima 1981: 3–26, 30–55; 1988: 102–20).

ASPECTS OF LATIN-AMERICAN SOCIETY

A BRIEF HISTORICO-POLITICAL SURVEY

In the late eighteenth century, the bishop of Michoacán, in New Spain, Manuel Abad y Queipo, moved by his very loyalty to the Spanish Crown, presented an invaluable diagnosis of the class situation in the colonial empire:

> New Spain contained approximately four million inhabitants, who may be divided into three classes: Spaniards, Indians, and *castas* [those of mixed racial origins]. The Spaniards made up one-tenth of the total population, and these alone hold almost the entirety of the property and wealth in the kingdom. The other two classes, which comprise nine-tenths, may be divided into thirds, two of them of *castas*, and one of pure Indians. The Indians and *castas* work in household service, in agriculture, and in commerce, crafts, and trades. That is to say, they are servants, serfs, or day laborers of the first class.... In America... there are no gradations: all are either rich or destitute, noble or base.... Given such a state of things, what interests could possibly join the latter two classes with the former, or all three with the laws and the government? (Quoted in Romero 1970: 40–41)

This description of Church authority held for the whole Spanish empire, except for the situation of Río de la Plata, where there was less wealth and consequently less Spanish cupidity, so that second-class whites, Creoles, had more leverage. The situation of Brazil was not radically different. The only difference was that Portugal lacked its neighbor's power, and thus was never able to develop a comparable military, administrative, and fiscal apparatus. But Portugal's conduct in the eighteenth century, even though it was then ruled by a representative of the Enlightenment, the Marquês de Pombal, shows that the policies of the two metropoles were identical. With the discovery of gold in 1698 and diamonds in 1701, Portugal transferred its capital to the city closest to the mines, Rio de Janeiro (1764), and made a fiscal and administrative center of Vila Rica, the major town in the mining region. From this identity of patterns derives the similarity of the relations, in Brazil and the Spanish-American colonies, between the colonial upper classes and the representatives of the mother countries, relations that were always fraught with tension—witness the failed insurrection in Minas Gerais in the late eighteenth century. Economic greed and political blindness made the two metropoles reserve posts of authority exclusively for white men born in Europe.

The consequences were dramatic in Spanish America: independence required military force. As Bolívar observed, "Americans have risen to power of a sudden, without having acquired knowledge previously; and, what is more evident, without having any practice in public affairs, [for] America was not prepared to break away from the metropole" (Bolívar 1942: 41). It should be noted that the future Liberator did not write this passage when, disenchanted with politics, he had doubts about the work he had accomplished. On the contrary, this evaluation appears in an analysis very much like Abad y Queipo's:

Americans, within the present Spanish system, and perhaps more markedly than ever, hold no place in society except for that of servants fit for work and, at the most, simple consumers; and even this is subject to shocking restrictions, such as the ban against cultivation of European fruits, the Crown monopoly on products, the Peninsula's power over factories, the exclusive privileges of trading in staples, the obstacles among American provinces, so that there may be no contacts, no understandings, no trade among them. (Bolívar 1942: 39)

What accident, then, could have caused insurrection throughout Spanish America, almost simultaneously? If we disregard rhetorical and sentimental arguments, we will conclude that in both Spanish and Portuguese America independence was brought about by the situation of Europe in the late eighteenth and early nineteenth centuries. More precisely, the cause was the clash of British and French interests, which led to Napoleon's intervention in the Iberian Peninsula. It also seems clear that the fate of Latin America, which has not changed drastically to this day, was determined by the outcome of the struggle between the two European powers. Since 1795 Spain had been an ally of France, and Spanish colonial trade had begun to decline because of attacks by English ships. The naval blockade climaxed with the British victory at Trafalgar (1805). The barriers to trade had an immediate impact on the colonial markets, which were unable to export their products on a regular basis: "Like the speculating merchants, the producers who were deprived of their markets by the vicissitudes of metropolitan politics increasingly saw the colonial ties as wholly disadvantageous; the freedom that would result from a trade policy set by the colonies themselves was a goal ever more desirable" (Halperin Donghi 1970: 81).

These feelings of discontent erupted in 1808, when Charles IV and the crown prince, the future Ferdinand VII, were imprisoned by Napoleon's army. Under the pretext of loyalty to the king, the Spanish colonies rebelled, overthrew the viceroys, and set up assemblies in which the Creoles were represented and sometimes formed the majority. Thanks to British eagerness to dominate the new market, the insurrection had begun a few years earlier in Argentina. In 1806, a British fleet arrived at Buenos Aires; when the viceroy fled for safety, Spanish merchants and Creoles had to organize the defense, and were able to defeat the invaders. In the following year, another British force appeared. Although successful at first, it was also defeated in Buenos Aires, by troops led by a French officer, Liniers, at the service of the Spanish king. A junta was then formed and swore allegiance to Ferdinand VII, apparently ignoring the change that had already taken place in the relations between Spanish-born and American-born whites. But in fact the struggle between the two class segments was already acknowledged, and it spread throughout Spanish America.

Meanwhile, in Brazil, John VI's flight to Rio de Janeiro, where he arrived in 1808, set the tone for a quite different process of independence. From the beginning, the king's opening of the colony's ports to "friendly nations" satisfied local merchants and British interests. As Manuel de Oliveira Lima wrote, although he was not referring specifically to relations with Brazil, "the United Kingdom was eventually to emerge from the Napoleonic epic richer . . . than it had been before the war, for its commerce and industry had reached a plethora, so that all that was lacking now for the organism to flourish was a good circulation" (Oliveira Lima 1945, 1: 39).

In Spanish America, the outcome of the struggle between Spaniards and Creoles was varied. The cases of Mexico and Argentina are opposite paradigms. In Argentina, Iberian power was never restored; increasingly

Creoles were the dominant force. If the initial step had been taken by a loyalist officer, by 1810 the situation had changed considerably. Liniers had already been shunted aside—he was to die later fighting the Buenos Aires forces—and the man who had replaced him, the last viceroy of Río de la Plata, resigned in favor of the ruling junta formed by the *Cabildo abierto* (May 25). The same process of replacement of metropolitan authorities had taken place a month earlier in Caracas, and would occur a few months later in Bogotá (July 20) and Santiago, Chile (September 18).

In Mexico, however, the process that led to independence was quite different from, and in some ways opposite to, the dominant pattern elsewhere in Latin America because it was conducted not by American whites, but by the Indian and half-breed masses, led at first by the priest Miguel Hidalgo. Consistent with Mexico's different social background, what was proclaimed was not simply political independence, but also the social independence of the most underprivileged sectors of society. This led to an alliance between Spaniards and Creoles, who defeated Hidalgo's troops in January 1811. However, a survivor, Father José Maria Morelos, kept up the fight, now as a guerrilla war. In November 1813, Morelos proclaimed, for the second time, the independence of Mexico. But it was not to last for more than two years. Like Hidalgo, Morelos proposed a program that contrasted with what had been done in all the other colonies, for it implied "the suppression of differences of caste and the division of large properties" (Halperin Donghi 1970: 126). Since a social revolution was involved here, maintenance of colonial order in New Spain did not depend solely on the defensive capacity of Spanish troops, as was the case in Upper Peru, Chile, and Venezuela, but on the alliance between the local upper classes and the representatives of the metropolis.

If their popular character made Mexican attempts at independence unique in the Latin American context, they failed at first, as did their counterparts in all other regions of Spanish America with the exception of Argentina, where national unity was proclaimed by the Congress of Tucumán in July 1816. (In Portuguese America, the presence of the court in Rio, the improvements that were necessarily introduced, and the articulation with British trade eliminated the possibility of motivations similar to those that had arisen among Brazil's Hispanic neighbors.) But Spain's calamitous situation, together with British domination, did not allow it to profit from its moderately successful military action. In 1810, anti-Napoleonic Spain was further reduced by the fall of Andalusia; all that was left was the city of Cádiz. The situation was made even more complex by the activities of the Spanish liberal movement, parallel to the struggle against the French invaders. In 1812, the Cádiz Cortes, which included representatives of the South American colonies, proclaimed a liberal constitution.

In Mexico, where the royalist alliance had preserved colonial status, the immediate consequence was that the rulers realized that independence was now the best way to protect their interests, for a liberal metropole might prove unresponsive. Led by a royalist former officer, Augustín de Iturbide, the independence of New Spain was proclaimed, ensuring—instead of the social measures undertaken by Hidalgo and Morelos—equality of Iberians and Creoles before the law. Thus, in the end Mexican independence conformed to the general Spanish-American pattern: it was accomplished by the bourgeoisie. The same process took place in the captaincy of Guatemala.

The about-face in Mexican independence, with the triumph of the politico-economic elite, is of fundamental importance for an understanding of the real character of the wars of independence. As the Argentine historian José Luis Romero has written: "Antiliberal sentiment, much more than loyalty to the metropole, was the force that led certain traditionalist groups to oppose the movement for liberation; so that, when the metropole yielded to the pressure of liberal groups, the traditionalists promoted independence precisely where they had managed to preserve subjection" (Romero 1970: 54). Also, it should be noted—as is well known and as Romero stresses—that the liberal revolution at Oporto in 1820 had the same effect on the proclamation of Brazilian independence. By comparison to the risks that liberalism posed for the politico-economic elites, it seemed safer to be ruled by a prince like Pedro I, who was soon to prove unresponsive to liberal demands.

Thus independence was a political process clearly steered by the local oligarchy, whose interests were hurt either by the privileges granted to Iberians or by Spain's political compromises and military defeats, which were detrimental to the export trade in raw materials. This oligarchy was favorable to social reforms only when the intensification of armed struggle made such a stand necessary. The liberation of slaves, for example, was often the price to be paid by landowners so that their former slaves could fight as their soldiers. Halperin Donghi observes: "The results of revolutionary radicalism are short-lived, since only organization for war is provided for; with the return to a peace economy power must be returned to landholders" (Halperin Donghi 1970: 141).

In 1825, when General Antonio José de Sucre defeated the Spanish in Ayacucho and the Republic of Bolivia was proclaimed (the name was a tribute to the Liberator), the period of Spanish-American wars of independence was over. In Haiti and Mexico, the popular masses had eventually taken over the command of the revolutionary process. The slaughter of white planters in Haiti greatly alarmed Creole elites, and in the late nineteenth century the episode was again recalled in Brazil by Joaquim

Nabuco, as a sobering reminder for those masters who were resisting the peaceful manumission of their slaves. In Mexico, as we have seen, the uprising of Indians and half-breeds forced the upper classes to find a compromise, even if a short-lived one.

Once independence had been won, after 1825, the new adversaries were the liberal and antiliberal currents. However, it should be remembered that both belonged to the same oligarchical groups, a fact that makes it quite difficult to establish their differences. Clearly, neither faction was interested in responding to social demands. But this is no reason why we should consider them identical, divided only for "psychological" reasons. Antiliberalism scored important victories in Paraguay, with the dictatorship of Dr. José Gaspar Francia (1814–40), continued by Solano López; in Argentina, with Juan Manuel de Rosas (1835–52); and in Ecuador, with the clerical dictatorship of García Moreno (1861–75). In brief, we may say that the general pattern was the adoption of authoritarian governments, determined to eliminate their opponents by any means whatsoever; governments that strongly emphasized discipline, tending to shut off their countries from foreign influence, favoring in theory and practice a militarized or—in the case of García Moreno—a religious state. Liberal governments, on the other hand, attempted to open their nations to European economic and cultural penetration, develop school systems, and adopt, with the necessary "adaptations," the style of advanced Western representative democracies. However, couched in such categorical language, the distinction between the two models is almost a lie. At the very least, it is a deceptive image, which cannot furnish a basis for an understanding of the drama of newly established nations. In order to do this, it will be necessary to return to the period I have just synthesized.

We have seen that the fate of newly independent nations was influenced by the outcome of the conflicts in Europe. Let me now elaborate on this statement, and examine the reasons why there was little difference between liberal and antiliberal governments in Spanish America. In this connection, it will be extremely useful to recall the political reflections of Simón Bolívar.

In an article dated June 9, 1814—the year in which his second expedition to Venezuela was defeated—Bolívar analyzed what America could expect from the conflict between France and Britain. Against those who foresaw an agreement between victorious Britain and the former metropole, Spain, that would lead to preservation of America's colonial status, Bolívar argued: "Given the vicissitudes of European politics, why should England wish America to remain a dependency of a Continental power, to increase with its riches and its immense population a force that can resist her?" (Bolívar 1950, 3: 831). Bolívar's argument is indirectly confirmed by one of Oliveira Lima's sources. Referring to the memoirs of the English admiral who commanded the British fleet that protected John VI in his flight to Rio, Oliveira Lima writes: "The admiral was the first to recognize that these [Brazilian] colonies would have been lost to the metropole if John had not emigrated to Brazil. The English would occupy them with the pretext of defending them" (Oliveira Lima 1945, 1: 74). If this was Britain's decision even as it was fighting Napoleon, why should it share the advantages it had gained after France's defeat?

Implicitly, Bolívar acknowledged the distance between political and economic independence. England would like to see all of Latin America independent in order to gain new markets for its products. This is not a conjecture; Bolívar himself says as much, at the end of his article: "Furthermore, America's circumstances are such that she cannot arouse any fear among those who engage in commerce and industry. For a long time we will necessarily remain an agricultural people, and an agricultural people able to furnish European markets with the most precious materials is the one most likely to establish friendly relations with merchants and manufacturers" (Bolívar 1950, 3: 832). Thus, at the very moment when it was feared that Ferdinand VII, after repudiating the liberal Cádiz constitution, might attempt to reconquer his old empire, Bolívar realized that the insurgent continent's fate was to be different: its political independence would be favored by the foreign power interested in seeing it divided into economically dependent nations. True, the passage quoted above has an optimistic tone that cannot be attributed to mere rhetoric. To the military leader and statesman, the commercial interchange seen as inevitable—America as an exporter of agricultural products, for a long time unable to "arouse any fear among those who engage in commerce and industry"—did not seem unfavorable in any way. Within the parameters of economic liberalism, Bolívar supposed that there was a balance between the prices of agricultural products and those of manufactured goods, so that Latin America's "vocation" as an exporter of agricultural products would not be negative for its development. What to him was a source of increasing concern, dismay, even despair, was the New World's political anarchy. That is why he tirelessly recommended the formation of confederations that might counter the already advanced process of fragmentation: "The states from the Isthmus of Panama to Guatemala might form an association. . . . New Granada will join Venezuela, if they are able to form a central republic" (Bolívar 1942: 49).

Such proposals, of course, foundered. Spanish-American balkanization not only failed to cease, but became even worse. How could it have been otherwise if there was no force to oppose the power of caudillos and generals? For the fragmentation had to do with the fact that the people were powerless. That is why Bolívar, even as he insisted on the need for unification, recognized that at the moment America could not aspire to a truly popular government, because in this case "the abuses that now occur would not be stopped, and our regeneration would be fruitless." Thus he proposed the following program for the nation to be formed by the union of Venezuela and New Granada (Colombia):

> Its government could follow the example of England, except that, instead of a king, there will be an elected executive office, at the most a lifelong but never a hereditary post, or it will not be a republic: a hereditary legislative chamber, or senate, which in political crises will mediate between the people and the government, and a freely elected legislative body, with no restrictions other than those of England's lower chamber. (Bolívar 1942: 50–51)

This program is softened in the "Angostura Address": although the lifelong tenure of senators is maintained, only the strength of the executive post is preserved. These proposals, criticized at the time, seen as proofs that Bolívar's ambition was to be king, seem in fact only consistent with Latin-American liberalism—that is, with the interests of a sector of society that intended to organize the life of the new nations by developing their "agricultural vocation," which necessarily depended on exports to the European market and imports of British manufactured goods.

It should be noted that, in spite of the specific character of Brazilian independence, in Brazil it was also necessary that the king assume powers beyond those enshrined in the principles of constitutional monarchy and act as a balancing force between parties, the so-called "moderative power." Note, also, that in the Brazilian empire the lifelong tenure of senators was justified by an argument similar to Bolívar's: the point was to ensure the decision-making power of a group of men supposedly above the interests and conflicts of parties.

Such coincidences cannot be explained solely by the economic aspects of Latin-American liberalism. Political aspects must be examined as well. Bolívar favored a strong government because the populace was not an active political agent. According to this interpretation, a strong government was indispensable because there was a power vacuum. But now the situation became more complex, and the distinction between the liberal-authoritarian project and antiliberal regimes disappeared in actual practice. In order to understand what happened then, it should be recalled that the immediate consequence of the fifteen years of wars of independence, in addition to the disastrous economic situation, was the militarization of Spanish-American society. (The men who built the Brazilian empire were aware of this danger, and did not let the military career become as prestigious in Brazil as it was in neighboring countries. But this policy could not be sustained after the war against Paraguay (1865–70). The establishment of military force began to threaten the stability of the empire.) Writing in our century, Ezequiel Martínez Estrada stressed the importance that the military had attained and the political consequences of this ascent: "As social structures took shape and solidified, though still cartilaginous, State and Army reached the plenitude of power together. The State was born armed with the sharpest defensive weapons with which to face a widespread danger, which existed, but whose whereabouts were as yet unknown; in short, it was no more than the Army's rest, its winter quarters" (Estrada 1968: 159–60). The widespread danger to political institutions could surface in the ambition of another general—and the lust for power of Bolívar's lieutenants is well known—situated in an important stronghold or on the country's frontier; or in the designs of some local boss in the interior; or in Spain's quite real intention to reconquer its former colonies. In the course of the century, these fears were not allayed, and another was added to them: the fear of invasion by some foreign power, increasingly identified as the United States, particularly after the war with Mexico and the annexation of Mexican territory. But the state, so feeble, threatened by such varied forces and beings, is, according to Estrada, also to be feared—because it knows no limits. It is feeble because it has no force of its own, and lacks sufficient legitimacy; it is fearsome because there are no limits to it. It is the army's "winter quarters" as long as there is no reason why the military should threaten it; but state and army pose a threat to each other when they clash. Civilian power is no more than an appendix of military power, either helped or victimized by it. In either case, whoever is not supported by the army is crushed.

Thus, when Bolívar proposed a strong executive branch, was he thinking of avoiding, of containing this hybrid nature? Since militarization was already taking place, the answer is yes. But what is the difference between such a state and a militarized state pure and simple? The difference, in fact, is nearly invisible: "A wise republican and liberal rhetoric disguised the establishment of a strong power, with no other limits than those imposed by the groups in power, whose spokesmen were the same ones who had secured seats in the parliaments that had been summoned" (Romero 1970: 95).

Would it then be fair to say that the numerous military dictatorships that have plagued Latin America are the practical actualization of the strong government envisioned by Bolívar, proof of his failure or of his shrewd political sense? No, such a conclusion would be a gross distortion. Here Tulio Halperin Donghi's position seems more reasonable: according to the Argentine historian, Bolívar's program cannot be identified with present Latin-American reality; in fact, it failed because it relied on a variable that proved unreliable: the role to be assumed by the urban elites, who, after the childhood disease of militarism, should have reestablished in the new countries the class structure that had existed before independence: "The urban elites, which [Bolívar] attempted to win over by handing them a share of power in the assemblies, had been weakened by the revolutionary crisis; the rural ones, whose makeup had been affected by the crisis, but whose power remained intact and even greater than before, tended to find support in the local military power, to which the revolution gave a decisive weight" (Halperin Donghi 1970: 173–74).

The failure of the urban bourgeoisie, therefore, corresponded to the rise of landowners, allied to the military. (In Brazil, the situation was different. One cannot speak of the failure of the urban bourgeoisie because it did not become an expressive force before the twentieth century. Landowners were in power during the empire, and did not share their power with the military. It was only after the republic was proclaimed that the military rose to power, a part of which, however, remained in the hands of the agro-exporting bourgeoisie. It was only after 1930 that the rural bourgeoisie lost its position as the sole or major ruling faction. In other words, it was only then that military had to forge a new pact.)

Does the failure of the urban bourgeoisie imply the utter failure of liberalism? Given the aims of Latin-American liberals, the answer is no. Revolutionary leaders, even when republican and liberal, had no intention of subverting the colonial order; all they wanted was to change the ruling elite, replacing Iberian officials with members of the Creole oligarchy. The strong government proposed by Bolívar was not a masquerade to distinguish his republicanism from the avowed monarchism of a San Martín; it did presuppose, though, that the urban bourgeoisie would dominate the legislative branch, and contain the brute force of regional caudillos.

Nevertheless, this failure does not affect the core of the social structure the Liberator envisioned. As a contemporary historian of ideas observes: "The freedom that revolutionary proclamations had mentioned acquired an increasingly limited meaning. . . . The single change that had been accomplished was that the Spanish dictator had been replaced by a national dictator" (Zea 1976: 67). To the landowners, who exercised power on the local level, and the military, who had the guns, a third power was added in the period immediately after independence: the Church. "Together, the Church and the military would soon establish the only order that was in their interest. This order was precisely the old Spanish order, with Spain left out" (p. 92). This was the restoration of the alliance that José Mariátegui saw as the reason for the weakness of Spanish dominion: "The weakness of the Spanish empire derived precisely from its character and structure as a military and ecclesiastical enterprise, rather than a political and economic one" (Mariátegui 1943: 8). But the old weakness disappears, because power now has the economic support of farmers and cattle raisers, and also because not even its adversaries favor a rival economic policy. The divergences are not profound.

This is apparent even in the intellectual sphere, as soon as such a thing begins to develop. Here, also, quite soon there was a split between critics of established power and those who saw it with "understanding." One of the former was the Chilean Francisco Bilbao, who wrote: "For half a century we have been independent of Spain. How many years of true freedom have there been in some of the new nations?" (Bilbao 1941: 39). The passion and the revolt are evident; but Bilbao, like various other critics of dictatorships, had no clear view of the reason why they succeeded. To many of them, the fault was in the Spanish heritage, seen almost as a hereditary trait; others blamed the barbarous condition of the majority. The arguments were so vague that the opposition followed the same political practice as whoever was in power at the moment. The theme of barbarism became increasingly dominant in the latter half of the century, with allusions to the races that made up the new nations. Bilbao did not go that far. To him, the paralysis of freedom was a consequence of the weight of religion: "Why does the Republic invoke dictatorship? Because your republican is a believer, and carries over into politics the nature, character, temperament, and logic of Catholic infallibility. . . . Opposition is heretical, despotism is sacred, obedience is a duty" (p. 40).

On the opposite pole we find Francisco García Calderón. It will be illuminating to examine his ideas, in order to see the issues that divided conservative intellectuals from liberal ones. In his important but unfortunately neglected work, *Las democracias latinas de América*, the Peruvian social historian begins with the reminder: "The founders of the Independence realized that only a strong regime could free the fledgling nations from the talons of demagoguery and anarchy, and preserve it from wars among generals and the premature ambitions of the provinces" (Calderón 1979a: 27). With apparent bitterness, the historian observes that the generosity of the purpose soon disappeared: "The genesis of these republics was as brave and heroic as a geste. Soon their history degenerated into a farce of petty interests, into a revolutionary orgy; such was the evolution of South America in the previous century" (p. 40).

But the bitterness is only rhetorical. In fact, the Peruvian diplomat does not share the pessimism of other authors. On the contrary, he believes that Latin-American dictatorships are the natural form of government for anarchical peoples. Thus he praises Venezuela's Guzmán Blanco, Argentina's Rosas, and Mexico's Porfirio Díaz. In relation to Guzmán Blanco his words reflect an ambiguous attitude of praise and irony: "A caudillo without clear political ideas, he loved power and his country. The state, the churches, the parties, and the riches were all his: they were the patrimony of this feudal baron" (p. 55). But his support of Rosas is clear: "Rosas's achievement is profoundly Argentinian. He accomplished three civilizing goals: he defeated isolated caudillos, conquered the desert, and founded an organic confederation.... Like Porfirio Díaz, he annihilated the provincial caudillos: he was a Machiavelli of the pampas" (p. 73).

As his metaphors make clear, what Calderón valued was the immediate establishment of national unity, once again couched in the language of biology: "organic confederation." However, his greatest enthusiasm is reserved for the Mexican Díaz. The very way he expresses his feelings is interesting, for his words convey an ideology that was not promoted by conservative intellectuals only: "Thus, the President, having stabilized the currency, balanced the finances and foreign gold, *founded a pragmatic republic*. He put an end to traditional revolutions, *to both Jacobin vehemence* and that which is proper to the race, with his utilitarian campaign: *he forged a silent State, where only the dim rumble of the factories was heard*" (p. 84; emphases added). Curiously—or ironically—enough, this very intelligent defender of conservative regimes insists on calling them democratic, just as he praises their leaders for suppressing mass movements, "Jacobin vehemence," and, above all, for creating a "pragmatic republic."

Seeing Bilbao and García Calderón as paradigms of the stands taken on the dictatorships of the post-independence period, we find that their differences are not such as to open an insurmountable political abyss between them. It is true that liberals struggled against the concentration of power in the arbitrary hands of arrogant chieftains and tried to create representative governments. But, implicitly or explicitly, they agreed that there was no such thing as active, legitimating masses. Thus, if for all their intellectual outrage they did not propose concrete political alternatives, this was not just because they shared or were contaminated by the spirit of the ruling oligarchies. One might even add that they were drawn into the oligarchical orbit because they did not believe that their nations contained any forces that could legitimate the sought-for representativeness. Bolívar's ghost still haunted the continent. The Liberator's failure was followed by the failures of his successors.

Thus, it was the actual social conditions, which blocked the formation of a middle class and a public opinion, that were responsible for the fact that the antagonism between liberals and conservatives in Latin America was almost a fallacy. For this very reason it is important to establish a link between this antagonism and another one: that between pragmatists and "idealists." Pragmatists held that the government should make the country work, whether or not it conformed to models that were perhaps no more than dreams. "Idealists," according to Oliveira Vianna's definition, were those who, fascinated by more advanced models, tried to import them.

Although in this case the opposing terms are better defined, again it would be a mistake to believe that an absolute contrast is involved here. No wonder that, on the one hand, not even the "idealists" of the nineteenth century could find *social* causes that might explain the failure of the independence movements, while, on the other, the pragmatists were forced to qualify as democratic the dictatorships they praised. Both facts seem to be related to the absence of any well-defined social alternative to oligarchical structure. Between the oligarchical minority and the popular masses there was a void. Thus the "idealist" could not achieve any effectiveness unless he compromised with oligarchical practices; and the pragmatist could not aspire to any intellectual respectability, be seen as more than a mere scribbler, unless he resorted to the adjectives employed by his opponents. As will become clear later, Latin-American intellectuals as such seemed disconnected from the class or sector of society they joined. Their speculations fell into the same void that swallowed public opinion.

But before I go any further into the question of intellectuals, let me emphasize the issue of public opinion. Writes José Luis Romero, commenting on a letter from Rosas to Facundo Quiroga:

Rosas observed that liberal liberalism broke the links with the old dual, paternalistic society; that freedom of opinion gave rise to politicized sectors that increasingly affirmed their rights in opposition to the old power structures; that freedom of consciousness weakened not so much religious feeling as the paternalistic influence of the Church. . . . Hostile to rationalism and all eighteenth-century political philosophy, he maintained that constitutional organization was not an effective solution—let alone the necessary solution—for the establishment of national order. . . . It was actually a conception sprung from the ideas of social romanticism; but it was also, for this very reason, a conception typical of the proprietary classes, deeply attached to the status quo and stubbornly opposed to change.

(Romero 1970: 74–76)

This rural, landowning orientation was quite different from Bolívar's own position, which emphasized the role of the urban bourgeoisie. However, if we return to Bolívar's reflections, we find an interesting aspect. While the 1814 article and the "Letter from Jamaica" show that he is well informed on the political and economic situation in Europe, in the "Angostura Address," in which he presents to Venezuelan legislators the principles for a constitution, Bolívar develops a purely legalistic argument—that is, as if he were unaware of the characteristics of the society the proposed constitution was meant for. In Oliveira Vianna's terms, the "Angostura

Address," if read in isolation, might appear to be the expression of a die-hard "idealist":

> The love of the Fatherland, the love of Laws, the love of Magistrates are the sole noble passions that should engage a Republican's soul. . . . To save our fledgling Republic from chaos, not even all our moral faculties will suffice, unless we fuse the mass of the people into a single whole: the composition of Government into a single whole: the Legislation into a single whole: and the national spirit into a single whole. Unity, Unity, Unity must be our motto. (Bolívar 1942: 87)

Why should legalistic rhetoric shy away from the social situation and require from all such a unity, such a love for country and law, as if all were equal or nearly equal in social status? How could Bolívar, sensitive as he was to the social reasons behind British policy and to the arbitrary rule South Americans had been subjected to during the colonial period, be unaware of the fact that the wars of independence had not diminished the blatant social differences? If it seems implausible that Bolívar was unaware of this, then how could he believe that the model of popular education he proposed in the same speech would ever be effective unless the causes of inequality were dealt with? In short, how could liberal legalism adopt what seems to be an angelic view, one that does not take into account the very real evils of earthly reality? Was it because Bolívar knew that, if he proposed any measures that might really attack the root of the problem, he would provoke the violent and effective opposition of the hacendados? The angelic tone, then, does not mean that Bolívar was unaware of the actual situation. Quite on the contrary, the abstraction was necessary because he was perfectly conscious of the actual state of society and did not think it would be politically expedient to attack its structure. Consequently, the legalist liberal had such a narrow range of action, even when he was as prestigious a man as Bolívar, that the strong government he proposed was little different from the pragmatic dictatorships.

The situation might have been different if the urban bourgeoisie had risen above its subordinate political and economic position, if urban centers had generated a middle class, and a public opinion had developed from the articulation between manifestations of classes. But even in the latter half of the nineteenth century the rural oligarchies preserved absolute power. One of the reasons for this was British domination of foreign trade. Weakened by the war, Creole merchants were unable to compete with the agents of British companies. "This defeat had irreversible effects: throughout Spanish America, from Mexico to Buenos Aires, the richest, most prestigious part of local trade would remain in foreign hands; within fifty years, in Buenos Aires or Valparaíso, there would be an abundance of English surnames among the local aristocracy" (Halperin Donghi 1970: 148).

Thus when the first half of the nineteenth century came to a close the social structure of the new nations remained intact. It was preserved under Rosas's dictatorship, under the Brazilian monarchy, in the political instability of Mexico. Given these conditions, the great problem for governments was to promote a certain degree of economic progress and preserve institutional stability without violating traditional parameters. Argentina achieved this under Rosas; in Brazil this was possible almost until the end of the century. In Mexico, stability was only obtained provisionally, under Benito Juárez (1876–80), and more lastingly with Porfírio Díaz, during his long "reign" (1884–1911). The only real change was that the continent was now dominated by a new master. The old Iberian metropoles were relegated to the background, where in fact they had rightfully belonged for centuries. Britain, with its industry, invaded the new markets.

However, an even newer master was beginning to flex his muscles. The revolution in Texas (1836) affirmed the advance of the slaveholding American South over Mexico, bled white by military coups. The war between the United States and Mexico, declared in 1845, ended with U.S. annexation of a large part of Mexican territory—New Mexico, parts of Colorado, Arizona, and Oklahoma. (However, U.S. domination was not always so explicit. As early as 1859, when Cuba was still a Spanish possession, 42 percent of Cuba's sugar production was acquired by the U.S. and only 12 percent went to Spain. Beginning in 1883, the U.S. presence became more visible, when Americans bought farms and estates in Cuba.)

While Mexico still struggled against political instability and felt the effects of a domination more explicit than British control, Argentina, after Rosas's defeat at Caseros (1852), took a different path. The position of monarchical Brazil, in between those of Mexico and Argentina, seemed to be an enviable tranquility; here there were no pronunciamentos or manifestations of social discontent. Slaveholding planters exported their tropical products, English establishments dominated trade, and in Parliament conservatives and liberals alternated in power. It was only with the close of the Paraguayan War, in 1870, that Brazilian elites began to realize that they were living in the same world as their Spanish-American neighbors.

After the fall of Rosas, the old Argentinian problem came to the fore once again: the conflict between the interests of the state of Buenos Aires, which boasted the country's only port and amassed the revenues from customs duties, and those of the desertic and impoverished interior. The general who had defeated Rosas, Justo José de Urquiza, favored a federative constitution, against the opposition of Buenos Aires, its rising middle classes, and the liberal publicists back from exile. There was a revolution, and Buenos Aires won. The federative plan seemed to have been defeated, for the Buenos Aires ruling classes favored either outright secession or a confederation that preserved their prerogatives. Defeated on the battlefield, the interior, however, won on the political plane. In spite of the opposition of the country's strongest state, the Argentine Confederation was established. In 1853, a constitution went into effect, establishing a strong executive branch, in order to ensure order and consequently the entry of European capitals, on the one hand, and on the other, to permit the economic exploitation of the undeveloped lands in the interior.

Under Urquiza, immigration and popular education were further encouraged. But the conflict with Buenos Aires flared once again into war, and the commander of Buenos Aires, Bartolomé Mitre, was defeated in 1859. But Buenos Aires remained a powerful state, and its customs privileges were preserved. There was a new confrontation in 1861, and this time, at the Battle of Pavón, Mitre was the winner. In 1862, the victorious general began his rule as a constitutional president. For six years, Mitre expanded the railroad network, started by his rival Urquiza, and favored British capital, the opening of public schools, and the strengthening of the university. His civilizing policies were continued by his successor, Domingos Faustino Sarmiento (1868–74). This was the most successful period of liberal-oligarchical rule in Argentina. In the next few decades, politico-military crises became less intense. From Mitre to the world crises of the 1920's, Argentina lived in political stability as a successful partner of the new colonial pact. In this period, General Julio Argentino Roca started a campaign (1878–79) against the Indians, whose fertile lands were then made available for agriculture and for speculation, to the benefit of big farmers. In addition, the conflict between Buenos Aires and the interior became a thing of the past. In 1880, the city of Buenos Aires was separated from the state of Buenos Aires and made the national capital. At the end of the century, Argentina was a rich country, with an economy based on exports of grain and beef.

Argentina was, then, the first Spanish-American country in which Bolívar's program was successful. Military caudillismo was pushed into the background; the popular masses were ignored; cultural institutions began to function; the urban oligarchy held politico-economic power; and, most importantly, integration with the Western world was achieved through the entry of capital—European, at this point—and the exports of primary goods. During his struggle against Rosas, Sarmiento had expressed the opposition between liberalism and caudillismo in the slogan "civilization or barbarism." But after the civilizing efforts of Sarmiento's government, one may well inquire what was the real meaning of his slogan:

Sarmiento's old formula was now freely translated in contemporary terms, opening the nation to foreign capital, introducing the country into the international market, populating the interior and cities with men from all parts of the world.

And the country began to become cosmopolitan, at least as to form, under the impact of the enlightened liberalism of its new oligarchy, and with the neglect of or contempt for the popular masses, hitherto of pure Creole descent and now little by little blending with the newly arriving masses of immigrants. (Romero 1965: 17)

The experience of the generation following that of the first liberals, such as Esteban Echeverría, Sarmiento, and Juan Bautista Alberdi, is based on "landowning, cattle-raising, close economic and cultural ties with Europe, the cult of an ill-defined 'progress'" (Jitrik 1968: 48). Thus, Argentina could only join the Western community if the position of active subject was restricted to its politico-economic elite. Liberal intellectuals helped to form the new oligarchy and belonged to it. The tradition of caudillos from the interior was relegated to backward countries, although the same oligarchical control was maintained. The middle classes that emerged in Buenos Aires in the last decades of the nineteenth century were not yet strong enough to change the political profile of liberalism.

At the moment when the intellectual history of Latin America began to acquire an identity of its own, a new idea was proclaimed: the notion of the unlimited progress of mankind. But before we turn to this issue, let us consider the major political problems. One of them involves three participants: Peru, Bolivia, and Chile. Peru had been one of the last strongholds of Spanish resistance, and the country's liberation had been largely an accomplishment of the military genius of the Argentine San Martín. Independence was proclaimed in July 1821, and San Martín was the first president. But he was in power for only one year. Having begun his term in early August 1821, immediately after a meeting with Bolívar in Guyaquil— the terms of which have never been clearly established—he returned to Lima and, on September 20, 1822, presented his resignation to the Primer Congreso Constituyente, which he had convened himself. Thus San Martín had the common fate of all the heroes of the independence. Before or after him, Francisco de Miranda, Simón Rodríguez, Bernardo O'Higgins, José Gervasio Artigas, Sucre, Antonio Nariño, Mariano Moreno, and, of course, Bolívar himself were branded as traitors, exiled, or, at the very least, forgotten.

Immediately after San Martín, Peru was controlled by an alliance of military officers and Lima aristocrats. These governments were marked by rebellions and military uprisings. In a sense, Bolívar had foreseen the plight of Peruvians when he wrote that Peru "contains two elements inimical to every fair and liberal regime: gold and slaves" (Bolívar 1942: 51). But immediately after independence, the country's mineral production was not enough to strengthen its economic situation. As Mariátegui was to stress, because Peru was more distant from Europe than other South American countries, at a time when the basic aim of British capital was to place its manufactured products on the Latin-American market, Peru's integration into Western economy was more difficult. It became possible only after the discovery of guano, a natural fertilizer, which began to be exploited in 1845, transported by British exporting firms. The duties accruing from guano allowed the Peruvian state to organize its finances, begin urbanization of Lima, and—as Roca had done before in Argentina—appropriate Indian land, thus destroying the Incan system of communal landholding. In addition, guano attracted foreign capital, so that the state increasingly became its debtor. The easy circulation of money from guano was short-lived; but by the end of the 1870's the exploitation of nitrate from the South allowed the same policy to continue in force. Prosperity came only to the small oligarchy holding the reins of the state, while the state itself depended on foreign concessionaires—mostly the French firm Dreyfus and the U.S. businessman Henry Meiggs. On the other hand, the persistence of the notion that the national treasury was the property of the individuals in power helped push the country to near insolvency.

In 1879, Chile, supported by foreign creditors, declared war on Peru and Bolivia, with the intention of appropriating Peru's nitrate deposits. Bolivia, which had experienced not even a brief moment of prosperity such as Peru's, had earned the antipathy of foreign creditors ever since General Hilarión Daza, in an attempt to increase public revenues, restricted the rights of concessionaires in nitrate concerns and extinguished the rights of others. The result of the War of the Pacific, disastrous for the defeated countries, had more than just economic implications for Chile. Bolivia lost its coastal region, and its economic insolvency gave to rise to a chronic instability that plagues the country to this day. (In *Pueblo enfermo*, Alcides Arguedas was to write that from 1825 to 1898 his country lived through more than 60 revolutions and had 6 of its presidents assassinated.) In Peru, as Mariátegui was to show in his *7 ensayos*, the creation of a national bourgeoisie was delayed, and with the suppression of the *civilista* movement that had begun with the exploitation of guano, the country returned to military caudillismo.

On the other hand, the outcome of the war was highly favorable to Chile. In the 1820's, Bernardo O'Higgins had seen his progressive authoritarianism fail before the intolerance of landholders, who were alarmed with his proposed reform of inheritance laws, and of the Church hierarchy, who wanted to retain its monopoly on religion. A succession of conservative governments followed, but beginning with that of Diego Portales these administrations were not wholly insensitive to popular demands. There was a relative liberalization—much praised by Sarmiento, then living in Santiago as an exile—made possible since 1831 by the rise of the mining bourgeoisie, which served as a counterforce to the conservative landowning class. The War of the Pacific was the apex of this flexible conservatism, not only because Chile won the war, but also because the army had proved to be "representative of the nation, and at the same time of the ruling faction" (Halperin Donghi 1970: 268–69). It was then that Chile acquired its aura of success and prosperity, which at the turn of the century it shared with Argentina. In both countries, though, it was less a real liberalization than the success—no more than provisional—of their oligarchies. "Liberalization did not mean democratization, since the extension of power reached no further than the economically or socially ruling class, and encompassed only the political plane; the upper class was, on the contrary, even more firmly in charge than before" (Halperin Donghi 1970: 270–71).

The other paradigmatic situation is that of Mexico. As we have seen, the Mexican struggle for independence at first was distinguished by a social makeup different from what was the rule elsewhere in Latin America. Because there was a large Indian and mestizo component in the population, Iberians and Creoles forged an alliance, which later came to favor independence when the liberal revolution in Spain seemed to threaten their interests. Thus Mexico was at first ruled by a monarch, Augustín de Iturbide (1822–23). After he was toppled, a republican constitution was adopted, and there was the short constitutional interregnum of Guadalupe Victoria (1824–28). Then came the predictable pronunciamentos. One of the men on horseback was the comical figure of General Santa Anna. Ever since the new constitution was proclaimed in 1836, Santa Anna acted as virtual dictator, with intermittent periods of exile followed by triumphal returns, until 1855.

Immediately after the fall of this landholder-general came the so-called age of reform; its earliest and most durable fruit was the 1857 constitution. In the same year, against conservative opposition, Benito Juárez was proclaimed constitutional president by the liberals in Querétaro. A civil war ensued; it lasted for three years and ended with the conservatives' defeat. In 1861 Juárez was elected president. Since the country's finances had been devastated by the economic chaos, Juárez decreed a two-year moratorium on the payment of foreign debts. European creditors resorted to military intervention, represented by French armies. They brought to Mexico the archduke of Austria, Maximilian of Habsburg, and had him proclaimed emperor. Thus it was that a plan nurtured by some of the first leaders of the independence movement—the idea of bringing in a European prince to rule in Spanish America—was finally implemented, though in rather peculiar circumstances. With the support of conservatives and the Church, Maximilian was anointed emperor in 1864, while Juárez and his troops retreated to the interior.

A new period of war began, now exacerbated by foreign presence.

Latin-American intellectuals, for whom France had been a compass and a mirror since independence, were outraged by the crudity of the intervention. In a tone reminiscent of Michelet, Bilbao exclaimed: "France, France, tell me, what flag was it that bombed Acapulco for three days? Or does His *Imperial Majesty* bear a different flag?" (Bilbao 1941: 54). What the great Bonaparte had been unable to achieve, the grotesque Napoleon III was now undertaking. But the conflict in Europe forced him to back out of his Mexican venture and withdraw his troops. In his delusion of heroism, Maximilian took his role seriously and refused to give up. In 1867, the second Mexican emperor was defeated by Juárez and executed by firing squad. The following year, Juárez, now a national hero, was reelected, and was finally able to govern. But in 1872 his heart failed.

In 1876, a pronunciamento by Porfirio Díaz brought to power one of the two governments—the other being Rosas's in Argentina—that inspired most pride and confidence in Spanish-American conservatives. Successively reelected, Díaz remained the Mexican strongman up to 1911. Although he paid lip service to the reform movement started by Juárez, the political stability he brought to his country had a clearly conservative stamp. However, he differed from Rosas in that he relied on institutionalized terror far less than on the affirmation of economic progress. Significantly, Porfirio Díaz was supported by the so-called *científicos*— that is, the positivists—who became his most effective ideologues. During his long regime, most of Mexico's railroad network was built, silver mining began again, and the production of sugar was increased. In the interior, the ancient agricultural community of Indian origin was destroyed in favor of large landowners. All these policies of *restoration* were naturally supported by Mexico's powerful northern neighbor and its European creditors. As in Argentina since the 1880's, an urban bourgeoisie was in the making, and its prosperity contrasted all the more vividly with the destitution of the majority of the population.

Thus, whether in liberal trappings, as in post-Rosas Argentina, or in conservative guise, as in Díaz's Mexico, a new colonial pact was established. In both cases economic progress was based on agricultural exports and the privileging of the international financial bourgeoisie, whose profits were multiplied by a government policy that facilitated the repatriation of dividends and, naturally, reduced to poverty the vast majority of the native population. Given the political blueprint of the first revolutionary generation, this was the best outcome that could be expected. If this best of possible outcomes may seem to present interpreters to be no more than a fraud, it must be remembered that limitations of space have forced me to describe only the "successful cases," which are very few indeed. Aside from Argentina, Uruguay, and Chile, apparently as stable as European bourgeois nations, and Mexico, where Díaz assumed the role of a civilized caudillo, only imperial Brazil seemed spared from the infernal cycle. As to the other countries, we are reminded of the argument with which Charles Gould, the Anglicized businessman in Conrad's *Nostromo*, justified his alliance with U.S. capital:

> What is needed here is law, good faith, order, security. Anyone can declaim about these things, but I pin my faith to material interests. Only let the material interests once get a firm footing, and they are bound to impose the conditions on which alone they can continue to exist. That's how your money-making is justified here in the face of lawlessness and disorder. It is justified because the security which it demands must be shared with an oppressed people. (Conrad 1917: 69)

Curiously enough, Conrad's character is a better incarnation of the businessman and pragmatic intellectual than any character in a work by a contemporary Latin-American writer. Should not this fact be seen as a symptom of the disconnectedness of Latin-American intellectuals, which I mentioned above?

Last, let us look at the situation of Brazil in the period. To begin with, why did the former Portuguese colony, unlike Spanish America, retain its unity and even increase it? Halperin Donghi believes that one of the reasons is the different effectiveness of the Spanish and the Portuguese colonial administrations. Spanish power was much stronger and more resistant, and thus much harder to defeat; this led to fragmentation of Spain's dominions. Granted that the geographical, climatic, and economic conditions—not to mention the sheer size of the territory and the obstacles to communication—hindered a complete unity of Spanish America, even so these factors alone do not explain why balkanization took place to such a degree. Or, conversely, if such factors indeed proved decisive, then they should have had the same effect in Brazil. Thus, Halperin Donghi argues, it was the force of resistance to the Spanish administrative-military apparatus that made the centrifugal force correspondingly stronger. The Portuguese administration, on the other hand, had to compromise with local power more than pursue its own interests, so that regional differences were attenuated when the libertarian reaction ensued.

This cause, though true enough, is insufficient by itself. We can arrive at a more satisfactory result if we add to it the factors presented by José Murilo de Carvalho. According to this historian, the decisive factor was the homogeneity of the Brazilian imperial elites:

> A powerful factor in the ideological unification of imperial policy was higher education, for three reasons. First, almost every member of the elite had a college education, which hardly anyone else had: the elite was a cultured island in a sea of illiteracy. Second, higher education was virtually synonymous with law school,

so that it produced a homogeneous core of knowledge and skills. Third, up to the independence it was concentrated in the University of Coimbra, and afterwards in four provincial capitals—or two, if we count only the law schools. The thematic and geographical concentration encouraged personal contacts among students from the various captaincies and provinces, instilling in them a homogeneous ideology within the strict control that universities were subject to under both the Portuguese and the Brazilian governments. (Carvalho 1980: 51)

While Brazilians studied almost exclusively at Coimbra, knew each other since college days, and received in nearly every case the same legal training, the Spanish-American elites were dispersed in the various universities that Spain had established from Santo Domingo to San Marcos, Peru, or Córdoba, Argentina. Besides, since in them the Jesuits had a dominant position, and since they were "ultramontanes and constitutionalists, even favorable to the idea of popular consent as the basis of the legitimacy of government" (p. 57), the influence of the Society of Jesus increased the heterogeneity of the future liberators and rulers.

But these factors surely would not have been as effective as they were if Brazilian independence had not been won by a coup d'état by the prince regent rather than by an actual libertarian movement. And since—in contrast with Mexico—Brazil saw no popular insurrection, Pedro I could count on the wholehearted support of the local tendencies in the beginning. Thus, in spite of the crises of the regime—Pedro I's abdication (1831) and the regency period (1831–40)—the Second Reign lasted almost half a century (1840–89), a stability that was not the same as paralysis. It was true, however, that the empire was supported by a conservative system, and the parliamentary system was based on parties with very similar programs. According to Nabuco, there was a saying at the time that "there is nothing more like a Conservative than a Liberal in power" (Nabuco 1949b, 1: 174). (The epigram, it seems, derives from Dr. Johnson's observation: "It has been said, that Tories are Whigs when out of place, and Whigs Tories when in place" (Boswell 1892, 1: 90).) This was because the Empire's institutional basis was extremely fragile: it depended on the support of large rural landholders. Their sugar mills and farms were manned by slaves, much to the indignation of the small intellectual elite, the meager academic world, and the emperor himself. But in the absence of a pragmatic motivation such as the Spanish-American civil wars, and in spite of British pressures, abolition could not be accomplished suddenly since this would have had the effect of destroying the economy or even the nation's unity. It should be noted that, in spite of the caution, even tardiness, of imperial legislators, abolition was one of the factors that brought about the republic.

But the proclamation of the republic came about in such a way that, although it did put an end to the monarchy, it did not satisfy the descendants of liberals of later periods. Since former slaves were given freedom without adequate preparation for salaried work, it became common to accuse abolitionist leaders of knowing nothing of Brazilian reality and having a purely bookish view of their country. However, if one analyzes the articles and lectures in Nabuco's O *abolicionismo* (1883), one sees that, as I have observed in connection with Bolívar, his legalistic, ethical, and sentimental arguments did not descend to more concrete matters because in this case they would necessarily have touched on such delicate issues as the distribution of land, which would surely have made it more difficult to pass the law. This, however, is not the place to go any further into this matter; suffice it to say that for Nabuco the problem of slavery did not end with emancipation. The oligarchical power base in Brazil, as elsewhere in Latin America, blocked the steps that should have followed. Thus freedmen were relegated to a marginalized condition in slums when they did not prefer to remain with their former masters.

In addition to making concessions to the interests of rural landholders, the stability of the Brazilian Empire also depended on keeping the army in the background. This was a fundamental point for the liberals, who during Feijó's regency, after separatist agitation had calmed down, furloughed a large part of the armed forces. But the empire was forced to revise this policy because of the war against López. When the conflict was over, the old tactic of weakening the army could no longer work. The military crisis of the late 1880's, which erupted when a prestigious general was transferred to a remote post, was aggravated by landowners' displeasure with abolition and by a conflict with the Church. The combination of the three crises, as Oliveira Vianna observed, led to the overthrow of the monarchy, a movement that met with no significant resistance.

With the republic, the military finally came into power, as had occurred in Spanish America long before. The days of the poor, struggling majors of Machado de Assis's stories were now gone. The army became the agent of the most powerful oligarchies. Civilian power, in fact, did manage to establish a republican environment, beginning with Prudente de Morais, in which the military did not remain constantly in the foreground. However, every time the stability of the revolving door of politics was affected, the armed forces affirmed their strength: thus they persuaded Washington Luiz to resign, supported the revolution in São Paulo in 1932, and, more effectively, shored up the new division of power under Getúlio Vargas's dictatorship.

In short, from the mid–nineteenth century to the crises of the 1920's, what is usually called a new colonial pact took root in Latin America. Foreign capitalists joined hands with rural landowners to exploit and export natural products, or to develop and export agricultural products or beef (Argentina and Uruguay). The pact either coexisted with the permanence of military governments, associated with the traditional oligarchy—the situation in most countries—or with parliamentary stability, in which case the rural oligarchy was allied with a sector of the urban bourgeoisie—particularly in Argentina—or else it brought about a change of regimes that left the socioeconomic structure unaffected—as in Brazil. In economically stronger nations, of which Argentina was number one, the middle class began to appear. It is to these richer, more stable countries that José Luis Romero's comment applies:

> Soon enough—toward the end of the century's last decade—out of the middle sectors of society an upper bourgeoisie had developed as a clearly differentiated economic and social class, with clear purposes that, in some aspects, did not coincide with those of the landed elite. The latter stuck to their basic convictions and political ideas, and when they came to accept their new role in the changing economy, they strove to preserve them even as they were helping to change the economic structure. This contradiction was highlighted in their relations with the new, liberal-bourgeois bourgeoisie, which became increasingly dominant. . . . The existence of two Rights became more and more evident. (Romero 1970: 104)

However, all of these nations had a common element: the permanence of the colonial economic structure. The most important new factor was the articulation with foreign capital, on which governments were increasingly dependent. If we leave out those elements that are specific to the more developed areas, the following passage from Martínez Estrada can apply to countries other than Argentina: "After the conquest of territory for the Crown there followed another absurdity, the conquest of food for the absent; and finally the third aspect, the present situation, just as logical as the others: the conquest of wealth for foreign capital in railroads, meat-packing plants, and grains trusts" (Estrada 1968: 23).

Such a situation presupposes the absence of a class or portion of a class able to upset the power structure. But, as we have seen, the presence of the United States was already felt, as a competitor of British capital. In the case of Brazil, by the mid–nineteenth century this competition was already beginning to look like a division of labor: "The financing came from Britain, the major creditor of Brazil's national debt; exports went primarily to the U.S. and Western Europe; imports came mostly from Britain, but up to World War I Germany was an aggressive competitor" (Fausto 1970: 88). The North American presence was conspicuous not only in the economy but also, more brutally, in military intervention. After proclaiming its independence from Mexico in 1836, Texas joined the Union in 1845. In addition to fighting the Mexican War (1846–48), the American government blocked the unity of Central America, a move that was still feasible at the time, fragmenting it into five countries. At the close of the century, in the Spanish-American War, the U.S. took Spain's last colonies, Puerto Rico and Cuba (1898). These military feats, the so-called "big-stick" policy, are merely the prelude to another, deeper, policy. Under the slogan "America for Americans," U.S. diplomatic policy meant in fact that all of America was to serve U.S. economic interests.

MIDDLE CLASSES AND PUBLIC OPINION

In North America, though colonization took place almost at the same time as in Latin America, the society that arose was sharply different. The colonists who arrived there had no possibility of returning to Europe; they were determined to build a society where they would not suffer religious persecution, and where there would be economic and legal mechanisms for the promotion of material progress and social homogeneity. Given these factors, the primary concern as to economic relations was the formation of a network of self-sufficient relationships. All these factors favored the establishment of a strong middle class, economically independent and founded on law. Thus the ideal of political freedom, as it arose, was supported by internal reasons: the desired political freedom was not to be dissociated from the economic interests of society, and revolution was a movement of society as a whole.

Latin-American societies, in contrast, were formed by adventurers, members of the lower nobility or ruined noblemen who dreamed of making a quick fortune, or by officials of the Iberian monarchies whose intent was to provide the governments they served with returns from their colonial enterprises. Both adventurers and officials extracted local resources and sent them back to Europe, to which they intended to return under the best possible circumstances. For labor they resorted to the surviving Indians, and later enslaved Africans, and they succeeded to the extent that, as individuals, they stood out in their communities. Consequently, rather than the development of a middle class, there was sharp social differentiation of classes and castes, as Bishop Abad y Queipo observed: the economy was geared not to the domestic market, but to European consumption. Similarly, the movement for independence did not integrate colonial society, but proceeded from an enlightened elite, stimulated, in the case of Spanish America, by the ideas of the cautious Enlightenment coming from the metropole—cautious because it did not touch on the question of religion and because, since it was developing after Napoleon's rise, it saw Caesarism as a consequence of Jacobin radicalism. Either because of this influence or because of fear of the masses that had not taken part in the movement for independence, the leaders of Spanish-American liberation adopted a cautious political position. If Rousseau inspired their republican ideal, it was a Rousseau tinged with legalism, that is, close to Montesquieu, from whom they adopted the "seductive set of principles of political philosophy and, above all, the constitutional technique, with the principle of the separation of powers as the fundamental element" (Romero 1980: 119). It was, then, because of the organization of Spanish-American colonial society that in the new nations formed after 1825 public opinion did not exist.

The first observations concerning the lack of public opinion and the consequences of this fact came rather early. Independence had not yet been accomplished when, in a letter to General Francisco de Paula Santander dated June 13, 1821, Bolívar complained of the opposition of Colombia's intellectuals. They did not understand that it was necessary for the army to fill in the void left by the absence of public opinion, in place of which the Liberator found all over America wild and hostile groups, unable to conceive of any sort of politics except the local variety:

These gentlemen believe that Colombia is filled with people bundled up in wool, warming before the fireplaces of Bogotá, Tunja, and Pamplona. They have never seen the Carib of the Orinoco, the shepherds of the Apure, the sailors of Maracaibo, the Bogas of the Magdalena, the bandits of Patia, the indomitable Pastuzos, the Guajibos of Casanare and all the savage hordes from Africa or America who, like deer, roam the wilderness of Colombia. (Bolívar 1950, 1: 565)

That is why Bolívar, though vehemently opposed to monarchy, always favored a strong executive branch as a way to neutralize the tendency to disintegration. Bolívar's stand on this issue derived not from his lack of ambition but from awareness of the new countries' situation. As he noted, if Napoleon had been unable to defeat the alliance of republicans and aristocrats, who in America could possibly found a monarchy "on a land where the brightest flames of liberty burn"? Thus Bolívar proposed an authoritarian policy, where the army would replace the nonexistent public. In the same letter to Santander he writes: "This policy, which is certainly not Rousseau's, will eventually have to be adopted lest these gentlemen cause our ruin once again" (p. 565).

As we have also seen, Bolívar supposed that military intervention would be provisional. Here he was mistaken, and this error destroyed the idealized version of his military authoritarianism. The absence of public opinion made independence a parade ground for the military. Caudillos and oligarchies flourished, both springing from the same source: the absence of middle classes, of public opinion and of men who represented it and were legitimated by it. In his well-known work *Evolución política del pueblo mexicano*, Justo Sierra observes, in connection with the instability of the 1823–35 period:

The rural masses, Indians and mestizos, who served as soldiers for whoever was strongest in a given place to dissolve rural families and scatter fathers and children, had no other guide, instinct, or program than his cures and superstitions; the urban popular masses obeyed their masters; both, then, were negative quantities; landowners, merchants, educated men, and professionals, relatively independent workers, formed the oligarchy, together with officials, army officers, and the clergy.
(Sierra 1940: 226–27)

As "negative quantities," both rural and urban masses encouraged oligarchical domination. From oligarchy it is only a small step to caudillismo. As Leopoldo Lugones wrote, "politics, in short, meant no more than a competition among oligarchs" (Lugones 1979: 54). The caudillo is only the most daring of the oligarchs, who by means of an act of force or shrewdness annihilates or neutralizes his rivals. Although he stands at the top of the pyramid, the caudillo, just like the oligarchical groups, is a consequence of the absence of public opinion. The Uruguayan novelist Eduardo Acevedo Díaz saw this quite clearly in 1888:

He was already someone among the people born in hardship, in the everyday struggle with beasts, a man who could tear the horns off a bull just as fearlessly as he could defeat an enemy with a dagger. . . . They were the ripened fruit of a system of force; among themselves they enforced the law of survival of the fittest, in order to apply it later, ruthless and united, to their common adversary.
(Acevedo Díaz 1968: 80–81)

As the end of the passage makes clear, the evolutionist explanation was incorporated into a justification of the political phenomenon. Instead of public opinion, there were the lonely wastes of the pampas, and this gave rise both to the caudillo and to the gaucho, on opposite poles.

It should be observed that the absence of public opinion also served to justify one-man rule, since allegedly there were no men able to exercise political leadership. The argument was skillfully employed by Rosas in 1834, when he still had to account for his acts to a possible competitor:

Given the deplorable situation of the Republic, which of the prominent men of the Federation will dare take over the General Government? Which of them will be able to avail himself of a body of representatives and ministers; who will provide him with the wisdom and cooperation necessary for him to acquit himself with due dignity, to play his part successfully, and not lose all his credit and reputation?
(Rosas 1978: 238)

Rosas went even further in his self-justification: though he had risen to power as a defender of federalist ideals, against those who wanted no more than the preservation of Buenos Aires's prerogatives, one of his first measures was to postpone the convening of the federative congress, arguing that "since among us so far there has been no unity or peace, better to have this Constitution than to suffer the disaster of its dissolution" (p. 240).

Thus, caudillismo—from the isolationist and conservative type represented by Rosas to the apparently liberal variety—derived from the fact that there was no group with any sociopolitical weight other than the oligarchy and its close allies. Therefore liberalism, as a theory and as a political program, was doomed to failure, to be no more than a fraud and mask with which the industrial bourgeoisie justified its enrichment to the exclusion of all other classes. But how did liberals themselves see this issue? Did the situation become clear only with hindsight?

One of the best accounts of the liberal view was written by one of its greatest representatives. In 1845, while living in exile at the time of Rosas's dictatorship, Sarmiento observed: "In such a society, where cultivation of the mind is pointless or impossible, where municipal affairs are non-existent, where the public good is a meaningless phrase, since there is no public, the exceptionally gifted man strives to educate himself, and for this purpose he adopts whatever means and paths he can find" (Sarmiento 1938: 69). Did Sarmiento believe that the defeat of the *gaucho malo*, represented in his book by Juan Facundo Quiroga and Rosas, implied the advent of the public? He may have been deluded by the same mirage as Bolívar. He certainly believed, like so many of his contemporaries, that the search for national salvation necessarily required a pedagogical effort; and on this account, at any rate, he cannot be said to have been contradictory: during his presidency, the Argentine school system was indeed expanded.

But one question remains: how did Sarmiento and his followers think education by itself could counter barbarism, violence, and dishonesty? Could they possibly have supposed education was enough to make men accept liberal values? Were they unaware of the role played by the economic conditions of students, which for most of the population would make learning impossible? Although he wrote much on the problem of education, Sarmiento never answered these elementary questions. However, the passage quoted above is noteworthy for a different reason. There it is stated that the absence of a public implies that gifted men must find in themselves the resources for self-improvement. That is, Sarmiento perceived a link between public opinion and what I will call internalization of the law, on the one hand, and the absence of public opinion and the need to open a path for oneself, on the other. But since this articulation is a delicate one, before exploring it let me mention other reflections on the problem of the absence of public opinion.

Shortly after, in Brazil, João Francisco Lisboa reached a conclusion very similar to that arrived at by the Argentine publicist. It should be noted that Lisboa's thoughts were not based on any experience of a major urban center. Up to that point he had never left the Brazilian North, and his theme was the political process in his native region. But the different environment is irrelevant here. Even in a province as distant from the court's practices as Maranhão, political parties were extremely repressive toward their opponents as soon as they came into power. But this did not make them any stronger: in fact, they dwindled away after a few victories. What was the cause of this deep-rooted interrelation between arrogance and weakness? How are we to explain the similarities between regions as far apart as Argentina and the Brazilian North? Lisboa ventures no opinion concerning other countries, but knows that his diagnosis holds for the whole empire:

> This part of the present considerations is perchance relevant beyond the borders of the province. None of [the parties] have any solid support in public opinion, nor are any of them rooted in the great masses of the population. And how could it be otherwise, if the population has become weary and disenchanted to the point of indifference; if in fact there is no such thing as public opinion?
>
> (Lisboa 1864: 1, 377–78)

Half a century later, in 1909, again on a different latitude, the same absence is noted by the Bolivian Alcides Arguedas. But this author belongs to a generation impregnated with the determinism derived from evolutionist sociology. To him, the climate is responsible for the "tropical" quality of public opinion, characterized by conversation, joking, and word-of-mouth transmission of news: "In a hot climate, there is the habit of going out of doors in search of the coolness of streets, of tree-shaded public squares. People gather under the shady lanes of squares, at the entrance of drugstores, there to kill time in idle talk, arguments, gossip" (Arguedas 1937: 70). Arguedas, who obviously adds race to the climatic factor and to his accusations against the Spanish legacy, can only reach a devastating diagnosis: "The Bolivian Parliament is, in short, made up of two groups: one that systematically attacks the government and one that supports it unconditionally. . . . The groups change their attitude, so that they support the government when their party is in power and oppose it when out of power, invariably, without exception" (pp. 100–101). With Arguedas, biological sociology offers a "scientific" explanation for the continent's political problem. Whereas Bolívar's and Sarmiento's liberalism believed in a solution that either failed or has proved to be "magical," and Lisboa's liberalism affirmed itself only in contrast with the description it offered, evolutionism and positivism attempted to reestablish the legitimacy of the authoritarian solution, but no longer by limiting it to specific circumstances.

However, Arguedas's determinism is too crude even for a conservative like García Calderón. In this Peruvian author we find a different relationship between absence of public opinion, oligarchical politics, and institutional anarchy. He wrote in 1912: "South American revolutions can be considered a necessary form of political activity. . . . The excessive simplicity of politics where opinion has no means of expression other than the tyranny of oligarchies on the one hand, and the rebellion of the defeated on the other, is the cause of the interminable bloody fighting of Spanish America" (Calderón 1979a: 204). This inevitably reminds us of the neglected Francisco Lisboa, who—as we have seen—associated the absence of a public with the passion for politics and the violence of unrepresentative parties. In such a vacuum, the only way to counteract the intolerance of political hordes was active military intervention. As Martínez Estrada has observed, the army will fill in the "empty honeycomb cells" of civilian institutions. The army took the place of the public; in any case, state and army "were formed before" the public.

Now, it is well known that this substitute power did not take over solely in order to contain the clash between passionate oligarchs. Although Dr. Francia's regime in Paraguay is an instance of authoritarianism that eventually came to oppose oligarchy, what usually formed was an alliance between the military and the hacendados. So the army not only replaced public opinion but also, and simultaneously, devised a policy whose purpose was to make it impossible for public opinion to develop; it not only filled in the void but also made sure that what should by rights fill it would never develop. Throughout the nineteenth century and the early decades of our present century, the army did so by acting as the ruling oligarchy's handmaiden. Later it became the dominant sector in a state-capitalist society.

In the Brazilian case, however, where the rise of militarism had been delayed by imperial policy, the absence of public opinion shows its effects in the episode of the liberation of slaves. Traditional historiography is content to stress the role played in the episode by the liberal romanticism of law students, the emotional voices of poets and street orators. This is indeed true. But if we leave it at that, we may arrive at the conclusion that students, poets, and orators amounted to something akin to public pressure. As Nabuco observed, public opinion was "dispersed, apathetic, intangible." For this very reason—although not for this reason alone—he emphasized that abolition must come from Parliament: "Emancipation must be achieved among us by a law with the external and internal requisites of all other laws. Thus, it is in Parliament, and not on farms or *quilombos* [communities formed by runaway slaves] in the interior, that the cause of freedom is to be won or lost" (Nabuco 1949a: 24–25). Though

Parliament proved responsive to the demands of poets and students, to British pressure and to the commitment of the royal family, it did not heed Nabuco's admonitions that the slave question should not end with emancipation. If, from the point of view of farmers, abolition was a catastrophe only in the North and Northeast—for in the South immigrant labor had already been introduced in coffee farms—coming to grips with the problem of former slaves, so as to prepare them for their transformation into salaried workers, was seen as an interference in the interests of the entire class of landholders. Thus it was not the proclamation of the republic that impeded the approval of these supplementary measures, but rather the fact that Parliament still failed to represent a public opinion. Emancipation was effected in such a way that Brazilian Negroes were relegated to the same destitution that, in Spanish America, had already been experienced by the Indians released from *mita* (labor tax) and other slaves.

There is another clear consequence of the absence of public opinion in nineteenth-century Brazil. The critic José Veríssimo, in a little-read essay, observed that among us literary expression enjoyed absolute freedom. This observation, however, was not part of any patriotic outburst. As the author himself explains, "not even the most mistrustful of governments could raise any objection to its absolute innocuousness. Only the poetry of the Empire's waning years waxed enthusiastic in republican, socialist, revolutionary, materialist stanzas. . . . Neither the government nor the people read it, and poets preached to one another" (Veríssimo 1903: 78). In short: there was no censorship because no one read books.

But the most comprehensive interpretation of the causes and consequences of the phenomenon in question is to be found in the work of a sociologist who, because of his authoritarian conservatism, had no reason to deplore this absence. In his major work, *Instituições políticas brasileiras*, Oliveira Vianna analyzed our sociopolitical history in an attempt to set the bases for institutions that would not be "idealistic," detached from the concrete conditions for their implementation. Not incidentally, he founded his proposal on an examination that began with pre-independence society: the preservation of the sociolegal structure not only legitimated his procedure but also seemed to justify his proposal of government by experts, with the outright exclusion of popular will. This had always been our tradition; the point, for Oliveira Vianna, was simply to "modernize" it. Let us follow his reasoning.

Vianna begins by observing that the process of settlement and colonization adopted by Portugal implied the creation of large, autarchic estates and the abolition of "community living, the cluster of homes—in short, the *village*, so common and generalized in the settlement of Europe and also in that of Spanish America" (Vianna 1955, 1: 150). Thus, he added,

"Brazilians are fundamentally individualistic; *more, far more than other Latin-American peoples*" (p. 153). This individualism was manifested in and socialized through the family. In turn, the family was not restricted to its basic core: rather, it was expanded through alliances, forming clans. The head of the clan was a potential caudillo, who imposed his will on the subjugated mass:

> Emerging from the great estates, opulent owners of land and slaves, these caudillos brought vitality to the assemblies of the colonial period, and later of the Empire; they, and not the popular masses. The latter were either excluded from the administration and the assemblies, as in the colonial period, or, when they did participate (as in the Empire), it was always as flunkies of these great potentates, never as an autonomous and independent entity—*as an organized democratic force.* (P. 180)

There was then both a similarity and a difference in relation to the Spanish viceroyalties. The similarity was that Creoles and mestizos were excluded from government; the difference was that the Portuguese colonial administration, weaker than its Spanish counterpart, particularly since the Bourbons had come into power, was forced to ennoble native patriarchs. Besides, since the clans had to take up arms against pirates and corsairs, runaway slaves, and members of rival clans, absolute authority and particularist law became the norm. The proclamation of independence affected this structure only superficially. If the clans were now no longer absolute, it was because they clustered around the newly formed political parties. In fact, clans became even larger, always under the unquestioned authority of patriarchs. They were transformed into voters' clans, in which the masses played a role: that of manipulated voters. "The popular masses, hitherto electorally insignificant, now gained significance ... and became the numerically dominant factor in the struggles and victories of electoral disputes" (p. 308). This change, however, did not affect the structure of power, as the author himself says. In short, life before independence, under the empire, the First Republic, and to a certain state Vargas's "New State" as well, was based on the dominance of rural landholders, on the decisive role played by the family in the socialization of individuals, and on the lack of public opinion.

Among the factors mentioned, the articulation between the prominence of the family and the absence of a public merits emphasis. In fact, it had already been the object of a brilliant analysis, in 1936—well before Oliviera Vianna wrote the work we have been quoting from—by Sérgio Buarque de Holanda. His book, although often cited, expressed a view that has not yet been quite understood. I am referring to the idea of Brazilian cordiality. Using J. G. Weber's concept of patrimoniality, Holanda noted that, among us Brazilians, there is no separation between the public and the private—that is, no bourgeois rationality:

In Brazil, one can say that only in exceptional cases have there been administrative systems and officials purely devoted to objective interests and based on such interests. On the contrary, one finds throughout our history the constant predominance of private wills, whose proper environments are closed circles that are hardly susceptible to temporal ordering. Of these circles, the family was undoubtedly the one that expressed itself most forcefully and freely in our society.

(Holanda 1969: 106)

This passage clearly relates the indistinction between the public and the private to the prominence of the family. This eventually came into conflict with urban development: given "the primitive type of the patriarchal family, the development of urbanization . . . was to bring about a social imbalance whose effects we can still feel today" (p. 105).

Before we attempt to understand the reason for this conflict, it is important to observe that, in raising objections to the role of the family in socialization and pointing to its lack of adjustment to urbanization, Holanda was opposing the thesis Gilberto Freyre had begun to develop in *Casa grande e senzala* (The Masters and the Slaves), published in 1933. Freyre believed that the patriarchal family was the institution that embodied the success and flexibility of Portuguese colonization in the tropics; an institution that had been able to soften the antagonism between races and fuse white and black, masters and slaves, into an affectiveness and a sensuality that was "above" the distinctions of class, and of setting a pattern of flexible conduct that explained how, in the Second Reign, landowners were able to overcome their prejudices and accept as sons-in-law poor mulattoes who had been dignified by a university degree.

Without mentioning this thesis explicitly, Holanda shows that it is no more than an idyllic fiction. "The development of urbanization . . . was to bring about a social imbalance" in patriarchal Brazil, he writes, apparently without proving his argument. But how could his readers fail to notice that the basis of his judgment is the type of socialization brought about by the family, which contrasted with the socialization made necessary by the bourgeois order, under which urban centers developed? This was so because patriarchal socialization was certainly unacquainted with the order that underlay Weber's rational official, and instead reaffirmed the "patrimonial" official. Cordiality, then, had been formed and preserved by the permanence of patriarchal socialization. But what did Holanda mean by "cordiality," a term that was to be so wildly misunderstood as to lead to the notion that the author was in fact a nostalgic defender of aristocratic rule? Holanda opposed cordiality to politeness, that is, a conduct guided by a "ritualistic view of life." Cordiality was defined as "aversion to social ritualism," a "mask" by means of which "the individual is able to preserve his mastery over sociality." In a note to later editions of *Raízes do Brasil*, he refines this definition, stressing that his concept is to be distinguished from the common notion of cordiality. Using Carl Schmitt's distinction between enmity and hostility, he wrote: "Enmity can be just as *cordial* as friendship, in that both of them spring from the *heart*, that is, from the sphere of the intimate, the familiar, the private" (p. 107). The concept, though subtle, was perfectly clear. To say that "the Brazilian contribution to civilization will be cordiality" was simply to say that, because socialization in Brazil was dominated by the patriarchal family, we are unable to distinguish between an impersonal, polite language, *proper to the public sphere*, and a personalized language, reserved for the sphere of private relations. Thus understood, the concept of cordiality has nothing to do with an *essentialistic* or patriotic view of Brazilians. It simply means that we are cordial because our sociopsychological formation is out of place in the age of the bourgeoisie.

But none of this was understood. And though such a misreading was reasonable enough at the time when the book was published, the fact that it survives to this day, even after Koselleck's studies on the absolutist state, Habermas's on the public space, and Richard Sennett's on its dissolution since the nineteenth century, suggests that the matrices of the misreading are still with us. What are these matrices? I think they can be reduced to a single factor: the strength of the documentalist position—that is, the idea that the function of the social scientist (as that of the historian) is to show how things were and are. Later we will see the impact of documentalism on the concept of literature. But I will anticipate my exposition to show how a subtle but precise sociopsychological concept was misunderstood because readers placed it against the wrong background. Thus the best way to understand Sérgio Buarque de Holanda's notion of cordiality is to explain it in terms of the authors mentioned above.

In *Kritik und Krise*, Koselleck shows how the absolute state, in order to legitimate itself, had to change the unique validity of moral judgment into a political ethics. In this way, policies that favored peace were positively judged, and those that led to (religious) war were negatively valued. Hence Hobbes's prominence as the theoretician of the new state: "Hobbes introduces the state as the entity that removes political consequences from private opinions. In Hobbes's political law, private opinions have no application in laws and laws have no application in the sovereign" (Koselleck 1976: 23). This subordination of private morality to politics, in turn, brought about a complete separation between the sphere of the private and that of the public: "Thus in Hobbes man is separated into two parts: a private half and a public half: actions and acts are wholly subordinated to the law of the state, while convictions are free, 'in secret free'" (p. 29). This is the space Enlightenment thinkers tried to occupy. They attempted to politicize that area which absolutism had left open for private convictions. Once morality is removed from the family nucleus where it had been confined, the individual is politicized, and the citizen is born: "Neutralization of conscience by politics favors secularization of morality" (p. 31).

Jürgen Habermas's thesis, like Koselleck's essay, is too well known for me to have to describe it in detail. I will emphasize a single point: the idea that bourgeois public space appeared at the same time as the need for the state to regulate exchanges, and is counterposed to it. Its use of reason has an impersonal character, since it assumes a collective aspect:

> Above all, bourgeois public space is to be understood as the sphere of private persons meeting to form a public; they claim for themselves a public space regulated by government and, later, employ it against government, in order to discuss with it the general rules concerning the exchange of goods and social work, in the essentially private sphere that nevertheless has public relevance. What is peculiar and has no historical precedent is the means by which this political discussion takes place: public use of reason [*das offentliche Rasonnement*]. (Habermas 1978: 42)

Bourgeois public space, Habermas adds, clashes with the state because it is not content to take part in it, but wants to subvert it, to adapt it to its concept of class. That is why bourgeois public space not only counterposes the private sphere to the domain of state administration but also places between them the "political public sphere," containing the organs able to pressure the state machinery. This political public sphere includes newspapers, reading rooms, salons, *Tischgesellschaften*, and cafés. The impersonal language that prevails in these places is not to be seen as a relief from the sphere of the private, as is the experience of a bar patron in our days, but rather as the exercise of reason, as interference in business, and thus as the formulation of the politics of the revolutionary class of the moment. These remarks, although sketchy, are enough to show how the absolutist neutralization of moral convictions is accompanied by the reaffirmation of these convictions—no longer as merely moral, but now as political convictions. The citizen is a political ethics.

Sennett, in turn, shows how this public space deteriorated during the nineteenth century. Once victory had been won, the bourgeoisie assumed a different conduct. Taking, for the sake of economy, Sennett's thesis as identical with Habermas's—though they are not identical—let us simply quote one of the reasons Sennett gives for the new privatization of social relations:

> The traumas of 19th Century capitalism led those who had the means to try to shield themselves in whatever way possible from the shocks of an economic order which neither victors nor victims understood. Gradually the will to control and shape the public order eroded, and people put more emphasis on protecting themselves from it. The family became one of these shields. (Sennett 1978: 19–20)

This detour through Koselleck, Habermas, and Sennett was necessary in order to bring out the intuition contained in *Raízes do Brasil*. What Sérgio Buarque de Holanda did was to formulate the sociopsychological consequence of the fact that in Brazil (in all of Latin America, perhaps?) the conditions were lacking for the modern experience of public opinion. And this lack, I repeat, is associated with the enduring presence of the family as the paramount means of socialization. In other words, the absence of a public, a fact noted by so many observers, had to do both with the absence of middle classes and with the preservation of a *family-centered* conduct that was inconsistent with bourgeois rationality. Now we can finally develop the line of reasoning we have been sketching out.

As we have seen, Sarmiento spoke of the "gifted man" as having to open a path for himself. Clearly, this could only mean that the law should be seen not as something that applies to all and must therefore be internalized, but rather as an obstacle to be overcome and turned into one's personal triumph. According to this hypothesis, then, the same causes that led to socialization through cordiality also led to a specific attitude toward the law: one's talent is tested by one's ability to take law as a foreign body and submit it to the sway of private interest. But what does this have to do with the question of the middle classes? However preposterous it may seem, the fact is that the connection between the two can be traced back to Tocqueville. Let me sketch it out.

The first thing that strikes the reader in Tocqueville is the *invisibility* that characterized American public opinion, in spite of the French observer's sharp-sightedness. He was impressed with the fact that, in early nineteenth-century America, the state seemed to be nowhere: "What particularly impresses the European traveler in the United States is the absence of what among us is known as government or the administration: in America one sees written laws; one is aware of their everyday enforcement; everything moves but no motor is to be seen. The hand that drives the social machine eludes one all the time" (Tocqueville 1839: 110). But Tocqueville is not about to create suspense. The mystery has an explanation, and the author himself presents it: "Europeans often see in a public official no more than the force; Americans see in him the law. It could then be said that in America no man ever obeys another man, but instead justice or the law" (p. 151). So complete is the internalization of the law that government became invisible. On the other hand, this internalization, instead of crushing public opinion, was its exact counterpart: "Thus in the moral world everything is classified, coordinated, anticipated, and decided beforehand. In the political world, everything is agitated, contested, uncertain; here passive—though voluntary—ambition prevails; there, independence, disregard for experience, and jealousy of all authority" (p. 68).

Between the moral and the political worlds there is a reciprocal interplay of the internalization of the law and the use of public opinion. Thus there is no longer the separation mentioned by Koselleck; instead, law and public opinion are linked. And this is particularly evident in Tocqueville because the author does not use this observation as the basis for indiscriminate praise of American society. As his readers have always observed—and Latin-American intellectuals have been keenly aware of this, even before Rodó—Tocqueville was not wholly uncritical of the society he described. If he was sympathetic to democracy, he nevertheless expressed the fear that the very condition of equality might lead to mediocrity, for if people "do not fear the great talents . . . neither do they appreciate them" (p. 46). Thus Tocqueville did not see what we call internalization of the law as an indication that the society in question was the best of possible societies.

Similarly, by pointing to the reciprocity between socialization through cordiality and the attempt to adapt the law to private interests I mean to do no more than call attention to a differential conduct. It would be mechanistic to conclude from this that the fight against oligarchical rule or any form of despotism in Latin America must necessarily imply internalization of the law. Thus, stressing that one should not interpret the relationship in question as anything other than an interpretive, nonevaluative instrument, I will close the section with a passage from a contemporary social scientist: "What best explains why before World War II Latin America did not have a strong, antiaristocratic, bourgeois, and capitalistic middle class is the absence of an industry strong enough to generate such a pressure group" (García 1970: 63).

Thus, if—in the words of Fernando Henrique Cardoso and Francisco Weffort—"economic and social development, national autonomy, and political democratization seem to be the ruling ideas in the problem of development as a problem of knowledge" (Cardoso and Weffort 1970: 17), it must be added that among these aspirations one should also include access to the means of expression of public opinion, at least in those places where public opinion is more than just a compliant puppet.

THE INTELLECTUAL PROBLEM

La grandeza del hombre es el flechazo, no el blanco.
(The greatness of man is the arrow's flight, not the bull's eye.)
—Lezama Lima, in "Interrogando a Lezama Lima," 1971

Latin America began to assert itself intellectually only after the wars of independence were over. Since Brazil had attained autonomy from above, Brazilian intellectual production was more active slightly earlier. By and large, however, up to the middle of the nineteenth century or thereabouts the most common model was romanticism, in conflict with neoclassical expression, which was championed and defined in Chile by Andrés Bello. Romanticism and liberalism went hand in hand in these writers, but their major aims were political rather than intellectual.

Sarmiento's *Facundo* can be considered the greatest work of the period. Fleeing from Rosas's *mazorca*, Sarmiento, like other Argentine liberals, became an exile, seeking refuge in Chile. Although Chile was in the hands of conservatives, the country had never experienced the horrors of caudillismo, and exiles there enjoyed freedom of expression, if not government approval. *Facundo* was originally published in pamphlets, to be circulated among Rosas's opponents. It is presented as the biography of a minor caudillo, presumably killed by order of Rosas; but Sarmiento's target was in fact Rosas himself. He tells the story of Facundo's life; analyzes his family background, the vicissitudes he faced until he became a *gaucho malo* and later a general, who helped to crush Buenos Aires liberalism; studies types representative of the interior and of the struggle between the seaport and the hinterland—in short, Sarmiento presents a general diagnosis of Argentine society. Thus his interpretation has a clear, immediate purpose: to discover the conditions that explain the phenomenon of caudillismo and to find a way to contribute to its defeat.

Many Latin-American works of the nineteenth century are like *Facundo* in this respect; one thinks of almost the entire production of José Martí, as well as of Euclides da Cunha's *Os sertões* (Rebellion in the Backlands). The predominance of political intentions highlights not only the importance of politics but also the precarious state of intellectual institutions. What Antonio Candido has written of Brazil applies to all of Latin America: writers gained social recognition for their "patriotic and sentimental" contribution to political and social causes (Candido 1973: 81). That is why for all Latin-American intellectuals, with the single exception of Machado de Assis, literary activity was not the major concern. This is true even of a writer who was to become as famous as José Hernández, whose *Martín Fierro* (1872), as a contemporary essayist observes, was written as a distraction from his important senatorial duties.

The primacy of politics and the fact that intellectuals were not conscious of themselves as intellectuals explain many of their works' characteristics, and not just in the nineteenth century. One of these is their comprehensive, generalizing intent. Another is their historical or historico-critical bent, carried sometimes to the point of proposing a program for national salvation. Another is the importance given to the study of national history; many politicians, of which Bartolomé Mitre is the most famous, were also historians. Yet another characteristic is the neglect of philosophical reflection, which required slow maturation and, in addition, seemed a pointless exercise for a committed intellectual. Hence the interest of the following passage from Juan Bautista Alberdi, published in 1842, in which the author sets forth the guidelines of his course on contemporary philosophy: "The duty to be incomplete so as to be useful has led us to examine only nineteenth-century philosophy; and even here we shall leave out everything that is less contemporary and less applicable to our countries' social needs" (Alberdi 1945: 303).

In contrast, the primacy of politics, with its defense of national interest, seemed to imply the praise of science, seen as an instrument of progress. But this was only an appearance. The pragmatic character of the envisioned program of science and the philosophical crudeness of its proponents led this intelligentsia to confuse theorization with bookish practice. It was assumed that to observe an existing thing or fact is the same as to formulate what it is. If the thing observed was seen to work—that is, if observation created the illusion that one knew reality—what more could one ask of it? But both in the elaboration of laws and in the creation of technical inventions the primacy of observation was surprisingly ineffective. Hence Manoel Bonfim's criticism and Oliveira Vianna's irritation: "It is [jurists'] conviction that all of these social realities can be eliminated or abolished overnight: by means of a new law, a new code, a new Constitution—or a coup. Why study them?" (Vianna 1955: 412). Facing such judicial and scientific absurdities, this intelligentsia decried the fact that we Brazilians were not as practical-minded as the Americans, or proposed that we fight all foreign imports and adapt as our institutions the centuries-old practices and costumes of our society (just as Oliveira Vianna justified the "New State"), or yet attacked the fetishism of writing in our country. That is, the primacy of observation, seen as a consequence of the cult of science, came, after the first few decades of the twentieth century, to be criticized for its effects. But in relation to literature and the arts the principle remained unchanged. There was a reason for this. Since the sole object of observation here was to tell us what we are and what we are like—that is, to illustrate some political view of reality—the praise of observation remained as before. This discussion became fruitful only when the social complexity and the questioning of the matrices of South American thought legitimated discourses outside the sphere of politics—that is, when it began to be seen that science, philosophy, and art have functions other than that of furnishing techniques for the mastery of nature or arguments for verbal confrontation. But this was still in the distant future during the period we are analyzing here.

The pragmatism and the primacy of politics that characterized the liberal-romantic period were further strengthened by the advent of positivism and evolutionism. In Argentina, Brazil, Chile, and particularly Mexico, Herbert Spencer's evolutionism and Auguste Comte's positivism gained fervent followers. In Mexico, positivism was introduced in 1867 by Gabino Barreda, who was inspired by it to implement an educational reform in his country. With its emphasis on order, positivism legitimated Porfírio Díaz's government and became a sort of official doctrine; it was to retain its authority up to the triumph of the Mexican Revolution. But the enthronement of positivism did not occur of a sudden, as one of its students observes: "French traditionalism, with its conservative spirit, eclecticism with its historical sense, Saint-Simonianism with its concern for society, the Scottish school and utilitarianism with their interest in the experimental and the positive, all paved the way for positivism" (Zea 1976: 76). In Argentina, evolutionism and positivism gained importance with the foundation of the Escuela Normal de Paraná, in 1870. In Brazil, the movement centered on the Escola Militar, where it played a key part, since it gave the military an intellectual tool with which to face civilian lawyers.

The impact of these currents of thought was felt even by already established writers. According to Leopoldo Zea, José Victorino Lastarria lamented the fact that, when he published his *Influencia social de la conquista* in 1844, he did not yet know Comte's work. The example of Sarmiento is particularly deplorable. In his unfinished *Conflicto y harmonía de las razas en América*, published in 1883, he justified his civilizing ideal with a veneer of biological sociology. He blamed his country's woes on miscegenation, which had been worse in Argentina than in Europe because the races that mingled were not homogeneous: "These races of different colors do not, nevertheless, form a homogeneous whole, as was the case in the mixture of Gauls and Romans, Saxons and Normans, Germans and Lombards, Goths, etc., or even Arabs and Saracens, which are all varieties of one and the same race, the Caucasian" (Sarmiento 1915: 113). The idea that some miscegenations are worse than others can be found in as late a work as the Mexican José Vasconcelos's *La raza cósmica* (1925), where the author, discussing the making of Spain, observed that there was no problem when the races mixed were kindred, but only when they were incongruent and thus unmixable.

Early in the twentieth century, the biological argument is no longer relied on absolutely. However, although the influence of the environment is also considered, the idea of race remains the basic principle in Carlos Octavio Bunge's *Nuestra América* (1903), where it is stated that "each physical race is a psychical race" (Bunge 1905: 102). The object of the author's biopsychological investigation was to propose a treatment for the nation's "disease": "To disseminate culture, to improve the economic situation, to make the conditions of physical life more wholesome ... that is, education in arts and sciences, finances, hygiene. In short, everything save upheavals and violence" (p. 6).

Also in Arguedas, the concept of race remains the determining factor, although the author does not construe it in a purely biological sense. But the emphasis he gives to the environment does not alter the kind of diagnosis offered, let alone the role intellectuals attribute to themselves. Intellectuals are the enlightening guides; instead of race in its purely biological sense, the environment is now the field where the reality that must be changed is *observed* and *documented*. The matrix is preserved, so that the change of basic concepts is secondary. Hence Bunge's adoption of the concept of psychical race seems to have no effect on Arguedas's diagnosis. Bolivia's poverty is a product of the Indian heritage: "If Indian blood had not predominated, from the beginning the country's life would have followed a more conscious orientation, adopting all kinds of perfections in the material and moral orders, so that today it would be on the same level as nations that were much more favored by immigratory waves from the Old World" (Arguedas 1937: 32). But that is not all. Miscegenation itself is harmful, for its product has the unhappy characteristic of incorporating only the negative traits of ancestors. Thus the *cholo* is described as follows: "From the white man he has inherited the despotic arrogance with which he sees his inferiors; and, like the Indian, he is submissive and servile, though not at all kind, toward his superiors. He favors all that is ostentatious, pompous, loud colors, all that glitters, thunders, or stuns" (p. 89).

All of these observations point to the same conclusion: the problem with America is its mixed-blood populations. These, as well as the "inferior" Indian and Negro, are seen as the cause of the continent's apathy, venality, and political immaturity. We have already seen the importance of the criticisms directed against the legacy of Spanish blood, by the liberal romantics and others, for the adoption of positivist, evolutionist, and transformist views in Latin America.* Here I would like to stress two points: First, the

---

*Even though positivism, evolutionism, and transformism are autonomous currents, in Latin America they have been so closely linked that one may use "evolutionism" or "transformism" or even "transformist evolutionism" as a general term. The following passages are pertinent here: (1) "The most vigorous and popular current of positivism followed the path opened by Mill, except that it led to Spencer's realism. That the latter is contradictory, dogmatic, ultimately even Scholastic; that the former's viewpoint is superior and more worthy of representing positivist criteriology in history, are reasons that cannot override this fact: the immense popularity of Spencer's criterion. Positivism was bound to become a popular philosophy; and every popular philosophy is realist, at least in part. Thus we find that Comte's notion of reality was replaced by Spencer's compromising formula, and this, in turn, gave way to Haeckel's concept of the known world as the only existing reality" (Ureña 1981: 66). (2) "The title of our book in itself indicated that—although one might disagree as to the formula of social laws, and some, following the Spencerian school, would assimilate them entirely with biological laws, while others would, following Giddings, consider them as essentially psychological, and perhaps most would see them, like Comte and Littré, as

close relationship between using blood as a metaphor for denunciation and using blood as a fact for explanation is evidence of the continuity of a form of thought that emphasizes the principles of documentation and observation (later we will see that the principle of essence should be added to these two). Second, the strength of transformist evolutionism was derived from the very fact that it provided a defense, albeit unconscious, for the "white" oligarchy. Two examples are in order.

In *La creación de un continente*, García Calderón blurred the distinction between the need to promote national unity and the need to maintain the "unity of the race":

> It is convenient to channel the invasion, to prevent the development of hostile colonies, of small states within the state. This is a task for vigilant nationalism. Distinct and prolific, blacks threaten the unity of the race in the United States.... In the New World no Russian or German or Japanese or Jewish enclaves can be allowed to develop, for they would add to native anarchy a new ferment of discord. Slowly these obscure centers of resistance become factors of disaggregation.
> (Calderón 1979b: 268)

A few years later, Leopoldo Lugones wrote of the gaucho: "His disappearance is good for the country, because he contained an inferior element in his share of Indian blood; but his definition as a national type emphasized in an irrevocable way—that is, ethnically and socially—our separation from Spain, endowing us with a personality of our own" (Lugones 1979: 51). In Lugones, the defense of the traditional structure seems even more *censored*, but it is none the less effective for that. The author welcomes the disappearance of the gaucho, with his biological inferiority, but at the same time praises him for his contribution to national identity (and here the question of national essence is implied). Would it, then, be an exaggeration to say that transformism became such a powerful idea because it provided justification for the oligarch and for the intellectual, who thus legitimated himself as one who observed our problems and proposed a "cure" for them?

Given the inferiority of natives, slaves, and half-breeds, it was necessary to encourage immigration, stimulate education, and keep the government in competent hands. Through positivism and evolutionism—never mind the conservatism of the former and the liberalism of the latter—intellectuals asserted their function as pedagogues and physicians of the people.

---

fundamentally historical—we all set out from the same concept: society is a living being, and therefore grows, develops, and changes" (Sierra 1940: 414). (3) "Twenty years earlier, around the 1880's, among intellectual circles in Sucre and La Paz, scientific positivism was already beginning to exert a powerful influence; Haeckel was translated, Darwin and Spencer were eagerly read" (Zum Felde 1954: 196).

And these physicians of politics, who were not acquainted with Machado de Assis's novella *O alienista*, a devastating satire on doctors, offered their own diagnoses and prescriptions. In 1899, César Zuneta published *El continente enfermo* in Venezuela and Agustín Alvarez his *Manual de patología política* in Argentina, followed by the Mexican Francisco Bulnes's *El porvenir de las naciones latinoamericanas*, in which the author argued that a diet based on corn necessarily gave rise to inferior offspring. In 1903, Bunge joined the debate with *Nuestra América*; Manuel Ugarte's *Enfermedades sociales* appeared in 1905 and Arguedas's *Pueblo enfermo* in 1909; as late as 1934 Salvador Mendieta published his *La enfermedad de Centro-América*.

Biologically oriented sociology reached an impasse in Euclides da Cunha's *Os sertões* (Rebellion in the Backlands). Perhaps because his "scientific" scheme had no a priori intention of justifying the domination of a given class faction, Cunha came to realize that the theory he espoused ran against insurmountable obstacles. Convinced that miscegenation was harmful, he had to explain how a group of half-breed rustics, inadequately armed, was able to resist and defeat two expeditions of the Brazilian army, freshly battle-hardened in the Paraguayan War. This made it necessary to amend the biological theory: *sertanejos* were strong because, isolated from the interbreeding of the littoral, they had had time to develop into a favorable biological type. But when he examined the government troops, Cunha found exactly the same sort of supposedly noxious miscegenation. So where was the biological superiority necessary for the country's leadership? With Euclides da Cunha, biological sociology reached, in theory, a crisis.

But none of the intellectuals of the period came to this conclusion. Although as early as 1865 Lastarria was saying that racial theory had been invented for the sole purpose of abolishing "all the individual rights we have conquered in our revolution" (Lastarria 1865: 411), and toward the end of the century Araripe, Jr., arrived at a similar position, racial theory continued to be pursued with a seriousness that cannot be seen as mere rationalization. Perhaps the explanation for this fact is akin to the one Noé Jitrik, in *El 80 y su mundo*, offers for the success of positivism: its belief in reason, its enthusiasm for science, and its hostility toward metaphysics and religion respectively implied belief in the enterprising individual, enthusiasm for the pragmatic (technique being confused with science), and the justification of the confusion between philosophy and ornamental rhetoric and defense of a secularized morality. Jitrik's explanation clearly does not conflict with the one I proposed above. Transformist evolutionism, as much as positivism, justified the rule of oligarchs and bourgeois entrepreneurs at the same time that it affirmed the legitimacy of the intellectuals who acted within those parameters. Little wonder, then, that the course of transformist evolutionism should have gone unchecked by any sort of inner questioning, except in the case of Mexico, as we have seen. If in the 1920's its adoption was restricted to a few epigones, this is mostly derived from the influence of Benedetto Croce, Giovanni Gentile, and Bergson, to which must be added the impact of Ortega y Gasset's two trips to Argentina (1916 and 1919), where he introduced the new German philosophy. But the absorption of trends that were critical of evolutionism and scientism did not imply any qualitative break. Scientism was replaced by a vague spiritualism: faith in facts gave way to the belief in intuition. There was no corresponding criticism of the documentalist matrix on which the emphasis on facts was based, nor was a theory of intuition developed. Things were merely combined in a pragmatic way.

This spiritualism is already apparent in José Enrique Rodó's widely read *Ariel* (1900). Until then, the United States had been an object of emulation, to be contrasted with the Iberian heritage; Rodó, however, turned the U.S. into a symbol of what Latin peoples should not be. Part of the reason for this change in attitude was the American intervention in Cuba in 1898. Another was probably the effect of European immigration, which was already beginning to have an impact in Argentina, where the rural oligarchy was beginning to contend with the fledgling middle classes. Be that it as it may, with Rodó a specific reading of Tocqueville is crystallized. In his *La Démocracie en Amérique*, Tocqueville on the one hand had explained the weight of public opinion in the U.S., and on the other had made ominous predictions concerning the power of numbers:

I see quite clearly two tendencies with equal force: one leading the mind of every man to new thoughts, and another that would gladly reduce him to the condition of not thinking at all. And I realize how, under certain laws, democracy would extinguish the intellectual freedom favored by the democratic social state, so that, having broken all the chains that classes or men had once imposed on it, the human mind would be narrowly confined by the general will of the majority.
(Tocqueville 1850: 11)

Rodó oversimplifies Tocqueville's argument, stressing only the risk of mediocrity posed by the democratic system: "In the environment of American democracy, the spirit of vulgarity finds before it no barriers that cannot be transposed by its ascending power, and expands and multiplies on a boundless plain" (Rodó undated [b]: 79). The complexity of Tocqueville's position is reduced to outright condemnation. No attentive reader of *La Démocracie en Amérique* can fail to acknowledge the author's emphasis on the superiority of democratic over aristocratic society, even though he is aware of the danger that it poses for marginal or deviant thoughts. Tocqueville writes in chapter 7 of the first volume: "In America, the majority draws a formidable circle around thought. Within these limits, the writer is free, but woe to him who dare overstep them! Not that he must face an auto-da-fé; but he is afflicted with all sorts of torments and everyday persecutions. . . . Everything is denied him, even glory" (Tocqueville 1839: 143). Tocqueville's argument works on two levels, so to speak: that of society in general and that of dissident thought. Reducing both to a single measure, Rodó replaces sociological investigation with a moral approach: a defense of an aristocracy of the spirit. "The civilization of a people draws its character not from the manifestations of its prosperity or of its material greatness, but from the higher ways of thinking and feeling that are possible in it" (Rodó undated [b]: 53). This may give the impression that the author is not defending traditional caudillismo, an impression reinforced by the fact that he lived in a country characterized at that time by prosperity and political freedom. One might add that, seeing Latins as the cultivators of imagination and creativity, as opposed to the cultists of activity and the material drive, the disciples of Caliban, Rodó rejected the strong pragmatic tradition, which had been favored among us by evolutionary optimism. But though this is indeed the case, one cannot help deploring the fact that intellectual activity should have been defended on such simplistic and misguided terms. The so-called aristocracy of the spirit is no more than a metaphor in bad taste. But Rodó's defect is not as much bad taste as it is his failure to go deeper into the issues he raises, indulging instead in a Manichaean sort of dualism.

Nonetheless, for all its flaws, *Ariel* had the virtue of opposing the solid majority who saw Latin America as a diseased continent, the "Frenchified Creoles" (to use Martí's term) who tended to see whatever was foreign as the ultimate in human ingenuity. The path started by the Uruguayan essayist was taken up by such talented writers as Alfonso Reyes and Pedro Henríquez Ureña, who made of Rodó's aristocratism a stimulus for intellectual research. Note, in this connection, Ureña's understanding of the issues of the Indian and of popular art. Concerning the former, he stresses the absurdity of transposing European interpretive schemes to the New World: "Indians are not the proletariat of industrialism. Indians live mostly in those countries that have been industrialized not at all or only to a very slight degree, such as Mexico, so that the solutions adopted in connection with them could not be fully socialistic" (Ureña 1978: 19). As to the latter, his formulation is extremely simple—the very opposite of simplistic—and has the richness of a pre-Socratic fragment. Popular culture is seen as indispensable not because it provides a field for folklore investigation or is the manifestation of the national "soul" or provides an illustration for some political tendency: "There should be no high culture, for it will be false and ephemeral, where there is no popular culture" (Ureña 1978: 5).

Thus, as the 1930's advanced, Rodó's spiritualism began to coexist with culturalism, Marxism and rightist thought, inspired by Charles Maurras or even directly by fascism. But this abundance of tendencies should not be overestimated. If on the socioeconomic plane to this date there has been no break with colonial structures in Latin America—with the single exception of Cuba—on the intellectual plane there has never been any break whatsoever with the matrix that began to take shape with the liberal romantics. The first characteristic of this matrix is the absence of an autonomous intellectual system, one not seen as subordinate to political activity. This has only apparently changed. Even in the social sciences, which have reached a level of production and recognition quite unknown in the field of literary studies, two outstanding researchers write: "Under these conditions, an analysis that would be a scientific explanation of reality often opens the way—as in the Enlightenment—to a critique of a reality that is seen as inconsistent with the postulates of reason and to the ideologization of science itself" (Cardoso and Weffort 1970: 20–21). However, the social and intellectual complexity already found in some Latin-American countries forces some of their interpreters to widen their discursive scope. That is, we are forced to recognize that the various discursive productions have each their own tempo and cannot be subordinated to the expression of a given reality, imposed equally on the most diverse fields. For such an omnipresent reality, to be documented and observed by agents of all kinds, could only be the product of a naive metaphysics—or, as a poet has written, of a terrible metaphysics.

Without undertaking a theoretical analysis of the issue, Halperin Donghi touches on it when he attempts to explain why in the 1960's Latin-American literature and sociopolitical interpretation presented such widely divergent views of the same object (see Halperin Donghi 1980: 3–18). While literary works presented a euphoric view of the continent, as if it were on the verge of something of great importance, such as a renewal of its promise of freedom—and here the author stresses the part played by the Cuban Revolution of 1959—social scientists, in contrast, were soberly pessimistic.

It does not matter if we reject the reasons he suggests, since this euphoric (or rather, burlesque) view had already been expressed in past decades, as for example in Oswald de Andrade's experimental novels, and in any case it was present only in part of the literary production of the 1960's. What is important is that the historian implicitly acknowledges the impossibility of adopting a single-cause scheme, as is often presented in both essentialist and Marxist explanations. But the need to recognize this discursive plurality and thus revise the documentalist matrix clashes with the practical monopoly of politics, now revived by the economic impasse in which dependent nations find themselves. Thus the urgent need for analytical diversification conflicts with the habit of seeing the most diverse discourses as "allegories" of reality, both valuing them according to their ideological options and interpreting them through their alleged socioeconomic conditioning. Hence the tragic tone of Octavio Paz's observation: "Modern poetry was and is a revolutionary passion, but this passion has been an unhappy one. Affinity and rupture: it was not the philosophers but the revolutionists who expelled poets from their republic" (Paz 1974: 69).

Of course, Octavio Paz is not referring only to Latin America. But in Latin America the unhappiness returns—and not only in the clamorous cases exploited by the media. The conflict is no longer only between those interested in the preservation of the status quo and disaffected intellectuals. This conflict is to be expected. But within the opposing groups themselves, and independently of their ideological options, a more subtle conflict arises: between those who would monopolize the demands and expectations of a discursive form and those who affirm the need to acknowledge that language not only bears witness to reality or documents it but is also part of its very makeup. Hence the different levels on which the various Latin-American discourses take place. Whereas Latin America's political science, sociology, and economic history, as well as part of its fiction, are deservedly renowned abroad, its philosophy, anthropology, and studies of fictional discourse run into major obstacles to their expansion. This is so because in these areas, as Fernando Henrique Cardoso and Francisco Weffort observe, there is a requirement to preserve "ideology as an intellectual style." The second part of this chapter is an attempt to overcome such obstacles, through an analysis of the conception of literature arising from the documentalist matrix.

THE CONCEPTION OF LITERATURE

One of the factors that make it difficult to investigate Latin America systematically is the segregation between Spanish-American and Brazilian studies. In fact, our mutual ignorance is astonishing. Very few Spanish-American scholars are able to write anything at all about neighboring Brazil, and very few specialists in things Brazilian can make knowledgeable comparisons between their field of study and its Spanish-American counterpart. But this leads to the question whether the systematic view I am looking for does not presuppose a unity that in fact does not exist—Latin-American unity. In *La creación de un continente* (1913), referring to Peru's attempt to achieve the political unification of Hispanic nations, García Calderón wrote: "In 1856 America was not a unified continent, nor is it one now. Deserts, unexplored lands, geographical fatalities separate the various peoples" (Calderón 1979b: 230).

These disparities cannot be denied. But just as the diversity of tempo among European countries—for example, between Iberian nations and the major powers—does not exclude the possibility of analyzing them as a group, Latin-American heterogeneity should not preclude a general approach. Such an approach is justified by the existence of similar conditions, which suggest comparisons and contrasts. Thus, for example, if the process of Brazilian independence was quite different from the Spanish-American pattern, this was not because Portuguese colonization was drastically different. The reason was that English pressure had the effect of saving the Portuguese king from the fate that awaited his Spanish counterpart, making him move to the colony and adopt a policy that both smoothed over the conflicts with the local oligarchy and indirectly paved the way for future political autonomy. Structurally, though, the position of all newly independent countries was the same: in all of them political autonomy failed to lead to economic autonomy; and in all of them merely political independence failed to cause any serious change in the structure of socioeconomic relations.

This homogeneity includes the function of the intelligentsia. Indeed, José Carlos Chiaramonte's shrewd observation applies to Latin America in its entirety: "This enlightened intelligentsia, and then the romantic one, often seems to subsist more on the support it gains from its position as a mediator toward the European social sectors with which their countries have economic relations than on a real political effectiveness in the Latin-American social environment" (Chiaramonte 1979: xxxix). Latin-American intellectuals have never been the "organic" expression of any sector or social class. Hence intellectuals' failure to lead certain groups "to certain models of social life and political action," as Chiaramonte observes. To this I would add: this isolated existence is the reason why we did not develop, in the nineteenth century, what I call an intellectual system. But what do I mean by "intellectual system"? Such a system—that is, one that is integrated into the general system—must necessarily contain a scale of values of its own, and thus a specific legitimation criterion. In other words: an intellectual system (or subsystem, more exactly, since its object is to be integrated with a larger system) can exist only if society acknowledges specific "signs" in its members—that is, a use of time different from that of members of other subsystems; a criterion of productivity different from that in other centers of production; a principle of loyalty different from that which characterizes, say, the members of a religious society, a sports team, or a political party. The classical Gramscian distinction between traditional and organic intellectuals can be understood only in terms of these parameters. But if organic intellectuals did not exist in nineteenth-century Latin America, neither did, strictly speaking, traditional intellectuals. If the former were changed into strayaways, the latter were rather like phantoms. Furthermore, since there was no solidarity among the members of the same would-be subsystem, intellectuals began to identify themselves by means of traits borrowed from other subsystems or copied from societies where effective intellectual subsystems did exist. In the first case, they are identified in terms of their adhesion or opposition to the system. (Even today, one may be totally unaware of what a Sarmiento actually wrote, and be content to know that he belonged to the generation of liberals who were in power after Rosas; one need not read what Euclides da Cunha wrote, but only know that he was a republican.) In the second case, they are called intellectuals by comparison with European societies.

These two criteria acted synchronically—and still do. The political criterion confers a local identity on intellectuals. (If one cannot attach a political label to an author such as Machado de Assis, one tends to be somewhat cautious about him, or tries to find "redeeming" passages in his work.) The second criterion allows one to "compare" them, see whether they are "in step with the times" or "backward," nativist or outlandish. Thus the strayaways and phantoms also reflect the structural unity of Latin America. But instead of treading such an all-embracing path, I will examine a specific problem: the conception of literature. Having pursued the matter in connection with Brazil elsewhere, I will concentrate on Spanish America here.

The idealization of tropical nature at the time of the discoveries and the conquest is a well-known fact. As José Luis Romero observed, in the European context this idealization served the important ideological function of countering the appeal of urban centers:

> Thus there arose—precisely at the time of the conquest of America—a vast nostalgic literature that may be called bucolic or pastoral, with a remote Hellenistic inspiration and following the Virgilian tradition. The evocation of the glories of life in nature, among woods, fountains, and gentle flocks, free from the anxieties of urban life, from the vain ambitions that animated courts and cities, nourished Politian's poetry and became the conventional stock-in-trade of an abundant literature.
> (Romero 1980: 91–92)

Transplanted to America, this ideological function suffered a sea change. Now it no longer simply idealized the countryside so as to defend the status quo and the exploitation of peasants, both of which were threatened by the appeal of urban and bourgeois relations. Instead it ensured that the tropics would update the topos "vision of paradise" (the term is Sérgio Buarque de Holanda's). As can be seen in the work of the Brazilian

Arcadian poets, Cláudio Manuel da Costa and Tomás Antônio Gonzaga, the tropics make their way into the pastoral landscape, sometimes in a negative way—when the poet complains that he misses the poplars and crystal-clear streams of Europe. Nature remains idealized, to be sure, but it loses the ideological exclusiveness that characterizes European pastoralism, and sometimes even serves as a backdrop for Indian characters—as in José Basílio da Gama's *Uraguai*, José de Santa Rita Durão's *Caramuru*, or Alonso de Ercilla y Zúñiga's *Araucana*. Therefore we are well advised to keep in mind its importance in the poetry of the colonial period before examining its role in post-independence literature. This is not to say that there was a simple continuity between the two. Quite the contrary, since literature then became the privileged channel for political expression, the effort to signalize independence was stronger in literary works than anywhere else. Besides, since literature was legitimated only in political terms, there evidently could not be the slightest semblance of continuity between the now-rejected products of the colonial period and the new literature. How did this rejection occur, and what were its consequences for the concept of literature that came into force? Both questions are related to the profile of colonial society, from which the intelligentsia of the new nations tried to dissociate itself.

Although in colonial Brazil the *reinóis* (i.e., those born in Portugal) were also hated because of their privileges, the Portuguese administration was too weak to exclude Creoles categorically, as the Spanish Crown did. In Spanish America, the Creole elites, although they shared in their parents' wealth—this was Bolívar's case, incidentally—they were relegated to a supporting role because, having been born in America, they could not be fully trusted. They were second-class whites. Zealously preserving the privileges that set them apart from mestizos and craftsmen, from the majority of the population, and disposed to fight and even rebel against any royal measure tending to weaken the rigid social structure, these elites could not but see with resentment the metropolitan lawyers and priests, the hated *gachupines*. Why should the Crown reserve for them the best posts, the bishoprics, the positions that brought the most prestige and profit?

These full-blooded Spaniards could not even complain of the lack of a decent education: in fact, the schools that the metropolitan government had founded all over its viceroyalties provided the same sort of education as was available in Spain, with the same emphasis on Latin, the same discussions that harked back to Scholasticism, the same distrust of anything that sounded heretical and modern. Following the rigid pattern of *quaestiones*, this sort of education favored gratuitous speculation—not to be confused with the taste for genuine, serious reflection—the art of casuistry, high-flown but shallow rhetoric. Also, the distrust of experimental science, only slightly softened in the expurgated version of Cartesianism adopted by the Jesuits (see Chiaramonte 1979: xxi), encouraged the empty display and vacant wordiness (for a long time erroneously confused with the legacy of Luis de Góngora) imported from Spain. Such an education could not possibly serve any purpose other than the pleasures of eloquence. Although philosophy was stressed, the taste for the dangerous business of thinking was surely not disseminated or encouraged when students knew from the outset that all verbal acrobatics were allowed as long as the rigid canons were observed. To be sure, control was not always effective. The sermons of a friar named Servando Teresa de Mier provide an example of one of these curious "deformations," in which the ingenious rhetoric is turned against its own propounders (see Jara 1979: 141–62). Even the deformations, however, serve to confirm the model: the eloquence taught in schools could be deviously used in a discursive sequence, but not in an expression of genuine philosophical thought.

The same was true of literature. Although the cult of language and the practice of the classics were emphasized, there was complete opposition to all that was not previously codified. For the Spanish model, which since the time of Philip II had been firmly entrenched against dangerous modern ideas, sterilized philosophy and controlled literature. In fact, the control was exerted over the entire sphere of the symbolic. As García Calderón aptly puts it: "For Spain, originality was as hateful as heresy; hence all costumes and beliefs, the hierarchy and privileges, had to remain unchanged; thus colonial life dragged on, sluggish and monotonous. . . . Festivities were decreed by means of posters: even merriment was an imposition" (Calderón 1979a: 22).

It was not to be expected that the leaders of independence would view their heritage in this way. They did not realize that the hated metropole, which until recently had consumed their lifeblood and destroyed their fortune, had inculcated into their minds a philosophy that was no more than a parody and a literature that had no blood. On the contrary, they, who had been brought up under the strictures of this emasculating education, considered the culture of their native lands, which they would liberate from colonial status, as too philosophical and literary. Inimical to the tradition they wanted to eradicate, nurtured with the reading of forbidden works, they emphasized the practical, the useful, everything that would free them from this rhetorical curse. In 1910, one of their illustrious descendants wrote: "Poets abounded; in schools and churches, there were countless literary festivities, in which the audience was served with verses in profusion, in Latin, Spanish, and Mexican in profusion" (Sierra 1940: 136). A similar observation can be found in the work of the Peruvian García

Calderón: "In the overseas democracies, men of letters abound and specialists are wanting.... The abundance of writers of prose and poetry and the scarcity of technicians in management and public administration are hindrances to American progress" (Calderón 1979b: 281).

Note that the authors we have quoted from, and indeed many others who dwell on this theme insistently, were by no means opposed to literature or philosophy. On the contrary, many were admirers of literature and even writers themselves. Nonetheless, they believed that an excessive literary taste had deformed American life. Post-independence generations were not opposed to literature or philosophy, but condemned their ornamental character and proposed instead their pragmatic use, in the service of the nation. As to philosophy, I have already quoted Alberdi on a proposal for a course of philosophy to be taught in Montevideo. But the pragmatic goal was not restricted to philosophy. Intellectual activity itself was to be subjected to it, through political commitment:

Lastarria, Bilbao, Montalvo, Vigil, Sarmiento took part in the struggle during this romantic period; for them, intellectual activity could not be divorced from politics. Lastarria and Bilbao fought Chilean authoritarianism; Montalvo and Vigil, clericalism in Ecuador and Peru respectively; Sarmiento, Rosas's tyranny. Their works are pamphlets; their theories always have a practical character, whether they aim at criticizing present reality or at building the city of the future.

(Calderón 1979b: 126)

This effort was not only understandable but also highly commendable. In these nations, where there was no such thing as public opinion, where individual activity had always met with the hostility of the colonial administration, where the risk of caudillismo and the possibility of additional political fragmentation were everyday facts of life, and where, furthermore, the example of North American success had such weight, it was to be expected that intellectuals should be encouraged to play a markedly political role.

Also, since there were no scientific or intellectual societies comparable to those of the cafés and salons of the French and British Enlightenment, intellectual exchange could only be seen either as purely ornamental or else as political. As René Jara observes, the process by means of which literary discourse became autonomous in Europe beginning in the late seventeenth century—the separation "of literature and political life"—had no counterpart in Latin America: "The urgency of the movement for independence, nevertheless, seems to have restored the old link in Latin America, starting a process that would lead to a more complex and heterogeneous conception of the literary phenomenon" (Jara 1983: 340).

If we add to this the parodistic nature of philosophical training, the lack of awareness of the confusion between rhetoric and speculation, and the nonexistence of critical discourse, in place of which there were programs imposed from above and received by popular masses who could only either follow them or reject them, we will have a fairly clear idea of the concept of literature that arose in Latin America. The topos of nature preserved its decisive role, although—as one might expect—it suffered a perceptible change. The question now was to articulate the praise of nature with the political purpose of expression of nationality.* What was the reason for this?

The answer seems quite simple. If in the European literatures that were the contemporaries of our colonial period nature served the ideological purpose of valuing rural life against the appeal of urban centers, when transplanted to America it served as a backdrop for an exaltation—though a cautious one—of "natural man." In addition, the leaders of independence had learned to admire in Rousseau not only his libertarian political ideal but also his taste for the sentimental praise of nature. Also, they were the contemporaries of Chateaubriand, and so were fascinated by the romantics' fusion of literary and historical discourses, their enhancement of local color, their effort to capture the popular soul in order to justify the existence of nationalities.

Thus, at least apparently, South American writers seem to have done no more than follow the lesson of *normalized* romanticism. And so it is that they are usually interpreted. But this overlooks a decisive difference. In early romanticism, particularly in Germany but also in Britain, the contemplation of nature gave rise to a specific dialectic, which involved observation and introspection. This was the source of both the early thematization of the imaginary—so evident in Coleridge, for instance—and the intense interchange between the poetic and the philosophical (one need only mention Novalis and Hölderlin, or Coleridge and Wordsworth). In Latin America, on the contrary, the articulation of romanticism with philosophy and introspection gave way to sentimentality, often rhetorical or merely lachrymose. The themes of *want* and social incongruency are privatized into nostalgia, exile, and idealization of women. The topos of nature, in fact, led not to a dialectical tension but to a laudatory description of its hugeness or variety, to emphasis on the description of the human types that appeared in it.

*Significantly, this canon seems to apply to prose only. I say "significantly" because poetry, particularly among those currents most consistent with evolutionism (realism and naturalism), was seen as a marginal activity. This, however, does not mean that it was exempt from the ban on fictionality. Poetry was seen as the expression of a self, which was valued to the extent that it harmonized with the values of the fatherland; this was only an "improved" version of romantic practice.

Sarmiento is a case in point. His contrastive analysis of the cities and the pampas, of the opposing forms of socialization, led to the dichotomy known even to those who have not read him: "civilization or barbarism." Used for political purposes, it served him and the party of exiled liberals as a banner against Rosas's dictatorship. Later, it also helped him in his defense of European immigration; with the pretext of intensifying the civilizing process, it indirectly contributed to economic dependence on England and justified the annihilation of Indian populations. In short, it served as the motto of Spanish-American liberalism until the intelligentsia of South America could rely on evolutionist transformism. Nonetheless, outside the sphere of politico-economic practice, the opposing terms civilization and barbarism were not polar opposites. In fact, the two terms of the dichotomy had a common ground: the fatherland. It contained not only the antagonistic forms of life but also, outside the politico-economic sphere, neutralized them and made it possible for even the barbarian or savage to assume a positive value, through the expression of the civilizing intellectual. Now, this transformation would not have been possible unless the barbarian had his roots in nature, were indeed one of its manifestations. Thus, to such an extent is nature the dominant factor in the formulation of the idea of fatherland that even the negative term, the barbarian, is admitted—nay, *must* be admitted—in the writer's speculations; for he could not be left out of what was seen as indispensable to national literary expression: "If for a brief moment national literature can shine in the new American societies, it will be the result of the descriptions of grandiose natural scenes, and above all of the struggle between European civilization and Indian barbarism, between intelligence and brute matter" (Sarmiento 1938: 47).

Thus the importance of "grandiose natural scenes" was not derived from mere subjection to the romantic canon, from an alleged imitation of Europe, which was in fact only a creation of lazy researchers. It was actually the product of a fundamentally political program: one whose purpose was to reveal the specificity of the nation that the writer helped to create with his pen. Nor was the specificity stressed in order to provide a basis for self-reflection. On the contrary, self-reflection was eschewed, for it would require readers to receive and develop it on their own, and encouraging such activity would be a historically unwarranted ambition that would necessarily disperse interest and attention. The effort to produce a literature dedicated to immediate political effect did not, however, derive solely from the anxious concern lest what little intellectual production and consumption there was be dispersed, but also from the pragmatic view to which we have already referred, according to which writers were useful only to the extent that they were politically effective.

Thus this effort, historically understandable and valid, contains nevertheless a certain degree of intolerance, which remains to this day. Because of this intolerance, even now there are obstacles to the rise of an intellectual subsystem with an identity of its own, and not just something considered good enough as long as it can yield political dividends. Since I cannot dwell on this point much longer, I will simply recall the reserve with which an author who was politically advanced in his time saw Pedro Henríquez Ureña: "Philology and philosophy, the highest forms of literary activity, in Latin America amount to applying cosmetic surgery to a cancer patient" (Sánchez 1941: 132).

The privilege granted to observation of nature had double and contradictory effects: first, it encouraged writers to participate in making their fatherland autonomous; second, it promoted the idea that this was the way to make intellectuals useful. The first effect, as we have seen, was not solely the consequence of a romantic-liberal option, but also a consequence of the very state of Latin-American society. Otherwise one could not understand how Sarmiento's judgment could possibly reappear in an author like Rodó, who was so averse to Sarmiento's defense of the primacy of the political. For all the discrepancies between the positions of the two, the Uruguayan essayist could write:

Our America today is a rather barren soil for the arts.... —True, we are still left with our superb Nature, and the original elements that find a refuge, increasingly restricted, in the life of the fields. —Except for these two sources of inspiration, the poets who would express, in a form universally intelligible to superior souls, ways of thinking and feeling entirely cultivated and *human*, must renounce the authentic seal of original Americanism. (Rodó undated [a]: 260)

Thus for Rodó nature and country life are the only elements that can stimulate art in these countries. Later I will return to Rodó's ideas; for the moment, let us observe that the emphasis on nature here is not accompanied by the idea that it must be captured by means of observation. Such a requirement would certainly have run counter to the author's aestheticizing purpose. In any case, nature is always highlighted.

If I am not to be accused of the very superficiality I have been criticizing, however, I must try to provide a better explanation for the two approaches to nature. I have said that to the observational approach there corresponded the outright political use of nature; in Rodó's nonobservational approach this political aim was replaced by an aestheticizing purpose. The question, then, immediately arises: what exactly was this aestheticizing purpose, and how was it manifested? And more: were these the only two concepts of nature? Let us begin with the second question.

Reading Martí, on the one hand we find a confirmation of the privileged role of nature and, on the other, we realize that it would be a mistake to hold that the political and the aestheticizing model are the only ones that exist. Let me elaborate on this point on the basis of a few passages. The first one is well known: "The government will be born out of the country. The government's spirit will be the country's. . . . —That is why in America imported books were defeated by natural man. . . . There is no struggle between civilization and barbarism, but rather between false erudition and nature" (Martí 1977: 107). In a direct reference to Sarmiento, Martí rejects his motto and proposes a new opposition instead: he substitutes "false erudition" for barbarism, as the negative term, and "nature" for civilization, as the positive term. This reformulation was doubtless influenced by Martí's political bent. The hero of Cuban independence repudiated not only Sarmiento's motto but also the form of the liberal project that had decisively contributed to the creation of a new colonial pact. Replacing the accusation of barbarism with the rejection of imported books, the symbol of false erudition, the Cuban emphasized the positivity of what is thought and done in the service of local needs and characteristics. In other words, civilizing liberalism is rejected in favor of a critical liberalism.

However, as a paradigm of the two views in question, the opposition between two pairs is not absolute. Two facts here call one's attention: first, the equivalence, in Martí's view, of imported books and false erudition; second, the common praise of nature. Since the first equivalence could not possibly be grounded in any logic and Martí's position was surely quite different from crude chauvinism, one can find his reasons only within a precise historical situation. Imported books aroused such a fascination for more advanced cultures, such mimicking of foreign ways, that intellectuals could indeed be accused of false erudition—that is, of proposing solutions not fit for their countries. Thus, although there are historical reasons for Martí's position, the way he formulates it is nonetheless revealing. He associates books with the colonial legacy, Spanish ornamentalism, which in Cuba, still subjected to the old conqueror, remained very much alive. In contrast, nature, and only nature, would allow intellectuals to overcome dependence and usefully serve the cause of independence. Therefore, however great the distance between Martí and the author of *Facundo*, the positive term in Martí's pair of opposites was based on the same factor as its counterpart in Sarmiento's scheme.

This, though, does not mean that nature meant the same for both. Nothing could be farther from the truth. For Sarmiento, nature implied the negation of the man who had been generated by it, who would have to be extirpated, replaced, or transformed by civilizing agents. Given this conflict between nature and aboriginal man, in Sarmiento the emphasis on nature implied observation of it. In Martí the terms are reversed. The positive term is made up of nature and natural man, so that there is no line dividing one from the other. One cannot grasp nature without grasping natural man. That is why the differences between Sarmiento's and Martí's programs are not restricted to the sphere of politics, but extend to a field to which neither of them ever made explicit reference: the field of the poetic. The observational strategy—in which the author regards nature as a territory to be conquered by political and intellectual action, nature yielding as its prize the knowledge that had helped the formation and the formulation of the fatherland—was opposed by what I will call the essentialist strategy: here the author regards nature as one with the man who works with it, apprehending the two in an active set, rather than simply describing their appearance.

We see, then, that in Sarmiento, Rodó, and Martí, nature is always taken as the marked term, the positive feature that must necessarily be incorporated into the expression of American writers. In each of the three cases, however, the expressive strategy favored is different. We have thus answered the second question posed above. Now we can proceed to answer the first. By referring to Rodó's aestheticizing purpose I mean that for him the emphasis on nature does not have a markedly political sense. That is, of the three authors in question Rodó is the only one who does not believe that political commitment is a necessary condition for Latin-American literature to exist as literature. In any case, Latin-American writers could not ignore nature, for the society they lived in contained very little else of any interest. Somewhat imprecisely, the Uruguayan essayist tried to give autonomous status to the aesthetic field of the ever-present politics. For him, it was as if the pragmatism implied by this link were not appropriate for the Latin "mind." If the purpose was theoretically valid, the form of his thought—incomplete, merely allusive, attached to such nebulous formulae as *latinidad*—provided ammunition for his critics. The fact is, wherever the autonomy of the aesthetic is proposed without analyzing its commitment to and confluence with other ways of relating to the world, the charge of escapism is inevitably made. That is why, for the purposes of our discussion, Rodó's position is the least interesting. I will concentrate on the positions that have greater consequences. To begin with, I will analyze Martí's essentialist position in more detail.

In an article published before the one I quoted from above, in 1884, he wrote: "Lest one be disheartened before it, because of a lack of spirit or a flaunting of false spirit, one would do well to feed, through memory or admiration, through judicious study or loving sorrow, on the fervent spirit of the nature into which one is born, heightened and vivified by that of men of all races who are born of it and who are buried in it" (Martí 1978: 221). Note, first, that here the praise of nature cannot be abstracted from the praise of the man who belongs in it, and that this man is not just American man. There is no chauvinism at all in Martí's vision. The "natural man" whom he praises is not natural because he was born in a place; rather, he becomes natural in consequence of the conduct he adopts. Second, notice that the "fervent spirit of the nature into which one was born" is stimulated by memory and admiration, and not by the "scientific" disposition of one who would describe it. This means that what I have called the essentialist position is closer than Sarmiento's to the path of self-reflection. But in order to demonstrate this and to understand why I am calling it "essentialist," it is necessary to make clear what Martí means when he speaks of "natural man."

In an 1888 article on Whitman, he wrote: "Universities and learned languages have placed men in such a position that they no longer know themselves . . . so that when they see before them man naked, virginal, loving, sincere, powerful . . . they flee as if they were fleeing their own conscience" (Martí 1978: 267). Martí professed a kind of Rousseauism: natural man was sincere and loving, reading in himself what nature had placed there and transposing it into a "natural book." That is, the man who could preserve his homogeneity with nature would be *essentially* good, free of the arrogance and artificiality produced by the instruments of erudition. It was not society as a whole but these wicked "learned languages" that made man stray from his original communion. Thus, outside of the political sphere, it seems that the difference between Martí and Sarmiento results from the difference between their *beliefs*: according to the Argentine, the races are characterized by their different potential for civilization; for Martí, who is both more romantic and more modern, there are no inferior or superior races: man is always the same, but he either remains faithful to nature or violates it.

However, if it all boiled down to a difference of beliefs, there would be nothing to discuss: we might accept one or the other, or decide in favor of yet a third one. Beliefs are by definition intransitive, immune to discussion. But that is not all there is to it. In Martí's short articles on art we can see that his belief in natural man had rational implications; and these implications are the sort of thing that can be discussed. Here is Martí writing on impressionist painters in 1886, emphasizing their indebtedness to Velázquez and Goya:

All of them derive from Velázquez and Goya. . . . Velázquez recreated the forgotten men; Goya, who as a child drew with all the sweetness of Raphael, descended, wrapped in a dark mantle, into the innards of man, and with the colors he found there he recounted his trip upon his return. Velázquez was the naturalist: Goya was the impressionist: with red and grayish blobs Goya made a "Madhouse" and a "Trial of the Inquisition" that chill one to the bone: there one sees, as a bloody and eternal portrait of man, the skeleton of deep vanity and evil. Through the rounded eyes of those hooded figures one sees the stairways to hell. He saw the court, love, and war, and naturally painted death. (Martí 1978: 295)

Martí had the ability—all the more striking because he was not an art critic—to perceive Goya's closer kinship with the art of his time. Obviously, the arguments with which he substantiates his praise of Goya are related to the secondary role he assigns to observation. This is evident once again in his article on an exhibition of paintings by Vasily Vereshchagin: "What stands out in this Russian painter . . . is that universal sin of contemporary art . . . the excesses . . . of the expressive faculty" (p. 305). It may be said that Martí's opposition to the "painting of exteriors, which requires only eyes for observing" is expressed in terms that are rhetorical rather than effective—what is desired is "that other kind of painting, in which the exterior is used truly in the state and forms that will produce that intimate caress . . . with which man in the presence of beauty, animate or inert, recognizes and values himself as a living portion of the universe, brother to all the others" (p. 305). Nevertheless, his expression serves quite effectively to show that the author did not subscribe to the notion that the function of art was to describe the natural beauties of one's country and use them as an allegory of a certain concept of reality.

It is not my intention to contribute to Martí's hagiography; every hagiography creates myths rather than saints. My purpose is merely to stress the little-noted discrepancy between Martí's positions and the canon on art and literature prevailing in all of Latin America. To be sure, compared with the production of the best critics of his time, Martí's brief notes are a minor contribution. But they played an important role in the Latin-American criticism of his time. And Martí's critical writings have more than merely historical interest: they are relevant to our present discussion.

We must, however, once again take care not to overestimate their value. If Martí's essentialism has the merit of remaining immune from the evolutionist scientism or the pragmatism of an earlier age, still it goes no further than the expressivism of ordinary romantic thought. Take the following passage, for instance: "Everything has already been said; but everything that is sincere is new each time it is said. What makes the world grow is not the discovery of how it is made, but the effort of each person to make this discovery" (Martí 1978: 329). Here Martí not only reaffirms his loyalty to the romantic view of the poet, whose expression is seen as dependent on his truthfulness, but also reasserts his essentialism: the act of creation is an act of *confirmation*. An observationist would not object to this axiom; but, unlike Martí, he would emphasize the image in the mirror, portrait, or reflection—that is, he would de-emphasize the role of individuality, which

Martí exalts. Thus, what from a European diachronic viewpoint would be an earlier conception—the affirmation of romanticism over the realist canon—is, in the Latin-American context, precisely the opposite: at the end of the nineteenth century, Martí *understands* romanticism, whereas "romantics" like Sarmiento interpret it much as realists do.

Contrary to what a linear sort of reasoning might lead one to expect, forerunners are not necessarily better than epigones. It all depends on what is anticipated or prolonged. But it should be understood that the epigonic character of Martí's criticism has a peculiarity: it is truly epigonic only from the superficial viewpoint of trends and literary schools, according to which our first real romantics were those who attacked the neoclassical ideas of Andrés Bello. However, unless I am mistaken, these Latin-American romantics were in fact closer to realism than to the romantic ideals they believed they espoused. When we classify intellectual currents according to European patterns, we run into difficulties of this kind. Thus Martí's criticism has the additional advantage of showing us the mythical sense we usually attach to such phrases as "more advanced conception" or "more antiquated conception." Once this crude misunderstanding is dispelled, we realize we are right to feel closer to Martí than to the defenders of the observational canon, who prevail to this day. Here is Martí's 1892 attack on naturalism:

> In short, naturalism is no more than a fancy name for a flaw: lack of imagination. Between naturalists and those who have no need to be naturalists there is the same difference as that found between painters who copy and those who create. A rigorous deduction of naturalism has the effect of demolishing it. If art is strictly adjusted to naturalist theory, the painter who copies a work of Raphael's is greater than Raphael. (Martí 1978: 409)

Unfortunately, Martí wrote his newspaper articles for money and never had the opportunity to elaborate his concept of imagination. But is it really right to say "unfortunately"? Perhaps the challenge he presents to us is the attempt to elaborate what he himself was unable to achieve. In any case, before attempting this, it is necessary to understand the meaning of the observationalist praise of nature.

To grasp the meaning given to the observation of the land and the costumes, it must be stressed that this perspective was the result of a set of factors that also included (a) the absence of an intellectual subsystem; (b) the related attribution of a single, political function to intellectuals; (c) the neglect of philosophical training; and (d) the strongly pragmatic bent that took the place of such training. This set of factors had a number of consequences, of which the primacy of observation, the basis of the documentalist view of literature, was only one.

In order to understand the features of the observational perspective, it helps to compare it with its effect on the social sciences. The economist Antonio García, for instance, observes that the way Adam Smith's ideas were received was reflected in the reception of other currents of economic thought of the same period: "This is the way—dogmatic and absolutist— that new ideologies are received in Latin America, whether Marxism or reformist trends of economic thought, such as Keynesianism: all propound formulae rather than methods of knowledge" (García 1970: 75).

Likewise, documentalism is, among us, a formula taken for granted in most statements, so that the need to substantiate it is simply not felt. One who runs across a statement like the following might expect to find a justification for it in the work of some other author: "Enough of pretense, enough of artificiality, enough of theater. We want air, we want light, we want nature" (Ugarte 1978: 268). But instead one is frustrated to find no more than rhetorical tirades, in which high-sounding phrases attempt to solve the most complicated questions. If, for instance, one asks what a certain author means by philosophy of history, one finds a respected essayist answering as follows: "It is that high judgment that gives each thing its time, and each time its prevailing costumes and laws" (Acosta 1908: 78). And if one asks what is the object of the historian of literature, one gets the following vicious circle for an answer: "It is a group of works that encompasses the vast field of human thought, and comprehends, in addition, all the genders found therein" (Rojas 1960, 1: 62). The Brazilian tradition is the same. The simple question "What is literature?," which José Veríssimo used as the title of one of his essays, brings on reactions of tedium and despair. And reviewers immediately speak of another "didactic" work. Hence the paradoxical nature of the documentalist conception of literature: the more this conception is left unexpressed, the vaster it is. Thus we have to look for it between the lines of discussions, or in general descriptions furnished by historians.

Such is the case of the two volumes that the Uruguayan Alberto Zum Felde devoted to Spanish-American essay and narrative, a work invaluable for the material it assembles. In the first volume, he emphasized the following factors as determinants of *americanidad*: "the characterizing primacy of the territorial, telluric, and human factor, in the phenomenality and problematicalness proper to all countries, within the diversity of their regional modalities" (Zum Felde 1954: 21). In the second volume he writes, consistently: "South American narrative is predominantly objectivistic, environmental, and mostly telluric, its proper field being the geosocial, and psychology being restricted to outlining character in function of the environment" (Zum Felde 1959: 144). Little or nothing is said about why this came to be so and what the consequences of this fact are for the literary essay and fictional practice. Documentalism is so pervasive that even the researcher's curiosity is inhibited. Positivist practice has taken root so deeply that the historian is content to compose a narrative that is in fact no more than a collection of annotated bibliographical notes. But to do justice to Zum Felde, it must be said that in one passage he offers a valuable observation: "And what the reader—the critic—of a Spanish-American novel requires is precisely this, above all: the typical, the characteristic, the geohuman, determined by the power of its telluric and ancestral reality; and not just in America, but abroad as well; what interests the European or U.S. reader is what is typically territorial, reflected in literature" (Zum Felde 1959: 35).

This observation is of great importance; documentality pleases not only South American readers and critics, but also the foreign market. On the domestic plane, the cult of observation serves as a form of atonement of *mauvaise conscience*: yes, I am a bourgeois, but my country's misery grieves me; yes, I work for a hateful government, but when I am not drinking myself to death I record all of my country's forms, types, and woes. Abroad, the same cult serves to gratify the metropolitan reader's yen for exoticism, offering him the heat, the sensuality, and the misfortunes of the tropics as a compensation for the cold climate and the internalized law of Europe, or as a good reason to find oneself lucky not to live in such an inferno of arbitrariness. In one sentence, Zum Felde captures the reason for the durability of the documentalist canon. However, such moments are extremely rare, which perhaps explains why the theme is hardly explored, and why, lurking in the protective shadows of implicitness, protected by the tedium of "complicated" questions, the canon remains practically intact, for all the changes in literary fashions and theoretical models. However, documentalism has very serious effects, except for those who are content to see literature as a practical example of something else. But why should its effects be serious? Because documentalism implies that "imagination" is a meaningless word, one that could be replaced by any other similar term, or even discarded as a mistake.

It is precisely in this second sense that the Bolivian Arguedas, in 1909, took the word, even though he himself was to become known as a telluric novelist:

I take imagination—following Miguel de Unamuno—as "the faculty of representing in a lively fashion, as if it were real, that which is not." . . . One might well hold that the people of Cochabamba are imaginative because they pretend that things are other than what they are, giving them a meaning that does not belong to them, and desire to accomplish feats that in their environment could not be achieved, simply because, on the one hand, the necessary elements are lacking, and, on the other, the absence of complexity in our social life does not favor the development of the capacity for observation, which is, one may say, the basis of the aspirations that are achievable in relation to the welfare of the community.

(Arguedas 1937: 69–70)

(At a recent symposium of Spanish-American scholars, I heard it said that the word "fiction" ought to be proscribed in literary discussions!) It is true that Arguedas is not a representative of the liberal-romantic type, but rather a product of evolutionist thought. But would his position have shocked Sarmiento, the first author we quoted as an example of the praise of documentalism? This question seems to be answered by the fact that Sarmiento himself, late in life, became an evolutionist.

In fact, it would be arbitrary to attempt to limit the practice and praise of observation to the followers of evolutionist trends. It comes as no surprise, then, to find in the work of Acevedo Díaz—an author who never identified himself as an evolutionist—how deeply the cult of observation had pervaded literary practice. In his 1914 novel *Lanza y sable*, we come across the following digression: "Everyone knows that the real literature of a people is in its origins, in the exact reproduction of the types, habits, and costumes that have become nearly extinct; in the study of primitive instincts, of how these instincts matured and to what extremes they were led by the initial spurt of change up to the first stage of progress" (Acevedo Díaz 1943: 18–19).

If, therefore, as in Brazil, Spanish-American evolutionism did not bring about a new literary canon, what it did was to reinforce, validate, and give a semblance of scientific foundation to an opinion that, among romantics, was justified as a documentation of nationality. Or, in more concrete terms, if after the wars of independence literature could only be legitimated by its political commitment, if this commitment brought about the primacy of observation of the land and the costumes of its inhabitants, evolutionism had the effect of reinforcing this principle, so that the writer of prose became a sort of ethnologist or practical biologist, recording the peculiarities and flaws of men, either simply for the sake of describing them or as part of the effort to change society. The ban on fictionality is then formulated more explicitly. Its control, exerted since colonial times, is now based on more solid foundations, and thus remains firmly intact. Note also that the justification is so comprehensive that it encompasses the practice of both conservatives and progressives. The former are content to be considered describers; the latter wish to be seen as whistle-blowers. In both cases, they are illustrators of reality, something that is such as it is, and to which they add no more than words so as to translate it.

Here, though, an objection might be raised: how can I say that the emphasis on observation was such that documentalism became a canon when so many foreign travelers and Latin-American essayists complained of the lack of local analyses, of the excessive authority attached to foreign books, which became veritable fetishes? An observation made by Manoel Bonfim, an essayist regrettably neglected in his own country, is applicable not only to Brazil but to other Latin-American nations as well: "These men, who ought to refer to their nation's real needs and draw their inspiration from them, live in ignorance of the facts, are blind to them; the present world, their environment, means nothing to them; they base their entire work on book learning" (Bonfim undated: 179). How, then, can I stand by my thesis, even after having written that observation and documentalism were part of a whole that also included pragmatism, the primacy of politics, the neglect of philosophical training? Doesn't the fact that all of these factors were present make my thesis even less tenable?

All of these objections would be correct, and I would be forced to retract my previous statements, if the cult of observation and documentation of national traits implied the actual adoption of a scientific attitude. That is, if, based on the observation of phenomena, the attempt were made to explain them through demonstration or experimentation, in order to arrive at a comprehensive theory that accounted for them. But observation implied none of this. Within an effective intellectual subsystem, legitimated as such, one would expect the praise of observation to imply, at the very least, the dawning of scientific curiosity. But this assumption is unwarranted in Latin America, just as it is unwarranted to believe there was an intellectual system here because there were schools and teachers, intellectuals and books. Among us, the praise of science was confused with the importance of acquiring machines and techniques in order to exploit the much-praised—and much-overdue—riches of the land. The passionate statements in favor of science never went beyond the elementary stage of admiring it for its usefulness. The idea that science, before the actual building of extractive machinery, required theoretical speculation and research was considered odd, even absurd. That is why our few true scientists, such as Florentino Ameghino, have never influenced our current ideas.

The admiration for science, seen as a useful and productive activity, was in fact admiration for technique. Hence our lack of flexibility in understanding theoretical currents, as Antonio García observed in a passage quoted above. The fact that such currents proved inadequate when transplanted to Latin-American reality was not necessarily their fault, but rather a consequence of the attitude in which they were—and are—received. In the period we are concerned with here (and even today), science was seen as no more than a legitimated practical activity, in which practical-minded men engaged.

This conception was reinforced by the absence of philosophical training and philosophical doubt; conversely, the latter was reinforced by the former. But its origin had an earlier cause: the rejection of colonial tradition, seen as justified by South American intellectuals. As we have seen, this rejection was the cause of their disdain for what they felt to be the excessive literary taste of the accursed colonizers. Thus Martí could write, in 1891: "Literary contests should award prizes not to the best ode, but to the best studies of the country one lives in" (Martí 1978: 28). Making the same assumption, García Calderón praised the Peruvian president Manoel Prado, whose "favorite daughter was the Faculty of Political Sciences, which trains administrators, rather than that of Letters, which breeds men of letters and philosophers" (Calderón 1979a: 59). For all their ideological differences, both counterposed the observation and study of technically useful subjects to ornamental eloquence, the business of poets and philosophers. But they failed to realize that the technically useful subjects were not the same as science, which was what they usually believed they were encouraging. Hence there was no paradox in the resulting situation: observation was praised, writers' practice reflected a documentalist view of literature, whereas at the same time books were fetishized, and no one had eyes to see freely.

It is precisely the adverb "freely" that is my whole point here. For what I have been trying to show is that the concept of literature in force in nineteenth-century Latin America, which remains dominant today, implies a ban on the fictional, which is reflected in the control of fictional production. If this legacy is common to Spanish America and Brazil, the former at least has the advantage of a possibility of escaping the canon in Martí, and secondarily in Rodó. (In Brazil the hope of escape is limited to a few passages in José de Alencar, a few articles by Machado de Assis.) Given, then, the pragmatic importance we have given to Martí's reflections, let us return to his ideas once again.

I have called attention to the fact that Martí rejected the cult of observation, replacing it with the exploration of an essentiality, that of "natural man"—that is, the man who had preserved in himself the fecundity of nature. But the vitality of this alternative is marred somewhat when we realize that the cult of essentiality in Latin America generated practices not at all positive, in politics and in art. In both cases, the search for national essence implied the purpose of formulating a constant nucleus that could both constitute the national identity and protect against alien influences. On the political plane, in the twentieth century, essentialism was incorporated into populism: "In the form of a populist political movement, nationalism took this doctrine of national essences—*peruanidad, bolivianidad, mexicanidad, argentinidad*—and applied it to the search for solutions to the great problems of the nation, solutions that went beyond traditional liberal formulas as well as those proposed by the Marxist left" (Romero 1970: 170). On the literary plane, the use of essentialism came earlier, serving as justification for regionalist currents:

> Nativism's false illusion of independence had set our literature in search of a new spirit, of themes furnished by the land and developing in the local environment. . . . After the illusion of the jungles had been dispelled, *the need to find local originality remained*, so that one looked to the fields, inhabited by that mixed race, already nationalized and integrated into the nation: the half-breed *sertanejo*.
> (Lima 1922: 138–39)

But the fact that essentialism was used first in the literary front did not mean that it could not be employed later in the aesthetics of the contemporary right. One of the leaders of Latin-American fascism defended the fusion of political and aesthetic essentialism. Attacking the cosmopolitanism of Oswald de Andrade's Antropofagia movement, Plínio Salgado wrote: "The same mistake that leads old fogies, academics, humanists, vassals of libraries, to live in settings that shut out the present age, leads the cosmopolite, indifferent to 'national feeling,' to the *minimum of humanity*, because of the lack of intensity of the contact between being and environment" (Salgado 1935: 32–33). Our intellectual independence, then, required delving into our roots, where "the intensity of life" "suggests a different rhythm, unique in the world" (p. 35). But what does this essentialism have to do with Martí's? Nothing, except for the fact that it is also a form of essentialism. And indeed, to return to the passage by Amoroso Lima quoted above, how can one differentiate it from the documentalist current? Didn't the various regionalisms profess the need to document what each region actually is like? Yes, they did, and they were nonetheless distinct for that.

We can see this in Martínez Estrada's thoughts on *Martín Fierro*. On the one hand, Estrada is clearly intent on denying the documentary character of Hernández's work: "The other gaucho poets wrote as they looked at the scene and the characters from outside. They observed the characters and made the scene speak by means of the system of dramaturgy. Hernández employs a different system (one very similar to ventriloquism)" (Estrada 1948, 1: 47). On the other hand, he no less clearly affirms the essentialist aspect of the poem he is analyzing: "What was perennial in the gaucho was his mind, not his dress, and what was perennial in the Indian was the tribal personality he acquired under the terribly hard conditions of his struggle for existence" (p. 231).

In fact, the relation between observational documentalism and essentialism cannot be properly determined if they are seen as radically diverging tendencies. Documentalism is content with describing the visible, and its commitment to perceptual reality is evident. It was no accident that the first example I gave was from Sarmiento, who believed that native populations could not be civilized because they could not adapt to the *modus vivendi* of civilization. The essentialist current, in contrast, assumes the form of a compromise between the perceptual and the imaginary, since to be restricted to the former would exclude meaning from the conjunction between nature and natural man. Thus, a documentalist would necessarily be irked by a delightful passage from Borges that would not offend an essentialist: "Gibbon observes that in the Arabian book par excellence, the *Koran*, there are no camels; I believe that, were there any doubt concerning the *Koran*'s authenticity, this absence of camels would be enough to prove that it is indeed an Arabian book. . . . Being an Arab, Mohammed did not need to worry: he knew he could be an Arab without camels" (Borges 1980: 219).

As a compromise, essentialism acknowledges that poetic production does not involve perception only, but also the activation of the imaginary. However, like the opposite tendency, it also supposes that every creation runs into, respects, and reinforces a constant, hard core, to which it must submit: the essence itself. As a compromise, essentialism does not ban the imaginary, does not create an absolute obstacle to the practice of fiction, but neither can it account for fiction's mobility. The fictional is admitted, as long as one can recognize the presence of this constancy in it. Thus a documentalist essentialism is possible with no violence to logic. And that is why, finally, if Martí's reflections merit the emphasis I have placed on them, one should not, however, rush to the conclusion that they are sufficient to change the documentalist canon. Essentialism can either tilt toward the observational tendency or work for a legitimation (at least a relative one) of the fictional.

This, however, is not to proclaim the autonomy of art, for in absolute terms this does not exist. Rodó's mistake was to believe that there was an autonomy of mind in regard to purely material interests. That is why his ideas were identified as conservative and abstentionistic. As one of his critics wrote, " 'novecentismo' or 'arielismo' was the ultimate, conservative consequence of modernism, the first ten years of which were marked by a tempo acelerato of rebellion and novelty" (Sánchez 1941: 40). Because of this flaw, Rodó and Spanish-American modernism were easily converted into instruments for the preservation of documentalism and its sequels. They were identified with art for art's sake, to which every decent man, conservative or progressive, ought to counterpose committed, or useful, art. Both directions are mistaken. The latter—which, as we have seen, is deeply rooted in the Latin-American tradition—leads to a situation where fictionality is accepted only as a facile allegory for a clearly or vaguely defined political program. Art for art's sake, when clearly presented as such, sets out from a real or feigned malaise in relation to the condition of society and ends up justifying the status quo. But this is a false dilemma. In order to expose it, I will conclude this chapter with a brief examination of two cases.

Published in 1872 and 1878 (first and second parts, respectively), and meeting at first with the indifference of cultured readers, José Hernández's *Martín Fierro* in time came to be recognized as one of the fundamental works of Spanish-American literature. In a 1916 essay that both marked the recognition of the work and canonized certain mistaken interpretations of it, Lugones wrote: "City people saw no more than amusement in that unruly, picturesque wordiness. They entirely missed its profound evolution, its value as an expression of the national character" (Lugones 1979: 126). Though Lugones saw the work as an essentialist exploration of *argentinidad*, he nevertheless took it as a representative of observationalism. Borges was to write that critics "affirm, with subtle inadequacy, that, for instance, *Martín Fierro* is a presentation of the pampas," even though a reading of the poem shows us that it contains little in the way of landscape description (Borges 1930: 124). The reason for this mistake is the fact that critics saw the description of *local color* as what fiction *ought* to do.

Borges's irony is taken up and expanded in Martínez Estrada's lengthy study of the poem. Although Estrada often disagrees with Lugones's interpretation and presents a matchless, exhaustive analysis, he strays not an inch from the essentialism of *El payador*. In fact, essentialism is the basis of his simultaneously sociohistorical and stylistic analysis of the poem. For even though Hernández's work cannot be appropriated by the observationalist canon, it still contains a profound reflection on his country's history, the life of the gaucho, the military conscriptions, the exploitation of convict labor in the frontier, the role played by livestock in pampa society, the anti-Indian policies. Since it excluded the merely descriptive and at the same time captured the parameters of everyday existence, *Martín Fierro* was a work able to generate a fictional tradition—that is, other works that included reality in the parameters of the imaginary. "Since the poem is elemental and takes an elemental state of social grouping, the cartographic lines of reality, which make up the channels of destiny, are apparent" (Estrada 1948, 2: 492). These "cartographic lines" work for the reader as the outline of a landscape to be filled in. As we have seen in connection with Martí, to the extent that it rejected the descriptivism stimulated by the cult of observation, essentialism allowed the analyst to see the fictional product neither as a mere testimonial (today "reflection" would be the word) of reality nor as an object that did not care to point to "external conditions."

This double negativeness allowed the essayist to achieve in his analysis of the poem a rare instance of ideological critique—all the more notable because it uses no categories other than those employed in the "aesthetic" examination of the poem. The category common to both is selection, according to which Hernández—whether consciously or not—excluded from his poem everything that was not strictly essential to his project. Thus the omission of documental details makes *Martín Fierro* an exceptional work in the so-called "literature of the land":

Because social, *gauchesco*, and environmental aspects make up the substance of the poem, its characters preserve throughout the text a vague, spectral imprecision: they have no will, no life of their own; they are activated and inhabited by these latent forces that . . . penetrate the poem in order to present a character, to make him act and lead him to death or oblivion. (Estrada 1948, 1: 295)

The spectral form assumed by the characters also has the effect of activating the imaginary. Though admittedly in an imperfect way, the same occurs in a later novel, José Eustasio Rivera's *La vorágine* (1924). I say "imperfect" because in this work, in contrast to what happens in *Martín Fierro*, men are turned into specters as the effect not of a strict principle of selection, which would be impossible in an author who cultivates landscape documentalism, but of the fact that the characters are merely will-less playthings of the prodigious force of the Amazonian world. In Hernández, in a more accomplished way, the principle of selection stresses on the written page the guidelines that orient the reader's response: this is a world where human violence, even cruelty, cannot mitigate the vaster cruelty of the world, which plays with men much as a gigantic cat plays with house mice.

This same principle of selection guides the author's ideological orientation. The poem, writes Martínez Estrada, is not a vindication of the gaucho, for "what Martín Fierro yearns for is the paternal protection of the government or the *estanciero*, this other orphanhood of those who have no fixed occupation" (Estrada 1948, 1: 316). This is so because the author "in the composition of his poem was limited by the prejudices of his clan, and because, deep in his soul, the social question was for him a political question" (p. 314). These prejudices are responsible for a constant censorship. Thus in his selective process Hernández excludes the caudillos and their role, and mentions Indians only in order to agree with the policies of his rival, Sarmiento: Indians are merely marauding bands that attack farms, filthy creatures who find refuge in the *desierto*, out of which they emerge as scourges of civilization. Ideology, then, acting as censorship, is the counterpart of the principle of selection.

Finally, the same principle can be seen in the relationship between the main character and his companion in the desert, Tadeo Cruz. Apparently, Tadeo Cruz is a *gaucho malo* like Martín Fierro. In fact, he is Martín's foil. A member of the police force sent to arrest or kill Martín, Cruz joins him when he becomes aware of his bravery; but the poem does not explain his exact motivation. If Fierro had killed, Cruz was also a murderer. If Fierro had stolen, Cruz was also a thief. But they are not two of a kind. Estrada shows clearly that Fierro begins to die when he meets Cruz, who is his double, his inimical face. The Martín Fierro who returns to white civilization after living among the Indians for years, and after his comrade's death, is only the shadow of a man. His vitality has been sapped by his vampirelike double.

This episode constitutes the limit for Martínez Estrada's sociostylistic approach. How could he deal with the problem of the double by submitting it to the necessary articulation with textual and sociohistorical approaches? This is the limit not just of Martínez Estrada's method but of the essentialist core that serves as his theoretical parameter. However, he is quite unaware of it. His treatment of Isidoro Cruz as Fierro's doppelgänger both extends and deepens what Borges had explored in one of his *ficciones*, "Biografía de Tadeo Isidoro Cruz (1829–1874)" (republished in *El Aleph*, 1957). Why, however, is the treatment of the double not consistent with Estrada's analytical vision? Why do I say that the former cannot be integrated into the latter? I do not mean to say that the theme of the double required an observational approach. Where, then, are the roots of the double, which make it impossible to assimilate?

The double is not part of the physical world, and an explanation of it could not possibly be completed by means of a sociohistorical approach. The double is a creation of the imaginary. It would be repetitious to go into a theoretical analysis of it (see Costa Lima 1976: 178–88). In order to understand it, we need only examine the source in question, Borges's apocryphal biography. As an essayist, Martínez Estrada was intelligent enough to realize that an exploration of Borges's approach was of decisive importance for the integration of the two parts of the poem. Something, however, is still missing, if one thinks about the theoretical model implicit in his analysis. It is the treatment of the double itself that rebels against the proposed analytical integration. How can one move from a study of Hernández's view of the gaucho, the Indians, the caudillos, frontier life, and the function of the army, to the question of the double, without having the feeling that the entire atmosphere has changed? The reader can go back as many times as he or she wants to without ever finding a connecting link. Not only is the double not placed on the same plane as those other elements, but also the mobility of the imaginary cannot combine with the fixity presupposed by the idea of essence.

Does this mean, then, that we have at our disposal two opposite analytical strategies—one documentalist in nature (as we have seen, essentialism is a variant of this type) and the other based on the exploration of the imaginary? That is indeed what I mean; but it is not the whole picture. It must be added that, although the converse is not true, exploration of the imaginary can include the material of the documentalist strategy—not only as documental matter but also as part of a world captured and elaborated by the imaginary. If one argues that thematization of the imaginary is unable to deal with the world of social relations, one would in fact be saying that the imaginary is not historical and is based on an archetypal foundation, part of man's eternal, unchanging essence.

The reader may want to verify my position by rereading Borges's text. It is structured so that the reader can fill in the *blanks* (to use Iser's term) on his or her own with the various aspects of Argentinian life that are implicit in that fictional biography. But, as Martín Fierro himself says,

> he conocido aunque tarde,
> sin haberme arrepentido,
> que es pecado cometido
> el decir ciertas verdades.
>   (Hernández 1981: 112)

> I've found, though it's nothing new,
> And I've no regrets today,
> Sometimes you sin when you say
> Things that are perfectly true.

One of these things that are perfectly true is my contention here, which will certainly clash with deep-rooted beliefs: that documentalism is indispensable for a non-"formalist" literature, that its opposite is the infamous marble tower, and so forth. Though I realize that the demonstration of a fact holds little weight against beliefs, particularly when the beliefs in question are the instrument of publicity, I have no means at my disposal other than demonstration and constant rectification; nor do I want any other. Let me, then, defend my position by examining a second example.

As recently as 1955, Juan Rulfo published his novella *Pedro Páramo*. Although it was acclaimed by the most discriminating Spanish-American critics, and compared to the best work of Borges, Alejo Carpentier, Guillermo Cabrera Infante, Julio Cortázar, and José Lezama Lima, with which it has in common its opposition to documentalist realism, curiously enough neither *Pedro Páramo* nor the works it was compared to provoked a systematic questioning of the canon they contradicted. Critics tend to opt for a more careful path. They see the variations of works as determined by history, and at best consider them a function of the relevant historical paradigm. Their caution has the effect of concealing a question apparently too difficult to answer: how, in fact, can we employ different evaluative criteria, appropriate to the very diversity of works, unless we accept the idea of the empathic method proposed by romantic hermeneutics? The question is all the more concealed because the caution of critics is combined with their lack of philosophical questioning: romantic hermeneutics, Schleiermacher, what does all of this have to do with literature? Rulfo, however, offers an invaluable opportunity to question Latin-American conceptions of literature.

If *Pedro Páramo* were a documentary-type narrative, it would be the story of a tyrannical latifundista and a cowardly curate. The latifundista constantly appropriates his neighbors' land and begets illegitimate children, until an unhappy love affair makes him apathetic and aware of his guilt. The priest, in turn, suspended from his ministry, cannot atone for the evils he has caused except by joining the 1910 revolution. All of this, however, would be no more than a very rough outline, and I doubt that anyone has ever attempted to read Rulfo's work in this way. But why not? Isn't this a fair description of the characters' behavior? Isn't the book set at the time of the Mexican Revolution? The answer is that this sort of summary would imply a kind of approach that is explicitly rejected by the work.

This is a story of the dead who never leave the earth. Auerbach observes that the dead who Dante and Virgil meet in the afterworld preserve their earthly passions and concerns. The same occurs in Rulfo. The difference is that here the dead do not "rise" to another world. The world where they remain is the same as that in which they once lived, but now it is seen from "the opposite margin"—that is, subjected to another form of thematization. If the living saw things in the world as *percepta*, the dead now "see" them from the vantage point of their annihilation—that is, outside the bounds of time and space; things remembered do not have the opacity of things perceived, but rather the translucent nature of imagined objects. Temporal translucency makes facts lose their chronological sequence, so that the desire felt by Pedro Páramo as a boy is simultaneous with his voice as a latifundista. The same translucency annuls space, so that the dead can see the world and comment on it from their coffins. Since the imaginary is thematized, the words and conversations are always heard, but they are soundless: "Now and then he heard the sound of words, and observed the difference. Because the words he had heard until then, until he became aware of it, had had no sound, were not heard but rather felt; they were felt, but soundlessly, like words heard in a dream" (Rulfo 1977: 51). This is not a passage carefully chosen to "demonstrate" a thesis. If such were the case, it would be no more than a curiosity. The words, although they are heard, are soundless, because the narrative is always conceived from the *other side*.

Let us see an explicit example. Susana, the woman Pedro has always coveted, is finally his. But she is only the ghost of the woman she once was. She is not just sick: she is mad. In the scene in question, Pedro has been told of her condition and watches her during an attack:

> Pedro Páramo opened the door and found himself by her side, letting a beam of light fall on Susana San Juan. He saw her eyes, firmly shut as though she were feeling an inner pain; the moistened lips, parted, and the sheets, drawn by unconscious hands until they exposed her body's nudity shaken by convulsions. —He walked the short distance to the bed and covered the naked body, which went on wriggling like a worm, in increasingly violent spasms. He moved close to her ear and spoke to her: "Susana!" And he repeated: "Susana!" (Pp. 114–15)

Later the reader is told that what Pedro took to be the expression of excruciating pain was in fact a dream in which the madwoman was experiencing an orgasm with the man she had loved. Thus the narrative adopts an external plane, and what the husband *perceives* is the opposite of what Susana experiences.

It is also on the *other side* that Pedro Páramo learns that Father Rentería has joined the rebels and is now an ally of Villa, Obregón, and Carranza. No wonder that, in his *position*, Pedro supposes he might co-opt the rebels. And doesn't the reader put himself or herself in the same position, if he or she fails to understand the narrative strategy? Only gradually does the reader realize that he or she is hearing a dialogue of the dead, that this is neither a horror story nor a mystery.

What, then, we have been describing as a narrative created from the *other side* means that the author pretends to speak of *percepta* when in fact his entire narrative focuses on the imaginary. By now it will probably be unnecessary to add that this thematization does not exclude material, historical reality; but it does exclude documentality. The imaginary in *Pedro Páramo* feeds on the injustice of social relations and guilt, arbitrariness, and orphanhood—on *want*. If we compare it with the so-called novels of the revolution—for instance, Mariano Azuela's *Los de abajo* (1916)—the difference between the two concepts of literature comes out even more sharply. It is not simply that Rulfo is better than his predecessors; it is not that his "technique" is necessarily more accomplished: the point is that Rulfo writes fiction without guilt. And he writes without guilt because for him there is no ban on fiction. One wonders when Latin-American critics will learn to write criticism this way.

CHAPTER FIVE

Diderot: Philosopher and Art Critic

OVERTURE 1

In our days, modernity has reached old age. Two centuries ago, the very word was unknown. How can its outline be sketched? However vague and diffuse, it is recognizable in the decades when Diderot was writing his works. It can be said that between the late 1740's—the *Lettre sur les aveugles* was published in 1749—and the late 1770's the Faustian theme was fermenting. What is the nexus between the Faustian theme and modernity? Of Goethe's *Faust* it has been said: "One of the most original and fruitful ideas . . . is the idea of an affinity between the cultural ideal of self-development and the real social movement toward economic development. . . . The only way for modern man to transform himself, Faust and we will find out, is by radically transforming the whole physical and moral world he lives in" (Berman 1982: 40). Indeed, *Faust* contains the myth of modernity. This, however, does not mean that modernity is to be conceived as a single whole. At least two phases can be distinguished: the first, expansive and optimistic, is the age of the philosophes; the second is critical and pessimistic, even escapist—critical with Marx and Nietzsche, pessimistic or escapist with Flaubert and Baudelaire.

Although there is a direct line running from Diderot's salons to Baudelaire's writings on art (see Pommier 1936), by and large the path between their eras had been interrupted, so that a century after Diderot the dream of Enlightenment had turned to mockery, pantomime, and death. So wide is the chasm that today a reader of Eliot and Pound, Joyce and Svevo, Musil and Kafka can immediately sense the contemporaneity of Baudelaire, Flaubert, and the *poètes maudits*, but finds it hard to discern in the multifarious work of Diderot. And this chasm is reflected not only in the perception of amateurs but also in that of scholars whose tastes are fundamentally classical. In the preface to his well-known *Die Struktur der modernen Lyrik*, H. Friedrich admitted that modern lyricism was not the object of his particular admiration. And Auerbach, although the author of some of the most penetrating essays on Baudelaire ever written, stated in his Princeton seminars that the poet of the *Fleurs du mal* was not among his favorites (see Fitzgerald 1965). Readers with modernist tastes, who can appreciate Flaubert and Baudelaire, feel closer to the metaphysical poets and baroque art than to the didactic and sentimental efforts of the eighteenth century. For beginning with Flaubert and Baudelaire, at the latest, modernity took a turn away from its earlier direction. Originally, the values of the bourgeoisie were seen as capable of generating individual freedom and dignity, which were denied in the actual practice of aristocratic society. The switch to a critical, pessimistic, or escapist direction came when the earlier project was demystified or seen to be an illusion.

But a new change seems to be taking place today. Concerning the mystique of art for art's sake professed by Gautier and Baudelaire and Comte's mystique of science, Berman writes: "They were at once perceptive and trenchant in their critiques of capitalism, and, at the same time, absurdly complacent in their faith that they had the power to transcend it, that they could live and work freely beyond its norms and demands" (Berman 1982: 119). For, in the phase most often identified with modernity, the artistic and scientific intelligentsia began to focus less on society itself and more on the construction of its various languages. (Thus it is that Marx is seldom mentioned in discussions of modernity: his critical version of it evidently remained closer to the heritage of Enlightenment.) But nowadays the construction of "pure" languages is no longer a convincing alibi. This change in thinking has led to the formation of "sanctuaries." Scientists, artists, and scholars generally have become acceptable in their little niches, from where they speak of values as exotic or negligible things compared with the pragmatic import of their discoveries. If a major physicist is a pacifist and his country is preparing for "star wars," the media are careful to downplay or even suppress his pacifist views, while the official agencies are busy financing the technicians who will use his calculations to make more potent missiles. If a respected novelist develops a language so personalized that it cannot be understood by educated native speakers who are not scholars, his "deviance" is eventually accepted because at the very least it will provide material for theses, glossaries, and academic symposia. Now, even if we remain emotionally and intellectually attached to the secular saints of modernity, we acknowledge that there is nothing heroic about sticking to one's values; the purity they defended, the refinement they attained in their languages, have been assimilated and now coexist with the generalized impurity of commerce and war. This realization provides us with a reason to turn our attention to what had previously seemed academic and remote. But we should not be so naive as to attempt to extend into the past the scope of contemporaneity. We should delve into the eighteenth century not to establish additional links of brotherhood, but rather to look for hitherto unsuspected roots that might reach into our soil.

But could there be anything in Diderot that still remains with us? How could we, so close to the aggressiveness and parodies of Baudelaire and Flaubert, find in our landscape points of contact with the praise of bourgeois virtue and honesty? In other words: how could we, instead of emphasizing the hiatus between the two phases of modernity, envisage a continuum reaching all the way to the present? The idea may seem odd indeed, but that is precisely what I am proposing. There is something in Diderot that, despite all historical differences, points to a connection between him and an issue still relevant today. This something—in addition to any other relevant traits—has to do with Diderot's discussion of the question whether or not art should be internally controlled.*

If this is my object, I must admit I am still quite far from making it tangible. Such is the purpose of the present chapter. At the end, the reader should be able to form an image of my immediate purpose.

OVERTURE 2

Let us think of the demon not as a divine being but as a psychological driving force. If this premise is accepted, then it follows that there are writers who seem to have been possessed by a single demon. Not that they never suffered any change, or that their writings show no diversity; but their earlier works seem to have a preparatory nature, that of rehearsals for a future performance. One thinks of Joyce's *Dubliners* and *Portrait of the Artist as a Young Man*; or of Proust's *Jean Santeuil*; or of Borges's leftist avant-garde poems. In other authors, such as João Cabral de Melo Neto, there seems to be no preparatory phase at all—the demon of antilyricism is already present in the poems of *Pedra do sono*. On the other hand, there is another family of writers, those who seem to have found in themselves a variegated coterie of demons, a conglomerate of distinct, even contradictory voices. Fernando Pessoa's "heteronyms" can be seen as

---

*I say "internally controlled" so that the control exerted by a concept of art that artists are expected to internalize is not confused with external control through institutionalized censorship. The existence of one does not necessarily determine that of the other.

a dramatization of this sort of diversity. For if Mondrian is the ideal type of the first family of artists, the Portuguese poet is the very embodiment of the second. It might be added that a playwright able to include in a single play different speech registers and different worldviews would be hard to classify according to this criterion. But let us leave Shakespeare out.

In a much less obvious way than Pessoa, Diderot was also possessed by conflicting demons. He himself complained of his tendency to feel attracted by such widely divergent interests as physiology, chemistry, geometry, poetry, and the visual arts. One may even establish a connection between this diversity of interests and his condition as a man without a profession, a writer who, during part of his life, was engaged in the most disparate literary projects. Recently, R. Darnton studied the reports of the police officer in charge of spying on writers living in Paris; this officer made a distinction between "men" and "boys." The distinction had nothing to do with age: "men" were those who, having written some sort of work, anything ranging from a pamphlet to a weighty treatise, and whatever they called themselves, had a definite status and occupation. "Boys" were those like Diderot, who, although he was about 35 years old, with a wife and child to support, kept changing jobs: "While the philosophes laid the foundation of the modern cult of the intellectual, the police expressed a more ordinary, down-to-earth view of their 'game.' Writing might embellish the career of a gentleman and lead to a sinecure for a commoner. But it was more likely to produce good-for-nothings" (Darnton 1984: 22).

But the relation between Diderot's "boyishness" and his lack of a profession is little more than a curiosity. Besides, the multiplicity of demons in his case was manifested not only in his various intellectual interests but also, more characteristically and forcefully, in the coexistence of conflicting positions within a given area. This fact would be uninteresting if it could be described in terms of phases. It is quite natural for a creative mind to suffer changes or even transformations in time. Thus one can account for the fact that Diderot originally conceived of genius as a surplus of feelings, emotions, and passions but later, in *Paradoxe*, presented a radically opposed view, seeing the genius as him who is capable of containing and distancing himself from the passions that seethe in his words (Diderot 1965a). In terms of phases, one can also account for the passage from the deism of the *Pensées philosophiques* to the full-blown materialism of later works. But sometimes no such easy explanations can be found. In some cases, Diderot's contradictory statements were made in the same period. This unruly richness is surely bewildering to the reader. We are apt to dislike dissonance, among other reasons because our writing method is linear. Thus we can understand why such Diderot scholars as Yves Belaval (1950) and David Funt (1968), using different arguments, should attempt to iron out the contradictions they found in his works. For—at least in Western thought—contradiction, whatever its source, is a crime of lèse-majesté. If, therefore, I believe that to explain away Diderot's contradictions does not solve the problem, I must find out the reason for them.

In the area I am particularly concerned with—Diderot's theoretical concept of art and his art criticism—the paradox is manifested in his simultaneously subscribing to the idea that art should be subordinated to the criteria of usefulness and ethical good and anticipating the possibility of a purely sensitive-textual analysis. In his *Lettre sur les sourds et muets*, for instance, Diderot both praises Racine's description as "a poetical picture that a painter might successfully imitate" (Diderot 1875, 1: 383) and analyzes a Homeric fragment showing that its value derives from the distribution of long and short syllables (p. 376). Similarly, in "Art de peindre de Watelet" he writes: "Painting, so to speak, has its own sun, which is not the same as the universe's" (Diderot 1980: 135). But, this observation notwithstanding, he remained attached to the theory of imitation. It was a stumbling block for his theory, not a refutation of it.

Admittedly, Diderot's statements are contradictory, but it must be added that the paradox is not to be attributed to his carelessness or immaturity. The notion of conflicting demons points to the presence of an inner, unconscious tension, which was never resolved. The fact that it took place below the threshold of consciousness made it all the more difficult for him to overcome it or suppress it. But what are the conflicting terms involved in this tension? In conscious terms, there is the (*dominant*) intention to keep art useful and the (*dominated*) impression, sharpened by Diderot's experience as a critic, that the criteria he used made it impossible for him to understand his object.

This conflict hardly seems plausible unless we consider Diderot's relationship to classical aesthetics. If he refused to preserve its evaluating criteria, he did accept that there must be parameters external to the work—that is, independent evaluative standards, without which no objective appreciation would be possible. In unconscious terms, the contradiction was formulated as the will to control in opposition to the awareness of the need to free artistic creation. If the will to control had the drawback of making it impossible to appreciate the value of certain works—and, again, Diderot's work as a critic reinforced this impression—the opposite feeling, of the need for freedom in art, could not supply a convincing answer to the question: for the sake of what should art be freed? Since he found his way obstructed in both directions, Diderot understandably could not resolve the contradiction.

Setting forth from different perspectives, my two overtures have led to the same point. This means that now they can be joined in a single analysis.

DIDEROT AND EIGHTEENTH-CENTURY VIEWS OF ART

Diderot's aesthetic reflections are contemporary with the clash between two currents: the continuation of the classical-rationalist tradition and the new emphasis on sentimentality. The first has Descartes as one of its foundations.* In his *Traité des passions*, Descartes had set up a correlation between our judgments of good and evil and the passions of love and hate, and another between our judgments of beautiful and ugly and the passions of pleasure and horror; he also added that these two series of passions were of unequal value from the viewpoint of knowledge. Thus, in Article 85 he explained that pleasure and horror acted upon the soul through the senses, and affected it more forcefully than those passions that are represented by reason. He concluded: "Of all passions these are the most misleading, and from them we should refrain most cautiously" (Descartes 1965: 127). That is, perception of the beautiful is the result of a factor that is disruptive of true knowledge of phenomena. In other words, the aesthetic experience is a lower logic. Even though Descartes himself did not attempt to consider the experience of beauty specifically, his views were taken up in Germany by Alexander Gottlieb Baumgarten, who saw aesthetics—a term he coined—as an inferior branch of logic. Thus, retaining the classical idea that beauty is derived from properties inherent in the object, the rationalist tradition reaffirmed the need to subordinate it to higher logical criteria.

How did Diderot react to this tradition? Here is his comment on Father André's *Essai sur le beau* (1752): "The only thing that his work may be found to want is an elaboration of the origin of the notions of relationship, order, and symmetry that are found within us; for given the sublime tone in which he speaks of these notions, one does not know whether he believes them to be acquired and nonnatural or whether he believes them to be innate" (Diderot 1965a: 415). Then Diderot proceeds to show quite clearly that he rejects classical-rationalist innatism. We are born, he writes, with the faculties of feeling and thinking; the needs "and the exercise of the most immediate of our faculties" are soon conjoined "to give us ideas of order, arrangement, symmetry, mechanism, proportion, unity; all of these ideas come from the senses and are not natural"; these notions "are experimental like all others" (p. 416). Thus Diderot made the phenomenon of beauty subordinate to experience, dependent on particularized situations. These passages seem to indicate that he was moving away from classical

---

*On Cartesian aesthetics, see D'Allones 1951: 50–55.

innatism toward the sensism of the Lockean tradition. This is even clearer in an earlier passage: "Father Batteux makes all the principles of the fine arts subordinate to imitation of beautiful nature; but he fails to tell us what *beautiful nature* is" (p. 406).

To be sure, Diderot was not alone here. Attacks on the criterion of imitation, by Hutcheson, Burke, Trublet, and Batteux himself, among others, already pointed to a crisis in the objectivism of the classical canon (see Folkierski 1925, esp. p. 117). But although he rejected imitation, Diderot did not embrace the opposite idea, based on the *feeling* of beauty. In the essay quoted above, he states his disagreement with the opposing view:

I daresay that every time a principle has been known to us from earliest childhood, and we apply it easily and immediately to objects outside us, we believe we are judging them with our feelings; but we are forced to acknowledge our mistake every time the complication of relationships and the novelty of the object make application of the principle impossible: then pleasure, in order to be felt, must wait until the understanding has decided that the object is beautiful.

(Diderot 1965a: 419–20)

In other words, for Diderot the phenomenon of beauty could not be explained in terms of a particular faculty, be it reason or feeling. The experience of beauty is based, first of all, on the plane of experience; that is, its principles are neither innate nor general. Because it is not preordered, prearranged, prestated, there is the impression that it is "plutôt une affaire de sentiment que de raison" ("a matter of feeling rather than reason") (p. 419). But this is just as false, for feelings are evoked only by objects containing familiar traits.

Diderot's rejection of the two views shows both his fascination for the act of thinking, that is, his willingness to get to the root of his object of interest, and the importance of aesthetic reflection in the latter half of the eighteenth century. Indeed, with the economic and political changes of the period, the criteria for evaluation of art changed accordingly.

Just as politico-economic thought was grounded on the assumption that it was necessary to try to theorize and struggle for a more just political organization and a more effective economic organization, aesthetic thought aimed at a more adequate form of appreciating art; justice, effectiveness, and adequacy were then conjoined with the earlier, more comprehensive principle of freedom. Having elsewhere characterized the classical mode as a form of control of art (see Costa Lima 1988 and Chapter 1, above), I now claim that Diderot proposed an aesthetic approach that critically recognized the artist's freedom. This is the approach from which my reading proceeds. But if Diderot refused the two traditions he had at his disposal, what third way could he propose? He tried to find such an alternative in his dialogue with Shaftesbury. In the English Platonist thinker, whom he translated, Diderot found the notion of enthusiasm for nature— not so-called beautiful nature, nature according to a model, which provided the basis for classical aesthetic precepts, but that nature which, by virtue of its inner organization, was a stumbling block for the cult of the God of revealed religion and the cornerstone for a natural deism. As Venturi aptly puts it, "for Shaftesbury, this concept of the unity of nature is a way to affirm the immanence of his philosophy, to subordinate the forms that the current of thought from which his philosophy was derived had abstracted from God and confer them on intermediate 'plastic natures,' in an ever profounder way" (Venturi 1967: 67).

But how was the philosophe to use nature for this purpose? As early as 1748, in his "Principes généraux d'acoustique," Diderot had conceived a notion whose development was to prove basic for his postulation. He wrote:

Perception of relations is the only foundation of our admiration and our pleasures; and it is thence that one must set forth for the explanation of the subtlest phenomena offered to us by the sciences and arts. The things that seem most arbitrary to us were suggested by relations; and this principle should serve as the basis for a philosophical essay on taste, if ever one is found with enough knowledge to apply it to all that it encompasses generally.   (Diderot 1875, 9: 104)

Diderot himself takes up this challenge in his essay of 1752. Beauty, he writes, is defined by its capacity to evoke relations in the receiver's understanding. These relations are not pure creations of our understanding itself—this would rule out their basis in the object—nor do they simply emanate from the thing that evokes them—which would be a rephrasing of the classical-rationalist principle. Rather than an exclusive "either . . . or," we have an inclusive "both . . . and": "Thus it follows that, although the relations exist in our understanding alone, as far as perception is concerned their foundation is in things nonetheless" (Diderot 1965a: 424). However, Diderot postulates the existence of two types of beauty, hierarchically arranged: "Thus of what is without me I call *beautiful* all that contains what arouses in my understanding the idea of relations; and of what is within me I call *beautiful* all that arouses this idea" (p. 418).

To use Diderot's own terminology, then, we can say that real or essential beauty is that beauty which imposes its presence on us, whereas perceived beauty is that beauty which is motivated within us so that it can be projected onto the object and recognized there. Although in the latter case the real or essential property of beauty is less evident, even here it would be more than a mere construct of the receptor's. Indeed, this would be the case of the third type of beauty, the lowest of all: "But there is yet a third type of relation: to wit, *intellectual or fictitious* relations: those that human understanding seems to ascribe to things" (p. 418). It should also be added that Diderot did not feel that these relations must necessarily be conscious in the receptor's mind:

> I do not insist that one who contemplates a piece of architecture should be in a condition to assert what the architect himself may not know, which part is to which as such a number is to some other number; or that the hearer of a concerto should in some cases be more aware than the musician himself that such a sound is in a relation to some other sound equal to that between two and four or four and five. It is sufficient that he should perceive and feel that the components of this work of architecture and the sounds in this musical piece stand in relations, either among themselves or with other objects. (P. 419)

This passage anticipates the development he was to present in a work written between 1774 and 1780, *Eléments de physiologie*:

> I am inclined to believe that all we see, know, perceive, and hear, from the trees of a large forest—nay, from the arrangement of the branches, the shape of the leaves and the variety of colors, the greens and lights; from the aspect of the grains of sand in a beach to the unevenness of the surface of the sea waves, whether stirred by a soft breeze or roughened and shaken by winds in stormy weather; from the multitude of human voices, animal shouts, and physical noises to the melody and harmony of all the airs, all the pieces of music in all the concerts we hear; *I am convinced that all of this exists within us without our being aware of it.*
> (Diderot 1875, 9: 366–67, emphasis added)*

Although this passage merits an extensive comment, I will simply observe that the idea of *real beauty* implied the adoption of a variant of the classical-rationalist view. And here the influence of Shaftesbury's Neoplatonism can be seen.

However, as Jacques Chouillet has noted, this essentialist position is gradually replaced by a biological-functional view (see Chouillet 1973: 53–66). The decisive text is the opening passage of *Essais sur la peinture*, published in 1766: "Nothing that nature does is mistaken. Every form, beautiful or ugly, has its cause; and of all the beings that exist, there is none that is not as it should be" (Diderot 1965a: 665). And in the long paragraph that follows he develops this idea, stressing the fact that each

---

*No longer in the peremptory tone in which he affirmed, in 1950, Leibniz's influence on Diderot—more precisely, the influence of Leibniz's notion of unconscious on the unity of Diderot's work—Y. Belaval, in a later essay, points to the above passage as possible evidence of Leibniz's influence. Although this evidence should be taken with the same reserve shown by Belaval himself, the passage clearly demonstrates the change from a hitherto purely intellectual concept of the beautiful to a greater acceptance of "unconscious perception" (see Belaval 1963: 435–51).

part of the body depends on the presence or absence of a given element. Thus if a creature should lose its eyes very early in life, its throat, neck, and shoulders would correspondingly be affected. And Diderot concluded: "If the causes and effects were evident, we would need do no more than represent beings just as they are. The more perfect the imitation, and the greater the analogy between it and the causes, the more completely satisfied we would be" (p. 666).

Clearly, the essentialist explanation had been replaced by a biological functionalism. Shaftesbury's Platonism had been discarded in favor of an alternative that, nevertheless, reinforced the model of nature even more emphatically. Justifying his rejection of the canon of *belle nature*, Diderot accepted the monstrous and the disproportionate—what might be termed the aesthetics of the ugly—as long as they were based on the reason of nature. But would it be correct to say that Shaftesbury's essentialism had been purified in the functionalism of the *Essais*? In Diderot's translation of the English thinker's work there is an extremely curious note. Though lengthy, it deserves to be transcribed here:

However misshapen a being may be . . . it will give pleasure as long as it is well represented. But this representation that enchants me does not imply that the thing represented must have any beauty: what I admire is the picture's conformity to the object. The painting is beautiful, but the object is neither beautiful nor ugly.—In order to reply to this objection, I will ask what is meant by a monster. If this term is taken to refer to a composite of parts assembled at random, with no connection, no order, no harmony, no proportion, I will venture that a representation of this being will be no less shocking than the being itself. Indeed, if in the picture of a head a painter should place the teeth below the chin, the eyes in the occiput, and the tongue in the forehead: if, in addition, these parts were figured totally out of proportion to one another . . . subtlety of brushwork could never evince admiration for this picture. *But*, one might argue, *if we do not admire it, it is because it is unlike anything*. This granted, I will repeat the question: What, then, is meant by a *monster*? A being that resembles something, such as a mermaid, a hippogriff, a faun, a sphinx, a chimera, or a winged dragon? But is it not evident that such products of the imagination are not at all absurd as to their configuration; that, although they do not exist in nature, they present no contradiction in terms of connection, harmony, order, and proportion? Further, is it not evident that, at the very moment that such pictures violated these ideas, they would cease to be beautiful? However, if these beings do not exist in nature, what determined the length of the mermaid's tail, the dragon's wingspan, the position of the sphinx's eyes, and the thickness of the faun's hairy thigh and cleft hoof? For these things are not arbitrary. One might answer *that, in order to call these possible beings beautiful, we wish, with no basis, that painting should observe in them the same relations that we find in actual beings; so that here, too, it is similarity that evokes our admiration.* Thus the question is, whether it is reason or whim that has made us insist that the law of real beings be observed in the painting of imaginary beings; and the question is settled when one observes that, in a painting, the sphinx, the hippogriff, the faun are either in action or are superfluous; if they are in action, they are placed in the picture, just as man, woman, the horse, and the other animals are placed in the universe: but in the universe, the duties to be performed determine the organization: the organization is more or less perfect depending on the greater or lesser ease that it confers on the automaton in order to perform its functions. (Diderot 1875, 9: 34–35)

If we compare the 1766 passage with the long note written in 1745, we will find that two seminal ideas appear in both: first, that the misshapen and monstrous are justifiable in a work of art, as long as they are organized in a way similar to some structure found in nature; second, in both nature and art, the functional criterion prevails. If this is indeed the case, how can one say that the author's analytical criterion changed? It so happens that the postulate of the *beau réel*, expressed in 1752, dispensed with the functional principle, relying instead on an ontological criterion. In other words, when he translated Shaftesbury, Diderot already anticipated the functionalist hypothesis, which he set aside in 1752, only to return to it in 1766. If the reader remembers my earlier observation about Diderot's demons, the "contradiction" will not come as a surprise. But the really decisive point is the fact that, whether resorting to an immanentist or a biological-functionalist argument, Diderot always affirmed the primacy of nature for the understanding of the beautiful, and expressed his contempt for everything "fictional"—the label he attached, as we have seen, to the lowest kind of relations that aroused the experience of the beautiful. Thus, while he was no longer following the classical-rationalist standard, Diderot had not severed all his ties with it.

In this he was not alone. Like Diderot, Edmund Burke was influenced by Lockean sensism, by the opposition to classical aesthetics, and in him this influence and this opposition led to an emphasis on the role of empathy in aesthetic experience. And from this emphasis on empathy Burke, like Diderot, drew the conclusion that the more realistic the imitation, the greater its emotional appeal (see Gita May 1960: 531). So both Burke and Diderot wound up counterposing the principle of imitation to the fictitious or imaginary product. For instance, Diderot writes: "However well made, the best, the most harmonious picture is no more than a tissue of falsities covering up one another" (Diderot 1957: 217). It is as if, in this period, Diderot the philosopher of art felt that, with the demise of metaphysical universals, perhaps there was no longer any possibility of finding an objective evaluative criterion for beauty; thus he was forced to maintain, based on new arguments, the old ban on the imaginary and the fictional. In short, then, the third way that Diderot sought turns out to have more explicit links with the tradition against which he rebelled than one might expect. Thus it is that we read, in the entry "Chinois" of the *Encyclopédie*, that "their drama is quite imperfect if it is true that in them a man's entire life is seen, beginning with the cradle, and that performances last several months" (Diderot 1976, 6: 431). And, as an art critic, Diderot insists that painters should obey the law of the three unities of the theater (see Chouillet 1973: 379–80).

Our conclusion, however, is rejected both by those who feel that Leibniz's notion of unconsciousness is the unifying key to Diderot's aesthetics and by other—perhaps more consistent—interpreters. The decisive evidence of this divergence seems to be Diderot's famous notion of poetry as a form of hieroglyph. Let us examine it with due caution. The argument appears in the *Lettre sur les sourds et muets*, in a speculative discussion concerning the phases of development of languages. From an initial state, in which they were made up of indeclinable words and gestures, they passed to a formative stage of oratorical signs that could express anything, and finally reached a state of perfection, in which the principle of harmony destroyed the natural order of the sentence. Through these stages, the analytic spirit gradually imposed itself, and linguistic expression gained precision even as it lost synthetic force. Thus ancient languages, such as Greek and Latin, could say in one word what modern languages, because of the need for decomposition, can only say using a number of words. In consequence, while "our *pedestrian* language [i.e., French] has over others the advantage of usefulness over agreeableness" (Diderot 1875, 1: 372), Greek and Latin, as well as Italian and English, are preferable for the expression of the passions (see p. 371).

Throughout this discussion, Diderot assumes that thought is distinguishable from expression; that expression, whether colorful or simply referential, is adequate according to the goal it intends to achieve. Thus clarity, verbal purity, and precision are sufficient in everyday conversation, while "the number and harmony of the period" must be added to those traits in order to attain a style adequate to academic discourse. But none of this is enough for poetry, marked by "a spirit that moves and vivifies all syllables"; this is because in poetry "discourse is not only a concatenation of energetic terms that express thought with forcefulness and nobility, but also a tissue of hieroglyphs disposed over one another. . . . In this sense, all poetry may be said to be emblematic" (Diderot 1875, 1: 374).

In order to understand the precise meaning of the passage, it is convenient first to recall that Diderot's point of departure was his emphasis on the distinction between thought and expression and his speculative history of languages. Poetry swims against the current, as it were: it opposes the communicative and analytic use of language, for which the French tongue was the best instrument; its sign is synthetic and nonlinear: it is a voluminal sign. As James Doolittle explained, "Diderot ... uses the term hieroglyph first because it designates a single sign pictorially expressing a complex of meanings. In contrast to verbal expression, which is successive, pictorial or plastic expression is simultaneous" (Doolittle 1952: 153). Thus in poetry the relations between expression and thought are different: while a psychological sensation ("l'état d'âme," as Diderot says) is formed in an immediate way, verbal expression can only express it in a linear succession. Thus "our *état d'âme* is one thing; acknowledgment of it, to ourselves or to others, is quite another" (Diderot 1875, 1: 369). This hiatus, however, does not exist in poetry, which reestablishes the immediacy of inner representation and becomes a "tableau mouvant" (p. 369). Doolittle adds: "The '*état d'âme*' is complex and simultaneous; it therefore follows that poetry must communicate it as nearly as possible simultaneously. This can be done only by means of a picture, a plastic representation, evoked in the hearer's imagination with the aid of sound and rhythm" (Doolittle 1952: 154).

All of this sounds surprisingly contemporary. But if we are to be faithful to Diderot's ideas, we must emphasize the difference that is his starting point: while the "prosaic" sign runs counter to the simultaneity of psychological representations, the hieroglyph captures its immediacy. The synthetic thickness of the poetic sign allows it to recover the visuality and concreteness that were lost in the commerce of prose. As we come to grasp his idea with greater precision, we realize how misleading it would be to read the passage in question as anticipatory of the contemporary notion that poetry operates on the plane of the signifier instead of simply on that of the signified. Diderot's comparison of poetry with hieroglyphs makes a different point, given the constant separation between thought and expression: poetry's role is to indicate the possibility of words' remaining close to their referents. Let us recall that, according to Diderot's speculation on the history of languages, in the first phase mimetic and gestural language coexisted with indeclinable words. Though this language was less perfect, it remained closer to its referents, actual things—that is, the sphere of the visual. In this context, Diderot returns to the subject of hieroglyphs in his discussion with Batteux. Raising against the priest's treatise the arguments he was to develop later in *Du Beau*, Diderot in his 1751 *Lettre sur les sourds et muets* objected to Batteux's definition of *belle nature* and added that this flaw could be corrected if Batteux had compared the hieroglyphs specific to each art (see Diderot 1875, 1: 385). Although Diderot himself does not state his conclusion clearly, his entire line of reasoning indicates that he anticipated a harmony among the hieroglyphs specific to each art—that is, elaborated by each art's specific means—and that this harmony was to be found in the laws that organize nature. In short, it is the order governing nature that ultimately justifies the artistic hieroglyphs, and these, differing only as to the artistic medium in which they are used, may be conjoined with hieroglyphs of other media—say, the painter's with the poet's—because all of them refer to something that is constant.

The reason why I have examined the passage quoted above in such detail becomes clearer when my conclusion is compared with those of other interpreters. Thus, for instance, Herbert Dieckmann writes: "Not only all new words and word-combinations are exclusively the work of the genius, but he also creates those expressions—Diderot calls them hiéroglyphes—which synthesize many things, thoughts and images into an indissoluble whole, and which constitute poetical beauty" (Dieckmann 1941: 177). Translating the hieroglyph as the synthesis of a compound of things, thoughts, and images and *not conceding any primacy to the visual*, Dieckmann overlooked the primacy of imitation and tailored Diderot's critical thought to contemporary trends. It comes as no surprise, then, to find Dieckmann's emphasis on genius in another text on Diderot published a few years later (see Walker 1944: 277–87).

The same temptation to "update" Diderot can be seen in a more recent essay, the quality of which is thereby compromised. Faced with Diderot's affinity for what would later be known as the "romantic" and the "realist" modes, Michael Fried convincingly demonstrates how his evaluative standard could swing both ways with no contradiction. According to Fried, the exploitation of themes that implied self-absorption of the characters as the dominant characteristic, which had peaked with Jean-Baptiste-Siméon Chardin, had begun to decline by the 1760's. It was replaced, both in painting and in criticism, by the emphasis on dramatic expressiveness. Although Fried, without exploring other possible causes, sees only the repudiation of rococo as the basis of this change, as a demonstration of a de facto situation his argument is novel and compelling. Thus Fried explains the flagrant difference between Chardin and Jean-Baptiste Greuze, the representatives of absorption and dramatic expressiveness respectively: "This development was part of a larger shift from the primacy of absorption toward the primacy of action and expression—more accurately, from the representation of figures absorbed in quintessentially absorptive states and activities toward the representation of figures absorbed in action or passion (or both)" (Fried 1980: 107). However, this change of evaluating standards is not an isolated fact; it corresponds to a much more drastic change in the relation between spectator and painting: "starting around the middle of the eighteenth century in France, the beholder's presence before the painting came increasingly to be conceived by critics and theorists as something that had to be accomplished or at least powerfully affirmed by the painting itself" (p. 93). That is, the change in the pattern of pictorial production is synchronous with the change in the criterion of reception.

At this point, though, the author makes a leap that is not substantiated by any evidence. The first part of his thesis concerning the position now assumed by the receiver followed from the earlier demonstration: the emphasis on states of self-absorption had been abandoned so that the picture might contain a dramatic charge expressive enough to capture the spectator's attention. Then Fried formulates the second part of his thesis: this dramatic charge was so intense that it dispensed with or even canceled the presence of the spectator: "In short, for Diderot pictorial unity was a kind of microcosm of the causal system of nature, of the universe itself; and conversely the unity of nature, apprehended by man, was like that of painting, at bottom dramatic and expressive" (p. 87). In other words, the painting was seen as autonomous and self-sufficient. Starting from correct premises—valuation of nature by means of a new criterion, in the passage quoted above—Fried treats Diderot and the painting of his time as contemporaries of Postimpressionist painting, a conclusion that must be rejected after a systematic analysis of the author of the *Salons*.

Whereas these authors emphasized the problem of creative genius and shunted aside the issue of nature as a model for imitation, Doolittle examined Diderot in terms of the question of the unconscious (and, we might add today, of the aesthetics of reception):

> We may ... define Diderot's hieroglyphs as a suggestion which the poet makes to the hearer's understanding, and particularly to his imagination, by means of sound and rhythm in conjunction with the vocabulary and subject matter of the poem. The poet's genius enables him, whether or not he is aware of the fact ... , to put the suggestions into his work; the genius of the hearer ... causes his organism to perceive the suggestions and his imagination to combine them into images.
> (Doolittle 1952: 155)

In the present case, the emphasis on the resources the genius has at his disposal is distinguished from the character of "plastic representation" that Doolittle himself had pointed out in his treatment of the hieroglyph. By means of omissions similar to those we have already mentioned, which were certainly not deliberate, it became possible to see Diderot as the forerunner of an aesthetics of the unconscious.

But this could be done only by ignoring the fact that the work of the unconscious is a production, something lacking the primacy of the stable plasticity and visuality in Diderot's hieroglyph. If there is in Diderot an inkling of the idea of the unconscious—and there is, indeed—it is of a passive rather than an active unconscious, more a reservoir in which nothing is lost than a medium for change. Only in this way can we understand Diderot's mistrustful stance toward the imaginary. Let us recall the following passage:

> Purely imaginary beings, such as the sphinx, the mermaid, the faun, the minotaur, the ideal man, etc., are those about the beauty of which there is least agreement, which should come as no surprise: these imaginary beings are in fact shaped according to the relations which we see in real beings: but the model which they should resemble, dispersed among the diverse productions of nature, is, properly speaking, everywhere and nowhere. (Diderot 1965a: 435)

Since the model on which purely imaginary beings are based is not specific to them, statements as to their beauty must necessarily be the most debatable. The imaginary could only be accepted, as it were, by means of a reprieve.

THE QUESTION OF NATURE

For all its meanderings, Diderot's thought has a few unmistakable constant elements. The most important of these is the almost obsessive search for a criterion of judgment and appreciation for works of art.

Here, much more than in his perorations in praise of virtue and of the mending of morals, his ethos can be discerned, an ethos that derived less from an internalized moral code than from his mental suppleness. Rather than merely give vent to his manifold demons, or simply apply himself to various lines of study, Diderot always tried to state the criteria by means of which his object of study could be appreciated in a nonarbitrary way.

There are two ways of being in harmony with the talents one has (or believes one has). One, the most common, is to become a virtuoso of one's talents, to express oneself through them, and not give a damn about the probable outcomes of one's acts and actions. The other—Diderot's way—is precisely the opposite. Although he witnessed the crisis of the ethos of the estate society and the new exaltation of the individual, from which the cult of genius evolved, to the theorization of which he himself was a major contributor, Diderot did not worship the individual *as such*. His very search for objective criteria was motivated by the fact that he was not content with simply affirming the individuality of an action or product. To him, the individual was valid, even worthy of exaltation, to the extent that his contribution was geared to the community. In other words, deviation was not valued as such, but only to the extent that it might provide an orientation for the entire community. In a passage quoted earlier we have already seen Diderot's concern for the receiver—his statement that the work of art requires the conjoining of two geniuses, that of the author and that of the receiver. The objectivity that fascinated him resulted from this political ethos, which recoiled from what was later to turn into aloof individuality, anomie.

From this trait another, which I have also mentioned before, is immediately derived: Diderot's unflagging willingness to pursue the solution of a problem rather than settle for solutions that are brilliant but inconsequent. Hence—in spite of the apparent paradox—his concern for the reader, which can be seen in the dedication of his *Lettre sur les sourds*: "I take care to do well whatever I do, even at the price of being less widely read" (Diderot 1875, 1: 347). The apparent paradox is clear: how could Diderot afford to lose any readers if for ethical and political (not to mention financial) reasons he depended on them? But the paradox is only on the surface. Although he is concerned with the reception of his works, Diderot will not shirk making it more arduous if current solutions do not seem satisfactory to him. Thus because of his ethos Diderot cannot feel satisfied with formulations that, though more accessible, gloss over the seriousness of problems. It is this ethos that can be found as a constant element throughout his variegated production.

This, of course, does not mean that I agree with all his postulations. Some of them are no longer pertinent or—more seriously—remain committed to precisely the sort of view of art that they intended to attack. But even if one can prove this was indeed the case, it would still be unfair to accuse Diderot of having devised another way of repressing art. When one studies a thinker of a relatively remote age, one's first impulse is to see him as a prophet or to attribute to him orientations that in fact did not become clear until later. For it is difficult or even impossible to accept that history, with its countless variables, can invest original lines of thought with meanings that could not have been originally foreseen. To avoid, then, depicting Diderot as a prophet or a conscious forerunner of evils we see around us, we must reconstruct his ethos and his radical questioning and apply them to his own work. There is material enough for such an undertaking: from his translation of Shaftesbury's *An Inquiry Concerning Virtue and Merit* to the many works he left unpublished, Diderot was constantly reflecting on the issue of art. Though his starting point was the Enlightenment, and though his reflections were a part of his struggle against religion and the privileges of absolutism, Diderot's thought was never disciplined by philosophical or political ideas. On the contrary, even when one disagrees with him, one cannot but admire his dignity as philosopher and art critic.

Having stated the premises on which I intend to base my investigation, I will begin by saying that the first element to be emphasized is the priority given to nature in Diderot's work. True, this priority is not an exclusive trait of his—nature is the object of concern of all pre-Kantian aesthetics (see Chouillet 1973: 300). But to establish this general truth is not enough. We must also ask why, precisely in Diderot, nature preserved this priority. To this question there can be no simple, immediate answer. The most elementary reason can be found in a quotation from the entry "Encyclopédie": "now that philosophy is advancing with giant strides; that it is submitting to its rule all the objects in its competence; that its tone is the dominant tone; and that it is beginning to shake off the yoke of authority and example and restrict itself to the laws of reason, there is hardly an elementary and dogmatic work with which one can feel entirely satisfied. One sees that such productions are based on the truths of men rather than on those of nature" (Diderot 1976, 7: 184). Here the chain formed by nature, reason, and good government is made explicit. Its significance is brought home when it is counterposed to the chain against which the philosophes were fighting: the one that began with God and, through theology, led to the legitimation of arbitrary government.

For nature had the political and emotional function of counterposing and replacing God in the central position. When, therefore, the records of Parisian police classified Diderot as a dangerous atheist (see Darnton 1984), this was no petty charge. If today we find it hard to imagine how a man's opposition to religion could be felt to be politically dangerous, it is perhaps because we are inclined to believe that placing nature as an alternative to the Christian God was no more than a strategy or a disguise. If we do so, we will fail to realize that in the early work of Diderot nature was made into a deity *because this implied a widening of possibilities for believers*: "Sometimes incredulity is the vice of a fool, and credulousness a wise man's flaw. The wise man's vision extends into the far distance, encompassing the immensity of the possible; the fool sees as possible no more than that which is the case. That, perhaps, is what makes the one pusillanimous and the other reckless" (Diderot 1965b: 28). The Christian God had been *disciplined* by the Church's officialization. His omnipotence, as it was affirmed, legitimated the de facto power of earthly lords. In addition, priests had to teach submission and respect for order. Consequently, the Catholic God had become timorous, attached to the ruling order—a conformist. In contrast, nature, whose riches were increasingly revealed by science, stimulated daring, challenged prejudices, and encouraged the imagination. Soon Diderot would discover that it was not necessary to deify nature for it to pose this challenge to man: on the contrary, seeing it in its full materiality required just as much courage. One might even add: deism implied emotional enthusiasm, admiration of nature by a sentimentalized worshiper—in short, it was somewhat reminiscent of Diderot's early concept of genius—whereas full-blown materialism was to correspond to the view of genius expressed in *Paradoxe sur le comédien*.

However, such an explanation is still incomplete. It depicts Diderot as a wild-eyed libertarian, in love with the possibilities of imagination—and this, as the reading of his works will show, is not the whole truth. At least in the field of art, where his thought attains a degree of complexity higher than that achieved in the realm of science, Diderot seems equally concerned with coordinating beauty and other values—or maybe even subordinating it to them. The primacy of nature will serve this additional purpose. It would, thus, be a mistake to take the primacy of nature either as a mere strategy for confounding his adversaries and spies, or as the way he had found, after freeing himself from a castrating orthodoxy, to give free rein to his enthusiasm and his inventiveness.

Having discarded the first of these hypotheses, I must complement the second with an additional formulation. The primacy of nature offered Diderot a focus on which he had to make two opposing lines converge: on the one hand, recognition of artistic invention; on the other, limits to it, or a model for it. But this formulation is not yet fully satisfactory. We must still ask what were the positions occupied by the opposite terms—the recognition of inventiveness and the attempt to set a limit or impose a model for it. Let us then examine our material.

The issue of the autonomy or dependence of the beautiful began to be approached in Diderot's conception of the relation between beauty and truth. We need only look at a few exemplary passages. The first is to be found in *Essais sur la peinture*. To the question "What is taste?" he answers: "A dexterity, acquired through repeated experience, in capturing the true or the good, together with the circumstance that makes it beautiful and of being promptly and vividly touched by it" (Diderot 1965a: 738). That is, the relationship that the beautiful establishes with the true or the good is not immediate. The difference, however, lies simply in a "circumstance." Beauty is thought of as near to truth, but still separated from it by an interval, which is not explained in the passage. But immediately after Diderot seems to suggest an answer: "Michelangelo gave the dome of St. Peter's, in Rome, the most beautiful shape possible. The geometer La Hire, impressed with this form, traced its cartoon and found that it was the curve of greatest resistance. What was it that inspired this curve in Michelangelo? His daily living experience" (pp. 738–39). The beautiful shape is also the most resistant geometrical form; it is not only truthful but also good (useful). The circumstance mentioned in the earlier passage, then, was the painter's intuitive discovery of truth. And such a great intuition could only be possible in an individual gifted with a special organization—a genius. The circumstance that separates beauty from truth could only be actualized by a genius's intuition. Later we will see the specific problem of genius; meanwhile let us examine our conclusion from a different angle.

What does it mean to say that, by different ways—one intuitive, the other intellectual—the geometer and the artist came to precisely the same form? Nothing less than that there is something prior to human experience, an order that is independent of it and that, being objectified, imposes itself on it. Surely Diderot did not think of nature as simply what is observable; in a great many passages he placed mere observers on a lower plane. Thus if the scientist and the painter were able to converge through nature, it could not have been the observation of nature that made this possible, but instead the structure that rules it. Here we seem to have a pre-structuralist Diderot before us. But the passages in the *Essais* are not conclusive. However, many years earlier, in his *Pensées philosophiques* of 1746, Diderot had written:

> In our churches there are pictures that, we are assured, were painted by angels or by God himself: if these pieces had been the work of Le Sueur or Le Brun, what could I object to in this immemorial tradition? Nothing, perhaps. But when I gaze on these heavenly works and I see that in every detail the rules of painting have been violated in the draftsmanship and in the execution, that the truth of art has been neglected throughout, since I cannot suppose that the artisan was ignorant, I can only conclude that the tradition is no more than a fable. (Diderot 1965b: 35–36)

In this passage, Diderot denies God the right to violate *les règles de la peinture*. Note that he does not write *l'art du vrai*, but rather *le vrai de l'art*. That is, the truth of art is conditioned by respect to its rules, which would necessarily be obeyed even by a superior being. Is this obedience the condition for acknowledging that intuition derives from genius? Is a genius one who does not need to learn in order to discover the order of nature? If we are not satisfied with mere speculation, it is useless to stretch the meaning of the passages. All we can do is point to the fact that both emphasize the existence of a road that is specific to art. But we do not yet know where this road leads. So it is better to place more pawns on our board. This can be done in two ways.

Twelve years after writing his *Pensées philosophiques*, in *De la poésie dramatique*, Diderot poses the same problem, and does not show much progress. In any case, the passage has the merit of stressing again that "artistic imitation is not justified as imitation pure and simple":

> There is a great difference between a jest in the theater and a jest in society. The latter would be far too feeble on a stage, and would have no impact whatsoever. The former would be exceedingly harsh in the actual world, and would cause offense. Cynicism, which is so odious, so unpleasant in society, is excellent on the stage. —Truth in poetry is one thing; truth in philosophy is quite another. If his discourse is to be true, the philosopher must conform it to the nature of objects; the poet must conform his to the nature of his characters. (Diderot 1965a: 251–52)

But the mystery has not been dispelled. The difference Diderot points to in the question of truth only restates, admittedly in a more explicit way, an earlier assertion. However, if placed in the context of Diderot's complete works, it does not warrant the inference that the poet's truth is simply the configuration of his characters' universe. For poetry and art, in Diderot, are never seen as autonomous, isolated fields. If, therefore, we know what must be denied, we have not yet found support for what must be affirmed. Let us then turn to a later text. This is a passage from Diderot's comments on the 1765 salon:

As to what kind of poetry is most rare, it is certainly that which brings fiction as close to truth as possible. If the subject of the letter in question is interesting and pathetic in itself, then it takes a hundred times more genius to keep it natural, so that we take it to be a letter actually written, than to make of it a piece of eloquence and virtuosity. The question of the cupola is different. First of all one would have to ask, What is a cupola? What does one propose to do when one paints a cupola? For if a cupola were, say, an epic machine or a part of an ode, then it would not require truth in poetry, but rather verve and delirium; the most beautiful delirium, the most sublime, would prevail over all. A painted cupola that could be mistaken for a real cupola would be no more than a cupola, that is, an object devoid of interest. (Diderot 1960: 159–60)

It is well known that Diderot was able to refine his aesthetic reflections when Grimm gave him the opportunity to comment on the painting salons from 1759 to 1781. But the passage quoted above shows that a certain tension, or even perplexity, still characterized his response to art.

This perplexity is clearly seen in the contrast between what is affirmed in connection with poetry and what is added concerning painting. At first, the quality of poetic fiction is subordinated to truth. Truth here is counterposed to rhetoric; it implies capturing the tone of everyday speech. (Note, incidentally, that genius is said to be a condition for this.) But then the argument becomes more sophisticated. A painted cupola imitating a real one would be an object devoid of interest; but if it is to be part of a poetic intention, then what is required is not truth, but verve and delirium. The perplexity manifested in this passage, however, does not seem to derive from an absolute contradiction. If we take "truth" here to mean "conformity to actual things"—that is, to the aspect of the world such as it presents itself outside of and before the production of the work of art—we may infer that the author is affirming that there can be no adequate general precept that applies to all arts. In a given case, what is adequate and interesting is to capture the tone of everyday experience (the example of the letter); in another, it might be to disregard the object's actual aspect and integrate it into the machinery of the poem (the example of the cupola). But what does Diderot mean when he writes "alors il ne s'agirait pas de vérité dans la poésie qu'elle exige" ("then it would not require truth in poetry")? I believe he means the following: in the example, what is required is not conformity to the visible appearance of the thing (the cupola), but rather to its function—that is, just as the real cupola has a function in relation to the building or temple of which it is a part, so the painted cupola has a function in relation to the object of which it is a part in the work of art.

In short, truth should be understood not as conformity to a single kind of thing or phenomenon—those that belong to the plane of the empirical and the visible—but rather as conformity to the totality of possibilities. Something is true to the extent that it is functional. Once again, it seems, we are surprised to find in Diderot a forebear of structuralism. But we cannot yet say we are satisfied. Though we have discovered much fascinating evidence, we should not yet say that we have pinpointed Diderot's thought. Otherwise we would have to conclude that Diderot arrived at a view of art quite different from a realist concept—a view implying the terrible consequence that a work of art is valid only to the extent that it duplicates a previously existing truth. But such a conclusion would be inconsistent with the vast majority of Diderot's production. Even the last passage we quoted furnishes an indication of this fact: whereas the term "fiction" is used only to be approximated and submitted to truth, the "liberated" cupola is not said to be fictional. This is so because Diderot always treats fictional and fictitious as synonymous, both being considered inferior achievements. With this caveat in mind, let us carry on our examination.

Is not what I have just written inconsistent with the notion, set forth in the *Recherches philosophiques* (1752), that the beautiful is the product of multiple relations, which are not even necessarily conscious? But the *Recherches* were written over a decade before the comments on the 1765 salon. It seems clear that the idea of truth as a bundle of relations, expressed in the *Recherches*, was close to the notion of poetry as a hieroglyphic or synthetic form, set forth in the *Lettre sur les sourds et muets* (1751), both concepts envisaging perception as the dominant faculty; however, the comment on the 1765 salon moved away from this interpretive scheme.

Was the change temporary or permanent? The answer is to be found in the texts written from the 1760's on. Hence the importance of the comment on the 1767 salon:

If nature is one, how does my friend explain the fact that there are so many different ways of imitating it, and that all of them are accepted? Is not this a consequence of the fact that, since it is admittedly, and perhaps fortunately, impossible to present it with absolute precision, there is a margin of convention on which art is allowed to ramble? That in all poetic productions there is always a bit of mendacity, the limit of which is not and never will be determined? Grant art the freedom of a deviation [*écart*] approved by some and proscribed by others. Once we acknowledge that the painter's sun is not and could not be the same as the universe's, we assume a commitment from which a great many consequences follow. The first of these is that one should not demand from art what is beyond its resources; the second is that we should be extremely cautious about appreciating every scene in which all is in harmony. (Diderot 1963: 195)

The now-famous sentence—"le soleil du peintre n'est pas celui de l'univers et ne saurait l'être" ("the sun of painting is not and could not be that of the universe")—is a more confident restatement of the idea we have already seen in the article on Watelet—"la peinture, pour ainsi dire, a son soleil, qui n'est pas celui de l'univers" ("painting, so to speak, has its own sun, which is not the universe's"). It is one of the *morceaux choisis* of those who see Diderot as a forerunner of contemporary aesthetics. However, placed in its context, it fails to dispel the perplexity I mentioned above. There are various and diverse ways of imitating nature, which is one, that are commonly accepted, because it is (perhaps fortunately) impossible to present nature with absolute fidelity. This is then a *necessary concession*. Unless I am mistaken, what the passage implies is the following: Since absolute precision is impossible, we ought to allow art a certain margin of convention. But the alibi thus granted to art makes it no less subject to the judgment of truth: "dans toute production poétique il y a toujours un peu de mensonge" ("in every poetic production there is always a bit of lying"), the limit of which must always remain undeterminable.

It is this indeterminacy that, coupled with the requirement of truth, makes the critic's work so difficult. The criterion of truth is not sufficient for him; and Diderot has been aware of this for decades. The critic must know the techniques of the medium he is analyzing, must learn from the artists themselves, just as the commentator of the salons was wont to do. Between pure truth and its artistic representation there is a gap, covered by truth. The critic's task is to avoid both the crude ideal of "faithful" imitation and what Diderot called mannerism. For the latter mistake is symmetrically opposite to the former. It was also the 1767 salon that provided Diderot with an opportunity to define *le maniéré et le faux*: "Rigorous imitation of Nature will make art poor, mean, petty, but never false or affected [*maniéré*]. —It is from the imitation of nature, be it exaggerated or beautified [*embellie*], that the beautiful and the true, the affected and the false, will arise; for then the artist is forced to rely on his own imagination: he is left without any precise model" (p. 399). Affected art is, in short, what results when the artist does not follow a precise model, and instead is adrift in his own imagination. Thus, although they may be fascinated by art, thinkers nonetheless can say that it is basically flawed: however skillfully done, a painting will always be "un tissu de faussetés" ("a tissue of lies") (Diderot 1957: 217). The philosopher of art cannot be content to acknowledge this fact; this would be as naive as for a biologist to be content to say that man is naturally unable to fly.

His task, then, is to investigate the gap that inevitably separates art from truth, keeping in mind that his ultimate aim is to discover how the two are articulated. As Diderot conceives it, this task would not provide a way out of his perplexity. Nevertheless, however strange the world into which he penetrates, Diderot never derives a different conclusion from it. Like Don Quixote returning from the grave of Montesinos, Diderot does not renounce what he had long thought to be true; his comments on the painting salons refine his evaluations, but do not imply any change in his ideas on the relations between art and truth. Effective art, necessarily separated from truth, is that art which, by means and not in spite of beauty, preserves its subordination to the truth of nature.

If one accepts the reasoning that led to this conclusion, one will accept with no suspicion some statements made by Diderot before his comments on the salons. In his *Essais sur la peinture*, for instance, he writes: "Take from Watteau his sites, his color, the grace of his figures and of their clothes; look at the scene only and judge it. The arts of imitation require something savage, something brutal, something formidable and huge" (Diderot 1965a: 714).

The appeal of the extraordinary, the defense of its specificity, did not compromise or affect the theory of knowledge of art that Diderot had already set forth.

The result we have arrived at must now undergo another test: an examination of the ways in which the beautiful is related to the good and the useful. Here, since these properties are subordinated to the question of truth, the author's position seems less marked by doubts.

In the *Lettre sur les aveugles*, attacking the idea that beauty is innate, Diderot writes: "For a blind man, if beauty is separated from usefulness, it is no more than a word" (Diderot 1965b: 83). He says much the same in the article on Watelet: "*On beauty*: The author sees it as a reflection of usefulness, and he is right" (Diderot 1980: 134). Jean Varloot, the editor of the volume in which this short article is included, observes that Diderot's professed utilitarianism can only be understood within a biological-functionalist frame of reference (p. 134 n. 36). The observation is correct, since it points to the philosopher's concern with the need for internal organization in a work of art. But we need not repeat that this internal organization has the function of covering the gap between beauty and truth. A work of art, then, is useful to the extent that it serves truth.

Diderot is equally consistent when he bases his "Eloge de Richardson" on the virtuous impulses that Samuel Richardson's books elicit in his readers: "I was, after I finished reading your book, what an honest man is after a day spent in doing good" (Diderot 1965a: 30). The moral service rendered by the English novelist is also associated with the realism it prefigures, which Diderot always praises:

> The world we live in is the setting; the basis of his plot is truthful; his characters are as real as they can be; his characters are drawn from society; the incidents are part of the customs of all civilized nations; the passions he depicts are just as I experience them ... he shows me the general course of the things that surround me. Without this art, my soul being subject to chimerical biases, illusion would be no more than momentary, and the impression no more than feeble and ephemeral.
> (Pp. 30–31)

Note that the praise of realism is associated with contempt for the fictitious and the imaginary because these are not guided by a precise model. To the sequence of negative terms a new one is added: *biais chimériques*.

Like the other terms in the sequence, "chimerical bias" also denotes something blameworthy, both from the viewpoint of truth and morality and from a strictly aesthetic one: were there no recognition of real scenes, the impression on the receiver would be weak and ephemeral. However, if a novelist learns the lesson taught by the author of *Clarissa*, he can do more than a historian, whose object "encompasses only a part of time, only a part of the world," whereas Richardson took for his model "the human heart, which has always been and will always be the same" (p. 40). Since the role of history as a standard for affirming the dignity of the novel is well known, it need only be added that Diderot was here introducing a variation of this familiar theme: now the novelist could not only learn from the historian but also go beyond him. Diderot is not just echoing Aristotle's *Poetics*, but following the Enlightenment tendency to see reason as a timeless value, when he places emotional reactions outside time.

The same harmony between the beautiful and the good reappears in a later text, on the 1767 salon: "Artists, if you would have your works endure, I advise you to stick to virtuous themes. Everything that preaches depravity to men is doomed to be destroyed, the more so the more perfect a work is" (Diderot 1963: 198). The fact that Diderot remained faithful to this position for so long shows, then, that the point is unproblematic; it would be uninteresting except that, first, it helps to confirm the result I had reached before concerning the relations between beauty and truth; and second, it provides a basis for Diderot's realist orientation in aesthetics. This realism exalted the novel's uplifting role: "If it is important for men to be persuaded that, regardless of any considerations that go beyond earthly existence, we have nothing better to do in order to be happy than to be virtuous, how well has Richardson served the human race!" (Diderot 1965a: 32). It is because of the realism of his paintings that Greuze, who specialized in depicting interiors of bourgeois homes, became one of Diderot's favorite artists. His praises are particularly elaborate in this comment on the 1765 salon: "Here is your painter and mine; the first among us who had the idea of introducing manners in art and putting together a chain of events with which one might easily write a novel" (Diderot 1960: 144). But immediately after writing this, he feels the need to differentiate himself from those who praise virtue for its own sake, and adds: "I hate all petty vilenesses, which betray no more than an abject soul; but I do not hate the great crimes, first because they are the stuff of beautiful paintings and beautiful tragedies, and also because great, sublime actions and great crimes are endowed with the same energy" (p. 144). Proclaiming the virtues of what would come to be called realism, Diderot takes pains to stress that his praise of a painting's moral quality is not to be confused with the praise of good intentions or holy souls. In life and in art, Diderot demands a capacity for daring—but only if it serves a useful purpose. Indeed, its positiveness may not be immediate, for it may depend, as the passage quoted above makes clear, on its providing a theme for a beautiful artistic representation. Mediately or immediately, only the exceptional is truly useful. (The exaltation of the exceptional already prefigures the role Diderot assigns to genius.)

This section cannot end without an investigation of Diderot's concept of a model. The term appeared in several of the passages quoted and was not the object of any sort of inquiry. In many of these passages, it seems to mean no more than conformity to the view of nature. However, if Diderot was aware that the mere act of imitation was very far from sufficing for the production of art, he could not but be forced to reflect on the concept of a model.

This becomes clear when we come upon the phrase "ideal model." In connection with the sculptures in the 1765 salon, Diderot wrote:

He who disdains the ancients in favor of nature runs the risk of becoming small, frail, and mean in draftsmanship, types, dress, and expression. He who neglects nature in favor of the ancients runs the risk of becoming cold, lifeless, with none of the hidden, secret truths that are to be found in nature only. It seems to me that one must study the ancients in order to learn to see nature.   (Diderot 1960: 207)

The phrase "ideal model" does not appear here, but it is nevertheless the idea behind the demand for the study of both nature and ancient art.

For, as J. Chouillet aptly puts it, "the great law on which the hypothesis of the ideal model is based" is that it is necessary to reduce the sensible matter of nature to "the condition of an idea." In other words, *the path that leads from the object to its representation passes through the idea* (Chouillet 1973: 178). The ideal model thus presupposes two agents: the natural object or phenomenon and its transformation in the mind of the artist. If either is missing, the outcome will be compromised. If the second one is lacking, the object will be uninteresting, for it will be no more than a copy; if the first one is absent, it will be chimerical and fictitious.

The notion of ideal model, with its twofold demand, was used by Diderot both in this art criticism and in his formulation of a realist aesthetics. But the passages we have seen are no more than a mere inkling of what the philosopher would come to write about the subject. The full-blown concept appears only in the reflections evoked by the comments on the 1767 salon. The most important of these is too long to quote in full; I will therefore summarize it.

Diderot presents a kind of dialogue between himself and a painter friend, the theme of which is the model of the painter's work. If the painter argued that he had taken for a model the most beautiful woman he knew, the worst of his students might then successfully argue that he had done no more than paint a portrait. A portrait, says Diderot, merely shows an individual face, and the artist is above producing a strict imitation of a single hair; if he neither adds nor suppresses, he is unable to produce an image, "a copy of truth," and his line is not "the true line, the line of beauty, the ideal line, but a line like any other, altered, deformed, imitative, individual." Against this view, which is derived from a crude notion of imitation, Diderot proposes his functional-biological conception of beauty: the functions performed by animate beings during their lives are reflected in the organization of their wholes—including their physical aspect—which are altered by these functions. Thus no creature can be mistaken for any other, no profile is like any other profile, and even one of the ends of a mouth is different from the other. That is why the artist who would rise above the minor status of a portraitist cannot choose as a model something outside himself: "Then you will agree that, when you create the beautiful, you do not create anything that is, not even that may come to be. . . . For the true line, the ideal model of beauty exists nowhere else except in the heads of the Agasiases, the Raphaels, the Poussins, the Pugets, the Pigals, the Falconnets" (Diderot 1963: 59–60). The ideal model of beauty can only be found in the mind of the genius, "who for a time shapes the spirit, the character, the taste of the works of a people, a century, a school" (p. 61).

If my summary can be trusted (the full passage is on pp. 56–61), the above extract unambiguously emphasizes the need for cooperation between the understanding of nature and the exceptional individual. Thus the notion of an ideal model sums up the basic lines of Diderot's art theory. It is clearly a theory of imitation, but it is patently different from both the classical and the later version, the latter being the canon followed by the entertainment novel of today. Now I seem to be treading firmer ground, and I can begin to focus on a more specific angle: the question of the relations between this theory of art and the problem of the control of the imaginary and the fictional.

In Chapter 2, we saw that during the heyday of absolutism the idea of verisimilitude was gradually dissociated from the idea of representation of truth, as it became subordinate to the principle of decorum, of appropriateness to the practices of good society. Diderot rejects this approach and denounces it when he showers irony on the principle of *belle nature*. Further, if it is recalled that, according to the first and ampler hypothesis put forward in *Control of the Imaginary*, ever since the decline of the Middle Ages there has been an attempt to tame art, with the immediate purpose of taming the individual, I may add that Diderot's emphasis on the subversive role of the genius assumed liberation from that control.

What is more, since the praise of genius is not disconnected from social function, Diderot's liberating theory did not enclose art in a sort of zoo or forest reserve, as is the case now. In other words, the attempt to harmonize the expression of properties of the world outside the individual and the individual's potential seemed to imply, in terms of the investigation I have been conducting since *Control of the Imaginary*, an attempt to do art justice without neglecting society, or even to contribute to social change without necessarily reducing the artist to the role of a mere illustrator of dogmas, programs, and ideas.

But it would still be premature to take this interpretation as definitive. It certainly seems to be reasonable; but other angles remain to be explored. At this point in our exposition, the only unquestionable point is that in Diderot the notion of imitation assumed a new shape. As H. Dieckmann wrote some time ago, "Diderot not only changed the concept of imitation but also raised the domain of 'realism' and 'naturalism' (to use terms of a later age) to the level of noble and serious genres" (Dieckmann 1959: 118). But, unless it is because of my modern distaste for the term "imitation," why do I still refrain from pronouncing a definitive judgment? For was not Diderot, having dissociated himself from classical standards, now ready to set art free?

But who ever said that Diderot had broken with classicism? Although his position could hardly be confused with Voltaire's aesthetic conservatism or Rousseau's sentimental moralism, it is quite evident that Diderot preserved elements of classical control—not because of their controlling function, but simply because he found them adequate to the object of art. Thus he writes: "In all arts, unity of imitation is as essential as unity of action; and to confound or associate two ways of imitating nature is a barbarous thing, in deplorable taste" (Diderot 1960: 211). In fact, the remnants of classical precepts in Diderot are serious only because they indicate a lack of distinction between truth and nature, and thus point to the need to preserve a center as ordinator of a theory of knowledge. Now, it seems clear that the notion of truth as an unquestionable center and thus a criterion for judging human productions leads to the favoring of one of these forms of production and the subordination of the others. It would be a mistake to believe that Diderot was unaware of this problem. In a little-known passage, he wrote: "The ideas of interest obsess me and disturb me in society, but they disappear in the sphere of hypotheses; there I am magnanimous, fair, merciful, because I can be so without any consequences" (Diderot 1875, 2: 392). This merits some thought. When he reflected on his art theory, Diderot tried to make it more magnanimous, strengthening it so that it transcended the plane of hypotheses; but, trying to act as *un citoyen honnête*, he was inevitably pressured by social interests. Thus, on the plane of hypotheses, when he understood that the beautiful was not directly theorizable on the basis of the notions of truth, good, and usefulness, he acknowledged that, if he did not investigate the gap where the beautiful is placed, he would only add to the misunderstandings concerning art.

Thus, from the viewpoint of the liberation of art, Diderot's functional theory was a major advance. But the pressure of social interests had the effect of making him turn back to the principle of the necessary correspondence between art and nature. Had he done otherwise, he would have abandoned the parameters of imitation. Now, since imitation referred to nature and since science had replaced philosophy as the discourse that proclaimed the truth of nature, scientific discourse eventually imposed itself as the foundation of truth. And with the establishment of the empire of science, the region of art could only become its colony. That is why Diderot's proposal of a liberating view of art was ultimately compromised. But this statement can be accepted as definitive only after we examine other angles. The most important of these is Diderot's theory of genius. Could it be that Diderot managed to undermine, at least in part, the terms of the final interpretation?

THE QUESTION OF GENIUS

Whoever reads Diderot for the first time is always astonished by the fact that the author is attracted by radically opposed aesthetic standards.

Briefly put, he is enthusiastic both about realism and about uncompromising individual self-expression. H. Dieckmann, for instance, associated this tension with a conflict in Diderot's personality: on the one hand, there was a tendency to impersonal objectivity, which made him plunge wholeheartedly into a collective effort such as the *Encyclopédie*, or the work of a friend such as Abbé Raynal or the poor theologian of Prades; on the other, he felt a strong urge to assert himself on every page he wrote (see Dieckmann 1959: 69). This conflict, it might be added, had its roots in the divergent answers he attempted to give to the classicist canon. For if classical art assumed the individual's anonymity, "that genius revealed itself only to reflection by means of purity and of the objectivity of his art" (Dieckmann 1959: iii), both orientations favored by Diderot clashed with the classical principle, even as they disagreed with each other. Realism, exalted in Richardson and Greuze, abolished the purification and beautification of nature that classicism aimed at. The emphasis on individual expression, in turn, violated the anonymity of the creator and made the exploration of his idiosyncrasies the very hallmark of art.

This point is well known, and I need do no more than compare two passages, written at about the same time. In his comments on the 1765 salon, Diderot interrupts his discussion of Chardin to observe: "This so-called genre painting should be the painting of those who are old or who were already born old. It requires no more than study and patience. No verve; little genius; not much poetry; much technique and truth; and that is all" (Diderot 1960: iii). And he writes of the 1767 salon:

A man of letters, not devoid of merit, held that the general and common epithets, such as great, magnificent, beautiful, terrible, interesting, horrible, which have a weaker hold on the reader's mind, since they give him, as it were, carte blanche, should always be given preference. I let him talk, but very quietly and deep inside I answered him: yes, when one is a poor devil like you, when only trivial images are painted; but when one has verve, rare conceits, a strong and original way of perceiving and feeling, the excruciatingly difficult task is to find the singular, individual, unique phrase that characterizes, distinguishes, pinpoints, and impresses.

(Diderot 1963: 196)

Evidently, the use of the term "verve" in both passages makes the antagonism between them less than absolute. Two points, however, should be observed: first, the frequent criticism of "genre painting" in the salon texts implied the praise of historical painting (see, for instance, Diderot 1967: 103); second, the 1765 passage associated absence of verve and genius with abundance of technique and truth. But in the 1767 passage the opposition is no longer between genre and historical painting, but rather between triviality and extraordinary expressive force. The idea of genius, therefore, stands at a crossroads, the historical moment when classical aesthetics turns obsolete.

Both realism and the emphasis on individual expression were clearly opposed to classical aesthetics, which could be reconciled neither with the nonidealized scenes of realism nor with the outpouring of individuality implied by the exaltation of the passions. If, as Paul Vernière observes, the exaltation of the passions was nothing new in the latter half of the eighteenth century (see Diderot 1965a: 10 n. 1), nonetheless Diderot overstepped the tradition that had developed since La Rochefoucauld. And this was so because he made the passions directly responsible for the excellence of the work of art. With the abandonment of the classical position—as expressed, for instance, in Descartes: "We see that [the passions] are all good in their nature and that there is nothing to avoid in them except abuse of them or their excesses" (Descartes 1965: 215)—the passions are turned into the instrument of individual exceptionality. It might be argued, of course, that the indiscriminate praise of the passions could be explained by the corresponding praise of enthusiasm and exaltation. For instance, in the entry "Génie," Diderot opposed genius and imagination to sangfroid (see Diderot 1965a: 16). Since this association is not only unmade but indeed inverted in *Paradoxe sur le comédien*, one might then say that the link between genius and the cult of the passions is at the most a characteristic of a phase in the author's career. Though it cannot be denied that the idea of genius in Diderot's thought went through two phases, it is also clear that in both of them genius was seen as a form of outpouring. The difference between the phases lies in the fact that in the first passion was still confused with extreme sensibility, whereas in the second it is measured by the effect it produces in the receiver.

A great actor, he writes in the *Paradoxe*, is not one who identifies with the character he plays to the point that his own emotions are aroused, but rather one who arouses the spectators' emotions. In either case, there is no genius without the arousal of emotion. It is no accident that genius was emphasized to the detriment of the principles of classical restraint. As I have been arguing from *Control of the Imaginary* onwards, the world of classicism—using the term to refer to the period from the beginning of the Renaissance to the demise of absolutism—had been marked by the effort to tame the individual, restricting him to the status he was born into, on the social plane, and submitting him to the truth taught by theology and philosophy, on the plane of art. For the emphasis on genius cannot be explained in historical terms without reference to the rebellion of the individual against the traditional society of the period. But how can it be reconciled with the formulation of what would come to be known as realism?

It might seem as if we were forced to agree with those who speak of a contradiction in Diderot between his political side, committed to the propagation of enlightenment, and his artistic side, geared to individualism. But I believe this view is anachronistic, for it projects onto Diderot's time a dilemma that would make sense only in the following century. Perhaps, though, the mistake is mine. For did not Diderot himself base his praise of Greuze and Richardson on their presentation of truth? And was not the realist standard praised precisely because it conformed to truth? And, finally, was it not because of its lack of truth that Diderot disdained romance, the work in which "things and characters" "differ excessively from what we are shown by experience or history" (Diderot 1965a: 214)? Although these doubts are well-founded, to conclude that there was an indissoluble contradiction here seems equally unwarranted.

Let us recall the passage quoted at the beginning of this section. Genre painting was deprecated because it was characterized as lacking in verve and genius, as having too little poetry and too much technique and truth. It would be arbitrary to conclude from this that Diderot believed genius was incompatible with the expression of truth. As we have seen, his theory of knowledge of art is based on the principle of the relations that, whether consciously or unconsciously, the artist *transposes* to his object. I say "transposes" because Diderot himself stresses that in this the artist is exactly like other men: "My understanding adds nothing to things and detracts nothing from them" (Diderot 1965a: 418). There is, then, a truth that is in general and common circulation, and that demands no special talent. This is the truth to which the genre painter and the writer of romance remain restricted. The former is content with an infrarealism— that is, an imitation in which little or nothing of the artist's own self is involved. The poet of the romantic and the fictitious, on the other hand, strays along a different path, and loses his way because he is entirely submerged in his flaming imagination (Diderot 1965a: 219). The genius is, then, the only one who masters the truth that discovers, that subverts the consensus rather than corroborates it. The truth of the genius is nonconformist. Thus the primacy of the genius is not an obstacle to, but the very condition for, the creation of a new art that will manifest reality rather than copy it or fantasize it, as in the cases of the deviant forms of genre painting and romance.

I am not saying that realism and the emphasis on individual expression were not results of one of the many tensions to which Diderot was submitted, or that these two trends became inimical to each other in the nineteenth century. But I do deny that they were already incompatible in Diderot's time. His inborn demons spurred him to find not a compromise solution, let alone a higher synthesis, but an effective and dynamic fusion. In the present case, where could he have found the area for such a fusion? Precisely in nature. Genius, he writes in the "Encyclopédie" entry, is defined by its "combining spirit" (Diderot 1976, 7: 223). If we associate this phrase with his theory of relations and recall his contention that relations were in things, it follows that genius was in the subject only for the purpose of finding nature. Or, should this line of reasoning be seen as unconvincing, perhaps it will be enough to read the following passage, about the poet:

> And the poet who pretends and the philosopher who reasons are equally and in the same sense consequent or inconsequent; for being consequent is the same thing as having the experience of the necessary concatenation of phenomena. . . . [The poet] has received from nature, in a higher degree, the quality that distinguishes the man of genius from ordinary man, and the latter from the stupid: imagination, without which discourse is reduced to the mechanical habit of applying combined sounds. (Diderot 1965a: 219)

Let me dispel a final doubt that might be raised by the ending of this passage: imagination is indeed praised, but only to the extent that it connects with the model of nature. Left to its own devices, imagination would remain negative, like a runner fantasizing the track without leaving his room.

To summarize, this section has not dissolved the contradiction between realism and individual expression, but rather reiterated the results arrived at in the preceding section. The criterion of objectivity on which Diderot attempted to base the knowledge of art referred, ultimately, to nature. Since religious and conventional illusions had been discredited, this was the only possible source of certainties left. Art was still a form of imitation. But the notion of imitation acquired a new meaning, derived from the new relation established with nature. For rather than sublimating nature—that is, making it decorous and inoffensive for delicate ears—art reveals those aspects of nature that were previously unseen and therefore unknown:

> In the man of genius, sometimes the imagination is merry; it busies itself with slight human imperfections, with everyday flaws and follies; for him, the opposite of order is no more than the ridiculous, but seen in such a novel way as to make it seem that it was the eye of the man of genius that made the object ridiculous, while in fact all it did was find it already there. (Diderot 1965a: 11)

This identification between genius and nature shows that Odo Marquard's remarkable observation concerning Schelling could be extracted from certain passages in Diderot: "Nature can no longer be copied as if it were preexistent, for what is preexistent—as artifact plus feeling—is the historical world; how can nature be imitated there? Obviously, only through an *imitatio* that is no longer a copy, but rather a succession: genius does not present nature, but rather presents as nature, *in likeness of* nature"

(Marquard 1968: 384). But Diderot apparently did not dare to go so far, and took the analogy implied by "as" and "in likeness of" in its weak sense: that is, genius does not *internalize* nature and act like nature, but rather discovers its hidden structure, its nonempirical face. Thus for him it was unthinkable even to accept the possibility of endowing with autonomy the area inhabited by the genius, as an artist: the area of aesthetics. A mediator between nature and the community of his fellowmen, the genius, as an artist, remained at the service of truth, the good, and the useful.

BOURGEOIS DRAMA

Around the mid–eighteenth century, classical French theater no longer attracted enough public to cover production expenses.* At the same time, new varieties of comedy were appearing—sentimental, moralizing, *larmoyante*—as well as an entirely new genre, *drame* (see Lough 1957: 185); all of these were associated with middle-class values. The historian whose research I have mentioned also observes that the predominance of the parterre declined in this same period; the judgment of the parterre had been decisive for the acceptance or rejection of plays in the classical theater (see Auerbach 1984b). Particularly after 1770, when the Comédie-Française moved to its new headquarters, the parterre was no longer frequented by students, artists, writers, minor legal clerks, and professionals, who had previously favored this section of the theater for its low admission prices and excellent view of the stage. As L. Sébastien Mercier wrote in *Tableau de Paris*, "the *parterre* then was much better than today. The *parterre* knew how to make an actor. Now that they no longer must face the useful censorship exerted by the students, actors are perverted by a crude *parterre*" (quoted in Lough 1957: 219). In its new building on the Rive Gauche, the Comédie was no longer accessible to its old patrons, and now there was a larger number of expensive seats, reserved for the aristocracy, who were interested less in evaluating the plays than in showing off.

It was in these circumstances that Diderot decided to try his hand at

---

*"It is notorious, for instance, that in 1746 the Duc D'Aumont, in his capacity as Gentilhomme de la Chambre, forbade the actors to perform any of Molière's five-act comedies until further notice. On 10 May of that year *L'Ecole des femmes* attracted a mere 35 spectators to the theatre, and *Tartuffe*, a few days later, only 32. On two occasions in June this latter comedy drew 91 and 84 spectators, while at another performance in this month *Le Misanthrope* was seen by only 170. In July *L'Ecole des femmes* was seen by a mere 99 spectators, and *Tartuffe* by 145. In the same month Racine's *Plaideurs*, played along with *Le Médecin malgré lui*, was seen by only 31 spectators. The Duke's order is dated 11 July 1746, and was made the day after *Tartuffe* had attracted only 145 spectators" (Lough 1957: 183).

play writing. In fact, his interest in the theater was short-lived, and resulted in no more than two plays, *Le Fils naturel* (1757) and *Le Père de famille* (1758), each accompanied by an analysis, respectively titled *Entretiens sur le fils naturel* (1757) and *De la Poésie dramatique* (1758). Probably because his first play was a flop, which folded after the first performance, and the second was successful only in the provinces (see Lough 1957: 251), Diderot soon gave up his theatrical career. No one who reads his plays today will lament Diderot's decision. In particular, *Le Père de famille* is marked by a stilted, sentimental tone that in no way contributes to the author's fame.

Though it is best to pass over Diderot's two plays in silence, the essays that accompanied them should not be disregarded. Both of them, particularly the first, were veritable manifestos, in which the author expressed his intention to fight for the renewal of the theater and explained how this should be done. Against conventional theater, respectful of decorum, Diderot proposed a realist program, which would arouse the interest of ordinary men: "Actual clothes, actual speech, a simple and natural plot. Our taste would indeed be degraded should such a spectacle affect us less than that of a man richly dressed, flaunting his jewels" (Diderot 1965a: 120). Further, the theme should be important, and the plot "simple, domestic, and close to real life" (p. 139). With these ingredients he intended to develop the *genre sérieux*. The new genre was to be placed between tragedy and comedy; it would avoid the classical prejudice of treating the two traditional genres as the depiction of nobles and humble folk, respectively, a prejudice that only Molière could not be accused of; and it would reject any approach that was not according to nature. For "painters and poets have the right to dare as much as they will; but this right does not extend to the license to fuse different species in a single individual" (p. 137).

What Diderot fails to add is that drama was to include, at least implicitly, the praise of bourgeois values. This is quite evident in the passage of *Le Fils naturel* in which Constance equates the justification of beauty with the need for virtue: "The effect of virtue in our souls is neither less necessary nor less powerful than that of beauty upon our senses" (Diderot 1819: 342). And in the short scene 5 of act 4, Clairville makes an explicit defense of the honesty of bourgeois life:

With my proud soul and my inflexible character, it is quite uncertain whether fortune will favor me as I need to be favored. What is achieved by scheming is quick but vile: by arms, glorious but slow: by talent, always difficult and paltry. There are other estates that lead to fortune quickly; but commerce is virtually the only one in which large fortunes are proportional to the work, the industry, the risks that make them honest. (P. 347)

Thus realism began its career as "progressive" art. It was, clearly, not just an aesthetic alternative—as we have seen, we cannot expect to find the absolute autonomy of the aesthetic in Diderot or any of his peers. It was equally clear that the play was linked to a social class whose ethos had not appeared onstage in the previous century. This connection is of decisive importance if we are to understand the restrictions to imagination that Diderot spells out in his statements. As in genre painting, imagination seemed to favor the marvelous, the trivial, even the frivolous, and thus did no more than provide entertainment or even encourage evasion. That is why, in *Entretiens*, Dorval, the character-author of *Le Fils naturel*, stresses the alleged factuality of his play: it was written by order of his father, who wished to see his entire family act out the drama of their lives. If the play had become somewhat autonomous as a work for the theater, it was only because his father died before he had time to finish writing it, and thus had to be replaced by an "actor." That is, Durval minimizes the theatrical "illusion" and emphasizes instead the staging of pure everyday existence. Thus if the actual events have suffered minor changes, he says, it was only in order to conform to the law of the three unities; and if a given passage seemed to be a particularly effective *coup de théâtre*, it was preserved solely for its strict factuality: "This is no fiction, but fact. For the good of the work, it was to be expected that things should have turned out quite differently" (Diderot 1965a: 92). It comes as no surprise, then, that Dorval is the real mouthpiece for the author's ideas.

Although Diderot himself is Dorval's interlocutor in *Entretiens*, his function is comparable to that of a prompter in today's theater: he merely suggests, hints, or provides Dorval with opportunities to say what he has to say. For this reason, Dorval's realist platform ultimately refers to nature. It is nature that separates what is proper from what is improper, what is adequate to the *genre sérieux* from what is no more than parasitic illusionism: "Dramatic art prepares incidents only for the purpose of concatenating them; and it concatenates them in its products only because that is how they are in nature. Art imitates even the subtle way in which nature conceals from us the connections between its effects (pp. 130–31). Dorval, Diderot's mask, even repeats almost literally one of the passages written in the entry "Encyclopédie": "There are no durable beauties but those that are based on the relations with the beings of nature" (p. 160). As is natural in a manifesto, the argument does not specify details and corollaries that might make the argument more complex and puzzle the reader. Thus the difference between Dorval's schematism and Diderot's realism is solely the result of a difference of expressive strategy. This much settled, it seems clear that the foundations of this realism also include the theorization of drama.

When one reads the *Salons* side by side with *Entretiens* and *De la Poésie dramatique*, one can see the difference between the developed version of a doctrine and a version of it aimed at the general public. The comparison between the two is revealing. It allows the analyst to understand better why Diderot saw fiction and imagination with such suspicion and why he commends history as the artist's guide:

> Poetry has been compared with painting, and with good reason; but a more useful and fruitful comparison would be that of history with poetry. This would provide more exact notions of the true, the verisimilar, and the possible; and thus the notion of the marvelous could be sharply and precisely defined, the marvelous being that which is common to all genres of poetry, and which few poets are in a condition to define properly. (P. 213)

For all the disguises that Diderot had learned to employ in his writing since he had been jailed for publishing his *Lettre sur les aveugles*, the direct, even schematic tone of the *Entretiens* and *De la poésie dramatique* could not have fooled his more perceptive readers. Perhaps the presence of noble characters in the two plays, M. D'Orbesson's condition as a rich bourgeois, and the aristocratic prejudice that made him demand that his son take up with a wealthy woman only are all intended to disguise the fact that the bourgeois ethos occupies a central position in the play. Perhaps, too, this disguise resulted from conformity to the taste of the time—John Lough observes that noble characters predominate in bourgeois drama even in the plays of such a consciously critical author as L. S. Mercier. Even if this is true, the disguise and the compliance were probably not enough to keep the aristocratic public and the critics who represented them from realizing the danger they were facing. A contemporary, Dominique-Joseph Garat, observed in his memoirs (which, it is true, were published only after the Revolution): "Tragedy was not supposed to be popular, for nature and the passions gave rise to so many tragical events among the people. . . . Poetics excluded the third estate from the tragic stage, just as the aristocracy excluded it from social honors. It was the same prejudice onstage and in the real world" (quoted in Lough 1957: 263–64). So that Diderot's failure as a playwright would seem to be a consequence both of his meager talent—surely he was no match for a Beaumarchais, whose *Mariage de Figaro* was to be a great box-office success—and of the pressure of the aristocratic public. But perhaps today we have yet another approach at our disposal.

If we admit that aristocratic control of art was partly the cause of the rejection of a proposal for a bourgeois aesthetics, was not the sort of drama that was then suppressed just as repressive? The reader of the present chapter is aware that this question is not new, and that it applies to both versions of Diderot's aesthetics—the developed one and the simplified one. In the former, control resulted from the subordination of beauty to truth, good, and usefulness. However, one might argue that the author carried out his investigation in such a radical manner that it became independent of the parameters it assumed. This argument is acceptable, particularly if we agree to eliminate not only the notion of service to truth but also the idea that art and beauty are synonymous. Not that Diderot himself ever did either one thing or the other; but a dedicated follower who adopted Diderot's radicalism might feel he had the right to go further than his master did. But what about the simplified, didactic version? One could also argue that the realistic drama he defended was justified both in terms of the struggle against the restrictions imposed by a status society and in terms of the wider expressive possibilities of art thus made possible. But a serious problem remains: how can we distinguish this realism from the limits that were imposed on it *from within*?

Indeed, this realism was identified with a class purpose, with the praise of its virtue and its professional honesty. Barthes once wrote, with his undeniable brilliance, that "it is not useful to say 'dominant ideology,' for this is a pleonasm: ideology is precisely the name given to an idea while it is dominant" (Barthes 1973: 53). Diderot's simplified aesthetics, at least, is a clear denial of this. Here is an ideology that at its time was dominated, and that nevertheless was just as controlling as the dominant ideology of its time. Classical control was based on a religious worldview. In order to vindicate art, one had to deny that it could be a center in its own right, and make it flexible and compliant with authorized truth. We have seen how, under Louis XIV, control slowly became secularized. During the period when the third estate had not yet taken over, it was in Diderot that the secular conception of art reached its most consistent formulation. But the controlling factor was retained.

It is hardly surprising that this fact was not evident at the time. George May, in a work that merits more praise than there is room for here, has shown that some time before the decades in which Diderot was active the novel as a genre had been violently attacked by the religious-aristocratic front. Both priests and aristocratic readers felt that its realism was offensive and threatening. In 1736, Père Porée called for rigorous repression of these fictions that "disturb men's spirits and fascinate their hearts." His diatribe was effective: "What makes Père Porée's speech exceptionally interesting is the fact that it came less than two years before an extraordinary legislative measure that seems to be its logical consequence: beginning in 1738, and in any case after 1737, publication of novels in France is submitted to exceptional measures that nearly amount to outright prohibition" (May 1963: 78).

Given these circumstances, Diderot's attacks on prevailing tastes, his defense of the dignity of the bourgeois family, his proscription of the burlesque and the marvelous, his defense of genius, the exceptional nature of which was based solely on itself, certainly sounded like liberating tactics, and that is what they were in fact. But with hindsight we see that, even though Diderot himself was unaware of it, they contained the germ of another form of control. Truth is never invoked without a purpose; it is always invoked, rightly or wrongly, in order to deny the right of what is opposed to it. The demand that human products be useful is only proclaimed when a clearly defined notion of usefulness is already in mind. The demand for the usefulness of art, as seen by the pragmatic bourgeois eye, could not but be transformed into a strict sort of pragmatism. In the heroic period of the class that it served, this pragmatism meant the defense of the self-made man and the struggle against the numerous aristocratic privileges. After its victory, it would mean no more than the subjection of art to the values imposed by the market. But if the pragmatic proposal was to succeed, it was necessary that the third estate destroy its rival first. In Diderot's lifetime, the control that was unconsciously proposed by him was confused with a dominated ideology, which was repressed by the implicit censorship mentioned in Garat's memoirs and the explicit censorship pointed out by May.

THE FORMS OF CONTROL

It would be a mistake to think that in France, in the latter half of the eighteenth century, the only conflict was that between the censorship of the *ancien régime* and the proposals of the Enlightenment. The root of the mistake is the confusion between Diderot's position and that of the philosophes in general. Among the latter, to begin with, there was no consensus. As to specific conceptions in the field of art, the contradiction is particularly evident in the disagreement between the Diderot who proposed the *genre sérieux* or who outlined the phenomenology of the actor in the *Paradoxe* and the Rousseau of *Lettre à M. d'Alembert* (1758) and the two prefaces to *La Nouvelle Héloïse*. Let us leave aside the specific circumstance that led Rousseau to write the *Lettre*—the publication of the article in which D'Alembert criticized the Geneva authorities for their recent prohibition of theatrical performances. Instead, I will concentrate on his central argument.

Rousseau is opposed to the notion that the theater can be morally useful. The theater, he says, has no power to change either feelings or customs, and the most it can do is follow them and beautify them. If he fails to obey this rule, the playwright will be left without a public. Since for this reason it is forced to reiterate values already in circulation, the theater is of no use whatsoever for the improvement of customs: "Thus the theater purges the passions one has not and promotes those one has" (Rousseau 1948: 28). Therefore, although D'Alembert believes he is working for the enlightenment of society, he is in fact making a fool of himself. Rousseau does not actually say as much, but he does what he can to ridicule his estranged friend. Not that he himself had grown disillusioned about his own long-fought campaign; it is only that he now acknowledged that the effectiveness of the political regeneration of nations depended on other instruments:

> I know of only three types of instruments with which one can affect the customs of a people, namely the force of laws, the empire of opinion, and the appeal of pleasure. Now, the laws have no access to the theater, for here the slightest pressure would arouse censure and not pleasure. Opinion, therefore, does not depend on it, for instead of making the law for the public, it receives it from the public; and as to the pleasure that can be found there, its full effect consists in making us return to it more often. (Pp. 28–29)

But Rousseau is not yet satisfied; he must proceed to demolish the theater utterly. His brilliant intelligence is coupled with his passionateness. Whereas the former trait might have allowed him to reach a view of art absolutely unique in his time, the latter truncated his argument and changed its direction. The two can be seen together in the following passage:

> The more I think about it, the more I am convinced that everything presented on the stage becomes not closer to us, but instead more distant. . . . If I were to enact an event that took place in Paris yesterday, I would think of myself in Molière's time. The theater has its rules, its maxims, its very own morals, as well as its language and its dress. It is rightly said that none of this is adequate to us, and that it would be just as ridiculous to adopt the virtue of its heroes as to speak in verse and dress in the Roman fashion. This, then, is almost the only use of all these noble feelings and all these glittering maxims that are so emphatically exalted: to be forever relegated to the stage and to show us virtue as a theatrical game, good for the amusement of the public, but which it would be folly to think of seriously transposing to society. Thus the most advantageous impression caused by the best plays lies in the reduction of all the duties of human existence to a few ephemeral, barren, and ineffective affections. (P. 34)

Rousseau understands that, in spite of the intentions of Diderot's bourgeois drama, the effect of the theater implies an immediate distancing. While the *genre sérieux* tried to win over its public by adopting themes, values, and a language closer to the bourgeois ethos, Rousseau realized that the plan was unworkable, for it was not adequate to theatrical space.

In this way, in place of imitation of reality, which would ultimately turn out to be illusory and conventional, the discovery of the distancing effect inherent in the theater might have led its author to conceive a theater different from the teary and moralizing efforts that characterized many of his contemporaries. Decades later, starting from a similar intuition, Nietzsche was to see the Greek chorus as an indicator of the separation between the area for the performance and the one reserved for the audience. And much later Brecht was to exploit this distancing to create a critical theater. I am mentioning these examples in order to emphasize the new trail that Rousseau opened but failed to explore. For his conclusion trivializes what he had been the first to see: because of the distancing that naturally occurs, the theater can only repeat what is already known.

It follows, then, that the theater should not be encouraged but rather suppressed, for its effect, if any, is to teach hypocrisy and propagate among people what should be kept hidden from them (see Rousseau 1948: 43). Hence Rousseau's conclusion: "I believe that these diverse considerations lead to the conclusion that the moral effect of spectacles and theaters can never be good or wholesome in itself: for even if one thinks of its advantages only, no sort of real usefulness can be found but contains inconveniences that override it" (p. 76).

What does the *Lettre à M. d'Alembert sur les spectacles* tell us? Besides highlighting the flagrant disagreement between Rousseau and his former associate Diderot, it shows us that the old control of poetry had not been exhausted, nor was it restricted to the defenders of the status quo. While the latter resorted to the police, appealed to the authorities, and wrote indignant accusations, in Rousseau control found an ally that would prove more efficient in the long run: the allegation that the theater was useless or even a bad example. If his attacks against the theater are compared with Diderot's defense of drama, it becomes clear that sometimes Rousseau's arguments demolish Diderot's contentions. Diderot recognized that imitation in art always contained an element of illusion; that the most accomplished of paintings was no more than "a tissue of falsities." Hence his attempt to cover the gap that separated the beautiful from the true, to conjoin them. Rousseau emphasized the same point, and—curiously assuming a much more rationalistic posture than Diderot—peremptorily proclaimed: "What matters the truth of imitation if illusion is present?" (p. 36). Fortunately for the philosophes, and unfortunately for art theory, the discussion was not taken up, Rousseau's attack being seen as the outcome of his recent quarrel with his former companions. In short, Rousseau remade the old control, furnishing it with new weapons.

Should we read the *Paradoxe sur le comédien* (1770) as a reply to Rousseau? Even if we don't have in mind an intentional reply, this hypothesis seems doubtful: the *Paradoxe* is not so much a philosophy of the theater as a phenomenology of the actor (and, ultimately, of the artist's work). Thus their perspectives are different. Besides, the *Paradoxe* does not stray from its author's philosophy of art. The relation between *Lettre à M. d'Alembert* and the aesthetics underlying the *Paradoxe* is, then, the opposition between two different tendencies in the sphere of control, one that takes up and renews the arguments of classical control and another that results from the emphasis on the bourgeoisie's pragmatic worldview.

The clash between the two forms of control becomes even more explicit in the two prefaces to *La Nouvelle Héloïse*. Since these texts had much more impact than the *Lettre*, my consideration of them here will certainly be far too skimpy. But the tone is so explicit that the reader can develop the argument.

The central problem in both texts is the same: what, after all, was Rousseau's role in relation to a novel of which he claimed to be no more than the editor? The issue would be only a curiosity if the author did not open the First Preface with the words: "Spectacles in large cities and novels are necessary for corrupted peoples" (Rousseau 1964a: 5). If the novel is aimed at corrupted audiences only, why should Rousseau be presenting a novel at all? Besides, since he claims to be the editor, what was his actual role in its making? The second paragraph of the First Preface both intensifies the problem and proposes the beginning of a solution for it: "Although I appear here as no more than the Editor, I have worked on this book myself, and I do not conceal this fact. Did I write all of it, and is the correspondence no more than a fiction? Why should you care, aristocrats? For you, it certainly is a fiction" (p. 5). For elegant society, it did not matter what "j'ai travaillé moi-même à ce livre" meant, for to them the book would be only "une fiction." For them, the noble cause would always be ruined. No, it had not been for such people that the book had been written; Rousseau must have been thinking of readers of another sort, like the characters of the novel themselves, "provincials—foreign, lonely, young, little more than children, who, in their romantic imaginations, take the honest deliria of their own brains to be philosophy" (p. 6). Only for those who are like them, who keep their distance from corrupted institutions and love nature, who deny glory and want peace, solitude, an egalitarian and simple life—only for these are works of imagination of any use (see Rousseau 1964b: 21).

For the two images of possible readers, the rejected and the cherished, are correlated with the negative and positive functions of imagination: "It is necessary that the writings of the Solitary speak the language of the Solitary.... When one aspires to glory, one must strive to be read in Paris; when one wishes to be useful, one must strive to be read in the province"

(p. 22). But his interlocutor seems to be particularly thickheaded, and he insists, as though he still failed to understand Jean-Jacques's point: "If all of this is no more than fiction, you have certainly made a bad book: but tell me that these two women really existed and I will reread this compilation for the rest of my life" (p. 29). However, Rousseau refuses to say he made up the whole book. According to his viewpoint, he is right. The tenor of his two prefaces may be summarized as follows: "Fiction is for corrupted minds. But there is a way to make it useful: to find readers as openhearted as I, who wrote the book." Thus one is faced with the same alternatives that will be offered in the *Confessions*: if the reader is as sincere and honest as the author, he or she will agree with him; if not, well . . .

The praise of feeling, of the *coeur mis à nu*, leads to the cult of sincerity. Only sincerity would be capable of redeeming fiction from its corrupted nature and making it useful. Thus control finds a different path. Only sincere expression could convert "letters" into "hymns."

If we want to check the impact of this sincere controller, we now have at our disposal the analysis of the correspondence of an actual—not at all ideal—reader (see Darnton 1984). From his analysis, the historian Robert Darnton concludes that "the quality of reading changed in a broad but immeasurable public toward the end of the Old Regime. Although many writers prepared the way for this change, I would attribute it primarily to the rise of Rousseauism. . . . His public probably applied an old style of religious reading to new material, notably the novel, which had previously seemed incompatible with it" (Darnton 1984: 251). Must I repeat that this new form of reading was new only to the extent that it legitimated a new control?

The discussion involving Diderot's ideas—whether directly or indirectly—did not end with the occasional clash with Rousseau's essay. Outside France, a lively debate was opened by Goethe. Indeed, Diderot's impact on Germany was comparable only to Rousseau's (see Mortier 1954). From Lessing to Hegel, by way of A. Schlegel, Schiller, and Goethe, besides dozens of publicists and minor writers, Diderot's example was imitated, criticized, praised, and reviled by the followers and opponents of the German *Aufklärung*. Among his admirers, none did more for him than Goethe, who translated *Le Neveu de Rameau* when the original text was still unpublished. But the role of an intellectual of Goethe's stature could not have been simply that of publicist. Goethe's partial translation of the *Essais sur la peinture* was accompanied by comments that deserve a more detailed examination. Since my interest here is to show how the author of *Faust* reacted to what I have interpreted as an implicit proposal for a new control over art, I will look at the fundamental passages only.

After translating the first paragraph of chapter 1 of the *Essais*, Goethe observes the following about the sentence "La nature ne fait rien d'incorrect": "One should rather say that nature is never correct! Correctness presupposes rules, and rules are established by man himself according to the feeling, the experience, the conviction and the pleasure, and concern the external appearance of a creature rather than its inner being: whereas laws, according to which nature acts, promote the strongest of organic cohesions" (Goethe 1954: 204). The author would probably not have emphasized his opposition were he not convinced that the concept of art always depended on its relations to nature. Thus, shortly after the passage quoted above, he adds:

> We should rather be concerned to present both [i.e., nature and art] separated in their results. Nature organizes a being indifferently alive, while the artist organizes one that is dead but meaningful—nature, a real being; the artist, an apparent being. Faced with works of nature, the spectator must himself invest them with importance, the ability of arousing feelings, thoughts, effects, and action in his own spirit; faced with works of art, he expects and deserves to find all of this already in them. An absolute imitation of nature is by no means possible; all the artist can be expected to do is to present the surface of a phenomenon. Why are artists needed? For externalization of the receptacle, for the throbbing whole, for that which speaks to all our spiritual and sensible forces, encourages our aspirations, elevates our spirit, in whose heritage we rejoice; for the life-force, for power, for the striving for perfection, for beauty. (P. 206)

We must then ask: if for Goethe (and also for Schiller) art does not imitate nature, where is its matrix? To which Goethe immediately replies: nature is in direct relation to knowledge, just as art is to pleasure. To subordinate art to nature, then, is to make the artist a collaborator of the scientist, whereas to associate it with pleasure is to place it in direct contact with the exploration of the individual's inner life:

> Yes, the artist must represent the external side of things [*das Aussere*]. But is the exteriority of an organic nature different from the ever-changing phenomenon of interiority? This external, superficial side is a multiple architecture, intricate, sensible, and intimate, so well adjusted as to change into an interiority, in which both inner and outer determinations maintain the most immediate relations, both in the state of greatest stillness and in that of greatest movement. (P. 217)

Since my point here is only the issue of control, we can now take another step forward. Clearly, Goethe did not accept the search for a reconciliation of truth (represented by the laws of nature) and the mode of being of art. It is just as clear that for him it was not enough—as it was for Diderot—to laugh at academic painting and suggest that live models be used: "To the painter, a live model is no more than a raw material, which he should not take as his limit but rather aspire to elaborate" (p. 219). His path is the opposite of Diderot's: art can find its true subject matter only in the exploration of man's interiority. And here it has no limits. Thus Goethe—like Schiller and the young Friedrich Schlegel, not to mention Kant's third critique—provides foundations not for a new control, but for the autonomy of art. And because, since the Brazilian edition of *Control of the Imaginary* (1984), I have been concerned with showing the metamorphoses of an ever-present control, it might seem that I have finally found the source that has nourished me all along.

But this is not the case. Not that I intend to deny the importance of the affirmation of the autonomy of art, an achievement—at least in intellectual terms—of German poets and philosophers. Perhaps the fact that they belonged to a backward nation, where the bourgeoisie could not possibly dislodge the inheritors of feudal privileges, indirectly made German thinkers see that the fictional would gain nothing with the hoped-for redemption of society through the victory of bourgeois ideas; perhaps, also, the fact that German intellectuals changed their view of the libertarian ideals of 1789 in the light of Napoleonic expansionism led them to adopt a concept of autonomy of art with an intimist and compensating orientation. Let us develop these provisional considerations a bit further, considering a recent essay by Jochen Schulte-Sasse.

The author observes that, because of the divisions of modern society already apparent by the early decades of the eighteenth century, new subsystems arose to satisfy differentiated social functions; in particular, the aesthetic subsystem had a basic compensating function. It should not be thought that Schulte-Sasse naively supposes that before the rise of the complexities of modern society there was an effective integrating wholeness; what he is saying is that the fragmented life of the present projected onto the past the ideal of unification. This experience and the project that resulted from it, then, explain why literature became a means for the actualization of feelings, emotions, and the organization of nature (see Schulte-Sasse 1985: 112). Thus Diderot's forebears, like Adam Fergusson and Charles Du Bos, on the one hand, and Diderot himself and the writers directly influenced by him, such as Lessing in *Hamburgische Dramaturgie*, on the other, all contributed to the creation of the compensating subsystem known as the field of aesthetic experience, based on the program of the Enlightenment. In other words, both the proponents of the new control (a concept that Schulte-Sasse does not use) and its opponents, German idealists, all ended up contributing to the same mystifying, unsatisfactory solution.

Thus summed up, the thesis, from a different angle than the one I have adopted, seems to reinforce an aspect that had been latent all the while.

To give historical treatment to the control that art has been submitted to does not mean that, after a given moment, such control will be found lacking. The "autonomy" of art was not socially accepted, except under the supposition that the role of literature was that of "*a means of mediating between the official view of the world* and the individual concept of new societies as the fulfillment of the promise of the Enlightenment, on the one hand, and among the reader's disparate everyday experiences (which diverge from one another)" (Gumbrecht 1985: 7). Now, this proposal assumed the effective implementation of tolerance, to be achieved in liberal society. But this was never actualized, for all the official statements of the spokesmen for the status quo. Thus it would be a mistake to suppose that the issue of control is now merely a historical question, or one that is relevant only in totalitarian countries. In liberal democracies, art is no longer officially controlled: it is simply included in a law common to all of society, which Marcuse called "repressive tolerance" (see Marcuse 1965: 96). That is why the concern with control does not reflect a merely historical interest. Having suffered one more metamorphosis, control is still alive. And now its irreducible feature is clearly shown: its political character.

The final pages of this chapter have taken a wild leap, vertiginous if not unjustified. My intention here—and once again let me stress the obviously provisional character of these pages—has been to show how close the question of control in the Enlightenment is to our contemporary scene. Elsewhere I have mentioned this fact, and criticized Theodor Adorno and Max Horkheimer for postulating a unanimity in the *Aufklärung* that depicted the differences among its participants as indistinct or secondary (see Adorno and Horkheimer 1986). In this chapter, I have tried to highlight these differences and provide as illustration a specific question posed by a single author. For if on the one hand Diderot contributed to the pragmatic and bourgeois control of art, on the other he also helped to locate it, through his doubts, waverings, and contradictory formulations. Thus the case of Diderot stands as a counterexample to Adorno and Horkheimer's excessively univocal conclusion. At the same time, by observing that the new control has come to depend less on a theory than on the way liberal political power deals with information, and by mentioning in passing the role of the monopolistic media, I have tried to drive home the point that the power of present-day control of the fictional is indistinguishable from the pervading, invisible control exerted over all of society.

But I will shy from such a conclusion, lest I compromise an investigation whose object is already far too wide. Let me then state a more modest conclusion: the control of the fictional seems to determine the character of fictional discourse. In Western modernity, fictional discourse, for all the praise lavished upon writers by governments and institutions, has always swum against the stream. Critical but unable to be doctrinaire, given the very limits of the discourse that mediates it, the fictional is useful to the extent that it cannot be useful, and is good for society to the extent that it has no programs to offer society. To see fiction, then, as the antagonist of an ever-changing control is not to sanctify it. Like all discourse, fictional discourse has its limits. To recognize its positivity, the critical spirit that develops in reaction to the very control to which it is submitted, is not necessarily to see it as a redeeming discourse. This would be to mystify it once more.

CHAPTER SIX

An Approach to Jorge Luis Borges

For Flora Süssekind

BORGES THE CONTROLLED AND BORGES THE CONTROLLER

The object of the present chapter is to examine Borges's prose from a single angle: its relation to the mechanisms of control of the fictional. My idea, then, is to make a cross section, with a single goal in mind, leaving aside everything else—admittedly a dangerous undertaking when dealing with such a complex writer. Though aware of the risks, I believe I am justified in adopting such an approach, since no attempt will be made to present an exhaustive appreciation of one of the best writers in the contemporary scene; I will concentrate on a rereading of his work in the light of the problems discussed in this book.

Two analyses will be undertaken: of a Borges whom the critics attempted to control, through substantive restrictions or even outright denial; and of another Borges who allows a reading according to his controlling manner.

The first analysis will come as no surprise to those who are aware of the prevailing ideas in Latin America. Although it seems interesting to link it with the problem of the control of the fictional and to bring to light what this control is (and was) exerted in the name of, the approach itself will not be particularly novel. But the second analysis is a different case. Borges the controller? The question immediately arises: Controller of what? Of the countless mediocrities that pop up and fizzle out in the international literary scene? If this were what I had in mind, the term would be incorrect; "asepsis" would surely be a better word than "control." But here there would be a different sort of difficulty: it would be arbitrary to attribute such a role to Borges only, for every work of quality inhibits those that are weaker, so that their fame gradually fades away. But "control" here is no misnomer. The second analysis will indeed treat Borges as the creator of a controlling work. If this proposition is to be taken as more than just a provocation, it will be necessary to turn to an internal analysis of Borges's poetics, its guidelines, the configurations it determines. Only then will the notion of controlling prose be seen as an idea with no sensationalist intent.

EARLY RECEPTIONS OF BORGES

In 1923 Borges published his first book, *Fervor de Buenos Aires*, a volume of poems, and two years later he made his debut as an essayist with *Inquisiciones*, a book he was later to repudiate. From the very beginning he aroused disparate reactions. Throughout the 1920's he was praised by Gómez de la Serna, Valéry Larbaud, and P. H. Ureña, among others, and he was awarded a literary prize in 1929; but most critics and reviewers reacted with irritation. What was so irritating about the young writer? Let us begin with a passage by an essayist who was always an enthusiastic defender of Borges. In a 1930 article, Nestor Ibarra, among sensible and perceptive observations, wrote the following:

In the last analysis, his lucidity in scrutinizing every hidden delusion, his sensuality as a gourmet of subtleties, a connoisseur of every hidden reticence, every delightful renouncement, irrevocably alienate him from his country, to such an extent that one wonders whether this Byzantine, this *précieux*, this near narcissist, is, for all his talent, what this country essentially needs. (Quoted in Bastos 1974: 91)

In an earlier passage of the same article, Ibarra observes that Borges "fabricates a country for himself, with which he is content." In Latin America, where the documentalist tradition was the most prestigious variety of essentialism (*argentinidad*, *mexicanidad*, etc.), to question a writer's national spirit was tantamount to denouncing him. To be sure, this was not Ibarra's tone, nor was his observation unfounded. But soon the point he had raised gave rise to other kinds of criticism.

In 1933 Anderson Imbert accused Borges of not being "even remotely a national critic or thinker" (quoted in Bastos 1974: 113), and added that for these two reasons persons like him "are absent from the country" (p. 114). In the same year, R. Doll went further, saying that Borges's prose was un-Argentinian! Why? Doll's argument is worth recalling:

First, because of his lack of affective tone, for whoever prefers, like him, to freeze one's entrails and mind rather than run the risk of betraying his emotions in a platitude or an overly revealing sentence may be influenced by the best European writers, but will never write an Argentinian page, with all its flaws, but with its charms too. His whole frigid expression, from which all emotion is deliberately anesthetized as soon as it is detected, is in fact an obsessive avoidance of platitudes, but to the detriment of the most genuine and authentic impulses of the self. It is an unfortunate sacrifice to petty literary concerns. If, then, we try to find our [Argentine] expression in Borges, we will find in his prose nothing but an intellectual wilderness, devoid of vital fluids or nourishment. (Doll 1978: 67)

Is such a criticism, based on an aesthetics of feeling, related to the documentalist criterion? Let us recall that, as I have said, documentalism is a variant of national essentialism (see Chapter 4, above). Let us also recall that the champion of sentimental aesthetics himself wrote that "if novels offered their readers nothing but pictures of objects around them, duties they could do, pleasures of their condition, novels would not drive them mad, but instead would make them wiser" (Rousseau 1964b: 21–22). However, the best justification of the link between sentimentality and documentalist aesthetics is to be found in a 1948 article by a no less inflamed critic, H. A. Murena:

The nationalist will, which demands that the "truly" national be dealt with and consequently involves turning to the past, the caudillo, the gaucho, the *compadrito*, or to traditional forms of interpreting the present, implies a reduction and impoverishment of the forms of present reality, forcing them into the narrow mold of past types; it implies denying the possibility of facing one's surroundings without prejudices, denying the possibility of experiencing the feeling that one's surroundings elicit, namely, the national feeling. (Murena 1980: 80–81)

Thus Murena felt that Borges's fixation on the past made him unable to see—that is, document—the forms of the present, and thus share in the national feeling!

How did Borges's defenders react to the accusations of documentalist essentialists? To one of the most illustrious of the defenders, the author of *Inquisiciones* showed "an orientation . . . new in Spanish, geared toward stylistics" and a "natural philosophical bent" (Ureña 1980: 29–30); and in a rare passage, Amado Alonso, discussing the story "Hombre de la esquina rosada," made a fine distinction between *costumbrista* documentalism and the transfiguration of orality: "Local color? The poetic problem posed and aptly solved here is a different one: it is that of achieving the feel of spoken language while at the same time preserving the highest literary dignity" (Alonso 1976: 51).

Their relative value aside—to say that Borges emphasizes stylistic procedures is to say very little of his creative process, whereas to speak of the transfiguration of facts and accidents is to address a characteristic of his that was to become increasingly evident—these arguments were too "literary" to carry much weight against the passionate "evidence" presented by Borges's adversaries. While the praise—whether appropriate or inept—was based on careful appraisal, the criticism was as roughshod as political invective. Whereas Ureña and Alonso saw the literary text as something that required a specific form of reading, the dominant tone of Latin-American literary criticism at the time was hardly different from that prevailing in campaign speeches. From the beginning, Borges disturbed the inheritors of the Latin-American tradition of romantic Enlightenment. Zealously guarding the fatherland and the "national feeling," this tradition quite justifiedly saw Borges as a threat and a challenge to the sort of banal allegory that it privileged. Therefore he was accused of neglecting native peculiarity, which must be felt and documented forever. Since he could not be accused of writing bad Spanish—another argument commonly wielded by traditional critics—he had to be banished from the circle of the elect for an even graver sin: Borges was a sheep whose color was not the same as that of the rest of the fold.

If as late as the 1940's this sort of criticism was still being made, the popularization of existentialism after the war made it somewhat unfashionable. It was Adolfo Prieto who refurbished the traditional line of attack, with the publication in 1954 of a short essay, significantly titled *Borges y la nueva generación* (Borges and the New Generation). The arguments set forth in this book came to have a numerous progeny. The forceful tone was evident from the prologue. Although by then Borges had already published *Historia universal de la infamia* (1935), *Historia de la eternidad* (1936), and, most importantly, *Ficciones* (1944) and *El Aleph* (1949), Prieto wrote, with a conviction that admitted no opposition: "Like Lugones, Borges is more a literary presence than the author of a work with intrinsic value" (Prieto 1954: 14). And he justified his evaluation by pointing to Borges's lack of contact with reality and his "absolute neglect of man." Borges's form, he adds, offers a specific kind of wonderment, the wonderment of emptiness. And his reflections involve nothing worthy of note (p. 20): "The stories and tales afford no more than amusement during the time spent in their reading. (I leave aside the metaphysical questions and theological entertainments, as well as the valuable task of popularizing foreign literatures.)" In addition, Prieto is annoyed with "the poet's impassive, watchful attitude, always standing on the sidelines of his subject, duly noting down external circumstances with the scrupulousness of a novelist" (p. 53).

Such remarks suggest that literacy is a much more restricted phenomenon than UNESCO statistics indicate. But *Borges y la nueva generación* was received so enthusiastically that the foreign reader may come to doubt his own understanding. We are too deeply involved to settle the issue.

In 1955, in an article the very title of which—"Borges y la nueva generación"—is an homage to Prieto, J. C. Portantiero shows how his master's idea has fallen on fertile ground: "Borges is, consciously, the literary provider of an entire elite, more or less connected with our cattle-raising aristocracy" (Portantiero 1980: 84). But he was not the only one to learn the lesson. In 1957, in "La imagen colonizada de la Argentina," J. J. Hernández Arregui linked Borges's lack of humanness (the influence of existentialism seemed to boil down to the call for humanity) and *argentinidad* to the cowardliness of a rootless elite: "Borgismo, as a literary tendency, is the manifestation of a superficial society whose culture is the epiphenomenon of a smug colonial financierism" (Arregui 1978: 110). The word "epiphenomenon" refers us to the well-known reflex theory, which can always be resorted to in order to set up the most unlikely connections. It is not at all surprising that the authors who use it do not take the trouble to mention it: since it is a presupposition of the old nineteenth-century documentalism, they could expect their readers to make the necessary association without the need for bibliographical references.

The reader, however, may feel I am handpicking representatives of the ever-present documentalism. For outside of Argentina who ever heard of the critics I have mentioned? The case of Ernesto Sábato shows that Borges's opponents were not necessarily stupid, and—what is surprising—that those who could not possibly be so labeled used the same arguments. Given its unexpectedness, the passage in question by the famous novelist deserves a wider circulation, for it highlights the importance of humanistic criticism in this context. In any case, in one aspect, at least, Sábato's criticism differs from those of the authors quoted above: he has actually read the texts he is discussing. Indeed, Borges's "fictions" seem to inhabit a *topos uranos*, devoid of human beings; I agree, too, that his literature contains a metaphysics only apparently; and it is just as evident his theology is that of a man who aims at nothing more than using it as the stuff of "a precious literature." Having established these points, Sábato joins the ranks of Borges's critics: it all points to a simulacrum, perhaps an infamous one: "And the dramas in which men of flesh and blood struggle and die, in the midst of chaos and contingency, are replaced by beautiful tales reminiscent of theorems" (Sábato 1980: 137). This much is clear to Sábato: a literature that does not focus on man and his misery—in short, a literature of *unbelief*—may well be precious, but none the less blameworthy for it. The novelist's intelligence arrives at arguments that Prieto himself never spelled out.

I am aware that my task is not an easy one. How, indeed, can one not feel indignant about the above-mentioned aspects of Borges? That here was a real problem, at least for the critical current in question, is indirectly shown by an essayist with no immediate political concerns. In her stylistic analysis of Borges, Ana Maria Barrenechea found it necessary to "destroy this nihilistic view" that her own study had been leading to (Barrenechea 1956: 144). No matter that she failed in this; her achievement is still important to the extent that it highlights the common assumption that good fiction must necessarily be in the service of mankind. What both this well-meaning defender of Borges and Sábato fail to question is why this should be so; that is, why the service rendered by fiction should be to deny nihilism and affirm some belief. True, every endeavor with an Olympic or godlike orientation is unpleasant. But why should the axiomatic apriorism of "humanists" be less obnoxious? They start from the assumption that the manipulation of cardboard figures—instead of flesh-and-blood creatures—by an unbelieving mathematician will lead to a "precious literature," where the adjective has a clearly derogatory sense. Thus the praise of man, the struggle against poverty, cruelty, and torture turns out to function as a form of control of literary production. No distinction is made between ethics and fiction; in both, the same sort of evaluation is employed. Sábato would certainly agree that good intentions alone do not justify a work of literature, but he would counter that lack of interest in the suffering of mankind certainly disqualifies it.

This discussion is to be expected here: the works of Borges arouse radical responses in their readers. In some, it is the radicalism of stupidity; in others, a radicalism that brings hidden assumptions into the open. In either case, regardless of the degree of intelligence involved, the situation is the same: in the name of a certain conviction, a conscious or unconscious attempt is made to control the fictional, and authors are told that this or that practice is objectionable because it disregards the national feeling or—more directly—the life of the population. A man of letters through and through, Borges challenges his readers to disclose their most cherished hidden assumptions. These, when revealed, throw into relief the mechanisms of control of the fictional that are in effect in Latin America to this day. (Much the same is true of Guimarães Rosa and Lezama Lima, official praise of their work notwithstanding.) Thus, from Anderson Imbert to Ernesto Sábato, regardless of the intellectual distinction of the critic, we see the metamorphoses undergone by Latin-American control of the imaginary, which has constantly remained in a central position. And this constant presence is all the more effective where it is least affirmed and where the axioms on which it is based are most "indisputable."

Now that scientism—like science itself—is being increasingly questioned, documentalism is seen either as outdated or, more commonly, as requiring a different kind of justification. So the old aesthetics of expression is once again revived, with the requirement—in the case of Borges's critics—that literary works should depict man. As often happens in areas where critical reflection is of little use, existentialism has been used here as a way of keeping the old Rousseauist position alive. Where the control of the fictional still holds, its manifestations can assume a wide range of forms, as we have seen. But the result of this control is always the same.

In short: an examination of Argentine responses to Borges shows that the persistence of nineteenth-century evaluative standards led either to a refusal to see him as an Argentine writer, and hence as a writer at all, or to a denial of the value of a literature that does not defend human values. In both cases, a certain a priori assumption is seen as unquestionable.

In the first case, the proposition, simply stated, is this: literature is not literature if it is not the expression of a nation. In theoretical terms, this statement harks back either to the romantic *Volkgeist* or to the various determinisms that eventually converge in the reflection theory. In the second case, the proposition is no less clear: unless it is dedicated to man as an instrument for his advancement, literature is an idle, even nefarious, pastime. In theoretical terms, this proposition is immediately linked to a reading of Sartre, and, more remotely, both to Rousseau and to the Christian tradition. History shows us that both propositions, for all the good intentions involved, have served as a basis for effective modalities of control. The first can be seen in the secularized control that began in the Enlightenment, whereas the second and older proposition was the basis for religious control, which prevailed up to the beginning of the Renaissance.

Following the plan outlined at the beginning of this chapter, I have now concluded the easiest stage of my undertaking. Now I must face a harder task. In order to arrive at the (paradoxical?) notion of Borges as controller, I will have to watch my step carefully. First of all, it will be necessary to take a cursory glance at the history of Christian heretical sects—specifically, Gnostic thought.

BORGES AND GNOSTICISM

This theme will not come as a surprise to the reader of Borges who remembers the frequent references to Basilides, occasional mention of Carpocrates and Valentinus, as well as specific references to gnosis and gnosticism in the earliest classical source on the sect: Irenaeus's *Adversus haereses*. However, aware of Borges's numerous "frauds," the reader may have taken these references as deceptive or even outright false. Such suspicions are unfounded; the summary of Basilides's doctrine presented in "Una vindicación del falso Basílides" (in *Discusión*) is in fact historically exact.

Just as authentic is the content of Borges's earliest reference to gnosticism, however unexpected its occurrence in the biography of Evaristo Carriego: "They are not puzzled by evil, nor do they indulge in speculation as to its origin; for the Gnostics have settled this issue directly by postulating a decadent or worn-out deity, improvising this world with adverse material" (Borges 1980: 54–55). Before the relevance of all this can be made clear, let us briefly summarize the Gnostic position.

The propagation of Christianity began at the same time as the reemergence of the Orient. The death of the ancient world was characterized by the decline of philosophical Logos and its replacement by religiously oriented conceptions. In the late Hellenistic phase, philosophical reason and its universalist orientation gave way to the resurgence of the East and the growing importance of myths in their religious function. This vogue of Orientalism contaminated the Hellenized world, and was, according to Hans Jonas, typically concerned with the salvation of man, the proposal of a transcendental concept of God, and the postulation of "a radical *dualism* of realms of being—God and the world, spirit and matter, soul and body, light and darkness, good and evil, life and death—and consequently an extreme polarization of existence affecting not only man but reality as a whole" (Jonas 1963: 31–32). It was in this period, particularly from the second century to the fourth, that Gnostic groups proliferated. This is not the place to examine the divergences among them or the different theses that have been put forth concerning their origins and the influences they suffered. Instead, I will concentrate on a few specific points.

First, with the dogmatization of Christian theology, its expounders found it necessary to rid biblical language of its mythical ballast. As Hans Blumenberg has written: "Thus the dogmatization of Christian theology, out of fear of contact with myth's orientation by means of images, produced a language different from the biblical one. Its consistency—consistency being the primary value in a structure of dogma—was achieved through the taking over, which was not concluded until the High Middle Ages, of ancient metaphysics" (Blumenberg 1985: 183). Gnosticism, on the other hand, even when it incorporated portions of the Greek heritage, particularly Platonism, remained firmly rooted in mythical narrative.

Second, Gnostic texts often include versions of myths that contradict their biblical counterparts. (Dogmatic theology and gnosticism are opposed to each other both in their respective approaches to myth and as to the versions of the mythical narrative that the former tolerates and the latter elaborates.) A good example of the extent to which these two versions could clash is the scene of the Fall. For the Ophites, the serpent was not responsible for man's expulsion from paradise, as Genesis has it. On the contrary, the so-called paradise had been reserved for man by the evil God, and what the serpent did was to confer on man the capacity for recognition (gnosis) of the divine spark—that is, the presence of *Deus alienus*—in himself. (The discovery of the Nag Hammadi Gnostic texts in 1945 brought to light the Apocryphon of John, containing the counterversion of the Jewish myth of the Fall.)

Third, for all of the differences among the many Gnostic sects—gnosticism never aspired to the status of a church—there is a characteristic common to all: the idea that the world was created by an inferior, antagonistic, and rebellious power, without the knowledge of the true God, who is not responsible for Creation. Out of the absolute God, devoid of any anthropomorphic trait, luminous beings had been born, such as Christ and Sophia. Now, Sophia, without the consent of the Spirit, her spouse, "wanted to bring forth a likeness out of herself" (*Apocryphon of John*: 104). Sophia's divine power and her spouse's disapproval had the combined effect: her will was done, but "a thing came out of her, which was imperfect and different from her appearance" (p. 104). Thus was born the archon one of whose names is Yaldabaoth. Out of the divine power he inherited from his mother he created "the likeness of the cosmos" (p. 105) and the angels destined to rule over it and to aid him in the creation of man. But as an inferior deity, Yaldabaoth unwittingly introduced in his creature something of the image of *Deus alienus*, which was reflected on water. Like the world itself, man was born of an error. Unlike the world, however, man is not irrevocably lost. For a repentant Sophia asked the absolute God that her sin be absolved. Yaldabaoth was tricked, and the emissaries of *Deus alienus* told him: "Blow into man's face something of your spirit and his body will arise" (p. 109). So it was that something of divine power penetrated the human creature, which could thus undo the mistake that had brought about its creation.

It was only then that the real struggle began. Yaldabaoth, after begetting Eve, implanted sexual desire in her and possessed her, engendering countless bodies prone to evil. There is a struggle for man, in man. Yaldabaoth and the angels who serve him try to preserve their control over their creation. Sophia, on the other hand, redresses her mistake. If the evil fruit, man, still has the ability to recognize the divine spark that the evil demiurge unwittingly blew into him, his body, like all matter, the cosmos and all it contains, is doomed to eternal perdition. According to the Apocryphon of John, "the spirit which originates in matter . . . is the ignorance of darkness and desire" (p. 110). And the *Gnostic Treatise on Resurrection* puts it even more aptly: since time is the category of the world and matter, it too is doomed to disappear, and therefore the world and time are simulacra and not real things. Thus "one ought to maintain that the world is an apparition, rather than resurrection" (*Gnostic Treatise*: 27).

In short, for the Gnostics the creation of the cosmos and man presents a radical duality: the Supreme Power, unnamed, external to time and space, the source of good and truth, is not responsible for our existence or all we know through our senses. Unlike *hyle* (matter), however, we have a chance to attain salvation, ascend through the concentric heavenly spheres—365 of them, according to Basilides—where the archons stand guard in order to keep us prisoners, and return to the Father, whose spark was inadvertently conferred upon us. This is the task of gnosis—to preach contempt for the perishable world, to deny the desires of the body, so that the psyche can return to its original dwelling-place. Thus the affairs of the world are to be despised. Just as time is a phantasm and not a real category, the sexual drive is also the phantasmal offspring of matter. Hence the two attitudes assumed by Gnostics toward sex: they either propose absolute abstinence from it, or else regard it with absolute indifference as something unworthy of attention or even as a power that must be expended by every conceivable form of promiscuity. Thus the followers of Nicolaus taught "that fornication is a matter of indifference and that one should eat the meats sacrificed to the idols" (Irenaeus 1961: 43).*

Fourth, an observation of Blumenberg's must also be considered in this summary, the only purpose of which is to provide a basis for a discussion of Borges:

> Gnosticism had been the most pronounced example of a nonmoral conception of the world. It has no need of the concept of freedom because in place of an intra-subjective decision between good and evil it provides the idea of a cosmic contest. If what is at stake in this contest is parts of the good that have fallen under the sway and the deluding influence of the powers of the world, then from the perspective of dualism this is only an episode. In relation to man's interest in salvation, the cosmic procedure is only a transaction surrounding him [*Rahmenhandlung*], whose reliability thus determines whether the event of the turning takes place, whether the recall arrives [*ob das Ereignis der Wendung stattfindet, ob der Rückruf ankommt*]. (Blumenberg 1985: 187)

As these observations make clear, the relation between man and his actual creator is not the ultimate key to our fate. On the contrary, we would be inevitably doomed if we could not see ourselves as the fruit of a struggle for which we are not responsible. Good and evil battle each other not in our hearts, but above our heads. Thus the world is none of our concern; our true concern is to distance ourselves from it. Whatever we do, evil lives within us; and, given the mythico-cosmic struggle that

---

*However, a specialist in gnosticism, Henry Chadwick, denies the contention, commonly accepted from Irenaeus on, that licentiousness was a rule often observed by Gnostics (see Chadwick 1980: 7).

rages above us, we are not guilty. The stern and revengeful God of the Old Testament has nothing to do with *Deus alienus*; Yaweh is seen as the incarnation of the inferior deity who created us. Since we are a priori free from guilt, our task is to find the way to free ourselves from the error that brought about our existence. And the power of the agents responsible for it is such that no human court could ever judge them. Human salvation, in short, consists in escaping the catastrophe associated with matter.

One final observation is in order. Both Jonas and Blumenberg emphasize the importance of myth in Gnostic thought. And Gershom Scholem writes: "Gnosticism, one of the last great manifestations of religious thought, conceived at least in part as a reaction against the Jewish conquerors of myth, bequeathed its language to Jewish mystics" (Scholem 1978: 119). What makes this quotation relevant here is its reference to the cabala. As Scholem observes, gnosticism exerted a powerful influence on Jewish cabalists, since they were also opposed to theological rationalism and favored a mythical reading of the sacred texts: "In the *Zohar* and in Isaac Luria, Gnostic and quasi-Gnostic symbols became for pious orthodox cabalists the deepest expression of their Jewish faith. In its first and crucial thrust the cabala was a mythical reaction in an area that monotheistic thought was clearing of myth with great difficulty" (pp. 118–19).

But none of this would be relevant here if Borges did not make frequent references to the cabala. Take, for instance, the poem "El Golem," included in *El otro, el mismo* (1964). What can these allusions to cabalistic elements and Gnostic formulae possibly mean? It would be ludicrous to suggest that Borges was an adept of either. At this point, it is worth quoting what Borges himself wrote on the subject, in "Una vindicación de la Cabala": "I do not want to vindicate the doctrine, but rather the hermeneutic or cryptographical procedures that lead to it" (Borges 1980, 1: 143). For him, the cabala and gnosticism were relevant as mythical means for his fiction, to provide him ammunition against a literary tradition based on a Logos that harks back to the Enlightenment rather than to Greece. As is well known, the Enlightenment set out to quash every kind of mythical infiltration. This struggle was associated with the emphasis on the idea of time as progress, and history as the field where reason proves itself and advances. And although the ideas of time and history no longer carry the same associations, the permanence of the Enlightenment in much of contemporary thought is also manifested in the suspicious attitude toward myth (see Blumenberg 1985, esp. pp. 34–57).

From the beginning Borges was interested in gnosticism and the cabala for the opposite reason: as stimuli for a literature against the grain, against the dogma of reason and feeling, against its optimistic view of historical time and in favor of a conception that sees time as having a mythical core. But this is still hardly enough. What, in fact, does it mean to say that a certain fiction, that of Borges, is rooted in myth? I will postpone the answer to this question. Right now, I would like to focus on one more aspect of the Gnostic tradition.

In a bold text, Harold Bloom establishes an opposition between two views of the meaning of texts, one originating in the heritage of Greek philosophy, the other in gnosticism. Both the Platonic and the Aristotelian traditions set out from the assumption that "literary texts were analogous to their interpretations, and since the Greek 'analogy' means an 'equality of ratios,' such an assumption allowed a literary text the status of a unity that might have a fixed meaning" (Bloom 1980: 66). As long as it was correct, the interpretation did not affect the unity of the original, the meaning of which was seen as constant. Textual univocity thus legitimated a priori the notion of a canon, so that divergent interpretations were branded as heterodox or even heretical. In other words, the written text contained a *single* truth, and the authorized interpretation was the one that brought it out, highlighting its contours. The assumption of cosmic harmony—an argument Bloom does not use—was implicit in this conception of correct reading. (Needless to say, it also potentially favored the principle of control and the consequent formation of various dogmas.)

The notion of reading that Bloom extracts from the most important of the Gnostics is precisely the opposite: "For Valentinus, the Demiurge is a liar, whose lie is both *about* Eternity and also *against* Eternity. Valentinus, in opposition, also lies, but his lie is not *about* time, but rather *against* time" (p. 67). The consequences of these opposing views of reading are evident. The immediate effect is that parody, appropriation, "counterfeiting," made-up sources are condemned by the view that favors the canon of faithfulness and made possible by the opposite view. For the moment, let us leave it at that. Later on in this chapter we will return to this question in greater detail.

The above summary allows us to take a small step forward. Gnosticism provides Borges with the assumptions requisite for a new fabulation; we see this, even before his memorable tales, in the closing passage of one of his versions of Zeno's paradox, "Avatares de la tortuga":

"The greatest wizard," Novalis memorably writes, *"would be one whose wizardry were such that he took his own phantasmagorias to be autonomous apparitions. Is not this our own case?"* I believe it is so. We (the undivided deity acting within us) have dreamed the world. We have dreamed it as resistant, mysterious, visible, ubiquitous in space, and stable in time; but in its architecture we allowed faint and eternal crevices of unreason, that we might know it is false. (Borges 1980, 1: 204)

Borges's gloss identifies us with the deity and makes the world a creation of the deity's (our) dream. The Gnostic stamp is evident in the negativity with which the created world is invested. But this is all. This version of gnosticism would not have been recognized by the Gnostics. To place the deity within ourselves is to identify it with us, and thus to discard from the outset the possibility of ascending through the concentric heavens of our prison. Besides, the entire Gnostic myth has been inverted here. We dream the world as ubiquitous and stable, if not good; its unreasonableness is indicated solely by tenuous threads. Borges not only breaks the link between classical Logos and Christian redemption but also eliminates the *religious* tenor of gnosticism. No communion is possible, only the acknowledgment of the bad product of a dream, an acknowledgment reached by the unreason that insinuates itself and gives the lie to what is dreamed. Nothing could be more alien to Borges than any kind of religiousness. Thus, as Paul de Man has observed, to compare his tales to Kafka's parables is misguided. Borges's characters are not the dwellers of a castle looking for its key; they live in an unending labyrinth, at the bottom of which Asterión or the detective Erik Lonrot find nothing but death. Religiousness is reduced to nothingness or to aesthetics. Aesthetics is the antidote to nothingness.

This aesthetic reduction allows Borges to revisit the story of Judas and propose a new interpretation for it. Judas's betrayal, he writes, is not well explained. You don't need a traitor to identify a man who preaches openly. It is even more unlikely that a chance denunciation should have determined "the most precious event in the history of the world." Thus, "Nils Runeberg" concludes that "it was a predetermined fact with its mysterious place in the economics of redemption" (Borges 1980, 1: 516). Relying on an authority who is in fact a character of his own invention, Borges, like the Gnostics, distorts the evangelical interpretation. But he goes one beyond the Gnostics when he makes Judas indifferent not only to the fate of the flesh, which is doomed in any case, but also to that of the spirit: "The ascetic, for the greater glory of God, debases and mortifies the flesh; Judas did the same to the spirit. He renounced honor, good, peace, the kingdom of Heaven, as others, less heroically, renounced pleasure" (p. 517).

The conclusion of this reinterpretation of the story of Judas is not at all arbitrary. The aestheticization of religion aims at a specific goal: the aesthetics of wonderment. The world is a mistake, the Gnostics said. Once the way to salvation is closed, Borges reads the world as a catastrophe, and the only proper response to it is the production of wonderment. With the conjunction of catastrophe as the given and wonderment as the goal, everything can be questioned. Thus, for instance, to take time as an a priori, as Kant does, is a necessary condition for the affirmation of the universality of which human knowledge is capable—that is, the affirmation of the legitimate possibility of recognizing oneself in the world. Once the link between man and world is broken, time becomes questionable.

In other words, the question of time is no longer the basis for a sought-after certainty. In *Inquisiciones*, the work Borges later repudiated, time was reduced to the present:

I am bound to this vertiginous present, and it is inconceivable that in its infinitesimal narrowness there should be room for the staggering thousands of other unconnected instants. If you do not wish to resort to miracles or to enlist, in defense of your frustrated thirst for unity, the help of an all-powerful God . . . , you will agree with me on the absolute vacuity of these portentous words: Self, Space, Time. (Borges 1925: 116)

Later, in "Tiempo circular," included in *Historia de la eternidad* (1936), Borges takes up this reduction again, relying on Schopenhauer. Elsewhere he writes that time is a category that exists only in nations with a short history (see Borges 1980, 1: 20 n. 2). But at the conclusion of "Nueva refutación del tiempo" he admits the hopelessness of denying time, or even of reducing it: "Our destiny (the difference between Swedenborg's hell and that of Tibetan mythology) is not amazing because it is unreal: it is amazing because it is irreversible and ironclad" (Borges 1980, 2: 300). What does this change mean? That he has finally convinced himself of the uselessness of his longtime obsession? Or that the seriousness of the demonstration is finally dispelled in a comic refutation? The real answer seems to be quite another: metaphysics, like religion, interests Borges in that it allows him to widen the range of possible aesthetic invention. Thus the conclusion he justifiedly draws—"To deny time is to deny two things: the succession of terms in a series and the synchronicity of the terms of two series" (p. 298)—provides a key to the conceptualization of many of his tales. Just as he does to religion, Borges aestheticizes metaphysics—that is, treats it as something valid only as fictional material.

Borges's indebtedness to the Gnostics is evident here. There is a passage by H. Jonas that points to the correspondence, as well as to the difference. The current deriving from Valentinus, writes Jonas, "makes no provision for a *present* on whose content knowledge may dwell. . . . There is past and future, where we come from and where we speed to, and the present is only the moment of *gnosis* itself, the peripety from the one to the other in the supreme crisis of the eschatological *now*" (quoted in Bloom 1980: 62). Whereas the Gnostic sect makes the present the dwelling in which the eschatology of each individual is prepared, Borges shuts it up inside itself, cuts it off from the past and the future, and makes it redeemable through the substitute of gnosis, that is, the fictional word. In so doing, he automatically negates history—not just as a discipline, but even as a possibility. But that is not all Borges negates. As a passage quoted earlier made clear, the refutation of time affects the constancy of the self. The negation of the constant self, another of Borges's obsessions, had already been formulated in *Inquisiciones*, where he relied on a translation of Schopenhauer: "An infinite time preceded my birth: who was I all this while? Metaphysically, I might possibly argue: I was always I; that is, all of those who throughout this time said 'I' were all I in actual fact" (Borges 1925: 93). Two consequences follow from this.

First, if, as an individual constancy, the self is an illusion, then individuality is equally false. This inference is clearly stated in what is perhaps Borges's most important story, "El inmortal":

Indoctrinated by an age-old practice, the republic of immortal men had achieved perfection in tolerance, and near perfection in indifference. They knew that, given an infinite length of time, every man experiences everything. For his past and future virtues, each man is worthy of all goodness, but also of every form of treason, for his infamies past and future. . . . No one is someone, a single immortal man is all men. (Borges 1980, 2: 8–9)

The passage omitted from the quotation above clearly indicates Borges's convergence and divergence vis-à-vis the Gnostics: "Thus envisaged, all of our acts are just, but they are also indifferent." Previously I observed that the postulation of indifference among the Gnostics applied to the body. Since the body was from the beginning doomed to sink back into the dust of matter, ascetic mortification or mundane dissipation was a matter of indifference. Borges transfers this issue from the field of ethics to that of fictional fabulation. When one considers that his original formulation dates from 1925, one realizes the extent to which Borges anticipated the attempts to temporalize the notion of self that have characterized the last two decades. (When, for instance, Foucault stresses the recent birth of man, he is simply stating in a provocative fashion the recent emphasis given to "the forces of finitude.")* But Borges would probably not have been delighted if his foresight had been acknowledged, for his path had nothing to do with that of the so-called social sciences. Not only that, but he assumed that other discursive areas were nothing but mere material for fictional elaboration. Thus the self he negated was meant to hold only in aesthetic experience.

The second consequence is less evident: the negation of the self implies the futility of psychology. That is why Borges always refers to Freud with contempt; depth psychology to him is no more than a secondary reelaboration of what the myths already knew. Let us examine this point. From the negation of the individualized self Borges extracts, to begin with, an

---

*Man is conceived when the force relations thematized are no longer those of infinity, which operated the God-form of classical thought, but those of finitude, life, work, and language (see Deleuze 1986: 131–41).

aesthetics for the writer. Flaubert, one of his heroes, is praised for the self-effacement he practices: "This superstition of language might have led another writer to concoct a petty dialect of bad syntactic and prosodic habits; but not Flaubert, whose fundamental decency saved him from the dangers of his own doctrine" (Borges 1980, 1: 214). This was to become Borges's own practice, as he indirectly acknowledges in "Borges y yo." So it would seem that the theme of the double, which often crops up in his work, did not spring from a problem of his individual psychology, but was rather the aesthetic precipitate of the search for a distancing from his own self.*

As an aesthetic drive, the negation of psychology has much wider effects than I have indicated so far. For all of Borges's work is a reply to this negation. The world of his characters is deliberately flat. Hence the difficulty of approaching them by means of so-called depth models, of which Freud is one of the major representatives in our times.

For Borges, avoiding psychological investigation of characters is a matter of asepsis and consistency, for he associates psychology with the sentimentality and intrigue of the nineteenth-century novel. As early as *Inquisiciones*, at the beginning of a chapter significantly titled "La nadería de la personalidad" (The Nothingness of Personality), he proposed an aesthetics "hostile to the psychologism we have inherited from the previous century" (Borges 1925: 84); five years later, in his praise of Evaristo Carriego, he excluded the declamatory poems, "which do not belong to literature but to crime" (Borges 1980, 1: 56). And it should not be thought that the contempt for psychology was solely a consequence of the attempts to refute time. For Borges, the relation between time and psychology is a close one. What they both share is the despicable taste for the dregs of the anecdotal, in which time indulges on the horizontal scale and psychology on the vertical scale. Thus the relatively few scenes set in the poor neighborhoods of Buenos Aires, the reflections on the pampas, the gaucho poems are not meant to convey any temporal view. Borges attacks the documentalist canon in his sober examination of *Martín Fierro*.

The importance and the sharpness of Borges's analysis are undeniable. But its virtues could not be recognized at the time of its publication, for the author's proposal assumed parameters that were foreign to contemporary Argentine criticism. There could be nothing in common between the documentalist canon, which still prevailed, as we have seen, and Borges's analytical practices. Even in the case of such a competent

---

*It is true that, against Borges's intention, one might argue that this conscious use would not be feasible, or fruitful in any case, without an unconscious personal motivation (see Costa Lima 1980, chap. 3).

essayist as Sábato, they remained worlds apart. While for the author of *El túnel* the raw materials of fiction are psychological and existential dramas, in Borges accidents and details are detached from temporality and made into an altar piece of petrified gestures, filled not with time but with static meaning. Referring to Estanislao del Campo's *Fausto*, Borges wrote, in "La poesía gauchesca": "*Fausto* does not belong to Argentine reality but rather—like the tango, *truco*, and Irigoyen—to Argentine mythology" (Borges 1980, 1: 117). The closing paragraph of "Parábola del palacio" underscores, perhaps unintentionally, the contrast between the mythical and historical ways of presenting a fact:

Others write history differently. There can be no two things alike in the world; if only (we are told) the poet pronounced his poem, the palace would disappear, as though abolished and annihilated by the last syllable. Such legends, of course, are no more than literary fictions. The poet was the emperor's slave and died as such; his work fell into oblivion because it deserved oblivion. (Borges 1980, 2: 340)

In opposition to the mythical presentation, expressed in the first version, the historical one, which takes into account the poet's condition as a slave, is banal and shallow. For according to Borges the antidote to the domesticity of psychology and the prosaism of history could lie only in mythical meaning or in themes of metaphysical import. Hence the vehemence with which he refers to a simple card game, *truco*: "From the labyrinths of painted pasteboard of *truco* we have approached metaphysics: the single justification and goal of all themes" (Borges 1980, 1: 69). But we also know that his emphasis on metaphysics, his reading of Schopenhauer, Berkeley, and Locke, did not aim at the elaboration of a philosophy. Nothing could be farther from his purpose. Why then should metaphysics matter to Borges? In order to prepare literature for the time of its own dissolution: "I do not know whether music can despair of music, or marble of marble, but literature is an art able to prophesy the time in which it will fall dumb, and rage at its own virtue, and fall in love with its own dissolution, and court its own end" (p. 138).

To summarize, then, we have seen that Borges's interest in gnosticism and the cabala, present from the beginning, had quite serious reasons. For him they were means of access to a set of parameters with which he might oppose the tradition made up of the Logos of classical Greek philosophy, monotheistic theology, and Enlightenment reason. The parameters he established allowed him to reject social time, as expressed in modern historical investigation, and subjective time, the basis of psychological investigation, in favor of myth. In making these decisions, Borges by no means privileged anything outside literature. Gnosticism might have interested him because it offered an alternative explanation for the existence of evil, pain, and death. Although his concern with death has been evident since his earliest known texts, we have no means of finding out whether at some point gnosticism was for him more than a source of intellectual fascination. In Borges, religion is always displaced in favor of aesthetic stimulation. And when he writes that metaphysics is a branch of fantastic literature, Borges is expressing an actual conviction. For metaphysics too is absorbed into aesthetics. In both cases, the omnipresence of aesthetics manifests itself in narratives following mythical patterns.

MYTHICAL DISCOURSE

In order to substantiate our argument, let us leave Borges aside for a moment. This pause is necessary to investigate, with Hans Blumenberg, what is characteristic of myth. From the outset, I must warn that those who tend to rely too much on classifications may find the following discussion frustrating. This is so, according to Blumenberg, because myth is never found in its pure or original state, but always after it has been polished by several successive generations, which remove from the mythical narrative everything that is not memorable. Also, this frustration will result from the fact that, contrary to what Enlightenment tradition holds, myth is not opposed to Logos or its ultimate incarnation, theory; indeed, theory's serene consideration of the world presupposes the age-old groundwork of myth (see Blumenberg 1985: 27). Finally, myth's true antagonist, dogma, through its repression of unorthodox questioning gives rise to a remythologization, in narratives that bring up the forbidden questions. Instead of a pure or autonomous discursive form—that is, one with a territory of its own—myth contains Logos and, conversely, is reborn out of Logos. Thus myth is not a discursive form, but rather a magma from which discursive systems emanate, and in turn give rise to new mythical veins.

These constant, dynamic metamorphoses would, however, prove deceptive if it were impossible to identify the mythical mass. It begins to take shape when we inquire about its function. The role of a mythical narrative is to offer an explanation for what would otherwise be seen as a purely arbitrary chaos. Therefore the organizing sense of myth can also be found in the discourses of religion and science. In addition, considering its function and its permeability, it is not an outdated discourse, to be consumed by new discourses fitted with theoretical trappings. That is why a mythical narrative will not flourish except where it gains collective significance (*Bedeutsamkeit*):

[Significance] is the form in which the background of nothing [*des Nichts*], as that which produces anxiety, has been put at a distance, whereby, without this "prehistory," the function of what is significant remains uncomprehended, though

present. For the need for significance is rooted in the fact that we are conscious of never being definitely exempted from the production of anxiety [*Ängstigung*].
(Blumenberg 1985: 110)

This significance, in turn, is signaled by a set of features. To begin with, it assumes that the mythical protagonists' goal will become more difficult, and that the difficulty is a result of the resistance they meet. If abstract concepts were used, it would be impossible to present in dramatic fashion the obstacles in the protagonists' path; thus the economics of myth requires the use of images. Also, myths, as narratives produced by images, with the object of assuaging or delaying human anxiety, do not attempt to explain particular cases, and thus appear as simultaneous. By "simultaneous" I take it that Blumenberg means that the elucidating power of myth is not aimed at a specific group, socially, spacially, or temporally delimited. (Otherwise, it seems to me, it would be impossible to distinguish myth from ideology, the functionality of which is always determined by a specific group or society.) This strength of simultaneous illumination is the reason why myth is indifferent toward chronological organization: "Myth doesn't even let indifferences arise. Significance makes possible a 'density' which excludes empty spaces and empty times, but it also makes possible an indefinitiveness of dating and localization that is the equivalent of ubiquitousness" (p. 96). This unconcern for chronology is only a specific case of a more general unconcern: myth is indifferent to time. "In myth there is no chronology, there are only sequences" (p. 126).

To these features we must add one more: the position assumed by myth in relation to the possibility of raising questions. Here its position is somewhat paradoxical. Although, as we have seen, its function depends on the significance it confers on the unreasonableness of existence, thus offering a shelter from anxiety, and although its specific form, narrative, by itself implies the imposition of a principle of order, on the other hand myth will not admit questioning: "Myths do not answer questions, they make things unquestionable. Anything that could give rise to demands for explanation is shifted into the position of something that legitimates the rejection of such claims" (p. 126).

Besides, since a mythical narrative is not set in a specific time, the objects it appropriates are abandoned at an immeasurable distance. In this, myth and dogma are alike. But the similarity is deceptive. From the communal viewpoint—the only one that really counts—myth offers no more than a proposed identity. To believe in the same myths is to be a part of the same community. As Gnostic myth exemplifies, the break with a given community—orthodox Judaism, in this particular case—is achieved by inverting the scheme prevalent in the community (for a number of examples, see Lévi-Strauss 1964). Dogma, on the contrary, shows an extremely rigid attitude: "Everything that dogma requires, myth exempts people from. It requires no decisions and no conversions, knows no apostates and no repentance" (Blumenberg 1985: 242). Whereas in the case of myth the interdiction of questioning brings about a new narrative, dogma's interdiction of questioning brings about the possibility of transgression, and consequent exclusion. Myth bypasses what it prohibits, inventing a new fabulation. Dogma protects the unity of the community, excluding the divergent.

Philosophical Logos creates a third position: "Philosophy, in opposition to myth, brought into the world above all restless inquiry, and proclaimed its 'rationality' in the fact that it did not shrink from any further question or from any logical consequence of possible answers" (p. 257). But its openness is apparent rather than real. Since it can only deal with concepts and demonstrations, philosophical Logos cannot tolerate the importance given to images; although it cannot despise them because of their poverty of language, it cannot structure itself by means of them. This constitutional requirement inevitably restricts its meaningfulness to the intellectual aspect. No Athenian would become a better citizen just by reading Aristotle; but familiarity with the tragic poets, inheritors of the ancient myths, would teach him to recognize the values and conflicts of the polis.

The openness of philosophical Logos to questions suffers from yet another restriction: since, on the one hand, concepts cannot be confused with images, but, on the other hand, there can be no thought without images, Logos must necessarily disguise those images with which it works, and which motivate its chain of demonstration.

Let me summarize this exposition, in which I did not limit myself to a mere paraphrase of Blumenberg. In the three cases analyzed, the question presents a common situation, a vulnerable and unsatisfactory one. Theoretical discourses, since they are the inheritors of *philosophical Logos*, or at any rate are influenced by it, characteristically repress alternative questions, as well as those that cannot fit into their systems, because of the seemingly exhaustive nature of their concepts and their apparent proscription of images. In the case of dogma, this vulnerability is even more visible, for the validity of the dogmatic statement requires the existence of the heterodox, who are to meet the fate reserved for heretics, renegades, traitors. In myth, finally, this is just as evident, for the principle of mythical narrative, its motivation in timelessness, leads only to the possibility of forming another myth. Taking myth, dogma, and philosophical Logos and the specific theoretical discourses derived from it as transversal forms of discourse—that is, as the seminal forms from which historical discursive formations are derived—we can then say that in all of them questioning has a precarious status, for this or that reason. That is, in none of them does questioning lead to definitive answers. We may think of questions as the most efficient and effective of human acts. But the questioning of discourses, in which questions themselves are of course included, only highlights the fact that all of them are suspicious of questioning.

By choosing *Arbeit am Mythos* as our major supporting text, I do not mean either to "introduce" Blumenberg's work—as an introduction, my summary would be both insufficient and distorting—or to propose a discussion of the function of myth. My intention is simply to present a few of the elements I will use in my analysis of myth in Borges. Likewise, my brief analysis of the relation between myth and Logos and of that between myth and dogma does no more than provide a background for the discussion I will present later in this chapter.

To link up what was said earlier with the considerations I have just set out, Borges's aestheticization of metaphysics and religion takes place through reliance on properties of mythical discourse. Borges's narrative excludes time in an attempt to reach a mythical significance. It makes narratives out of metaphysical and religious issues in order to divest them of their pretentions to conceptual or intellectual sufficiency, changing them into formulaic images of catastrophe, wonderment, and parody. The catastrophe is of the world; the wonderment is the goal of the sequences that tell of it; the parody is aimed at the limits of (religious or metaphysical) systems. But mention must be made of an aspect so simple it may be seen as trivial: this translation of metaphysics and religion into aesthetic experience is not only a change of discursive register but also a loss. The myth that oriented him has a communal inspiration, which Blumenberg was obviously not the first to detect. Here it will be useful to recall Borges's tale "El informe de Brodie."

It is the story of an English missionary who lived for a time in a community of rude, primitive men. One of their few amusements was the identification of the poet: In an assembly, a participant would get up and combine six or seven words, generally enigmatic ones. If no one was moved, nothing happened. If, however, the words struck a chord in the group, everyone would get up and walk away, without speaking to the poet. From then on he knew he was excluded and could be killed by anyone. In "El informe" the transfiguration of mythical narrative reaches its limit, where myth no longer recognizes itself: the narrative follows a path unknown to real myth.

If the strength of myth lies in its communal interest, the aestheticization of myth reaches a different goal: myths are now created for the written page; the community now is that of random, scattered readers. The aestheticization of myth is a parody of myth. Myth is incorporated into literature, and is thus shorn of its original liveliness. Indeed, the Gnostics could not have conceived such a successor: the community, too, is part of corruptible matter. If there is no longer a God—whether *alienus* or revealed—to which one can aspire, the new Gnostic can only wait for the page on which he will write "six or seven words, usually enigmatic ones." Literature has taken the place of the gnosis of old. In spite of the loss, however, something has been preserved of the old community of myth. Contrary to what many of his interpreters have written, from P. H. Ureña to Paul de Man, Borges does not confuse literature with the concern to create a style. In 1930 he identified the worship of style with the exalted values of the uncultured: "The miserable state of our literature, its inability to attract, has generated a superstition of style, a casual reading of partial attentions" (Borges 1980, 1: 135). Though like Mallarmé he often says that the world must end in a book, Borges is aware that style and book are not the only parameters: "A literature differs from a later or earlier one less on account of the text itself than on account of the way in which it is read" (2: 272). The stray reader, exiled from his community, like the poet in "El informe," is the survivor of the ancient assembly that listened to the narrative and was made coherent by adhering to it. Therefore Borges could not have intended to restore the form defeated by philosophical Logos and dogma. For he knows that, in a quite literal sense, no restoration is ever possible. By reducing time to the present, every reading of the past—and here I agree with H. Bloom rather than with de Man—is a misreading. Thus Borges's Homer has forgotten the Greek language and his own works. His catastrophic view of the world makes any form of continuity unthinkable.

We seem to have taken another short step here. Like Zeno's tortoise, we linger over minutiae, so small, even insignificant, that they fit into a few short sentences: In the Gnostics, Borges found a way of unreading tradition. And he unread it by discarding privileged figures: historical time, psychological investigation, the teachings of haughty reason; and by emphasizing something that, we had been told, has been exhausted: myth. But just as he had distanced himself from the Gnostics by ignoring their goal, so he distances himself from myth by denying its value as an instrument of social identity. Myth is formed and dispelled on the page of a literary work. But what sort of literature is this?

In an article to which I will return, Paul de Man wrote that Borges's prose was like the philosophical prose of the eighteenth century. This can be accepted, as long as we add that in this case the philosopher has no intention of teaching anything. Nothing could be more repugnant to Borges than didactic or committed prose. The philosopher is here in order to be unread, in sequences that change his seriousness into a proposal of wonderment. If this much is accepted, we can see that our tortoise has a peculiarity that Zeno had not thought of: he is not only slow but also cautious; he takes infinitesimal steps only the better to turn his head back and see the ground he has covered. What the tortoise sees now is that what we have done so far has not yet clarified what must be clarified. For what is this literature that Borges has created?

BORGES AND *ANTIPHYSIS*

The practice of literary analysis shows that the fascination with great authors typically leads to questions that the analyst is unable to answer from his or her previous knowledge. If the analyst is unaware of this fact or disregards it, he or she will use words only to confirm what is already known, a scholarly version of parasitism.

Given his proposal, which subverts tradition, Borges demands strenuous effort from the analyst. So far I have done no more than try to identify his orientation. What conclusions can be drawn? It is always advisable to set out from a relatively well settled starting point.

When we discussed the classical conception of the world, to which gnosticism was opposed, we called attention in passing to the fact that the classical worldview assumed a well-ordered cosmos, contemplation of which (theory) would make its harmonic structure explicit. Naturally, there were various paths by which to reach such a cosmos. According to the Platonic conception, which agrees with the Gnostic to a certain extent, the world of ideal, absolute, constant, and incorruptible forms was beyond *physis*. The philosopher's effort consisted in moving away from the shadow of *doxai* (opinions) toward the geometry of eternity. Although the world was impure, the fact that the philosopher could educate himself pointed to the possibility of commerce with perfection. For Aristotle, on the other hand, perfection is not beyond *physis*, but in it. *Physis* includes not only what is manifest, what is actualized, but also what exists in things as potential. Thus, for all their divergences, both Plato and Aristotle saw the world as perfectible.

Divergence and convergence characterize the relation between Plato's and Aristotle's conceptions of mimesis. According to Plato, the poet had a narrow range at his disposal. As an imitator of copies—that is, the objects in the world—the poet could not aspire to the status of a philosopher. In any case, if he accepted the only role that the philosopher reserved for him and devoted himself to singing of dignity, his place in the republic would be assured. For Aristotle, on the contrary, the poet's dignity lies not in subordination to the ethics propounded by the legislator, but rather in capturing the latency of form and thus actualizing an object according to its inner energy. Thus he condemned deus ex machina and, conversely, praised the five-legged horse if his five legs were functional within the context of what was represented. In both cases, then, mimesis was adequate to a well-made cosmos and contributed to its greater perfection.

But what would happen if the assumption of cosmic harmony were dropped? If, instead of being seen as the image of perfection, the world were conceived as the product of an inferior, perverse, and ignorant deity? Since we do not know any literary works directly inspired by gnosticism, we cannot answer this question. But the question can be posed in relation to this peculiar Argentine Gnostic, who from an early stage found in Gnostic thought a special stimulus for his work.

The immediate conclusion is almost trite: the mimesis based on classical parameters *recognizes* the world; it can mock the world, attack it with terrible invective as the Greek tragedians did, or suspect that we are no more than a pastime for bored gods; but in any case it always acknowledges, and thus refers to, the world of *physis*. How is the world seen by one who starts out from the opposite assumption? Can one properly speak of mimesis if the notion presupposes the acknowledgment, albeit transfigured, of something previously given and potentially well made? Let us assume that the answer is yes. It will be necessary to add, though, that in this case what we have is mimesis of an *antiphysis*—that is, a *physis* based on the premise that we have no sure evidence that the world is well made; the premise that the world is a simulacrum or an illusion, or even that the world ought to be replaced by another world. It might be argued, however, that all of this, though admissible, is inconsequent. My answer would be that it isn't when we are discussing Borges. If this hypothesis is accepted, it will come as no surprise that Borges's first affirmation of *antiphysis* should appear in a passage where he is discussing the Gnostic doctrines: "What these narratives have in common is what matters: our reckless or blameworthy improvisation by an inept deity, using inadequate material. . . . Salvation, according to this disenchanted heresy, is a mnemotechnical effort of the dead, just as the Savior's torment is an optical illusion—two simulacra that mysteriously coincide with the precarious reality of their world" (Borges 1980, 1: 148–49). The world, Borges writes at the close of "Avatares de la tortuga," is the false product of a dream. This refusal or condemnation of the existing world, however, is not to be found solely in texts dealing directly with gnosticism. In his book on Carriego, reflecting on such a realistic and trivial subject as a game of cards, Borges writes: "This is a narrow world, I know: a phantom of parochial politics and pettiness, a world invented by wizards and corner witches, but which is nonetheless a substitute for this real world, nonetheless inventive and devilish in its ambition" (Borges 1980, 1: 68–69). The need to fashion another reality is present even when Borges considers a game apparently devoid of any transcendence. The game's own space, in which the rules that govern everyday interrelation with the world are temporarily suspended, indicates that even unpretentious *truco* players feel the inadequacy of *physis*; and thus that it is necessary to conceive an *antiphysis*.

This is the undeclared primordial myth of Borges's *inventio*. Since he had no religious or ideological commitments, clearly there was no reason why Borges should not disseminate it in his purely fictional texts. However, faithful to the logic of myth—that is, its ability to preserve its basic structure, however radical the inversions it may suffer—the structure of Gnostic myth is preserved even in inventions that no Gnostic would subscribe to. Thus the hell and the heaven of the heresiarch Hakim do not correct the corruption of matter, but rather culminate it:

> Hakim's heaven and hell were no less desperate. *To those who deny the Word, to those who deny the Jewelled Veil and the Face* (here he pronounced a curse on the Hidden Rose, which has been preserved), *he promised a marvelous Hell, where each of them is to reign over 999 empires* of fire. . . . The paradise is less concrete. *It is always night, and there are stone fonts, and the happiness of this paradise is the happiness of leave-takings, of resignation, and of those who know they are asleep.* (Borges 1980, 1: 287)

We may then take "El tintorero enmascarado" as the paradigm of the first type of Borgian *ficción*. This type of text starts out from an argument with clear Gnostic influences, but develops in such a way that it strays from or even contradicts Gnostic doctrine. Then there is a second type of *ficción*; "Tlön, Uqbar, Orbis Tertius" may be taken as its paradigm. Here there is no discernible element of Gnostic origin; the invention is entirely of Borges's making. But the same rule is operative: the model of the fundamental myth is still acknowledged. Thus, in the fictional city of Tlön, all philosophy is considered a mere approximation, an *als ob*, and therefore metaphysicians "seek not the truth, not even verisimilitude, but wonderment" (p. 416). And they do not seek truth for the plain reason that the idea of truth presupposes the possibility of a coincidence between what is said and the reality being spoken about, while in Tlön it is precisely the distinction between the real and the fantastic that is denied. That is why the story of the retrieval of the lost coins is met with skepticism or even outrage: "They insisted it was a verbal fallacy based on the rash use of two neologisms, unauthorized by usage and alien to all rigorous thought: the verbs *find* and *lose*, which involve *petitio principii*, since they presuppose the identity of the earlier nine coins with the later" (p. 417).

Once the solid, material ballast of *physis* is discarded, an even more remarkable phenomenon becomes possible in the fantastic city: to think of something, to desire it or covet it, may be a way of creating it. Thought interferes with reality. Thought is not ideally contemplative, as the Greeks believed, with their valuing of theory, but rather a sort of womb. So the archaeologists of Tlön begin to find evidence of a past created by the sheer desire of the excavators. And the past becomes "no less plastic and docile than the future" (p. 420). For *antiphysis* is no redeemer. Nothing could be further from it than a *paradis artificiel*, a passive use of the imaginary such as fantasy. If for the Gnostics human reality still contained a mixture, in which the dross of reality was agglutinated around a divine spark, in Borges's elaboration of the Gnostic myth *antiphysis* generates phantoms, simulacra, an unstable and mendacious reality. (The very word "mendacious" is improper here, for it necessarily evokes its opposite.) *Antiphysis* is the ultimate nightmare. It makes the nightmare our fundamental experience. That is why, in "Las ruinas circulares," the unnamed protagonist improves the action of dreams in such a way that he is able to conceive a son. The son has all the marks of common men. But he is a simulacrum, and fire cannot destroy him. A shadow made substantial, the simulacrum of a being, the son does not know he is a mere phantom—just like the one who created him, who is also impervious to fire.

What could be behind the new Adam if not *antiphysis*? In the rejected *physis*, death is a source of anguish. As soon as they acquire language, children are terrified of the idea of death. They have not yet learned what adults know, that the only defense against this horror is to convince oneself that death is an accident to which only others are exposed. In the spectral world of *antiphysis*, death is a blessing that new creatures long for. In "El inmortal," the immortals, after they have built their city, realize their mistake; they subvert it and opt for a mindless existence. Time is no longer an expense, but a burden.

That is why Joseph Cartaphilus, who is visiting their land and has inadvertently also become immortal, wishes to drink water from the river that would make him mortal again. Paradoxically, time is a reality only for those who are free from its yoke. To mortals, the unreality of all time except the present is confirmed by the objects in Tlön that are products of the desire to find them, or by the drastic change that takes place in *Don Quixote* when Pierre Menard copies it. For the irony of "Pierre Menard, inventor del Quijote" lies in the deceptive nature of the common conception of time: the past is not fixed, and the historian's task is unfeasible; the phrase "what happened" is meaningless; the past is as plastic as the future. *Antiphysis*, having converted metaphysics into "a branch of fantastic literature," undermines the bases of history and psychology. The former was founded on the possibility of recapturing the identity of past events; the latter starts out from the equally deceptive identity of the self. Thus both history and psychology proceed from the same assumption as Greek mimesis: the analogy between something being investigated or created and the final product of investigation or creation.

We then return to the question posed above: How could the violence of *antiphysis* allow mimesis to take place? There is, of course, a trivial answer: if mimesis presupposes an analogy between a "referent" and its representation, as long as there is a referent, however absurd it may seem to the logic of *physis*, it is always possible to find an analogue for it. If Borges's "referents" imply a radical unfolding of Gnostic myth, which provides the basis for the world of *antiphysis*, then Hakim, Menard, Homer, Funes, the universe of Tlön, and so on, are still mimetic products in relation to this fictional world. Here mimesis would be rooted in the redundancy that is necessary for all language. But this would still be a simplistic answer. I must either give up this path or find a better argument.

Beginning with *Mimesis e modernidade* (1980)—more precisely, with the essay on Borges included in the book—I have been consistently describing the phenomenon of mimesis in such a way that the idea of a referent with the status of reality is discarded. Only in this way, it seems to me, can "mimesis" be freed from its deceptive and restrictive identification with the Latin term *imitatio*. Clearly *imitatio* is conditioned by the previous existence of an actual model; mimesis, however, must be conceived fundamentally in terms of the expectations of the receiver. The primary importance of expectations derives from the fact that things do not become significant or even recognizable simply because they are there, placed before a human subject. As Borges himself writes, "the eyes see what they are used to seeing. Tacitus did not perceive the Crucifixion, though he duly records it in this book" (Borges 1980, 2: 280). "The very fact of perceiving, of considering, is selective in nature: every attention, every focusing of our consciousness contains a deliberate omission of the uninteresting. We see and hear through memories, fears, anticipations" (Borges 1980, 1: 155).

Evidently one's stock of expectations varies according to one's time, culture, and reference group. These factors set the conditions for one's individual reaction. A product is not mimetic because of any objective traits it may have. Objectivity is said to exist as a function of the similarity (analogy) between what was expected and what is perceived. This is the first trait of the activity by means of which mimesis is recognized, but it is not sufficient. It is also necessary that the agent have enough mental flexibility to recognize the presence of significant differences between the two, within the basic analogical frame. Without the vector "difference," a mimetic product would be indistinguishable from a copy or a double, which are simply special and anomalous cases of mimetic production. Thus it is that allegory is made possible—that is, the decoding of a set of apparently autonomous indices that point to a cultural "referent"; it is through this connection that the object acquires autonomous status. This form of mimesis I have labeled *mimesis of representation*. Such a representation—given the similarities and differences between it and the previously internalized expectations, it being understood that the differences do not nullify the similarities—is not a mere repetition, but rather the actualization of a configuration the outline of which may be meaningful for some receiver. The reader of *Les Fleurs du mal* who sees nothing but the similarity between Baudelaire's diction and classical alexandrine fails to understand the difference between Baudelaire and Racine; but the reader who notices only the absence of the topos of *douceur du foyer* in these poems will not realize the uniqueness of Baudelaire's position. The spectator at a performance of Chinese drama who sees only an actor walking across the stage holding the representation of a butterfly lacks the necessary analogical basis to understand that the passage of time is being indicated.

These examples, chosen at random, indicate that in most mimetic products expectation does more than just make it possible to understand what is going on. In mimesis of representation, the act of understanding is not restricted to the decoding of the text's immediate sense. This first level of understanding opens into a horizon that, in principle, is undetermined.

One of its limits is allegory. In allegory, the segments of the text make up a presence taken to be analogous to a certain absent being. The cross is both a signal of torture and death and a signal of the sacrifice that a god made for man. But allegory is not the only limit of mimesis of representation. Its other limit, antipodal to allegory, is the limit of the performative. A given scene does not simply mean such and such a thing; it *is* such and such a thing. Thus, in J. L. Austin's familiar example, the authority who says "I declare you man and wife" legitimates the marriage by the very fact of pronouncing the appropriate ritual words, just as it often happens that passages included in mimesis of representation do not *represent* moments of life but instead *create* such moments.

The situation is quite different in the case of what I have named *mimesis of production* (for a more detailed discussion, see Costa Lima 1980: 168–83). This assumes a divergence between the meaning of a text and the way a given horizon of expectations tends to interpret similar indices; the divergence is such that one either misses the point altogether or lends the text a quite inappropriate meaning. Thus, for instance, if Guimarães Rosa's "Meu tio o Iauretê"—in which a jaguar hunter changes into a jaguar, the metamorphosis being indicated in the narrative sequences by the very language, which gradually becomes filled with Tupi words—is read as an allegory of, say, the character's progressive animalization, Rosa's story acquires a rather crude meaning. Such a reading will fail to see, as Haroldo de Campos pointed out (Campos 1976, chap. 6), that the change is not referred to, but rather produced on the level of narrative itself.

Since this is not the proper place to pursue the subject any further, let me simply observe how close this is to the performative limit of mimesis of representation. The difference between the two seems to lie in the fact that in mimesis of production the performative thematizes itself—that is, the form with which it is accomplished makes its process evident. Thus the difference between the two forms of mimesis may be said to lie in the different position occupied by the performative: in mimesis of representation, the performative is the lower, subordinate limit; whereas in mimesis of production it is the higher, dominant limit.

For our present purposes, what matters is how all of this can help us to understand Borges's *antiphysis*. Perhaps the reader has already anticipated my answer: Borges's reliance on *antiphysis* eliminates the dominant presence of the allegorical. By this, though, I do not mean that Borges's stories are mostly instances of performativeness. Let me put it more clearly: while in mimesis of representation allegory is the "higher" limit—that is, that to which the interpretive process tends—in Borges allegory is displaced: more often than not it is no more than a starting point for the communication of the text. The following observations on "La lotería de Babilonia" also apply to his other, denser, narratives.

After reading "La lotería," one may think: although there is no Babylonian lottery in our societies, we are subject to the arbitrary power of similar companies. Like the Company in the story, these corporations rule, with equal rigor and arbitrariness, over death and glory, scorn and praise. Such a reading is a reduction of Borges's story. The reader who thinks of "La lotería" in this way is not very far from the critic who accused Borges of being the representative of a shallow and cowardly society. For allegory here is not the goal, but only the beginning of the story: just as in our world, in Babylonia men did not separate fear from hope, and were willing to pay the necessary price, even if it meant risking their lives. Once this banal analogy is made, the story develops by inverting or ignoring all our relevant habits and common expectations. In other words, beginning from an allegorical common element, the machinery of *antiphysis* is set in motion—a motion that does not refer to it, but actualizes it. *Antiphysis*, then, does not produce allegories; rather, it signifies the ironical and paradoxical exploration of the inversions of our world of *physis*. It proceeds by means of performative chains—that is, by performing acts and actions rather than merely describing or observing them.

For this process Borges avails himself of his previous elimination of history and psychology. His characters are not made distinct by specific psychological complexities or historical specificities; that is, the motivation of their behavior is not conditioned by any aspects of this or that historical moment. Their characters are not only outside time: they assume a non-time. The coupling of an initial allegorical clue with a sequence of performatives aims at the continuous production of wonderment. An unenthusiastic reader may well wonder: What is this all about? What does it tell us? Borges's fiction, in fact, does not contain the so-called grand themes; in this sense it is deliberately insignificant. As Maurice Blanchot says, in the most enlightening text I have ever read on Borges: "This indefinite power of reverberation, this unlimited, shimmering multiplication—which is the labyrinth of light and, save for that, nothing—is all we will ever find, vertiginously, at the bottom of our desire to understand" (Blanchot 1971: 141).

If, then, we expect to find in Borges's infinite labyrinths a "lesson" for our everyday existence, one that represents it or, in particular, allegorizes it, we are inevitably frustrated. Perhaps this is what annoys his detractors, who react in such an aggressive, passionate way. In fact, few writers have courted the attack of controllers so much as Borges. For few have ever attacked so systematically, in such cold blood, and consequently with such irony, the common expectations about the function of literature. But aggressiveness is not necessarily a merit in an author. One of the first surprises Borges gives the reader is that in the 1930's he had already realized that literature was changing its path. As John Updike wrote at the close of his long note on Borges: "Ironic and blasphemous as Borges's hidden message may seem, the texture and method of his creations, though strictly inimitable, answer to a deep need in contemporary literary art— the need to confess the fact of artifice" (Updike 1965: 246). His literature discards as contemptible all the illusionism that has been perpetuated all the way to realism, and is preserved today in every would-be best-selling novel. Borges's fiction is manifestly of the painted-cardboard type, a fake that proclaims itself to be just that. No better way of provoking misunderstandings and outrage could have been found.

But even his admirers are just as prone to commit the same mistakes. One of the most illustrious of these, for instance, writes: "His stories are about the style in which they are written" (de Man 1964: 9). Now, Borges himself scoffed at the excessive valuing of style. But in spite of this lapse, Paul de Man made a decisive observation: "Poetic invention begins in duplicity, but it does not stop there. For the writer's particular duplicity (the dyer's image in 'Hakim') stems from the fact that he presents the invented form as if it possessed the attribute of reality, thus allowing it to be mimetically reproduced, in its turn, in another mirror-image that takes the preceding pseudo-reality for its starting-point" (p. 9).

The mirror image mentioned by de Man is, as everyone knows, one of the fundamental motifs in Borges's work. Not only that, but it also allows us to determine precisely the author's convergence with gnosticism and the difference between them. In "El tintorero enmascarado" we find the sentence: "Mirrors and paternity are abominable because they multiply and affirm the earth" (Borges 1980, 1: 287). Though the Gnostics detested procreation because it multiplies our misery, at no time did they ever compare it to mirrors. And in "Tlön, Uqbar, Orbis Tertius," Borges reaffirms this equivalence: "Then Bioy Casares recalled that a heresiarch of Uqbar had declared that mirrors and copulation were abominable, because they multiply the number of men" (p. 409). Why do mirrors acquire this status in Borges? Aren't they the very iconic representation of *antiphysis*, of a world that does not imitate, but simulates the one we live in and feel we know? If, thus, the labyrinth stands as a model for the initial allegory, mirrors provide the basis for the ideation of the sequences that follow. Actually, the separation between the two is only approximate. Mirrors and labyrinths fuse with each other and support each other in their multiplication. This mutual support does not aim at making the reader's task any easier; on the contrary, it increases the possibility that he or she will be led astray.

Take, for example, the ending of "El inmortal." Cartaphilus, the author of the manuscript that describes the discovery of the city of the immortals, casts doubt on the veracity of his tale when he observes that it contains Homeric references and expressions. Since Homer himself had been his character, the doubt expressed by Cartaphilus has to do with the identity of one vis-à-vis the other. As Jacques Reda shrewdly observed, Cartaphilus's hesitation both opens and disguises a final labyrinth. The difference of identities is mirrorlike in nature: Cartaphilus and Homer, like all individuals, after all, are projections of a mirror that deceives them (Reda 1963: 449). Artifice and simulacrum are the counterparts of deception and parody. Together they form the two sides of the Borgian coin.

THE BORGIAN COIN

In which realm does this coin circulate? In the realm of aesthetic emotion. But is it enough to speak of aesthetic emotion to agree as to the subject's value? This would seem to be a strange idea, at the least. My intention is to exploit Reda's words beyond his original intention: "Its power [i.e., of aesthetic emotion] (as its weakness also) lies perhaps in the fact that it is indeed revealing, but all it reveals is itself" (Reda 1963: 443).

I have already emphasized the common fate religion and metaphysics find in Borges's hands: that of fruitful raw materials for fictional fabulation. Thus his work is characterized by the "attempt at intellectual reduction of the ecstasy that legitimates it and gives it depth" (p. 444). Therefore the world is dignified when—more precisely, *only* when—it is in the service of the aesthetic experience. In a conversation with Richard Burgin, Borges himself said (though he was speaking only of certain poems of his and not of his entire work): "I mean if art is perfect, then the world is superfluous" (Burgin 1969: 80). Admittedly, it would not be reasonable to see in this statement more import than Borges himself invests it with. Even so, the question is still pertinent: since the world is no more than a fertilizer for art, is the unequivocal value of fiction secure? Blanchot broaches this question at the beginning of his essay: "The experience of literature is perhaps fundamentally close to the paradoxes and sophisms of what Hegel rejected by naming 'the bad infinity'" (Blanchot 1971: 139). If the opposite of Hegel's bad infinity is the understanding of infinity as becoming (see Hegel 1929, bk. 1: chap. 2, C), since becoming is not only identified with progress but also declared by History, it seems that Borges can only be seen as an instance of bad infinity. But is this conclusion inevitable? I believe not. Let me try to show why.

When fiction is shorn of everything that is not fiction, it changes into pure textuality. It is no accident that so many analysts have said that in Borges there are no differences between essay, criticism, and fiction proper. Everything he touches becomes fiction. Thus fiction is his practical and theoretical parameter. Having been controlled for centuries, fiction is now the controller: any given thing becomes acceptable only if it serves as raw material for fiction. If its traditional control, be it religious or secularized, has hardly ever been thematized, this quite recent inversion has been explored even less. What further obscures it is the insistence on pure textuality that characterizes a certain trend in contemporary thought. Very few analysts, indeed, are as lucid as David Carroll, who despite his avowed debt to Derrida is opposed to the sort of textualism that deconstructionalists engage in: "The conflicts and contradictions between theory and fiction are not resolved when fiction takes on the project to be its own theory of itself, to be only 'pure,' visible textuality" (Carroll 1982: 199–200). Borges's uncontested and well-deserved fame both nourishes and capitalizes on the textualist inflation that proliferates in some major centers these days. I am not saying that he is famous because of this coincidence, but rather calling attention to the little-noted fact that his invention is clearly self-enclosed: whatever is not fiction is of value only if it can feed fiction. As often has been the case in history, the victim is now the jailer; the controlled has become the controller.

Thus I see Borges not as a colonized writer, as his detractors have done, but as the founder of a new colonization. One may well question Borges's *argentinidad*—indeed, question the validity of concepts of this kind. But it seems clear that through Borges Argentina avenges itself for having been colonized, and contributes to a new kind of colonization, spearheaded by textuality or—to use the favored term—*écriture*, in which the entire range of discursive possibilities is contained. Whereas the nineteenth-century novel had to imitate history in order to legitimate itself, Borges has made a decisive contribution to the opposite mode: the historian, and maybe even the philosopher, have to become fictionists. This monism of the fictional is just as authoritarian and controlling as any other. True, the fictional cannot see itself as the depository of truth, or it would deny its own statute. That is, the limit of the urge to control in Borges lies in the fact that he aspires to be no more than a fictionist. But this limit can easily be transposed by the philosopher who, denying the validity of discursive boundaries, accepts no more than the constitution of textualities. The privilege of the text institutes a new hierarchy, another power—in short, another control.

Any society committed to mitigating the evils of inequality must see discursive plurality as no less necessary than the plurality of opinions and ideas—all the more so because it does not believe in any redeeming utopias, and so should not defend any form of monism. The monism of the controllers of fiction was based on the primacy of some form of reason, on which the corresponding form of truth was erected. Those who reduce everything to fictional *inventio* are just as monistic. More than most, Borges has helped to make Latin America less poor. But to defend the exclusive value of his position would be to encourage a new form of control.

The core of the present chapter is made up of two movements. In the first, we tried to show Borges's aesthetic appropriation of the Gnostic tradition. Being aesthetic, this appropriation consisted in adopting a position that for the Gnostics had a religious meaning in order to swim against the current of Western fiction, particularly since the Enlightenment, which neglected the marvelous and the metamorphoses of myth in favor of the basic categories present in the Greek concept of *physis*. Thus by attacking the idea of *physis* Borges came to abandon the equation:

$$\text{time} : \text{history} :: \text{space} : \text{nation}$$

In the second movement, I tried to articulate Borges's appropriation of gnosticism with the trend that, beginning with Flaubert, has now culminated with deconstructivism, its major representative. This consists in the systematic criticism of serious discourse, the discourse of truth, proposing instead fiction as the only humanly legitimate discourse because it is unhampered by discriminatory dilemmas such as true/false, representative/nonrepresentative.

At the end of this movement, and of the chapter, I present Borges as the stimulator of a trend, very active these days, which focuses on the categories text and structure, with the avowed purpose of abandoning the hierarchy of discourses, and winds up reaffirming it, only placing the formerly dominated discourse in the position of ruler. Elsewhere, someday, I intend to return to Borges and show how his work is more than what I have said. While it cannot be understood without a consideration of its ironic and devastating critique of the pretentions of the discourse of truth, it cannot be reduced to a mere deconstructivist trap. There is another dimension in it. I believe that the key here may be to establish a relation between Borges and the effect of *unheimlich*, the strange familiarity that Freud speaks of. Borges's *unheimlich* is the way in which the author goes further than a mere critique of truth criteria, allowing us to represent the world outside of the strict coordinates of time and space. If this hypothesis is plausible, then Borges's "gnosticism" has a revolutionary dimension beyond the field of art: if time and space are only parts of a certain construction of the world by men, then man can construct other worlds. And, just as we are not inexorably limited to the dimensions of *physis*, we are not limited to no other destiny, no other form of slavery. In short, in this summary I am only outlining a possible reading of Borges that has not yet been accomplished.

CHAPTER SEVEN

A Proscribed Concept: Mimesis and Avant-Garde Theory

For Sebastião Uchoa Leite

PROLEGOMENON

It is well known that *imitatio* occupied a unique position in the various poetics proposed from the sixteenth century to the mid–eighteenth century, approximately. It was seen not only as a basic category for artistic practice—and in this it was to be replaced by decorum and then by verisimilitude—but also, on the basis of an ancient tradition that began with Aristotle, as the result of a gregarious force. Its nobility, then, was all the greater for deriving from man's very nature. Thus Edmund Burke stated, in a work begun in 1747:

> It is by imitation far more than by precept that we learn every thing; and what we learn thus we acquire not only more effectually, but more pleasantly. This forms our manners, our opinions, our lives. It is one of the strongest links of society; it is a species of mutual compliance which all men yield to each other, without constraint to themselves, and which is extremely flattering to all.   (Burke 1968: 49)

Although Burke cannot be strictly identified with the tradition of the immediately preceding centuries, and although he anticipates what will later be called the preromantic sensibility, significantly he does not find it necessary to define what he means by "imitation." This is so because Burke was writing at a time when this issue, which dated back to the Italian

Renaissance, still occupied a central position, and to the public he wrote for, imitation was a living concept.

Nevertheless, Burke is already distancing himself from the notion. This is made evident when he discusses the relation between *imitatio* and poetry. In the short section 6 of the fifth and last part of his book, Burke serenely declares:

> Hence we may observe that poetry, taken in its most general sense, cannot with strict propriety be called an art of imitation. It is indeed an imitation so far as it describes the manners and passions of men which their words can express.... There it is strictly imitation; and all merely *dramatic poetry* is of this sort. But descriptive poetry operates chiefly by substitution; by the means of sounds, which by custom have the effect of realities. Nothing is an imitation further than as it resembles some other thing; and words undoubtedly have no sort of resemblance to the ideas for which they stand. (Pp. 172–73)

Here we have two archaeological strata, as it were, of the understanding of the poetic: the earlier layer sees poetry as imitation of the world; that is, it sees words as belonging to the same sphere as things; whereas the upper layer defines poetry as a form of language, by means of which—the romantics would soon proclaim—the self expresses its feelings and proves their truthfulness. Burke, however, does not say so; and his qualification has a merely logical weight. That is, outside of drama, properly speaking poetry is not imitation because it relies on words, and since words do not indicate the ideas they convey in a transparent way, they appear to be imitative solely because of the convention that associates a certain name with a certain thing.

We say that the restriction is merely logical because users of words fail to see the difference between word and thing. The fact that the word "tree" stands for the idea of tree simply because of a convention would not seem to the man in the street to be revolutionary in relation to current thought. That is, outside of scholarly or specialist circles, Burke's qualification would not be seen as an argument against the view that poetical practice should be seen in terms of imitation. Burke's treatise indeed proves that the classical explanation was losing ground, but this fact was not yet so noticeable as to indicate that an alternative theorization was already present.

It was not, however, only *imitatio* that retained its central position. The *contiguity of the social* also remained present in every reflection concerning the poetic. This was so because the cult of *imitatio* understood it as a form of communication—that is, it still took for granted the existence of a certain form of society. More explicitly: whenever the authors of classical treatises set out to justify *imitatio*, society was immediately mentioned—

either in reference to the service that poets must render it by submitting to decorum and verisimilitude, or, as in Burke's case, in reference to the empire of communal force. This was so because there was a solidarity between the established social order and the legitimate exercise of poetry. This solidarity meant that one could not think about poetry without taking into account the expectations of society. Thus to treat poetry as *imitatio* was to see it as a *form of communication*—or, more precisely, a *communicative situation*.

To us, who live in the postromantic culture, this seems so amazing that I must dwell longer on the point in order to be fully understood. What sort of society was this, so comprehensive and inclusive, so extensive, as to be invoked and manifest even when it came to discussing a discourse we are used to seeing as marginal, deviant, related only to the darkest side of the individual self, tending to a personal idiolect? Would not such a society be recommendable for us moderns, who are so devoid of links?

By bringing up such questions, we can dispel serious misunderstandings. It is true that the privilege of *imitatio* occurred in a society that included the poetic; but it is no less true that the structure of this society was such that today it would be experienced as repressive rather than desirable. To put it quite clearly, the society that took the poetic into consideration by emphasizing *imitatio* was the one in which the estate system prevailed. The historian José Antonio Maravall has described this system as follows:

> In it, the stratum or estate to which one belongs becomes a criterion by means of which to each and every one of its members—that is, individuals—a single social role is homogeneously attributed, a *social role* that indicates to each the function that corresponds to his position, fixes the status that is conferred on him by dint of that function, in principle equal to that of all others in the same stratum; confers a rank that may and should be publicly displayed, an *esteem* or *prestige* derived from his position, and, last, a social *compensation* or *retribution* assigned to him; and this entire set culminates in the acknowledgment of the right to an *honor*—to which he must respond and in respect of which he may direct at others the most severe exigencies. (Maravall 1978: 9)

Thus the estate system does not consider the individual, for—in addition to the observations in the passage above—it "usually finds expression above all in the requirement that all that are part of a given social category should lead a specific way of life and adopt a behavior common to it" (p. 11). Further, the estate system excluded the primacy of the economic criterion, on which the fledgling bourgeois society was being built. This, however, does not mean that no economic considerations had any place in it. Noblemen, who were benefited by the system, enjoyed privileges that were directly or indirectly economic, for, as the Spanish historian observes, "the condition of nobility was ... above all a fiscal benefit" (p. 23), to which other sorts of privileges were added, such as those of a "judicial nature," "military exemptions," and "oligopolistic control of posts" (p. 23).

I emphasize this aspect in order to counter the common and mistaken tendency to conceive the estate system in isolation from any economic considerations—a mistake that has led to many a misreading of Max Weber. But what is even more important for my present purposes is to highlight the *insignificance* of the individual as a psychologically oriented being. The fact that the individual so conceived did not exist implied that poetry could and should rely on a common, conventional stock—that is, the topoi on which it fed and on the basis of which it was understood and theorized. In other words, *imitatio* prevailed as an objective criterion of explanation and evaluation of art because it was a convention that had general circulation in society, linking authors and receivers. Thus *imitatio* expressed, in the field of art, the social pact of the estate society, and was at the same time a coercive instrument for the preservation of the system. To the extent that it helped socialize producers and receivers of art—particularly poetry and the visual arts—it discouraged individual exploration of dissident values, thus favoring the maintenance of a rigidly stratified society.

In short, poetry could be seen as a form of communication as long as the *horizontality* of its circulation was preserved—that is, as long as it was kept within the bounds of the estate from which it proceeded or to which it was addressed. In other words, it was seen as a form of communication less because it had a theorization specific to it than because it was the by-product of a strongly stratified idea of society. For this reason, one may well associate classical theoreticians' emphasis on the communicative aspect of poetry with their concern—none the less effective for being unconscious—with taming the fictional. As I tried to show in *Control of the Imaginary*, the intention was to subordinate the fictional to the principles of common sense, making it conform to both the social and the perceptual order. Hence, for instance, the law of the three unities, to be followed in the theater; hence the hostility for the marvelous; hence the erudite Don Quixote's antipathy toward Sancho's folksy and "irrational" refrains.

The situation was more complex in the visual arts. Because of the enthusiasm for the works of antiquity—a decisive component of the Renaissance attitude—and the general lack of erudition among artists, the Humanists played an important role in subordinating the fictional to common sense not only by assisting the artists but also by writing treatises and practical manuals describing the traits and properties associated with each mythological being and pagan god. Jean Seznec, who studied this problem in detail, shows that this gave rise to a controversy. On the one hand, artists and Humanists emphasized the importance of the classical heritage; on the other, the Church denounced the rising neopaganism. But such denunciations, writes Seznec, could not be too categorical because the religious authorities themselves, as men of culture, shared the same admiration for antiquity. Nonetheless, artists felt threatened, and were forced to devise excuses and compromises: "Painting and sculpture, they replied, do not perpetuate idolatry; there is no risk whatsoever in preserving the memories of the gods, now that superstition has vanished from the world" (Seznec 1972: 268). Since this excuse sounded reasonable to Church authorities, their most sophisticated representatives became indispensable for artists, not only as consultants but also as commissioners of works (see Seznec 1972: 265).

But Seznec, who wrote in 1940, did not carry his examination to the point that would seem necessary today. The artist's desire or need for compromise is not the whole story. Nor was finding an excuse that put churchmen's conscience to rest the only factor involved. A more rigorous frame was needed. This was supplied by the authors of classical poetics, veritable masterpieces of deliberate compromise. On the one hand, *imitatio*, verisimilitude, and decorum legitimate the authority of ancient models, while on the other they submit this authority to the parameters of the rationalism of common sense. Therefore the instruments of classical art theory both permit its practice and control it. (It was not in Seznec but in Auerbach's "La Cour et la ville" that we found the inklings of the solution to this problem.)

The explanations above will not seem excessive or unnecessary when one considers that without them I might give the impression that an investigation of mimesis could afford to ignore the kind of society in which *imitatio* took root. If, then, the society in which *imitatio* prevailed was fundamentally of the estate rather than the class type, then three consequences follow. First, the demise of the domination of *imitatio* must have corresponded to the birth of a new kind of society. Second, the reconsideration of the question of mimesis, as I have been developing it since *Mimesis e modernidade* (1980), must proceed from the assumption that mimesis cannot be identified with its apparent Latin counterpart, *imitatio*. Third, if this investigation is to bear any fruit, it will be necessary at some point at least to suggest the outline of a different social formation, or else a different way of conceiving the world and society. I will leave this third point aside, for this is surely not the place to go into the matter, and concentrate instead on the first two. More emphasis will be placed on the first point, and it is to be hoped that clarifying this issue will put us in a better position to understand the second point.

THE PROSCRIPTION OF MIMESIS

Few concepts have elicited such unanimous responses from literary theorists as *imitatio*. Not even the most intransigent defender of realist aesthetics would dare invoke it, fearful of his professional reputation. Indeed, from the beginnings of romanticism *imitatio* has been relegated to the ash heap of history. Schlegel and Novalis, Coleridge and Wordsworth, and somewhat later Stendhal, in *Racine et Shakespeare*, and Hugo, in the preface to *Cromwell*, all spoke of *imitatio* as an enslaving, external norm and a violation of the right to individual expression. The romantics, in fact, aimed at a radical change. They felt that the artist, rather than incorporate a standard, should explore the paths of nature and subjectivity: hence the notion of genius, the extraordinary individual who converts his own errancy and waywardness into a source of art. Instead of socialized models or themes, inducive to communication, the singularity of the individual was emphasized.

The self, as M. H. Abrams showed in his admirable works *The Mirror and the Lamp* (1953) and *Natural Supernaturalism* (1971), came to take the place of God, while the religious experience became secularized and developed in the *Bildungsroman*. (If in the *Bildungsroman* happiness is only a passing phenomenon, this is not because it was thought to be less individualizing than misfortune, but because it was self-sufficient and therefore did not require sublimation into art.) It is true that this self, the young artist's object of exploration, did not have a single, univocal meaning. For Friedrich Schlegel, a reader of Fichte and a critic of novels that were purely confessional or that presented themselves as variants of historical narrative, the individual self should be *magnified* and unfolded into what it did not contain itself, whereas for most later romantics—Shelley and Byron, Musset and Vigny—it is the little self, with its petty miseries, contingencies, and passions, that turns into the beacon that casts its light in the poem.

This aesthetics, evidently, had its sources; between the aesthetics of *imitatio* and it there were transitional figures such as Abbé Dubos Burbe and, above all, Rousseau. Similarly, between the estate system and romantic individualism there was the development of capitalist relations, as well as the early enthusiasm over and later disillusionment with the French Revolution. Again, it is unnecessary to go into the growing importance of historiography and its effect on the development of the novel. Although

I do not imply that these problems have been satisfactorily settled, right now my concern is to emphasize that, with the triumph of romanticism, a new quest was consolidated—that for a new orientation based on the self—and that since then *imitatio* has been buried so deep that it seems to have lost all links with anything or anyone.

But what replaced *imitatio*? What are the changes that took place so that literature—a term that only then came into use—was legitimated? To think of it as the discourse that seeks to express individuality would be an arbitrary formula, which at best gives a vague idea of what the romantic search actually was, and fails to discriminate between symbolists, realists, and expressionists. In fact, the centering on the self, beginning with Baudelaire, is changed into hostility toward common expectations and common language. It is as though poetry, having broken out of the prison of *imitatio*, were striving to master experiences and a language marked as *abnormal*, as though it had identified as its enemy the numerous community of well-adjusted people. Clearly this tendency is not the result of internal workings of the poetic, for it is the consequence of life in the interior of capitalist relations. I will take this for granted and concentrate on another aspect: the phenomenon of the poet's distancing, in search of his irreducible expression. This phenomenon can be stated as follows: Ever since the poet lost the estate society as his horizon, increasingly he elected the exploration of his own means of expression as the legitimating center of his activity; this also sharpened his sensitivity to what was repressed and ignored by common use. That is, language itself became the basic object of exploration, and its conquest was evaluated according to the degree to which it incorporated what was ignored, despised, or feared by those who served established society, willingly or not. This process snowballed from romanticism to the advent of the avant-gardes of the early twentieth century.

I will now examine some of the statements and the personalities that are representative of avant-garde art, and then proceed to explain why I feel that it is important to return to the question of mimesis. It should then be clear that this chapter has a wider intention. The idea is to study the ideas of the avant-garde as the most recent development of an *episteme* that has been taking shape since romanticism. For it is between romanticism and the era of the avant-gardes that the artistic and intellectual reception of modernity was solidified—an era that Nietzsche aptly qualified as that of "active nihilism." Let us now turn to the proscription of mimesis in avant-garde thought.

My examination need not be factually exhaustive. And I will leave out Mallarmé's *idéias*, though logically their analysis would belong here both because in his time he could not yet see himself as part of an avant-garde and because it would be impossible to do justice to Mallarmé in a single chapter. This much being understood, I now add that it will be necessary to revise this survey only if some representative of the avant-garde presents a contrary thesis.* I will concentrate on the ideas of Apollinaire, Huidobro, Klee, and Breton, arriving at Duchamp and examining the development of his theses on a philosophical plane by Gilles Deleuze.

Apollinaire was already an established poet when, in 1913, he published his essay on the cubist painters. By so doing, he came with his prestige to the defense of a movement seen by official circles as just another provocation. The light tone of the short sentences, the aphoristic rather than dissertative structure, the elegant turns of phrase, all clearly contributed to the impact of this essay-manifesto. Reading it, the cultured bourgeoisie—even as its standards of taste were being attacked—could feel that only one of their own could reach such heights of mundane lightness. But what do we find if we scratch the text's varnished surface?

The first thing that comes into view is the break with the pact between the conformist painter and nature. The time of impressionism was gone. Meadows, flowers, picnics, the interplay of light and shadow—such things had already conquered the peace of museums. For Apollinaire, this was well deserved. The compromise with the feast of nature, although reduced to a Sunday walk in a garden, still harked back to the ancient *imitatio*. Hence Apollinaire's scathing criticism: "Let workers master nature; and gardeners have less respect for nature than artists do.—It is time to master it [*Il est temps d'être les maîtres*]" (Apollinaire 1950: 8). The author of *Alcools*, with the (bad?) habits of a literate man, does not require much from his reader's reasoning, and to make sure of his effectiveness expresses his thoughts in well-crafted sentences, such as this gem: "This side of eternity the mortal forms of love dance, and the name of nature sums up their accursed discipline" (p. 8). *En deçà de l'éternité* refers to the sphere to which the average man can aspire—the man who is unable to rise to the daring heights reserved to potential immortals. The ordinary man remains walled in between the "mortal forms of love" and the nature that contains them. Life circulates between two watertight compartments. Below are those who, limited to mortality, can only follow nature's steps. Above, the transmission of life takes place—the life that the heroes of yore communicate to today's elect: "Painting purifies itself, in the West, with this ideal

---

*According to my friend Karlheinz Barck (oral communication), such a counterposition can nevertheless be found in the essays of R. Desnos and in the group of dissenting surrealists formed around G. Bataille and the magazine *Documents*, who intended to associate formal innovation with the search for communicability.

logic that ancient painters handed down to the new, as though they had given them life" (p. 8).

It might be objected that I am overinterpreting the passage, that the accusation against the painting of nature has nothing to do with the problem of imitation. But Apollinaire himself dispels any doubts, making his point quite explicitly: "Verisimilitude no longer has any importance, for the artist sacrifices all to the truths, to the needs of a higher nature, which he supposes without discovering" (p. 13). "What distinguishes cubism from old painting is the fact that it is not an art of imitation, but one of conception tending to rise to the sphere of creation" (p. 26). The two passages, in addition to making their point, also throw light on some parallel themes that accompany the theorization. Verisimilitude is rejected for the sake of truth and of the need for a *nature supérieure*—that is, a nature that acts as *essence*, as opposed to one reduced to the condition of *appearance* and superficiality. Thus the idea of essence lives on in spite of the condemnation of *imitatio*, although the relation between essence and imitation seems to be quite close. (Later we will see this link reappear in a much more elaborated reflection.)

The parallel theme implied by the second passage is even more evident: *imitatio* is further condemned because it prohibits creation. By escaping subjection to the referent and to nature, the cubist painter no longer aims at sketching out some biographical incident, as does thematic painting, much less at capturing some emotional chaos; rather, he wishes to create *un art de conception*—that is, to proclaim a constructivist principle. To Apollinaire it seemed self-evident that mimesis had broken its ancient ties with *poiesis*, in such a way that it was necessary to abjure the former in order to defend the latter. But this is not the only place where the legacy of romanticism can be seen in Apollinaire's text; it also shows in the ambivalent meaning of the creative work: now it amounts to the expression of the self, now it has to do with something beyond the self. Thus, on the one hand the self is deified: "First of all the painter must present himself with his own divinity, and the paintings he offers to the admiration of men will confer on them the glory of also being able to exert momentarily their own divinity" (p. 10). "Every deity creates according to his image; so it is with painters. And only photographers manufacture the reproduction of nature" (p. 11). On the other hand, Apollinaire declares, exposing himself to the charge of being self-contradictory: "Greek art had a purely human concept of beauty. It took man as the measure of perfection. The art of the new painters takes the infinite universe as its ideal, and it is this ideal that provides a new measure of perfection, which allows the artist-painter to give the object proportions that are adequate to the degree of plasticity that he wishes to attain" (p. 18).

Actually, the obvious ambiguity of these passages does not imply a contradiction. If we compare them (i.e., those on his pp. 10 and 11) with another, previously quoted passage, we will arrive at a curious conclusion: since the artist has access to a "higher nature," the existence of which he supposes without discovering, and thus relegates mundane nature to "photographers," the artist is the one who denies (contingent) nature the better to remain faithful to (essential) nature, which has been preserved in him and nowhere else. The artist's specificity consists in having preserved the capacity of reading nature, whereas other men know only how to recognize its appearance. The self that is deified here is just as invisible to common eyes as this essential nature is. What is valuable (the deified self, higher nature) is thus hidden to *common* eyes, in the two senses of the word "common." We then see, though at the cost of an ambiguity that remains intact, that the passages are not contradictory. Taking the "infinite universe" as a "new measure of perfection" does not contradict the deification of the self, because both are related to a hidden reality that common eyes cannot see. It might even be said that, for Apollinaire, the avant-garde painter does not depict anything, not because nothing can depict anything, but because, except for the artist himself, no one knows what it is that he depicts. But this complication would not be in the taste of the poet's sugared words.

This brief comment certainly fails to do justice to the historical importance of *Méditations esthétiques*. But for this very reason I found it necessary to point out what the work contains and expresses even in a reading that is far from exhaustive. In any case, the validity of this comment will depend on the resonance it acquires in the transcriptions below, the first of which are of texts by Vicente Huidobro.

Even before he arrived in Paris, in 1916, and began to mingle in avant-garde circles, the Chilean poet already had some experience in writing manifestos. In "Non serviam," in 1914, he wrote: "I will not be your slave, Mother Nature; I will be your master. You will make use of me; that is very well. I do not wish to avoid that, nor can I help it; but I will make use of you as well. I will have my trees, which will not be like yours, I will have my mountains, I will have my rivers and my seas, I will have my sky and my stars" (Huidobro 1976, 1: 715).

Let us leave aside the declamatory tone of Spanish-American rhetoric. But the date of publication is significant, because it shows that the young poet was aware of a discussion that might be thought to be exclusively European at that time. Here, too, though without the European elegance of Apollinaire's sentences, creation is opposed to imitation of nature. The fact that Huidobro's manifesto came out almost at the same time as *Méditations esthétiques* is not exceptional; it simply indicates the young Chilean poet's ability (which is indeed exceptional) to reflect on the post-Baudelairean poetic tradition and even appropriate it. (In later statements, Huidobro mentioned texts and lectures of his, written before "Non serviam," in which his "creationist" position was already formulated. Unfortunately they are not to be found in the edition of his "complete" works.)

It is directly from this tradition, particularly Mallarmé's essays, that the vehement attack on referential language is derived: "The value of poetic language is directly proportional to its distance from spoken language. This is what common people cannot understand, because they will not accept that the poet should want to express only the inexpressible" (p. 716). There is a logical connection between the refusal of *imitatio* and the refusal of referentiality, which limits the semantics of words to the sphere of their pragmatic use. The passage from "Non serviam" transcribed above assumes such a connection. But it must not be forgotten that the attack on referentiality poses for the artist a problem much more intractable than the mere refusal of imitation. So it was that the romantics discarded *imitatio* but did not dare, either in theory or in practice, to question the words of the tribe. It seems clear that the contempt for referentiality was conditioned by the aggravation of the causes that had led, since the latter half of the eighteenth century, to the abandonment of *imitatio* and the exploration—ambiguous, as we have seen—of the self; and, since the latter half of the following century, to the making of poems as an act of aggression against bourgeois expectations and values. That is, the backdrop for the questioning of referents is the artist's feeling that, as an artist, he could transcend the obstacles posed by a profit-based society only by exploiting areas of expression unknown or opposed to those in which *raisonneurs* and common men move.

This, then, is the social conditioning of the question; but we have not yet seen the full set of necessary inferences. The survival of a discursive formation may depend on its exclusion from the language of the public square, the court, and the market; but if it is to be a form of discourse at all, it will necessarily require the attention of the *other*—the nonproducer or nonartist, who might be interested in it as a consumer, for one. Thus Mallarmé's ambition to "donner un sens plus pur aux mots de la tribu" ("give a purer meaning to the words of the tribe") (Mallarmé 1956: 189) implied the task of undermining the wall of referentiality, a task that could be successfully accomplished only if it were possible to draw out of the circle protected by the wall those—no matter how few—who were worthy of reaching the *sens plus pur*.

When he attacked referentiality, proposing a language freed of its fetters, Huidobro was using an argument that was in the air, although he was unaware of the risk it implied. I am not blaming him for it. As we will see, even more clear-sighted avant-gardists did not find it necessary to investigate the matter any further. The intellectual circles of the first decades of our century were marked by such enthusiasm over the challenge to pragmatic reason and its institutions, schools, museums, and academies that they failed to see or take seriously the need to reflect on the biggest obstacle to their proposals, from the point of view of the indispensable circulation of their products. (Janick and Toulmin's *Wittgenstein's Vienna* [1973] shows that this search for a purified language was not restricted to artistic circles, but was also carried out by philosophers, who sought a formalized, mathematicized language, uncontaminated by the imprecision of everyday speech—which, in turn, I might add, was parallel to Saussure's definition of a *langue* as distinct from the vocalization of *parole*, and to Freud's exploration of the *mare magnum* of the unconscious. The intelligentsia of the period was going through a sort of modified Enlightenment, minus the pedagogic intent, but retaining the purpose of radical change. The artistic, scientific, or political avant-garde found itself compelled to elaborate a more precise and refined language—one that would resist the mystifications of speech and that would be independent of the agent's deliberate motivation—as well as forms of action that could demolish the status quo. As to the masses, all that had to be done was to make them understand and follow the path opened by the avant-garde.) The problem of communication was never faced *directly*, as if receivers had to tread the road opened by the producers, whatever their sphere of activity. The poet had only to recognize the new America he was helping to conquer. In the words of an enthusiastic interpreter of the inventors of the period:

The "plot" of the poem is that mind's activity, fetching some new thing into the field of consciousness. The action passing through any Imagist poem is a mind's invisible action discovering what will come next that may sustain the presentation—what image, what rhythm, what allusion, what word—to the end that the poem shall be "lord over fact," not the transcript of one encounter but the Gestalt of many, from the Metro traveller's to that of Koré in the underworld.

(Kenner 1975: 186)

Although Hugh Kenner was writing 50 years after Huidobro and was in a position to weigh the positive and negative legacies of the generation he was analyzing, he did not consider the risk that the avant-gardists' project had to face: the danger that their distance from common language might lead, at best, to a monologue with shadows, or to a sober, isolated museum room. Indeed, it was only much more recently that the trap modernity set for itself was acknowledged:

And yet, it seems to me, we don't know how to use our modernism, we have missed or broken the connection between our culture and our lives. Jackson Pollock imagined his drip paintings as forests in which spectators might lose (and, of course, find) themselves; but we have mostly lost the art of putting ourselves in the picture, of recognizing ourselves as participants and protagonists in the art and thought of our time. Our century has nourished a spectacular modern art; but we seem to have forgotten how to grasp the modern life from which this art springs.

(Berman 1982: 24)

This complaint sounds so natural today that it is hard to realize that it became a commonplace only recently—so difficult has it been to accept that the very authors we admire were among those responsible for the break, at least to the extent that they believed communication was a minor problem, of purely technical or commercial interest.

With his antireferential proposal, Huidobro sees realism as his great adversary: "Realism in the usual sense of the word, that is, as a more or less skillful description of preexisting truths, does not concern us and we will not even discuss it, for artistic truth begins where the truth of life ends" (Huidobro 1976, 1: 722). With better arguments, countless others joined him in this attack. This identity of positions explains how it was that Huidobro discovered on his own what posterity has come to identify as the principle of estrangement developed by Russian formalists: "A poem is a poem when it contains the unusual. From the moment that a poem is changed into something usual, it no longer moves, no longer astonishes, no longer disturbs, and thus is a poem no longer" (p. 730). The aim of art, Viktor Shklovsky had written a few years earlier in "Art as a Procedure," is to break the automatism that causes things no longer to be seen, but only recognized. Automatism and estrangement oppose each other just as realism and "creationism," or imagism, or vorticism, or surrealism.

If there is a logical consistency in the sequence formed by the fight against referentiality, against realism, against the usual, we may borrow Foucault's term "*epistemic* consistency" to describe it. Its central point is the refusal of "representation" understood as image—or rather, imagetic fixation—of what is presented, of what is *outside* the self. Out of this core refusal derived the alternative I have already mentioned: the generating nature of the outside world is negated, in order either to exalt the absolute invention of the self or, to quote Apollinaire, to reach "the infinite universe." Given these two options, the Chilean poet made the more common choice. Concerning the title of the book *Horizon carré*, he wrote: "Square horizon. A new fact invented by me, created by me, which could not exist without me" (p. 739). Faithful to his avant-garde origins, vain to such a degree that his work suffered by it and his time was wasted in absolutely futile polemics, Huidobro consistently saw himself as the principle and center of creation. As he wrote in his most important poem, "I am Altazor / Altazor / Shut up in the cage of his fate."

It might be argued, though, that Apollinaire and Huidobro are poets rather than thinkers, and that for this reason my argument has the serious flaw of trying to reconstruct paradigmatic points of the avant-garde based on texts that are not intellectually representative. This objection will clearly stand unless I am able to find comparable statements in the writings of artists with greater analytical ability, such as Klee and Breton.

The role of Paul Klee's reflections on art has been compared to that of Leonardo da Vinci's. One could even say that the comparison fails to do justice to Klee, for Leonardo's writings found a wider public only long after his death. As a modern artist who was interested less in asserting himself as an avant-gardist than in actually being one, Klee from the outset disqualifies *imitatio*: "Like a man, a painting also has a skeleton, muscles, and skin. A painting may be said to have its particular anatomy. A painting with the theme 'Naked Man' is figured not according to human anatomy but to the anatomy of the painting" (Klee 1957: 241). The differences of tone—his language is dry and precise, rather than flowery and mannered like Apollinaire's—and intended public—Klee is writing a diary, not a manifesto—do not imply any major discrepancies. Instead, Klee's sharp wording—he uses his pencil as he does a burin in his work as an engraver—aims straight at the bull's-eye, with no roundabouts or flourishes. When he writes that a picture of a naked man must be figured according to the painting's visual requirements and not to the anatomy of the human body, Klee is asserting the need to break with the concerns and the very character of the work of Leonardo, an ancestor of his whom he had studied intensely and whom he greatly admired. Again, he writes: "Light, seen graphically. To represent light by clarity is like the snows of yesteryear. Now, light as chromatic movement, that is something new" (p. 263). Here Klee is explicitly affirming the urgent need to distance himself from the achievement of the impressionists. The denial of all imitative form is emphasized as the basic condition for access to modernity, for acceptance of its Faustian challenge, and not as submission to the taste of his potential consumers; on the contrary, it implies a refusal of what they would like to buy.

Like Apollinaire and Huidobro, Klee abjures realism in the most unequivocal way. Referring to the "natural forms of phenomena" (*natürlichen Erscheinungsformen*), he writes: "[The modern artist] does not feel very much attached to these realities, for he does not see these finished forms as the essence of the natural process of creation. For he is more interested in formative energies than in finished forms" (Klee 1945: 43). This means that, on a much more rigorous and effective level, Klee is reaffirming the opposition between imitation-realism and expression-creation. What does he place at the center previously occupied by *imitatio*? I have said that this place was taken up either by the pure self or by something that transcended it. Given these terms, Klee's position is just as unequivocal. Not for him Huidobro's notion of the artist as "a little God"; not for him the self-pity or heroic posturing so typical of the romantics. The opposite of *imitatio* is not the praise of the self, but rather the use of the self as a passage: "In the position of a trunk, he [the artist] does no more than collect and pass on what comes from the depths. Neither serve nor dominate, simply transmit" (p. 13). Klee has absolutely no doubts concerning the self—an attitude that contrasts with the ambiguity I have shown to be common in avant-garde thought. His firmness and incisiveness are intensified by his readings of Freud. "What is aroused by these drives [*Treiben*]," he writes in his 1945 essay, "dreams, ideas, fantasies, is of any value only when it is completely connected to the plastic means adequate to the work [*Gestaltung*]" (p. 49). This means that the exploration of the unconscious will not be plastically fruitful if there is no deliberate mediation of formativeness (*Gestaltung*). Thus, while in Apollinaire and Huidobro the problem of form was a private question, perhaps because it was difficult to submit it to a conceptual treatment, so that it did not appear in published texts, in Klee it is the fundamental question, in his lectures as well as in his diaries. So Paul Klee's place among the masters of contemporary art is not a function solely of his artistic production, but also of his theoretical production on the problem of the technical ascesis necessary in order to reach the modern *Gestaltung*.

It seems natural, then, that the painter of *Angelus Novus* should not restrict himself to repeating paradigmatic points already present in the writings of others. Instead, he thematizes other points. The first of these results from a reflection on the abandonment of representationalism: "When a certain figure grows larger before our eyes, an association can all too easily step in to play the role of the tempter as to the meaning of the object. For, with a bit of fancy, each complex figure can be compared with some figure known from nature" (p. 29). This text raises a point that will be developed more fully in the last section of this chapter: that the freeing of art from forms commanded by "representational" figuration—that is, forms subordinate to those known from nature—is not ensured by the a priori decision to paint noncomparative forms. For the elaboration of a free and productive figuration can at any time be caused to deviate by the intervention of an association of ideas that leads the figure (*Gebilde*) back to its representational format. But the imminence of this "tempter" could only derive from the presence, in each individual, of a stock of expectations by means of which things, even the strangest and least "representational," gain a meaning. Indeed, it is by means of this stock of expectations that we approach natural and cultural phenomena and select them so that we can evaluate them. The internalization of this stock, then, is not an individual "option," but a consequence of the fact that the individual is part of the group in which he is socialized.

Therefore, what stands before us—the object, the phenomenon—is not exactly *before* us; what we see has already been shaped by our expectations. In actual fact, it is not an object or phenomenon that places itself before us; rather, our expectations place it there. Depending on our expectations, the object or phenomenon is perceived as *identical* when nothing in it diverges from the organizing expectation; as *similar* when it more or less allows an analogy with our expectations; as different when the discrepancy outweighs the expectations; and as hostile when the structure of what stands before us cannot be codified by our expectations.

Perhaps every contact between a human being and what is found around him or her—"phantom" things or other beings—takes place within these parameters. To "perceive" a phenomenon as identical, then, means to decode it as totally expectable (redundant). This does not mean that the phenomenon is so in itself—that is, that its configuration is indeed identical to what the subject that observes, appreciates, or analyzes expects from it; it means simply that it is selected in such a way that only the coincidence is perceived. If, for instance, someone sees me as pale and depressed and greets me with a smile, my absentmindedness may cause me not to perceive the irony contained in the greeting and to take it as the normal behavior I *expect* to see in an acquaintance. On the other hand, if, in the same situation, I see nothing but the irony in the greeting, I may feel that I am being attacked and may fail to recognize the fact that, whatever the irony involved, the acquaintance did greet me after all.

Certainly Klee did not have such matters in mind, for what concerned him specifically was the creation of a form of pictorial language that left no place for such associations. As we will see later, my discussion is based on assumptions that Klee did not share. Bearing in mind that I am submitting Klee's reflections to a different sort of consideration, I will continue my attempt to see how they can be "translated." By now this seems easy enough: the result of the association between a nonrepresentational form and a form known from nature is seen by Klee as harmful to the very process of creation because it restricts formativeness to the expectation of the *identical*, or of the *similar* at least—that is, the predictable, from the point of view of the producer himself. Klee was sharp enough to realize the trap the nonimitative painter might run into; but he failed to thematize the act of communication—that is, to ask himself whether the association would not have been just as inescapable on the side of the receptor as on that of the producer, for otherwise there would be no attribution of meaning.

However, it might be argued that the attribution of meaning to the visual object was precisely what Klee was striving to avoid. More simply put: Could it be that Klee privileged form to such an extent that he was horrified at the possibility that any sort of content would creep in? Even if we use such a simplistic and exhausted dichotomy as form-content, the answer to this question must be no. This becomes obvious in a later passage: "Proportions on the plane of linearity may, for instance, refer to the angle: zigzag movements, in sharp angles, in contrast with a horizontal succession of lines, provoke correspondingly opposite resonances of expression" (Klee 1945: 37). Here, I believe, Klee's idea is that the association of ideas plays a negative role when it imposes an arbitrary—that is, unmotivated—content on the formativeness of what is being processed. Or, conversely, formativeness must provide the basis, the *scheme*, on which its appropriate thematization, its content, is structured. Thus, in the last passage quoted, "opposite resonances of expression"—that is, opposite thematizations—are constituted on the basis of differentiated formal organizations. The following passage can be read in the same way: "What counts the most in evaluation is not whether what is represented is a dog, cat, etc., or 'nothing' (what does not exist), but rather whether what shows itself [*die Darstellung*] makes use of means adequate to the making of the painting or of means that are external to it" (Klee 1956: 72).

In short: Klee is not so naive as to suppose that the painting he practices and on which he theorizes should contain a barrier against any sort of semantics. All he wants is that meanings should not be imposed on a visual work of art by means of a connection that is automatic, irreflective, or arbitrary in relation to the formative principle of the work itself. Returning for the last time to my typology of expectations, if it is clear that Klee was hostile to the first two kinds—the expectations that generate identity and similarity—it is no less clear that his statement was directed at a figure close to the third type—the one that generates difference. In fact, however, this is only an approximate result, for Klee's theorization did not take into account the dispositions of the receiver, but only the qualities of production itself.

So far I have dwelt on the first distinctive characteristic of Klee's thought. Let me now take up the second, which has to do with the problem of the communication necessary to the artist. I have said that the enthusiasm over the new land to be explored made the post-Mallarméan tradition blind to the risks implied by its proposals. Again, Klee's position is divergent, at least to a certain extent. Referring to his teaching experience at the Bauhaus, which by then had been destroyed by Nazism, he wrote, in a half-nostalgic, half-combative tone, toward the end of his essay on modern art: "Nothing can be done quickly. The work must grow, higher and higher, and when its time comes, so much the better! We must still search for it. We find parts, but not yet the whole. We do not yet possess this final strength, for we are not followed by an entire people. —But we do search for a people, we began this search with the Bauhaus public" (Klee 1945: 53). But one must not overestimate this passage. As the Weimar Republic lay in its dying throes, Klee's work at the avant-gardist Bauhaus gave him the feeling that, together with his fellow artists, he was helping to create the community that contemporary intellectuals need. But the stimulus he received was not enough to change the dominant tenor of his writings. Klee is too great to need to be "rescued"—particularly by an essayist from the tropics. If only to avoid mythicizing him, it must be acknowledged that Klee's thought is a capital formulation of the *immanentism* of contemporary art. As an immanentist, Klee believed the essential questions in art had to do with the process of its formativeness. In this theory there is no room for any thoughts concerning the receiver. Implicitly, the immanentist theorist takes for granted that, if the work responds to its time in a creative way, sooner or later someone will be able to appreciate it and understand it. But this is tantamount to making the historical lag between time of production and time of effective reception into a necessary, substantial, intrinsic condition of art.

If, on the contrary—particularly with the theorization of Wolfgang Iser in mind—one introduces the figure of the receiver in the very structure of the fictional work, there is an inevitable clash with immanentist views. Thus, Klee writes: "As to the question of what is abstract, it is fundamental to consider direction [*die Behandlung von Vor und Zuruck*]. If one places yellow in front and blue behind, this is abstract. —It is the opposite if we use lighting to stress or downplay the positions in front and behind" (Klee 1956: 72–73). From the viewpoint of a theory interested in the communicative action of art, one might counterargue that if in a picture we grasp only the differential impression of the colors, what the painter meant to be "abstract" will be perceived as merely ornamental. In the same way, the precious opening sentence of Klee's "Schöpferische Konfession" (1920)— "Art does not reproduce the visible, it makes visible"—is sufficient only for an immanentist position, which takes into consideration solely the terms "artist" and "object to be produced." If, however, we introduce the receiver as an integral part of the structure of the fictional work—that is, if we affirm that fictional discourse has no stable inner properties, but depends on an observer able to see it as such—it remains to consider how the receiver's stock of expectations is actualized, and how—influenced by what type of expectation—he or she will react to the shapes and colors that make up the painting. If the receiver simply apprehends syntactic relations—that is, the differential position of colors—the painting will be "read" as ornamental. True, to the 1920 passage quoted above we must add later passages in which Klee moderates the opposition I have referred to. When he speaks of the fantastic and the fabulous of the imaginary character, Klee touches on a decisive issue, which is nearly always skirted. Formativeness is not achieved if the receiver's imagination is not fired.

But although he did approach the position in which the communicative action proper to art takes place, Klee does not really formulate the problem in this direction. The imagination he has in mind is that of the producer, perhaps because of a residual essentialism in his own theoretical reflections. Here is what Klee has to say on the difference between contemporary painters and the impressionists: "Our antipodes of yesterday, the impressionists, were right in their time to live with the roots and the underbrush of everyday appearances. —But our throbbing heart leads us below, to the depths of the original soil" (Klee 1945: 47). What could this primeval soil (*Urgrund*) be, this gulf in which the self loses itself, if not a form of abyssal essence?

Doubtless, one may look at this differently, and see this primeval gulf or abyss as the region of the nonself. To one, for instance, who knows absolutely nothing of Oriental thought (such is my own case), the Buddhist attack on thinking centered on the self is bewildering. In his unfinished journal written during his travels in the East, Thomas Merton presents a number of quotations that quite amaze me. Here is the paraphrase of one of these maxims: "The self is merely a locus in which the dance of the universe is aware of itself as complete from beginning to end—and returning to the void" (Merton 1968: 68). It would then seem as if my reflections, which aim simply at a better understanding of fictional discourse, corresponded to what in the East was developed centuries ago as a more comprehensive kind of thought, philosophical and religious.

But it would certainly be arbitrary to set up some sort of correspondence with Klee's reflections. Thus it seems impossible to erase the boundary line that separates us. In any case, I must emphasize that, without Paul Klee's paintings and theoretical writings, our passage would have been more hazardous. Apollinaire may have helped to consolidate the appreciation of cubism, but without Klee it would have been more difficult for me to maintain my profound sympathy for the work of the avant-gardists at the same time that I affirm my theoretical differences with them. And all of this applies equally to Breton.

When one reads the manifestos and essays of André Breton, his fictional prose and his poetry, one realizes why he is one of the great catalysts of contemporary literature. Without Breton it would be impossible to understand what literary experience became in the twentieth century, and the dilemmas it had to face. In addition, as Lévi-Strauss observed in his *Leçon inaugurale* at the Collège de France, surrealism inaugurated a new kind of cognitive relation with the world, and is thus much more than just another "ism" in contemporary art.

With Breton and the young artists of the early decades of the century, the divorce between artist and public, evident since Baudelaire, was further intensified. The self-imposed exile of the romantics had grown with the poet of *Fleurs du mal*, who learned that he could identify only with such outsiders as the *flâneur*, the dandy, the casual passerby. This process became even more intense with Jules Laforgue, Tristan Corbière, and the symbolists, who were aware that they had to listen to what was deviant, to move away from the world around them, where the only option open to the *voyant* was Rimbaudian abandon or Mallarméan schizophrenia. The poet's progressive displacement toward a life of anonymity, to which he is driven by the expansion of industrial society and its ruling values, leads, in the First Surrealist Manifesto, to an angry attack on the growing mediocrity of literature:

> The realist attitude, inspired in positivism, from Saint Thomas to Anatole France, appears to me to be hostile to all intellectual and moral activity. I see it with horror, for it is made up of mediocrity, hate, and self-sufficiency. It is this attitude that is now generating these ridiculous books, these insulting plays. It unceasingly draws strength from the newspapers, and neutralizes the efforts of science, of art, doing its utmost to flatter opinion, in its lowest tastes.   (Breton 1955: 9–10)

"Realism" is, in short, the word that links the contempt for intellectual adventure to the satisfaction of the reader who finds, on each page, his own image: "That is just what I would do in a situation like that." This attitude of contempt and repulsion for daring dominates logical discourse itself, reducing it to narrow good sense: "We still live under the domain of logic. . . . But in our days logical procedures are applied only to problems of secondary interest. The absolute rationalism still in fashion does not allow consideration of anything except facts that apply strictly to our own experience" (p. 12). (This, one should remember, was written ten years before Breton got to know the U.S.)

Consider the difference between Breton's fury and Huidobro's superficial enthusiasm. While the Chilean poet identified poetry with the "language of creation" and the "challenge to reason" (Huidobro 1976, 1: 176), Breton, almost alone in the midst of the anti-intellectualism that marked avant-garde groups, does not confuse reason with the use of this castrated logic, which is fearful of losing contact with the solidity of "reality." On the contrary, his struggle aims at endowing it with the necessary daring to validate the effort of using it.

However, for the purposes of this chapter, it is less important to stress the differences in intellectual force between the artists I am examining than to point to the gap that all of them were pointing at. However they might differ as to their respective speculative talents, for all of them the urgent task was to break down the invisible but effective wall of good sense, the prejudices of factualism, the middle ground that was the aim of realism; to attack, by every possible means, the "civilized" taming of mind and life. Thus it makes sense that avant-gardists should tend to take radical stands in politics. While Filippo Tommaso Marinetti and, unfortunately, Ezra Pound adhered to fascism, much more frequently other artists tried to reconcile their avant-garde positions with Marxism. This, again, was nothing new: since romanticism, the reason and the *modus vivendi* of the bourgeoisie had been seen with distaste by artists, even those whose dissent eventually led to conservative, even reactionary positions. What is important about this antibourgeois radicalism is that the reason of calculation, the rationality of surplus value, as they become increasingly comprehensive, forced the poet to move his expression away from the circuit of communication.

For Breton, Freud's discoveries—his curiosity being sparked by his medical and psychiatric training—had been since the 1920's the royal road for the liberation of poetry. Thus he postulated a poetry that, rescued from the logic enslaved to fact and calculation, would contain "as exactly as possible the *spoken thought*" (Breton 1955: 22). This was the origin of automatic writing. According to Anna Balakian's convincing argument, Breton picks it up not from Freud, though he always mentioned Freud as his source, but from Pierre Janet, whose works he had studied as a psychiatric student. Automatic writing, as its creator saw it, allowed the agent to distance himself from the self's heritage, which amounted to the various social pressures he suffered, and at the same time gave him access to a liberated and liberating language. Thus Breton, influenced by Janet and Freud, affirmed the existence of a paralyzing gap between thought and expression, a consequence of the incorporation of the *other* and his logic, tamed by its service to society. If, however, this gap were filled in, it would be possible to restore a truly productive flow.

These assumptions are present in the very definition of the movement: "*Surrealism, n*. Pure psychical automatism by means of which one proposes to express, in spoken or written language or in any other way, the actual working of thought. A dictate of thought, in the absence of every control exerted by reason, outside of every aesthetic or moral concern" (Breton 1955: 24). The definition makes it clear that surrealism, according to its propounder, was deliberately placed outside of literature, if we think of literature as a discourse with an aesthetic intention. Aesthetics and morals are for Breton links by means of which we perpetuate the closed circle of "master and slave." This statement was reiterated in 1953, in a sort of memento of the movement:

Nowadays it is generally known that surrealism, as an organized movement, originated in an ambitious operation directed at language. In this connection, it cannot be overemphasized that its creators did not advance any aesthetic criterion whatsoever. From the moment that the vanity of some of its members found a place for such a criterion, as soon was the case, the operation was doomed.

(Breton 1955: 117)

Similar observations have been made both with critical and with laudatory intent. My purpose here is neither. Surrealism will have nothing to do with literature because it sees itself as an instrument for the liberation of domesticated man, and because it conceives this liberation *outside of any considerations concerning communication*. The circuit of communication, whatever its type or tenor, was itself corrupted, and itself amounted to the beginning of a surrender to those who controlled life.

To defend my view, I will begin by observing that in Breton, as in Klee, there are traces of essentialism. If automatic writing is liberating, isn't it because it provides access to abyssal depths the way to which had been scarred over by the castrating action of social reason, which encouraged mediocrity? The social was identified with paralyzing logic, with tamed reason, whose scope of action—luckily for us—is restricted. That is why deep inside us there remains a diamond; in the floor of the psychical sea creative energy remains intact. What could this be, at least according to Western tradition, if not an essence? The very way in which Breton opposes the noxious effects of social alterity and the fruitfulness preserved by the deep sea of the psyche shows that Breton's residual essentialism is part of a conception that sees communication as the cancer that corrodes language.

With this argument in mind, let us return to the definition of surrealism and pose the question of how the product of this psychical automatism can be communicated—that is, under which conditions it can circulate among subjects. Though Breton might reject or ignore such a notion, the fact is that here he parted company with Freud. In psychoanalysis, it was and is to be expected that the analyst's "floating attention" should be able to reveal the logic behind the meandering, contradictory, and irregular trajectory of the patient's discourse. It would certainly be a mistake to suppose that the analyst's floating attention was to *grasp the truth* of the facts, as if psychoanalysis were committed to the positivist conception of history. The analyst merely *interprets* the way in which something has been experienced, that is, symbolized, by the patient. Therefore psychoanalytical practice requires an "artificial" environment, in which the analyst acts as a mediator between the unconscious and actual discourse (a *contaminated* mediator, in fact, for rather than simply acknowledging the meaning of what he is told, he introduces himself, affirms his presence as a subject to this discourse he listens to and interprets). How are we to assume the existence of some parallel between this discourse and automatic language, which is ultimately addressed to the page one is writing and to someone who, one hopes, would care to open it? Who will then act as *tertius*, or mediator? How are we to judge whether it is "pure"—that is, attuned to the discourse of the psychical abyss—or a "literary" mystification?

Breton never posed this problem directly. On the contrary, as early as the First Surrealist Manifesto we come across the passage I quote above, concerning the contempt for communication. Praising the practice of unaffected conversation for its "effort at sociability" and by the "habit it teaches us," Breton says about its interlocutors:

> Each one simply goes on with his soliloquy, with no attempt to derive any specific dialectical pleasure from it, or to impose the least part of it upon his neighbor. The resolutions made do not, as is usually the case, aim at the development of a thesis, however insignificant it might be; they are as disinterested as possible. As to the response it elicits, it is in principle totally indifferent to the self-esteem of him who announced it. Words and images are offered as no more than springboards to the mind of the hearer. (Breton 1955: 33)

The author seems to have in mind something like an enlarged version of an analyst's office. This, however, would be either naive or contradictory. Naive because, in the analyst's absence, who would replace him? And, if someone took his place ad hoc, how would the desired position of parity between interlocutors be maintained? And contradictory because, without a recognized interpreting authority, a playful mood would prevail, and we would have a sort of theatrical happening, a "laicized" aesthetic experience, so to speak—which would run counter to the surrealist principle against any aesthetic interference.

Since he could not think of communication as anything but a negative interchange, the interference of compromise, exhibitionism, or mental restriction, it is no wonder that Breton also praised estrangement. He did not present a typology of surrealistic images, but merely observed: "For me, the strongest is the one that presents the highest degree of arbitrariness, I admit; that which takes most time to translate into practical language" (p. 33). This preference for deviance from language norms necessarily implied—the more so because it was not restricted to the literary medium—the refusal of the public: "The public's approval should be avoided above all. It is definitely necessary to prevent the public from *coming in*, if we are to avoid confusion. I will add that it is necessary to keep the public exasperated at the door, by means of a system of challenges and provocations" (p. 89).

Although Breton was unaware of the problem or avoided it by means of statements that only made it the more serious, it would not be fair to conclude that he simply did not care. Breton did not share the *épater* mentality common among avant-gardists, who always believed that a serious question can be solved by means of an improvised gag. In his moving Prague conference of 1935, Breton, who took seriously his double condition as a leftist militant and avant-garde poet, defended the surrealist ideal against the hostility of socialist realism: "Art, which for centuries has been pressured to stick to the paths opened by the ego and the superego, cannot help being eager to explore in all senses the immense and nearly virgin expanses of the id" (Breton 1935: 58). What he proposed was no less than politicizing the unconscious. But how could this be done if communicative action was identified with the circuit that repressed the mind and the individual? How could one conceive a political action if the *other* was seen a priori with mistrust?

In a way, Walter Benjamin understood Breton's problem, in one of the most perceptive essays ever written about the meaning of surrealism. After aptly observing that the French poet and militant dispatched the cult of the self and of individuality—language "has precedence. Not just in relation to meaning. Also in relation to the self" (Benjamin 1974: 1, 297)—the essayist points to the Achilles heel of the movement: the excessive enthusiasm over the "state of surprise" and the joy of language: "The aesthetics of the painter, of the poet 'en état de surprise,' of art as a response to the surprising, implies a commitment to fatally romantic prejudices" (Benjamin 1974: 1, 307).

Is there anyone who still finds it arbitrary to associate this indiscriminate praise of the state of surprise, of what shocks usual practices, with the praise of estrangement—that is, the praise of a language that congratulates itself for running counter to common language? Or for limiting itself to seeing communication as the fluid that permeates a community of slaves and masters, in which the slaves, as Nietzsche wrote, are only preparing to assume the role of masters? A strange contradiction indeed for a movement that, as one of its analysts observes, always defended the connection between art and life and always attempted to "make social experience compatible with fantasy" (Barck 1979: 198). But the contradiction seems less strange when we recall the epistemic pressure that mounted when *imitatio* died. It is as though several successive generations had taken for granted that communicative situations are a priori doomed to justify the slaveholders; as though the masses—whatever their numbers—left to their own devices were unable to receive anything except for what catered to their lowest appetites—as though, in short, we ought to leave the problem of communication to the technicians of manipulation. But surely this thought has occurred to everybody at one time or another—the idea that the solution lies solely in the receiver of the future, *en retard*, as Duchamp would put it. But before closing this discussion, let me examine, albeit briefly, the case of Marcel Duchamp.

DUCHAMP AND THE QUESTION OF PAINTING

The best description of modernity is one that stresses its contradictory traits. On the one hand, it is characterized by a Faustian dynamism. Never before had human history known such forceful global change; whatever was maintained by routine, supported by tradition, legitimated by the authority of the ancients, was destroyed, banished, or changed into a tourist reserve. On the other hand, this Faustian dynamism clearly results from a pact with the devil: capital is its only stable monarch, a rational and consistent tyrant who ignores the limits of his own greed. We are all his subjects, all benefit him or are exploited by him, all are hypocrites or deluded innocents.

Within modernity, the artist, active in a specific symbolic medium, has manifested a specific kind of behavior. From Baudelaire to Joyce, from the streets of Paris to the remembered streets of Dublin, he has been aware that he has nothing left to do other than delve deep into everyday reality, cast off the aura of heroism that was once his mark, and accept mud and exile. This urge to be part of his time, however, has not led him to defend the governments he lives under. Particularly in modernity, the artist has learned that politics requires forms of compromise that inevitably have a noxious effect on his own work. That is why, however widely individual positions may diverge, in the last analysis the only thing that can be properly said of all modern artists is that they belong to the tradition of negativity.

The tradition of negativity finds its limit in Marcel Duchamp. As Octavio Paz has said, "Duchamp is at the same time the artist who takes the tendencies of the avant-garde to their ultimate consequences and the one who, as he consummates them, turns them on themselves and thus inverts them" (Paz 1973: 101). This radicalization, which leads to the inversion of the aims of avant-garde painting, took place in a relatively short period, basically between 1912, when he painted *Nude Descending a Staircase, No. 2*, the short series of nonrepresentational nudes and virgins, and 1923, when he abandoned work on his most famous piece, the *Large Glass, or The Bride Stripped Bare by Her Bachelors, Even* (1915–23), a synthesis of his small output. In between, Duchamp produced a few ready-mades, the most important of which is perhaps *Fountain* (1917). Apparently gratuitous, or only part of a provocation—"a common object promoted to the dignity of a work of art by the artist's mere choice," according to his own definition (Duchamp 1975: 49)—the ready-made had a more concrete justification for the artist. It was part of the struggle against "retinal art"—that is, art that is content to be a beautiful form for the eyes, which he attacked both for its superficial sensuality and for its use as a medium for aesthetic experience.

The apparently gratuitous nature of the ready-made in fact had a meaning, which is best apprehended when placed in its context. Thierry de Duve shows that it was contemporary with two other tendencies: the search for a pure language, which characterized such widely different painters as Klee and Kandinsky, and the attempt to create a functional (or industrial) art. Both are marked by optimism, yet the two also diverge. On one hand, the optimistic search for a pure language, which can ultimately be traced to Mallarmé but, as we have seen, was not restricted to the sphere of art, intended to establish a code *au dessus de la mêlée*, free of the mistakes and imprecisions of ordinary communication. On the other hand, the optimism of industrial art presupposed and tried to encourage the full integration of art into practical life:

> The functionalist "resolution," from Morris to Gropius and beyond, is the history of the acceptance—slow and reticent at first, then falsely triumphalistic—of the death of the craftsman, and of the consequent murder of painting. But it is also nourished by the illusion of the tabula rasa, the dream of a total transfer of power from the ancient artist craftsman to the new conceiver-designer, the dream of the complete and almost instantaneous transfer of what had been acquired by an ancient tradition now defunct to a culture yet to be born, which so far had no tradition whatsoever. (Duve 1984: 168)

The ready-made, not only ironical but downright sarcastic, turned its back on these noble purposes and parodied art itself, of which it preserved no more than the name: "The ready-made also proclaims the material, the making, and the utility, but as a means of isolating the only value instituted in the name of art, to the detriment of every aesthetic value and every use-value, both of them being neutralized" (p. 162).

Was this a new use of the old strategy of the libertines, of whom it was said that they loved the bedrooms of the powerful the better to attack them? Was the artist to turn into a mere satirist, ridiculing art by offering it urinals? No; Duchamp's gesture cannot be explained by these "daring" images. As he himself said, his distaste for modern painting—and not just that of his contemporaries—his dissatisfaction with its retinal and aesthetic character, resulted from his intention to return to a painting that deals with ideas; put less equivocally, a thinking painting. But what was it to think of? Was the ready-made an allegory? With its brute displacement from the world of useful objects to that of art, the ready-made proposes a sudden change: the abandonment of sensual aesthesis in favor of an exercise in ascesis. Does that mean a religious experience?

As Octavio Paz aptly put it: "Differing from the practices of the mystics, it aims not at union with the deity nor contemplation of the ultimate truth: it is a meeting with nothingness, and it aims at noncontemplation" (Paz 1973: 41). The spectator is invited to take the object that has been removed from its pragmatic destination and change it into a scheme for a reflection that has no starting point and no goal. This is a proposal against ornamental painting, against illustrative painting, which leads to a truth already known, and for a painting conducive to thought. Duchamp paints, or produces, or displaces—one may pick the verb one prefers—for the spectator, but not for the spectator's delight, and even less for the delight of the contemporary spectator. Faithful—though he may not know it—to the gesture common to all avant-gardes, he sets his hopes on the future and expects communication to be effective *en retard*; but still he believes in it.

This aspect of a painting of ideas, which summons the receiver to an act of reflection that is neither aesthetic nor religious but rather meaningless, leads me to a very brief comment on Duchamp's most famous work. I will not offer any precise description of it because either the reader already knows it or, if he doesn't, he will not be able to form an idea of it with a mere description unaccompanied by a reproduction. About this work André Breton observed, in a pioneering essay, that it presented a mechanistic and cynical view of love: the transition from the condition of virgin to nonvirgin was seen without any sentimentality, as though by a nonhuman being (see Breton 1959: 92). And Paz wrote: "The *Large Glass* is an infernal and buffoonish painting on modern love, or, more clearly, on what modern man has done to love" (Paz 1973: 67).

But if the reader has never seen the painting before and then attempts to read it according to these interpretations, he may find himself, if not angry with, at least baffled by the ingenuousness of the two essayists. How were they able to identify the bride and the bachelors, nine of them? How did they—not to mention countless other interpreters—identify the bride's transmission of messages to the mechanical males and understand their replies as shots that damage part of the glass? How did they identify, in the mysterious signs on the bottom right of the picture, observers of the scene? Actually, interpretations such as the ones quoted above are neither arbitrary nor wholly dependent on the interpreter's talent. On the contrary, they are determined by Duchamp's own notes, collected in the so-called "Boîte Verte" (1934) and now printed in Duchamp 1975: 39–104. For instance, Duchamp writes "the bachelors, who must serve," and "the bride is at bottom a motor." Resorting to the "Boîte" is not an idea of Duchamp's analysts; they simply followed the artist's explicit instructions: Duchamp specified that the "Boîte" should be consulted at the same time that the *Large Glass* was seen. The explicit purpose of avoiding aesthetic appreciation explains why the bride, on the left-hand top, appears as a dummy or skeleton, and why all the figures are represented as machines. The idea is to avoid the receiver's identifying with the scene and thus having an aesthetic experience. Instead, the instructions contained in the "Boîte" make us understand the erotic experience as an (incomplete) set of "desiring machines." The nonrepresentational nature of the painting aims at evoking in the spectator's mind only the representation of a concrete situation, conceived and criticized at the same time.

But, Paz asks, how can a painting of ideas be intended if we no longer have ideas as collective representations? If our time has reduced the universals of yore to simply this: the idea of criticism? Since this is our only universal, the Mexican essayist concludes, Duchamp makes criticism his constituent principle. And another critic adds: since criticism has no limits, in Duchamp's paintings "there is no eroticism, but a critical eroticism" (Chénieux 1979: 218). But what is the idea that is represented? For it is not enough to speak of criticism, for there must be something that is being criticized. To overcome this difficulty, Paz resorts to the Hindu myth of Shiva. Just as I was unable to describe the painting, I cannot describe the comparison with the Hindu image. But this is not fundamental for our purposes. It is the conclusion that matters: "Unlike the Hindu exegete, Duchamp rejects the metaphysical explanation and is silent. The Bride is a fourth-dimensional projection, but the fourth dimension is, by definition, the unknown dimension" (Paz 1973: 65). That is, if the painting of ideas is not to be *closed*—is not to have a final, ultimate explanation—it is necessary not only that its commentator be silent but also that the painting itself remain incomplete. Thus, although he refuses to submit his work to the aesthetic sensation, Duchamp retains from aesthetics its nature as a scheme to be supplemented by the receiver.

If, however, in this way the receiver is integrated into the structure of the work (that is, the structure does not work without him), does this mean that Duchamp's break with the avant-garde tradition still implies its thematization of the communication itself of the work of "art"—even if the thematization here is critical, mocking, parodistic? If so, could Duchamp be taken as the starting point for a reconsideration of a problem that has been neglected ever since mimesis was proscribed? But although the hypothesis seems reasonable, it does not seem to be right. Communication directed simply by criticism and its variants—irony, fraud, parody—arrives at noncommunication. For, as Paz says, "the *Large Glass* . . . is a work that turns on itself, striving to destroy precisely what it creates" (p. 73). But he arrives at a conclusion contrary to mine: comparing the *Large Glass* and *Étant donnés* (1946–66) and emphasizing the reciprocity of the two works, he writes: "The wooden door and the glass door: two opposite faces of the same idea. This opposition is resolved into an identity: in the two cases we see ourselves seeing. Operation Hinge. The question What is what we see? sets us face to face with ourselves" (p. 100).

Here I disagree. To face oneself is not a communicative act (it might be, at best, a preparation for such an act—or its preclusion). In itself, reduced to the act proper, facing oneself is quite the opposite: an act of pure solipsism. In short, if I understand Duchamp properly, his gesture does radicalize, but it remains in the field of the very same *episteme* I have been analyzing.

DELEUZE AND THE PHILOSOPHY OF *DIFFÉRENCE*

Among the decisive influences on the philosophical work of Gilles Deleuze are Nietzsche's rethinking of philosophy and the lesson he extracted from modern art. To limit my discussion to the problem I am concerned with, both lead to the same denunciation of the world of representations and the habitual misunderstanding of the categories of difference and repetition: "When the modern work of art . . . develops its interchangeable series and circular structures, it shows philosophy a path that leads to the abandonment of representation" (Deleuze 1968: 94). "The eternal return cannot mean the return of the identical, for it presupposes, on the contrary, a world (the world of will to power) in which all previous identities are abolished and dissolved. To return is to be, but only the being of becoming" (p. 59).

The critique of representation is fundamental for Deleuze because he sees it as tributary to the privilege that Western ontology has attributed, since Plato, to the identity of the concept. Hence the basic purpose of *Différence et répétition*: to destroy the primacy of identity, of unity as a solar figure, in order to recover difference, hitherto determined as negation: "In its essence, difference is the object of affirmation, it is itself affirmation" (p. 74). Thus a hierarchy is established beginning with the enthroned identical—which asserts and condenses itself in the concept and in law. From it derives the protecting shadow where its lieutenants find shelter: *representation* and the *figure of the self*. At the lowest end of the hierarchy are the negative forms of difference and repetition. The aim of the French philosopher is to upset this state of affairs, bringing to philosophical reflection the same subversion that characterizes modern art. In order to follow the discussion, let us first see how Deleuze characterizes his basic terms.

Contrary to what is proclaimed by the view that privileges the identical, repetition does not mean the return of the *same*, the reiteration of a situation. This is the enemy's rhetoric. The emphasis on the identical brings about the search for generality, and when generality is reached the singular loses its aspect of singularity. Thus repetition defines itself in opposition to generality: "Thus generality, as *generality of the particular*, is opposed to repetition, as *universality of the singular* (p. 8, emphases added). That is why repetition asserts itself as a power that subverts the law: "If repetition is possible, it is against the moral law, just as it is against the law of nature.... Repetition belongs to humor and irony; it is by its very nature transgression, the exception that always manifests a singularity against the particulars submitted to the law, a universal against the generalities that become laws" (p. 12). On the other hand, it is distinguished from difference by their respective positions in relation to the concept. The principle of difference is characterized "as difference in concept" (p. 21), while "repetition appears ... as difference without concept ... a potency proper to the existing, an obstination of the existing intuition, which resists every specification in the concept, however far the latter may be carried" (p. 23). If instead we remained content with the ontological structure in which Leibniz and Hegel still operate, we would be forced to take the path that leads away from any questioning of what is deepest: "Let us say not only that difference in itself is not contradiction 'yet,' but that it refuses to be led back and reduced to contradiction, because the latter is less deep, not deeper, than the former" (p. 73).

That is—reading this passage in the light of the passage from the First Surrealist Manifesto quoted above—commitment to the established ontology implies complicity with a mentality that favors only pragmatic reason. Thus Deleuze sets out from the same premise as Breton, though, being a philosopher, he places it in a much denser context. For all the differences of tone, both point in the same direction: it is necessary to reconsider the entire structure of intellectual elaboration of Western thought. This would require not only that repetition and difference be no longer stigmatized, not only that Hegel's commitment to the primacy of the concept be denounced, but also that those figures that are in solidarity with identity be deconstructed.

The first of these is representation. "Representation is the name given to the relation between the concept and its object, in this double aspect, as it is effected in this memory and in this self-consciousness" (p. 21). "What is objectionable about representation is the fact that it remains subordinate to the form of identity, in the twofold relation of the thing seen and the seeing subject" (p. 94). Thus representation stiffens movement, transforms flight into a fixed portrait, while repetition, which does not submit to the concept, conforms to the movement itself, speaks of the motion that takes place between phenomenon and subject: "*Repetition changes nothing in the object that repeats itself, but changes something in the mind that contemplates it*" (p. 96). "Re-petition is opposed to re-presentation; the prefix changes its meaning, for in one case the difference is said only in relation to the identical, while in the other it is the univocal which is being said in relation to the different" (p. 80).

Repetition, located this side of the zone of light to which the philosophy of the identical is limited, laughs at the idea of a fixed, restored, and recaptured center, which is implied by the principles of essence and truth: "The true subject of repetition is the mask. It is because repetition differs from representation as to its nature that what is repeated cannot be represented but only meant, masked by what it means, itself masking what it means" (p. 29). For this reason, there is no possibility of an agreement between the two projects. Consciously and consistently, the philosopher, like the avant-garde artist of past decades, braves tradition and does not fear its weight: "The theater of repetition is opposed to the theater of representation, as movement is opposed to the concept and to the representation that refers to the concept" (p. 19).

It is because of this confrontation that Freud's thought, although it interests Deleuze, does not inspire him to produce a pious exegesis or a definitive concordance. In his well-known later work, *L'Anti-Oedipe*, written in collaboration with Félix Guattari, Deleuze was to write that Freud elaborated his theory of the psychical apparatus thinking of the image of representational theater, even though he already had access to avant-garde theater. But it is unnecessary to resort to this later work: the book we are discussing already contains a formulation of the about-face Deleuze intended to do in relation to psychoanalysis: "I do not repeat because I repress. I repress because I repeat, forget because I repeat. I repress because from the outset I cannot experience certain things or certain experiences outside of the mode of repetition" (p. 29).

Deleuze's opposition to Freud might seem strange, even arbitrary, if we considered only Deleuze's critique of the primacy of the self as a figure derived from the primacy of identity: obviously a Freudian psychoanalyst would find nothing objectionable in Deleuze's attack on the alleged unity of the self, taken as a *je fêlé*. At the same time, it would seem likely that at least those Freudians who accept Lacan's legacy would agree with Deleuze's opposition to the idea that the function of the analytic treatment is to restore the *truth* of the patient's questions: "No answers or solutions can ever be original or definitive: only questions-problems can, in favor of a mask previous to every mask and of a displacement previous to every place" (p. 142). But if these points do not put Deleuze outside the Freudian camp, whence his combativeness? His disagreement with psychoanalysis seems to derive from his oft-repeated denunciation of representation, taking it as indissolubly linked to the centrality of the self. In short, it is the importance of *Vorstellung* for Freud that shows that the ontology of identity has crept into his theoretical edifice, and this is what causes it eventually to crumble. That is why Deleuze's thought cannot be reconciled with a development of psychoanalytic reflection such as André Green's. His disagreement must center on the function associated with representation.

Indeed, it begins with the very way he characterizes the phenomenon. While Deleuze constantly subordinates representation to the primacy of identity—"The primacy of identity, however it may be conceived, defines the world of representation," he states on the opening page—Green stresses its character of productivity, nonpassivity: "Representation, to the extent that it is not a perception passively received but rather a created form, is a product of the transformation of perception, the result of a psychical elaboration of thought" (Green and Donnet 1973: 249). Now, this production, which according to Deleuze is in the service of the rigidity of the self and of the myth of its identity, shows that it cannot be exhausted or contained in a negative function. Instead of a debate in purely deductive terms—which would not be a real debate, but an infinite running along parallel lines—Green offers a discussion of the space of the psychotic. Green writes:

> The functioning of the ego takes place in the space of the id: the ego *in* the [*dans le*] id. In other words, the functioning of the contents of the ego has a container that concerns the id. Thus the struggle takes place in a double place: against external reality, which emits incitements that, from the moment they emerge, are subverted by the space of the id, which adapts them to its will, and against the representatives of reality in the ego ("ideas and judgments"), of which thought is the result. Thought is then negativized; that is, it suffers a destructive negativization at the hands of the space of the id, which leads us to negative hallucination of thought, which replaces the subject with subjectivity. (P. 260)

Having established these points, Green concentrates on the type he calls white psychosis. It is characterized by the subject's inability to elaborate the real—that is, transform it into a symbolic structure that can make life livable. This is the role that from the beginning is played by the internalization of the oedipal structure: "The Oedipus is a structure whose fate is to be *destroyed and transposed*, that is, to be replaced by this investment in the real that marks the break with the parental images and brings about the existence of new figures in the child's life" (p. 266). But the psychotic, Green's major concern, has no access to it. The white psychotic cannot *represent* the parents' role because this role has become "unpalatable"—that is, not symbolizable:

> The object is unthinkable because it is bad, and thus is marked for expulsion; the subject can no longer think because thinking would amount to having to think of an unthinkable object. The bad breast is indigestible because it is inedible; all that can be done to it is to destroy it, but it is indestructible, for to destroy it is to destroy oneself. The first stage is this paralysis of thought. (P. 269)

Representation is not ephemeral or oscillating. It is simply impossible, and its impossibility is directly derived from the paralysis of thought. And thought cannot be articulated because it would have to create, as a stock, simply inconceivable figures. Representation, in short, is shown to be connected to a process of vital production. Its whiteness reveals the drastic impossibility of directing itself—that is, of elaborating.

In short, analytical practice undermines the philosopher's peremptory tone. It shows that the prohibition of representation ends up compromising the very existence of the subject, making him unable to elaborate alterity. This inability begins in relation to the parents, who, excluded from oedipal symbolization, are confused with antagonistic qualities, paralyzing the very moment of their elaboration—that is, the force that makes it possible to think of them. So it is that the outright rejection of the representation of the family triangle ultimately makes the psychotic unable to establish a *solitary* space, that is, a space inhabited by his thoughts and representations. And without solitude no contact with the other is possible. Empty inside, unable—as in the Amazonian myth analyzed by Lévi-Strauss—to have a "stomach" in which the "food" ingested could be stored, he is unable to participate in situations of communication.

Let me interrupt this exposition to ask: Is it really true that the inevitability of representations implies the inevitability of a complete self, which thus ought to be reinforced, fondled, and encouraged, reproducing the ideal of the ontology of identity? No, this is not my position, nor is it Green's. Representations presuppose a seat, a cleft seat, the *cleft self* that Deleuze referred to; cleft because it is crossed by opposing and conflicting flows. Therefore I may side with Green and at the same time agree with his opponent:

> There is no ultimate term, our loves cannot be traced back to the mother; it is just that the mother occupies, in the series that constitutes our present, a given place in relation to the virtual object, a place that must necessarily be filled by another character in the series that constitutes the present of another subjectivity, always bearing in mind the displacements of this object = X. (Deleuze 1968: 139)

The only difference is that, whereas Deleuze thinks it is necessary and urgent for us to undertake this journey into the depths of the individual night, I am forced to acknowledge that, if such a journey is not to become a passage among obsessive shadows, there must be stops—that is, a unity must be established, even if only a provisional one. In short, the representations subsumed into the self—into the cleft self—are multiple and conflicting, and every organization they submit to in a self is, in principle, provisional. But to discard them categorically, for the sake of the exclusiveness of repetition and difference, would lead, as in the exemplary case analyzed by Green, to the paralysis of thought—or, what is even more serious, to providing arguments in favor of a society in which the absence of the individualized self would only correspond to an amorphous mass of cataloged sets, masses of electronically stimulated voices.

Deleuze's thought, then, seems to be the philosophical extension of an impasse that avant-garde art has made us familiar with. More radically than avant-garde art, it poses the impossibility of thematizing intersubjective experience. For how would it be possible to conceive communication, other than the exclusively playful and disinterested communication between partners, if not as the ostracism of representation? If representation in itself is neither all positive nor all negative, simply to banish it from intellectual elaboration leads to an even greater divorce between the productions of modernity and the ability to recognize their motivation in our everyday experience.

All the analyses presented have served to allow me to return, with a firmer grounding, to the differential theorization of the poetic along the lines I have been exploring since *Mimesis e modernidade*. What follows is one more turn of the screw. As such, it should be read against the background of what I have said in earlier works or in the previous chapters of the present book.

MIMESIS AS NON-*IMITATIO*

The estate society understood the Greek category of mimesis in terms of similarity. In a world that saw itself as well ordered, in an age when religion was a decisive element, art was required to multiply similarity. On the other hand, the making of the class society led to the atomization of the estates, the emphasis on the enterprising individual, the reinforcement of the self and its exploration—an exploration that has been ambiguous, as we have seen, now taking self as a surrogate for the deity, now as a path leading to the depths of the unconscious. I have tried to show that communicative action became problematic at this point, to the extent that thought was not inclined to ratify the values and standards prevailing in the contemporary world. In a class society, where at any rate power is not exerted by agents whose entitlement to the positions they hold is legitimated a priori, the justification of power requires a persuasive force all the greater for being subtle.

Thus the accusations against the taming of the mind that have been raised by poets since Baudelaire are justified. Hence the praise of nonautomatized language. It is praised for not having been tamed, and it is expected, in spite and because of its strangeness, to make a vital contact with another subjectivity. Between the expectation and the result another deviant language appears, which will then live in the necessary limbo, until it is accepted for communication, so that another deviant language must arise, and so on. That is, the refusal to consider with due seriousness the question of communication, within the parameters of a nonimitative theory of art, assumes that, although with an inevitable lag, something in human nature will always allow the extraordinarily gifted artist to break through the blockade of established standards and reach his spectator, however belatedly.

But how can one fail to perceive that to hold such a view of human nature is, at the very least, to see the universe as a lottery, or that its corollary is the suicide of fiction? How can we be sure that the "happy few" Stendhal wrote for will rejoice in the deviant work of art instead of losing interest in this "ideolect"? Or that they will accept the innovation instead of seeing it as no more than an item to be preserved in a museum or library? Instead of persisting in such a belief, it seems reasonable—particularly after the immanentist attempts to define the poetic have proved unable to reach the desired scientific goal—to see whether the ancient boat of mimesis cannot be used by other Argonauts.

I believe it can, provided that it suffers a radical change as to those of its aspects that were affected by classical poetics. Mimesis, in spite of what the mistranslation *imitatio* seems to imply, is not the production of similarity but of difference. But this difference remains within a given horizon of expectations of similarity. To make this point clear, let me elaborate on an idea introduced earlier in this chapter. I have said that apparently every phenomenon is received by a human agent according to a set of expectations, based on the specific culture of which the agent is part. That is, in the subject-object relation, the object is captured by means of a net that is not the invention of an individual, but that imposes itself on all as a condition for their socialization. (Of course, this is not to deny that there are individual variants within the common net.) However great the variability of each individual response or internalization, each member of a culture—and, within a culture, of each of its segments—is recognized in opposition to the "foreigner," that is, the one who has been given a different form of socialization.

To say this is not the same thing as to affirm the primacy of the self or of the category of identity. Similarity—that is, the actualization of an internalized stock of expectations—acts as a selector, sometimes more flexible, sometimes less, that enables us to convert experiences into representations. Similarity allows us to find echoes in the world, the basis of that redundance without which everything would seem strange to us. We use this selector in order to classify the information we receive as relevant or secondary, secondary or hardly noticeable. Whereas the socialization of each individual is based on this selector, the motivation and talent of each responds in a new, unprecedented way. In this context, an unprecedent response is distinguished from one that would do no more than actualize an *identical* expectation in the other.

But what does it mean to respond in a new, unprecedented way? It means to respond positively to a situation in which two other possibilities exist, both negative: (1) the negativity of the identical response; that is, one that would decode the proposed question so as to reduce it to the level of the already expected; (2) the negativity of entropic noise, or the inability to see the problem except as totally beyond any expectation of dealing with it. While expectation of the identical sees the world as a toothless mouth, unable to bite any longer, entropic expectation transforms the world into a region inhabited by monsters and ghosts. The former changes the mimetic relationship into an automatized relation; the latter converts it into a relation of terror. Therefore, seeing mimesis as the production of difference assumes that a random phenomenon is treated by the subject as discordant with one's horizon of expectations, but not as aggressively entropic in relation to it. Further, to consider mimesis within a theory of communicative action means to approach this production of difference both from the viewpoint of the producer and from that of the receiver. But before I go any further, I must ask in what way all of this is distinguished from estrangement, which, as we have seen, has paradigmatic value in the theorization that proscribes mimesis.

The answer to this question can already be found in Wolfgang Iser: estrangement, he writes, sees the world as thematized in terms of *perception*. In this world phenomena are categorized as familiar (tending to automatization) or unfamiliar (potentially strange). That is why, as Shklovsky wrote, the text valued for its deviance will not be valued indefinitely, for its very success will tend to make its favorite procedures turn into automatized products in the works of epigones. The approach I have been developing assumes that mimesis is the privileged space for the opposite view, which does not see the world in terms of perception, but rather organizes it in terms of the imaginary. This is so because its production is not exhausted in the verbal medium in which it is actualized, nor is the poet the single active agent involved. (Here I am focusing on mimesis from the viewpoint of poetic production only. But it should be kept in mind that its scope is much vaster: see the final section of Chapter 3 above). If there is to be production of difference, the partners in poetic communication must be equally active—that is, both must activate the imaginary. "Usually . . . the various fictional signs do indicate that what is operated through them is not something in opposition to reality, but rather something the alterity of which cannot be understood from the habits that prevail in the world of life [*Lebenswelt*]" (Iser 1983: 397). Since the receiver's actualization of the imaginary is as much a part of the work as the author's, it is imperative that both should see literary discourse as something made from the "néantisation du monde" (Sartre), as a suspension of the conventions that govern the "finite province" (Schütz) of everyday reality so as to receive it as an irrealization to be once again realized, as a finite province submitted to a key different from the one that rules the world of everyday pragmatic relations.

Thus it is not an indispensable condition that the work of art should resort to a use of language that, in its strictly verbal aspect, is antithetical to its current use. The imaginary does not necessarily require deviance in order to be activated. As we have seen, this praise of deviance is a characteristic of a view of art that still clings to the notion of essence. Deleuze's questioning of this sort of thinking proved unsatisfactory because it preserved and even radicalized the impossibility of considering communicative action. We need a theorization that satisfies both aspects: one that rejects the essentialist vision and that is able to illuminate the communicative process taking place in the various "finite provinces" of reality. I stress my disagreement with those conceptions that emphasize deviance, seeing it as necessary to the language of art, because from the viewpoint of the conditions of actualization of the imaginary they are arbitrary or out of place. Borges's "normal" Spanish activates the imaginary just as much as the ideolect of *Finnegans Wake* does; the same applies to Samuel Beckett's "normal" English and French as opposed to the visual poems of e. e. cummings. In order to postulate the idea of communication proper to the fictional (not just the poetic, but the artistic in general, and even in areas not recognized as artistic, such as comic books), that is, in order to change aesthetics from a system of normative values into a branch of anthropological investigation *aiming at understanding the poetic experience*, we must give up the principle that tended to or was actualized in an immanentist poetics: the dominance of deviation, the rejection of the shopworn words of pragmatic discourse, a principle that led to the position that linguistics was the science of the poetic par excellence.

It should be observed that the proposal that the fictional should be seen as a specific form of communication, involving other *marks* different from those present in the communication of everyday life, science, religion, and so on, is not to be understood as a sociology of the reader, which at best would be an auxiliary science here. Also, and more importantly, the communicational orientation does *not* necessarily lead to a revival of the concept of mimesis, though it was a reconsideration of it that allowed us to arrive at the idea of communicative situation. Although I take the aesthetics of effect and of reception as the trends most dedicated to the development of the notion of a communication proper to the fictional, it should be stressed that neither Iser, the major representative of these currents, nor Hans Robert Jauss, their best-known expounder, would agree to the need for such a notion. For Iser, a treatment of the work's fictional character is enough for aesthetic experience. I myself, however, tend to feel that it is necessary to differentiate between the mimetic process—the scope of action of which neither begins nor ends in fictional production—and the fictional result. The latter, at least in the West, is evaluated in two opposite ways: it is negative or not subject to evaluation in all cases of discourses not aiming at the aesthetic experience—thus, to say of a scientific demonstration or a religious or philosophical exegesis that it gives evidence of a fictional talent would not be understood as praise—and positive only when there is aesthetic intent.

In conclusion, I will repeat that to define mimesis as the production of difference within a horizon of similarity means, from the viewpoint of the fictionist (poet or prose writer), that he creates "unrealities," and not recognitions, but always on the basis of what he experiences as *reality*; and, from the viewpoint of the receiver, that he, on the basis of the similarity recognized in what is read, seen, or heard, realizes the "unreality" of the object he is in contact with. It is this irreducible unreality that he will supplement with his reading, or interpretation. Thus, at least in a rudimentary form, it is possible to discard the optimistic conformism present in postromantic theorization and exacerbated by avant-garde thought. There is no reason why the production of difference should be recognized only belatedly, if only because we cannot be sure of any future. Communication may occur here and now, or never.

I have been reiterating the need to connect this reconsideration of mimesis with the idea of a specific form of communication, but so far have said nothing as to what such a form would be like. This is so because I feel this question should be developed by others. Nevertheless, I will venture a few observations, although no more than provisional.

When I speak of "communication," I do not mean a phenomenon characterized by the exchange of information liable to be quantified and thus industrialized. This way of thinking transforms communication into a process with a single structure, so that investigation of it is identified with investigation of the (mostly verbal) code in which information is actualized. Now, this single-code principle, borrowed from communication theory, from the outset makes any concept of discourse impossible. In order to make the categories discourse and communication compatible, it is necessary to think of the latter along the lines of Austin's philosophy of language. Since it is no longer necessary to describe his theory in detail, I will limit my discussion to a few basic points.

First, we must distinguish between the object of linguistics and the object of speech-act theory. The object of linguistics is the sentence, while that of speech-act theory is the utterance. The two differ as to various types of claims associated with one or the other. While sentences contain a claim to understandability, which is linguistically expressed in the norm of well-formedness, the utterance requires three other claims in order to be valid: "The three general pragmatic functions—with the help of a sentence, to represent something in the world, to express the speaker's intentions, and to establish legitimate interpersonal relations—are the basis of all the particular functions that an utterance can assume in specific contexts" (Habermas 1976: 33). Linguistics must bracket off everything that does not concern what can be detached and formalized as pure linguistic matter, for the purpose of reconstructing the codes actualized on the level of the sentence or on any level below it; whereas speech-act theory hinges on what Austin called illocutionary force. Habermas's definition of the concept will do here: "The illocutionary force of a speech action consists in fixing the communicative function of the content uttered" (p. 34). It is the illocutionary force that determines how a certain utterance is to be received—as an order, a request, an admonition, and so forth. While linguistics delimits its material so as to make it conform to the purity of its object and thus liable to formalization, speech-act theory takes as its basic unit a composite aiming at human interaction. In this way, human interaction can no longer be defined as a simple exchange of information, for communicative interaction is not achieved by means of mere utterances; understanding it implies understanding the *positions* of the interlocutors, analyzing the power relationships present in the act of utterance. The utterance is made within "patterns of pre-established relationships" (Habermas), and depending on whether they are known and accepted or not, the utterance will be successful or not—that is, will or will not be received as legitimate, false, or preposterous.

Now, this agreement or lack of agreement with preestablished patterns means precisely that the continuum of speech, from the viewpoint of effective communication, cannot be understood simply as a function of grammaticality. If the claim to understandability corresponds to a grammatical structure that the utterance must present as a first condition, the claims associated with the speech act point to a second structure, which may be labeled semiologic (see Costa Lima 1980: 67–74). Whereas the first structure, which is within the competence of the linguist, has as its object the continuum of speech, which contains sentences, the semiological structure decomposes the continuum of speech into discrete regions, which are separated by patterns of relations and give rise to differentiated expectations. These discrete regions are discourses. The category "discourse," which derives not from speech-act theory but from Foucault, seems to me an indispensable tool for the analysis of what transcends the dimensions of the linguistic method. (See the first section of Chapter 1 above).

A theory of literature as I conceived it, since it takes as its object the verbal modality of fictional discourse, is necessarily related to the development of speech-act theory, although one should not expect that the relation between the two must converge. From the outset this seems unlikely, given Austin's—and John Searle's—reluctance to characterize fictional speech acts. For strategic purposes, then, rather than expect much from this interchange, I prefer to approach speech acts specific to fictional-literary discourse from the premise that the theoretical justification of this discourse as a communicative act feeds on diversified sources: Foucaultian analysis of the relations between knowledge and power, Erving Goffman's analysis of the territoriality of everyday life, and developments in speech-act theory. In this way I delimit my area and acknowledge the authors I will probably rely on. But those who know the area I work in will appreciate that even with this delimitation the domain is so wide as to make it almost impossible for a single researcher to cover it. However narrow we wish to make the confines of our chosen field, they are still much too ample for any single individual. But just as the question "What's the use of so much effort?" leads to discouragement, the question "What can I do alone?" encourages conformity. One must be rather brash to keep on sailing against the wind.

CHAPTER EIGHT

Oblique Fiction and 'The Tempest'

Throughout the sixteenth and seventeenth centuries, the travel writings of those who dared to go beyond the confines of Europe revolutionized the Western conception of man, and also affected the assumption that, ideally at least, narrative should be truthful.* In particular, the discovery of America, the contact with Indian societies, and the beginning of the process of colonization forced European thought to reformulate its view of human society. "Our world has lately discovered another (and who will assure us that it is the last of its brothers, since the Daemons, the Sybils, and we ourselves have been ignorant of this till now?)" (Montaigne 1952: 440).

Until this widening of the known world took place, Aristotle's view of a constitutive human constancy still held: men are by nature freemen or slaves.† In the late seventeenth century, however, this notion gave way to "a wider anthropological and historical relativism" (Pagden 1982: 1), which was later to provide a basis for evolutionary doctrine. (Incidentally, I am not saying that evolutionism actually *revoked* the principle of constancy to which the human race and hence human society—according to classical thought—were subject, but only that it attempted to make it more flexible, through the phases that all peoples must undergo.)

The reference to Anthony Pagden's essential work has two specific purposes here: First, my examination of *The Tempest* will consider the prob-

---

*The importance of travel literature for the consolidation of the status of fiction is amply demonstrated by Percy G. Adams (1983). However, as often happens in such studies, the author fails to notice that the abundant evidence he presents points to the control to which fiction was subject—it was accepted as a useful form of entertainment, in the service of morality—rather than to its *ex-centric* position vis-à-vis truth.

†On natural slaves, see *Politics*, I, 1254b 21–22.

lem of fictionality in the light of Aristotle's statement concerning human nature and elaborations on it by Bartolomé de Las Casas (1474–1566), Francisco de Vitoria (c. 1492–1546), and José de Acosta (1540–1600). Second, I will find out whether my task is consistent with the conceptions of the imagination prevailing in the period. These considerations will ground my study of the status of fiction in Shakespeare's play, of how it is directly related to conceptions of the roles of reason and imagination. In this way, I will indirectly emphasize the importance of the discovery of America for the making of modern fiction, through the curiosity provoked by the writings of travelers and colonizers. Although this articulation may not be new, it seems of the utmost importance to return to it, for previous treatments have minimized or even neglected the control that denied fiction its specific status.

Let us begin with an unproblematic assertion: because Aristotelian tradition remained tied to the aporia of human constancy, interpretive practice was unable to acknowledge and understand difference.*

This contention is simple enough, and only a few supporting instances will be called for. The first has to do with the horror inspired by cannibalism:

Human sacrifice may not, Vitoria conceded, be unnatural—for the urge to pay homage to God, even if that God is not the true one, is undeniably strong—but its practice by the Indians indicated once again that they possessed only a blurred vision of reality, that on crucial matters they had failed to interpret correctly the prima *praecepta* of the law of nature. (Pagden 1982: 90)

Precisely because it holds to the Aristotelian view, the Spanish theologian's interpretation implies that human sacrifice cannot be understood except as a deviation from true nature. This view, therefore, has a high price: "cannibal peoples" must be expelled from the human universe.

A quite different sort of observation leads to the same result. The anthropologist Bernadette Bucher attempts to account for the frequency of "sagging breasts" in the iconography of America by showing that the sagging-breasted woman is the counterpart of the young woman represented by "statuesque bodies and Roman profiles" (Bucher 1981: 49); thus nature's "excessiveness" is opposed to the model of culture. Personifying evil and good respectively, both representations resort to the traditional iconic repertory: the sagging breasts are derived from medieval images of the deformed and grotesque, whereas the image of the good woman comes from Roman-Renaissance sculpture.

A third example points to an association between the suppression of

---

*This can be seen in Aristotle himself, for whom perfection is not given to women, children, and slaves. See *Politics*, I, 1260a 28–34.

difference and the treatment of the imagination. As late as 1765, Charles de Brosses could write, in his *Traité de la formation méchanique des langues*, that "the languages of 'savages' were rich in metaphor precisely because such peoples were more dependent on 'passion' than 'reason.' They speak, he said, the 'language of imagination and the passions,' a language which, because it is not concerned with *explanation*, with science, depends not on abstract ideas—for these are the modes for rational expression—but on 'material images'" (Pagden 1982: 184). Just as the cannibal was seen as deficient in basic precepts of natural law, so the use of metaphor was interpreted as an indication that wholesome reason was "devoured" by the voracity of a forceful imagination. The light of reason does not shine among savages; cannibalism and an overabundance of images are homologous signs of inferiority. The mark of constancy implies that deviating from the enunciative modality is a sign of inferiority.

Even before we investigate the impact of this mark on the fiction of the period, let us recall that it can be seen in the proliferation of images of monsters. This is a well-known fact. Teratology—and the image of sagging breasts is one of the least shocking examples—is a product of the clash between the raw perception of difference and the cultural impossibility of elaborating it mentally. The first exchange between Trinculo and Caliban is paradigmatic. At first the jester does not know what to call him. "What have we here? a man or a fish?" (II, ii, 26). Upon closer investigation, he decides: "This is not a fish, but an islander" (II, ii, 38). Since difference cannot be acknowledged, contact with it is a shocking experience for the eyes, for the nose, for ethical and aesthetic sensibility. The monstrous figure fills offended space and is displayed as the revenge of its victim.

By determining the place of the monstrous figure, we learn something about the question of fiction in the period. Before we began to formulate the hypothesis of control of the imagination, William Nelson had the merit of pointing out that narratives neither true nor false, already a problem for ancient thinkers, became crucial in the Renaissance: "It was characteristic of the Renaissance attitude . . . to depreciate the value of the narrative component of the work, to refer to that component, *with a tolerance something bordering on contempt*, as a concession to human weakness of no real worth save as it lured the reader to partake of the solid nourishment he might otherwise reject" (Nelson 1973: 59; emphasis added). Indeed, given an *episteme* that made no room for difference, fiction could only be admitted by a conscious act of tolerance—the solution adopted in antiquity, according to Nelson—or by delimitation of an area where it would be permissible (see Nelson 1973: 45).

With all due respect for Nelson's findings, I feel, however, that there is more to say on the subject. Nelson is, of course, right to observe that authors might be aware of the restrictions imposed on them, and accordingly make fun of or manipulate the requirement that their stories be documented and true. He also notes correctly that this gesture gave rise to a differentiation among readers: those who were more knowing would perceive the authors' cunning, whereas the majority would accept their truth claims or simply be entertained. But this is not enough to determine the status of fiction in the period. Rather, these are parallel effects, which seem to blur the very formulation of the question. To bring it into focus, I must begin by stressing that travel narratives increased the pragmatic need to control those accounts that could not be classified as either true or false. This was so for two reasons.

First, their authors' extravagance and the fact that it was impossible to verify their stories, when they did not claim to be actual witnesses, resulted in a generalized unreliability of texts:

For your better bred sort of men are much more curious in their observation, 'tis true, and discover a great deal more, but then they gloss upon it, and to give the greater weight to what they deliver and allure your belief, they cannot forbear a little to alter the story; they never represent things to you simply as they are, but rather as they appeared to them. . . . I would have every one write what he knows, and as much as he knows, but no more. (Montaigne 1952: 93)

Second, the preservation of an *episteme* rooted in the affirmation of man's constancy implied that a text could only be seen as either true or false. It is at this point that the hypothesis of control shows its explanatory potential. To control fiction did not mean to forbid it. Censorship, let us stress, is only the visible, superficial tip of a much larger body. Censorship declares or makes explicit the impossibility of coexistence. For those who hold power, it is much more convenient to keep their sword poised than to bring it down. Thus, from the viewpoint of those in power, control, whenever feasible, is to be preferred. Controlling fiction meant tolerating it as long as it respected certain limits. The controllers, mostly authors of treatises of poetics, were aware that works of imagination did not correspond to the plain statement of truth, that therefore they sinned against the discourse of truth, that in this way they somehow interfered with the exercise of power, since all power is based on some truth-discourse. But they were also aware that, for this reason, works of imagination were not necessarily to be seen as merely false. By establishing requirements for the circulation of this strange hybrid—which did not conform to truth but could not be labeled false—the preceptists tried to reconcile the unreliable narrative with the *episteme* to which they belonged. What, then, was the status of fiction?

By now we can formulate a less simplistic argument than the one we have been developing so far. We have been saying that because of the privilege given to constancy in Aristotelian poetics, interpretive practice was unable to deal with difference. We can now reformulate this statement as follows: Modern fiction, as it appeared in the seventeenth century with the publication of the first part of *Don Quixote* (1605), had an inevitable oblique character; this was so because explicit thematization was then impossible. The conception of human nature in terms of a constancy that explained the makeup of human society, the impossibility of conceiving difference, and the existence of control mechanisms for regulating fiction—that is, for justifying and providing an evaluation criterion for texts that were neither true nor false—these were the variables that produced this result.

Let me proceed to flesh out my idea of oblique fiction by means of a few brief references to *Don Quixote*. Although my previous considerations (see Chapter 1) might be of use here, it will be more enriching to return to Cervantes's book with a different approach. We will single out chapters 12 to 14 and chapter 51 of Part I, and chapter 58 of Part II, all of which question the conventions of pastoralism. Within this subset, we can make a distinction between chapters 12 to 14, on one hand, and chapter 58 on the other; chapter 51 marks the transition.

In the first case, throughout the story of Chrysostom and Marcela, pastoralism has to do with a poetical convention—the "shepherds" abandon urban life so that the mountains and woods may resound with their lovers' complaints. In the second case (Part II, chapter 58), when Don Quixote meets the young gentlefolk who decorate the woods with pastoral symbols and who have memorized eclogues by Garcilaso and Camões, poetical convention has become a pastime for good society. The difference lies in the *setting*: the poetic space where convention is practiced is changed into the physical space of a make-believe activity. But Marcela's intervention breaks the symmetry. She contradicts Chrysostom's friends, and in support of the discreet Vivaldo, she rejects any responsibility for the "shepherd's" suicide: "I told him that my purpose was to live in perpetual solitude, and that the earth alone should enjoy the fruits of my retirement" (Cervantes 1952: 38). In other words, Marcela preferred the country not because she followed the pastoral convention, but for purely personal reasons. Here the convention loses its predictable, harmless aspect, its lack of contact with reality, which the controllers imposed on it. Marcela has become a shepherdess as a consequence of her misanthropic nature. But as we realize that the introduction of reality implies the destruction of artifice, are we not forced to admit that the destruction had already taken place, at the beginning of the chapter? How else should we understand Chrysostom's suicide? If convention was accepted as poetic, it was precisely because those who accepted it were supposed to keep their distance from reality. Since actual misanthropy and actual death were not foreseen, their appearance had the effect of transgressing the convention.

For the while, let us settle for this partial result: in *Don Quixote*, narrative proceeds so as to overstep the boundaries that Renaissance poetics imposed on fiction. The rule is broken when a short circuit is formed between poetic convention and the element that until then had been kept at a distance: reality. According to Renaissance rules, reality could only be approached through statements of truth; in Cervantes, reality is mingled with fantasy and madness.

If we now turn to chapter 51 of Part I and chapter 58 of Part II, this mixture of reality and convention is further verified. Anselmo's companion, in Part I, chapter 51, tells the reader of the "pastoral Arcadia" made up of real and imagined rejected suitors of Leandra, who pass their time upbraiding Leandra for the sorrows she has inflicted on them. The narrator is clearly poking fun at pastoral convention, which creates *malades imaginaires*, and, more seriously—as we see in Part II, chapter 58—provides an outlet for the bored children of idle noblemen, who don costumes and decorate the hills in an indolent masquerade.

Cervantes's satire, however, has a far greater effect than humorous mockery. The demolition of convention makes way for reality, the raw, sharp reality that does not confuse goatherds with shepherds, nor woods with garlands; a demolition that necessarily brings about the end of the franchise hitherto conferred on fiction. The novel, as created by Cervantes, becomes the genre that thematizes everyday reality; not because, as it will be said much later, it has a "realist" calling, but because it belongs to a discursive form that can only justify itself to the extent that it raises problems.

This, then, was the decisive step that established the theme appropriate to fiction. But is fiction's character oblique or direct? In order to arrive at a conclusion, we must once again turn to chapters 12–14. It is easy to see that here a parallelism is established between two madmen: one is an out-and-out lunatic; the other is mad because he trusts conventions. Each in his own way is spurred to action by his beloved. In addition, each is related to a conventional poetic form, the two forms being distinguished one from the other solely by their different connections with time. The convention adopted by Don Quixote, the romance of chivalry, is a dead convention, which could only be revived by a madman. The other one, however, is very much alive, even fashionable. Establishing a parallelism in a comical and satirical situation, Cervantes raises the possibility of questioning the relationship between *disguise* and *truth*. And he profits from the fact that the novel as a genre has not been codified.

The pastoral component of Don Quixote is thus sufficient for a verification of the interconnections between disguise and truth. These terms become mutually permeable; they no longer occupy discrete spaces, but rather are seen as existing in one and the same place, everyday reality.

With the benefit of hindsight, we can say that here the specificity of fiction is already established: its ability to question habits, customs, and values—that is, what society holds to be true. Although the conclusion is correct, we should not see in Cervantes what is not yet there: explicit and direct thematization of fictionality.

By overstepping the allowed boundaries of poetic fiction by means of procedures similar to the parallelism we have mentioned above, Cervantes devises a strategy that separates his novel from Renaissance fiction. The latter still attempted to solve the problem of imagination by giving it a semblance of direct or indirect observation of facts—that is, investing it with verisimilitude. The follower of a convention no longer socially alive, Don Quixote actualizes a form of interpretation that immediately elicits the reader's mockery. For him, "the distinction is not between fact and fantasy but between intelligibility and non-intelligibility" (Williamson 1984: 100). How could the contemporary reader fail to perceive the protagonists's madness if "whatever reminds him of the books of chivalry is seized on as a providential sign of romance identity and proclaimed as such in the teeth of any evidence to the contrary" (p. 99)? The distinction, now attributed to the madman, between the intelligible—and liable to become verisimilar—and the unintelligible had been a continuation of medieval allegory, which made it unnecessary or even unthinkable to control imagination. This control, therefore, was motivated by the acknowledgment of the autonomy of facts, against the medieval notion that facts were previously invested with meaning. At this point we must be more explicit, even if this incurs a digression.

In one of his most valuable essays, Auerbach shows that the central category of medieval interpretation was the idea of *figura*. As developed by the Church Fathers, the *figura* ensured that a fact or event was simultaneously seen in its particular historico-real density and as part of a teleological view of the world. "*Figura* is something real and historical which announces something else that is also real and historical" (Auerbach 1984a: 29). In this manner, the Old Testament could be seen no longer as "a book of laws and a history of the people of Israel," but rather as "a series of figures of Christ and the Redemption, such as we find later in the medieval theater and in the cyclic representations of medieval sculpture" (p. 52). Thus a *closed* series was created—"a connection between two events or persons, the first of which signifies not only itself but also the second, while the second encompasses or fulfills the first" (p. 53)—which abandoned the merely abstract and unearthly use of allegory and gave medieval realism its peculiar tone: the particularities of both events and creatures were seen as localized inscriptions, even as their meaning still remained on a timeless plane.

Auerbach's interpretation is reinforced by the concept of "symbolic realism"—the relation between "every earthly event" and "a transcendental order"—which Hugo Kuhn drew from German medieval texts dating from before the late twelfth century (Kuhn 1969: 66). Now, this date coincides with the results of the wider interpretation undertaken by Howard Bloch. This American medievalist has shown that for grammarians and encyclopedists of late antiquity, as well as for Abelard and twelfth-century nominalistic philosophers, there was a homologous conception of etymology and genealogy. It can be said that in both cases, to use Auerbach's terms, a figural principle of interpretation was in force. Indeed, one can see the affinity between the *figura* principle and the description given by Bloch:

Names, as signs, bear prospectively the mark both of their meaning and of their historical effects; understood through time, they fulfill the promise—complete the genealogy—that they contain. Language constitutes, in this respect, a kind of genetic code in which the future in germ is inscribed but which remains indecipherable until its genesis has become historically realized. (Bloch 1983: 37).

The consequences of this fact are magnificently exploited by the author in connection with the earliest French heroic poetry. Here it need only be observed that in this way it became possible to justify the lack of "distinction until the fourteenth century between 'estoire' and 'roman'" (p. 98). The figural model legitimated the concrete inscription of events and at the same time removed their temporal autonomy. As we have seen, Cervantes's problem falls outside this previous semantic saturation of the event, the strength of which had been undermined by the diffusion of travel writings.

It is in this context that the importance of Cervantes's criticism of pastoralism becomes apparent. He made fun of pastoralism, but at the same time widened the scope of his criticism. But what was the rationale, the basis of this criticism? The difficulty faced by his interpreters derives from the fact that they fail to take into account the previous existence of the control mechanisms and their setting of limits within which the discourse of disguise would not violate "truth." Unconsciously—it would be ludicrous to claim that Cervantes actually intended to do what he did—he overstepped the boundaries of accepted convention, giving it what was not allowed to it, namely, contact with reality, and thus created a new discursive space: that of fiction. But the best proof that Cervantes does not thematize it explicitly lies in the very fact that interpreters find it hard to understand what the author actually does in his text.*

In Cervantes, modern fiction appears only indirectly—that is, by overstepping the limits imposed on Renaissance genres: limits that separated thematizations of fancy from those of reality. This implies that modern fiction is born with an oblique character. Its basic procedure will be to explore ambiguous situations. This is what we will see in *The Tempest*. Since the text is well known, I need only remind the reader of a few of its ambiguities to provide the point of departure for an unconventional approach.

The very material condition that gives rise to the story is ambiguous: the tempest is as real as any storm, but is also the product of effective magic. Let us turn to a less obvious confirmation of our thesis. In Prospero's first dialogue with his slave, we are told that Caliban, among his other unsavory qualities, has once attempted to rape Miranda. Caliban's response to this seems to confirm that he is unredeemingly wicked: "O ho, o ho! would't had been done! / Thou didst prevent me; I had peopled else / This isle with Calibans" (I, ii, 349–51). Unable to take in his master's teachings, Caliban is ugly both physically and morally. And yet, as Stephen Orgel observes, "imperial rapes, once they get into history, are a source not of shame but of national pride" (Orgel 1987: 55). Thus Caliban's criminal intention is unequivocal only because his attempts at revenge always fail. Human action is not intrinsically univocal, in spite of what Prospero says. But is not Prospero himself an ambiguous figure too? He tells Miranda that he failed as a ruler just because his excessive interest in the "liberal arts" left him helpless before the machinations of Antonio, the usurper of his dukedom. Prospero, however, is no less a usurper, for he has made use both of his magic and of his powers of seduction in order to become lord of the island. It is Caliban who speaks, and his contention goes unrefuted:

> This island's mine, by Sycorax my mother,
> Which thou takest from me. When thou camest first,
> Thou strokedst me and madest much of me, wouldst give me
> Water with berries in't, and teach me how
> To name the bigger light, and how the less,
> That burn by day and night: and then I loved thee

---

*This is the difference between Cervantes's problem and the realist pattern systematized beginning with the eighteenth-century English novel. Whereas the Spanish author was concerned with opening a space for the treatment of fictionality, eighteenth-century realism no longer relied solely on the legitimation of the autonomous observation of facts—and thus of everyday and Everyman's life—but also on the internalization of the mechanisms of control of the fictional. Both were effects of the criterion of truth proposed by the natural sciences.

And show'd thee all the qualities o' the isle,
The fresh springs, brine-pits, barren place and fertile.
(I, ii, 331–38)

Since it would be pointless to go on listing examples, let me simply stress that "the world represented in *The Tempest* is shown to us with all the uncertainties that might arise in the mind of an Elizabethan reader of some travel narrative. Shakespeare thematizes and, as it were, projects these uncertainties on the entire play, which becomes a discourse about the world and a discourse about itself" (Marienstras 1972: 35).

This statement seems sufficient for the relationship we are trying to set up between ambiguity as a procedure and the obliqueness with which fiction is thematized. The ambiguity has to do both with the plane on which the event takes place—is the tempest real or magically induced?—and with the values in question—is Prospero a usurped duke fighting for his right or a usurper exploiting the legitimate master of the island? Is Caliban a physical and moral monster or a helpless innocent facing the malice and operative power of the whites? The ambiguity is never resolved, in the sense that neither alternative is ultimately affirmed. The tempest is real, although magically induced; the shipwreck is real, although the sea water does not affect the castaways' clothes; Prospero is both usurper and usurped; Caliban is both lecherous and naive, and so forth. The play draws on this procedure in order to create the "objective correlative" of the expectations of the public it was written for. In this way, it cannot be taken as a travel narrative or as a fantasy based on such writings: the ambiguity affects the very relationship between fantasy and reality. As Sebastian, Alonso, Antonio, and Gonzalo will learn at the banquet offered by Ariel, one cannot tell a priori whether succulence is real or induced.

Thus the ambiguity allows the author to see the travel narrative from a distance, in perspective, to examine it critically, without disrespecting the magical character of "romance" and pastoral. In other words, ambiguity is in the service of an uncontrolled fiction. It will not do to say that Shakespeare *points* to a permissive convention and then to underscore the passages that bear this out. His *fictional detachment* subverts the wholeness of his text.

However, even though this is fiction free of control, it is still oblique: as a whole, the play does not thematize its own condition; it uses it as a theme for reflection, but does not yet lay it bare.

Could this obliqueness be a consequence of the fact that, given the mentality of the historical period in question, it would have been impossible to become aware of difference? The oblique fiction of Cervantes and Shakespeare draws on the doubts, misgivings, and skepticism inspired by the official truth. As all fictional discourse, oblique fiction opens the way for itself as it endeavors to see truth in perspective—that is, from a distance, without mingling with or committing itself to its discourse.* In other words: like all fictional discourse, oblique fiction does not propose a different sort of truth. Its merit is also its limitation. Both merit and limitation, in the case of the oblique fiction we are examining, are contrasted with evolutionism, which, as mentioned above, was to fertilize the same soil. Evolutionism, preserving the mark of the constancy of human nature, does not simply reemphasize the *naturalness* of the opposition between freemen and slaves. Slavery and inferiority are no longer justified as requirements of nature. Instead, they are temporalized: they are products of stages to be outgrown. Thus, in relation to ancient thought, evolutionism represents a certain way of postulating difference. Now, oblique fiction did not yet contain this "certain way"; that is, it did not propose a different sort of truth. This means that in itself it could not come to the aid of slaves in their struggle for freedom.† But this limitation of oblique fiction was also its merit: the questioning of truth brought about by oblique fiction was more critical than the evolutionist position would later be, if only because it was uncommitted to the primacy of constancy.

Having reached the first goal of this chapter, let us now see whether a reading of *The Tempest* can tell us something about the relation between reason and imagination in the seventeenth century. There is apparently no evidence in support of our hypothesis. According to such an eminent interpreter as Frank Kermode, the fundamental opposition in the play is that between Art and Nature: "The main opposition is between the worlds of Prospero's Art, and Caliban's Nature. Caliban is the core of the play; like the shepherd in formal pastoral, he is the natural man against whom the cultivated man is measured" (Kermode 1961: xxiv). But the obviousness of Kermode's point has the disadvantage of all that is obvious: it blinds us to the existence of other paths, which though less evident may be fruitful. Nevertheless, Kermode's undeniable contribution to the understanding of the play—his examination of the magician Prospero—will be fundamental for the opening of one of these untrod paths. Indeed, it is to Kermode that modern readers are indebted for the comparison between

---

*Thus Williamson, for instance, explains Cervantes's criticism of pastoral in terms of an ethical criterion: "What Cervantes is attacking in both pastoral and chivalric romance is not so much the desirability of these ideals in themselves as the means by which romance represents their fulfillment" (Williamson 1984: 94). In this way, the uniqueness of *Don Quixote* cannot be understood.

†For an in-depth study of the status of fiction and its unique relation with the question of truth, see Iser 1983: 121–51.

Prospero and the occultist philosophy of Cornelius Agrippa (1486–1535). Such is the English critic's conviction that there is a connection between Prospero and Agrippa's thought that he quotes passages from *De occulta philosophia* as justifications for the magician's activity: "He is 'divinorum cultor interpres,' a studious observer and expounder of divine things," and his Art is "the absolute perfection of Natural Philosophy" (p. xli). In conformity with Agrippa's conceptions, Prospero's magic implies the possibility of summoning celestial beings to influence the elemental world. This means that magic is not only effective but also ascensional. Thus, as a good practitioner of magic, Prospero is opposed to the emissary of the lower, subterranean world, Sycorax, who is impregnated by a demon to conceive Caliban. The magic that Prospero dignifies with his studies involves the invocation of heavenly effluvia—hence the attention he gives to his star—and therefore favors the Deity himself in the elemental order of matter. Through ascensional movement, achieved by slow and continuous intellectual effort, magical gnosis strengthens the links between the divine and the sublunary. In this way, according to the teachings of Agrippa, the magician—friend, cultivator, and propitiator of heavenly bodies—should not be regarded by the Church with suspicion.

The approximation of Prospero and Agrippa's occultism was given historical substance by Frances Yates. On the basis of the established fact that the play was staged during the festivities accompanying the palatine elector's wedding to Princess Elizabeth, Prince Henry's sister, Yates associates the tone of *The Tempest* with the hopes that the prince would restore the Protestant, Reformational spirit that had characterized the reign of the late Elizabeth I and had been interrupted under the timorous leadership of James I. But these hopes were dashed quite soon with the prince's unexpected death. The palatine elector returned to Germany, and the mathematician and occultist John Dee, a possible link between Agrippa's thought and Shakespeare, fell out of favor. Thus *The Tempest* bears the mark of a revival that did not come to be: "Prospero is poles apart from the witch Sycorax and her evil son. Indeed, Prospero as the good magus has a reforming mission; he clears the world of his island from the evil magic of the witch; he rewards the good characters and punishes the wicked. He is a just judge, or a virtuous and reforming monarch, who uses his magico-scientific powers for good" (Yates 1975: 94).

But Yates's development interests me less for its historical hypothesis than for its peripheral considerations about the link between "good" magic and science in the Renaissance. In her *Giordano Bruno and the Hermetic Tradition*, she had already shown that at the time there was no gap between genuine science and magical hermetism for Cornelius Agrippa, or for Giordano Bruno, or for a mathematician such as John Dee. Thus, for instance, the close relation between magic and mathematics was explained as follows: "Mathematics are most necessary in magic, for everything which is done through natural virtue is governed by number, weight, and measure" (Yates 1978: 134).* In short, leaving aside the historical hypothesis, about which I have nothing to say, what interests me in Kermode's and Yates's examinations of the figure of Prospero, a magician, is, first, the virtuous justification of his calling and, second, the close relation between his magic and a certain ideal of science, which—although not peculiar to a few philosophers—derived its inspiration mostly from Cornelius Agrippa. In a word, Prospero's good magic is best defined as *virtuous reason*. As reason, his work presupposes scientific knowledge of nature; being virtuous, it implies that the ethically positive character of its practitioner cannot be underestimated.

This characterization allows me to enrich the Prospero-Caliban opposition. If Caliban represents the savage, he is—as Kermode observes—the very opposite of Montaigne's idea of a savage. Prospero calls him dull, ungrateful, a liar, and says he is unable to learn the good lessons he is taught. Apparently Caliban cannot defend himself. Since the only good he derived from the language he learned from his master was knowing "how to curse," it seems natural that he should not defend himself in any way. But his actions tell the reader a different story. They tell us, first, that Caliban cannot control his appetites or calculate his risks. Lecherous, he is not restrained by the consideration that Miranda is the daughter of his powerful master, and that therefore his attempt would only cause him harm. Later he is easily deceived. Cherished by Prospero at first, he shows the magician the treasures of the island—"The fresh springs, brine-pits, barren place and fertile" (I, ii, 338); then, seduced by Stephano's wine, he is willing to worship him and serve him as a loyal vassal—"I'll swear upon that bottle to be thy true subject" (II, ii, 129–30). In short, Caliban is clearly dominated by his own imagination. His imagination is clearly undeveloped, unable to devise any but the most elementary plans, to impel him to anything other than immediate reaction: it is the sort of imagination that Aristotle attributed to animals. His opposition to Prospero is nothing less than absolute. Whereas Prospero has the strength necessary to devote years to the study of magic, and the success of his plans shows his excellence in his craft, Caliban has only brute strength, immediate desire, a quickly impressionable soul. As to his imagination, the opposition

*We must, however, keep in mind that the affirmation of what a discursive form in itself can do is valid only as a logical exercise. In actual fact, discursive forms do not appear in isolation, but rather in confluence, interaction, and conflict with others, in particular with the one that is historically conceived as the way to affirm truth.

here is the same as the one Aristotle found between the animal's sensitive imagination and man's calculative imagination: "Inasmuch as an animal is capable of appetite it is capable of self-movement; it is not capable of appetite without possessing imagination; and all imagination is either calculative or sensitive. In the latter all animals partake" (*On the Soul*, III, 433b 29–30).

This antagonism between forms of imagination is projected onto the ethical antagonism of the protagonists. Whereas Caliban, one might say, has "no thinking or calculation but only imagination" (III, 433a 11) since his soul is quickly suggestionable, Prospero, once he overcomes all obstacles, can even forgive his enemies; endowed with "calculative imagination," he is sensible to the sway of reason: "Though with their high wrongs I am struck to the quick, / Yet with my nobler reason 'gainst my fury / Do I take part" (V, i, 25–27). Thanks to his "calculative imagination"—that is, his ability to place imagination in the service of his deliberation—Prospero occupies the highest place along the axis of reason, whereas sensitive imagination relegates Caliban to the lowest end of the axis of imagination.

Though this conclusion may not seem to require further justification, it is worthwhile pointing out that, in the case in question, the value of a term depends on both operative and ethical considerations. As may be apparent by now, ethical value is particularly sensitive to sexuality. Thus if Caliban's primitiveness is responsible for the attempted rape, Prospero's noble nature makes him warn Ferdinand against trying to possess Miranda before the wedding (IV, i, 14–19). Reiteration of this point underscores the variables involved in the treatment of imagination in *The Tempest*. This becomes even clearer when we examine the actions of Antonio.

When Prospero describes Antonio's plot that cost him his dukedom, he stresses less Antonio's treachery than the evil force of his imagination:

> Like one
> Who having into truth, by telling of it,
> Made such a sinner of his memory,
> To credit his own lie, he did believe
> He was indeed the duke.
> (I, ii, 99–103)

By repeatedly lying to himself, Antonio made a sinner of his memory and came to believe that he was indeed the duke. Clearly, we do not know whether what is involved is "fancy" or "imagination." But would it be reasonable to question that it is Antonio's action that is being discussed? Nevertheless, we can see that imagination here is quite different from what it was in Caliban: calculating yet not subject to reason, it gives operative force to evil. This qualification will be enough for now.

The second conspiracy in which Antonio takes part shows the source of his malignity even more clearly. Prospero's magic, through the effective agency of the airy spirit Ariel, had dispersed the castaways around the island, seeing that Alonso, Sebastian, Antonio, and Gonzalo remained together. The fact that Ferdinand is separated from them and cannot be found is the necessary condition for Antonio's act, foreseen by Prospero. The group is discussing the late events and the possibility of finding the king's heir when Prospero's loyal spirit causes them to fall asleep, all save for Antonio and Sebastian. Experienced in such matters, Antonio tries to convince the king's brother to allow him to kill the sleeping Alonso. His argument is crafty and effective—one of the king's heirs is away from Naples and the other, Ferdinand, they believe to be dead. Sebastian, though seduced by the will to power, has enough scruples to ask Antonio about his conscience. But Antonio reassures him on this point:

> But I feel not
> This deity in my bosom: twenty consciences,
> That stand 'twixt me and Milan, candied be
>   they
> And melt ere they molest!
>   (II, i, 277–80)

Antonio simply despises his conscience, because it would not be practical to heed it. As he says, "if 'twere a kibe, / 'Twould put me to my slipper" (II, i, 276–77). Thus Antonio is the man who musters his imaginative force and dissociates it from the plane of virtue so that it is purely instrumental. What distinguishes him from the old witch Sycorax is, to his own detriment, only his contempt for the connecting power of the imagination with which he was naturally invested; what distinguishes him from the conceited Sebastian is only the active use of imagination, which in Sebastian remains passively receptive.

Though the two events end differently, the usurpation of Prospero's dukedom and Sebastian's seduction imply the same quality in Antonio: he is the man who activates his imaginative capacity and, ridding himself of virtue, uses imagination to further his ambitious designs. In this sense, he is both similar to and different from Caliban. The savage is the actively inept subject of his own imagination; Antonio is the ultimate master of imagination disconnected from the sway of reason. But they are similar in that reason is alien to both. (We might now subject Sebastian and Caliban to a similar examination. However, let us simply observe that, while both are actively inept, Caliban is naturally so, whereas Sebastian, having been educated, is conceivably an apprentice of Antonio's "art.")

Prospero is distinguished from all the others. Could it be that he is devoid of imagination? We already know the answer to this question. He does have imagination, but he has learned to connect it with efficient reason, the propitiator of celestial forces. The very personification of the "moral reformer," to quote Yates's apt image, Prospero combines the qualities of magician and scientist—he knows how to use and develop his talents along the right path, so that not even forgiveness is neglected. Thus he uses imagination in a human way, rescuing it from merely animal appetites.

In short, the characters and situations in the play can be placed along two basic axes. The first of these is the axis of reason, which covers two areas—the ability to manipulate material elements and celestial forces, and the area of ethical righteousness. On the noble axis of reason we are to place both its higher representative, Prospero, and his lower counterpart, Gonzalo, a faithful vassal who, however, is not interested in the "liberal arts."

The second axis is that of imagination, which also occupies two corresponding areas—that of manipulative ability and that of ethical want. Its first representative is Sycorax, doubly negative because she activates a magic purely of the earth, which makes her imprison the airy spirit, and because she will consent to sexual intercourse with a demon. Its maximum representative is, however, Antonio and not Caliban, who, as a "natural man," has no understanding of the laws of nature and thus cannot subject his imagination to "nobler reason." Therefore it is the presence of an unequivocal ethical ingredient that ultimately determines the placement of characters along this or that axis. This is the role of ethics, because it assumes the capacity to resist the body's will and subject it to the principle of reason. Thus Caliban is less evil than Antonio because his ineptness, according to Prospero and to Aristotelian tradition, is innate. Ethics is therefore the element that permeates the positive axis of reason and the negative axis of imagination. Where ethics is present, imagination is deliberative; where it is lacking, merely sensitive. In the latter case, one may still distinguish between innate ethical deficiency (Sycorax, Caliban) and willed absence of ethics (Antonio, Sebastian). Finally, this volition can be active or passive.

For my interpretive purposes, this analysis would be pointless if I did not link it in the end with my earlier discussion of the function of ambiguity. It is because of ambiguity that *The Tempest*—particularly when it thematizes the opposition between Prospero and Caliban—cannot be reduced to a mere justification of the colonization of the "brave new world." As we have seen, the usurped Prospero is also a usurper. His possession of the island and his use of Caliban are necessary conditions for the recovery of his rights. Only in this manner can he succeed as a "moral reformer."

As we have also seen, it is to the extent that oblique fiction is rooted in the exploration of ambiguity that ambiguity invests Shakespeare's play with more than documentary or "parochial" interest. Further, it shows an interpreter who is uncommitted to a European viewpoint the need to go beyond the allegorical reading to which *The Tempest* has been subjected from Rodó's *Ariel* to Fernández Retamar, Aimé Césaire, and George Lamming.* In order to do this with some effectiveness, we must also realize that if the uncertainties that pervade the play are an "objective correlative" of the way contemporary readers reacted to travel narratives, *The Tempest* is more than that: it is the perspectivization of this uncertainty—that is, its configuration from a given point in discursive space—that will not admit certainties, and instead feeds on its own fluctuation, its questioning of established truths. Thus the perception of Shakespeare's obliqueness can be used for the purpose of freeing him from habitual interpretive practices. Since it does not rely on violent manipulation of the text itself, as allegorical readings are accused of doing,† the perception of obliqueness allows a vision that is not only historically informed—because seventeenth-century fiction had to pay its dues to the principle of the constancy of human nature—but also able to account for difference.

This chapter began as an investigation of the workings of fiction in a seventeenth-century text, and ended referring to the problem of imagination vis-à-vis the realm of reason. But I will distort this final and vital development if I take it as no more than an illustration of a thesis I have been proposing. Let me clarify this point.

We have seen that, as Yates observes, in certain Renaissance circles magic was strictly interrelated with the exact sciences. Should we now add that Shakespeare's play demonstrates that science, legitimated by magic, threatened to become as controlling as science armed against magic? The answer to such a question would be trivial, if not disastrous. In itself—that is, in its assumed capacity to overstep the boundaries of the sublunary—magic did not despise imagination; it did imply, however, an ethical purification that could transform it into virtuous reason.

This consequence is confirmed and stimulated by a source we have not yet referred to. In his remarkable *Saturn and Melancholy*, Panofsky and his co-researchers discuss the impact of the magical philosophy of Cornelius Agrippa and Marsilio Ficino on the Protestant mind of Albrecht Dürer:

---

*For additional material on this topic, see Yates 1979.

†On the allegorical appropriation of *The Tempest* by third-world writers, see Nixon 1987: 557–58.

Dürer, more than anyone, could identify himself with Agrippa's conception; contemporary in thought with Agrippa, and opposed to the older Italian art-theorists such as Alberti or Leonardo, he, more than anyone, was convinced that the imaginative achievements of painters and architects were derived from the higher and ultimately divine inspiration. . . . Alberti's and Leonardo's speculations on the theory of art were totally unaffected by the Florentine Neoplatonists, and laid the foundations of an "exact" science as defined by Galileo. They assigned to pictorial art that place in culture as a whole which we to-day are accustomed to allocate to "sober science." (Panofsky et al. 1979: 360–61)

The main point here is that in the study of the relations between the Renaissance concept of science and the status of the visual arts, we find two clearly divergent positions. One way of justifying art was to see it as consistent with the Galilean view of science; thus for Leonardo da Vinci the dignity of painting derived from the fact that it was a path to rigorous knowledge. Dürer, on the other hand—less in his theoretical reflections than in his artistic practice—preferred Agrippa's magical philosophy and, through it, arrived at the praise of imagination, expressed in *Melancholia I*. This second way is congruent with the basic structure of *The Tempest*: analyzing the concept of imagination implied in the play, we find that it points to a different way of seeing its relation to reason, an approach that has been lost.

However, if I went no further than this, my conclusion would once more be insufficient. Thus I must add: the examination I have now concluded suggests that control is the result of a specific historical-ideational configuration, one that might well have been different, might even have not come to be at all, if history had opted for Agrippa rather than Galileo. Further, it suggests that the presence of control is not automatically proved by any text from this historical period. To affirm otherwise would be to do violence to Cervantes's novel and to Shakespeare's play, and to compromise the questioning capacity allowed by the ambiguity of fiction: the capacity for critical questioning. For when fictional discourse interacts with analytical discourse, the latter is given a precious possibility of showing that fiction, precisely because it does not propose any truth, is a questioner of truths. To require any more than that from fiction is to indulge in mystification; to require any less is to settle for mere aestheticism.

REFERENCE MATTER

References Cited

Abelard, Peter. 1964 [1132–36]. *The Story of Abelard's Adversities*. Trans. J. T. Muckle. Toronto: The Pontifical Institute of Medieval Studies.
Acevedo Díaz, Eduardo. 1943 [1914]. *Lanza y sable*. Montevideo: G. Garcia and Cia.
———. 1968 [1888]. *Ismael*. Montevideo: Centro Editor de América Latina.
Acosta, Cecilio. 1908 [1877]. *Influencia del elemento histórico-político en la literatura dramática y en la novela*. In Cecilio Acosta, *Obras*, vol. 2. Caracas: Empresa El Cojo.
Adams, Percy G. 1983. *Travel Literature and the Evolution of the Novel*. Lexington, Ky.: University Press of Kentucky.
Adorno, Theodor, and Max Horkheimer. 1986 [1947]. *Dialectic of Enlightenment*. Trans. John Cumming. New York: Continuum.
Alberdi, Juan Bautista. 1945 [1842]. "Ideas." In José Gaos, ed., *Antología del pensamiento de lengua española en la edad contemporánea*. Mexico City: Editorial Séneca.
Alonso, Amado. 1976 [1935]. "Borges, narrador." In J. Alarazki, ed., *Jorge Luis Borges*. Madrid: Taurus.
Apocryphon of John. 1977. In F. Wisse, ed. and trans., *The Nag Hammadi Library in English*. New York and San Francisco: Harper and Row.
Apollinaire, Guillaume. 1950 [1913]. *Les Peintres cubistes, Méditations esthétiques*. Geneva: Editions P. Cailler.
Arguedas, Alcides. 1937 [1909]. *Pueblo enfermo*. Santiago, Chile: Ercilla.
Aristotle. 1984. *The Complete Works of Aristotle: The Revised Oxford Translations*. Ed. J. Barnes. Princeton, N.J.: Princeton University Press.
Arnaud, Charles. 1888. *Les Théories dramatiques au XIIe siècle. Etude sur la vie et les oeuvres de l'abbé d'Aubignac*. Paris: A. Picard.
Arregui, J. J. H. 1978 [1957]. "La imagen colonizada de la Argentina." In Juan Fló, ed., *Contra Borges*. Buenos Aires: Galerna.
Auerbach, Erich. 1984a [1940]. "Figura." In Auerbach, *Scenes from the Drama of European Literature*.
———. 1984b [1951]. *Scenes from the Drama of European Literature*. Trans. R. Mannheim. Minneapolis: University of Minnesota Press.

Baltrušaitis, Jurgen. 1978. *Le Miroir.* Paris: Seuil.
Barck, Karlheins. 1979. "Differenzierung der Beziehungen zwischen künstlerischer und politischer Avantgarde. Blickrichtung: französischer Surrealismus." In K. Barck, D. Schlenstedt, and W. Thierse, eds., *Künstlerische Avantgarde.* Berlin: Akademie-Verlag.
Barras, M. 1933. *The Stage Controversy in France from Corneille to Rousseau.* New York: The Institute of French Studies.
Barrenechea, Ana Maria. 1956. *La expresión de la irrealidad en la obra de Jorge Luis Borges.* Mexico City: Colegio de Mexico.
Barthes, Roland. 1961. Introduction. In Roland Barthes, *Maximes et reflexions.* Paris: Le Club Français du Livre.
———. 1973. *Le Plaisir du texte.* Paris: Seuil.
Bastos, Maria Luisa. 1974. *Borges ante la critica argentina* (1923–60). Buenos Aires: Edic. Hispamérica.
Belaval, Yves. 1950. *L'Esthétique sans paradoxe de Diderot.* Paris: Gallimard.
———. 1963. "Note sur Diderot et Leibniz." *Revue des Sciences Humaines,* Oct.– Dec., pp. 435–51.
Benjamin, Walter. 1974 [1929]. "Der Surrealismus. Die letzte Momentaufnahme der europaischen Intelligenz." In Walter Benjamin, *Gesammelte Schriften,* vol. 2. Frankfurt a. M.: Suhrkamp Verlag.
Berman, Marshall. 1982. *All That Is Solid Melts into Air: The Experience of Modernity.* New York: Simon and Schuster.
Bilbao, Francisco. 1941 [1862]. *La América en peligro.* In Francisco Bilbao, *La América en peligro. Evangelio americano. Sociabilidad chilena.* Santiago, Chile: Ercilla.
Blanchot, Maurice. 1971 [1959]. "L'Infini littéraire: L'Aleph." In *Le Livre à venir.* Paris: Gallimard.
Bloch, R. Howard. 1977. *Medieval French Literature and Law.* Berkeley: University of California Press.
———. 1983. *Etymologies and Genealogies: A Literary Anthropology of the French Middle Ages.* Chicago: University of Chicago Press.
Bloom, Harold. 1980. "Lying Against Time: Gnosis, Poetry, Criticism." In B. Layton, ed., *The Rediscovery of Gnosticism, 1, The School of Valentinus.* Leyden: E. J. Brill.
Blumenberg, Hans. 1985 [1979]. *Work on Myth.* Trans. R. M. Wallace. Cambridge, Mass.: MIT Press.
Blunt, Anthony. 1956. *Artistic Theory in Italy 1450–1650.* Oxford: Clarendon.
Boccaccio, Giovanni. 1930 [1375]. *De genealogia deorum gentilium.* Books 14 and 15. In Giovanni Boccaccio, *Boccaccio on Poetry,* ed. and trans. C. Osgood. Princeton, N.J.: Princeton University Press.
Boileau, Nicolas. 1966 [1674]. *L'Art poétique.* In F. Escal, ed., *Oeuvres complètes.* Paris: Pléiade.
Bolívar, Simón. 1942. *Ideario político.* Buenos Aires: El Ateneo.
———. 1950. *Obras completas.* Havana: Editorial Lex.
Bonfim, Manoel. Undated [1905]. *A América Latina: Males de origem; o parasitismo social e evolução.* Paris and Rio de Janeiro: Garnier.

Borges, Jorge Luis. 1925. *Inquisiciones.* Buenos Aires: Editoral Proa.
———. 1980. *Prosa completa.* Vol. 1. Barcelona: Bruguera.
Bossuet, J.-B. 1828 [1694]. *Maximes et réflexions sur la comédie.* In J.-B. Bossuet, *Oeuvres complètes,* vol. 12. Paris: N.p.
Boswell, James. 1892 [1741]. *The Life of Samuel Johnson, together with the Journal of a Tour to the Hebrides.* 5 vols. London: George Bell and Sons.
Brecht, Bertolt. 1967. *Gesammelte Werke.* Vol. 5. Frankfurt a. M.: Suhrkamp.
Breton, André. 1935. *Position politique du surréalisme.* Paris: Editions du Saggitaire.
———. 1955. *Les Manifestes du surréalisme.* Paris: Le Saggitaire.
———. 1959 [1935]. "Phare de la mariée." In Robert Lebel, *Marcel Duchamp,* trans. G. H. Hamilton. London: Trianon.
Bruss, Elizabeth. 1976. *Autobiographical Acts: The Changing Situation of a Literary Genre.* Baltimore, Md.: The Johns Hopkins University Press.
Bucher, B. 1981 [1977]. *Icon and Conquest: A Structural Analysis of the Illustrations of de Bry's Great Voyages.* Chicago: University of Chicago Press.
Bunge, Carlos Octavio. 1905 [1903]. *Nuestra América (Ensayo de psicología social).* Buenos Aires: Valerio Abeledo Editor.
Burckhardt, Jacob. 1960 [1860]. *The Civilization of Renaissance in Italy.* Trans. I. Gordon. New York: Mentor Books.
Burgin, Richard. 1969. *Conversations with Borges.* New York: Holt, Rinehart and Winston.
Burke, Edmund. 1968 [1757]. *A Philosophical Enquiry into the Origin of Our Ideas of the Sublime and Beautiful.* Ed. J. T. Boulton. Notre Dame, Ind.: University of Notre Dame Press.
Calderón, Francisco García. 1979a [1912]. *Las democracias latinas de América.* Caracas: Bibl. Ayacucho.
———. 1979b [1913]. *La creación de un continente.* Caracas: Bibl. Ayacucho.
Campos, Haroldo de. 1976. "A linguagem de Iauretê." In Haroldo de Campos, *Metalinguagem.* São Paulo: Cultrix.
Candido, Antonio. 1973. *Literatura e sociedade.* São Paulo: Cia. Editora Nacional.
Canetti, Elias. 1982 [1980]. *The Torch in My Ear.* Trans. J. Neugroschel. New York: Farrar Straus Giroux.
Cardano, Geronimo. 1930 [1643]. *The Book of My Life.* Trans. J. Stoner. New York: E. P. Dutton.
Cardoso, Fernando Henrique, and Francisco Weffort. 1970. *América Latina. Ensayos de interpretación sociológico-político.* Santiago, Chile: Editorial Universitaria.
Carroll, David. 1982. *The Subject in Question: The Language of Theory and the Strategies of Fiction.* Chicago: University of Chicago Press.
Carsten, F. L. 1961. "Introduction: The Age of Louis XIV." In F. L. Carsten, *The New Cambridge Modern History,* vol. 5. Cambridge, Eng.: Cambridge University Press.
Carvalho, José Murilo de. 1980. *A construção da ordem.* Rio de Janeiro: Editora Campus.

Cassirer, Ernst. 1963 [1927]. *Individuum und Kosmos in der Philosophie der Renaissance*. Darmstadt: Wiss. Buchgesellschaft.

Castiglione, Baldassare. 1983 [1528]. *The Book of the Courtier*. Trans. C. Singleton. New York: Anchor Books.

Cellini, Benvenuto. 1946 [1728]. *The Life of Benvenuto Cellini Written by Himself*. Trans. J. A. Symonds. New York: Doubleday.

Cerquiglini, Jacqueline. 1980. "Le Clerc et l'écriture: Le *voir dit* de Guillaume de Machaut et la définition du dit." In H. U. Gumbrecht, ed., *Literatur in der Gesellschaft des Spatmittelalters*, suppl. to *Grundriss der romanischen Literaturen des Mittelalters*, vol. 1. Heidelberg: Carl Winter-Universitatsverlag.

Cervantes, Miguel de. 1952 [1605–15]. *The History of Don Quixote de La Mancha*. Trans. J. Ormsby. Chicago: Encyclopaedia Britannica.

Chadwick, Henry. 1980. "The Domestication of Gnosis." In B. Layton, ed., *The Rediscovery of Gnosticism, 1, The School of Valentinus*. Leyden: E. J. Brill.

Chastel, André. 1945. "Art et religion dans la renaissance italienne." *Bibliothèque d'Humanisme et Renaissance*, 7: 7–61.

Chénieux, Jacqueline. 1979. "L'Erotisme chez Marcel Duchamp et Georges Bataille." In J. Clair, ed., *Marcel Duchamp: Tradition de la rupture ou rupture de la tradition?* Paris: 10/18.

Chiaramonte, José Carlos. 1979. Introducción. In José Carlos Chiaramonte, *Pensamiento de la ilustración. Economia y sociedad iberoamericanas en el siglo XIX*. Caracas: Bibl. Ayacucho.

Chouillet, Jacques. 1973. *La Formation des idées esthétiques de Diderot*. Paris: A. Colin.

Collingwood, R. G. 1982 [1939]. *An Autobiography*. Oxford: Clarendon.

Conrad, Joseph. 1917 [1904]. *Nostromo: A Tale of the Seaboard*. New York: Holt, Rinehart and Winston.

Corneille, Pierre. 1971 [1660]. *Discours du poème dramatique* and *Discours des trois unités*. In Pierre Corneille, *Théâtre complet de Pierre Corneille*, ed. G. Couton. Paris: Garnier.

Costa Lima, Luiz. 1976. *A perversão do trapezista: O romance em Cornélio Penna*. Rio de Janeiro: Imago.

———. 1980. *Mimesis e modernidade*. Rio de Janeiro: Graal.

———. 1981. "Da existência precária: O sistema intelectual no Brasil" and "A crítica literária na cultura brasileira do século XIX." In Luiz Costa Lima, *Dispersa demanda*. Rio de Janeiro: Francisco Alves.

———. 1984–85. "Social Representation and Mimesis." *New Literary History*, 16: 447–66.

———. 1986. *Sociedade e discurso ficcional*. Rio de Janeiro: Guanabara.

———. 1988. *Control of the Imaginary: Reason and Imagination in Modern Times*. Trans. Ronald W. Sousa. Minneapolis: University of Minnesota Press.

D'Allones, Revault. 1951. "L'Esthétique de Descartes." *Revue des Sciences Humaines*, Jan.–Mar.

Darnton, Robert. 1984. *The Great Cat Massacre*. New York: Basic Books.

D'Aubignac, F. H. 1644. *Dissertation sur la condemnation des théâtres*. Paris: N.p.

———. 1971 [1663]. *Troisième dissertation concernant le poëme dramatique*. In

Pierre Corneille, *Théâtre complet de Pierre Corneille*, ed. G. Couton. Paris: Garnier.

Deleuze, Gilles. 1968. *Différence et répétition*. Paris: PUF.

———. 1986. *Foucault*. Paris: Minuit.

de Man, Paul. 1964. "A Modern Master." *The New York Review of Books*, vol. 3, Nov.

———. 1988. *Critical Writings 1953–1978*. Ed. Lindsay Waters. Minneapolis: University of Minnesota Press.

Descartes, René. 1965 [1634]. *Les Passions de l'âme*. Ed. G. Rodis-Lewis. Paris: J. Vrin.

Díaz del Castillo, Bernal. 1933 [1632]. *Historia verdadera de la conquista de la Nueva España*. Vol. 1. Madrid: Espasa-Calpe.

Diderot, Denis. 1819. *Oeuvres complètes*. Vol. 6. Paris: N.p.

———. 1875. *Oeuvres complètes*. Vols. 1, 2, and 9. Ed. J. Assézat. Paris: Garnier.

———. 1957. *Salons*. Vol. 1. Ed. J. Seznec and J. Adhémar. Oxford: Clarendon.

———. 1960. *Salons*. Vol. 2. Ed. J. Seznec and J. Adhémar. Oxford: Clarendon.

———. 1963. *Salons*. Vol. 3. Ed. J. Seznec and J. Adhémar. Oxford: Clarendon.

———. 1965a. *Oeuvres esthétiques*. Ed. P. Vernière. Paris: Garnier.

———. 1965b. *Oeuvres philosophiques*. Ed. P. Vernière. Paris: Garnier.

———. 1967. *Salons*. Vol. 4. Ed. J. Seznec and J. Adhémar. Oxford: Clarendon.

———. 1976. *Oeuvres complètes*. Vols. 6 and 7. Ed. J. Lough and J. Proust. Paris: Hermann.

———. 1980. *Oeuvres complètes*. Vol. 13. Ed. J. Varloot. Paris: Hermann.

Dieckmann, Herbert. 1941. "Diderot's Conception of Genius." *Journal of the History of Ideas*, 2, pt. 2: 151–82.

———. 1959. *Cinq leçons sur Diderot*. Geneva: Droz.

Doll, R. 1978 [1933]. "Discusiones con Borges." In Juan Fló, ed., *Contra Borges*. Buenos Aires: Galerna.

Doolittle, James. 1952. "Hieroglyph and Emblem in Diderot's *Lettre sur les sourds et muets*." In O. E. Fellows and N. L. Torry, eds., *Diderot Studies*, 2. Syracuse, N.Y.: Syracuse University Press.

Droysen, Gustav. 1971 [1868]. *Historik*. Ed. R. Hübner. Darmstadt: Wiss. Buchgesellschaft.

Duchamp, Marcel. 1975. *Duchamps du signe: Écrits*. Ed. M. Sanouillet. Paris: Flammarion.

Dumont, Louis. 1978. "La Conception moderne de l'individu." *Esprit*, Feb.

Duve, Thierry de. 1984. *Nominalisme pictural: La peinture et la modernité*. Paris: Minuit.

Elias, Norbert. 1983 [1969]. *The Court Society*. Trans. E. Jephcott. New York: Pantheon Books.

Erasmus, Desiderius. 1908 [1538]. *Ciceronianus*. Trans. Izora Scott. New York: Teachers College, Columbia University Press.

Estrada, Ezequiel Martínez. 1948. *Muerte y transfiguración de Martín Fierro. Ensayo de interpretación de la vida argentina*. 2 vols. Mexico City: FCE.

———. 1968 [1933]. *Radiografía de la pampa*. Buenos Aires: Losada.

Fausto, Boris. 1970. *A Revolução de 30: Historiografia e história*. São Paulo: Brasiliense.
Ferguson, W. K. 1939–40. "Humanist Views of the Renaissance." *American Historical Review*, 45: 1–28.
———. 1968 [1951]. "Interpretation of Renaissance." In P. O. Kristeller and P. P. Wiener, eds., *Renaissance Essays*. New York: Harper and Row.
Ferraro, R. M. 1971. *Giudizi critici e criteri estetici nei Poetices libri septem (1561) de Giulio Cesare Scaligero rispetto alla teoria letteraria del rinascimento*. Chapel Hill, N.C.: University of North Carolina.
Fitzgerald, Robert. 1965. *Enlarging the Change: The Princeton Seminars in Literary Criticism (1949–51)*. Boston: Northeastern University Press.
Folkierski, Wladislaw. 1925. *Entre le classicisme et le romantisme: Étude sur l'esthétique et les esthéticiens du XVIIIe siècle*. Cracow and Paris: N.p.
Foucault, Michel. 1982. "The Subject of Power." *Critical Inquiry*, 8, pt. 4: 777–95.
Fried, Michael. 1980. *Absorption and Theatricality: Painting and Beholder in the Age of Diderot*. Berkeley: University of California Press.
Funt, David. 1968. *Diderot and the Aesthetics of the Enlightenment*. In O. Fellows and D. Guiragossian, eds., *Diderot Studies, 11*. Geneva: Droz.
García, Antonio. 1970. "La estructura social y el desarrollo latinoamericano." In Fernando Henrique Cardoso and Francisco Weffort, *América Latina. Ensayos de interpretación sociológico-político*. Santiago, Chile: Editorial Universitaria.
Gilson, Etienne. 1964. Preface to Abelard. In Peter Abelard, *The Story of Abelard's Adversities*, trans. J. T. Muckle. Toronto: The Pontifical Institute of Medieval Studies.
Giuliani, Oscar. 1977. *Allegoria retorica e poetica nel Secretum del Petrarca*. Bologna: Pàtron editore.
Gnostic Treatise on Resurrection. Trans. B. Layton. In F. Wisse, ed., *The Nag Hammadi Library in English*. New York and San Francisco: Harper and Row.
Goethe, J. Wolfgang. 1954 [1799]. "Diderots Versuch über die Malerei." In J. W. Goethe, *Gedenkenausgabe der Werke, Briefe u. Gespräche*, vol. 13, ed. E. Bentler. Zurich: Artemis-Verlag.
Gombrich, E. H. 1978 [1972]. "Botticelli's Mythologies: A Study in the Neo-Platonic Symbolism." In E. H. Gombrich, *Symbolic Images*. Oxford: Phaidon.
Gray, H. H. 1968 [1963]. "Renaissance Humanism." In P. O. Kristeller and P. P. Wiener, eds., *Renaissance Essays*. New York: Harper and Row.
Green, André, and Jean-Luc Donnet. 1973. *L'Enfant de ça. Psychanalyse d'un entretien: La psychose blanche*. Paris: Minuit.
Gumbrecht, Hans Ulrich. 1985. "Déconstruction deconstructed: Transformationen franzosischen Logozentrismus-Kritik in der Amerikanischen Literaturtheorie." Unpublished.
Gusdorf, Georges. 1980 [1956]. "Conditions and Limits of Autobiography." In J. Olney, ed., *Autobiography: Essays Theoretical and Critical*. Princeton, N.J.: Princeton University Press.
Habermas, Jürgen. 1976. *Communication and the Evolution of Society*. Trans. T. McCarthy. Boston: Beacon.

———. 1978 [1962]. *Strukturwandel der Öffentlichkeit.* Darmstadt: Luchterhand Verlag.
Hall, Vernon. 1950. "Life of Julius Caesar Scaliger." *Transactions of the American Philosophical Society*, 40, pt. 2: 87–169.
———. 1959. *Renaissance Literary Criticism: A Study of Its Social Content.* Gloucester, Eng.: Peter Smith.
Halperin Donghi, Tulio. 1970. *Historia contemporánea de América Latina.* Madrid: Alianza Editorial.
———. 1980. "Nueva narrativa y ciencias sociales hispanoamericanas en la década del sesenta." *Hispamérica*, vol. 27 (Dec).
Havelock, Eric. 1963. *Preface to Plato.* Oxford: Blackwell.
Hegel, G. W. F. 1929 [1812–16]. *Science of Logic.* Trans. Haldane of Cloan. London: George Allen Unwin.
Heller, Agnes. 1978 [1967]. *Renaissance Man.* Trans. R. E. Allen. New York: Shocken Books.
Hernández, José. 1981 [1872, 1879]. *Martin Fierro.* Madrid: Alianza Editorial.
Holanda, Sérgio Buarque de. 1969 [1936]. *Raízes do Brasil.* Rio de Janeiro: José Olympio.
Huidobro, Vicente. 1976. *Obras completas.* 2 vols. Santiago, Chile: Editorial Andrés Bello.
Huizinga, J. 1938–39 [1920]. "Le Problème de la renaissance." *Revue des Cours et Conférences*, Dec. 1938–Mar. 1939, pp. 163–74, 301–13.
Irenaeus. 1961 [2nd century]. *Adversus haereses.* In R. M. Grant, ed., *Gnosticism: A Source Book from the Heretical Writings from the Early Christian Period.* New York: Harper and Brothers.
Iser, Wolfgang. 1980. Interview. *Diacritics*, 10, pt. 2.
———. 1983 [1979]. "Akte des Fingierens. Oder: Was ist das Fiktive im fiktionalen Text?" In Wolfgang Iser, *Poetik und Hermeneutik*, vol. 10. Munich: W. Fink Verlag.
Jara, René. 1979. "El criollismo de Fray Servando Teresa de Meir." *Cuadernos Americanos*, 222, pt. 1.
———. 1983. "Crítica de una crisis: Los estudios literarios hispanoamericanos." *Ideologies and Literature*, 4, pt. 16.
Jitrik, Noé. 1968. *El 80 y su mundo.* Buenos Aires: Jorge Alvarez.
Jonas, Hans. 1963 [1958]. *The Gnostic Religion: The Message of the Alien God and the Beginnings of Christianity.* Boston: Beacon.
Kenner, Hugh. 1975 [1972]. *The Pound Era: The Age of Ezra Pound, T. S. Eliot, James Joyce and Wyndham Lewis.* London: Faber and Faber.
Kermode, Frank. 1961 [1954]. Introduction. In William Shakespeare, *The Tempest.* Cambridge, Mass.: Methuen and Harvard University Press.
Klee, Paul. 1945. *Über moderne Kunst.* Bern and Bumpliz: Verlag Bentili.
———. 1956. *Das bildnerische Denken. Schriften zur Form- und Gestaltungslehre.* Ed. J. Spiller. Basel: B. Schwake.
———. 1957. *Tagebücher.* Ed. Felix Klee. Cologne: Verlag M. DuMont Shauberg.
Koselleck, R. 1976 [1959]. *Kritik und Krise.* Frankfurt a. M.: Suhrkampf.

Kristeller, P. O. 1944–45. "Humanism and Scholasticism." *Byzantion*, 17: 346–74.
Kuhn, Hugo. 1969 [1959]. "Stil als Epochen-, Gattungs- und Wertproblem in der deutschen Literatur des Mittelalters." In Hugo Kuhn, *Dichtung und Welt im Mittelalter*. Stuttgart: J. B. Metzler.
La Bruyère, Jean de. 1962 [1694]. *Les Caractères ou les moeurs de ce siècle*. Ed. R. Garapon. Paris: Garnier.
La Rochefoucauld. 1950 [1662–1731]. *Oeuvres complètes*. Ed. L. Martin-Chauffier. Paris: Pléiade.
Lastarria, José Victorino. 1865. *La América*. Buenos Aires: N.p.
Le Goff, Jacques. 1981. *La Naissance du purgatoire*. Paris: Gallimard.
Leonardo da Vinci. 1952 [c. 1490]. *Selections from the Notebooks of Leonardo da Vinci*. Ed. J. P. Richter. London: Oxford University Press.
———. 1954 [c. 1490]. *The Notebooks of Leonardo da Vinci*. Ed. and trans. Edward MacCurdy. New York: Braziller.
———. 1970 [c. 1490]. "Paragone." In Leonardo da Vinci, *Literary Works of Leonardo da Vinci*, ed. J. P. Richter. London: Phaidon.
Lévi-Strauss, Claude. 1962. *La Pensée sauvage*. Paris: Plon.
———. 1964. *Le Cru et le cuit*. Paris: Plon.
Lima, Alceu Amoroso. 1922. *Afonso Arinos*. Rio de Janeiro and Lisbon: Anuário do Brasil.
Link, Jürgen. 1984. "Einfluss des Fliegens! Auf den Stil selbst!" In J. Link and W. Wülfing, eds., *Bewegung und Stilstand in Metaphern und Mythen*. Stuttgart: Klett-Cotta.
Lisboa, João Francisco. 1864. *Obras completas*. 4 vols. São Luís, Brazil: Tipografia B. de Matos.
Lough, John. 1957. *Paris Theatre Audiences in the Seventeenth and Eighteenth Centuries*. London: Oxford University Press.
———. 1961. "France Under Louis XIV." In *The New Cambridge Modern History*, vol. 5. Cambridge, Eng.: Cambridge University Press.
Lugones, Leopoldo. 1979 [1916]. *El payador y antologia de poesía e prosa*. Caracas: Bibl. Ayacucho.
Luhmann, Niklas. 1983. *Liebe als Passion. Zur Codierung von Intimitat*. Frankfurt a. M.: Suhrkamp.
Machiavelli, Niccolò. 1954 [1520]. *Dell'arte della guerra*. In Niccolò Machiavelli, *Opere*, ed. M. Bonfantini. Milan: R. Ricciardi Editore.
Mallarmé, Stéphane. 1956 [1945]. *Oeuvres complètes*. Ed. H. Mondor and G. Jean-Aubry. Paris: Gallimard.
Mandel, Barrett J. 1980 [1972]. "Full of Life Now." In J. Olney, ed., *Autobiography: Essays Theoretical and Critical*. Princeton, N.J.: Princeton University Press.
Maravall, José Antonio. 1978. "La función del honor en la sociedad tradicional." In *Ideologies and Literature*, 2, pt. 7 (May–June).
Marcuse, Herbert. 1965. "Repressive Tolerance." In Robert Wolff, P. Barrington Moore, Jr., and Herbert Marcuse, *A Critique of Pure Tolerance*. Boston: Beacon.
Mariátegui, José Carlos. 1943 [1928]. *7 ensayos de interpretación de la realidad peruana*. Lima: Amauta.

Marienstras, R. 1972. "La Littérature élisabéthaine du voyage et *La Tempête* de Shakespeare." In R. Marienstras, *Le Voyage dans la littérature anglo-saxonne*. Paris: Libr. M. Didier.

Marquard, Odo. 1968. "Zur Bedeutung der Theorie des Unbewussten für eine Theorie der nicht mehr schönen Kunst." In H. R. Jauss, ed., *Poetik und Hermeneutik*, 3. Munich: W. Fink Verlag.

Martí, José. 1977 [1891]. "Nuestra América." In José Martí, *Nuestra América*. Caracas: Bibl. Ayacucho.

———. 1978. *Obra literaria*. Caracas: Bibl. Ayacucho.

May, George. 1963. *Le Dilemme du roman au XVIIIe siècle*. Paris: PUF.

May, Gita. 1960. "Diderot and Burke: A Study in Aesthetic Affinity." *PMLA*, Dec., pp. 527–39.

Merton, Thomas. 1968. *The Asian Journal of Thomas Merton*. New York: New Directions.

Misch, Georg. 1950 [1907]. *A History of Autobiography in Antiquity*. Trans. E. W. Dickes. London: Routledge and Kegan Paul.

Monroe, Paul. 1908. Introduction. In Erasmus, *Ciceronianus*, trans. Izora Scott. New York: Teachers College, Columbia University Press.

Montaigne, Michel de. 1952 [1580–95]. *The Essays*. Trans. C. Cotton, ed. W. C. Hazlitt. Chicago: Encyclopaedia Britannica.

Mortier, Roland. 1954. *Diderot en Allemagne (1750–1840)*. Paris: PUF.

Müller-Freienfels, Richard. 1919. "Der Begriff der Individualitat als fiktive Konstruktion." *Annalen der Philosophie*, 1: 270–318.

Murena, H. A. 1980 [1948]. "Condenación de una poesía." In Juan Fló, ed., *Contra Borges*. Buenos Aires: Galerna.

Nabokov, Vladimir. 1966. *Speak, Memory. An Autobiography Revisited*. London: Weidenfeld and Nicolson.

———. 1973 [1955]. *Lolita*. London: Corgi Books.

Nabuco, Joaquim. 1949a [1883]. *O abolicionismo*. São Paulo: Progresso Editorial.

———. 1949b [1899]. *Um estadista do império*. São Paulo: Progresso Editorial.

Nelson, William. 1973. *Fact or Fiction: The Dilemma of the Renaissance Storyteller*. Cambridge, Mass.: Harvard University Press.

Nixon, R. 1987. "Caribbean and African Appropriations of *The Tempest*." *Critical Inquiry*, 13, pt. 3: 557–78.

Novalis. 1978 [1797–98]. *Bluthenstaub*. In H.-J. Mahl and R. Samuel, eds., *Werke, Tagebücher und Briefe*, vol. 2. Munich: Carls Hanser Verlag.

Oliveira Lima, Manuel de. 1945 [1908]. *D. João VI no Brasil*. 3 vols. Rio de Janeiro: José Olympio.

Orgel, S. 1987 [1981]. "Shakespeare and the Cannibals." In M. Garber, ed., *Cannibals, Witches, and Divorce: Estranging the Renaissance*. Baltimore, Md.: Johns Hopkins University Press.

Pagden, A. 1982. *The Fall of Natural Man: The American Indian and the Origins of Comparative Ethnology*. Cambridge, Eng.: Cambridge University Press.

Panofsky, Erwin. 1954. *Galileo as Critic of the Arts*. The Hague: M. Nijhoff.

———. 1971 [1943]. *The Life and Art of Albrecht Dürer*. Princeton, N.J.: Princeton University Press.

Panofsky, Erwin, and Fritz Saxl. 1933. "Classical Mythology in Medieval Art." *Metropolitan Museum Studies*, 4, pt. 2: 228–79.

Panofsky, Erwin; Fritz Saxl; and Raymond Klibansky 1979 [1964]. *Saturn and Melancholy*. Neldeln, Liechtenstein: Krausprint.

Pascal, Blaise. 1952 [1670]. *Pensées*. Trans. W. F. Trotter. Chicago: Encyclopaedia Britannica.

Pascal, Roy. 1960. *Design and Truth in Autobiography*. Cambridge, Mass.: Harvard University Press.

Paz, Octavio. 1973. *Apariencia desnuda: La obra de Marcel Duchamp*. Mexico City: Ediciones Era.

———. 1974. *Los hijos del limo*. Barcelona: Seix Barral.

Petrarch (Petrarca, Francesco). 1968a [1342–58]. *Il conflitto secreto dei miei affanni*. In Petrarch, *Opere di Petrarca*, ed. G. Ponte. Milan: Mursia.

———. 1968b [1342–58]. *Il secreto dei miei affani*. In Petrarch, *Opere di Petrarca*, ed. G. Ponte. Milan: Mursia.

Pommier, Jean. 1936. "Les Salons de Diderot et leur influence au XIXe siècle: Baudelaire et le salon de 1846." *Revue des Cours et Conférences*, nos. 12 and 13: 290–306 and 437–52.

Portantiero, J. C. 1980 [1955]. "Borges y la nueva generación." In Juan Fló, ed., *Contra Borges*. Buenos Aires: Galerna.

Prieto, Adolfo. 1954. *Borges y la nueva generación*. Buenos Aires: Letras Universitarias.

Racine, Jean. 1980 [1677]. *Théâtre complet*. Ed. J. Morel and A. Viala. Paris: Garnier.

Reda, Jacques. 1963. "Commentaire de *L'Immortel* de Jorge-Luis Borges." *Cahiers du Sud*, Feb.–Mar., pp. 435–55.

Reiss, Timothy. 1982. *The Discourse of Modernism*. Ithaca, N.Y.: Cornell University Press.

Renza, Louis. 1980 [1977]. "A Theory of Autobiography." In J. Olney, ed., *Autobiography: Essays Theoretical and Critical*. Princeton, N.J.: Princeton University Press.

Riley, E. C. 1962. *Cervantes's Theory of the Novel*. Oxford: Clarendon.

Rodó, José Enrique. Undated (a) [1899]. "Rubén Darío." In José Enrique Rodó, *Cinco ensayos*. Madrid: Editorial América.

———. Undated (b) [1900]. *Ariel*. Valencia: Prometeo.

Rojas, Ricardo. 1960 [1917–22]. *Historia de la literatura argentina*. Buenos Aires: Editorial G. Kraft.

Romero, José Luis. 1965. *El desarrollo de las ideas en la sociedad argentina*. Mexico City: FCE.

———. 1970. *El pensamiento político de la derecha latinoamericana*. Buenos Aires: Paidós.

———. 1980. *Las ideologías de la cultura nacional y otros ensayos*. Buenos Aires: Centro Editor de América Latina.

Rosas, Juan Manuel de. 1978 [1834]. "Carta de la hacienda de Figueroa." In Juan Manuel de Rosas, *Pensamiento conservador* (1815–98). Caracas: Bibl. Ayacucho.

Rousseau, Jean-Jacques. 1948 [1758]. *Lettre à M. D'Alembert sur les spectacles*. Ed. M. Fuchs. Lille and Geneve: Giard-Droz.

———. 1964a. *Oeuvres complètes*. Ed. B. Guyon, J. Scherer, and C. Guyot. Paris: Pléiade.

———. 1964b [1761]. "Seconde préface" to *La Nouvelle Héloïse*. In Rousseau, *Oeuvres complètes*, ed. Guyon, Scherer, and Guyot, vol. 2.

———. 1969 [1764–89]. *Oeuvres complètes*. Ed. I. B. Gagnebin and M. Raymond. Paris: Pléiade.

Roy, Claude. 1972. *Nous. Essai d'autobiographie*. Paris: Gallimard.

Rulfo, Juan. 1977 [1955]. *Pedro Páramo*. Mexico City: CFE, Biblioteca Popular.

Sábato, Ernesto. 1980 [1963]. "En torno de Borges." In Juan Fló, ed., *Contra Borges*. Buenos Aires: Galerna.

Salgado, Plínio. 1935. *Despertemos a nação*. Rio de Janeiro: José Olympio.

Sánchez, Luis Alberto. 1941. *Balance y liquidación del novecientos*. Santiago, Chile: Ercilla.

Sarmiento, Domingo Faustino. 1915 [1883]. *Conflicto y harmonía de las razas en América*. Buenos Aires: La Cultura Argentina.

———. 1938 [1845]. *Facundo. Civilización o barbarie*. La Plata: N.p.

Scholem, Gershom G. 1978 [1965]. *A Cabala e seu simbolismo*. Trans. H. Borger and J. Guinsburg. São Paulo: Perspectiva.

Schulte-Sasse, Jochen. 1985. "Art and the Sacrificial Structure of Modernity: A Sociohistorical Supplement to Jay Caplan's *Framed Narratives*." In Jay Caplan, *Framed Narratives*. Minneapolis: University of Minnesota Press.

Scudéry, George de. 1639. *L'Apologie du théâtre*. Paris: N.p.

———. 1862 [1643]. *Observation sur Le Cid*. In Pierre Corneille, *Oeuvres de Pierre Corneille*, ed. Marty-Laveaux, vol. 12. Paris: Hachette.

Sennett, Richard. 1978 [1977]. *The Fall of Public Man*. New York: Vintage Books.

Sentiments de l'Académie sur Le Cid. 1862 [1637]. In Pierre Corneille, *Oeuvres de Pierre Corneille*, ed. Marty-Laveaux, vol. 12. Paris: Hachette.

Seznec, Jean. 1972 [1940]. *The Survival of the Pagan Gods*. Trans. B. F. Sessions. Princeton, N.J.: Princeton University Press.

Shakespeare, William. 1984 [1623]. *The Tempest*. In *The Annotated Shakespeare*, ed. A. L. Rowse. New York: Greenwich House.

Sierra, Justo. 1940 [1910]. *Evolución política del pueblo mexicano*. Mexico City: FCE.

Spender, Stephen. 1980 [1962]. "Confessions and Autobiography." In J. Olney, ed., *Autobiography: Essays Theoretical and Critical*. Princeton, N.J.: Princeton University Press.

Starobinski, Jean. 1966. "La Rochefoucauld et les morales substitutives." *Nouvelle Revue Française*, nos. 163 and 164 (Jul. and Aug.): 16–34, 211–29.

Thomas, Henry. 1920. *Spanish and Portuguese Romances of Chivalry*. Cambridge, Eng.: Cambridge University Press.

Tocqueville, Alexis de. 1839 [1835]. *De la démocratie en Amérique*. Vol. 1. Paris: Charles Gosselin.

———. 1850 [1840]. *De la démocratie en Amérique*. Vol. 2. Paris: Pagnette Editeur.

Ugarte, Manuel. 1978 [1908]. *La nación latinoamericana*. Caracas: Bibl. Ayacucho.
Updike, John. 1965. "The Author as Librarian." *The New Yorker*, Oct. 30.
Ureña, Pedro Henriquez. 1978. *La utopía de América*. Caracas: Bibl. Ayacucho.
———. 1980 [1926]. "Sobre Inquisiciones." In Juan Fló, ed., *Contra Borges*. Buenos Aires: Galerna.
———. 1981 [1909]. "Positivismo independiente." In *Obra critica*. Mexico City: FCE.
Vasari, Giorgio. 1967 [1550]. *Le vite di piu eccelenti pittori, scultori e architettori*. Ed. R. Bittati. Florence: Sansoni Editore.
Vauvenargues, L. de C. 1857 [1746]. *Oeuvres de Vauvenargues*. Ed. D.-L. Gilbert. Paris: Furne et Cie.
Venturi, Franco. 1967 [1938]. *Jeunesse de Diderot (1718–53)*. Trans. J. Bertrand. Geneva: Slatkine Reprints.
Veríssimo, José. 1903. *Estudos literários*. 3a. série. Paris and Rio de Janeiro: Garnier.
Vianna, Oliveira. 1955. *Instituições políticas brasileiras*. 2 vols. Rio de Janeiro: José Olympio.
Voltaire. 1968 [1751]. *Le Siècle de Louis XIV*. In Voltaire, *Oeuvres historiques*. Paris: Pléiade.
Walker, Eleanor. 1944. "Towards an Understanding of Diderot's Esthetic Theory." *Romanic Review*, 35, pt. 4: 277–87.
Weber, J. G. 1974. "The Personae in the Style of La Rochefoucauld's *Maximes*." *PMLA*, 89, pt. 2. (Mar.): 250–55.
Weintraub, Karl. J. 1978. *The Value of the Individual. Self and Circumstance in Autobiography*. Chicago: The University of Chicago Press.
Weisinger, H. 1944. "Who Began the Revival of Learning? The Renaissance Point of View." *Papers of the Michigan Academy of Science, Arts, and Letters*, 30: 625–38.
———. 1968 [1945]. "Ideas of History During the Renaissance." In P. O. Kristeller and P. P. Wiener, eds., *Renaissance Essays*. New York: Harper and Row.
Williamson, E. 1984. *The Half-way House of Fiction: Don Quixote and Arthurian Romance*. Oxford: Clarendon.
Yates, F. 1975. *Majesty and Magic in Shakespeare's Last Plays: A New Approach*. London: Routledge and Kegan Paul.
———. 1978 [1964]. *Giordano Bruno and the Hermetic Tradition*. Chicago: University of Chicago Press.
———. 1979. *The Occult Philosophy in the Elizabethan Age*. London: Routledge and Kegan Paul.
Zea, Leopoldo. 1976 [1965]. *El pensamiento latinoamericano*. Barcelona: Ariel.
Zum Felde, Alberto. 1954. *Indice critico de la literatura hispanoamericana. Los ensayistas*. Mexico City: Guarania.
———. 1959. *Indice critico de la literatura hispanoamericana. La narrativa*. Mexico City: Guarania.
Zumthor, Paul. 1975. *Langue, texte, énigme*. Paris: Seuil.

Library of Congress Cataloging-in-Publication Data

Lima, Luiz Costa, 1937–
 [Selections. English]
 The dark side of reason : fictionality and power / Luiz Costa Lima ; translated by Paulo Henriques Britto.
   p.   cm.
 Translation of selected chapters from Sociedade e discurso ficcional and O fingidor e o censor; contains an additional chapter never published before.
 Includes bibliographical references.
 ISBN 0–8047–1976–4 (alk. paper) :
  1. Literature and society.   I. Title.
 PN51.L53213 1992
 809—dc20   91–24853
                                                       CIP
                                                       Rev.

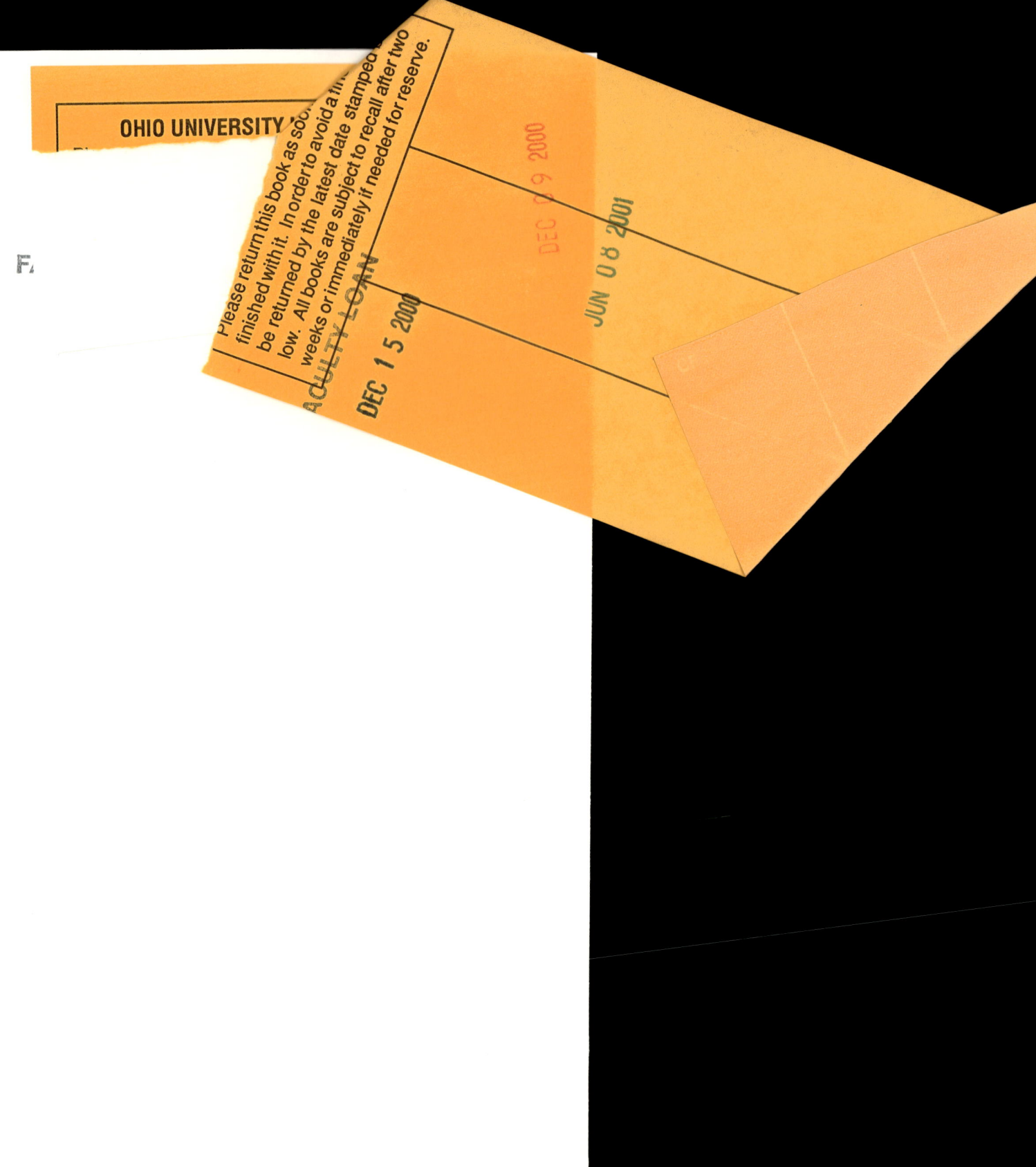

The EDEN-EISENHOWER *Correspondence, 1955–1957*

The EDEN-EISENHOWER *Correspondence,*
1955–1957 EDITED BY PETER G. BOYLE

THE UNIVERSITY OF NORTH CAROLINA PRESS   *Chapel Hill & London*

© 2005

The University of North Carolina Press

All rights reserved

Designed by Richard Hendel

Set in Scala by Keystone Typesetting, Inc.

Manufactured in the United States of America

The paper in this book meets the guidelines for permanence and durability of the Committee on Production Guidelines for Book Longevity of the Council on Library Resources.

Library of Congress Cataloging-in-Publication Data

Eden, Anthony, Earl of Avon, 1897–

The Eden-Eisenhower correspondence, 1955–1957 / edited by Peter G. Boyle.

p. cm.

Includes bibliographical references and index.

ISBN 0-8078-2935-8 (cloth: alk. paper)

1. Eden, Anthony, Earl of Avon, 1897–Correspondence.
2. Eisenhower, Dwight D. (Dwight David), 1890–1969—Correspondence. 3. Great Britain—Foreign relations—United States. 4. United States—Foreign relations—Great Britain.
5. Prime ministers—Great Britain—Correspondence. 6. United States—Foreign relations—1953–1961. 7. Presidents—United States—Correspondence. 8. Great Britain—Foreign relations—1945– I. Eisenhower, Dwight D. (Dwight David), 1890–1969. II. Boyle, Peter G. III. Title.

DA566.9.E28A4   2005

327.41073′09′045—dc22   2004027158

09 08 07 06 05   5 4 3 2 1

CONTENTS

Acknowledgments vii

Abbreviations ix

Introduction 1

The Personalities 7

The Issues 53

CORRESPONDENCE, PART I

*From Eden's Accession to the Outbreak of the Suez Crisis,
April 1955–July 1956* 79

CORRESPONDENCE, PART II

*The Suez Crisis and Eden's Resignation,
July 1956–January 1957* 149

Conclusion 191

Bibliographical Essay 211

Index 219

A section of illustrations follows page 142.

ACKNOWLEDGMENTS

I am grateful to John S. D. Eisenhower for permission to publish the letters of his father, President Dwight D. Eisenhower. The letters of Prime Minister Anthony Eden to President Eisenhower in the Prime Ministers' Papers in the Public Record Office in the National Archives in Kew, Surrey, are Crown copyright, which, thanks to recent liberalization of access to information, no longer requires formal permission for reprinting material. I am grateful to Lady Avon for permission to conduct research in the Papers of Lord Avon (Anthony Eden) in the Special Collections of the University of Birmingham Library and to quote briefly from these papers.

I am obliged to the British Academy for a research grant in 2003 and to the University of Nottingham for a sabbatical semester in 2003.

I am grateful to my editor, Charles Grench, senior editor at the University of North Carolina Press. I am also grateful to his predecessor, Lewis Bateman, who first suggested to me the idea of an edition of *The Churchill-Eisenhower Correspondence, 1953–1955* and who encouraged me to follow this up with an edition of *The Eden-Eisenhower Correspondence, 1955–1957*. I am grateful to the archivists in the Dwight D. Eisenhower Library, especially David Haight, the archivists in the Special Collections of the University of Birmingham Library, especially Chris Penney, and the archivists in the Public Record Office in the National Archives in Kew.

I am very grateful to Christine Worthington for assistance in editing and for typing the manuscript.

I am very appreciative of the assistance of three of my colleagues at the University of Nottingham, Robert Frazier, Spencer Mawby, and John Young, who read the entire manuscript and made useful suggestions for improvements. I am likewise very obliged to the two anonymous University of North Carolina Press readers for very helpful suggestions for improvements.

With regard to a number of matters I am grateful to Richard Aldrich, Angela Chandler, Oliver Daddow, Hugh Goddard, Rhodri Jeffreys-Jones, Paul Lashmar, Scott Lucas, Ann McQueen, Ritchie Ovendale, Ian Scott, Helen Taylor, Stephen Twigge, and Laura Wurzal.

Assistance from many quarters has saved me from many mistakes. For those which remain I take full responsibility.

ABBREVIATIONS

Text

AIOC	Anglo-Iranian Oil Company
Clarissa	Clarissa Eden
Foster	John Foster Dulles
Harold	Harold Macmillan
Mamie	Mamie Eisenhower
NATO	North Atlantic Treaty Organization
Nuri	Nuri al-Said
OSS	Office of Strategic Services
RAF	Royal Air Force
SACEUR	Supreme Allied Commander, Europe (commander of NATO forces)
SCUA	Suez Canal Users Association
Selwyn	Selwyn Lloyd
Winthrop	Winthrop Aldrich

Notes

AP	Papers of the Earl of Avon (Anthony Eden), Special Collections, University of Birmingham Library, Birmingham, England
AWF	Ann Whitman File, Dwight D. Eisenhower Library, Abilene, Kans.
DDEL	Dwight D. Eisenhower Library, Abilene, Kans.
FO	Foreign Office
FRUS	*Foreign Relations of the United States, 1955–1957* (Washington, D.C.: U.S. Government Printing Office, 1985–1993).
NSC	National Security Council
PP	*Public Papers of the Presidents: Dwight D. Eisenhower, 1953–1961*, 8 vols. (Washington, D.C.: U.S. Government Printing Office, 1958–1961).
PREM	Premier (Prime Minister)
PRO	Public Record Office, National Archives, Kew, Surrey

INTRODUCTION

"There is no one better fitted than you to seize the opportunities inherent in your new office for helping to guide the world towards the goal we all earnestly seek. On the more personal side, I cannot tell you how delighted I am that my old friend Winston has been succeeded by an equally valued friend in an office in which friendliness and genuine readiness to cooperate can mean so much to my own country." In these words in the first letter of his personal correspondence with Anthony Eden on April 8, 1955, President Dwight D. Eisenhower warmly welcomed Eden's appointment as prime minister of Britain. Eisenhower concluded his letter with an expression of "my confident belief in the brilliant career ahead of you." Eighteen months later, however, the relationship had degenerated into the deception and disagreements over Suez, which culminated in Eden's resignation in January 1957. The Anglo-American relationship during the Eden-Eisenhower years, 1955–57, is, therefore, a dramatic tale of initial high hopes and promising potential, which ended in tears and in ashes. The development of the relationship from its early promise to its final collapse is vividly revealed in the personal correspondence between Eden and Eisenhower during the period when they were simultaneously in office, April 6, 1955, to January 9, 1957.

The tradition of personal correspondence between the prime minister of Britain and the president of the United States was begun by Winston Churchill and Franklin Roosevelt during World War II.[1] In 1952, following Eisenhower's election as president, Churchill, who had become prime minister of Britain again in 1951, suggested to Eisenhower that they should engage in a similar personal correspondence in addition to normal government-to-government exchanges. Eisenhower agreed to the suggestion and throughout the period when they were simultaneously in office as prime minister of Britain and president of the United States, from January 20, 1953, to April 5, 1955, Churchill and Eisenhower engaged in a correspondence in which letters were less frequent than between Churchill and Roosevelt but were generally longer and more reflective.[2] Eden was keen to continue this tradition and to have a similar correspondence with Eisenhower. On April 11, 1955, he wrote to Eisenhower, thanking him for his complimentary comments and adding, "I hope that you will allow me from time to time to address you where there is some particular aspect of a problem which I would like to present to you and that you won't hesitate to tell me of any reflections or criticisms you may have." The Eden-Eisenhower correspondence thereby duly commenced and continued on a regular basis, with occasional lapses, until the end of Eden's premiership.

Eden, a well-educated diplomat, was, of course, very experienced in the art of letter writing and in expressing himself in a lucid, fluent fashion. Eisenhower was in his way also an experienced and gifted letter writer. As a soldier who was frequently away from home, writing and receiving letters was an important part of his life. He was of a generation to whom the writing of letters was one of the social graces to be acquired as well as a form of communication. Indeed, by contrast to e-mail and the coarser forms of instant communication of later times, the correspondence between Eden and Eisenhower raises a yearning for a lost art and a gentler, more courteous means of interchange of views and ideas.

Eisenhower was, moreover, intelligent and reasonably well educated, and he became accustomed to writing reports throughout his military career. Eisenhower's lucidity of expression and at times surprising reflectiveness had been demonstrated not only in the correspondence with Churchill but also, for example, in his lifelong correspondence with his friend Swede Hazlett.[3] Eden and Eisenhower had known one another very well since the war years, so their correspondence is not simply between two political leaders but between two figures who had become closely acquainted during a time of great historic importance.

Eisenhower was not so close to Eden as he had been to Churchill, however, and this is reflected in the extent to which the letters were written personally by Eisenhower and Eden. With regard to Eisenhower's letters to Churchill, Eisenhower's son, John S. D. Eisenhower, writes that "DDE was close to WSC throughout the war and obviously felt much closer to him than to Eden. I'm sure that he personally drafted all his messages to WSC."[4] Ann Whitman, Eisenhower's personal secretary, supports this, writing that Eisenhower's method of composing letters to Churchill was that "he dictated; I made a draft; he edited if necessary; I had the final version typed. He did not, in these letters, consult with, or show them to, any associate in the White House or State Dept."[5] Andrew Goodpaster, Eisenhower's staff secretary, makes the qualification, however, that although a number of Eisenhower's letters to Churchill were composed entirely by Eisenhower and dispatched without consultation with anyone else, many were based on drafts submitted by the State Department, which were often extensively reworked before dispatch, or were composed by Eisenhower and shown to Dulles for comment before the final draft.⁶ With regard to Eisenhower's letters to Eden, a number were likewise largely or wholly composed by Eisenhower without consultation, but the degree of input from the State Department was generally greater, especially with regard to letters on such technical matters as trade or Cyprus.⁷ This was most crucially the case with regard to the letters relating to the Suez crisis. Andrew Goodpaster records that "the key point that I recall is that Eisenhower and Secretary of State John Foster Dulles were in very close, substantive, almost daily contact over the issue of the Suez Canal. . . . In the interest of full coordination between Secretary Dulles' negotiations and Eisenhower's letters to Eden, I do recall that Eisenhower wrote from State Dept. drafts provided by Dulles. These of course conformed to the basic policy Eisenhower had laid down and Dulles was pursuing. The result was a difference between Eisenhower's method in this case and the way he prepared his letters to Winston Churchill, which, as Ann Whitman informed you, was very much his own, often shown to Dulles for comment before finally sending them."⁸ On Eden's side, Eden worked from drafts prepared in his private office, and Ivone Kirkpatrick, permanent undersecretary at the Foreign Office, was heavily involved in Eden's letters to Eisenhower on the Suez crisis.⁹ Nevertheless, as Roger Makins, British ambassador to the United States from 1953 to 1956, observed, "Churchill virtually weighed every word of his important speeches and important outward correspondence, and Eden, in this case, would certainly have done the same."¹⁰

Copies of the letters are in the Prime Minister's Papers in the Public Record Office in the National Archives, Kew, Surrey, and in the Ann Whitman File in the Dwight D. Eisenhower Library in Abilene, Kansas.¹¹ The original letters from Eisenhower to Eden are in the Prime Ministers' Papers in the Public Record Office, along with copies of letters from Eden to Eisenhower. The original letters from Eden to Eisenhower are in the Ann Whitman File in the Eisenhower Library, along with copies of letters from Eisenhower to Eden.¹² The collection of letters in the Ann Whitman File in the Eisenhower Library is complete. The collection in the Prime Minister's Papers in the Public Record is virtually complete, omitting only copies of a few short, unimportant messages from Eden to Eisenhower. The collection in the Public Record Office also does not include drafts of letters that were not sent. There are several very interesting drafts of letters in the Eisenhower Library which were written by Eisenhower during the Suez crisis, but any such drafts which were not sent are not included in this edition.¹³ Ann Whitman conducted a very thorough search in June 1956 in an attempt to ensure that the State Department could be provided with a full set of the Eden-Eisenhower letters. In a cover letter when transmitting this set of copies to the State Department, Ann Whitman wrote to John W. Hanes Jr., special assistant to the secretary of state, "Here is the book of the Eisenhower-Eden correspondence, which—insofar as we can determine—is now complete and up to date."[14] Subsequent to June 1956, the extremely important letters throughout the period of the Suez crisis were very carefully kept. It would seem fairly certain, therefore, that there are no additional letters which have been lost or misfiled.

The letters were normally received a day after they were sent. The letters were transmitted through the embassies, from Eden to the British embassy in Washington, D.C., to be delivered to the White House and from Eisenhower to the American embassy in London to be delivered to 10 Downing Street. Eden normally addressed Eisenhower as "Dear Friend" and closed "Yours ever, Anthony." Eisenhower normally addressed Eden as "Dear Anthony" and closed with "D.E.," "D.D.E.," "DE," or "DDE." Some letters were sent as personal messages without salutation or closure.

Many of the letters in the Eden-Eisenhower correspondence have been open to historians since the mid-1980s when, in accordance with the thirty-year rule, British records for the mid-1950s were opened. Some of the most important letters had already been published in the memoirs of Eden and Eisenhower.[15] Virtually all of the letters between Eden and Eisenhower during the period of the Suez crisis, from July 26, 1956, to November 1956, were included in the volume of *Foreign Relations of the United States* on the Suez crisis, which was published in 1990.[16] Most of Eisenhower's letters to Eden for the period of the correspondence were printed in 1996 in the relevant volumes of Eisenhower's published papers, but these volumes do not include Eden's letters to Eisenhower.[17] Three of Eden's letters to Eisenhower before July 1956 were published in the volume of *Foreign Relations of the United States* that covered Anglo-American relations between 1955 and 1957.[18] Most of Eden's other letters to Eisenhower before July 26, 1956, have not previously appeared in print. Moreover, many letters between the two leaders, such as those on intelligence operations, remained closed until the mid-1990s. Then, as a result of the Waldegrave initiative conducted by William Waldegrave, minister of state at the Foreign Office in Britain in the 1990s, a more liberal policy of opening British records was introduced, which allowed the opening of all of the letters between Eden and Eisenhower.[19] The letters that were declassified in the 1990s are contained in the collections of the Public Record Office and in the Eisenhower Library. There is also a copy of the Eden-Eisenhower correspondence in the Avon Papers, the personal and political papers of Anthony Eden, Earl of Avon, in the Special Collections section of the library at the University of Birmingham, although this collection does not include the letters which were declassified in the 1990s.[20]

With the opening of all of the previously classified letters, this edition is able to present the entire Eden-Eisenhower correspondence, 1955–57. Moreover, the previously published letters were printed as individual letters in the midst of a mass of other documentation in *Foreign Relations of the United States* and in Eisenhower's published papers. This edition gathers together the letters between Eden and Eisenhower into an accessible, chronologically arranged volume, providing a focus on the development of the relationship between Eden and Eisenhower.

In editing documents of such great historical importance, the editor's approach is to attempt to be as unobtrusive as possible. Brief annotations and presentations of background information are provided where it is considered to be necessary. Of greater length is the introductory material, which tries to set the scene of the time at which the correspondence commences in April 1955. This material covers in some detail the personalities of Eden and Eisenhower and their careers up to 1955. Discussion is also given of John Foster Dulles, U.S. secretary of state and close adviser to Eisenhower, whose relationship with Eden was strained. Discussion is then given of the major topics that had arisen in the Anglo-American relationship up to 1955, in particular: the nature of the "special relationship"; relations with the Soviet Union; nuclear issues; intelligence; colonialism; the Middle East; the Far East; Europe; and economic issues. Questions are raised with respect to the personalities and issues, which the reader may wish to consider while reading the correspondence. The editor will not, however, signal in advance passages of particular significance and prejudice the reader's response to the material.

In the Conclusion, the editor offers an evaluation of the significance of the correspondence, both its general significance and insights on particular issues and personalities. Any such evaluation, however, is of secondary importance and is liable to be transitory. The correspondence itself, on the other hand, between two figures of such significance at the height of the Cold War and in the midst of the most serious crisis in Anglo-American relations in the post–World War II period, is a unique collection, which will provide historical evidence of very great importance for as long as history is studied.

NOTES

1. Warren F. Kimball, ed., *Churchill and Roosevelt: The Complete Correspondence*, 3 vols. (Princeton, N.J.: Princeton University Press, 1984).

2. Peter G. Boyle, ed., *The Churchill-Eisenhower Correspondence, 1953–1955* (Chapel Hill: University of North Carolina Press, 1990).

3. Robert Griffith, ed., *Letters to a Friend, 1941–1958* (Lawrence: University of Kansas Press, 1984).

4. John S. D. Eisenhower to Peter G. Boyle, July 24, 2002, personal correspondence in editor's possession.

5. Ann C. Whitman to Peter G. Boyle, October 21, 1987, personal correspondence in editor's possession.

6. Andrew J. Goodpaster to Peter G. Boyle, November 17, 1987, personal correspondence in editor's possession.

7. Louis Galambos and Daun Van Ee, eds., *The Presidency: The Middle Way*, vol. 16 of *The Papers of Dwight D. Eisenhower* (Baltimore, Md.: Johns Hopkins University Press, 1996), 1052 n.1, 2056 n.1.

8. Andrew J. Goodpaster to Peter G. Boyle, August 8, 2002, personal correspondence in editor's possession.

9. D. R. Thorpe, *Eden: The Life and Times of Anthony Eden, First Earl of Avon, 1897–1977* (London: Chatto & Windus, 2003), 495–96.

10. Lord Sherfield (Roger Makins) to Peter G. Boyle, April 18, 1995, personal correspondence in editor's possession.

11. PREM 11/1177, PRO.

12. AWF, International Series, boxes 20–22.

13. Drafts, Eisenhower to Eden, October 31, November 1, and November 5, 1956, AWF, International Series, box 21, Eisenhower to Eden (5)-(6).

14. Ann Whitman to John W. Hanes Jr., June 21, 1956, AWF, box 22. This collection of copies of the Eden-Eisenhower correspondence is in Department of State, Presidential Correspondence: Lot 66, D204, National Archives, College Park, Md.

15. Anthony Eden, *Full Circle* (London: Cassell, 1960); Dwight D. Eisenhower, *Waging Peace, 1956–1961* (Garden City, N.Y.: Doubleday, 1965).

16. *The Suez Crisis, July 26–December 31, 1956*, vol. 16, FRUS.

17. Galambos, *Papers of Dwight D. Eisenhower*, vols. 16–17.

18. *Western Europe and Canada*, vol. 28, FRUS.

19. Richard J. Aldrich, "The Waldegrave Initiative and Secret Service Archives: New Documents and New Policies," *Intelligence and National Security* 10 (January, 1995): 192–97.

20. Prime Minister's personal telegrams to and from President Eisenhower, AP 20/27/1-105.

THE PERSONALITIES

Anthony Eden and Dwight D. Eisenhower were in some respects an odd couple. One was a refined English gentleman of aristocratic background, educated at Eton and Oxford. The other was a German-American son of a dairy creamery mechanic who grew up on the wrong side of the tracks in a small town on the plains of America. Yet, in their differing ways, they were embodiments of developments of momentous significance at a crucial time in the histories of their two countries. Each played a role of extreme importance (Eden as British foreign secretary, Eisenhower as supreme Allied commander) in the most glorious chapter of his nation's history, as their two nations fought side by side in the climactic struggle for freedom and defense of Western civilization in World War II. Each went on to lead his country in a period when the partnership between their two nations became increasingly less equal, with America's growing preeminence and Britain's relative decline.

Eden was born in 1897 at Windlestone, the family home near Bishop Auckland in County Durham in the north of England. The family could be traced back to Robert de Eden in the reign of Edward III in the fourteenth century. The Edens fought on the Royalist side in the English Civil War in the 1640s and were rewarded after the restoration of the monarchy in 1660 by the conferment of a baronetcy. One of the family, Robert Eden (1741–84), became governor of Maryland in 1768. Anthony Eden's father was the seventh baronet. Eden's elder brother, Timothy, succeeded to the baronetcy as the eighth baronet. His sister, Marjorie, married the Earl of Warwick, adding to Eden's aristocratic connections.

Eden's father was notorious for demonstrations of eccentric behavior, and Eden was never close to him. Moreover, his mother had numerous affairs. According to Eden's official biographer, Robert Rhodes James, there is doubt as to whether Anthony Eden was in fact the son of Robert Eden or an offspring from one of his mother's liaisons.[1] If the benefit of the doubt is given to Eden's legitimacy, he was the third of four sons. He went to a preparatory school in London at the age of eight, then to Sanroyd School in London, and at the age of thirteen to Eton College. He was conscientious in his studies, a good all-rounder at games, and was well liked at school.

With the outbreak of the First World War, Eden's brother John enlisted and was killed in France in 1914. His brother William was killed as a midshipman at the battle of Jutland in 1916. His brother Timothy was taken prisoner and interned for two years. Anthony Eden joined the army as soon as he left school in 1915. As a young officer he acquitted himself efficiently and bravely. He was promoted to captain and won the Military Cross.

At the end of World War I, Eden went to Christ College, Oxford. He studied Persian and Arabic, and he graduated with first class honors. He had learned German as a child when he had a German governess, and he spoke French. His felicity in languages and his interest in the Middle East inclined him toward a career as a diplomat. Instead he decided on a political career, though his interest in politics was always in the field of foreign affairs. In the general election of 1922 he ran as the Conservative candidate for Spennymoor, a mining constituency in County Durham, but he lost to the Labour candidate, an ex-miner. In 1923 he was elected at a by-election in Leamington Spa in Warwickshire, a constituency which included Warwick and Stratford-on-Avon as well as Leamington Spa. In the same year, 1923, he made a very suitable marriage to Beatrice Beckett, whose father was a banker, chairman of the *Yorkshire Post*, and Conservative member of Parliament for North Leeds. Eden's prospects appeared to be excellent. As David Dutton has put it, "With his distinguished service on the Western front, he was the knight errant of the survivors from the so-called 'lost generation,' the most perfect gentleman in British politics."[2]

His maiden speech in Parliament was on the need for Britain to have adequate air defenses; his speeches were for the most part on issues of foreign affairs and defense. In 1925, he traveled around the world to represent his father-in-law's newspaper, the *Yorkshire Post*, at a conference in Melbourne, Australia. He traveled by way of Canada and New Zealand, and returned via Ceylon. He wrote a series of articles for the *Yorkshire Post*, which became a book, *Places in the Sun*, published in 1926 with a foreword by Prime Minister Stanley Baldwin.[3] He was appointed parliamentary private secretary at the Foreign Office under Foreign Secretary Austen Chamberlain.

In 1929, in the first British election in which women aged twenty-one to thirty were allowed to vote, the young, handsome, debonair Anthony Eden campaigned extensively and was considered to have benefited the Conservatives considerably in any constituency he visited. Eden himself benefited from the "flapper vote," with a comfortable margin of victory in his own constituency. The Conservatives lost the election, however, in this year of the Great Crash, and a Labour government under Ramsay MacDonald came to power. Eden continued to speak in the House of Commons on various topics in the field of foreign affairs, especially the League of Nations, which was becoming his specialty.

In 1931, with the economic situation becoming increasingly serious, a National Government was formed. Ramsay MacDonald continued as prime minister, but the government was no longer a Labour government, as in 1929–31, but rather a coalition in which the Conservatives predominated. Eden was appointed undersecretary of state for foreign affairs in the new government. In 1934 he was appointed to full ministerial rank as Lord Privy Seal, which had no departmental duties, allowing him to be seconded to the Foreign Office and to serve as principal delegate at the League of Nations. In 1934 he traveled to Berlin and to Rome and, in 1935, to Moscow. He met Hitler in Berlin and reported to Stanley Baldwin that "he is a surprise. Without doubt the man has charm."[4] In Moscow, Eden was received with great ceremony as the first Western statesman to visit Stalin; a subway station in Moscow was named after him.

As a result of the election in 1935, Baldwin replaced MacDonald as prime minister of the National Government. Sir Samuel Hoare became foreign secretary and Eden was appointed to the cabinet as minister without portfolio, with special responsibilities for League of Nations affairs. In October 1936, the League of Nations was put to a severe test when Italy invaded Abyssinia, with an ostentatious display of bluster on the part of the Italian Fascist leader, Benito Mussolini, and the brutal use of bombs, tanks, and mustard gas. The League of Nations named Italy as an aggressor and applied economic sanctions but made a fatal compromise by omitting oil from the list of embargoed goods. A further compromise was made by Hoare and the French foreign minister, Pierre Laval, whose Hoare-Laval Plan gave Italy control of over two-thirds of Abyssinia and established a League of Nations protectorate over the rest of the country. Together with the lack of Western resistance to German reoccupation of the Rhineland in the same year, the feeble League of Nations response to Mussolini over Abyssinia symbolized craven Western impotence in the face of growing Fascist arrogance. Hoare was forced to resign, and Eden became foreign secretary. He was thirty-eight.

Eden's star had been on a constant rise, taking him to a great height at a very early age. His personal life had, however, run into difficulties. Two sons had been born, Simon in 1924 and Nicholas in 1930. But incompatibility had developed in his marriage, and both Eden and his wife, Beatrice, began to have affairs. Eden now also began to face serious difficulties in his professional life. In 1937, Stanley Baldwin was replaced as prime minister by

Neville Chamberlain, with whom Eden had a less close relationship, and there followed a series of events which led to Eden's resignation as foreign secretary in February 1938. His resignation was later regarded as an act of courage and statesmanlike opposition to Chamberlain's policy of appeasement. The historical reality is, however, more complex than the simplistic mythology, which was created in later accounts, especially in Churchill's historical writing. In *The Gathering Storm*, the first volume of Churchill's history of the Second World War, Churchill wrote that Eden's resignation gave him one of the few sleepless nights of his life. Churchill was horrified by the departure of "the most resolute and courageous figure in the Administration," the "one strong young figure standing up against long, dismal, drawling tides of drift and surrender."[5] In fact, Eden's position was much more ambivalent. He had hoped to achieve an accommodation with Hitler, and he did not regard Nazi Germany as beyond the diplomatic pale. His disagreement with Chamberlain was not so much over policy as over tactics and resentment over Chamberlain's interference in Foreign Office affairs. There was a serious difference between Eden and Chamberlain over a secret proposal from Franklin Roosevelt on January 11, 1938, suggesting that FDR should call for a conference including Britain, France, Germany, and Italy in order to reduce international tensions. Eden was in France at the time, and Chamberlain, without consulting Eden, replied in a dismissive tone to FDR that the proposal would cut across Chamberlain's own efforts for peace. Eden was shocked when he received news of Chamberlain's reply, and he vigorously protested. Chamberlain then agreed that a telegram should be sent to Washington urging that FDR's proposal be more fully explored. On January 18, however, FDR himself decided to defer his offer. It would be quite inaccurate to suggest that Eden resigned over a lost chance to bring America at that point into the forces of resistance to Fascism. After some further disagreements with Chamberlain over policy toward Italy in January and February 1938, Eden tendered his resignation on February 20. In his resignation speech on February 21, he said that differences over "outlooks and methods" rather than over fundamental principles had led to his resignation, and his admirers found it somewhat difficult to understand exactly why he had resigned. In many respects he had been outmaneuvered by Chamberlain, who wanted him to go, and as David Dutton has argued, issues of *amour-propre* as much as of principle brought about his resignation.[6] In the course of time, nevertheless, the Churchillian myth of Eden's resignation as an act of courageous protest against Chamberlain's policy of appeasement gained widespread acceptance rather than the more complex reality.

In 1938–39 Eden was at the centre of a group of about thirty mainly young MPs who were referred to as the Eden group and who, in common with but distinct from the Churchill group, pressed for more vigorous policies from the government, such as the introduction of conscription. After the outbreak of war in September 1939, Chamberlain appointed Eden as secretary of state for the Dominions. It was not a cabinet office, although Eden was invited to attend cabinet meetings on relevant occasions. Eden described this as a "somewhat anomalous position. . . . It is always disagreeable to be neither fish nor fowl."[7] It was a much lower office than Eden had hoped for. But in his eight months in this post he was successful in coordinating the war efforts of the Commonwealth, and he won a high degree of respect, especially in Australia, New Zealand, and Canada.

In May 1940, Chamberlain was replaced as prime minister by Churchill. Eden was appointed secretary for war, a post which he held for seven months. In December 1940, on the death of Lord Lothian, the British ambassador to the United States, Churchill appointed the Earl of Halifax, the current foreign secretary, as the new ambassador and named Anthony Eden the new foreign secretary. Thereafter throughout the war Eden was clearly Churchill's right-hand man, even if Clement Attlee, leader of the Labour Party, was deputy prime minister in the wartime coalition government. In November 1942, Eden took on the additional post of leader of the House of Commons, which added considerably to his responsibilities. Churchill advised King George VI in 1942 that, in the event of Churchill's death, Eden, "the most outstanding Minister in the largest political party in the House of Commons, should be invited to form a government."[8] Indeed, to some extent Churchill's relationship with Eden was paternal; as Churchill had said to him on one occasion in 1941, "I regard you as my son."[9] Churchill, who was sixty-four in 1940, with one son and three daughters, no doubt saw in Eden, who was forty-three in 1940, the qualities which Churchill would have wished for in a son. Churchill's rather hapless son, Randolph, bitterly disliked Eden, clearly at least partly due to a feeling of resentment over his displacement in his father's affection and esteem by Anthony Eden.[10]

Eden shared Churchill's broad approach to foreign affairs. However, whereas Churchill tended to look at the broad sweep, Eden was more professional as a diplomat in looking at the details. Moreover, while Churchill tended to place the greatest emphasis by far on relations with the United States, Eden paid more attention to other nations, especially to France and to the Soviet Union. Eden and Churchill had some of their strongest disagreements during the war over Eden's insistence on building up France as a postwar ally. With regard to the Soviet Union, Eden demonstrated his skill in diplomacy with the negotiation of the Anglo-Soviet Treaty in 1942. Eden took a realistic approach toward the issue of Soviet territorial issues, recognizing that the massive Soviet contribution to the war effort and Soviet occupation of disputed territories made it unrealistic to have a split with the Soviets over the Baltic States and over parts of Poland which had been acquired in the Nazi-Soviet pact. But Eden hoped that the rest of Eastern Europe would not necessarily fall under Soviet control.

With regard to the United States, Eden realized that the American alliance was crucial for Britain's survival and victory in the war. But Eden did not have the same instinctive emotional attraction to America, which, for example, Winston Churchill and Harold Macmillan felt. It has been suggested this may be because Churchill and Macmillan both had an American mother, while Eden's American connection was a distant ancestor who had been governor of colonial Maryland in the eighteenth century. It should be noted, however, that Neville Chamberlain had an American mother, which did not lead him to take an endearing attitude towards the United States, so that aspects of outlook and experience were perhaps as important as maternal influence in determining the attitudes of British statesmen toward America.

In the wartime alliance, especially as the balance of power gradually shifted from equality to increasing American dominance as the war progressed, Churchill, pro-American as he was, found himself frequently exasperated by the need to defer to the American position.[11] Eden, with his less natural warmth toward Americans and his more highly strung personality, found deference to the United States even more exasperating. He wrote to Churchill in October 1942, for example, that dependence on American aid meant that "the United States makes a policy and we follow, which I do not regard as a satisfactory role for the British Empire."[12] In July 1944 he cried out, "Can't we have a foreign policy of our own?"[13] He made frequent complaints about the Americans, writing to Viscount Cranborne in 1942, for example, that the Americans were becoming "increasingly tiresome" over French–North Africa "as well as over almost everything else."[14] Eden had strong reservations with regard to FDR. After the Cairo conference in 1943, Eden noted in his diary that "FDR was a 'charming country gentleman,' but business methods were almost non-existent."[15] Eden, with his professional approach to diplomacy, was appalled by Roosevelt's tendency to pull far-fetched and ill-considered schemes out of the air. Roosevelt, for example, who was irritated by the French in general and by Charles de Gaulle in particular, suggested that, rather than France regaining its independence after the war, a new state of Wallonia should be created out of Northern France, Alsace-Lorraine, Luxembourg and part of Belgium. Eden commented that "Roosevelt was familiar with the history and geography of Europe. Perhaps his hobby of stamp-collecting had helped him to this knowledge, but the academic yet sweeping opinions which he built upon it were alarming in their cheerful fecklessness."[16] On the other hand, Eden realized that, as Roosevelt aides such as Harry Hopkins indicated to him, Roosevelt tended to float such ideas as trial balloons and in practice was more cautious. Overall, Eden's professional wartime relations with American colleagues were good, while he was held in high regard in America. He was very well-received, for example, during his visit to the United States in 1943. In London, Eden had constant dealings with American military and political figures in the preparations for the invasion of North Africa in 1942 and even more so for D-Day in 1944. The most important of those Americans was, of course, Eisenhower, whom Eden came to know and with whom he established a good relationship. Nevertheless, as Robert Holland puts it, "Of all the major British statesmen of the Second World War Eden had been the least integrated into the machinery of the Anglo-American alliance."[17] Moreover, although Eden had fought in the First World War and had been secretary for war, he was not inclined toward the camaraderie of the military. He always wore the diplomat's pinstripe suit and Homburg hat, while Churchill loved to dress up in military uniform. As Evelyn Shuckburgh, who was later Eden's private secretary, put it, "He is remarkably unsympathetic to the ordinary masculine simplifications of the English mind. He dislikes bishops, boy scouts and almost all soldiers except Eisenhower."[18]

While Churchill played the more visible role when attending high-level wartime meetings in Casablanca, Washington, Moscow, Quebec, Cairo, Tehran, Yalta, and Potsdam, Eden pursued quiet diplomacy, along with Soviet Foreign Minister V. I. Molotov and U.S. Secretary of State Cordell Hull, in setting up the machinery for allied cooperation, such as the European Advisory Commission, which later divided Germany into four zones, and the Four Power Declaration, which led to the establishment of the United Nations. Together with his duties as leader of the House of Commons, this meant that Eden's workload was enormous. This was no doubt one reason why his marriage relationship became even more troubled. Moreover, his wife became involved in a relationship with C. D. Jackson, Eisenhower's psychological warfare advisor. Eden's frequent travels abroad added further strains to his marriage. The end of the war in Europe found him, typically, abroad in San Francisco at a meeting concerning the establishment of the United Nations, celebrating the end of the war at a dinner dance on May 11,

1945, very elegantly attired in his black dinner jacket, dancing the night away with some of San Francisco's most attractive women.

The end of the war was a difficult time for Eden. On his return from America in May 1945, he felt unwell. A duodenal ulcer was diagnosed, and he was ordered to rest for six weeks. It was the beginning of a succession of health problems. In 1948 he had appendicitis, and in 1949 he collapsed while making a speech at the United Nations Association. His ill health became chronic, even before his well-publicized health problems in 1953. Moreover, in June 1945, his mother died, and news was received that his son, Simon, was missing in action in Burma. On July 22, 1945, it was confirmed that Simon was dead.

Meantime, political developments brought the heavy blow of the landslide Labour victory in the British general election in July 1945. The massive Labour majority of 393 indicated plainly that although the British people were very grateful to Churchill (and to Eden) for wartime leadership, their focus was now on postwar issues such as reconstruction, housing, and health and education, matters in which Conservative policies seemed to be deficient or nonexistent. Not only were the Conservatives out of office, but their prospects of a return to office in the foreseeable future seemed bleak.

Eden strongly considered leaving British politics to become the first secretary-general of the United Nations. He would have reserved to himself the possibility of a later return to British politics when Conservative fortunes were more promising, but the matter did not arise, since the new Labour prime minister, Clement Attlee, did not support Eden for UN secretary-general. Eden then considered resigning from Parliament to make money in business. He was not a wealthy man. He decided, however, to remain in politics but to improve his financial position by taking on a number of directorships, which he had time to do in opposition. In 1949 he was tempted by the prospect of becoming the first secretary-general of the North Atlantic Treaty Organization (NATO), but the post was not offered to him. Meantime, his private life almost brought his political ambitions to an end. Simon's death was perhaps the final blow to his marriage. In December 1946, he and Beatrice and their remaining son, Nicholas, sailed to America in an attempt to hold the family together. Soon afterwards Beatrice decided to leave him. She went to America and resumed her relationship with C. D. Jackson. Jackson, however, was married and decided not to leave his wife but to end the relationship with Beatrice, who then formed a relationship with a New York surgeon, whom she subsequently married. She and Eden were divorced in 1950. In the late 1940s Eden became involved with Countess

Beatty, an American socialite who was married to Earl Beatty, a former Conservative MP who had aspirations to political advancement. When Eden did not assist Beatty in his ambitions, Beatty threatened to name Eden as corespondent in divorce proceedings, which could have tarnished Eden's reputation and endangered his future career. Churchill's intervention led Beatty to back off from his threat, and Eden in any event decided to end his relationship with Countess Beatty.[19]

Churchill was leader of the opposition, but he spent more of his time writing his war memoirs and attended the House of Commons irregularly. Eden was burdened with many routine administration duties in which he was little interested. He was also not particularly interested in the major issues of domestic policy, such as the nationalization of various industries and of the health service. His interest in politics was revived, as always, by issues of foreign affairs. He established a good relationship with the new foreign secretary, Ernest Bevin. They had been colleagues in the wartime cabinet, in which Bevin had served very effectively as minister of labor. Bevin's background made him seem a strange choice for the post of foreign secretary; an illegitimate child from the West Country with a very limited education, he had become a dock worker in Bristol and made his career in the trade union movement. But Bevin was a great success as foreign secretary, winning the respect of the Foreign Office establishment, which had strongly doubted his suitability. Eden agreed with Bevin's view on the emerging Cold War, with an initial attempt to establish a working relationship with the Soviet Union in 1945–47 but then concentrating on containment by means of the Marshall Plan, NATO, and participation in the Korean War. Eden assured bipartisan support for these policies. Britain's weakened postwar position reduced its influence relatively and made it more dependent on the United States. Eden tended toward the view, however, that Britain's position had only fallen to a slight extent and that the decline need only be temporary. He continued to be resentful of dependence on the United States. "We cannot become permanent pensioners of the United States," he said. "We have a role of our own to play at the heart and centre of a great Empire."[20]

The social reforms of the postwar Labour government, such as the introduction of a national health service, were generally popular, but Britain's poor economic performance, which resulted in a continuation of rationing, led to a weakening of Labour's support and new opportunity for the Conservatives. In the election of 1950 Labour won, but with a majority of only five, which created the prospect of another election within a short period of time, in which the Conservatives had reasonable prospects of success. As a result of by-elections in 1950–51, Labour lost its majority, and another general election was held in May 1951 in which the Conservatives were returned to power. Churchill became prime minister again but there was an unwritten agreement that he would retire and hand over to Eden in the near future. After Eden's gloom over his future in the late 1940s, in 1951 at the age of fifty-four he resumed his post as foreign secretary and as heir apparent to the office of the prime minister.

Eden was welcomed back to the Foreign Office. His private secretary, Evelyn Shuckburgh, records that "his return to office seemed to be everywhere greeted with delight and relief, as if a popular cricket captain had returned to the field."[21] At the same time, his personal life took a turn in a brighter direction. In 1952 he married Clarissa Churchill, niece of Winston Churchill, daughter of Jack Churchill, Winston Churchill's only brother. Winston Churchill was best man at the wedding. Despite the wide age difference between Eden and his thirty-two-year-old new wife, his marriage to Clarissa was both politically very suitable and personally very successful. The marriage seemed to be very happy and Clarissa was a source of great support to Eden for the rest of his life.

Eden's counterpart as U.S. secretary of state in 1951 was Dean Acheson. They appeared to be very similar in outlook. Acheson was from an East Coast establishment background, son of an Episcopalian minister, educated at Groton and Yale and a very close friend of the British ambassador, Sir Oliver Franks.[22] Not only in background and outlook but even in physical appearance, Eden and Acheson appeared to be very similar. In their respective memoirs, they were very complimentary to one another. "Eden and I worked easily together," Acheson wrote, "and agreed on basic matters, where he was a resourceful and strong ally."[23] Eden described Acheson as "above all a loyal colleague. I would never hesitate to go tiger-hunting with him."[24] Eden conceded, however, that there had been disagreements between them. "If there were occasional squalls in our dealings," Eden diplomatically phrased it, "our relations gained from them."[25] The record suggests that there were in fact serious clashes over such issues as Korea and Iran, while the meeting between Truman, Churchill, Acheson, and Eden in Washington in 1952 was not very successful. Lester Pearson, Canadian minister for external affairs, wrote of Eden and Acheson that "these are two people who shouldn't be left alone in the same room to argue."[26] Evelyn Shuckburgh wrote that "the fact is that, when you scratch this elegant and civilised Acheson, he turns out to be just another tough guy."[27] The disagreements between the two did not essentially arise from their personalities but over the increasing degree of

American predominance and British frustration. As D. R. Thorpe puts it, "The central theme of Eden's Foreign Secretaryship was that of maintaining Britain as a front-rank power in the face of superpower competition and economic difficulty."[28] In these circumstances, Eden was irritated by "Acheson's imperiousness. Relations between the two were not easy."[29]

In 1953 Stalin's death opened a new phase in the Cold War. Churchill was eager to attempt a dramatic breakthrough in relations with the Soviet Union, especially by means of a summit meeting with the new Soviet leaders. Eden, however, took a different approach, in which he was closer to Eisenhower than to Churchill, aiming at step-by-step progress rather than spectacular, sudden achievements. As John Young has put it, "Where Churchill wished for a leaders' Summit, Eden quite naturally preferred foreign ministers' talks; where Churchill wished to talk around an open agenda, Eden preferred narrow discussions on precise topics; where Churchill's taste was for grand gestures to end the Cold War, Eden preferred smaller incremental advances."[30] As Eden expressed it himself, "If we could take a number of definite, but limited problems . . . and seek to solve even one of them . . . we might . . . move into a . . . more hopeful field."[31] Eden's approach was demonstrated most fully in 1954, when there was a remarkable series of negotiations on Germany, Austria, Indochina, Trieste, Egypt, Sudan, the European Defense Community, and West Germany's admission to NATO. The year 1954 was regarded as Eden's *"annus mirabilis."* On some of the problem areas, such as Indochina, Germany, and Austria, the outcome was either controversial or a stalemate. On others, however, such as the tricky dispute between Italy and Yugoslavia over Trieste, Eden showed great skill in helping to create a solution which was acceptable to all parties. Above all, over the potentially explosive issue of German rearmament, Eden produced a diplomatic tour de force to bring about a solution. Since 1952, when Acheson had insisted upon German rearmament as part of the buildup of Western European military strength, the proposed solution to the political problems of fears over German rearmament, such as in France, had been the European Defense Community (EDC). This was a rather complicated scheme for the integration of the military forces of Western European countries, which Churchill, for example, derided, picturing "a bewildered French drill sergeant sweating over a platoon made up of a few Greeks, Italians, Germans, Turks and Dutchmen, all in utter confusion over the simplest orders."[32] Reluctance on the part of Western European governments to ratify the EDC treaty created growing tensions between Europe and the United States, reaching a climax in August 1954, when the French National Assembly rejected EDC. Eden immediately took the initiative to fly to each of the major capitals of Europe and added a sweetener of a British commitment to maintain indefinitely four RAF squadrons in Germany. A means was agreed upon by September 1954 to admit West Germany into NATO, which the other nations considered a more acceptable way of enabling West Germany to contribute to the defense of Europe, while keeping possible German aggressive tendencies in check. Eden's admirers poured praise on his achievements in 1954. Acheson, who in his retirement became increasingly more of an admirer of Eden, wrote to him that "I have watched with intense admiration and joy your superb work all through the year. If there was one thing you could have done better it has escaped me."[33] Eden's critics, however, suggested that his achievements amounted only to successful crisis management and that he lacked broader vision. Anthony Nutting, for example, minister of state at the Foreign Office, wrote that Eden was "a mediator par excellence. He was not a strategist who set a course for . . . years ahead. . . . He was essentially a tactician who planned his advance in limited moves."[34] More fundamentally, Eden's term as foreign secretary from 1951 to 1955 has been criticized as a period when Eden strove too hard to maintain Britain's great power status, which overstretched Britain's resources and was responsible for its economic decline and consequent political problems. As always, in suffering the frustrations of Britain's growing weakness, Eden expressed resentment towards the Americans. During the Geneva conference on Indochina in 1954, for example, Eden told his private secretary that "all the Americans want to do is to replace the French and run Indochina themselves. They want to replace us in Egypt too. They want to run the world."[35]

During his term of office as foreign secretary, 1951–1955, deficiencies of Eden's temperament were commented upon with growing regularity, although these characteristics had always existed to a greater or lesser extent. David Dutton writes that "observers who admired his calm negotiating skills might have been amazed by the violent bouts of temper to which his personal staff were often subjected. In different situations Eden was as renowned for his outright rudeness as for his polished charm."[36] Roderick Barclay, parliamentary private secretary in the Foreign Office, noted that "Eden's impatience and irritability . . . made life very difficult for his close associates."[37] There was a frenetic atmosphere around him constantly, which was liable to lead the highly strung Eden, with his brittle temperament, to explode. Gladwyn Jebb, Eden's parliamentary private secretary, wrote that "Eden lives in a constant whirl, people rushing in with papers and doors opening and shutting in all directions, like the best French farce."[38] Harold

Macmillan noted of Eden that "he'd have a mass of people round when he was trying to write a speech. How he ever wrote it I can't imagine. Everybody talking; a tremendous flap went on. . . . He was always very excitable, very feminine-type, very easily upset, easily annoyed."[39] David Dutton notes that "a striking number of observers drew attention to a feminine streak in Eden's make-up. . . . His habit of addressing male colleagues as 'my dear' was disconcerting, especially for Americans."[40] In fact, to some extent these were oddities of northern English expression, which had no particular significance. Eden, moreover, was very much a ladies man and showed no inclination toward homosexuality. The allegedly "feminine" characteristics which many commented upon were, above all, a tendency toward highly strung brittleness in temperament, which was liable to end in explosions. This was particularly the case, for example, when Eden felt that there were intrusions upon the foreign secretary's prerogatives, especially by the prime minister. Churchill's private secretary, Anthony Montague-Browne, records that messages from Eden "not infrequently conveyed personally by telephone, were wont to end: 'And tell Winston that I'm at the end of my tether.'" Montague-Browne adds that "our internal philosophical comment with a sigh was: 'The Foreign Secretary's at the E. of his T. again.'" Montague-Browne recalls that "I remember remarking to Eden's Private Office: 'The difference between us is that I work for a great historical figure, and you work for a great hysterical one.'"[41]

Critics of Eden suggest that these deficiencies of temperament revealed severe limitations not only of personality but also, for example, in organization, such as overabsorption in detail and unwillingness to delegate. Some critics have suggested that Eden was superficial—a dashing, debonair figure with charm and good dress sense to match his good looks, but essentially a vain, insubstantial prima donna. Frank Roberts, a long-serving Foreign Office official, observed that Eden was "a great stickler for details" who "took the closest personal interest and at times drove us to distraction by insisting on commas being adjusted and adjectives changed, as we thought, unnecessarily."[42] Sir John ("Jock") Colville, one of Churchill's private secretaries, records that Churchill "complained that his Foreign Secretary was indecisive, too much given to compromise and obsessed by details."[43] John Young concludes that "as a negotiator Eden was confident and commanded every detail; his reputation for liberty and fairness and his commitment to conciliation and discussion, combined with his affability and impeccable manners, helped him resolve even the most complex problems. Yet these skills went hand-in-hand with a concentration on detail and reluctance to delegate, which added to his tiredness and impatience."[44]

Eden's defenders, however, argue that these temperamental lapses were relatively superficial. D. R. Thorpe suggests that "many performers, artistic as well as political, need cathartic release. Though Eden could lose his temper alarmingly . . . he did not let the sun go down on his wrath, and his public performances had a quiet dignity."[45] Nicholas Henderson, who worked in Eden's private office when Eden was foreign secretary, writes that while Eden was "given to gusts of impatience and prone to constitutional irritability, he was nevertheless a most considerate man to those dependent on him. Indeed, his occasional outbursts had the effect of rendering his politeness more human."[46] Henderson notes further in Eden's defense that "nobody realises the difficulty of being Foreign Secretary with Winston butting in all the time."[47] Among effusive statements of praise for Eden is, for example, the assessment of Hastings Ismay, Churchill's chief staff officer in World War II, who wrote of Eden that "I had always liked and admired him, but I had hitherto been inclined to think that he was one of fortune's darlings . . . and that his meteoric success had been primarily due to charm of manner and a lucky flair for diplomacy. I now saw how wrong I had been. His hours of work was phenomenal. . . . Nothing was too much trouble and he never went to a meeting without making sure he had every aspect of the problem at his finger tips."[48] Evelyn Shuckburgh, who was critical of Eden in many ways, wrote in his defense that "he is like a child. You can have a scene with a child of great violence with angry words spoken on both sides and ten minutes later the whole thing is forgotten. This is not possible with grown-ups, but it is the regular thing with A.E."[49] Shuckburgh's overall assessment of Eden was that he was "one of the great operators on the post-war international scene, an acutely sensitive and skilful player of the diplomatic game."[50]

Two further matters substantially affected Eden's equilibrium during his period as foreign secretary, namely, his health and Churchill's vacillation in yielding the succession as prime minister. With regard to his health, Eden's problems became more serious in the early 1950s. In 1952 he had an attack of jaundice, which had lingering consequences. Shuckburgh records that "he was constantly having trouble with his insides. We used to carry round with us a black tin box containing various forms of analgesic supplied by the doctor, varying from simple aspirin to morphine injections, and we dealt them out to him according to his degree of suffering."[51] In early 1953 he felt unwell and x-rays revealed gallstones. On April 12, 1953, he had an operation for removal of gallstones, which was a relatively routine operation and did not constitute major surgery. Disastrously, however, the surgeon performing the operation allowed his knife to slip and cut Eden's bile duct, which resulted in the spread of poison around his body and caused fever. On April 29, a further operation was required to remedy this damage, but the operation caused Eden to bleed profusely and he almost died, while the operation itself was not successful. Eden learned that a surgeon in Boston had perfected a technique to deal with his type of condition, and in June 1953, Eden went to Boston for surgery, which was successful.[52] In 1954, Clarissa began to insist that he take more rest from work, especially on weekends. It is a debatable matter how far Eden's health problems affected his judgment and his performance in office. It would seem a little harsh to suggest that, as a critic such as Anthony Montague-Browne puts it, Eden's health problems "added to his endemic feverish petulance."[53] Nevertheless, health problems were clearly a factor which affected Eden throughout his career with increasing severity and constituted an element of considerable significance as he entered into the office of prime minister.

The date when Eden would enter into the office of prime minister would be determined by Churchill, whose postponement of his departure from office exasperated Eden. Churchill had said in 1951 that he would retire a year after the election. In February 1952, however, King George VI died, and Churchill said that he should stay on until the coronation of the young Queen Elizabeth in 1953. Then after Stalin's death in March 1953, Churchill made it his last great goal as a political leader to initiate détente in East-West relations, especially by means of a summit meeting with the new leaders of the Soviet Union. More generally, Churchill's feelings of indispensability made him reluctant to relinquish power. Some of Eden's critics suggest that Eden's inability to persuade Churchill to yield office demonstrated weakness on Eden's part and was an indication of the fundamental lack of the qualities which were required of a successful prime minister. Others suggest that simply the process of being an heir apparent for such a long time in itself weakened the ability of the successor when he eventually came to power. As Harold Macmillan put it, "It may really be that he had been Prince of Wales too long."[54] On the other hand, in Eden's defense, he was aware that his career had greatly benefited from Churchill's reflected glory. A badly handled maneuver to force Churchill out against his will would have had serious political repercussions, while at the same time Eden did not wish to act in a manner that would have shown a lack of gratitude or an insensitivity toward Churchill. As Robert Bruce Lockhart put it, "Anthony is completely loyal to Winston, but waiting for the premiership is playing on his nerves."[55] The more serious consequence of Churchill's delay in departing was to raise suspicions that Churchill felt that Eden was the loyal, able and long-serving

Number Two, but that he was not suited to become Number One. Such suspicions were indeed justified. After the farewell dinner for Churchill at 10 Downing Street on April 4, 1955, Churchill said to his private secretary, Jock Colville, "I don't believe Anthony can do it."[56]

As Eden at last entered office as prime minister on April 6, 1955, he seemed in one way to be eminently well-qualified for office. His brilliant early career had been followed by long years of office in challenging times, giving him a wealth of experience to prepare him for the premiership. In other ways, however, there were doubts as to whether underneath his undoubted qualities there were serious deficiencies that were liable to come to the surface in the highest office and that he was indeed a first class servant but an inadequate master. It remained to be seen, in Churchill's memorable phrase, whether Anthony could do it.

Dwight David Eisenhower's career had followed a rather different path. Eisenhower was purely German-American in his ethnic origin. His ancestors came to Pennsylvania in the mid-eighteenth century. Eisenhower's grandfather, Jacob, moved west to Kansas in 1878. His father, David, ran a general merchant store in a small hamlet named Hope in Kansas. In 1885 he married Ida Storer, who was of German-American background from Virginia. Her mother had died when she was a child, leaving her father with eleven children to raise on his own. He parceled out some of the children to relatives, and Ida was brought up by her maternal grandparents. When two of her brothers moved west to Kansas, Ida decided to go with them. She studied music at Lane University in Lecompton, Kansas, where she met David, who was also a student there. They decided to marry and to drop out of college without completing their degrees. David opened a general merchant store in Hope, and their first son, Arthur, was born in 1886. David's business partner and a lawyer engaged in dishonest financial dealings, and the business failed, so David went to Denison, Texas, where he worked with the Missouri-Texas-Kansas Railroad. While the family was in Denison, two more sons were born, Edgar in 1889 and Dwight David in 1890.

In 1891 the family returned to Kansas. David began to work as a mechanic in the Belle Spring Creamery in Abilene. The family lived in a modest home south of the railroad tracks on the outskirts of Abilene. Three more sons were born, Roy in 1892, Earl in 1898, and Milton in 1899. Moreover, grandfather Jacob made his home with the family from the time of his wife's death in 1890 until he died in 1906. There was some land around the house for crops, vegetables, and animals, which allowed the family to be almost self-sufficient, which, together with David's income, enabled the family to live modestly. They were a hardworking, God-fearing, German-American family, though with the boisterous atmosphere inevitable in a family of six boys. In religion they were River Brethren, a Mennonite sect that practiced baptism in rivers, and David and Ida were both pacifists.

At school, Dwight acquired his nickname, "Ike," which apparently arose from a natural transformation of the first syllable of Eisenhower and which was applied to many by the name of Eisenhower, including several of his brothers; only in his case did it stick as a lifelong nickname.[57] He was reasonably intelligent, but not particularly academically oriented, having more interest in football. Nevertheless, when he graduated from Abilene High School, the yearbook predicted his future as a history professor at Yale. He always had quite an interest in history, but his prospects of studying in college, let alone teaching in college, were restricted, not only by relatively modest academic attainment but by financial impediments. He graduated in the same class as his brother Edgar, and it was financially impossible for both of them to go on to college. Edgar went to the University of Michigan while Ike went to work at the Belle Springs Creamery.

After a year working at the creamery, during which he helped to support Edgar financially, the suggestion was put to Ike by his friend Everett ("Swede") Hazlett that he should apply to a military academy, since this would enable him to obtain a college education free of charge. Swede Hazlett had applied to the Naval Academy at Annapolis. Ike followed up the suggestion, and after passing the required tests and obtaining the recommendation of a Congressman, he was accepted at the West Point Military Academy. Ike was extremely grateful to Swede for the suggestion, and they engaged in correspondence as their careers progressed. Swede advanced rather modestly, while Ike, with pacifist parents and an attraction to the military academy mainly as an opportunity for a free education, went to the very top.

Entering West Point in 1911, Ike was an average student, and he remained one. He was ranked sixty-first in a graduating class of one hundred and sixty-four. Most of his courses were in science and technology. In his one combined English and History course, he was tenth in his class and displayed a natural ability in writing. His roommate, P. A. Hodgson, who became a lifelong friend, noted in a letter home that Ike had "naturally a very direct and pleasing style of writing."[58] He continued to be a very keen football player. By his second year, he was the varsity team half back. Unfortunately, however, he suffered a serious knee injury, which ended his playing career.

After graduation from West Point in 1915, Eisenhower was posted to Fort Houston in Texas. There he met Mary Geneva ("Mamie") Doud, the daughter of a wealthy meatpacker from Denver, whose family wintered in San Antonio, Texas. They were married in July 1916, and in 1917 their first son, Doud Dwight ("Icky") was born. Eisenhower became involved in training recruits, especially in tank warfare, a matter in which he took a special interest. His work became all the more important when the United States entered the First World War in April 1917. In 1918, two British officers came as advisers on tanks. "This began my connection with allies," Eisenhower later wrote, "a word that was to become vitally important to me as the years rolled on."[59] Eisenhower was stationed at Fort Meade, Maryland, and rented a family home in Gettysburg, Pennsylvania, an area where he felt very much at home as the land in which his ancestors had lived for generations and to which he would eventually retire. Eisenhower was very keen, however, to be sent overseas on active service, but he was of more value to the army training recruits in tank warfare in the United States. Eventually he persuaded his commander to allow him to go to France with the next contingent of troops whom he trained, and he received orders to embark from Fort Dix, New Jersey, on November 18, 1918. The armistice on November 11, 1918, led, of course, to the cancellation of these orders, so that Eisenhower was not on active service in World War I, a fact which he felt would impede his future career.

In the years after the end of World War I, Eisenhower, who was promoted to the rank of major in 1920, continued to be involved in training at various army camps in the United States. In 1920 he suffered a serious blow in his personal life when Icky died. Ike and Mamie had hired a maid who had recently been ill with scarlet fever and had not fully recovered; Icky caught the disease and died. The Eisenhowers blamed themselves for the tragedy, and Ike felt the loss for the rest of his life.

In 1922, however, another son, John, was born, who would be their only other child. In these years Eisenhower worked alongside Major George Patton, who was very interested in the use of greater mobility and speed in the employment of tanks in warfare. Patton introduced Eisenhower to General Fox Connor, who had a great influence on Eisenhower's career. Connor was impressed by Eisenhower and appointed him as his chief of staff in the Panama Canal Zone. While Eisenhower served in this post from 1922 to 1924, Connor encouraged him to read widely in military strategy, military history, and more generally in history and philosophy. Connor then helped Eisenhower to be admitted to the infantry command and general staff school at Fort Leavenworth, Kansas, which Eisenhower attended from 1925 to 1926, graduating first in his class of 275. Connor's mentorship was undoubtedly an element of considerable significance in Eisenhower's development. More generally, however, as Matthew Holland has shown, Eisenhower in the interwar years applied himself with great diligence to the development of his considerable innate talents in military leadership and acquired a remarkably wide range of experience in an impressive career.[60] In 1928 Eisenhower went on to the Army War College in Washington, D.C., where he again graduated first in his class. This was followed by his first assignment in Europe, working on a Battle Monuments Commission booklet, which involved touring the World War I battlefields in France. Eisenhower then returned to Washington, D.C., to serve as an assistant to the secretary of war, 1928–32, which gave him experience in such matters as budgets, congressional liaison, and federal government administration. In 1932 he was appointed as an assistant to Army Chief of Staff Douglas MacArthur. One of his first tasks, which Eisenhower found very distasteful, was to stand at MacArthur's side in clearing out of Washington the Depression-ravaged, unemployed veterans who had set up a camp on waste ground while they petitioned Congress for full payment of their World War I bonus. Eisenhower continued as MacArthur's assistant in Washington until 1935. This brought Eisenhower into contact with the New Deal, especially such programs as the Civilian Conservation Corps in which the army was involved. He was critical of such programs as wasteful of public money. This increased his innate dislike of federal bureaucracy and influenced his political philosophy.

In 1935, MacArthur became military advisor to the president of the Philippines, and he took Eisenhower along as his assistant. Eisenhower enjoyed the experience, but in 1939, with war looming on the horizon, Eisenhower returned to the United States. In 1941 Army Chief of Staff George Marshall organized war maneuvers with a war games battle between the Second and Third Army. Eisenhower had command of the Third Army and won the war games battle. Marshall was very impressed and brought Eisenhower to Washington as head of the War Plans Division. Following American entry into World War II in December 1941, when the decision was taken that American forces should become engaged against German forces in 1942, Marshall's choice as commander of the expedition, over large numbers of more senior American military leaders, was Eisenhower.

In June 1942 Eisenhower arrived in London to prepare for the campaign which would be fought in North Africa, November 1942–May 1943. Eisenhower demonstrated the main characteristics of his military leadership. He had sound technical knowledge of strategic and practical details. He had an unpretentious manner, which made him popular with his troops as well as his colleagues, while he had at the same time a quiet authority which led him not to shrink from difficult decisions, such as replacement of ineffective subordinates. Above all, however, Eisenhower's skill lay in his ability to bring people to work together, including prima donnas and prickly personalities, and especially to facilitate cooperative working relations between allies. His experience in Washington had developed his skills as a political military leader. His years with MacArthur had improved his ability to work with people with outsized egos. His need to cooperate with the British brought out Eisenhower's diplomatic skills in dealing with other nationalities. In the course of the war, Eisenhower, from his pacifist, potentially isolationist, German-American, Great Plains background, became a very strong Anglophile. Partly this was due to common ideals and values and from personal experiences and relationships, but it was also, of course, to a very important extent, due to an appreciation of the practical necessity for effective Allied co-operation in order to win the war. Eisenhower later wrote that "history testifies to the ineptitude of coalitions in waging war. . . . The Allied task was to utilize the resources of two great nations with the decisiveness of a single authority. There was no precedent to follow, no chart by which to steer. . . . The true history of the war . . . is the story of a unity produced on the basis of this voluntary co-operation. Differences there were, . . . but these faded into insignificance alongside the miracle of achievement represented in the shoulder-to-shoulder march of the Allies to complete victory in the West."[61]

The differences of views on many issues between the Americans and the British were, in fact, very considerable. As Mark Stoler has demonstrated, the degree of suspicion of the British within the American Joint Chiefs of Staff was very deep.[62] There were constant disagreements over such issues as strategy and resources. Nationalistic rivalry went well beyond friendly banter. Eisenhower's son, John, records that even after the British and Americans had worked together for nearly two years in the Combined Chiefs of Staff, in November 1943, "The Combined Chiefs of Staff could still meet below the Pyramids of Egypt in an atmosphere so acrimonious that one witness was not ruling out a fist fight, even hoping for it."[63] Eisenhower made every effort to eliminate nationalistic differences and to emphasize Allied cooperation. When it was reported to him that an American, while drinking, had boasted that the Yanks would teach the limeys how to fight, Eisenhower reacted furiously and ordered the man to be sent home. On another occasion he was told of a fracas between a British and American officer and ordered the latter to be reduced in rank and sent home. The British officer protested that the American had only called him a son of a bitch, and he understood that this was a fairly innocuous American slang expression. Eisenhower replied that "I am informed that he called you a *British* son-of-a-bitch. My ruling stands."[64] These deliberately well-publicized incidents were intended not only as a warning to American servicemen but as a signal to British civilians of Eisenhower's awareness of their sensibilities, as American soldiers began to pour into Britain in increasingly large numbers. At the highest level, Eisenhower's relations with the British were helped considerably by his relationship with Winston Churchill. Churchill and Eisenhower disagreed strongly on many issues, especially on Churchill's aversion to a cross-Channel invasion. But the personal rapport between the two was strong. As John Eisenhower puts it, "There was something about the chemistry of the two men that gave them a mutual affinity from the start."[65]

In the North African campaign, Eisenhower faced not only formidable military problems in organizing amphibious landings and in engaging German troops but also extremely difficult diplomatic issues in relations with the French authorities in French Morocco and Algeria. A plan was made for General Henri Giraud, a World War I hero, to be smuggled out of Vichy France to meet Eisenhower in Gibraltar. Very difficult negotiations took place between Eisenhower, Giraud, and Charles de Gaulle, the leader of the Free French in London. Giraud, however, lacked sufficient authority to command a cease-fire by French forces in North Africa when the Americans landed on November 8, 1942. By coincidence, Admiral Jean Darlan, second in command to Marshall Henri Pétain in Vichy France, arrived in Algiers on November 9 to visit a sick son. Negotiations were conducted with Darlan by General Mark Clark, which produced an agreement that Darlan would order a cease-fire and lead the civilian government in Algeria while Geraud commanded the armed forces. The cease-fire largely held, which reduced American casualties to small numbers and eased their military problems, but since Darlan was regarded as a Fascist collaborator who ruled in an authoritarian manner in Algeria and persecuted Jews, the agreement with Darlan was ferociously condemned in many circles in Britain and America. As events transpired, Hitler moved in and occupied Vichy France on November 11, and Darlan was assassinated on December 24. Eisenhower had been required to participate in very difficult decisions, involving serious moral compromises. He felt that pragmatically the correct course had been followed. With British progress in Egypt and Libya, following victory at El Alamein in November 1942, the British and American forces met up in Tunisia in May 1942, driving German and Italian forces out of North Africa.

In the North African campaign, Eisenhower benefited greatly from cooperation with his British allies. In preparations for the Torch landings at Casablanca in Morocco and Oran in Algeria in November 1942, Eisenhower wrote that "the British and Americans were unconsciously, in their absorption in common problems, shedding their shells of mutual distrust and suspicion."[66] Robert Murphy, Consul-General in Algiers and Roosevelt's political advisor on North African affairs, briefed Eisenhower on the complicated situation in North Africa and later wrote that "the General seemed to sense that this first campaign would present him with problems running the entire geopolitical gamut—it certainly did."[67]

Eisenhower's relations with British military leaders grew steadily closer, particularly with Colonel James Gault, who was assigned as Eisenhower's British personal assistant, Sir Andrew Cunningham, General Sir Hastings Ismay, and Field Marshall Alan Brooke. In his relations with the French, Eisenhower benefited considerably from the assistance of Harold Macmillan, who was appointed minister resident, the political advisor to the armed forces in North Africa, and with whom Eisenhower struck up a close friendship which lasted through to the days of Macmillan's term of office as British prime minister in the late 1950s. Macmillan's assistant, whom Eisenhower also came to know well, was Roger Makins, who later served as British ambassador to the United States, 1953–1956. Makins was, moreover, an important link between Eden and Eisenhower. Makins served as assistant to Eden on his work on the League of Nations in the 1930s. He then worked with Eisenhower in North Africa during the Second World War. Makins formed such a sufficiently informal relationship with Eisenhower that when they met again in Washington in January 1953, Eisenhower exclaimed with pleasure and good humor, "Christ, Roger, what are you doing here?"[68]

Another friendship of a somewhat different nature which deepened in the course of the North African campaign was Eisenhower's relationship with his personal assistant, Kay Summersby. She had been assigned as a driver to Eisenhower when he arrived in London in June 1942. She was the daughter of an Irish landowner and cavalry officer and an English mother. She had been brought up in County Cork but came to England in 1924 at the age of sixteen when her parents separated. She moved in London's society circles of balls, debutantes, and parties. She married and divorced a young publisher, Gordon Summersby, and worked as a model for Worth of Paris. With the outbreak of war, she joined Britain's Motor Transport Corps, which, as she later wrote, was "*the* volunteer corps that the debutantes and post-debutantes flocked to when war was declared."[69] She experienced some of the harsh realities of war, however, as a driver in London during the Blitz. In 1942 the American Embassy requested the services of drivers for Americans, and Kay was assigned as a driver to Eisenhower. Eisenhower was attracted to the thirty-three-year-old Kay's Anglo-Irish good looks and charming vivacity, and he saw her frequently in the course of her duties as his driver, which included driving Eisenhower on weekends to Chequers, the prime minister's country residence in Buckinghamshire. Gossip began to spread about Eisenhower's relationship with Kay, especially after an article in *Life* magazine appeared featuring Eisenhower's personal staff—"he calls it his family"—with a photograph which included "Kay Summersby, a pretty Irish girl who drives for General Eisenhower."[70] This caused a certain amount of concern to Eisenhower's wife, Mamie.[71] Eisenhower, in his letters to Mamie, which he wrote regularly during the war, gave strong reassurances of his love and fidelity. "You are all that any man could ask as a partner and a sweetheart," he wrote. "If anyone is banal or foolish enough to lift an eyebrow to an old duffer such as I am in connection with WAACs, Red Cross Workers, nurses and drivers, you will know that I've no emotional involvement and will have none."[72] Mamie, moreover, could be reassured that Kay was engaged to a young American officer, and Mamie felt that in any event the relationship would end when Eisenhower went to North Africa. However, when Eisenhower had established headquarters in Algeria, Kay was among the staff who came out from London. Moreover, her fiancé was killed in action. Kay became Eisenhower's personal assistant and, although she was a British citizen, Eisenhower arranged for her to be commissioned in the American Women's Army Corps. The relationship may have been quite innocent, implying no more than that Kay fitted in well with Eisenhower's office team and that her vivacious charm was a boost to morale, while her appointment as personal secretary was to some extent motivated by kindness to give her duties to keep her mind occupied after the loss of her fiancé. If the relationship was becoming more serious, however, it was hazardous for Eisenhower's future, both personally with respect to his marital relationship and politically with regard to any potential political career to which he might aspire.

After the North African campaign, Eisenhower had command of the campaigns in Sicily and Italy. This involved to an even greater extent a joint operation by British and American forces under a single command. Eisenhower later wrote with regard to Sicily that "one of the valuable outcomes of the campaign was the continued growth and development of the spirit of comradeship between British and American troops in action."[73] When controversy arose over General Bernard Montgomery's slow progress towards Messina in northeast Sicily, while Patton advanced rapidly in the northwest, Eisenhower avoided public criticisms and smoothed out the disagreements as well as possible. After successful landings in Italy, attention turned to the most important campaign, Operation Overlord, the cross-Channel invasion of northern France. It had been expected that Marshall would be given command of this campaign, but Roosevelt decided that he needed to keep Marshall in Washington. When Roosevelt consulted with Churchill at the conference in Cairo in November 1943, with respect to the command of Overlord, Churchill told him that the British "had the warmest regard for General Eisenhower and would trust our fortunes to his direction with hearty good will."[74]

Following his appointment as supreme Allied commander, Eisenhower came to London in January 1944 to prepare for the cross-Channel invasion. He met regularly with Churchill, for lunch on Tuesdays and dinner on Fridays at Chequers. Churchill was very apprehensive over a cross-Channel invasion and continued to suggest alternative approaches, such as through the Balkans or by means of a massive air bombardment. As Churchill not infrequently told Eisenhower, his nightmare was the repulsion of a cross-Channel invasion and thousands of British and American dead bodies in the English Channel. Eisenhower was very respectful of Churchill's concerns and appreciated the enormous dangers and difficulties involved in a landing in France. But Eisenhower demonstrated inner self-confidence as well as impressive organizational and leadership skills in his command of the forces, which not only successfully landed on D-Day but avoided becoming bogged down in France and instead advanced quite rapidly to liberate Western Europe.

Eisenhower continued to be the popular commander who felt that it was important for morale for him to make visits frequently to ordinary soldiers, while as supreme commander he made the difficult final decisions on overall strategy and on issues which arose between the British and Americans. Montgomery not infrequently exasperated him, while Churchill was feisty on such matters as advancing to Berlin before the Soviets, despite earlier agreements. As John Eisenhower wrote, Eisenhower was "the one high leader whose position as Supreme Commander carried no national label. When issues became deadlocked along national lines, therefore, the deciding vote tended to fall to him."[75] Eisenhower, however, won the confidence and respect of those under his command and was regarded as fair-minded as well as effective. After the German surrender at Rheims on May 8, 1945, Churchill wrote to Harry Truman, who had succeeded Roosevelt as president, expressing his "admiration of the firm, far-sighted and illuminating character and qualities of General of the Army Eisenhower" and adding that "in him we had a man who set the unity of the Allied armies above all nationalist thoughts."[76] In a speech at the Guildhall in London on June 12, 1945, Eisenhower spelled out the firm convictions which he deeply held on the Anglo-American bonds which had led to victory and which bound the two nations together: "I am not a native of this land. I come from the very heart of America. To preserve his freedom of worship, his equality before law, his liberty to speak and act as he sees fit, subject only to provisions that he trespass not upon similar rights of others—a Londoner will fight. So will a citizen of Abilene. When we consider these things, then the valley of the Thames draws closer to the plains of Abilene and the farms of Texas. . . . No petty differences in the world of trade, traditions or national pride should ever blind us to our identities in priceless values."[77]

Eisenhower returned to the United States as a war hero. He gave an address to a joint session of Congress. A ticker tape parade was held for him in New York, and he went on a triumphant tour by train across the country.[78] His immense prestige and popularity, together with his photogenic smile, inevitably increased speculation that his next step would be the presidency of the United States. Eisenhower denied that he had political ambitions. At Potsdam in July 1945, Truman, who was a great admirer of Eisenhower until they fell out later in the election campaign in 1952, said to him, rather extraordinarily, "General, there is nothing that you may want that I won't help you get. That specifically includes the presidency in 1948."[79] Eisenhower replied that he had no intention of seeking the presidency in 1948. It was nevertheless widely rumored at the end of the war that Eisenhower would be a future president. He firmly denied such ambitions. His denials, however, were interpreted as coyness and were not taken as final.

A potential impediment within his personal life stood in the way of any political career in Eisenhower's future. According to Truman, at the end of the war Eisenhower wrote to General George Marshall stating that he intended to seek a divorce in order to marry Kay Summersby. By the social standards of the time divorce was unacceptable for a presidential candidate; even more important, much of the gloss would have been knocked off Eisenhower's image if he had divorced the wife who had waited for him at home and married a younger woman, who was not an American, whom he had met overseas. Truman said in an interview for an oral biographer in 1973 that "right after the war was over, [Eisenhower] wrote a letter to General Marshall saying that . . . he wanted to come back to the United States and divorce Mrs. Eisenhower so that he could marry this Englishwoman." In response, according to Truman, "Marshall wrote him back a letter, the like of which I never did see. He said that if . . . Eisenhower even came close to doing such a thing, he'd not only bust him out of the Army, he'd see to it that never for the rest of his life would he ever be able to draw a peaceful breath." Truman then rather astoundingly related that "one of the last things I did as President, I got those letters from the file in the Pentagon and I destroyed them."[80] In her account, Kay Summersby writes that she did not know of this specific letter but that her relationship with Eisenhower had become emotionally very deep by the end of the war, making divorce and remarriage a distinct possibility, even if Eisenhower did not specifically raise the matter with her.[81]

The veracity of these accounts is open to question. Although rumors of Eisenhower's letter to Marshall circulated in political circles, no copy has ever been discovered, while Truman's report of his action in destroying such documents seems somewhat incredible. John Eisenhower denies that such a letter existed and dismisses Truman's story as "spiteful falsehood."[82] With regard to Kay Summersby's version of events, John Eisenhower writes that "her imagination played a stupendous role."[83] John Eisenhower concludes that "there is no evidence that divorce ever seriously crossed Dad's mind."[84] Whatever the nature of Eisenhower's relationship with Kay Summersby during the war, on his return to America after the war, Kay essentially disappeared from his life and he reestablished his marital home with Mamie. His son John was married in 1947, producing a grandson, David (after whom Eisenhower later named Camp David), and three granddaughters. By the time Eisenhower entered the political arena, any possible skeletons in his personal life had been firmly locked in the closet, and he had the strong credentials of a family man with a popular wife and young grandchildren.

Eisenhower had planned to retire from the army after the war, but in the autumn of 1945 Truman sent Marshall to China to try to mediate an end to the civil war there, and Eisenhower was appointed to take Marshall's place as Army chief of staff. In November 1945 Eisenhower, without much enthusiasm, took up this post and over the next two years presided over the problems of demobilization. He regularly appeared before congressional committees and came to know quite well the leading political figures in Washington, many of whom urged him to run for president. In 1947, however, he decided to retire from the army to engage in writing and to accept the post of president of Columbia University. His writing, which he did without a ghostwriter, consisted of *Crusade in Europe*, an account of his wartime experiences and an enormous bestseller, bringing him for the first time in his life a reasonable amount of money, which, along with assistance from friends, he used to buy a farm near Gettysburg in Pennsylvania. In the late 1940s, however, he lived in New York as president of Columbia University. His duties at Columbia brought him into contact with wealthy and influential men such as Thomas Watson of IBM and Paul Hoffman of Studebaker, who encouraged him to consider a bid for the presidency of the United States. These figures, as well as some Republican politicians, wished Eisenhower to be the Republican candidate in 1948. Eisenhower, however, had never had a party affiliation during his military career, and it was not known which party he would support. Many Democrats wished him to be the Democratic candidate in 1948. Truman's political stock had fallen steadily since 1945, with the Republicans gaining control of Congress in 1946, with breakaways from the Democratic Party by Henry Wallace's Progressive Party and Strom Thurmond's Dixiecrats, and with Truman's rating in opinion polls sinking to 22 percent by 1948. Leading Democrats, including liberal Democrats such as Hubert Humphrey and Arthur Schlesinger Jr., wished to dump Truman and to nominate Eisenhower as the Democratic candidate. Eisenhower, however, declined the invitation of both parties. Truman was renominated by the Democrats and, against the expectations of all political commentators, was surprisingly reelected as president, defeating his Republican opponent, Thomas Dewey.

Churchill wrote to Eisenhower with regard to his decision not to run in 1948 that "my feeling is that you were right not to intervene on this occasion. Because if you had stood as a Democrat, it would have looked like going to the rescue of a party which has so long held office and is now in difficulties. On the other hand if you had stood as a Republican it would have been hard on the party whose president you served. However, luckily there is plenty of time."[85]

In fact, Eisenhower did not really have plenty of time. Eisenhower later recorded that he had voted for Dewey in 1948—the first vote that Eisenhower had cast in an election.[86] If Dewey had won in 1948, as was widely anticipated, and had been reelected in 1952, Eisenhower would have been sixty-six in 1956, with World War II receding into history. By narrow political calculations, the year 1948 would have seemed to have been the time for Eisenhower to seek the presidency when it was offered to him on a plate, whereas delay carried with it a very real chance that the opportunity would not arise again. After the election of 1948, however, the pressure was unrelenting on Eisenhower to run as a Republican candidate for president from many circles within the Republican Party. The surprising Republican defeat in the presidential election in 1948, together with Republican defeat in the congressional elections in 1948 after the victory in 1946, led many Republicans to look to Eisenhower the war hero as the only possible Republican savior. As he later wrote in his memoirs, the drive for him to run for president began "almost within hours of Truman's defeat of Dewey."[87]

Eisenhower encountered frustrations as president of Columbia University. He felt that he was too remote from faculty and students and too much involved with fundraising and administration, while many intellectuals sneered that the soldier whose favorite reading material was Westerns lacked the qualifications desirable for the presidency of an elite Ivy League university. He was not unwilling to leave Columbia in 1950 when Truman asked him to return to active military service as supreme Allied commander in Europe, following the formation of NATO. Taking up this post in February 1951, Eisenhower enjoyed the experience of living in Paris and working with some of his old military and political colleagues as well as new ones in an enterprise to which he was fully committed. This also made him increasingly aware of the strength of isolationist opposition to internationalist engagement on the part of the United States. In political terms this was embodied by the progress of Senator Robert Taft, who was inclined towards isolationism and unilateralism, in the contest for the Republican nomination for president in 1952. The strongest single element which led Eisenhower to decide to run for president was his conviction that America must continue to pursue an internationalist policy and that a victory by Taft and a shift towards isolationism would be disastrous for America and the world. At the same time, Eisenhower felt that Taft's image as an extreme right-winger on domestic affairs would doom the Republican Party. Eisenhower wished the Republican Party to be seen as the middle course in American politics. It became increasingly clear that Eisenhower had no inclination toward the Democratic Party, which he viewed as overcentralizing and bureaucratic in its approach and by 1952 tarnished by dissension and scandals. Eisenhower was ready to be persuaded to run for president in 1952, and leading Republican politicians, such as Senator Henry Cabot Lodge, made the necessary arrangements for him to become a candidate.[88] He defeated Taft for the Republican nomination, though with some difficulty, and he went on to defeat his Democratic opponent, Adlai Stevenson, governor of Illinois, winning thirty-nine of the forty-eight states and bringing in a sufficient number of Republicans on his coattails for the Republicans to gain a very narrow majority in both houses of Congress.

By the time of Churchill's retirement and Eden's accession to the premiership in Britain in April 1955, the main lines of Eisenhower's presidency had been set. His goals were peace, prosperity, calm, contentment, and moderation. He was a reassuring figure in an age of anxiety. America had suffered the traumas of the Great Depression and the Second World War, followed by a series of shocks in the early Cold War years, such as the Communist victory in China, the Soviet development of an atomic bomb, and the outbreak of the Korean War. Fear of another Great Depression and of nuclear war lay just below the surface within American society. Eisenhower's presence in the White House was a major factor in enabling Americans to come to terms with these fears and to come to enjoy the benefits of their position as the richest and most powerful country in the world. Eisenhower's first priority was peace, and in July 1953 a truce in Korea brought an end to the fighting. When a recession occurred in 1954, Eisenhower pursued Keynesian policies of increasing government spending and allowing deficit spending in order to bring the country out of recession. Eisenhower showed that, although he was no New Dealer, neither was he a Herbert Hoover. The economy grew, suburbs expanded, babies boomed, Disneyland opened, and for the majority of Americans it seemed a golden age of simple values and the fulfillment of the American dream.

Critics charged that this was an age of complacency and materialism, as Americans blinded themselves to underlying problems and indulged in supernationalistic self-congratulation, and that Eisenhower embodied and encouraged this sense of complacency. It is clearly true that Eisenhower had no wish to be an activist reformer and that his endorsement of small-town values was in keeping with the national mood of the time. As revisionist accounts of Eisenhower's presidency since the 1970s have made plain, however, the image of Eisenhower as a genial, idle figurehead who spent more time on the golf links than in the Oval Office is quite false.[89] Although Eisenhower took a somewhat Whiggish approach to the presidency and felt that many initiatives should be left to Congress, he was direct and orderly in his style of executive leadership, holding regular meetings with congressional leaders as well as meetings of the cabinet and National Security Council, while also restoring greater decorum to the office of president. This gave an aura of calm and orderliness in contrast to the more frenetic atmosphere in the presidency of Truman and ever more so of Roosevelt. At the same time, Eisenhower demonstrated a much greater degree of cunning in his political approach than might have been expected. In order to reunite the Republican Party after the struggle against Taft, Eisenhower was willing to choose as his vice-presidential running mate Richard Nixon, a thirty-nine-year-old right-of-center Republican who had made his name as a prominent member of the House Un-American Activities Committee, and to use Nixon as a link to try to appease the McCarthyist, red-baiting wing of the Republican Party. He did not confront Senator Joseph McCarthy directly, since he felt that this would split the Republican Party. Instead, he employed the tactic of what Fred Greenstein has called "the hidden-hand presidency." Eisenhower worked behind the scenes to undermine McCarthy and to give him enough rope to hang himself. As Nixon wrote, Eisenhower "was a far more complex and devious man than most people realized."[90]

With regard to foreign policy, Eisenhower was fully committed to peace, but a peace which preserved freedom and was attained at an affordable cost. A somewhat surprising feature of Eisenhower's policy, as a former general, was his emphasis on the economy as the first line of America's defense and his insistence on the maintenance of a balance between security and solvency.

Eisenhower spoke with remarkable eloquence on the tragic waste of resources in their diversion from civilian to military purposes. "Every gun that is made," he said in the most memorable speech of his presidency in April 1953, "every warship launched, every rocket fired, signifies in the final sense, a theft from those who hunger and are not fed, those who are cold and are not clothed. . . . This is not a way of life at all, in any true sense. Under the cloud of threatening war, it is humanity hanging from a cross of iron."[91] He expressed the hope that the day would come when "the world may turn its energies and resources to serving the needs, rather than the fears, of mankind."[92] Eisenhower believed, however, that the Soviet threat necessitated the investment of sufficient resources to deter Soviet aggression. He accepted containment as the most realistic policy for the West in the belief that in the course of time Soviet communism would disintegrate from within, though this was not likely to occur in the near future. He felt, therefore, as he said at a meeting of the National Security Council, that "we would have to stick to a system of defense that could be sustained for forty years if necessary."[93] In these circumstances, Eisenhower emphasized that defense policies must be economically sustainable over the long term. "Our problem is to achieve adequate military strength within the limits of endurable strain upon our economy," he said. "To amass power without regard to our economic capacity would be to defend ourselves against one kind of disaster by inviting another."[94] Eisenhower warned that overly excessive expenditures on defense would not only gravely damage America's economy but would create a "garrison state" which would undermine American liberty. "If we must live in a permanent state of mobilization," he said, "our whole democratic way of life would be destroyed in the process."[95] Eisenhower constantly grappled with the "great equation" of attaining a level of defense which was sufficient to contain the Soviet Union but which was not so great as to cause undue damage to the American economy.

A vital aspect of this matter was the role of America's allies. From his experience in World War II and as SACEUR from 1951 to 1952, Eisenhower instinctively placed high store on the importance of allies. He argued strongly in favor of the Mutual Security Program. On most matters in the budget he was always looking for cuts, but he denounced as a false economy reductions in the Mutual Security Program which were imposed by congressional budget-cutters. He said that "We should never forget that in defending Europe with $6 billion of Mutual Security assistance we are getting a very great deal for our money, because we are avoiding the necessity of using our own troops. The money in this program was not merely 'giveaway' money."[96] According to National Security Council documents, Eisenhower stressed that "if the Communists succeeded in gaining control of Europe the world balance would be hopelessly upset against us.... That Western Europe not fall to the Communists was a sine qua non.... Bringing back our divisions in any abrupt way would not improve European morale but completely destroy it. Speaking with great emphasis, the President pointed out that the United States divisions in Europe had done marvels in restoring Europe's faith in itself."[97] Moreover, aside from the vital practical advantages of allies as sources of substantial support, Eisenhower argued that America's moral position of world leadership necessitated the involvement of allies. He said that "the concept of leadership implied associates. Without allies and associates the leader is just another adventurer, like Genghis Khan."[98]

With such views on the crucial importance of allies, Eisenhower's natural inclination was to turn first to his right-hand ally, the British. With regard to the Anglo-American special relationship, Eisenhower, as Robin Renwick has put it, "was deeply imbued with it, though remarkably unsentimental about it."[99] Eisenhower was, therefore, aware that times had moved on from the wartime period. The NATO alliance had been formed, West Germany had become an important ally, and Britain's power had declined. Churchill, Eisenhower felt, was in many ways still living in the past. Eisenhower's affection and admiration for Churchill was profound, but by the time of Eisenhower's inauguration, when Churchill was seventy-eight years old, very hard of hearing and suffering the effects of several strokes, Eisenhower felt that the time had come for Churchill to move on and to give way to a younger man. When he met Churchill in January 1953, Eisenhower noted in his diary that Churchill "had developed an almost childlike faith that all of the answers are to be found merely in British-American partnership."[100]

Eisenhower did not accept Churchill's pressing invitation, which was frequently repeated, to come on a visit to Britain, where Eisenhower would not only have been assured a very warm welcome but where he would have been subjected to the seductions of Anglo-American dominance as in wartime days. Eisenhower expressed severe irritation over differences with the British in the early to mid-1950s over such issues as China, Egypt, and Guatemala. When the British government gave only lukewarm support to the CIA overthrow of the left-wing government of Guatemala in 1954, for example, Eisenhower noted that "the British expect us to give them a free ride and side with them on Cyprus and yet they won't even support us on Guatemala. Let's give them a lesson."[101] Nevertheless, fundamentally Eisenhower felt that "unless the English-speaking peoples can live relatively close together and can set something of a model for the necessary cooperation among free peoples, then we are truly in for desperate troubles. However, no such special relationship can be maintained or even suggested, publicly. In public relationship all nations are sovereign and equal."[102]

In Eden, Eisenhower saw a figure who had vast experience since he had stood at Churchill's right hand for so long, but who, aged fifty-five when Eisenhower was inaugurated in 1953, was younger than Churchill and more in tune with modern ideas in the postwar world. Although Eisenhower had met Eden on innumerable occasions during the war, they had not worked directly together. In the early 1950s, they met on various occasions while Eden was foreign secretary. Of particular significance was a visit by Eden to Washington in March 1953, when he had spent quite a lot of time in conversation with Eisenhower after being impressed that Eisenhower had sent him a note that he could have "as much time as I wanted here, and I think that he meant it."[103] Eisenhower wrote to Eden after his visit expressing how useful he felt that their conversation had been and that it had brought out that America regarded Britain as her principal ally but that "we must, by all means, avoid the appearance of attempting to dominate."[104]

In April 1955 Eden still had to prove himself as a leader. Eisenhower was in a more self-assured position. Eisenhower had wielded enormous responsibility as a military leader. As a political leader, he had won election as president by a comfortable margin and established a record as a popular president who symbolized peace and prosperity. He had many critics, especially among intellectuals at home and abroad, who derided his folksy style and questioned his qualifications. Eisenhower, however, was a fundamentally self-confident man who was able to withstand such criticisms. But he knew the importance of allies. In Anthony Eden he saw an ally with whom he had every confidence that he could work closely and cooperatively. He was undoubtedly very genuine in his first letter's warmth of expression of congratulation and welcome to Eden on his accession to the post of prime minister. There was, however, another figure of great significance who complicated the Eden-Eisenhower relationship, namely, Eisenhower's secretary of state, John Foster Dulles.

In many respects John Foster Dulles seemed an ideal choice as Eisenhower's secretary of state. In other respects, however, Dulles had certain characteristics and convictions that created difficulties in his dealings with many people. Anthony Eden had a very uneasy relationship with Dulles, which, while the personal aspects should not be overstated, was a background factor of major significance in Anglo-American relations in the Eden-Eisenhower period.

John Foster Dulles almost seemed to have been born to be secretary of state. His grandfather, John W. Foster, had been American minister to Mexico, Russia, and Spain and served as secretary of state for the last eight months of Benjamin Harrison's administration in 1892–93, while Dulles's uncle, Robert Lansing, was secretary of state, 1915–20, during the presidency of Woodrow Wilson. His paternal grandfather, the Reverend John W. Dulles, had served as a missionary in Madras before settling in Philadelphia. Dulles's father, the Reverend Allen M. Dulles, was a Presbyterian minister, pastor of a church in Watertown in upstate New York, where Foster, as he was generally known, grew up. Foster was extremely bright and had a brilliant academic and professional career. Born in 1888, he went to Princeton University at the age of sixteen, where he took a course in constitutional government from Professor Woodrow Wilson. He took a year off from his studies at Princeton to serve as a secretary at the Second Peace Conference at The Hague in 1907, at which his grandfather, John W. Foster, was a delegate. The conference, like the First Peace Conference in 1899, was a somewhat fruitless exercise in idealistic discussion of theoretical concepts of peace, but it was a fruitful learning experience for the nineteen-year-old John Foster Dulles. He remained close to his grandfather, who invited him to Washington for frequent visits where he met senators, ambassadors, and State Department officials. The family also had a summer lodge in Henderson, New

York, on Lake Ontario, where distinguished visitors often came, such as William Howard Taft, Andrew Carnegie, and Bernard Baruch. After graduation, Dulles engaged in further study at the Sorbonne in Paris and in Leipzig and Gottingen in Germany. In 1909 he entered George Washington University Law School from which he graduated with outstanding grades. He accepted a post in the Wall Street law firm of Sullivan and Cromwell and rose rapidly in his legal career, becoming a senior partner at the age of thirty-eight. Meantime, in 1919, he served on the Reparations Commission at Versailles, which instilled deep Wilsonian instincts within him. In the 1920s he was an adviser on the Dawes Plan in 1924 and the Young Plan in 1929 on the problems of reparations and war debts. He became a member of the Council on Foreign Relations and contributed several articles to its journal, *Foreign Affairs*, and he participated in other internationalist organizations, such as the Carnegie Endowment for International Peace, the American Society for International Law, and the International Chamber of Commerce.

In the 1920s and 1930s he rarely attended church and was only a nominal Christian. In 1937, however, he attended a conference at Oxford at which he chaired a subcommittee on the potential of Christianity for mitigating international animosity. This produced spiritual renewal within him, and he thereafter not only became a very firmly committed Christian but also became very active in church organizations. He was very involved in the Federal Council of Churches, publishing articles on the Christian perspective on international affairs, and his reputation was further enhanced with the publication in 1939 of his book, *War, Peace and Change*.[105]

Dulles was not interested in party politics, but he did not trust Franklin Roosevelt, whom he regarded as unprincipled, and he came to admire Tom Dewey, governor of New York. He supported Dewey for president in 1944, when Dewey had little chance of success. He gained further experience in foreign policy as a delegate to the conference at San Francisco for the founding of the United Nations and at the first session of the United Nations General Assembly in London in 1946. At the invitation of Secretary of State James Byrnes, in order to add bipartisanship, he also attended meetings of the Council of Foreign Ministers in 1945 and 1946, when the foreign ministers of the United States, the Soviet Union, Britain, and France met every three months to try to resolve East-West differences. In 1948, when Dewey was again the Republican nominee for president and when his chances of success seemed excellent, Dulles was Dewey's foreign policy advisor, and it was assumed that he would have been appointed secretary of state if Dewey had won the election. Although Dewey was surprisingly defeated in the presidential election, he continued to be governor of New York and in 1949 appointed Dulles to the U.S. Senate, when Senator Robert Wagner resigned. Dulles, however, failed in his Senate reelection bid in 1950. In 1951 he was appointed by President Truman to lead the negotiation of the peace treaty with Japan. Dulles's success in this task not only illustrated his talents as a negotiator but also the regard in which he was held as a respected bipartisan figure.

In 1952 Dulles was instrumental in writing the foreign policy plank of the Republican Party platform. Given the competition between Taft and Eisenhower for the Republican nomination, this was a task which required considerable skill in drafting in order to prevent a split in the party between isolationists and internationalists. When Eisenhower was elected president, Dulles was the obvious candidate for secretary of state. Eisenhower had a great deal of knowledge of the broad issues of foreign policy, but he needed the assistance of a secretary of state with experience in the technical matters of negotiation, drafting agreements, and suchlike. With his immense range of experience in drafting legal documents, treaties, and party platforms, and with his extremely distinguished record in law and in foreign affairs, Dulles was not only the natural choice for secretary of state in 1952, but he seemed to be the best-qualified candidate ever to enter that office in the history of the United States.

There was, however, another side to John Foster Dulles. For all of his training and experience as a diplomat, he seemed to be deficient in certain basic diplomatic skills. His appearance, with his steel-rimmed spectacles and aquiline nose, exuded austere, stern gruffness. Herbert Parmet writes that "he carried with him an aura of forbidding righteousness and . . . a pompous shell of aloofness."[106] He did not make good eye contact in conversation but tended to look up high around the room, which created the impression of the adoption of a superior, pontificating manner rather than engagement in genuine dialogue. Moreover, this appearance seemed to be accompanied by a simplistic moralism and self-righteousness in his attitude. For all of his intelligence, learning, and sophistication, he came across, as Richard Immerman puts it, "as a fire and brimstone anti-Communist fanatic."[107] He seemed like a figure from the Old Testament or from the Counter-Reformation. Also, he had a penchant for the use of chilling expressions such as "brinkmanship" and "massive retaliation," which filled his allies with alarm. On occasion he was spectacularly undiplomatic, such as in his attitude to Chinese Foreign Minister Zhou En-lai at the Geneva Conference on Indochina in 1954. Not only did he refuse to shake hands with Zhou when they first met, he refused to sit at the same table as Zhou, which caused considerable logistical problems at the meeting. As Townsend Hoopes put it, Dulles conducted himself at the Geneva Conference with the "pinched distaste of a puritan in a house of ill-repute."[108]

Even Eisenhower, for all his regard for Dulles's intellect and experience, worried, as Richard Immerman expresses it, "about his propensity for hyperbole and oversimplification."[109] Eisenhower noted in his diary that Dulles "seems to have a curious lack of understanding as to how his words and manner may affect another personality."[110] As Robin Renwick has noted, "Eisenhower actually liked Dulles, but in this respect he was virtually unique. Nearly everyone else found Dulles impossibly pompous, priggish and unbearably dull. He loved to give sermons, moralize and monopolize conversations."[111] This dislike of Dulles seemed to be particularly prominent among British figures who encountered him. Alexander Cadogan, who was a Foreign Office official accompanying Eden when Eden first met Dulles during the war, wrote of "J.F.D., the woolliest type of useless pontificating American . . . Heaven help us!"[112] Harold Macmillan wrote that Dulles was "the most dunder-headed man alive" and that his "vanity more than equalled his talents."[113] Churchill, above all, loathed Dulles. Churchill's private secretary, Anthony Montague-Browne, writes that Churchill "objected to almost everything about him, in particular his lack of humour and his 'great slab face.' "[114] Churchill denounced Dulles frequently, saying that "this fellow preaches like a Methodist minister and his bloody text is always the same. . . . Dulles is a terrible handicap."[115] Dulles, Churchill ranted on another occasion, is a "chill, unimaginative, uncomprehending, insensitive man. So clumsy. I hope he will disappear."[116]

Recent historical evaluations of Dulles have treated him much more sympathetically. Revisionists of Eisenhower's presidency have clearly established that Eisenhower, rather than Dulles, set the main lines of American foreign policy. As Fred Greenstein put it, "They jointly perfected policies, but Eisenhower made the final decisions and Dulles executed them."[117] There is no validity in the old view that Dulles pulled the strings of American foreign policy and that Eisenhower was a pawn in his hands—as Khrushchev put it in his memoirs, for example, "That vicious cur Dulles was always prowling around Eisenhower, snapping at him if he got out of line."[118] The British ambassador to the United States, Roger Makins, noted that "one thing I quickly learned was that Dulles never took an important step or replied to representations on major issues, without first consulting with the President."[119] Revisionists of Dulles's career, such as Richard Immerman and

Frederick Marks, have argued that, for the most part, Dulles executed American foreign policy with considerable skill and sophistication and that his blemishes have been exaggerated.[120] Immerman writes, for example, that the evidence and arguments in his book on Dulles "cast doubt on the image of Dulles as the inflexible moralist, the bombastic ideologue better suited for the ministry than the State Department."[121] Marks argues that "it is the rigid side of the Secretary that has been featured with little or no attention paid to his flexibility."[122] These historians suggest that Dulles had subtle purposes behind his apparently rigidly moralistic standpoint. Dulles was aware of the need to maintain the support of Congress and public opinion, which his predecessor, Dean Acheson, had failed to do, ultimately rendering him ineffective. Dulles also realized that, from a narrow partisan political point of view, a staunch anticommunist position was politically advantageous in the political climate of 1952, enabling the Republicans to win support, for example, from ethnic Americans of Eastern European ethnic origin, who normally voted Democratic. As John Young puts it, "His frequently crude, frightening public statements were probably designed to meet a number of needs: to neutralise the McCarthyist right, distance the administration from Truman's containment policy, impress the American public and make the Communists cautious."[123] Moreover, Dulles, like Vice President Richard Nixon, acted as a lightening rod and enabled Eisenhower to take the political high road and to appear more moderate and restrained, while he benefited at the same time from Dulles's more extravagant rhetoric. Sophisticated political observers had a better understanding of Dulles's approach and realized that his apparent extremism and intolerance were to some extent for domestic consumption to protect the administration politically, while in practice a more pragmatic foreign policy was pursued. British Foreign Office and embassy officials, for example, who were very knowledgeable observers of the American political scene, took a more benign view of Dulles. Roger Makins, who formed quite a good relationship with Dulles, wrote to Eden in 1954 that Dulles was "an awkward old buster" but "for all his clumsiness . . . a sincere believer in Anglo-American understanding."[124] Makins later wrote that "out of the office, he was friendly and genial and a good companion who took his bourbon with the best of them."[125]

Eden first met Dulles in 1942 and had taken a dislike to him. Dulles had not been taken by Eden either, disliking Eden's form of address of "my dear."[126] The two clashed again during the negotiation of the Japanese peace treaty in 1951, when Eden felt that Dulles was duplicitous in making it seem that Britain supported American pressure on Japan not to recognize Communist China.[127] Eden was aware of Dulles's reputation as an extreme hardline anticommunist, and he was told by Herbert Morrison, foreign secretary in the Labour government in 1951, that Dulles also took an anti-British stance.[128] When Eisenhower ran for president, therefore, Eden, like Churchill, did not wish Eisenhower to choose Dulles as secretary of state. At a meeting in Paris in May 1952, when Eisenhower was about to resign as SACEUR and return to the United States to begin his campaign for the presidency, Eden later recorded that "when we were breakfasting . . . alone for a confidential talk at his suggestion, he asked me what I knew of various possible candidates for Secretary of State. I praised Dewey and said I felt he would be good. I said that I did not know Dulles . . . indicating that I therefore had no view of him myself, but admitting the difficulties which Morrison had reported to me that he had had with Dulles." Eden rejected "the foolish tale now abroad that I had volunteered an opinion against Dulles to Ike. That is not true."[129] Eden's innocuous account is disputed by John Wheeler-Bennett, who expressed surprise that so skilled and experienced a diplomat as Eden had on this matter employed "so clumsy, tactless and generally 'ham-fisted' an approach."[130] After the American presidential election in 1952, Eden was in New York for a meeting at the United Nations and reported to Churchill that, with regard to Eisenhower's consideration of the choice as secretary of state, "the man we don't like is making all the running."[131] After the appointment of Dulles as secretary of state was announced on November 20, 1952, Eden met Eisenhower, who, Eden reported, "was almost apologetic about the appointment. Says it is for a year anyway."[132] It was hardly an auspicious beginning for a relationship between the British foreign secretary and the U.S. secretary of state.

As pragmatic statesmen, Eden and Dulles attempted to work together effectively. When Eden came on a visit to Washington in March 1953, he found Dulles "very friendly."[133] At the Bermuda conference in December 1953, Eden and Dulles went for a swim together each day and Eden said that "I came to like him more and more."[134] Their working relationship was reasonably satisfactory through 1953, but in the course of the major negotiations on many issues in 1954, the relationship became increasingly strained, especially at the Geneva Conference on Indochina. Shuckburgh wrote that, after the first few days of the Geneva Conference, "there is no doubt that Dulles and A.E. have got thoroughly on each other's nerves and that both are behaving rather like prima donnas."[135]

Eisenhower optimistically wrote to Churchill after Churchill and Eden's visit to Washington in June 1954 that "one of the major advantages we may have gained from it is what seems to me an obvious drawing together of Anthony and Foster in their thinking and relationships."[136] Churchill was not convinced. At one point during the meeting in Washington Eden and Dulles had gone off together and were a long time in rejoining Churchill and Eisenhower, which led Churchill to remark, not wholly in jest, that perhaps they had "quarrelled and killed each other."[137] Dulles graciously wrote to Eden after Eden's successful diplomacy in bringing West Germany into NATO following the collapse of EDC that "you gave wonderful leadership to the Lancaster House Conference. . . . I feel that we are, more than ever before, working closely together, both in terms of basic objectives and in terms of their implementation. We must keep this up."[138] But this was untypical, and further difficulties arose especially over Quemoy and Matsu, the islands offshore from China, in late 1954 and early 1955. By the time Eden succeeded Churchill as prime minister in April 1955, therefore, Eden's relationship with Dulles had a long history of strain.

At the end of his premiership, Eden wrote very bitterly about Dulles. "He was against everything in which the UK and perhaps above all self could take a lead," Eden wrote in January 1957. "A meanly jealous man."[139] It was "easier to deal with Ribbentrop or Laval," he wrote on another occasion, "than with Dulles."[140] In his memoirs, he denounced Dulles as a "preacher in the world of politics," who appeared to have "little regard for the consequences of his own words."[141] Eden wrote that "my difficulty in working with Mr. Dulles was to determine what he really meant and in consequence the significance to be attached to his words and actions."[142] In fact, the denunciations were influenced by Eden's soured view of matters after 1957. As a veteran diplomat, Eden could appreciate Dulles's skills in what Frederick Marks describes as "expertise in the art of ambiguity," such as "draft communiqués designed to paper over differences and to accommodate diverse points of view."[143] Moreover, as a seasoned observer of American politics, and with the reports from the British embassy and the Foreign Office's North American department, Eden appreciated that Dulles's rhetoric was in many ways geared to domestic public opinion and that in practice he operated more pragmatically. More revealing were complaints such as by Eden at the Geneva Conference in 1954 that "I think they are jealous of our authority and following here. They like to give orders, and if they are not at once obeyed they become huffy. That is their conception of an alliance—or Dulles' anyway."[144] As Robert Murphy noted, "It seemed impossible for Eden to keep in mind how much Britain's power had diminished in relation to the United States and Russia. Dulles never forgot this."[145] Dulles believed, moreover, that America's superior strength in nuclear weapons and greater willingness to engage in more confrontational policies toward the Communist powers had the result that Anglo-American problems to some extent "derived from the growing danger of atomic war. In light of this our 'tough' policy was becoming increasingly unpopular throughout the free world, whereas the British 'soft policy' was gaining prestige and acceptance both in Europe and Asia."[146] Fundamentally, Eden's difficulties in his relations with Dulles were not due to personality but to the changing power relationship between Britain and the United States. Dulles's demeanor and some unfortunate mannerisms made him seem the quintessential embodiment of the American Century. Eden's resentment and frustration over Britain's fading power and America's growing dominance, rather than the quirks of John Foster Dulles's personality, were at the heart of the difficulties which developed in the Anglo-American relationship in the Eden-Eisenhower period.

In summary, then, with regard to the overall world view and strategic goals of Eden and Eisenhower at the beginning of their simultaneous periods in office as leaders of their countries in 1955, there were broad areas of similarity in outlook, yet in some respects there were significant differences, at least in emphasis. Eden had to an important extent the mindset of a foreign secretary, with skill in tactical maneuvering and smoothing out disagreements. This was based, however, on a set of fundamental goals and values. As a staunch antiappeaser, Eden believed in a firm stance in the containment of Soviet communism. As a realist, Eden accepted that for Britain this necessitated a close alliance with the United States, but this was based not only on narrow considerations of British self-interest in order to gain American protection against the Soviet threat but also on principled commitment to the values of Western civilization, which the two leading English-speaking nations embodied. Yet, to an even greater extent than Churchill during World War II, Eden resented that Britain's power had declined so greatly relative to the United States. The hope that Britain would make a swift recovery from World War II exhaustion had been exposed as illusory by the mid-1950s. At the same time, the pace of the movement toward the end of empire had accelerated rapidly. Eden struggled to come to terms with these unwelcome developments. Eden was relieved that under Eisenhower's leadership America had firmly renounced reversion to isolationism, and Eden appreciated the importance to Britain's security of the American nuclear umbrella and of America's commitment to international involvement. Yet, Eden shared the somewhat schizophrenic attitude of many of his British contemporaries in appreciating the need for American international involvement and American nuclear protection while on the other hand fearing that American inexperience and zealousness might create confrontation and conflict, which in an age of nuclear weapons of rapidly increasing power could culminate in catastrophe. Eden hoped, however, that Britain remained sufficiently strong as to enable it to exercise a significant amount of influence within the Western alliance. He hoped, moreover, that in Eisenhower there was an American leader who stood for values and policies with which Britain largely agreed and who was well disposed toward Britain and open to British advice with regard to the most prudent course to follow.

Eisenhower's military background as supreme Allied commander predisposed him toward a greater sense of wider strategic objectives. Yet Eisenhower had always been a military leader who had involved himself in tactical details and diplomatic maneuverings in order to achieve consensus, and this characterized his approach to the conduct of foreign policy as president. He was self-consciously strongly committed to international involvement on the part of the United States. He was more virulently anticommunist and anti-Soviet than Eden and more inclined to view the world in stark, Manichean terms of the evil of Communist tyranny versus the virtue of Western democracy. In a world so sharply divided, Eisenhower was deeply afraid of the possibility of war. His appreciation of the power of nuclear weapons made him aware of the calamitous consequences of the outbreak of war. In order to keep the peace and to contain communism, Eisenhower set great store on America's need for allies, with Britain foremost among them. Eisenhower's World War II experience had produced a strong affinity toward Britain, which was not only personal but also based on a deep belief in the values and traditions that the two nations shared. Yet, Eisenhower realized that Britain's relative decline and the importance of other allies in NATO and elsewhere meant that he needed to avoid too close and exclusive an alliance with Britain.

The areas of agreement and of difference become more apparent in a consideration of the particular issues which Eden and Eisenhower faced in 1955.

NOTES

1. Robert Rhodes James, *Anthony Eden* (London: Weidenfeld and Nicholson, 1986), 14–18.

2. David Dutton, *Anthony Eden: A Life and Reputation* (London: Arnold, 1997), 3.

3. Anthony Eden, *Places in the Sun* (London: J. Murray, 1926).

4. Dutton, *Eden*, 35.

5. Winston S. Churchill, *The Gathering Storm*, vol. 1 of *The Second World War*. (London: Cassell, 1948–54), (London: Cassell, 1948), 190, 201.

6. Dutton, *Eden*, 99–108.
7. Anthony Eden, *The Reckoning* (London: Cassell, 1965), 63.
8. Churchill to King George VI, June 16, 1942, AP 19/1/10.
9. J. Harvey, ed., *The War Diaries of Oliver Harvey* (London: Collins, 1978), 50.
10. Randolph Churchill, *The Rise and Fall of Sir Anthony Eden* (London: McGibbon and Kee, 1959).
11. Warren F. Kimball, ed., *Churchill and Roosevelt: The Complete Correspondence*, 3 vols. (Princeton, N.J.: Princeton University Press, 1984).
12. Eden to Churchill, October 19, 1942, AP 20/1/22.
13. Harvey, *War Diaries*, 348.
14. Eden to Cranborne, December 21, 1942, AP 20/39/42.
15. Diary, November 25, 1943, AP 20/3/5.
16. Eden, *Reckoning*, 374.
17. Robert Holland, *The Pursuit of Greatness: Britain and the World Role, 1900–1970* (London: HarperCollins, 1991), 268.
18. Evelyn Shuckburgh, *Descent to Suez: Diaries, 1951–56* (London: Weidenfeld and Nicholson, 1986), 42.
19. Ben MacIntyre, "Eden's Secret American Beauty," *Times*, June 3, 2000.
20. Anthony Eden, *Days of Decision* (Boston: Houghton Mifflin, 1949), 24.
21. Shuckburgh, *Descent to Suez*, 13.
22. James Chace, *Acheson: The Secretary of State Who Created the American World* (New York: Simon and Schuster, 1998); Michael F. Hopkins, *Oliver Franks and the Truman Administration: Anglo-American Relations, 1948–1952* (London: Frank Cass, 2003); Peter G. Boyle, "Oliver Franks and the Washington Embassy, 1948–1952," chapter 6 in *British Officials and British Foreign Policy, 1945–50*, ed. John Zametica, 189–211 (Leicester: Leicester University Press, 1990).
23. Dean Acheson, *Present at the Creation: My Years in the State Department* (New York: W. W. Norton, 1969), 578.
24. Anthony Eden, *Full Circle* (London: Cassell, 1960), 200.
25. Ibid.
26. Lester Pearson, *The International Years, 1948–1957*, vol. 2 of *Memoirs* (Toronto: University of Toronto Press, 1973), 328.
27. Shuckburgh, *Descent to Suez*, 56–57.
28. D. R. Thorpe, *Eden: The Life and Times of Anthony Eden, First Earl of Avon, 1897–1977* (London: Chatto and Windus, 2003), 362–63.
29. Ibid., 375.
30. John W. Young, *Winston Churchill's Last Campaign* (Oxford: Clarendon Press, 1996), 50–51.
31. *Parliamentary Debates*, 5th ser., vol. 494 (1951–52), cols. 34–37.
32. Acheson, *Present at the Creation*, 598.
33. Acheson to Eden, Nov. 1, 1954, AP 14/3/506A.
34. Anthony Nutting, *No End of a Lesson: The Story of Suez* (London: Constable, 1967), 25.
35. Shuckburgh, *Descent to Suez*, 187.
36. Dutton, *Eden*, 6–7.

37. Roderick Barclay, *Ernest Bevin and the Foreign Office, 1932–1969* (London: Latimer, 1975), 108.
38. Ben Pimlott, ed., *The Second World War Diary of Hugh Dalton, 1940–1945* (London: Jonathan Cape, 1986), 348.
39. Alistair Horne, *Macmillan, 1894–1956*, vol. 1 of *Macmillan* (London: Macmillan, 1988), 375.
40. Dutton, *Eden*, 463.
41. Anthony Montague-Browne, *Long Sunset: Memoirs of Churchill's Last Private Secretary* (London: Cassell, 1995), 132.
42. Frank Roberts, *Dealing with Dictators: The Destruction and Revival of Europe, 1931–1970* (London: Weidenfeld and Nicholson, 1991), 163.
43. John Colville, *The Fringes of Power: Downing Street Diaries, 1939–1955* (London: Hodder and Stoughton, 1985), 632.
44. Young, *Last Campaign*, 46.
45. Thorpe, *Eden*, 451.
46. Nicholas Henderson, *The Private Office: A Personal View of Five Foreign Secretaries and of Government from the Inside* (London: Weidenfeld and Nicholson, 1984), 15.
47. Ibid., 15–16.
48. Hastings L. Ismay, *Memoirs* (London: Heinemann, 1960), 327.
49. Shuckburgh, *Descent to Suez*, 73.
50. Ibid., 15.
51. Ibid., 14.
52. James, *Eden*, 362–66.
53. Montague-Browne, *Long Sunset*, 208.
54. Horne, *Macmillan*, 352.
55. Kenneth Young, ed., *The Diaries of Sir Robert Bruce Lockhart* (New York: St. Martin's Press, 1974), 720.
56. Colville, *Fringes of Power*, 708.
57. Kenneth S. Davis, *Soldier of Democracy, a Biography of Dwight Eisenhower* (Garden City, N.Y.: Doubleday, 1945), 15.
58. R. Alton Lee, *Dwight D. Eisenhower: Soldier and Statesman* (Chicago: Nelson Hall, 1981), 34.
59. Dwight D. Eisenhower, *At Ease: Stories I Like to Tell to Friends* (New York: Doubleday, 1967), 147.
60. Matthew Holland, *Eisenhower Between the Wars: The Making of a General and a Statesman* (Westport, Conn.: Praeger, 2001).
61. Dwight D. Eisenhower, *Crusade in Europe* (Garden City, N.Y.: Doubleday, 1948), 4.
62. Mark Stoler, *Allies and Adversaries: The Joint Chiefs of Staff, the Grand Alliance, and U.S. Strategy in World War II* (Chapel Hill: University of North Carolina Press, 2000).
63. John S. D. Eisenhower, *Allies: Pearl Harbor to D-Day* (Garden City, N.Y.: Doubleday, 1982), xxiii.
64. Stephen E. Ambrose, *The Supreme Commander* (Garden City, N.Y.: Doubleday, 1970), 80–81.

65. Eisenhower, *Allies*, 103.

66. Eisenhower, *Crusade in Europe*, 89.

67. Robert Murphy, *Diplomat among Warriors* (Garden City, N.Y.: Doubleday, 1964), 104.

68. Saul Kelly, "A Very Considerable and Largely Unsung Success: Sir Roger Makins' Washington Embassy, 1953–1956," chapter 8 in *Twentieth Century Anglo-American Relations*, ed. Jonathan Hollowell, 125–27 (London: Palgrave, 2001).

69. Kay Summersby Morgan, *Past Forgetting: My Love Affair with Dwight D. Eisenhower* (London: Collins, 1977), 17.

70. *Life*, November 9, 1942.

71. Susan Eisenhower, *Mrs. Ike: Memoirs and Reflections of the Life of Mamie Eisenhower* (New York: Farrar, Straus and Giroux, 1996), 193–94.

72. John S. D. Eisenhower, ed., *Letters to Mamie* (Garden City, N.Y.: Doubleday, 1978), 104–5.

73. Eisenhower, *Crusade in Europe*, 179.

74. Winston S. Churchill, *Closing the Ring*, vol. 5 of *The Second World War* (London: Cassell, 1952), 418.

75. John Eisenhower, *Allies*, xiii.

76. Churchill, *Triumph and Tragedy*, vol. 6 of *The Second World War* (London: Cassell, 1954), 476.

77. Herbert S. Parmet, *Eisenhower and the American Crusades* (New York: Macmillan, 1972), 4.

78. Stephen E. Ambrose, *Soldier, General of the Army, President-Elect, 1890–1952*, vol. 1 of *Eisenhower* (New York: Simon and Schuster, 1983), 412–13.

79. Eisenhower, *Crusade in Europe*, 444.

80. Merle Miller, *Plain Speaking: An Oral Biography of Harry S. Truman* (New York: Putnam's, 1973), 339–40.

81. Kay Summersby Morgan, *Past Forgetting*, 16, 263–64.

82. Eisenhower, *Letters to Mamie*, 11.

83. Ibid., 12.

84. Ibid.

85. Churchill to Eisenhower, July 27, 1948, in *Columbia University*, vol. 10 of *The Papers of Dwight D. Eisenhower*, ed. Alfred D. Chandler Jr. (Baltimore: Johns Hopkins University Press, 1978), 686.

86. Parmet, *Eisenhower and the American Crusades*, 59.

87. Dwight D. Eisenhower, *Mandate for Change, 1953–1956* (Garden City, N.Y.: Doubleday, 1963), 10.

88. William G. Pickett, *Eisenhower Decides to Run* (Chicago: Ivan R. Dee, 2000).

89. Stephen E. Ambrose, *Eisenhower: The President, 1952–1969* (New York: Simon and Schuster, 1984); Fred I. Greenstein, *The Hidden-Hand Presidency* (New York: Basil Books, 1982); Robert F. Burk, *Dwight D. Eisenhower: Hero and Politician* (Boston: Twayne Publishers, 1986); Charles L. Alexander, *Holding the Line: The Eisenhower Era, 1952–1961* (Bloomington: Indiana University Press, 1975); Blanche W. Cook, *The Declassified Eisenhower: A Divided Legacy* (New York: Doubleday, 1981); Lee, *Eisenhower*; Parmet, *Eisenhower and the American Crusades*.

90. Richard M. Nixon, *Six Crises* (Garden City, N.Y.: Doubleday, 1962), 161.

91. "A Chance for Peace," address delivered before the American Society of Newspaper Editors, April 16, 1953, PP, 1:182.

92. Special Message to the Congress on the Mutual Security Program, May 5, 1953, PP, 1:257.

93. 210th Meeting of NSC, August 12, 1954, AWF, NSC Series, box 5.

94. Annual Message to the Congress on the State of the Union, February 2, 1953, PP, 1:17.

95. 138th Meeting of NSC, March 25, 1953, AWF, NSC Series, box 4.

96. Special Meeting of NSC, March 31, 1953, AWF, NSC Series, box 4.

97. 165th Meeting of NSC, October 7, 1953, AWF, NSC Series, box 4.

98. 194th Meeting of NSC, April 29, 1954, AWF, NSC Series, box 5.

99. Robin W. Renwick, *Fighting with Allies: America and Britain in Peace and War* (Basingstoke: Macmillan, 1996), 392.

100. Robert H. Ferrell, ed., *The Eisenhower Diaries* (New York: W. W. Norton, 1981), 223.

101. Robert H. Ferrell, ed., *The Diary of James C. Hagerty: Eisenhower in Mid-Course, 1954–55* (Bloomington: Indiana University Press, 1983), 75.

102. Ferrell, *Eisenhower Diaries*, 232.

103. Diary, March 4, 1953, AP 20/1/29.

104. Eisenhower to Eden, March 16, 1953, AP 20/16/25A.

105. John Foster Dulles, *War, Peace and Change* (New York: Harper Bros., 1939).

106. Parmet, *Eisenhower and the American Crusades*, 187.

107. Richard H. Immerman, *John Foster Dulles: Piety, Pragmatism and Power* (Wilmington, Del.: Scholarly Resources, 1999), 44–45.

108. Townsend Hoopes, *The Devil and John Foster Dulles* (Boston: Little, Brown, 1973), 222.

109. Immerman, *Dulles*, 44.

110. Ferrell, *Eisenhower Diaries*, 237.

111. Renwick, *Fighting with Allies*, 187.

112. David Dilks, ed., *The Diaries of Sir Alexander Cadogan, 1938–1945* (New York: Putnam's, 1972), 462.

113. Horne, *Macmillan*, 272–73.

114. Montague-Browne, *Long Sunset*, 146.

115. Lord Moran, *Winston Churchill: The Struggle for Survival, 1940–1965* (London: Constable, 1966), 540.

116. Ibid., 580.

117. Greenstein, *Hidden-Hand Presidency*, 87.

118. Strobe Talbott, ed., *Khrushchev Remembers* (London: André Deutsch, 1971), 361.

119. Roger Makins, unpublished memoir. Quoted in Kelly, "A Very Considerable and Largely Unsung Success," 127.

120. Immerman, *Dulles*; Frederick W. Marks, *Power and Peace: The Diplomacy of John Foster Dulles* (Westport, Conn.: Praeger, 1993); Richard H. Immerman, ed., *John Foster Dulles and the Diplomacy of the Cold War* (Princeton, N.J.: Princeton University Press, 1990).

121. Immerman, *Dulles*, 265.
122. Marks, *Power and Peace*, xi.
123. Young, *Last Campaign*, 122.
124. Makins to Eden, June 18, 1954, FO 800/842, PRO.
125. Makins, unpublished memoir. Quoted in Kelly, "A Very Considerable and Unsung Success," 127.
126. Renwick, *Fighting with Allies*, 194.
127. Eden, *Full Circle*, 19–20; Acheson, *Present at the Creation*, 603–5.
128. Young, *Last Campaign*, 83.
129. Eden to John Wheeler-Bennett, July 22, 1970, AP 33/4/190.
130. John Wheeler-Bennett, *Semblance of Power: The Political Settlement After World War II* (London: Macmillan, 1972), 619–20.
131. New York to Foreign Office, November 12, 1952, PREM 11/352/T 212/52, PRO.
132. Shuckburgh, *Descent to Suez*, 55.
133. Diary, March 4, 1953, AP 20/1/29.
134. Cyrus L. Sulzberger, *A Long Row of Candles: Memoirs and Diaries, 1934–1954* (New York: Macmillan, 1969), 934.
135. Shuckburgh, *Descent to Suez*, 186.
136. Eisenhower to Churchill, July 7, 1954, in *The Churchill-Eisenhower Correspondence, 1953–1955*, ed. Peter G. Boyle (Chapel Hill: University of North Carolina Press, 1990), 152.
137. Moran, *Struggle for Survival*, 368.
138. Dulles to Eden, October 3, 1954, AP 14/3/587.
139. Diary, Jan. 1, 1957, AP 20/2/5.
140. Eden to Lord Hailes, Sept. 27, 1958, AP 23/34/3A.
141. Eden, *Full Circle*, 64.
142. Ibid., 63.
143. Marks, *Power and Peace*, 123.
144. Eden to Salisbury, May 16, 1954, AP 20/17/118A.
145. Murphy, *Diplomat among Warriors*, 379.
146. 204th Meeting of NSC, June 24, 1954, AWF, NSC Series, box 5.

THE ISSUES

The major issues that faced Britain and America in 1955 and that would concern Eden and Eisenhower in the years of their correspondence, 1955–57, while they were respectively prime minister of Britain and president of the United States, were: relations with the Soviet Union; nuclear issues; intelligence; colonialism; the Middle East; the Far East; Europe; economic issues; and the overall Anglo-American relationship, which all of the other areas touched upon. A brief consideration of the development of the issues up to 1955 should help to provide context for the correspondence.

The most important single issue in the world of the mid-1950s was relations with the Soviet Union. The Cold War was at its height and the Soviet threat seemed frighteningly menacing. In 1953 the Soviets tested a hydrogen bomb. This followed the Soviet development of an atomic bomb in 1949, which was much sooner than the West had expected. Moreover, Western intelligence revealed that Soviet progress in missile technology for the delivery of nuclear weapons was well advanced. At the same time, the Soviet economy was growing at an impressive rate. Soviet propaganda pointed to Soviet central Asia, for example, with a modern city such as Tashkent in Uzbekistan, as a model for third-world countries of successful, rapid economic development, especially for countries emerging from colonial rule, rather than the allegedly irrelevant, immoral, and inefficient model of free enterprise capitalism. Stalin died in 1953, but the new Soviet leadership did not appear to have altered in any way the basic goals of Soviet foreign policy. There had been a struggle for power in the Soviet Union after Stalin's death, with Lavrenti Beria tried and executed in 1953, Georgi Malenkov overthrown in February 1955, and Nikita Khrushchev, first secretary of the Communist Party of the Soviet Union, appearing to emerge by mid-1955 as the new leader, although he was officially in a collective leadership along with the chairman of the Council of Ministers, Nikolai Bulganin, and Stalin's closest henchman, Viacheslav Molotov, who continued to be Soviet foreign minister. Khrushchev seemed in some ways to be a jovial, peasant figure who was inclined toward liberal reform. But he was also a mercurial character who had been a longstanding associate of Stalin and was a true believer in the inevitable triumph of communism and the collapse of capitalism.

In the face of this Soviet threat, Britain and America felt a strong need for one another. Britain had a basic need of America for security, while America needed allies and naturally looked first to her closest ally, Britain. One of Britain's underlying fears was that America would revert to isolationism and leave Britain alone in the face of the Soviet menace. Britain had a strong memory of America in the First World War crusading to make the world safe for democracy and to fight the war to end wars, then swinging to the other extreme after the war and retreating into isolationism. The result had been that when new threats arose in the 1930s, Britain was left to stand alone against them, especially after the fall of France to Hitler's blitzkrieg in 1940, while America remained on the sidelines until, very reluctantly and somewhat fortuitously, the United States was at last drawn into the conflict and compelled to assume her international responsibilities. During the Second World War, Britain had been very afraid that after its conclusion America might act in the same manner as after World War I. Throughout the war Britain engaged in an extensive, surreptitious propaganda campaign in the United States to try to ensure against a postwar American reversion to isolationism. At the end of the war, Britain was worried that America was overoptimistic in its hopes of accommodation with the Soviet Union and would demobilize too extensively and fail to play a proper part in holding back the Soviet threat. Even when America became more fully involved in the Cold War after 1947 with the Truman Doctrine, the Marshall Plan, and NATO, Britain continued to harbor a deep-seated fear that America would not stay the course but would swing back to isolationism. The strong support in America for Robert Taft, with his tendency toward isolationism, confirmed British fears of the potential inclination of America to retreat to a "Fortress America" policy. With Eisenhower in office, these fears were allayed to a considerable extent, but the deep habitual British fear of American reversion to isolationism never fully disappeared.

On the American side, the United States had a strong sense of nervousness and uncertainty as world leadership was thrust upon America in the post–World War II era. The majority of Americans after the war would have preferred, as Averell Harriman put it, "to watch a movie and drink Coke."[1] America in some respects acted in a domineering fashion and manifested an arrogance of power in its new role as world leader. But in many other respects America did not welcome its new role and was unsure of itself and of its proper role in world affairs. American leaders felt a need for allies and looked to their most natural ally, Britain. This was above all the case when hostilities broke out, as in Korea in 1950. As Oliver Franks, British ambassador to the United States, expressed it, there was in America a steady and unquestioning assumption that Britain was "the only dependable ally and partner" and that it was, therefore, essential for Britain to send troops to Korea as a substantial sign of reassurance to the United States of British support when America was making a decisive commitment to international involvement.[2]

While Britain was afraid of America swinging back into isolation, Britain also feared, however, an American swing in the other direction to extreme aggressiveness, especially in light of American attitudes towards communism. British Foreign Office officials frequently commented that Americans were mercurial and were inclined to swing from one extreme to the other. By comparison, those officials felt, the British were mature, stable, worldly wise, and very experienced in the conduct of the foreign policy of a great power. The British felt that their role should be to act as a mentor to the Americans and in a subtle manner to guide America in the right direction. As Bernard Gage, an official in the North American department in the Foreign Office, put it in August 1945, "The Americans seem moved at present mainly by enthusiastic and self-congratulatory emotion and they are probably in one of their more irritating cockahoop moods. But we can no doubt 'take it' as we have often had to before. . . . In due course it will no doubt be borne upon Americans that we, with our long experience, can be of some assistance in the proper application of their power."[3] John Donnelly, another official in the North American department in the Foreign Office, expressed it, in a characteristically supercilious manner, that "whenever we tactfully can . . . we should, I think, try to induce in the Americans something of that historical sense which they so sadly lack."[4] To a certain extent, Britain succeeded in helping to guide America in the late 1940s, in the direction of the Marshall Plan and NATO, for example, which were as much British initiatives as American. To a much greater extent, however, no matter how subtle the British felt they were in guiding the Americans, Britain's design was very obvious to the Americans, who either resisted it strongly or dismissed it as further evidence of British jealousy that its declining power left it increasingly impotent as America superseded it.

With the election campaign of 1952 and the accession of the new Republican administration, British fears grew sharply of American impulsiveness and extreme anticommunism. When Churchill received the news of Eisenhower's election, he said to his private secretary, Jock Colville, "I think this makes war much more probable."[5] Given Churchill's strong admiration for Eisenhower, this may seem surprising. Churchill's fear, however, was not of

Eisenhower himself but of the right-wing elements within the Republican Party, which Churchill feared Eisenhower would not be able to control and might push him into dangerous and reckless policies. The Republican appeal to "liberation" in 1952, implying policies to achieve the liberation of Eastern European countries from Communist rule, seemed to many in Britain a very good example of the immaturity of Americans. George Kennan had advocated a policy of "firm but patient" containment of the Soviet Union in the belief that in the course of time the Soviet Union would collapse from within. Right-wing critics such as James Burnham dismissed Kennan's policy as passive and negative. "Let History do it," Burnham wrote contemptuously of containment.[6] Burnham advanced the argument, which had superficial plausibility, but which was fundamentally extremely dangerous, that America should take the initiative in the pursuit of policies that would bring about the liberation of Eastern Europe. These ideas were then written into the Republican platform in 1952 in the vivid language of John Foster Dulles. Such language, combined with Dulles's stern, imperious demeanor and his reputation as a narrowly moralistic, staunchly anticommunist son of a Presbyterian minister, filled many British hearts with grave apprehension. The British Foreign Office and knowledgeable commentators, as observed earlier, had sufficient understanding of the American political system to appreciate that many of the statements were for domestic consumption in a political campaign and would not be enacted in policy. They worried, however, with reasonable justification, whether in Moscow there was sufficient sophistication to realize that these words should not be taken at face value and whether as a result the Republican campaign in 1952 could heighten tensions with the Soviet Union. This inclined the British more in the direction of seeking greater engagement in dialogue with the Soviets. Above all, this was the position taken by Churchill.

Having established his reputation as the original Cold Warrior with his speech in Fulton, Missouri, in March 1946, Churchill's great aim in his last years in office in the 1950s was, when the strength of the West had been rebuilt by rearmament in the early 1950s, to parley with the Russians and to achieve a modus vivendi in the Cold War. After the election of 1951 which brought him back into office, Churchill was keen to try to arrange a summit meeting with Stalin. Even more so after Stalin's death in March 1953, Churchill advanced the case with passionate conviction that a summit meeting with the new Soviet leadership was the vital opportunity to seize as the first step towards détente. In his correspondence with Eisenhower, Churchill pressed his case with considerable eloquence and lucidity. "I have the feeling," Churchill wrote to Eisenhower on March 11, 1953, "that we might both of us together or separately be called to account if no attempt were made to turn over a leaf so that a new page would be started with something more coherent on it than a series of casual and dangerous incidents at the many points of contact between the two divisions of the world."[7] Eisenhower replied, however, that "I tend to doubt the wisdom of a formal multilateral meeting since this would give our opponent the same kind of opportunity he has so often had to use such a meeting simultaneously to balk every reasonable effort of ourselves and to make of the whole occurrence another propaganda mill for the Soviets."[8] Churchill persisted with his argument, writing in March 1954 that "I recur to my earlier proposal of a personal meeting between Three. Men have to settle with men, no matter how vast, and in part beyond their comprehension, the business in hand may be. I can even imagine that a few simple words, spoken in the awe which might at once oppress or inspire the speakers might lift this nuclear monster from our world."[9] Eisenhower maintained his view, however, that, as he replied to Churchill, "I doubt whether the progress on which we are engaged would at this moment, be advanced by a meeting of heads of government. In fact, I can see that such a meeting might inject complications."[10] Churchill became exasperated and wrote with passion that "it will seem astonishing to future generations— such as they may be—that with all that is at stake no attempt was made by personal parley between the Heads of Government to create a union of consenting minds on broad and simple issues. . . . Fancy that you and Malenkov should never have met, or that he should never have been outside Russia when all the time in both countries appalling preparations are being made for measureless mutual destruction."[11] But Eisenhower maintained his position that "while I would like to be more optimistic, I cannot see that a top-level meeting is anything which I can inscribe on my schedule for any predictable date."[12]

With the domestic political situation in America of McCarthyism at the height of its power and the pronouncements which had been made on liberation in the election campaign, Eisenhower was in no position to participate in a summit meeting with Soviet leaders. Eisenhower argued that a gradual step by step approach was required, with Soviet displays of good faith, such as assisting to bring about peace in Korea and signing a peace treaty with Austria. As a former SACEUR, Eisenhower was aware that European public opinion was very vulnerable to siren songs of peace from Moscow, which could lead to unrealistically high expectations and to a lowering of support for the necessary level of defense expenditure and to less cohesion within NATO.

Eden largely agreed with Eisenhower on the issue of a summit. Eden had been closer to Eisenhower's position on the matter than Churchill's and he had not supported Churchill's attempt to arrange a summit in 1953 or 1954. By 1955, however, the Soviets had shown some signs of good faith, such as the Korean armistice and moves toward an Austrian peace treaty, as well as reconciliation with Yugoslavia. Furthermore, Eden realized that a summit meeting, as a symbol of better prospects for peace and détente, was popular with public opinion in Britain. An election would be due in Britain within a year of his accession as prime minister in April 1955. The Conservative government in 1951–55 had achieved some modest successes in producing greater prosperity and economic stability, but Eden's electoral prospects would be improved if he placed more emphasis on his strong suit, foreign policy, and an action such as a summit meeting made him seem the candidate for peace. Eisenhower by 1955 no longer needed to fear McCarthy, after McCarthy's condemnation by the Senate in December 1954. Also, Eisenhower was beginning to look towards reelection in 1956 and hoped to strengthen his chances by running as a man of peace. There were, therefore, domestic political reasons as well as foreign policy considerations moving both Britain and America in the direction of a greater degree of dialogue and possibly a summit meeting with the Soviet Union, even though basically both Eden and Eisenhower were fundamentally very skeptical and suspicious of the Soviet Union and regarded the Soviet threat as extremely dangerous and not susceptible to any easy solution in the foreseeable future.

Aside from the general issue of relations with the Soviet Union, there were more particular matters relating to nuclear issues which were of great concern to Britain and the United States. One particular reason why the United States needed Britain as an ally was America's need for air bases from which to launch nuclear strikes against the Soviet Union. Britain provided, in Duncan Campbell's phrase, an "unsinkable aircraft carrier."[13] Britain thereby gained the benefit of a nuclear deterrent in a very visible form, but at the price of becoming the prime target for Soviet nuclear retaliation in the event of war. As Churchill put it in 1951, "we have made ourselves the target, perhaps the bull's eye, of a Soviet attack."[14]

The U.S. Air Force left Britain at the end of World War II, but within a year an agreement was signed for its return to British bases from which atomic attacks could be made. In 1946, Strategic Air Command (SAC), the bomber component of the U.S. Air Force, was created, with capability for the delivery of atomic bombs from aircraft its most important responsibility. In June 1946, General Carl Spaatz, the American commander of the air force, came to Britain and reached an agreement with Air Chief Marshall Lord Tedder, the RAF chief of staff, for the designation of a number of RAF bases for use by American B-29s, the planes which were capable of carrying atomic bombs. In accordance with the Spaatz-Tedder agreement, five bases were assigned— Lakenheath, Mildenhall, Scrampton, Marham, and Bassingbourne. In 1948 the first squadrons of B-29s arrived in Britain, at the time of the Berlin crisis. A clear diplomatic signal was thereby sent to the Soviets by the arrival of these six squadrons of planes which were known for their capability to carry atomic bombs. In fact, these B-29s had not been converted to carry atomic bombs, though that detail was not known to either the Soviet or the British government. In 1950 the first B-29s which were converted to carry atomic bombs arrived in Britain. Four new bases were assigned that year— Greenham Common, Upper Heyford, Fairford, and Brize Norton—which, together with four of the bases assigned by the Spaatz-Tedder agreement— Lakenheath, Mildenhall, Scrampton, and Marham—became the principal SAC bases in Britain. After the outbreak of the Korean War in 1950, the nonnuclear components of nuclear weapons began to be stored in Britain, with only the nuclear core to be flown over from America in an emergency. In 1953 Eisenhower decided that complete nuclear weapons should be stored on British bases. In addition to the eight SAC bases for B-29s, which were superseded by B-47s in 1953, the United States established a large number of storage facilities and command and communications centers, so that by 1953 there were forty-three American bases in Britain with a force level of 45,000 in addition to 28,000 dependents and around 3,500 civilians. The Soviet Union did not have a transcontinental air capacity, which made American bases in Britain (and obviously, in consequence, Britain itself), as Churchill had said, the "bull's eye" of a potential Soviet retaliatory attack.

In this situation, a matter of vital importance was the degree of British control over an American decision to launch a nuclear attack from a British base. In the Quebec Agreement of 1943, Roosevelt and Churchill agreed that neither Britain nor the United States would use atomic weapons against a third party without each other's consent. But this was a secret personal agreement whose validity was open to challenge, and in any event in the so-called modus vivendi between Attlee and Truman in 1948, Britain gave up any claim to a veto over American use of atomic weapons. The United States did not wish to have any restriction by another power on its use of atomic weapons, especially in an emergency situation when time was of the essence. No American president would have wished to suggest to Congress any agreement that gave a foreign power any control over America's sole use of nuclear weapons, even if those nuclear weapons were stationed on the territory of another power. But Britain was conscious of a loss of sovereignty if Britain had no control over an American decision to launch a nuclear attack from British soil. This could have devastating consequences for Britain, especially if in the particular situation in which an American attack was made, Britain did not wholly agree with the American decision. Various attempts were made to reach an agreement which would at least give Britain some right to be consulted while not hampering the American capability to use nuclear weapons instantly in a crisis. The problem proved to be fundamentally insolvable. The formula that was arrived at was worked out by Oliver Franks, British ambassador to the United States, and General Omar Bradley, chairman of the U.S. Joint Chiefs of Staff, on September 14, 1951, in which it was agreed that the use of air bases in Britain "remains a matter for joint decision in the light of the circumstances at the time."[15] This was hardly an assured guarantee to Britain against possible irresponsible use of bases in Britain by the United States, but Britain could do nothing other than accept these terms in order to gain the protection of the American nuclear umbrella.

An even deeper grievance on Britain's part with regard to nuclear issues had to do with the sharing of atomic information. In 1941, even before America entered the Second World War, Britain and the United States began to cooperate on nuclear research. Britain was at this stage more advanced in nuclear physics than the United States and had more to contribute. There was, however, hesitation and reluctance on both sides in 1941 and 1942 to engage in full-scale cooperation. Some Americans, especially General Leslie Groves, the director of the Manhattan Project, which was the American code name for the atomic bomb program, were skeptical of the value of the British contribution and suspicious that Britain aimed to acquire nuclear information from America which would be of value for postwar commercial nuclear development. Following meetings between Churchill and Roosevelt at Quebec in 1943 and Hyde Park in 1944, the level of cooperation increased, with many British scientists coming to Los Alamos in New Mexico to work on the project that produced the Hiroshima and Nagasaki atomic bombs. After the war, despite the understanding that Churchill felt he had reached with Roosevelt, America was very unwilling to transmit information on nuclear matters to any other country. America wished to prevent the proliferation of nuclear weapons and in the Baruch Plan of 1946 proposed the international control of nuclear energy by the United Nations. When this proposal proved unworkable, Congress passed the McMahon Act, which imposed a blanket ban on the transmission of information on nuclear matters to any foreign country. The British were very bitter over this matter and felt that the United States had reneged on wartime agreements. In January 1947, a secret British cabinet committee decided that Britain would need to work on its own to construct an atomic bomb. There were some alterations of the provisions of the McMahon Act in subsequent years. In exchange for an increase in the supply of uranium from Canada and Britain, the United States in the modus vivendi of 1948 released some nuclear information to the British, and in 1951 an amendment to the McMahon Act relaxed its provisions a little further. Eisenhower was sympathetic to the British case on the matter. He said at an NSC meeting "that he had a great deal of sympathy with the British position and that their complaints were legitimate. The 1946 law ought to be modified, and he was willing to do all that he could to obtain the modification."[16] In 1954 the Atomic Energy Act allowed wider U.S. collaboration with allies on atomic weapons. In 1952 Britain successfully tested an atomic bomb, and in 1955 Britain deployed the V bomber, which was capable of carrying nuclear bombs. The British nuclear program had been developed, however, at a vastly greater cost and with more delays as a result of the denial of information from the Americans that the British felt had been due to them. On the other side, the Americans had a very ambivalent attitude toward the development of an independent British nuclear deterrent, whatever its cost.

A matter on which there was a much closer degree of Anglo-American cooperation was intelligence. During the Second World War there developed what Bradley Smith has called "the most secret special relationship."[17] As with nuclear research, Britain had more to offer at the beginning of the war, and there was hesitation and reluctance in the exchange of information in the early war years. But in the later years of the war there was full cooperation, especially on such matters as the exchange of Ultra and Magic, that is, code messages from Germany deciphered by Britain and code messages from Japan deciphered by America. After the war there was reluctance to cease this cooperation, which continued, though at a somewhat reduced level, in 1945–46. In 1947 the Central Intelligence Agency (CIA) was established in the United States, with an input of British advice regarding its organization, and from 1947 to 1952 a number of secret agreements were made with the British on intelligence cooperation. There remained some degree of hesitation with regard to exchange of information. Whereas the British had looked down on the Americans at the beginning of World War II on account of the lack of any intelligence establishment in the United States compared to a long British tradition of expertise in this field, by the late 1940s the CIA regarded itself as much more professional than the more amateurish gentlemanly style of

British intelligence in the mode of John Buchan and Ian Fleming. As Ray Cline, a CIA liaison officer with British intelligence in the early 1950s, put it, "There was a feeling that they were stuffy, British old boy stuff."[18] This was particularly the case with regard to Communist infiltration into government, especially into the intelligence services. The British derided the excesses of the red scare in America, with its ludicrous search for reds under the bed and suspicions of the Communist leanings of such figures as Charlie Chaplin. The Americans, however, rather more seriously, were aghast that lax internal security procedures allowed the penetration into the British government of a figure such as Donald MacLean, a British Communist and Soviet agent who became first secretary in the British embassy in Washington, as well as others such as Guy Burgess and Kim Philby, with suspicions of even more. This led some Americans to regard the British as careless and unreliable, but others, such as Ray Cline, emphasized the "unique case of the Cambridge cell—Blunt, Philby, Burgess and MacLean. It could happen in America too: feelings of utopianism, alienation, depression in the 1930s. It was an historical accident."[19] The degree of cooperation between the intelligence services of the two countries continued to be very extensive. The two countries were bound together for Signal Intelligence purposes, with regard to such matters as electronic spying, surveillance, and code-breaking, dividing up different areas of the world and sharing intelligence and information. As John Ranelagh puts it, "The British Secret Intelligence Service has always been the CIA's foremost partner, not simply because of the war alliance and its help in creating OSS and the CIA but also because Britain operates the only other friendly international network."[20]

There was clearly a great need to gather intelligence on the Soviet Union, yet the opportunities to do so were very limited, which added further incentives for Britain and the United States to cooperate. The most important source of human intelligence on the Soviet Union came from German sources, particularly German military targeting plans and German soldiers who had been prisoners of war in the Soviet Union. When these German sources dried up or became dated, further human intelligence provided very little information. Soviet counterintelligence was so ruthless and well organized that few Western agents who went to the Soviet Union or native Soviet sources survived for long. Embassy and consular officials in the Soviet Union were very restricted in their movements, while large parts of the country were totally closed. All the implements of a totalitarian society were put into operation to maintain a totally controlled society.

The main sources of intelligence on the Soviet Union were, therefore, necessarily technological. One source in which there were dramatic new developments was aerial photography. The technology of aerial photography had advanced considerably from its earliest days in World War I and World War II. In the late 1940s and early 1950s cameras became increasingly sophisticated and were able to take sharp and detailed photographs. Since the Soviets, however, were protective of their border and their airspace to the point of paranoia, Western aerial reconnaissance flights close to the Soviet border, let alone penetrating across the border, were extremely hazardous, risking the danger of the plane being shot down and the creation of a serious incident, resulting in vigorous Soviet diplomatic protests and adding to the tensions in relations with the Soviet Union. Throughout the late 1940s and early 1950s, however, both Britain and the United States, with varying degrees of daring, engaged in extensive aerial reconnaissance around the borders of the Soviet Union, using oblique cameras which were capable of photographing dozens of miles within Soviet territory and gathering vast amounts of intelligence on Soviet border installations and defenses, probing soft spots and selecting wartime targets. The British were bold in risking penetration of Soviet airspace, sometimes assisted by American equipment to enable them to do so and to evade Soviet defenses. The fruits of this intelligence, as well as the massive amount of intelligence that was constantly gained through electronic sources by Government Communications Headquarters in Cheltenham, England, and by the National Security Agency in Washington, D.C., were shared between Britain and America.[21]

By the mid-1950s two new means of engaging in aerial photography were about to become operational. First, the U.S. Air Force had developed balloons which could be fitted with cameras and could fly unmanned across the Soviet Union. Although the balloons could fly at 50,000 feet, it was uncertain whether they would be beyond the reach of Soviet defenses and whether they might be blown off course. Moreover, there was some question about whether the quality and usefulness of the pictures that the balloons could take on an uncharted crossing of Soviet territory would make the project worthwhile. Much more sophisticated was the CIA project of a new plane, the U-2, which could fly at 70,000 feet, which was thought to be beyond the reach of Soviet defenses, either antiaircraft missiles or fighter planes, and which possibly would not be detected on Soviet radar. It would be possible, therefore, for the pilot of a U-2 to fly at will across precise sites in the Soviet Union from a base in Western Europe, such as Britain. Such overflights were, however, manifestly breaches of Soviet airspace and Soviet sovereignty, which, if discovered, would be liable to produce Soviet protests of the most vigorous nature and strenuous Soviet efforts to shoot down the intruder. As the Eden-Eisenhower era opened in the spring of 1955, both the balloon project and the U-2 were fast moving from the drawing board to the production stage, creating the possibilities of exciting new intelligence sources of dramatic capabilities but also of commensurate risks.22

A longstanding issue of contention between Britain and the United States was colonialism. Anthony Eden, like Winston Churchill, was of a generation which took great pride in the British Empire, which, it felt, had brought order and good government as well as greater prosperity and the fruits of civilization and the Christian religion to millions of backward people across the globe. Although India had become independent in 1947, and steps toward eventual self-government had been taken in many other colonies, many in Britain envisioned in the early 1950s that a long future lay ahead for the greatest empire that the world had ever known and on which the sun never set. Most Americans took a very different view, with an innate dislike of colonialism and a strong expectation that the countries of the British Empire would become independent in the very near future. From their own national mythology, ideology, and historical tradition, Americans were imbued with a spirit of republican self-government, which made distasteful to them the imposition of colonial rule upon another people by a foreign monarchy. Americans were disappointed that the example which they had set in 1776 had not been followed throughout the rest of the British Empire. Instead the Canadians remained loyal to Britain, and the other white dominions of Australia and New Zealand developed as British dependencies, while the empire expanded in every corner of the globe, including India, Burma, Malaya, and Hong Kong in Asia; the Gold Coast, Nigeria, Kenya, South Africa, and other colonies in Africa; British Guyana, British Honduras, the West Indies, and the Falkland Islands in the Caribbean and Central and South America; and the acquisition of Cyprus and Malta in the Mediterranean, a mandate in Palestine and Transjordan in 1919, and informal control over the Persian Gulf and much of the rest of the Middle East.

A small number among the American elite, such as Theodore Roosevelt, Alfred T. Mahan, and other such jingoist imperialists in the late nineteenth century, felt that, as America's power grew, the United States should act like Britain and, in Rudyard Kipling's phrase, "take up the White Man's burden." America's major experiment in colonialism, however, in the Philippines, which involved a suppression at considerable cost in casualties of a Filipino revolt between 1899 and 1901 as well as long-term foreign policy complications in relations with Japan, dampened enthusiasm for an American empire even among the minority of supporters of American colonialism. America promised that the Philippines would be granted independence in 1945 and, even in the disruptive circumstances of World War II, kept that promise. Much more typical of American attitudes towards colonialism than Theodore Roosevelt was Franklin Roosevelt, who detested colonialism and who constantly jibed Churchill with regard to British colonialism. In the Far East during the Second World War, Anglo-American relations were soured by American suspicions that Britain's strategic objectives in the Far East were not simply to win the war against Japan but to restore British colonial rule in colonies which had been conquered by the Japanese and to safeguard the interests of Britain's other colonies in Asia. The American Joint Chiefs of Staff commented that SEAC was not an abbreviation for South East Asia Command but Save England's Asian Colonies.[23] In the post–World War II world, with the founding of the United Nations and Soviet exploitation of colonialism as a propaganda issue, American pressure on Britain was strong to move in the direction of independence for Britain's colonies.

Eisenhower expressed his views on colonialism most explicitly in a letter to Churchill in 1954.[24] "Colonialism is on the way out as a relationship among peoples," he wrote. "The sole question is one of time and method."[25] Eisenhower suggested that colonial rule now faced a rising spirit of fierce nationalism. If colonial powers attempted to repress this nationalist fervor, "it would," Eisenhower wrote, "burst through the barriers and could create havoc."[26] If, on the other hand, the assurance of self-government at some point in the future was given, "within a space of twenty-five years (or some other agreed upon, definite date)," colonial peoples would be diverted from a nationalist struggle for independence to cooperation with the colonial powers on the practical issues of development and of preparation for self-government, and they would be inclined in fact to wish to delay self-government as they realized the burdens and responsibilities which self-rule would bring. Eisenhower, then, showed himself to be relatively moderate on the issue of colonialism.[27] He shared the basic American distaste for colonial rule. He favored, however, a gradualist approach to bringing about an end to colonial rule, one which might vary from one colony to another but which would, above all, dampen intense nationalism that could lead to violence and create opportunities for exploitation by Communists both within the colonies and from the Kremlin.

Churchill was not impressed by Eisenhower's views on colonialism.[28] "As a matter of fact the sentiments and ideas which your letter expresses," he wrote in reply to Eisenhower, "are in full accord with the policy now being pursued in all the colonies of the British Empire." Churchill conceded that "in this I must admit that I am a laggard. I am a bit sceptical about universal suffrage for the Hottentots even if refined by proportional representation." Churchill proclaimed his belief with regard to "colonialism, namely: bringing forward backward races and opening up the jungles. I was brought up to feel proud of much that we had done."[29]

In fact, by the mid-1950s, developments were well under way in most of Britain's colonies which would lead to their independence within a decade or so. In some respects, the differences between the British and the Americans over the issue of colonialism were not so much about the issue in itself as over the attitudes that the issue brought out on both sides—an American perception of a British sense of arrogant superiority, which grew out of a class-ridden, privileged, undemocratic society, and, on the other side, a British perception of American self-righteousness, prejudice, and ignorance, which grew out of a shallow, supernationalistic, traditionless society. These differences were apparent in disagreements over policy with respect to the subject in Anglo-American relations that was the most important by far in the Eden-Eisenhower era, namely, an area which was not formally part of the British Empire but where Britain exercised informal control—the Middle East.

Britain's main interests in the Middle East were oil and the route to India. Most of the Middle East had been for centuries part of the Ottoman Empire, whose power and authority steadily declined. Britain protected its interests in the Middle East in the eighteenth and nineteenth century by the exercise of influence with the sultan in Constantinople. In 1798 Napoleon aimed to break British influence in the Middle East by attaining French control over Egypt, constructing a canal linking the Red Sea and the Mediterranean, and ultimately replacing the British with the French in India. Admiral Horatio Nelson's destruction of the French fleet at the Battle of the Nile in 1798 ended Napoleon's ambitions. But French interest in Egypt had been awakened and grew steadily in the nineteenth century. French archaeologists began the modern study of Egyptology in the early nineteenth century. Even more significantly, a French diplomat in the embassy in Cairo, Ferdinand de Lesseps, was asked by the pasha of Egypt, Mohammed Ali, to serve as tutor for his son, Mohammed Said. When Mohammed Said succeeded as pasha in the 1850s, he granted a concession to de Lesseps for the formation of a Suez Canal Company, to fulfill de Lesseps's dream of the construction of the Suez Canal. The shares of the Suez Canal Company were owned mainly by French financiers and the Egyptian government. In 1869 the canal was opened and was a great success. Mohammed Said, however, had become mesmerized by the great wealth which canal tolls might bring in and had begun to engage in wild profligacy even before the canal opened, while his son, Ismail Pasha, had even more extravagant tastes. Consequently, in 1875 Ismail Pasha was desperate to raise money and was willing to sell the shares in the Suez Canal Company of the Egyptian government. The British prime minister, Benjamin Disraeli, seized the opportunity with alacrity and bought up Egypt's shares for the British government. Thereafter, the Suez Canal Company was a joint enterprise, consisting of French financiers and the British government. In 1876 Queen Victoria acquired a new title, Empress of India, which put even greater emphasis on India as the jewel in the crown of the British Empire and made the Suez Canal, the key to the route to India, even more a symbol of British imperial might.

In 1882 when troubles arose in Egypt over increasingly impotent attempts by the Ottoman Empire to wield authority, British forces moved in to quell the troubles. They remained there for over seventy years. Under such proconsular figures as Lord Cromer, Egypt was ruled as an informal part of the British Empire. British colonial influence grew as the British surpassed the French in the field of Egyptology, with major excavations and spectacular discoveries by such figures as Lord Carnarvon and Howard Carter, including the tomb of Tutankhamen in the Valley of the Kings near Luxor in 1922. Many of the treasures of Egypt were shipped off to the British Museum in London, although others, such as the contents of the tomb of Tutankhamen, were put into the Cairo Museum. Egypt became a fashionable wintering spot for the British, to visit the Pyramids at Giza or to drink gin and tonics in the gardens of the Cataract Hotel in Aswan, where Agatha Christie wrote *Death on the Nile*.

Despite the hopes of Lawrence of Arabia for self-government for Arab countries after World War I, British rule continued in Egypt. A 1922 treaty formally recognized Egypt's independence in theory, but Britain retained many rights and powers. In 1936 a new treaty, which was negotiated by Anthony Eden, specified the situation more precisely, especially with regard to the very large military base which the British had built on the west side of the Suez Canal. This base was of vital importance in World War II, when Field Marshall Erwin Rommel attempted to succeed where Napoleon had failed by taking over control of Egypt and the Suez Canal and destroying British rule in India. The British Eighth Army under General Bernard Montgomery won as glorious a triumph at El Alamein as had Nelson at the Battle of the Nile, and Rommel was driven out of Egypt and in due course out of North Africa. During the war there were a number of signs of nationalist protest in Egypt, which were suppressed, but which were indicators of trends for the future.

Of increasing importance to Britain in the Middle East, however, was oil. In the first decade of the twentieth century explorations for oil were conducted in Iran, and the Anglo-Iranian Oil Company (AIOC) was founded, which exercised considerable economic influence over Iran. Britain did not exercise direct political control over Iran, but in Iraq, in which large quantities of oil were discovered, Britain gained influence and a large measure of control over the rulers In the same way that Britain acquired control over other parts of the Middle East, such as Transjordan, Kuwait, and the sheikdoms on the Persian Gulf such as Abu Dhabi. The United States made its entry into the world of Middle Eastern oil in 1933, when Standard Oil of California acquired a concession in Saudi Arabia and created a subsidiary to develop it, the Arabian American Oil Company. Britain was suspicious of American ambitions with regard to oil in the Middle East. This was increasingly the case in the post–World War II period. When in 1951 a left-wing nationalist government in Iran led by Mohammed Mossadeq nationalized AIOC, Britain planned to overthrow Mossadeq by covert action but was restrained by the United States on the grounds that this would seem a colonialist-style intervention. In 1953, however, the CIA took covert action in Iran, stirring up the mob in Tehran, to bring down Mossadeq and to restore to power Shah Reza Pahlavi, under whose rule American influence in Iran increased, while British influence and control over the oil industry diminished. British and American interests in the Middle East differed also on other matters, especially the status of Palestine and policies to keep the Soviet Union out of the region.

Palestine had been part of the Ottoman Empire for centuries. In the late nineteenth century the Zionist movement developed, pressing for a homeland for the Jews. The Zionist cause was given a major boost with the proclamation in 1917 of the Balfour Declaration, a statement of support by British Foreign Secretary John Balfour for a Jewish homeland in Palestine. This became particularly significant when Britain acquired a mandate for rule over Palestine at the Versailles Peace Conference in 1919. Britain was very aware, however, of the deep hatred of the Jews on the part of the Arabs, who regarded Jews as foreign, European invaders bent on taking over land on which Arabs had lived for centuries. Britain, therefore, wishing to maintain good relations with the Arabs, did not allow many Jews to immigrate to

Palestine in the interwar years. The Holocaust in World War II changed the situation, creating strong worldwide sympathy for the Jews, especially among the Americans. Many Jews had immigrated to America and became politically influential, especially in the key electoral states of New York and California. American Jews put pressure on the administration of Harry Truman to persuade the British government to allow increased Jewish immigration into Palestine, which Britain was reluctant to concede. The situation became disorderly when many Jews immigrated illegally to Palestine; many Americans regarded them as heroic figures of the Exodus returning home, but the British attempted to deport them in order to allay Arab protests. Facing Jewish terrorist activity against British soldiers in Palestine as well as severe economic problems, Britain decided in 1948 to give up the Palestine mandate and to hand the matter over to the United Nations. In May 1948, the Jews in Palestine declared the state of Israel. Neighboring Arab countries went to war against Israel, but Israeli military prowess held the Arab states at bay, and in January 1949 a truce was signed. This brought a ceasefire, but no Arab nations recognized the state of Israel.

The United States had been the first nation to recognize Israel, and in the 1948 presidential election the Jewish vote was regarded as crucial to Truman's surprising reelection. The British were wary of the influence of the Jewish lobby in American politics. In 1950 the United States, Britain, and France issued the Tripartite Declaration, stating that problems in the Middle East should not be resolved by force and that nations should not make arms sales to any nation in the region that would upset the military balance in the area. In 1952 Eisenhower's election brought in a Republican administration which was less beholden to the Jewish vote than the previous Democratic administration. The Eisenhower administration worked with the British government to attempt to bring about a settlement of the Arab-Israeli dispute, especially the Alpha Project in 1955, a secret plan to settle the Middle East conflict by some border adjustments and Western financial support for the resettlement of Palestinian refugees, who had fled from or been driven out of Israel in 1948. The British felt that the Eisenhower administration was more evenhanded toward Israel and the Arab states than Truman had been, but the British were afraid that the political pressures of the Jewish lobby would lead the Eisenhower administration, especially in election years, to favor Israel and to further alienate the Arabs.

The United States and Britain had a common interest in trying to keep the Soviet Union out of the Middle East, but the American and British approach to this matter differed. Britain aimed to maintain its political dominance and military strength in the region, especially in Egypt, where King Farouk was a weak leader susceptible to British control and where Britain had a very large base with 80,000 troops on the west bank of the Suez Canal. Growing nationalist resentment against the British in Egypt, however, led in 1949 to the repudiation of the Treaty of 1936 by the Egyptian government, while terrorist activity, together with the financial burden, made the maintenance of the Suez base increasingly difficult. The British position became even more difficult after 1952, when Farouk was overthrown by the Young Officers Movement, which was fronted by General Mohammed Neguib but whose real leader was Colonel Gamal Abdel Nasser, who assumed power in 1954. The development of nuclear weapons had in any event made Britain's Suez base vulnerable to a Soviet nuclear attack. Britain, therefore, began to develop a strategy to keep the Soviets out of the Middle East by building up an alliance of countries in the northern tier, such as Iraq and Turkey. This produced the Baghdad Pact in early 1955, signed initially by Iraq and Turkey and joined by Britain and Pakistan.

The United States was not averse to leaving to Britain the pursuit of policies to keep the Soviets out of the Middle East. On the other hand, America felt that Britain's colonialist attitudes were liable to alienate the Arab nations and to provide opportunities for Soviet penetration. The United States pressed Britain to withdraw from Egypt. The Churchill administration, which had come into office in 1951, was very reluctant to withdraw from Egypt, but after lengthy and difficult negotiations Britain agreed in 1954 to withdraw from the Suez base, with the last troops to leave in the spring of 1956. The United States realized that Arab radical nationalists created problems and dangers for the West, but America hoped that a figure such as Nasser, who had ambitions to unite all Arabs under his leadership and to throw off the yoke of colonialism, could be courted and kept in the Western camp rather than being alienated by colonialist policies which could drive him towards the Soviet Union. The CIA and the State Department both realized that Nasser was a dangerous radical, but he was not a Communist, and the United States took steps both by covert and overt action, including supplying arms to Nasser, to try to develop good relations with him. The British agreed that policies such as economic aid to Egypt were desirable and justifiable in order to try to gain at least a measure of Egyptian goodwill and to keep out Soviet influence. But the supply of American weapons to Egypt, at a time when British soldiers were being killed by Egyptians, incensed the British, who were at the same time irritated by sanctimonious American expressions of anti-imperialism and by what the British considered to be

American naïveté and stupidity in its foreign policy in an area in which the United States had no knowledge or experience. The British were also displeased that the Americans, somewhat paradoxically, did not choose to join the Baghdad Pact. The United States believed that American participation in the Baghdad Pact would further alienate Nasser, who disliked an alliance that brought an Arab nation, Iraq, into a Western-oriented security organization instead of into an all-Arab union under Nasser's leadership. At the same time, the Jewish lobby in America was opposed to American participation in a security alliance that included an Arab nation while Israel was not a member of any such collective security alliance. Thus, although Britain and America had many common interests in the Middle East, they also had many differences, which made them suspicious rivals as much as close allies in the region.[30]

While Anglo-American differences over the Middle East simmered in the background in the 1940s and early 1950s, differences over the Far East were much sharper and more prominent. During World War II, the Anglo-American alliance in the Far East was much less close than in Europe and in the Mediterranean. In the Far East in World War II, Britain and the United States were "allies of a kind," in the phrase of the leading historian of the subject.[31] The British could not understand the American obsession of attaching such prominence to China, while the Americans were suspicious that Britain's main interest in China was simply to regain her colony in Hong Kong. Following the Communist revolution in China in 1949, there were bitter Anglo-American disagreements when Britain gave diplomatic recognition to the government in Beijing and the United States did not. In Korea, the British supported the initial intervention in June 1950 to prevent a takeover of South Korea by North Korea, which was seen as a move instigated by the Soviet Union, manipulating its puppet, North Korea. In the autumn of 1950, however, when the North Koreans had been driven out of South Korea and the forces of General Douglas MacArthur invaded North Korea, bringing the Chinese into the war, the British were eager to reach a settlement with the Chinese and to make concessions. This infuriated the Americans, who felt that a strong, united stand against Chinese aggression was imperative. In Indochina, Eden felt that the Geneva Conference of 1954 brought an end to hostilities on the best terms available, given the West's weak bargaining position after the French defeat at Dienbienphu. Many Americans, however, especially Dulles, believed that the British had pulled the rug from under Dulles's United Action plan, which might have deterred the Communists in Indochina. Instead, the result was that a settlement had been made which resulted in a Communist regime in North Vietnam that threatened to expand communism into South Vietnam and elsewhere throughout Southeast Asia. Dulles fumed that "far from thinking their policy a failure, the British believed it a glowing success."[32] In the crisis in the Taiwan Straits in 1954–55, Britain advocated the abandonment of the offshore islands of Quemoy and Matsu, which seemed indefensible, lying within ten miles of the coast of China, and concentration on the defense of Taiwan, which was a hundred miles from China. The United States, however, took a rigid stance in arguing that since Quemoy and Matsu were part of the territory of Nationalist China, abandonment of these small offshore islands would demoralize the regime in Taiwan and send a dangerous signal of appeasement to Communist China. The British were alarmed that the United States threatened the use of nuclear weapons in the defense of Quemoy and Matsu, and Churchill and Eisenhower engaged in extremely strong disagreements in their correspondence over the issue.[33]

European unity was another issue on which Anglo-American divergence was strong, though manifestations of disagreements were less sharp than over the Far East. Many Americans had developed a firm belief that the fundamental solution to the conflicts in Europe, which had led to two world wars, lay in European unity, following the American model of federation and cooperation. The British, however, felt that their worldwide connections, particularly the empire and commonwealth and the special relationship with the United States, made British participation in a united Europe undesirable. Some British leaders, such as Churchill, spoke out strongly in favor of unity among the continental European nations, but these leaders believed that the British role should be to encourage unity among those other countries rather than to become directly involved, as that would entail the loss of a degree of British sovereignty. Anthony Eden, though modern and sophisticated in his outlook on Europe and with vast experience in diplomatic contacts in Europe, tended to emphasize Britain's worldwide position and consequently to be unenthusiastic over British entanglement in Europe. Eisenhower, especially after his term as SACEUR in 1950–52, was a strong supporter of cooperation and unity in Europe, particularly in defense and the economy, and he felt that Britain was thinking too much in terms of the past with respect to worldwide connections and that the British should become more involved with modern European statesmen, such as Jean Monnet, and new European institutions, such as the Coal and Steel Community. Eisenhower realized, however, that there had been constant American pressure since World War II to push Britain into a united Europe, which many in Britain resented.

The final issue on which there were severe Anglo-American tensions was the economy. Britain exhausted herself economically in the Second World War, and postwar economic recovery was very slow. An important underlying source of British resentment was that America had benefited economically while remaining on the sidelines in 1939–41, as in 1914–17, and indeed as in the wars of the French Revolution and the Napoleonic era. Americans, on the other hand, believed that they had shown great generosity in their aid to Britain, even while the United States was still a neutral, and that America had been generous in its programs of postwar aid, such as the British loan in 1946, the Marshall Plan, and continuing military assistance. The British, however, felt that they should have received a grant instead of a loan in 1946. They resented some of the conditions attached to the Marshall Plan and even more so the humiliation of being placed in a position of being a supplicant and a recipient of American charity. With regard to military assistance, Britain resented that, after embarking on a huge program of rearmament in the early 1950s on the understanding that very large sums of American military aid would be forthcoming, American aid was much less in practice, resulting in a serious overstraining of Britain's financial resources. This was an important reason for Britain's slow economic growth compared to her European rivals such as France or, even more galling, West Germany.

There were, moreover, some particular issues, especially relating to trade, which produced sharp clashes between Britain and the United States. In the immediate postwar years the United States set out with a zeal, which the British regarded as somewhat messianic, to impose a new world trading order, which would establish free trade and remove restrictions such as those imposed by cartels, bilateral agreements, and imperial preferences. Britain did not disagree with the fundamental objectives of these policies but felt that the United States used its economic dominance to impose conditions which were favorable to the United States and which allowed exceptions for the United States, such as high American tariffs on some goods, while forbidding such exceptions to other countries such as Britain. Sharp differences also arose over trade with Communist countries. Britain took a more tolerant view on this matter and felt that trade was a useful channel to normalizing relations; trade with Eastern bloc countries also enabled Britain to import goods such as timber from a nondollar area, which helped Britain's economic situation. The United States took a much more rigid stance, regarding trade with Communist countries, in Eisenhower's Defense Secretary Charles Wilson's phrase, "like selling firearms to the Indians."[34] Right-wing congressional backwoodsmen had extremely strong feelings on this issue. In 1951 Representative Laurie C. Battle sponsored the Mutual Defense Control Act (the Battle Act) which linked American aid to observance of export restrictions. Truman and even more so Eisenhower were willing to be more flexible on trade, but they were under strong domestic political pressure as well as legislative restrictions to try to prohibit trade by the allies with Communist countries. At an NSC meeting in 1954, "the President commented, with evident heat, that we were allowing a bunch of damned idiots to force us into policies with respect to trade that were absolutely foolish."[35] Eisenhower said that "to his way of thinking, barring trade was just about as silly as censorship."[36] He argued that "we had better make up our minds to be pretty generous and go along as far as possible with British requests for relaxation of controls of some items."[37]

There was general agreement among Western countries that they should not trade in military goods with Communist countries. There was disagreement, however, on nonmilitary goods, especially the large number of goods which could possibly be used for either military or nonmilitary purposes. In 1949 the Coordinating Committee of the Paris Consultative Group of Nations, or COCOM, was formed to try to establish regulations by the United States, Western Europe, and Japan with regard to acceptable and prohibited items for trade with the Soviet Union and Eastern Europe. After the Communist takeover in China, the Coordinating Committee established a similar mechanism, CHINCOM, to try to regulate and restrict trade with Communist China. But it was a matter on which there was endless wrangling, and no acceptable consensus could be reached.[38]

In 1955, then, Eden and Eisenhower inherited a long tradition with respect to the general issue of the Anglo-American relationship as well as the evolution of areas of agreement and disagreement with regard to particular issues. In some respects, the Anglo-American relationship was justifiably regarded as a special relationship. America, for all its emphasis on uniqueness, derived not only its language but a great deal of its political, economic, and cultural traditions from Britain. America's ideology and the American political system had not sprung from the heads of the Founding Fathers but had evolved from the constitutional struggles in England, from Magna Carta to the conflicts between monarch and parliament in Tudor, Stuart, and Hanoverian times. The American economic system owed much to Adam Smith as well as to the economic system which had developed in colonial times. American culture was strongly influenced by English writers such as Shakespeare and Dickens. America had been populated largely by British people until the mid-nineteenth century, and European immigrants in the subsequent years had learned the English language and, in the most important essentials, conformed to established Anglo-American institutions. With these foundations, the two nations had undergone an intense bonding experience in World War II, which, despite disagreement on details of strategy, had created a profound sense of unity of purpose in saving Western civilization from Nazi barbarism and in safeguarding the West against the new threat from Soviet imperialism. There might, then, be disputes over such matters as trade or Taiwan, but such disagreements were superficial and fundamentally there existed a very special relationship.

In other respects, however, the Anglo-American relationship did not seem so special at all. The earliest post–World War II writings on Anglo-American relations by such historians as Harry Allen and Herbert Nicholas emphasized the closeness of the Anglo-American partnership.[39] More recent historians, such as David Reynolds, William Roger Louis, Robert Hathaway, Robin Renwick, and others have suggested that the special relationship has been somewhat mythologized and sentimentalized.[40] These historians emphasize that Britain and the United States have not always been friends but that the deeper tradition is of rivalry and at times hostility. After the conflicts of the War of American Independence and the War of 1812, America concentrated on internal development, overtaking Britain in population in the 1840s and surpassing Britain's industrial production by the 1890s. There were many disagreements throughout the nineteenth century over such issues as boundary disputes in the Oregon Territory and disputes during the Civil War over maritime rights and possible British recognition of the Confederacy. At the end of the nineteenth century there was a rapprochement and the development of an Anglophile elite, but the shallowness of this improved relationship became evident at Versailles in the bitter disputes over colonies, reparations, and other such issues. In the interwar years there was a deep Anglophobic feeling that America had been deceived and been used by the British in World War I, which was one of the major elements within American isolationism in these years. Naval rivalry and disputes over war debts brought Anglo-American relations in the 1920s and 1930s to a new low. The Second World War partnership, against that background, had the semblance almost of an alliance of convenience, while the postwar relationship had its strongest glue in the mutual security requirements of the Cold War.

An evaluation of the issues in Anglo-American relations in the correspondence between Eden and Eisenhower, 1955–57, should help to cast some light on the nature of the Anglo-American relationship in that period. This can be assessed by an evaluation of the evidence from the correspondence on such issues as trade, intelligence, relations with the Soviet Union, and, in a category by itself, the Suez crisis. Assessment can also be made of what evidence the correspondence provides with regard to Eden's capability in his conduct of the office of prime minister and with regard to the revisionist view of Eisenhower's presidency, which portrays Eisenhower as a much more engaged and capable president than earlier interpretations suggested.

It may be helpful, for the reader's greater appreciation of the correspondence, to bear these issues in mind while reading the correspondence. An evaluation of these issues will be presented in the Conclusion. On the other hand, the main purpose in an edition of correspondence is simply to present the correspondence to the reader.

NOTES

1. Walter Isaacson and Evan Thomas, *The Wise Men: Six Friends and the World They Made: Acheson, Bohlen, Harriman, Kennan, Lovett, McCloy* (New York: Simon and Schuster, 1988), 19.

2. Oliver Franks to Ernest Bevin, August 16, 1950, FO 800/517/106, PRO.

3. Minute by Bernard Gage, August 21, 1945, FO 371/44538/AN2505/4/45, PRO. (In British government documents, the term minute, which is commonly used, means a marginal comment or brief note.)

4. Minute by John C. Donnelly, May 17, 1946, FO 371/51607/AN1515/1/45, PRO.

5. John Colville, *The Fringes of Power: Downing Street Diaries, 1939–1955* (London: Hodder and Stoughton), 654.

6. James H. Burnham, *Containment or Liberation* (New York: J. Day, 1953), 43.

7. Churchill to Eisenhower, March 11, 1953, in *The Churchill-Eisenhower Correspondence, 1953–1955*, ed. Peter G. Boyle (Chapel Hill: University of North Carolina Press, 1990), 31.

8. Eisenhower to Churchill, March 11, 1953, in *Churchill-Eisenhower Correspondence*, 32.

9. Churchill to Eisenhower, March 9, 1954, in *Churchill-Eisenhower Correspondence*, 124.

10. Eisenhower to Churchill, March 19, 1954, in *Churchill-Eisenhower Correspondence*, 126.

11. Churchill to Eisenhower, August 8, 1954, in *Churchill-Eisenhower Correspondence*, 166–67.

12. Eisenhower to Churchill, December 14, 1954, in *Churchill-Eisenhower Correspondence*, 182.

13. Duncan Campbell, *Unsinkable Aircraft Carrier: American Military Power in Britain* (London: Michael Joseph, 1984).

14. *Parliamentary Debates*, 5th ser., vol. 484 (1950–51), col. 630.

15. C. J. Bartlett, *The "Special Relationship": A Political History of Anglo-American Relations since 1945* (London: Longman, 1992), 52.

16. 203rd meeting of NSC, June 28, 1954, AWF, NSC Series, box 5.

17. Bradley Smith, *The Ultra-Magic Deals and the Most Secret Special Relationship, 1940–1946* (Shrewsbury: Airlife Publishers, 1993).

18. John Ranelagh, *The Agency: The Rise and Decline of the* CIA (New York: Simon and Schuster, 1986), 253.

19. Ibid., 254.

20. Ibid., 253.

21. Richard J. Aldrich, *The Hidden Hand: Britain, America and Cold War Secret Intelligence* (London: John Murray, 2002); Paul Lashmar, *Spy Flights of the Cold War* (Stroud: Sutton Publishing, 1996); William E. Burrows, *By Any Means Necessary: America's Secret Air War in the Cold War* (New York: Farrar, Straus and Giroux, 2001).

22. Curtis Peebles, *Shadow Flights: America's Secret Air War against the Soviet Union* (Novato, Calif.: Presidio Press, 2000); Gregory W. Pedlow and Donald E. Walzenbach, *The* CIA *and the* U-2 *Program, 1954–1974* (Washington, D.C.: Center for the Study of Intelligence, Central Intelligence Agency, 1998); Michael Beschloss, *Mayday: Eisenhower, Khrushchev and the* U-2 *Affair* (New York: Harper and Row, 1986); Norman Polmar and Mike Haenggi, eds., *Spyplane: The* U-2 *Declassified* (Asceola, Wis.: Motorbooks International, 2001); Chris Pocock, *The* U-2 *Spyplane: Toward the Unknown: A New History of the Early Years* (Atglen, Pa.: Schiffer Publications, 2000).

23. Mark A. Stoler, *Allies as Adversaries: The Joint Chiefs of Staff, The Grand Alliance and U.S. Strategy in World War II* (Chapel Hill: University of North Carolina Press, 2000), 244.

24. Eisenhower to Churchill, July 22, 1954, in *Churchill-Eisenhower Correspondence*, 162–65.

25. Ibid., 163.

26. Ibid.

27. Ibid., 164.

28. Churchill to Eisenhower, August 8, 1954, in *Churchill-Eisenhower Correspondence*, 166–68.

29. Ibid., 167.

30. Ritchie Ovendale, *Britain, the United States and the Transfer of Power in the Middle East, 1945–1962* (Leicester: Leicester University Press, 1996); Peter Hahn, *The United States, Great Britain and Egypt, 1945–1956* (Chapel Hill: University of North Carolina Press, 1991); Matthew F. Holland, *America and Egypt: From Roosevelt to Eisenhower* (Westport, Conn.: Praeger, 1996); Robert McNamara, *Britain, Nasser and the Balance of Power in the Middle East, 1952–1957* (London: Frank Cass, 2003); Ray Takeyh, *The Origins of the Eisenhower Doctrine: The United States, Britain and Nasser's Egypt, 1953–1957* (Basingstoke: Macmillan, 2000).

31. Christopher Thorne, *Allies of a Kind: The United States, Britain and the War against Japan, 1941–1945* (New York: Oxford University Press, 1978).

32. 204th Meeting of NSC, June 24, 1954, AWF, NSC Series, box 5.

33. Boyle, *Churchill-Eisenhower Correspondence*, 189–98.

34. Philip J. Funigiello, *American-Soviet Trade and the Cold War* (Chapel Hill: University of North Carolina Press, 1988), 76.

35. 187th Meeting of NSC, March 4, 1954, AWF, NSC Series, box 5.

36. 205th Meeting of NSC, July 1, 1954, AWF, NSC Series, box 5.

37. 191st Meeting of NSC, April 1, 1954, AWF, NSC Series, box 5.

38. Burton I. Kaufman, *Trade and Aid: Eisenhower's Foreign Economic Policy, 1953–1961* (Baltimore, Md.: Johns Hopkins University Press, 1982); Funigiello, *American-Soviet Trade*.

39. H. C. Allen, *Great Britain and the United States: A History of Anglo-American Relations, 1783–1952* (London: Odhams Press, 1954); H. C. Nicholas, *Britain and the United States* (London: Chetto and Windus, 1963).

40. David Dimbleby and David Reynolds, *An Ocean Apart: The Relationship between Britain and America in the Twentieth Century* (London: Hodder and Stoughton, 1988); William Roger Louis and Hedley Bull, eds., *The "Special Relationship": Anglo-American Relations since 1945* (Oxford: Clarendon Press, 1984); Robert M. Hathaway, *Great Britain and the United States: Special Relations since World War II* (Boston: Twayne Publishers, 1990); Robin W. Renwick, *Fighting with Allies: America and Britain in Peace and War* (Basingstoke: Macmillan, 1996); Bartlett, *"The Special Relationship"*; Coral Bell, *The Debatable Alliance: An Essay in Anglo-American Relations* (London: Oxford University Press, 1964); Bruce M. Russett, *Community and Contention: Britain and America in the Twentieth Century* (Westport, Conn.: Greenwood Press, 1983); Donald Cameron Watt, *Succeeding John Bull: America in Britain's Place* (Cambridge: Cambridge University Press, 1984); John Dickie, *"Special" No More: Anglo-American Relations: Rhetoric and Reality* (London: Weidenfeld and Nicholson, 1994); Alan P. Dobson, *Anglo-American Relations in the Twentieth Century* (London: Routledge, 1995); John R. Charmley, *Churchill's Grand Alliance: The Anglo-American Special Relationship, 1940–1957* (London: Hodder and Stoughton, 1995); Jonathan Hollowell, ed., *Twentieth-Century Anglo-American Relations* (Basingstoke: Palgrave, 2001).

CORRESPONDENCE, PART I
From Eden's Accession to the Outbreak of the Suez Crisis, April 1955–July 1956

EDEN TO EISENHOWER
April 7, 1955
Dear Mr. President,

I want to send this letter to thank you for the kind and generous things you said in your statement on my appointment as Prime Minister.[1] They have encouraged me so much.

The memory of all the work done together with you in utter confidence and trust was always an inspiration to my great predecessor. It will be so to me as well.

I look forward to the closest co-operation with you and your administration at all times. I will do everything in my power to ensure that the good purposes which our two countries share as friends and members of the Atlantic community are steadfastly pursued.

Kindest regards.

Yours sincerely,
Anthony

1. On April 6, 1955, Eisenhower issued a public statement welcoming Eden's appointment as Churchill's successor as prime minister of Britain.

EISENHOWER TO EDEN
April 8, 1955
Dear Anthony,

Through this note I send my salute to you as the Prime Minister of Her Majesty's Government of the United Kingdom. It gives me tremendous satisfaction to do so, a fact concerning which I am sure you have not the slightest doubt.

I most earnestly hope that your Premiership will be notable in the history of your country and of the world by the progress toward world peace that will be achieved. I know there is no one better fitted than you to seize the opportunities inherent in your new office for helping to guide the world toward the goal we all so earnestly seek.

On the more personal side, I cannot tell you how delighted I am that my old friend Winston has been succeeded by an equally valued friend in an office in which friendliness and genuine readiness to cooperate can mean so much to my own country.

With my confident belief in the brilliant career ahead of you, and my very best wishes and warm regard,

As ever,

DE

P.S. Won't you please convey my warm greetings to your Lady?

EISENHOWER TO EDEN

April 9, 1955

Dear Anthony,

Your letter of the seventh apparently crossed in the mails with one I dispatched to you on the following day. I merely repeat that it is a tremendous satisfaction to me that you and Harold Macmillan will be the old friends with whom Foster and I will be working as we attempt to concert our actions and thinking in reaching for our common goals.[1]

With warm personal regard,

Sincerely,

D.E.

1. Harold Macmillan was appointed foreign secretary when Eden became prime minister. John Foster Dulles was U.S. secretary of state, 1953–59.

EDEN TO EISENHOWER

April 11, 1955

My dear Mr. President,

It was more than kind of you to send me such a heart-warming salute. I am sure that you can have no doubt of the sincere admiration I have felt for so many years for the services you have rendered not only to your own country but to the world. More particularly I recall those dark days in Europe in the early nineteen-fifties when your name and leadership were the compelling factor in the first building of Western defence.[1]

You will know that I will do everything I can to help the course of the relations between our two countries run smoothly. In the many anxious problems which face me here, nothing gives me more pleasure than to know that our common friendship will help us to find the joint solutions we seek.

I hope that you will allow me from time to time to address you where there is some particular aspect of a problem which I would like to present to you and that you won't hesitate to tell me of any reflections or criticism you may have. Foster and Harold will I am sure build up a close understanding and friendship.

Clarissa joins me in warmest greetings to Mrs. Eisenhower and yourself.[2]

Yours ever,

Anthony

1. Eisenhower was the first supreme Allied commander, Europe, (SACEUR), 1950–52, after the formation of NATO.

2. Eden's second marriage was to Clarissa Churchill, niece of Winston Churchill, in 1952.

EDEN TO EISENHOWER

May 5, 1955

Dear Mr. President,

You will have heard, no doubt, of our proposal to the joint meeting of officials in London that the time has come when "top level" talks, between heads of Government, could play a useful part in the reduction of world tension. This may be rather a surprise to you, but I do pray that you may give it earnest consideration. Of course we don't believe that everything can be settled in a few hours or days conversation. But I do really think that to arrange such a meeting would have great advantages.

After a full and frank review of the problems, a further programme of work could be drawn up, with a far better chance of success than by any other means, if only because the imagination of all the peoples of the world will have been stirred. Meetings of Foreign Ministers could follow, and any lines of progress explored. But to start off with such discussions may be the best hope of getting progress later. I do hope you will be willing to try this. The hopes of so many people, on both sides of the iron curtain, have been raised and a kind of mystique surrounds the idea. This may be foolish, but it is human. If our meeting was publicly represented more as a starting point than as a final solution these hopes would be kept alive. I must also tell you that much in our country depends upon it; this is not a party question here, but responds to a deep desire of our whole people.[1]

Of course our Foreign Secretaries could have an earlier meeting to arrange the form of our talks if you thought this necessary. In any event they would come with us. Our meeting, so far as the principals are concerned, need not last more than a very few days. A great advantage would be that it would give us time—and we need time for things to quieten, especially in the East. I do not think that anyone would precipitate trouble and try rash adventures while such a meeting was in the air.

This would help us all. Moreover, I believe if we issue the invitation promptly it may get in ahead of any tiresome Soviet approach to the Germans. Of course, if the Russians turn it down, our people and the other peoples of our alliance would feel that at least we have tried. And a fresh and much needed impulse would be given to N.A.T.O. and the efforts of each member state.

Could you consider this, and Foster could discuss it further with Harold in Paris.[2]

With kindest regards,

Anthony

1. A general election was due to be called in Britain within the next year. Eden was eager to seek a fresh mandate soon after his accession. A summit meeting was felt to be a popular proposal, which, at least in the short term, it was hoped, would create an atmosphere of improving the prospects for peace. This would be helpful to Eden and the Conservative Party in an election, which was held on May 26, 1955.

2. Dulles was scheduled to meet Macmillan in Paris on May 7–13, 1955, at a meeting of the North Atlantic Council and at subsequent meetings that would include French Foreign Minister Antoine Pinay.

EISENHOWER TO EDEN

May 6, 1955

Dear Anthony,

While we are a bit surprised that you have gone so far in your thinking as to present your idea as a definite proposal, nevertheless Foster and I have together spent some hours on it, and I give you my immediate reactions as follows:—

We appreciate the importance to you of this project under existing circumstances, and are naturally disposed to do everything we can to further it. On the other hand, you will understand that we also have our local problems, including public opinion, to consider. We believe that it would be wholly impractical to have such a meeting with a previously announced specific agenda covering a global variety of subjects. At the other extreme, we think it would be most unwise to meet without giving the world some clear intimation of the generality of the subjects to be discussed. The reason for this is that almost every nation in the world will believe its interests are in some way to be affected by such a conference and would therefore be resentful at its lack of representation.

If there were to be a meeting, general subjects to be talked about might, we suppose, include some or all of the following:—

Exploration of ways and means of eliminating or minimizing atomic
   activity and armaments;
the general subject of disarmament by the large nations;
the limitation of forces in continental Europe that belong to nations
   outside that area; and, possibly,
a general limitation of armaments in the European area.

Another subject that might be added would be the reunification of Germany, but for this one the announcement should specify that Germany would be represented. To this of course could be added the perennial question of lessening of world tensions.

Even if such a procedure could prudently be followed, it would seem to us most unwise to attempt to hold a meeting without some form of preparation through our Secretaries of State. If those officials could meet informally, possibly when they are in Vienna, and discuss this matter and each suggest to his own government that these or similar subjects might be well talked about "at the summit" in order to discover whether or not there was a general willingness to proceed on an honest search for some answers, such a meeting would probably make sense even to the die-hard opponents of any contact with the Communists.[1] I wonder whether such a scheme could be implemented without delaying too long the ability to issue the invitation, which delay might defeat the purposes you may be seeking.

In any event, Foster and I have discussed this at such length that he will be far more capable of clarifying our views to Macmillan and possibly to you than I can do in this hastily written cable.

With warm personal regard,

As ever,

D.E.

1. The foreign ministers of Britain, France, and the United States were scheduled to be in Vienna on May 15, 1955, for the signing of the Austrian State Treaty, which ended the Soviet occupation of the eastern zone of Austria and restored Austrian unity and independence within the framework of a neutral state.

EDEN TO EISENHOWER ———————————————

May 8, 1955

Dear Mr. President,

Thank you so much for all the trouble you have taken. I am sure that we can now leave it to Harold and Foster to work something out. Your understanding help is so valuable to me.

Yours ever,

Anthony

EISENHOWER TO EDEN ———————————————

May 27, 1955

My dear friend,

My enthusiastic congratulations.[1]

Dwight D. Eisenhower

1. In the British general election on May 26, the Conservatives retained power with a majority of fifty-eight seats in the House of Commons.

EDEN TO EISENHOWER ———————————————

May 29, 1955

Dear Mr. President,

Thank you so much for your kind message. These results have exceeded our expectations. But nothing in them gives me more pleasure than to know that we can go on working together.

Anthony

EDEN TO EISENHOWER ———————————————

May 29, 1955

Dear Mr. President,

I have had a personal message from Nehru giving a brief account of Krishna Menon's talks with Chou En-lai.[1] He tells me that Krishna Menon will give us a detailed report when he comes to London shortly. Meanwhile Nehru makes reference to the release of four United States airmen. The following is an extract from his telegram:

> In response to my request, the Chinese Government agreed, "as a first step," to release four U.S. airmen of the Fischer group. This opens the way to further efforts towards final solution of the issue of U.S. nationals in China.
>
> The initial response which the U.S. President and other responsible

statesmen make to the announcement of the release of the four airmen will, if helpful, definitely contribute to further and similar steps.

Announcement in respect of the four airmen will be made in Peking on the evening of the 30th May. Until then the decision must be treated as secret.

I am sure it would be helpful if you felt it possible to express some satisfaction at this news, if it materialises as Nehru foreshadows.[2]

Yours ever,
Anthony

1. Jawaharlal Nehru, prime minister of India; Krishna Menon, foreign minister of India; Chou (Zhou) En-lai, foreign minister of China.

2. Eleven American airmen, who had been shot down during the Korean War when they flew over Chinese territory, were put on trial in Beijing and in November 1954 were found guilty of espionage and sentenced to long terms of imprisonment, ranging from four years to life. Since all but two of the airmen had been in uniform and since the Korean armistice agreement of July 1953 specified that all prisoners of war should be returned, the conviction and imprisonment of these American airmen raised an outcry of protest in the United States and a demand for retaliation against Communist China. The United States made representations through the United Nations, and behind the scenes diplomacy through Britain and India played a part in leading to Chinese agreement in May 1955 to release four of the American airmen: Harold Fischer, Rowland Parks, Lyle Cameron, and Edwin Heller. Later in the summer of 1955 the remaining airmen were also released.

EDEN TO EISENHOWER

May 29, 1955

My dear Mr. President,

Harold is sending Foster a reply to his helpful message about the Four-Power talks. We are in entire agreement with you about the need for adequate preparation by the Western Powers. It is essential that we should all have clear ideas as to our joint attitude on the questions which will be raised.

The proposed programme of talks at the official level and between Foreign Secretaries seems good to me and well planned. But I also feel that we should be wise to have a talk ourselves before meeting the Russians. You have on occasion said that you might be able to visit this country again. Nothing could give greater pleasure in Britain and you would certainly receive a heartfelt welcome from everyone. Is there any possibility that you could come here before the first round of top-level discussions, perhaps in July? We could ask Faure over to join us.[1] It would be a real help to me to talk over our general attitude and the tactics which we might adopt. Nor would it do any harm to display the unity of the West.

I have also been thinking about the length of time that the first round of talks should take. These are to be purely exploratory and intended to find some basis on which further discussions can go on at other levels and at such length as may be necessary. I therefore agree that, apart from practical and personal considerations, we should not allow them to be dragged out. But I am a little apprehensive of our tying ourselves too firmly and rigidly to an exact timetable. We are after all meeting to test the temperature and see what openings there are for useful discussions and an improvement in relations. In my experience it is the informal contacts which are often the more useful with the Russians. This should be especially true if, as I believe, they are—whether for internal or other reasons—more ready for serious discussion now than they have been since the war. Even so they are deeply suspicious and slow-moving animals. I hope therefore that we shall leave ourselves a day or two in hand to extend the talk should this seem desirable at the time. In any event I trust that we shall have a minimum of four to five clear days.

Yours ever,
Anthony

1. Edgar Faure, prime minister of France.

EISENHOWER TO EDEN
May 30, 1955
Dear Anthony,
Thank you very much for your cable. I will be answering it soon.
D.D.E.

EISENHOWER TO EDEN
May 31, 1955
Dear Anthony,
Our recent public statement of satisfaction over the release of four United States airmen conforms, I think, to your suggestion as to what we should do along that line.

I agree that the three Western powers should have a clear accord among themselves as to their joint attitude on questions which will likely be raised at the Conference. I doubt, however, that it will be possible for me personally to undertake attendance at a preliminary meeting which would have as its purpose the formulation of such joint attitudes. It is always an awkward thing for the President to leave this country for more than a day or so, and at this particular time it seems more difficult than is usually the case.[1]

However, it is clear that we must make arrangements that will bring about the desired accord. Possibly Foster and Harold should work on this.

As to the length of the "Summit" meeting, there are several reasons why we do not want it unduly prolonged. The first of these is, again, the difficulty I have mentioned above. The second is that long and laborious meetings, discussing substantive questions, will inevitably lead the public to expect concrete solutions to the specific problems that obviously trouble the world. A meeting of a very few days could logically be accepted by the people as an effort to ease tensions and to outline means and methods of attaching the tough problems we have to face. But a prolonged meeting would lead to expectations which cannot possibly be realized either quickly, or in this kind of meeting. Thirdly, we feel that we must be particularly careful that the meeting and the note on which it ends shall neither raise false hopes among our own people nor create despair among the captive nations.[2]

We are, of course, quite ready to take what time is necessary in such a conference to discuss general attitudes and general methods to be followed in the solution of problems. To attempt more than this and at the same time try to devise a final communiqué that would convince the world that an easing of tensions has actually begun, would, I think, most certainly create confusion. Possibly it might lead the peoples of Eastern Europe to believe that we had finally and irrevocably accepted the status quo with regard to them. This, of course, we must not do.

If necessary, I think I can manage the "clear four to five days" that you believe will be required. But we would want to know that you were prepared to stand with us in preventing the development of long drawn-out, profitless arguments which could have nothing as their purpose except propaganda.

With warm personal regard,

D.E.

1. Eisenhower was referring to the provision in Article I of the U.S. Constitution that the president of the United States must sign or veto bills within ten days; otherwise, if Congress was in session, the bills automatically became law, or if Congress was not in session, they fell by default, which was known as a pocket veto. The president could not sign or veto bills when he was out of the country. Difficulties had arisen over this matter when Woodrow Wilson had been out of the country for a long time for the negotiation of the Treaty of Versailles in 1919 and had returned to Washington in February 1919 in order to sign bills. This had created great difficulties in his relations both with Congress and the negotiating parties at Versailles.

2. The Communist nations of Eastern Europe were routinely referred to in the United States as "the captive nations."

EDEN TO EISENHOWER

June 3, 1955

Dear Mr. President,

Thank you so much for your message. Naturally I am disappointed that you do not feel able to come to this country for preliminary talks, but I quite understand how difficult it would be for you to get away. I am sure excellent preparations will be made by the Foreign Secretaries but I hope that you and I, perhaps with Faure, will have some chance of a talk when we arrive in advance of our meeting with the Russians.

I am very glad that you think you could manage the four to five clear days for the meeting at the summit. I understand your reasons for wanting to identify the problems and discuss methods of work rather than enter into a discussion of solutions. This is our own approach also. It follows that, if we are to carry public opinion with us, the meeting should be presented as a first of a series at various levels to handle the problems confronting the world. For this reason I think it important that we neither in our minds nor in anything we say publicly exclude the possibility of further meetings at the top level if that seems useful.

Yours ever,
Anthony

EISENHOWER TO EDEN

June 3, 1955

Dear Anthony,

My calendar reminds me that in a matter of days you will celebrate the anniversary of your birth, your first as Prime Minister.[1] I know that the occasion will be an especially happy one for you, coming as it does so closely after the events of the past two months. I hope that in the year to come you will know the utmost measure of personal accomplishment and that we all will have the satisfaction of taking a long step forward in our goal of a secure and lasting peace for all the world.

I look forward to seeing you—and in the meantime my felicitations and warm regard.[2]

As ever,

D.E.

1. On June 12, 1955, Eden celebrated his fifty-eighth birthday.
2. Eisenhower and Eden were due to see one another at the summit meeting in Geneva, which had been arranged for July 18–23, 1955.

EDEN TO EISENHOWER

June 10, 1955

Message from Prime Minister to President.

Krishna Menon, who, as you know, has been to Peking to see Chou En-lai, has left here for Washington. I very much hope that amidst all your preoccupations you will be able to find a few minutes to see him. I have had several long talks with him here, and I am sure that his intention is a helpful one. His main idea, after talking to Chou En-lai, is to find ways of reducing tension in the Far Eastern area without discussing any particular solution to the Formosan problem.[1] It seems to me that this approach could avoid some difficulties and may be worthy of pursuing. I know that if you could manage to see him it would give a great deal of satisfaction to India.

1. China claimed Formosa (which was also called Taiwan), an island ninety miles off the coast of China, as part of China and denounced the Nationalist regime in Formosa of Chiang Kai-shek. The United States did not recognize the Communist government of China but recognized Chiang Kai-shek's Nationalist regime as the legitimate government of China.

EDEN TO EISENHOWER

June 12, 1955

Dear Mr. President,

How very kind of you to think of sending me a birthday message. At the moment my birthday is being greeted by the foulest day we have seen this year, pouring rain and blowing a gale.

I am really looking forward to our talks. I think we have the whole business in the right perspective so that nobody will be disappointed if we do not make much progress at one bound, and most will be pleased if we make any.

With many thanks, and best wishes,

Yours,

Anthony

EISENHOWER TO EDEN

June 13, 1955

Thank you for your telegram. I have already set up an engagement with Krishna Menon and Foster Dulles for tomorrow morning, the fourteenth. I shall, of course, be glad to see Mr. Menon.

D.D.E.

EDEN TO EISENHOWER ─────────────────

June 29, 1955

Dear Mr. President,

Harold has told me of your telephone conversation with him at San Francisco.¹ I am delighted to know that you will be in Geneva early on Sunday July 17 and look forward to good talks with you then as you suggest. Harold and I are therefore arranging to reach Geneva by Saturday evening and I will get into touch with you as soon as you arrive.

We are bringing Gault with us and he will be available to you in any way you wish.² He is most happy to come. He will appear with General Brownjohn on our delegation list, suitably disguised.³

Yours ever,
Anthony

1. Harold Macmillan came to the United States at the end of June 1955 to attend a meeting in San Francisco to mark the tenth anniversary of the founding of the United Nations. Eisenhower also attended and met and talked briefly with Macmillan.

2. Brigadier Sir James Gault served as a military assistant to Eisenhower during World War II and also during Eisenhower's term as SACEUR in 1950–52. Eisenhower and Gault had become very good personal friends.

3. General Sir Nevil Brownjohn was chief staff officer, Ministry of Defence.

EDEN TO EISENHOWER ─────────────────

June 30, 1955

Dear Mr. President,

I must approach you about two decisions which are causing us much concern here and which I understand may be shortly taken in the United States. One concerns the award of further contracts for the Chief Joseph Dam, and the other is in regard to the application for increased duties on bicycles.¹

It is my earnest hope that it will be possible to avoid any action in these cases which would run counter to the liberal trade policies we have both been pursuing. Any such action would, in my sincere view, be likely to cause quite disproportionate harm in this country and in Western Europe. Adverse public reaction here and in Europe must hinder the efforts we are all making to expand trade both ways with the United States.

My colleagues and I have been much encouraged by your success in getting the recommendations of the Randall Commission accepted.² The first fruits of this have been the renewal of the Reciprocal Trades Agreement Act for a further three years.³ I do feel, however, that any action, especially at this time, which would throw doubt upon the determination of your great country to pursue liberal trade policies would go far to destroy the hopes in the free world which no one has done as much as you to build up.

I know how difficult these questions can be, but do please help us in these two issues if you can.

Yours ever,
Anthony

1. The English Electric and Export Company made a bid for a contract to install six generators and three transformers for the Chief Joseph Dam on the Columbia River in the state of Washington.

2. Clarence Randall, special consultant to the president, chaired the Commission on Foreign Economic Policy, which was commonly referred to as the Randall Commission. Composed of representatives of the executive branch and of Congress, the commission was established in August 1953, and in January 1954 it published a report on foreign economic policy, which recommended relatively liberal trading policies on the part of the United States.

3. On June 21, 1955, Congress extended for three years the existing trade agreements program with a number of countries, including Britain, and provided new authority for the president to reduce tariffs through trade agreement negotiations.

EISENHOWER TO EDEN

July 1, 1955
Dear Anthony,

I shall, of course, give sympathetic consideration to your letter. Possibly I can do something that you will at least partially approve. I hope so.

I am truly grateful to you for making arrangements to bring Brigadier Gault to Geneva with you.

As ever,
D.E.

THE GENEVA SUMMIT MEETING

The leaders of the United States, Britain, France, and the Soviet Union met in Geneva on July 18–23, 1955, represented by Eisenhower, Eden, Prime Minister Edgar Faure of France, and Nikita Khrushchev, first secretary of the Communist Party of the Soviet Union, and Nikolai Bulganin, chairman of the Council of Ministers of the Soviet Union. Khrushchev and Bulganin were supposedly joint leaders of the Soviet Union, but it became clear that Khrushchev was the effective leader.

The main issues that were discussed at the formal sessions of the conference were German unification, European security, disarmament, and East-West trade and cultural links. No significant progress was made in negotiations at the formal sessions, but there were many opportunities for informal interchanges, at dinner each evening and at lunches and other breaks. These informal meetings, which the Americans had been particularly keen to encourage through such casual events as buffet lunches, helped to create a fairly relaxed and friendly atmosphere, which came to be referred to as "the spirit of Geneva." It did not lead, however, to substantial developments of significant importance. It was agreed that matters of detail should be dealt with at a meeting of the foreign ministers of the four nations in October 1956. At this meeting, matters became bogged down in disagreements, and clashes arose along similar lines to discussions at most Big Power meetings since 1945.

The only unexpected matter which arose was Eisenhower's proposal of open skies, namely, unlimited aerial reconnaissance by the United States over the Soviet Union and by the Soviet Union over the United States, which would give sufficient information on the state of readiness of each side to reassure them against the possibility of surprise attack. The Soviet leaders were unprepared for this proposal. At an informal session, however, Khrushchev said emphatically to Eisenhower that the proposal was unacceptable to the Soviet Union, which rejected any such surveillance as spying in its territory.

It had been hoped that the Geneva conference would initiate a process of regular summit meetings of the four Big Powers, including France, which had not been included in the Big Three meetings at Tehran, Yalta, and Potsdam. In fact, however, this proved to be the first and last Big Four summit meeting. The next such summit meeting in Paris in May 1960 was aborted by the U-2 incident, and subsequently the United States engaged in bilateral U.S.-Soviet summit meetings, ignoring Britain and France, from the Kennedy-Khrushchev meeting in Vienna in 1961 through the Nixon-Brezhnev, Reagan-Gorbachev meetings and beyond.

One result of the Geneva Conference that reflected Britain's continuing relative importance, however, was Soviet acceptance of an invitation to Khrushchev and Bulganin to make a visit to Britain. At one of the breaks at the conference, Bulganin said to Eden that, although as foreign secretary Eden had been to the Soviet Union in the 1930s and during the war, he had not been to the Soviet Union for a long time and that he should come again on a visit. Eden replied that it might be difficult for him to find time but that since no Soviet leader had ever come to Britain, perhaps Bulganin and Khrushchev could come on a visit. Khrushchev joined in the informal conversation and the matter was agreed.

EDEN TO EISENHOWER

July 23, 1955

Dear Mr. President,

Following our conversation about tanks for Iraq, I write to let you know that the United Kingdom Government would be prepared to play their part in providing these, and would accept an expenditure of half a million pounds.[1] As a Centurion with spares costs about £50,000, this would produce ten tanks.

Iraq requires about eighty Centurions. The gift of ten tanks by the United Kingdom would be complementary to the supply of the remaining seventy by the United States under off-shore purchases.[2]

I agree with you that it is important that the shipment of the tanks should begin at the earliest possible moment, and I am giving the necessary instructions so that we can get moving the moment we get the all clear from you.

Yours ever,

AE

1. Tanks for Iraq was one of a large number of items that were discussed at a breakfast meeting between Eisenhower, Eden, Dulles, and Macmillan on July 20, 1955, in the course of the Geneva summit meeting.

2. Offshore purchases referred to purchases by the United States of military equipment that was manufactured by another country for supply to the armed forces of the United States or an American ally.

EDEN TO EISENHOWER

July 26, 1955

It is with the deepest regret that I have learned of the death of Cordell Hull, whose long service and tireless endeavours in the cause of peace will long be remembered in Britain.[1] I grieve for the loss of a personal friend.

Anthony Eden

1. Cordell Hull, U.S. secretary of state, 1933–44.

EISENHOWER TO EDEN

July 26, 1955

Thank you for your message on the death of Cordell Hull. Our nation mourns the loss of a distinguished statesman.

With warm regard,

As ever,

DDE

EISENHOWER TO EDEN ─────────────

August 3, 1955

Dear Anthony,

"Life" for August first contained a number of colored photographs taken at the Geneva Conference that I thought were excellent. The Editors have very kindly made for you a set of two of them, and suggested that I forward the pictures to you as a memento of the event. I am delighted to do so.

If you would like to acknowledge the photographs, a note could be addressed to Mr. Edward K. Thompson, Managing Editor, Life, Rockefeller Center, New York 20, New York.

With warm regard,

As ever,

D.E.

EDEN TO EISENHOWER ─────────────

August 17, 1955

Dear Mr. President,

On my return from a brief holiday in the country I found waiting for me the excellent photographs of Geneva which you sent. I am very glad to have this record of our time together and it was most kind of you to think of sending them to me.

I shall, of course, arrange to thank the Managing Editor of "Life."

I still think that Geneva worked out as well as we could expect but October will show how far such progress is possible.[1] I hope you have had some holiday. We have basked in a wonderful summer here.

Yours ever,

Anthony

1. At the Geneva summit in July 1955, it was agreed that the foreign ministers of the Soviet Union, Britain, France, and the United States should meet in October 1955.

AERIAL RECONNAISSANCE BALLOONS

In the summer of 1955, the U.S. Air Force was ready to put into operation a project of sending reconnaissance balloons on overflights of the Soviet Union. Presidential approval was sought, and since one of the launching pads for the balloons was in Scotland, Eisenhower consulted with Eden about the matter.

Extensive research and development had been conducted in the United States on the balloon project since the idea was first advanced in 1950. Researchers realized that the jet stream could carry balloons from launching pads in Western Europe all the way across the Soviet Union. Extensive work was carried out on cameras which could be fitted into the gondolas of the balloons and on the means of recovering the cameras and the balloons when they exited on the eastern side of Soviet airspace. By 1955, the U.S. Air Force reported that it had solved all of the technical problems involved and had devised a viable project which could gather vast amounts of valuable intelligence from the cameras on the balloons.

The balloons were made of polyethylene and could fly at 50,000 feet, which, it was thought, was beyond the maximum altitude capabilities of Soviet fighter aircraft or antiaircraft shells. The cameras were capable of taking very precise photographs from each side. The balloons were equipped with radio beacons which would be activated after the predicted time it would take a balloon to pass from west to east across Soviet airspace (approximately three days). Once the beam was switched on, the recovery process would come into operation. A specially equipped American C-119 recovery plane would home in and begin to circle far below the balloon. The balloon's gondola was equipped with a device which would cut the camera package free by radio command, and the falling gondola, slowed by parachute, would be snatched out of the sky by grapples which trailed from the C-119, and the camera would be recovered.

The proposed plan was to launch hundreds of balloons in waves over a short period of time, such as over a few weeks. It was thought that this could maximize the photographic coverage that the balloons could obtain, while keeping the Soviets off balance and giving Soviet armed forces less time to rally their defense system against these bewildering intruders.

Balloons and their launch crews were taken to five launch sites in Europe: Evanton, Scotland; two sites in West Germany; and one site each in Norway and Turkey. Fifty C-119 recovery planes were deployed in Okinawa, Japan, and Alaska. A cover story was devised that the balloons were being deployed for weather research in connection with the International Geophysical Year. The project was initially given the codename Grayback, which was later changed to Genetrix.

Eisenhower was uneasy as to whether the potential benefits of the project were worth the risks, but he reluctantly gave the go-ahead in December 1955. On January 10, 1956, the first balloons were launched from West Germany and Turkey. On January 12, balloons were launched from Scotland. On January 13, the first balloons that had survived the journey through Soviet airspace were recovered by C-119s.

The Soviets became aware of the balloons immediately. MIG-15 fighters were just capable of reaching a height of 50,000 feet, while some heavy Soviet antiaircraft artillery pieces were capable of firing shells to that height. Many balloons were, therefore, shot down, while others malfunctioned or were blown off course across the Black Sea or into China.

The Soviets, although enraged by this invasion of their airspace, were reluctant to reveal publicly that the Americans had been able to intrude upon them in this way. On February 4, however, the Soviet government made an official protest to the U.S. ambassador in Moscow. The United States issued its cover story of weather research. But on February 6 Eisenhower ordered an end to the project. On February 9 the remains of fifty balloons were put on display in Moscow, and the Soviet Union denounced the United States for its provocative action in engaging in peacetime aerial espionage and illegally violating Soviet airspace.

A total of 516 balloons were launched over the month-long project, of which forty-six were recovered. Only one site of major significance was discovered, a nuclear materials complex. Some other useful findings were made on Warsaw Pact radar networks, ground-controlled interception techniques, high altitude wind currents, and the altitude at which the Soviets were capable of making interceptions. Moreover, the project provided photography of about one tenth of Soviet territory. The positive results of Project Genetrix were far outweighed, however, by its political liabilities, namely, the protests from the Soviet Union. Nevertheless, it produced some useful intelligence, particularly for the U-2 program.

EDEN TO EISENHOWER ───────────────────────

August 19, 1955

Dear Mr. President,

I have just been told about an operation which your Air Force have been planning for some time and propose to carry out from November 1 onwards. I have been asked to agree that we should provide facilities for some of the launchings to be made from Scotland.

I am greatly impressed by the ingenuity of this project and the success attained in the experimental trials. I do not doubt that it might yield valuable results. And, as you know, I am always anxious that we should work together in these matters.

I am, however, concerned about the timing. If anything goes wrong, the real purpose of the operation is likely to be known. Our action will then be contrasted with what we said at Geneva. In particular, it will be related to your own offer of reciprocal facilities for aerial reconnaissance.[1] And this may happen at the very moment when our Foreign Ministers are meeting in Geneva.² It would not be difficult for the Russians, if they chose, to make effective use of this—and I fear that we might not emerge from it with any great credit.

I do not know whether you were aware of the intention to start this operation on November 1. I should, however, be grateful if you would consider its timing, in the light of what I have said. I hope that you will agree that it would be wiser to postpone it for the present.

Yours ever,
Anthony

1. At the Geneva Summit, Eisenhower had proposed open skies, that is, unrestricted aerial reconnaissance by the United States and the Soviet Union in each other's airspace. The Soviet Union rejected the proposal since it was unwilling to give up its sovereign right to control its own airspace and since it wished to maintain a rigidly closed society.
2. The foreign ministers of the United States, Britain, France, and the Soviet Union were due to meet in Geneva in late October and early November 1955 for a follow-up to the summit.

EISENHOWER TO EDEN
August 23, 1955
Dear Anthony,

I have your message about "Grayback."¹ I agree with you that November first would be inauspicious from the standpoint of timing. Indeed I think that it is probably better to plan to do nothing until we can judge the temper of the foreign ministers' meeting, and then decide whether or not it is desirable to proceed. I am giving instructions accordingly and will get in touch with you again after we know about the foreign ministers' conference.

Faithfully yours,
D.E.

1. "Grayback" was the initial codename for the project of balloon overflights over the Soviet Union. The codename was later changed to Genetrix.

EDEN TO EISENHOWER
August 23, 1955

I am profoundly grieved at the news of the disastrous floods which have caused so much devastation and damage in the North Eastern States. Please accept my sincere sympathy and that of my colleagues.

Anthony Eden

EISENHOWER TO EDEN ———————————————
August 23, 1955
I have your kind message in regard to the recent disastrous floods in this country and am grateful to you and your colleagues. I know the people of the area as well as the entire country will deeply appreciate your expressions of sympathy and interest.
Dwight D. Eisenhower

EDEN TO EISENHOWER ———————————————
August 25, 1955
Dear Mr. President,
I agree. Thank you so much.[1]
Anthony

1. Postponement of Operation Grayback.

EDEN TO EISENHOWER ———————————————
August 30, 1955
Message from Prime Minister to President.
We shall shortly be sending to your Administration a formal notification of our intention to send two long-range maritime aircraft of the Royal Air Force to Canton Island for a few days, and asking that necessary facilities may be provided at the airport which as you know is operated by Pan American Airways.[1] I should like you to know that the purpose of these flights is to carry out a photographic reconnaissance of certain British islands in the Central Pacific which may be suitable as sites for testing thermo-nuclear weapons. This will not of course be publicly announced; and if questions are asked we shall say that our information about British islands in the area is out of date and that we are taking the opportunity of combining navigational training exercises for some of our long-range maritime aircraft with a photographic reconnaissance of these islands.
It is of course most important to us that knowledge of the real purpose of these flights should be confined within the narrowest possible circle, but we should be glad that Admiral Strauss and Admiral Radford should know.[2]

1. Canton Island is a small atoll in the central Pacific, nine miles long and four miles wide at its widest point. Pan American Airways, the U.S. civilian airline, built a runway on Canton Island in 1938, which it used as a port of call for flights between the United States and New Zealand.
Canton Island was discovered in the nineteenth century by American whaling

boats, one of which, the *Canton* from New Bedford, Massachusetts, ran aground on a reef on the island in 1854 and gave the island its name. The island later fell under the jurisdiction of the Gilbert and Ellice Islands, a British colony. The British tried to maintain their jurisdiction over this remote outpost of the colony, but in 1937 President Franklin Roosevelt placed Canton, along with some neighboring islands, under the jurisdiction of the U.S. Department of the Interior, and a small group of Americans landed on the island in March 1937. An agreement was reached between London and Washington in 1939, which placed Canton Island under joint British and American control for fifty years. Pan American Airways, like many American corporations, was willing to allow the use of its facilities for intelligence purposes, though the airline, of course, received remuneration from the British for the use of its airport at Canton Island. In 1957–58 Britain conducted a series of atomic tests on Christmas Island in the central Pacific.

2. Admiral Lewis L. Strauss, chairman of the Atomic Energy Commission; Admiral Arthur W. Radford, chairman of the Joint Chiefs of Staff.

EISENHOWER TO EDEN

September 1, 1955

Personal Reply from the President to the Prime Minister.

I have received your Note and assure you that this Government has no objection to you carrying on the aerial explorations from Canton Island that you have described. We shall take no public notice of the matter and so far as the true purpose of reconnaissance is concerned, knowledge will be confined in this country to myself, the secretary of state, Admiral Strauss and Admiral Radford. If and when you come to any positive conclusions we would be interested to know of them.

EDEN TO EISENHOWER

September 6, 1955

Thank you so much. I will keep you posted.

Anthony Eden

EDEN TO EISENHOWER

September 25, 1955

I am most deeply distressed to hear the news of your illness.[1] I send you my heartfelt wishes for a quick recovery.

Anthony

1. On September 24, 1955, Eisenhower suffered a heart attack while he was on vacation in Colorado. He remained in the hospital in Denver, Colorado, for six weeks. Vice President Richard Nixon chaired meetings of the cabinet and of the National Security Council.

EDEN TO EISENHOWER ───────────────────────────────

October 14, 1955

Many happy returns and every possible good wish.[1]

Anthony and Clarissa

1. On October 14, 1955, Eisenhower celebrated his sixty-fifth birthday.

EDEN TO EISENHOWER ───────────────────────────────

November 11, 1955

This is indeed wonderful news. The whole of this country joins in your welcome back to Washington.[1]

I was so delighted to hear good accounts of you from Winthrop,[2] and from Foster through Harold.

Every possible good wish from

Clarissa and Anthony

1. On November 11, 1955, Eisenhower left the hospital in Denver and returned to Washington, D.C. He spent much of his time up to Christmas recuperating at his farm in Gettysburg, Pennsylvania, but he gradually resumed his duties. He made a good recovery from his heart attack, and the prognosis which he received from his doctors was good.

2. Winthrop Aldrich, U.S. ambassador to Britain.

EISENHOWER TO EDEN ───────────────────────────────

November 12, 1955

Dear Anthony,

Thank you so much for the message that I received on my return here yesterday evening. The good wishes of yourself and Clarissa, and of many of my British friends, have touched me deeply during the last seven weeks.

Now that I am back in the East communication is much easier. Please do not hesitate to get in touch with me whenever you so desire.

DDE

EDEN TO EISENHOWER ───────────────────────────────

November 19, 1955

Dear Mr. President,

Thank you so much for your message. I am very happy that we can talk again.

I do not think we should take too gloomy a view of the Geneva failure.[1] It was hardly to be expected that our summer weather could have been continued into the winter.

The worrying part of this business is its effect on West Germany. It cannot be good for Europe that a great country should be divided for an indefinite period. I think we must do all we can to bring the Bear to understand how dangerous is the part he is playing in this.[2] If Bulganin and Khrushchev do come here in April you may be sure that we shall do all we can in this sense.[3]

Kardelj has just been here.[4] The Yugoslavs seem to take a sensible and balanced view of Europe and urge that we should give time for these German-Russian problems to be solved. They were delighted with Foster's visit.[5]

Thank you so much for your help in my calculated indiscretion about the Israelis and the Arabs.[6] I really think we have a chance to bring about a settlement in this area. The Arabs seem now to accept that there must be an Israeli State and the Israelis would be wise to accept that a peace guaranteed by us both is worth more than an armistice. As far as we can see the position militarily the Israelis could win all the battles, but would they win the war? And even if they did, how could they survive without any trade with their Arab neighbours? Nuri has sent me an encouraging message and Nasser does not seem entirely negative.[7] If the Israelis will move a little we may yet pull off an agreement on the Trieste model.[8] The trouble with this particular problem is that it is likely to get worse rather than better if we cannot eliminate it.

Forgive these random thoughts. You will know what sincere good wishes go with them.

ANTHONY

1. The foreign ministers of the Soviet Union, the United States, Britain, and France met in Geneva, October 27–November 16, 1955. The meetings produced no agreements. The Western foreign ministers attributed the lack of progress to a persistently negative attitude on the Soviet part.

2. The Bear, derived from the Russian bear, was a nickname for the Soviet Union.

3. Negotiations were in progress for a visit to Britain by Nikolai Bulganin, chairman of the council of ministers, and Nikita Khrushchev, first secretary of the Communist Party of the Soviet Union, in April 1956.

4. Eduard Kardelj, first vice president of the Federal Executive Committee of Yugoslavia, visited London, November 14–19, 1955.

5. U.S. Secretary of State John Foster Dulles visited Yugoslavia on November 6, 1955.

6. In a speech at the Guildhall in London on November 9, 1955, Eden stated that if the Arabs and Israelis reached an agreement on boundaries, Britain and also, Eden suggested, the United States and perhaps other powers would be prepared to give a formal guarantee of these boundaries to both sides.

7. Major General Nuri al-Said, prime minister of Iraq.

8. The city of Trieste and its hinterland was disputed between Italy and Yugoslavia

at the end of World War II. The area had been awarded to Italy at the end of the First World War as a reward for Italian entry into the war on the Allied side in 1915, but most of the population in the southern part of the area were Yugoslavs. In 1945, Yugoslavian forces occupied this southern part, while British and American troops occupied the northern half. After years of disputatious negotiations, Eden was instrumental in achieving a settlement in 1954, whereby a permanent boundary was fixed, with the Yugoslavs retaining the southern part of the area while the northern part, including the city of Trieste, was awarded to Italy.

EISENHOWER TO EDEN

November 19, 1955

Dear Anthony,

It is good to have your thoughts. You are of course right in saying that to keep Germany divided is dangerous business for Europe and the world as well. We made some progress, however, at Geneva in impressing this point on the Russians. At the least I believe we have made clear to everyone that the Soviet policy concerning Germany is designed to preserve the GDR as the keystone of their satellite position rather than Russian security.[1]

I quite agree with you that the only real solution to the dangerous situation in the Middle East is an Israel-Arab settlement. The prospects do look brighter at the moment than they have for some time. We must do everything we can to follow through effectively.

With warm regards,

As ever,

DDE

1. German Democratic Republic, the official name of East Germany.

EDEN TO EISENHOWER

November 23, 1955

Dear Mr. President,

I should so much welcome a chance to talk to you again. On the other hand, I do not want to be an importunate visitor. I have therefore been wondering whether it might be acceptable to you if I was to propose myself for a brief visit to the United States at some date convenient to you in the second half of January.[1] The main purpose would be to talk over the world scene together. I would not suppose that anything in the nature of an official agenda would be necessary. I do however attach importance to our having to talk together well in advance of the visit of the two Russians here in April. We should show the world that we are in full agreement and that nothing can divide us before they descend upon us.

I would hope that Harold could come with me, and I should much look forward to seeing Foster again.

Please do not hesitate to let me know exactly how you feel about all this. Of course I would not want to make any suggestion that could put any strain upon your health.

Kind regards,
Anthony

1. Agreement was reached for a visit by Eden to Washington on January 30–February 3, 1956.

THE ASWAN DAM

Since ancient times, the flood waters of the Nile had created fertility along the banks of the river, which had been the economic foundation of ancient Egyptian civilization. The annual flooding and receding of the river waters, however, which followed the melting of the snow on the mountains deep in Africa in the upper waters of the Nile, created grave problems, which were incompatible with a modern economy. The solution appeared to be the construction of a dam which would control the flood waters of the Nile. Since the river was not navigable south of Aswan, on account of cataracts, the most suitable location for such a dam was Aswan. The British had in fact built a dam at Aswan at the beginning of the twentieth century, but it was not sufficiently large to perform the massive task of adequately controlling the flood waters of the Nile. In the post–World War II period, with the development of modern technology, Egypt's dream was the construction of a massive high dam at Aswan, which would control the flood waters of the river while also creating a very large lake and producing massive amounts of electricity. The construction of the high dam was, however, beyond the economic resources of Egypt without assistance from abroad.

Since the United States wished to encourage modernization and economic development in countries such as Egypt and considered economic aid to be a means of gaining political influence in such countries and steering them in a non-Communist direction, the Aswan High Dam seemed to be an excellent example of a project worthy of American aid. The British also, despite their difficulties with Nasser, saw the advantages of gaining political influence over Egypt by giving economic aid for a very worthy cause. Moreover, the project appeared not only to have tremendous economic possibilities but also had an appeal to the imagination, which could illustrate the successful application of modern technology to the solution of an age-old problem, which had been beyond the resources of the pharaohs. Both the

British and the Americans were, moreover, very eager to ensure that Nasser did not turn for funding to the Soviet Union. In 1953 the president of the World Bank, Eugene Black, went on a fact-finding tour in Egypt and reported very favorably and enthusiastically on the possibilities of funding the construction of a high dam at Aswan, with a combination of Egyptian resources, a World Bank loan, and grants and loans from the United States and Britain.

Protracted negotiations on the project took place over two years, 1953–55. The potential benefits to the United States and Britain continued to seem considerable. It was estimated that the dam would take ten years to construct, which would create good opportunities for gaining influence over Egypt. On the other hand, Nasser proved increasingly difficult and slippery as a negotiating partner and seemed to be trying to play off one side against the other in the Cold War. In September 1955, the Egyptian decision to import Eastern bloc arms through Czechoslovakia seemed ominous. Meanwhile, within the U.S. Congress, opposition grew to American economic aid to Egypt for the construction of the Aswan Dam. Southerners were opposed to a scheme that would increase Egyptian cotton production and create greater competition for Southern cotton. Representative Otto Passman, chairman of the House Appropriations Subcommittee on Foreign Aid, was an inveterate skeptic concerning the value of the expenditure of American taxpayers' dollars on foreign aid schemes. Senator Wayne Morse from Oregon argued that the money would be better spent on a project on the Snake River in Oregon rather than on the Aswan Dam. The Jewish lobby exerted its considerable influence against aid to Israel's leading enemy. The Senate majority leader, Lyndon Johnson, the minority leader, William F. Knowland, the speaker of the House of Representatives, John McCormack, as well as powerful figures such as Hubert Humphrey and Estes Kefauver were all inclined to oppose American aid for the Aswan Dam, while John Foster Dulles was increasingly exasperated by Nasser's lack of response to efforts to bring about an Arab-Israeli settlement and his sly overtures toward both sides in the Cold War. The British meanwhile felt that mounting tensions in relations with Nasser made British commitment of aid to Egypt for the Aswan Dam an anomaly.

Nevertheless in December 1955, a tentative agreement was reached that the World Bank would lend Egypt $200 million for the construction of the Aswan Dam, while the United States and Britain would make initial grants of $54 million and $14 million respectively, with the possibility of further British and American loans and grants at later stages in the development of the project. Nasser, however, wished to make some changes to the terms of the agreement, though Black tried to assure him that many of the conditions in the agreement were standard commercial conditions of any loan. Further haggling over terms against a background of mounting opposition in Britain and America to aid for the Aswan Dam culminated in the conclusion of Dulles and British Foreign Secretary Selwyn Lloyd, when they met for a NATO meeting in Paris in May 1956, that the matter of aid for the Aswan Dam should be left to wither on the vine. A few days later, Nasser recognized the Communist government of China, which was a red rag to the bull to the Americans and increased suspicions of Nasser's pro-Communist tendencies. On June 20, 1956, Black flew to Cairo to present Nasser with a final offer. Nasser's continuing equivocation and attempts to alter the terms provided Eisenhower with the opportunity to withdraw the American offer. Dulles informed Roger Makins, British ambassador to the United States, that he would call in the Egyptian ambassador and inform him that the American offer of support for the Aswan Dam had been withdrawn. Meanwhile, however, the Egyptians decided to accept the terms of the agreement which had been negotiated in December. On July 19 the Egyptian ambassador to the United States was stunned by Dulles's statement to him that the offer of support for the Aswan Dam was being withdrawn. Moreover, the Egyptian ambassador felt that Dulles was abrasive and unfriendly in the meeting and that he rubbed salt in the wound by making a public statement of the American decision before the ambassador had had time to inform Nasser. At the same time, Dulles had brushed aside the Egyptian ambassador's statement that funding from the Soviet Union was on offer to Egypt. On the next day, July 20, the head of the Middle East section in the Foreign Office, Harold Caccia, called in the Egyptian ambassador to Britain and informed him that the British offer of support for the Aswan Dam was also being withdrawn.

On July 26, 1956, Nasser announced the nationalization of the Suez Canal, which, considering its timing, seemed to have been brought about by the cancellation of British and American support for the Aswan Dam. Nasser stated that funds from the dues paid by ships using the Suez Canal, which would now be paid exclusively to Egypt, would pay for the construction of the Aswan Dam. In fact, the dues from the Suez Canal did not raise amounts of money anywhere near sufficient for the building of the Aswan Dam. Instead, Egypt accepted the Soviet offer of assistance. The massive project took fifteen years, reaching completion in 1971. Nasser died in 1970, a year before the completion of his great project. The huge lake which was created by the construction of the high dam was named Lake Nasser. The historic sites of ancient Egypt, such as Pilae and Abu Simbel, which would have been covered by the waters of Lake Nasser, were painstakingly moved to other locations in a huge operation supported by UNESCO and many individual countries. A commemorative monument in the shape of a very large stone lotus, the flower associated with Egypt, was erected at the top of the high dam as a mark of gratitude to the Soviet Union for its assistance in building the dam for the Egyptians. The economic impact of the high dam, however, although very beneficial in controlling the flood waters of the Nile, was less spectacular than some of the projections, with regard, for example, to its capability in generating electricity. Moreover, the Soviets gained a poor return in political influence for their enormous financial commitment to the construction of the dam. In 1972, a year after the completion of the dam, Nasser's successor, Anwar Sadat, who had found the Soviets rather overbearing, ordered the Soviets to leave Egypt, and Sadat began a process of orienting Egypt toward the United States.

EDEN TO EISENHOWER ─────────────────────
November 26, 1955
Dear Mr. President,

Harold has telegraphed to Foster details of very disturbing information which we have just received about the likelihood of an Egyptian-Russian deal over the Aswan Dam. If the Russians were to succeed in this they would of course be ruthless with the Sudan and abuse their control of the Nile Waters. The outlook for Africa would then be grim indeed. Kaissouni and Hilmi are now in Washington negotiating with the International Bank for a loan to enable a Western consortium to build the Dam.[1] A preliminary contract has been signed with Alexander Gibb, a British firm, as consultant engineers. I understand that the main difficulty the International Bank has in helping the Egyptians is that they should pay some regard to their usual rule of international tendering.[2] If this is insisted upon and the Egyptians leave Washington without agreement, I fear the Russians are certain to get the contract. Poland will act as a stooge in this case as Czechoslovakia did for the arms.[3] The Bank are not unnaturally anxious about the position of the Egyptian economy over the next thirty year outlook and want to be assured that there is some outside finance in addition to the money which the Bank will themselves put up. We are prepared to do our small part in supporting our share of the consortium and there is also the question of the other two Governments involved namely the French and the German Governments. We believe that they will play their part. It would be invaluable to get the help of your Government, it being always understood that in that event an American firm would take part in the operation.

I hate to trouble you with this but I am convinced that on our joint success in excluding the Russians from this contract may depend the future of Africa. I hope to have the chance of a talk with you when it suits you about the whole of this situation but meanwhile we must avert the disaster of the two Egyptians leaving Washington without the conviction that agreement is going to be reached.

Yours ever,
Anthony

1. Abd al-Moneim Kassouni was the Egyptian minister of finance. Samir al-Hilmi was a military associate of Nasser from the time of the Young Officers Movement in 1952.
2. This point is elaborated upon in Eden's subsequent letter to Eisenhower on December 15, 1955.
3. On September 27, 1955, Nasser announced an agreement for the supply to Egypt of a large quantity of arms from Czechoslovakia, which in reality meant that the arms were supplied by the Soviet Union.

EDEN TO EISENHOWER
December 10, 1955
Dear Mr. President,

The Russians are tempting the Indians with offers of aircraft. I am sure you will agree that we must do all we can to prevent any further increase of Russian influence in this sensitive part of the world. We have offered the Indians British aircraft and they are inclined to take them. We think that the matter would be clinched in our favour if we could offer them a fighter armed with a guided weapon. We have such a weapon, known as Blue Sky, which will not go into operational service with the Royal Air Force, since we have a better one coming along close behind. It would however provide a great increase of fighting power to any aircraft which carried it. The weapon is only graded "Confidential" and contains no information of American origin. Under normal practice we should be free to tell the Indians about it. However, in view of our close collaboration with the United States on guided weapons research and development and of the fact that the weapon contains a V.T. fuze, I think you should know about it before we commit ourselves.[1]

Time is very pressing since the Indians are most anxious to settle within a week. I hope that you will see no difficulty in what we propose.

Kindest regards,
Yours ever,
Anthony

1. A VT (variable time) fuze, which was also known as a proximity fuze, emits a radio signal and goes off when it detects that enough of this signal is being reflected back from a hard object.

EDEN TO EISENHOWER

December 15, 1955

Dear Mr. President,

I have had a full report from Makins on the latest discussions about the High Aswan Dam. We must surely press home and clinch the agreement now we have got so far.

The main point outstanding is the way in which the contract for the first phase of the work is to be placed. The Egyptians want to give it to the Consortium in the interests of speed. Your people have said that if Congress is to vote a share of the money, American firms must have at least the chance of getting orders at every stage.

So far as our commercial interests are concerned, I quite understand that. We do not ask for more than a fair field and no favour. We ourselves are prepared to be at risk for five and a half million pounds in dollars on the first stage, and you know what that means to us. We are perfectly willing to face this risk because it is a political rather than a commercial matter. The Egyptians are convinced that competitive tender means a year's delay and it would be a tragedy if we broke down with them on this point. Hilmi, as you know, has great influence with Nasser and may easily persuade him to break with us and go to the Russians instead.

I know how seriously you would take the possible consequences of this, as I do. Surely some compromise can be found, for example on the lines of the latest Egyptian suggestion for the first tranche. Nearly everything else, as I understand it, is agreed.

Kindest regards,
Anthony Eden

EDEN TO EISENHOWER

December 24, 1955

Message from Prime Minister to the President.

I agree that the operation should take place and we will make available all the facilities to do our share.[1] I understand that March 31 is the last possible date for the conclusion of the operation. It would be helpful if in fact a slightly earlier conclusion were possible.

For your guidance we have in mind possible Soviet reactions and would prefer these to be registered, if at all, a little while ahead of the projected visit of Bulganin and Khrushchev.

1. Operation Grayback, balloon reconnaissance overflights over the Soviet Union.

EDEN TO EISENHOWER
December 26, 1955
I am greatly distressed to learn of the disastrous floods in the States of California, Oregon and Nevada.
Please accept my sincerest sympathy and that of all my colleagues.
Anthony Eden

EISENHOWER TO EDEN
December 30, 1955
I have just received your message of sympathy for the victims of our recent floods. Those who are suffering, as well as the nation as a whole, will be deeply grateful for your thoughtfulness.
DE

EDEN TO EISENHOWER
January 16, 1956
Dear Mr. President,
I think that I must approach you about the situation which is rapidly developing in the Middle East, particularly in regard to the activities of Saudi Arabia and the bribery in which she is indulging. This is going on so fast that I felt I must telegraph before we meet. No doubt much of our information will be available to the State Department from the same sources as we receive it. Saudi money has been subsidising newspapers in Syria, Jordan and in the Lebanon, some of them extremely left and Communist or near-Communist papers, which they keep going. Many Ministers and Deputies are also being bought up.

Now has come a move, of which you will be aware, to supplant us in Jordan by making payments similar to those which we have been making all these years. Our payments to Jordan last year have cost us twelve million pounds. Nominally, the new offer comes from Egypt, Syria and Saudi Arabia. However, the first two have no money.

There now appears to be a new development, as we learn from Jordan. The Russians are behind this whole plan to subvert the country. The Soviet Ambassador has approached the Jordan Charge d'Affaires in Cairo, with presumably the full knowledge and support of the Egyptians and Saudis, and offered him "everything" that he wants, including arms, provided Jordan denounces her treaty with us.[1] The Jordan Government also has information that the Russians have offered to pay five years subsidy in advance.

In the light of all this it becomes increasingly clear that the Saudis, the Russians, the Egyptians and the Syrians are working together. If we don't want to see the whole of the Middle East fall into Communist hands we must first back the friends of the West in Jordan and Iraq. This we are trying to do. It is equally important to find some way of regulating the Saudi use of their money and of stopping them playing the Russian game.

I understand full well all the difficulties this means for you, but if the Saudis go on spending and behaving as at present there will be nothing left for anybody but the Bear, who is already working in their wake.

Yours ever,
Anthony Eden

1. Britain and Jordan had signed a mutual defense pact in 1946.

EISENHOWER TO EDEN
January 26, 1956
Dear Anthony,

The Soviet Ambassador handed me yesterday a long personal letter from Bulganin. I have not had a chance to study it carefully but it appears to be a recapitulation of the Soviet position on peace, disarmament, and relaxation of tensions. It concluded with the suggestion that the Soviet Union and the United States conclude between themselves a treaty of friendship and a draft text of such a treaty was enclosed. I will show you the letter and enclosure when you reach Washington, but I wanted to get you word promptly of its general tenor. I surmise that its delivery was timed with an eye to our meeting and for this reason the manner of delivery was designed to promote wide speculation as to its contents.

Sincerely,
Dwight D. Eisenhower

EDEN TO EISENHOWER
January 27, 1956
Dear Mr. President,

Thank you so much for your information about Bulganin's personal letter to you. I feel sure that you are right in your judgement of its purpose.

Chou En-lai has also sent Selwyn Lloyd, as one of the Chairman of the

Geneva Conference, a request for a fresh meeting because of delay in arranging elections.[1] I am asking Makins to show this to Foster.[2] I should guess its purpose is in part the same as that of Bulganin's message to you.

Greatly looking forward to our meeting.

Yours,

Anthony

1. On December 20, 1955, Eden reshuffled his cabinet, appointing Selwyn Lloyd as foreign secretary, while Harold Macmillan became chancellor of the exchequer. Chinese Foreign Minister Zhou En-lai had written to Lloyd requesting a reconvening of the Geneva Conference that had in 1954 reached a settlement of the Southeast Asia conflict, including a provision that elections should be held in Vietnam within two years. The government of Ngo Dinh Diem in South Vietnam, supported by the United States, refused to hold elections, claiming that the Communist regime of Ho Chi Minh in North Vietnam would not permit free elections. The United States calculated that Ho Chi Minh would win an election in the whole of Vietnam and therefore supported Diem's decision to refuse to hold elections. Britain and the Soviet Union had been cochairs of the Geneva Conference in 1954. The conference was not reconvened and elections were not held, leaving Vietnam divided into Communist North Vietnam and non-Communist South Vietnam.

2. Roger Makins, British ambassador to the United States.

EDEN TO EISENHOWER
February 1, 1956

Dear Mr. President,

Since I left you last night, I have had the following message from Rab Butler on behalf of the Cabinet.[1] We have been having a real struggle with the Indians to get them to buy our Canberras rather than the Russian ILGs.[2] The Russians have made them most generous offers. As a result, to get the order, we have cut our prices mercilessly and switched Canberra bombers due for delivery to the R.A.F. We shall lose about half a million pounds if we get the order. The Cabinet think this delay and cost for ourselves should be accepted to keep Russian bombers out of India. I think they are right.

There is however one difficulty. We need your agreement for the supply of certain specialised bombing equipment with which our Canberras are being fitted. Do you think you could help us in this? There is no question of money in this, but only of security. The joint advantages seem considerable.

General Whiteley has full technical details of the equipment concerned and I would gladly send them to you if you wished, or to anyone you may appoint.[3]

Yours ever,

Anthony

1. R. A. Butler, popularly known as Rab, was leader of the House of Commons.

2. The Canberra was the first British jet bomber, with advanced equipment to enhance capability with regard to speed and altitude. The IL-28 was a Soviet Iluyshin bomber with similar capabilities. "ILGs" is an unusual abbreviation of "Iluyshins."

3. General Sir John Whiteley was chairman of the British Joint Services Mission in Washington, D.C. During World War II he served as British deputy to Eisenhower's chief of staff, General Walter Bedell Smith.

EISENHOWER TO EDEN

February 2, 1956

Dear Anthony,

This note is merely to acknowledge your communication of late yesterday. As soon as we can have the matter adequately studied, we will be in touch with you about it.

With warm personal regard,

As ever,

DE

EDEN TO EISENHOWER

February 2, 1956

Foster has given me your most helpful message in which you agreed to supplying certain specialised bombing equipment for the Canberras for India. Thank you so much.

We will now do everything we can to keep the Russians out of India in this field. I will let you know if I may the final outcome.

Yours ever,

Anthony

EDEN TO EISENHOWER

February 3, 1956

Dear Mr. President,

I really don't know how to thank you for all your help, kindness and hospitality in these days.[1] Hitherto I have always looked upon conferences as in the nature of an ordeal (I guess that you have too). But this one I have truly enjoyed from the beginning, and I really feel that we have been able to do a "solid" (to quote the communiqué!) piece of work for peace and understanding in the world. This is due above all to you and the part you played.

On more personal matters, I feel that our friendship is closer than it has ever been. I value that immensely. You have both always made me feel so much at home at the White House, that I long for an occasion to show you some hospitality at home. Maybe one day the chance will come.

Meanwhile thank you for all.

Yours ever,

Anthony

1. Eden visited Washington, January 30–February 3, 1956.

EISENHOWER TO EDEN

February 5, 1956

Dear Anthony,

I deeply appreciated the handwritten note that you sent me shortly before your departure from Washington. Although I don't in the slightest underestimate the official importance, to both our countries, of your visit here, I value equally the warm personal friendship that is renewed through such an event.

With affectionate regard to Clarissa and, as always, the best to yourself.

As ever,

Ike

EDEN TO EISENHOWER

February 17, 1956

Dear Mr. President,

We are faced with an urgent problem in deciding our future tank production programme. The very large capacity which we built up after the Korean war has played its part with the help of your off-shore orders in facilitating the expansion of our own Army and of many other NATO forces. Now that our requirements, and those of our customers, are contracting we have to decide how much capacity to retain.

Much turns on your views about the supply of further tanks to Iraq, a possible order for Holland, which we understand may have your support, and most of all the possibility of a large order from Germany.

The German requirement is particularly important. First, from the military point of view, there would be great operational and logistic advantages if the German forces under Northern Army Group Command were equipped with the same type of tank as the British forces; and the Centurion, as I think you will agree, is at least the equal of the M.47.[1] Secondly, an export order of this size would help us in the great difficulties which, as you know, we are facing in our balance of payments difficulties in which Germany is playing no small part.

You have already given the Germans enough M.47s to cover half their requirements. We hope that, for the reasons which I have indicated, you will be ready to agree that we should now supply the balance of their requirements.

Our position was set out in detail in an *aide-mémoire* which was left with the Deputy Assistant Secretary for European Affairs on 28th January. I should be most grateful for your help in settling this matter.

Yours ever,
Anthony

1. The M-47 was the main tank used by the U.S. Army.

EISENHOWER TO EDEN
February 20, 1956
Dear Anthony,
I have your message and will have it thoroughly studied at once. I should be able to give you my views no later than the beginning of next week.
Warm regard.
D.E.

U-2

At the Geneva summit in July 1955, Eisenhower had proposed open skies, which would have permitted unrestricted reconnaissance by American and Soviet aircraft over one another's territory and which would thereby provide mutual re-assurance against the possibility of a surprise attack. Khrushchev, however, rejected open skies, which he regarded as an unacceptable intrusion into Soviet airspace. Eisenhower decided, therefore, particularly after the unsatisfactory results of the Genetrix balloon project, to authorize the deployment of the U-2, which could fly at a very high altitude over the Soviet Union beyond the range of Soviet interception and which, whether acceptable to the Soviet Union or not, would provide the United States with vital intelligence information with regard to Soviet military capabilities and, above all, the possibility of a Soviet surprise attack.

Eisenhower, however, felt very uneasy about U-2 flights, since he realized that the Soviet Union would be antagonized and that there was the danger that a U-2 would be shot down or be involved in an accident over the Soviet Union. The U-2 program was developed by the CIA, not by the air force, since Eisenhower considered that an intrusion into Soviet airspace by an American military plane was technically an act of war. The CIA sought to reassure the president with regard to the dangers of a mishap. Richard Bissell, CIA director of operations, informed Eisenhower that since the U-2 flew at

70,000 feet, it would not be detected on Soviet radar and that, if the Soviets did detect the U-2, they were incapable of shooting it down at such a height. Moreover, pilots would be issued a suicide pill, which they were not required to take but which would be available to them, while a destruct button was installed which would blow up the plane seventy seconds after the pilot pressed the button. There was, therefore, the CIA assured, virtually no possibility that the Soviets would capture either a pilot who was alive or a plane which was anything more than unrecognizable small fragments of wreckage. In the unlikely event of a mishap, the cover story that the U-2 was a weather plane that had gone off course could not be disproved in the absence of a pilot or pieces of the aircraft that revealed its true purpose.

Eisenhower was by no means fully convinced by these reassurances, but in spite of his misgivings, he approached Eden in March 1956 with regard to the use of a British base for U-2 flights over the Soviet Union. Eden was apprehensive, but he agreed to cooperate. Bissell was pleased to have the involvement of America's closest ally, not only for the practical need of a base in a country within a U-2's flying distance to and from the Soviet Union, but also because it was intended that British pilots would fly on some U-2 missions. Bissell hoped an agreement could be reached such that either the president of the United States or the prime minister of Britain, depending on the nationality of the pilot, could grant permission for a U-2 flight over the Soviet Union, or, if the president was unwilling to allow any flight without his permission, even by a British pilot, Eisenhower would be even more eager for heavy British involvement in the program, which might provide him with greater opportunities for credible deniability in the event of a mishap.

In April 1956, U-2 planes arrived at Lakenheath under cover of the "1st Weather Reconnaissance Squadron, Provisional," and a number of practice flights took place in preparation for the commencement of operational flights over the Soviet Union. During the visit of Khrushchev and Bulganin to Britain in April 1956, however, an incident occurred which led Eden to reverse his position and to withdraw permission for the use of British bases for U-2 flights over the Soviet Union and for British involvement in the U-2 program. Khrushchev and Bulganin came to Britain by sea in a Soviet cruiser, which docked in Portsmouth harbor. British naval intelligence was interested in obtaining information about this cruiser, the *Ordzhonikidze*, which had elaborate sonar equipment and devices to ensure quieter running. Soviet divers had spied on British ships when they had made an official visit to Leningrad, so the Secret Intelligence Service (SIS) wished to return the compliment. Eden had, however, issued specific instructions forbidding any underwater spying, since he was fully aware of the damage which would be inflicted on his diplomatic efforts to ease relations with the Soviet Union if a British intelligence operation was carried out that was discovered by the Soviets. Due to an administrative bungle, SIS did not receive word of Eden's prohibition. SIS employed a frogman, Commander Lionel "Buster" Crabb, whom SIS had used for various missions previously, to dive under the *Ordzhonikidze* when it was docked in Portsmouth and to gather information from its hull regarding its electronic equipment. Crabb, however, although he had a distinguished World War II record as a diver who had worked on underwater bomb disposal and had been awarded the George Medal, was now a little old for a hazardous mission, while his lifestyle as an eccentric, bisexual alcoholic had taken its toll. On April 19 Crabb made a dive under the *Ordzhonikidze* in Portsmouth harbor, but he needed to come up to add more weight. He was seen by Soviet sailors aboard the cruiser. He dived down a second time and did not resurface.

Within days there was press speculation about the mysterious frogman. On May 4 the Soviet government lodged a formal protest and made the matter public, and questions were raised in the House of Commons. The Admiralty offered the lame explanation that Crabb had been on a training exercise, and his proximity to the Soviet vessel was a coincidence, but this account lacked credibility. As Eden had feared, loose cannons in the intelligence services had caused an incident which severely undermined his diplomatic efforts to improve relations with the Soviet Union through the visit of Khrushchev and Bulganin to Britain. (On June 10, 1957, Crabb's body was discovered by fishermen on a sandbank at the mouth of Chichester harbor. Crabb was identified by his wetsuit, since much of the body, including the head, was missing, which added further to the bizarre, mysterious nature of the episode.)

As a result of the Crabb affair, Eden decided that he could not risk a further mishap over another intelligence operation, and he consequently reversed his position with regard to the U-2. Eisenhower accepted Eden's reasons, and the U-2s were moved from Lakenheath to Wiesbaden in West Germany. The first U-2 operational mission over the Soviet Union flew out of Wiesbaden on July 4, 1956. Several further flights took place over the next week. Thereafter, flights took place intermittently. The Soviets detected the flights and protested through diplomatic channels. The Soviets were, however, unable to shoot down a U-2 at its high altitude, and the Americans disregarded Soviet diplomatic protests.

When Macmillan succeeded Eden in 1957, at his first meeting with Eisenhower in Bermuda in May 1957, agreement was reached for Britain to become involved again in the U-2 program. RAF pilots went to the United States for training in the American U-2 program at a base in Nevada. British pilots were then based at Incirlik in Turkey, where they joined seven American pilots and shared four U-2s. Two U-2 flights over the Soviet Union in 1959 and 1960 were undertaken by British pilots. In March 1958, Eisenhower temporarily halted U-2 flights, since he feared that the Soviets might have developed the means to shoot down a U-2. In 1959, however, a small number of U-2 flights were permitted. In 1960, the Defense Department and the CIA were very eager to discover more precise information about Soviet military capabilities in advance of the summit meeting in Paris in May 1960. Eisenhower therefore reluctantly authorized two further U-2 flights in April 1960, one on April 15, the other, delayed by bad weather, on May 1, 1960; this was the final, fatal U-2 flight, piloted by Francis Gary Powers. The Soviets had developed the capability to shoot down a U-2. When Powers's plane was hit by an antiaircraft missile, he chose not to take the lethal poison with which he had been provided but to eject from the plane. Moreover, because of damage to the plane, Powers was unable to push the destruct button before he ejected. Powers was apprehended as soon as he parachuted to the ground, while the plane crashed with much of its equipment still intact. Unaware that the pilot was alive and that the plane had not been blown up and destroyed, Eisenhower issued the cover story that a weather plane had gone off course over the Soviet Union. Khrushchev triumphantly announced that the pilot was alive in Soviet custody and that the remnants of the plane revealed unmistakably its purpose as a spy plane. Eisenhower was totally humiliated. When the summit met in Paris on May 16, 1960, Khrushchev demanded that Eisenhower ban further U-2 flights and apologize. Eisenhower was willing to ban further U-2 flights, but he refused to apologize. Khrushchev therefore walked out of the summit meeting. He also cancelled an invitation to Eisenhower to visit the Soviet Union in the spring of 1960, and when Khrushchev came to a meeting of the United Nations in New York in September 1960, he took off his shoe and banged it on the table to express his anger and to protest further. Instead of Eisenhower's presidency ending with a successful summit meeting that might initiate a process of détente, Eisenhower's final months as president were marked by severe tension in U.S.-Soviet relations and a general sense of chaos and farce. The damage was extremely severe not only to U.S.-Soviet relations but to Eisenhower's historical reputation. Eden's concern in the spring of 1956 that a risky intelligence operation might destroy the beneficial results of a summit meeting proved ultimately to have been very prescient.

EDEN TO EISENHOWER
March 1, 1956

Since my return from Washington I have been told about a secret operation which your airmen are to carry out.[1] I understand that you know of this and favour it in principle. It is suggested that one of our service aerodromes should be used for the purpose.

I confess that I am concerned about the risk which seems to me to be involved. If one of the aircraft had for any reason, engine trouble or otherwise, to come down to a level at which it could be intercepted, we should be confronted with a serious international incident for which the blame would be laid upon the West.

The last thing I should want is to be separated from you in anything you think to be really necessary, but I would like to feel certain that you are personally satisfied that this operation will give us value which outweighs the risk involved.

Yours ever,
Anthony

1. U-2 flights over the Soviet Union.

EDEN TO EISENHOWER
March 1, 1956
Dear Friend,

I am so happy to hear that you are really well again.[1] This will rejoice millions of people all over the world and especially your many friends in this country.

The rest of yesterday's news it would not be proper for me to comment upon so I must pass it over in silence.[2]

Kindest regards,
Anthony

1. Medical reports appeared to indicate that Eisenhower had made a very good recovery from his heart attack of September 1955.
2. On February 29, Eisenhower announced in a radio and television broadcast that he would run for a second term as president.

EISENHOWER TO EDEN ─────────────

March 2, 1956

Dear Anthony,

I most deeply appreciate your personal message. Concerning the other point you mention, I shall take the silence of my British friends as approval.[1]

With warm regard,

As ever,

DE

1. The reference is to Eisenhower's announcement of his decision to run for a second term as president.

EDEN TO EISENHOWER ─────────────

March 5, 1956

Dear Friend,

I am asking Selwyn Lloyd to discuss with Foster developments in the Middle East which are causing me much concern.[1]

There is no doubt that the Russians are resolved to liquidate the Bagdad Pact.[2] In this undertaking Nasser is supporting them and I suspect that his relations with the Soviets are much closer than he admits to us. Recent events in Jordan are part of this pattern.[3]

Our policy should surely be to encourage our friends who will now come under heavy pressure. This means urgent and effective measures to shore up the Bagdad Pact and Iraq in particular.

We are considering the allotment to Iraq of some of the very considerable aid we have given to Jordan—over £12,000,000 a year. If the United States could accede to the Bagdad Pact the effect would be tremendous. On a lesser scale it would greatly help Nuri if you could agree that we should let him have very soon the further Centurion tanks which we discussed last month.[4]

I feel myself that we can no longer safely wait on Nasser. Indeed if the United States now joined the Bagdad Pact this would impress him more than all our attempts to cajole him have yet done.

Certainly we should accept, I think, that a policy of appeasement will bring us nothing in Egypt. Our best chance is to show that it pays to be our friends.

I send you these reflections because events are moving fast and I am anxious to keep in touch.

Yours ever,

Anthony

1. Dulles and Lloyd were due to attend the Southeast Asia Treaty Organization Council meeting in Karachi, Pakistan, on March 6–8, 1956.

2. The Baghdad Pact was formed by Iraq and Turkey in 1955 and was joined by Britain and Pakistan. Its purpose was to create a northern tier of states to contain the Soviet Union. The United States endorsed those goals and gave support to the Baghdad Pact but did not join. The United States was concerned that American membership would alienate Egypt, which wanted Arab countries such as Iraq to join an Arab pact led by Egypt, while Israel would at the same time be offended by an American security commitment to an Arab nation, Iraq, when Israel was not a member of a similar pact with a similar security guarantee.

3. Nasser had been employing various means to try to turn Jordan against Britain, including financial inducements, which, it was suspected, had Soviet backing.

4. Nuri al-Said, prime minister of Iraq.

EISENHOWER TO EDEN ——————————————————————
March 5, 1956
Dear Anthony,

The project of which you write is one from which we expect much.[1] In developing this general idea, we had hoped that we would be supported by your professionals. Of course, we are making very thorough tests here in order to be sure that the equipment is reliable. I fully appreciate the concern you express and my own directive for this project will ensure that it will be conducted prudently.

There would be certain advantages, particularly from the point of view of efficiency and security of operation, in initiating this project in close cooperation with your people but we will not press this upon you now. Assuming we have success in our activities elsewhere, we shall thereafter come to you for a full discussion before again requesting the use of a facility in your country.

Sincerely,

DE

1. U-2 flights over the Soviet Union.

EISENHOWER TO EDEN ——————————————————————
March 6, 1956
My immediately preceding telegram refers to AQUATONE.[1]

1. Aquatone was the code name for U-2 flights over the Soviet Union.

EDEN TO EISENHOWER

March 6, 1956

Dear Friend,

Thank you so much for telegraphing as you have done. I accept to the full the assurances you give me of the trouble that has been taken in this matter and the prudence with which it would be carried out. I would much prefer in the light of what you say that the project should be initiated in cooperation with our own people. I highly value your consideration of my misgivings, but as I told you last time we are not going to be parted in this way.

Yours ever,
Anthony

EISENHOWER TO EDEN

March 6, 1956

Dear Anthony,

In your letter of February 18 you requested my assistance in settling some questions relating to the supply of tanks to Iraq, the Netherlands, and Germany.

In line with our previous discussions, I propose to request of Congress, in connection with the Mutual Security Program for the Fiscal Year 1957, funds to supply Iraq with forty additional Centurion tanks.[1] This is being done only because there are firm understandings that these tanks will not be used for any purpose except defense of the area in connection with the Baghdad Pact. I would not want this information to become known until the program has been presented to the Congress, and then it should be handled in such a manner as not to increase tensions in relation to the Arab-Israeli dispute. It is extremely important that this matter be considered as secret pending further discussions between us.

We do not at present have any plans to supply additional tanks to the Netherlands from any source. The Netherlands should therefore provide a market for Centurion tanks with respect to any additional tank requirements for which the Netherlands Government may decide to place contracts.

As far as Germany is concerned, it will be our general policy to encourage the Germans to satisfy their equipment requirements insofar as it is possible and practicable from European sources, including of course the United Kingdom. A study which I have directed to be undertaken with specific regard to the problem of tank availabilities and requirements for Germany has not yet been completed. I am informed, however, that on the basis of a preliminary assessment, the magnitude of the German requirements for medium tanks is likely to be such as to provide a substantial market in Germany for British tanks.

If the final results of the study lead to any important revision of the above assessment, I shall be glad to communicate them to you.

Sincerely,

D.E.

1. Eden had requested seventy tanks for Iraq.

EDEN TO EISENHOWER ─────────────────────────

March 8, 1956

Dear Friend,

Thank you so much for your reply about tank orders, which Winthrop has now given me.¹ Your intentions will be of much benefit to us, as I explained in my earlier message. I shall be glad to hear about the final results of the study on tank availabilities and requirements for Germany in due course.

Yours ever,

Anthony

1. Winthrop Aldrich, U.S. ambassador to Britain.

EISENHOWER TO EDEN ─────────────────────────

March 9, 1956

Dear Anthony,

I share your concern over the current developments in the Middle East and know that Foster has discussed them with Selwyn Lloyd.

We face a broad challenge to our position in the Near East and to our objectives of strengthening our ties with those countries. I believe that our reaction should consist not of isolated moves, but a carefully thought out program.

The Soviets have made abundantly clear even in their public statements their intentions toward the Near East. It is of course true that some of the moves made by Nasser, though for different reasons, have the effect of assisting the Soviets. It may be that we shall be driven to conclude that it is impossible to do business with Nasser. However, I do not think that we should close the door yet on the possibility of working with him. For one thing, such a decision would cancel out any prospects of obtaining now an Arab-Israel settlement.

I agree thoroughly with you on the necessity of aiding our friends and have written you separately with respect to the additional Centurion tanks for

Iraq. However, I question whether adherence by the United States to the Baghdad Pact now is the right answer. Measures apart from actual accession to the Pact such as our recent decision to increase aid to Pakistan and Iran may be more effective support for our friends. This is particularly true when drawbacks to adherence are considered, such as the effect on the other Arab States and probable demands for arms and a security guarantee to Israel.

I do not believe that our assessment of the situation in Jordan is firm enough to permit useful comment on your suggestion that you allot to Iraq some of the aid currently given to Jordan.

I am pleased that you sent me your preliminary thoughts and shall be waiting to hear the results of the discussions between Selwyn Lloyd and Foster.

Sincerely,
Dwight D. Eisenhower

EDEN TO EISENHOWER
March 15, 1956
Dear Friend,

I send you herewith a most secret note of Egyptian intentions of whose authenticity we are entirely confident.[1] I thought you should see it even though it adds nothing startlingly new to what we both suspected. It does, however, confirm the wide range of Egyptian ambitions against the Saudis, as well as Iraq and Jordan. May I ask you to treat it as highly confidential?

Of course I would expect Foster to see it.

Yours ever,
A.E.

1. Egyptian plans for a United Arab States, appended below.

EGYPTIAN PLANS FOR A UNITED ARAB STATES
(JANUARY 1956)

We have absolutely reliable information that at the Conference of Egyptian Ambassadors and Ministers to the Arab States which ended in Cairo on 30th January, 1956, it was agreed that the following policy should be adopted by Egypt in her relations with other Arab States:—

(a) The ultimate aim was to form United Arab States with no Customs, a common educational and economic system and an Arab Currency Bank which would control the financial affairs of all the Arab States.
(b) This United Arab States must consist of Republics amongst whom Egypt would naturally play the leading part.

(c) To this end the following steps were necessary:
  (i) The unseating of Nuri El Said, the Iraqi Prime Minister, and the frustration of the Bagdad Pact.
  (ii) The overthrow of the Hashemite families in Iraq and Jordan.[1]
  (iii) The overthrow of the monarchy in Libya and the establishing of purely Arab republics in Tunis, Algeria and Morocco. If this could be done, Egypt could strengthen her claim to be an Arab State rather than an African country outside the Arab orbit.[2]
  (iv) Whilst Saudi Arabia would be encouraged to partake in Egyptian moves against Iraq and Jordan, the long term policy was first to isolate Saudi Arabia as the only remaining Monarchy in the Eastern Arab States and then to remove King Saud. To this latter end Egypt was already in touch with many of the more powerful sheikhs in Arabia.
(d) This anti-monarchical policy was receiving full support from the U.S.S.R., which was sending so-called "technicians" to help in the organisation of intelligence services throughout the Arab World.
(e) In order to implement this policy, Egypt was despatching educational missions to all the Arab States. Several of the personnel of each mission had been trained as intelligence agents before their departure. Their general instructions were to recruit refugees and dissidents and to establish contact with anti-Government movements; but the direction of their activities was the responsibility of the Egyptian Ambassador or Minister to the Arab State in which they were operating.

1. Members of the Hashemite family had, with British support, become monarchs of Jordan and Iraq in 1921. Egypt regarded them as pliant monarchies of the British.
2. Most Arabists and Arab nationalists defined Arabism in cultural terms and regarded as Arabs all whose native language was Arabic. A number of Egyptians dissented on cultural grounds and did not regard Egyptians as Arabs. Furthermore, Egypt had held itself somewhat aloof politically from the wider Arab world before the revolution in 1952. Those factors were obstacles in the way of Nasser's pursuit of his goal for Egypt to assume leadership of the Arab world.

EDEN TO EISENHOWER ─────────────────
March 18, 1956
Dear Friend,
We are under strong pressure here in Parliament to say something about the progress of our talks in Washington on carrying out the Tripartite Declaration.[1] Naturally we could not say anything about military measures, but I should like to make a statement in general terms fairly soon.

Apart from this, I am becoming increasingly worried at the absence of any definite Anglo-American plan for dealing with aggression from either side in the Arab-Israel dispute. We should both be in a position of the utmost embarrassment if an attack occurred and we had to confess that in spite of all we have said about the Tripartite Declaration, no plan had been made for meeting it. I should be more than grateful for anything you can do to speed up the present talks.

Kindest regards,
Yours ever,
Anthony

1. The Tripartite Declaration (or Tripartite Agreement, as it was alternatively referred to) was proclaimed by Britain, France, and the United States on May 25, 1950. It was designed to prevent another war in the Middle East by promising the support of the three powers to Israel or to any Arab state that was attacked, and agreeing not to make arms sales of sufficient volume to either Israel or Arab nations that could upset the balance of power in the Middle East.

EDEN TO EISENHOWER
March 19, 1956
Message from the Prime Minister to the President.

Thank you for your message about the Middle East. The following is just to keep you in touch with our thoughts about the growing dangers in that part of the world.

Selwyn Lloyd discussed these matters with Foster in Karachi. Since then he has visited the other capitals of the Bagdad Pact countries and Israel. In consequence of his report to us we have made a careful re-examination of our policy towards Egypt. Selwyn is sending to Foster a detailed analysis of the situation as we see it. I am sure you will agree that it is essential that we should act together in these matters, and I hope that we shall be able speedily to evolve a common line. I need not emphasise to you the urgency of this task: the situation can deteriorate so rapidly.

EISENHOWER TO EDEN
March 20, 1956
Dear Anthony,

The enclosure you sent me with your letter of March fifteenth is a most interesting report on the intentions of the Egyptian Government. Assuming that the information therein contained is completely authentic, it seems to me to give a clue of how we—your Government and ours—might operate with the greatest chance of frustrating Soviet designs in the region.

Foster will return in a couple of days, and he and I will then go over this document and a good deal of other information which we have on this subject. In the meantime, thank you very much for sending it to me.

With warm personal regard,

As ever

DE

EISENHOWER TO EDEN ———————————————————

April 5, 1956

Dear Anthony,

When you were here we mentioned the forthcoming visit to London of our Russian friends(?) and you were good enough to say that if I had any suggestions to make, you would be glad if I would drop you a line on the subject.[1] I have been giving this matter some thought, but I believe your thinking and mine are so close together on the matters that are likely to come up that any suggestions from me would be superfluous.

Of course, at the back of our minds must be the very grave threat in the Middle East. We are, I think, both of us fully alive to what this could do to the well-being and indeed safety of Western Europe, and most particularly the United Kingdom. Whether or not you bring that up must be for you to decide in light of the circumstances. I fully agree with you that we should not be acquiescent in any measure which would give the Bear's claws a grip on the production or transportation of the oil which is so vital to the defense and economy of the Western world.

I shall be following your encounter with intense interest, and I hope that it will result in awareness on the part of the Russians of the dangerous nature of the game they seem to be playing.

As ever,

DE

1. The visit of Bulganin and Khrushchev to Britain had been arranged for April 18–27, 1956.

EDEN TO EISENHOWER ———————————————————

April 18, 1956

My Dear Friend,

I am grateful for your message about the Russian visit, and for your generous expression of confidence.

We expect the Middle East to come up in the course of a general review of world affairs. We propose to take up the Russian thesis that Palestine questions should be handled in the United Nations and see if we cannot get an undertaking from our visitors not to use their veto in the Security Council to block a resolution identifying the aggressor in the event of trouble. I have not high hopes of getting it, but I am sure you will agree that it is worth going for.

We shall make it very plain that our Middle Eastern oil supplies are a vital interest and that any attempt to deny them to us will create a most dangerous state of tension, since the British are not the kind of people to let themselves be quietly strangled. If the Russians suggest four-power consultation about arms for Egypt or Israel, we shall be very cautious and consult you before we give any reply.

I had a word about all this with Winthrop last week. We shall of course continue to keep in close touch with him throughout the talks, and I know that you and Foster will not hesitate to let us know if anything occurs to you that we could do for our common cause.

Yours ever,
Anthony

EISENHOWER TO EDEN ———
April 18, 1956
Dear Anthony,

Thank you very much for your cable. I agree with every word you have to say. I am sure that throughout the time of the meeting, Foster and Selwyn Lloyd will find some way of keeping in fairly close touch with each other.

As ever,
DE

EISENHOWER TO EDEN ———
April 27, 1956
Dear Anthony,

We have had quite a few discussions here these last days about the COCOM and CHINCOM trade controls.[1] Foster wrote to Selwyn Lloyd a few days ago and he will be talking further with Selwyn at Paris next week.[2] In the meantime I want to let you know how much I hope that you can find it possible to get copper wire back on the embargoed list.[3] All the information I get from our military, intelligence and economic people is that these exports are seriously interfering with our common objectives in a number of unfortunate ways. On the other hand, we are inclined to believe that it is also consistent with our common objectives to acquiesce in liberal use of the exception procedure for rubber and a number of other items on the CHINCOM list as Foster will explain further to Selwyn in Paris.

I am sorry that we have been so slow about this matter but it is full of all sorts of complications for us.

I congratulate you on the way you emerged, at least in public opinion, from your encounter with the Bear.[4]

With warm regard,

As ever,

D.E.

1. COCOM (the Coordinating Committee of the Paris Consultative Group of Nations) had been formed in 1949 to try to establish regulations with regard to items that could be traded with the Soviet bloc by the United States, Western Europe, and Japan. CHINCOM was the mechanism of the committee for the regulation of trade with Communist China. The United States sought to impose very restrictive regulations on trade with Communist countries, whereas other countries, such as Britain, wished to have a much more liberal approach to trade with both the Soviet bloc and Communist China.

2. Dulles and Lloyd were due to meet in Paris on May 4–5 at a meeting of the North Atlantic Council.

3. The United States believed that copper wire was a commodity in particularly short supply in the Soviet Union, so that a ban on its export to the Eastern bloc would therefore be damaging to Soviet military development. The British were skeptical of the impact of a ban on the export of this item and did not wish to cause damage to the economy of Rhodesia, a British colony, which was a major exporter of copper.

4. The visit of Bulganin and Khrushchev to Britain, April 18–27, 1956.

EDEN TO EISENHOWER

May 1, 1956

Dear Friend,

Here are a few random reflections from the visit of the bears. We were soon agreed that the main purpose of our meeting was serious talk. They made no attempt to escape from this and accepted without demur all the arrangements for the meetings, heavy as these were. They were considerate guests and made little attempt at propaganda. This may have been in part because the public behaved with such admirable restraint. They got no encouragement to attempt any such tactics as playing off the people against the Government, even if they had had them in mind.

From such exchanges as they had they seemed to prefer Her Majesty's Government to Her Majesty's Opposition.[1]

There was no effort at wedge-driving between us and you may think that this was clever on their part. I am inclined to think that it was an acceptance of the facts. They made few references to the United States and always spoke with respect of you.

Some of our earlier discussions were tough, especially an argument about colonialism, and a corresponding one about Eastern Europe. I think both were useful and instructive to each of us. Khrushchev was emphatic that we ought to understand that although the Russian influence with the satellites was considerable, the latter could be touchy and the Russians could not just order them about. There may well be something in this.

I was impressed by the grasp that these two men had of all the topics we discussed. I hardly saw them with anything that amounted to a brief. They were confident about their own country but I did not think that they were arrogant about their economic situation.

In the Middle East talk I made plain to them that we had to have our oil and that we were prepared to fight for it. They accepted this and though they continued to inveigh against the Bagdad Pact (or the Eden Pact, as Bulganin told me they called it in Moscow) I think that they may have begun to understand that it is a protective pad for our vital interests and not a dagger pointing at their guts.

I believe that war in the near future has no place in their plans. Their country seems to me to be going through a fairly normal post-revolutionary phase, Stalin having played the part of Napoleon in their story. These men seem to me to want to get on with their work at home, and why should they not? Therefore they do not want a flare-up, even in the Near East. I had to explain to them that this would happen if we did not align our policies.

I feel sure that the whole business was useful, although I confess I had some anxious moments at times. As the days went by I found these men more ready to admit other points of view than any Russians I have known, which does not of course mean that they accept them. It seems strange that they should exercise so much power. At times one wonders how long it can last.

Yours ever,
Anthony

1. At a dinner on April 23, 1956, given in honor of Bulganin and Khrushchev by the leaders of the Labour Party, there were sharp exchanges between the guests and their hosts over human rights in the Soviet Union.

EISENHOWER TO EDEN ──────────────

May 2, 1956

Dear Anthony,

Thank you very much for your interesting report on your recent visitors. Comparison of their conduct in Britain with the deportment of these same two individuals in Yugoslavia a couple of years ago does at least show that these men are capable of learning from experience.[1]

I am delighted that you made your views so utterly plain to them. At least in some areas we should be able to avoid emergencies that could arise out of misunderstanding or miscalculation on their part.

Foster left for Europe last evening, but I believe that on this trip he is not counting on stopping in London, so he will not get to see you.

With warm regard,

As ever,

DE

1. On a visit to Yugoslavia in May 1955, Khrushchev engaged in heated verbal exchanges with the American ambassador to Yugoslavia.

EDEN TO EISENHOWER ──────────────

May 2, 1956

Dear Friend,

Thank you for your letter of April 27 about trade controls. I must frankly tell you that your suggestion of adding to the embargoed list presents most serious difficulties for us. I do not see how we could agree to this now.

As to the CHINCOM list, we greatly need appreciable relaxation, particularly because of progress towards self-government in our colonial territories. A country like Malaya simply does not understand why it has to accept restrictions which are not in operation in, for example, Ceylon.

But Selwyn will talk all this over with Foster in Paris in the next few days.[1]

Kindest regards,

Yours ever,

Anthony

1. Dulles met Selwyn Lloyd in Paris where they were attending a meeting of the North Atlantic Council on May 4–5, 1956, but they failed to resolve the issue of copper wire and other issues of trade controls. In spite of American objections, Britain continued to export copper wire to Eastern bloc countries.

EISENHOWER TO EDEN

May 2, 1956

Dear Anthony,

I regret that the copper wire items offers for you such a problem. There is no question in our minds that this is the most important thing that the Bears and their associates now get from us.

As to the rest of your telegram, I think that Foster will be able to propose something that will ease the situation for you. I do hope that he and Selwyn Lloyd can work out something that will be satisfactory.

As ever,

D.E.

EDEN TO EISENHOWER

May 17, 1956

Dear Friend,

I am very reluctant to trouble you again about the secret operation on which we exchanged messages in March.[1] But I now find myself in new and embarrassing difficulties about this. You will have seen from the press the trouble we have had here about the incident of the frogman in Portsmouth Harbour.[2] This was a bad business. Though I have declined in the public interest to disclose the facts, most people here have deduced that it was a Secret Service operation. As a result both press and public in this country will for a time be very much on the alert for anything of this kind. Indeed they are likely to ask questions about your unusual aircraft as soon as it is seen in the air.

In these special circumstances I do not think that at present we can run any further risks from here with operations of this kind. I am sure that your people would take every possible precaution but, even so, there must remain some risk of mishap, whether from engine failure or other cause. At the end of my speech in the House of Commons debate on the frogman incident I said that I intended to safeguard "at all costs" the possibility that my recent discussions with the Soviet leaders might prove to be the beginning of a beginning towards better relations. I believe very sincerely that there may be some prospect of a lessening in international tension, and I may perhaps be forgiven for thinking that this is not the moment at which to risk anything which might impair that prospect.

I am told that the cover plan for the operation is high altitude weather reports. The aircraft already here is I believe ready to start its experimental flights. I should be greatly relieved if it could be decided that these initial flights should be confined to that meteorological purpose and that the other operation should be postponed. This would not wholly stultify the preparations that have already been made, and it would give substance to the cover plan. Certainly it would relieve me of my anxieties for the time being.

I am very sorry indeed to have to suggest this postponement. I hope you will appreciate the very real difficulties in which I find myself and that you will recognise that, if it had not been for these, I would not think of re-opening the matter.

Yours ever,
Anthony

1. U-2 flights over the Soviet Union.
2. On April 19, 1956, Commander Lionel "Buster" Crabb, employed by the Secret Intelligence Service, dived to inspect the electronic equipment on the hull of the Soviet cruiser in Portsmouth harbour on which Bulganin and Khrushchev had sailed to Britain. The Soviets became aware of Crabb's activities and lodged a diplomatic protest. Crabb disappeared, and his body was found a year later on a sandbank in Chichester harbour.

EDEN TO EISENHOWER ─────────────────────────

May 17, 1956
Dear Friend,
The code name of the operation is Aquatone.
Yours ever,
Anthony

EISENHOWER TO EDEN ─────────────────────────

May 17, 1956
Dear Anthony,

I understand your embarrassment under existing circumstances and have postponed Aquatone for the time being. All U.K. flights will be confined to bona fide weather activity and training over friendly territories. If we should finally conclude that the Soviet change of attitude is on the surface only, we can make new plans. In the meantime, I agree with you that we should do everything possible to determine the authenticity of friendly gestures from the other side and to encourage the growth of any that appear genuine.

As ever,
DE

EDEN TO EISENHOWER

May 19, 1956
Dear Friend,

I am grateful for your understanding reply. I am glad that you agree that the crucial point at the present time is to do nothing to discourage any possibility of an improvement in our relations with the Soviet Union. While there is any hope of this I should not be willing to authorise anything beyond the *bona fide* weather tests, and I am happy that you feel the same way.

Meanwhile your Air Force people here are getting enquiries about these aircraft since they have already been seen flying near their base. They therefore want to release a statement to the press describing their weather research programme. I am telling them that I have no objection to this. Of course, it will now correctly describe a *bona fide* weather operation.

Yours ever,
Anthony

EISENHOWER TO EDEN

June 4, 1956
Dear Anthony,

On my desk this morning I find a reminder of your approaching birthday anniversary.[1] I do hope—even though as I say it I recognise its impossibility—that for a day you will be able to shed all the worries of state and celebrate the occasion happily and properly.

At the same time I must remark upon the gratitude I feel for the good fortune that gives the two of us a long and deep personal friendship. As I look back upon the events of the past year, I cannot but believe that that relationship has been even further solidified.

With best wishes for the finest of birthdays, and, as always, my warm regard,

As ever,
Ike

1. On June 12, 1956, Eden celebrated his fifty-ninth birthday.

EDEN TO EISENHOWER

June 7, 1956
Dear Friend,

John Harding is here and we have had some long talks over this anxious Cyprus business.[1] I would like to give you for your own personal information one or two conclusions which emerge. First, as to the security situation. We have now reached the stage at which we are able to hit back at the terrorists, and to continue this process. Our forces had a marked success against the guerrilla bands about a week ago. The whole operation was planned with great care and was well executed. As a result we have broken up two of the bands and have captured the leaders of two more. Harding estimates that there are probably five or six more bands, of moderate size, in various parts of the island, but their total strength is probably not more than sixty full-time terrorists. Therefore this aspect of security should continue to show improvement over the next few months.

On the other hand, there has always been a real anxiety about Greek and Turkish communal riots in Cyprus. Though the Turks say less than the Greeks it does not mean that they feel less, and their anxiety about their future has put them into a highly excitable state. They are violently determined against Enosis.[2] There is also a considerable population of Turkish-Cypriots in Turkey itself which plays its part in moulding Turkish opinion. I believe they number a quarter of a million or more. If anything in the nature of widespread communal disturbances were to break out this would put a heavy and most disagreeable task upon our forces which would have to try to keep the parties apart and restore order. This could be more costly in casualties than anything we have to cope with now, and would divert our forces from operations against the terrorists.

We are of course also discussing the various political aspects of this problem. The truth is that the offer which we made to Makarios at the end of our last negotiations went beyond what the Turks themselves thought we should have offered.[3] This the Turkish Prime Minister has said publicly. To attempt to get results by offering more in this direction would inevitably entail strong Turkish reactions which would have very serious consequences for the security and stability of the Middle East as a whole. Nor would I feel confident of facilities in Cyprus under present conditions unless we had control of internal security. Athens radio has made it plain enough that the Greeks would not in any event be willing to allow our facilities in Cyprus to be used for any purposes connected with the Middle East. That is just what we might want them for. A N.A.T.O. base by itself would meet only part of our needs.

I do not think that either of our countries would be really happy if we were only able to counter a threat to vital oil supplies in the Persian Gulf from landing grounds in Arab lands.

You will know that Kuwait by itself has now twenty per cent of the proved oil reserves of the world, and all the indications are that the economy of Western Europe will increasingly depend on oil supplies from that area over the next twenty years or more. I just cannot take the risk of finding ourselves unable to protect these supplies should the need arise. But I did want you to know that I am working hard and will attempt to find some means of reconciling our needs with rival Greek and Turkish aspirations in the island.

If any new thought emerges from all this effort I will not hesitate to let you know, and of course Selwyn Lloyd will keep in touch with Foster.

John Harding asks to send you respectful greetings.

Kindest regards,

Yours ever

Anthony

1. Field Marshal Sir John Harding, governor of Cyprus. Britain had ruled Cyprus since 1878, and British bases on Cyprus were of great importance to Britain in the defense of British interests in the eastern Mediterranean and the Middle East. The majority of the population of Cyprus were Greeks, who wanted an end to British rule and either the union of Cyprus with Greece or independence. There was, however, a substantial Turkish minority, which was adamantly opposed to union with Greece and which feared suppression by the Greek majority in an independent Cyprus. Britain sought a compromise solution, which would enable Britain to maintain its bases and achieve an acceptable constitutional settlement for the Greeks and Turks. In 1955, violence broke out, with terrorist tactics employed against British soldiers by the National Organization for the Cyprus Struggle (EOKA), which pressed for union with Greece.

2. Union of Cyprus and Greece.

3. Archbishop Makarios III was not only a Greek Orthodox religious leader as primate of the Church in Cyprus but the leading political figure among Greek Cypriots. Britain had made an offer of a constitution for Cyprus with one house of the legislature determined by population, the other divided equally between Greeks and Turks, and with a security treaty leaving defense in British hands. The constitution needed acceptance by both Greeks and Turks. The British felt that Makarios was unwilling to accept a compromise settlement and that he was implicated in EOKA terrorism, so Makarios was exiled to the Seychelles in March 1956. Two years later Makarios was released and in 1960 Cyprus became independent, with a compromise settlement and Makarios as its first president. In 1974 Turkey invaded Cyprus to protect the Turkish minority, resulting in the de facto partition of Cyprus.

EDEN TO EISENHOWER

June 8, 1956

Clarissa and I are deeply concerned at the news.[1] We send you both all heartfelt thoughts and sympathy.

Anthony

1. Eisenhower had become ill with ileitis, an inflammation of the ileum, part of the small intestine.

EDEN TO EISENHOWER ─────────────────────

June 12, 1956

My dear Friend,

So glad at the steadily improving news. I know that such an operation can be a horrid business even at the best and we feel so much for you.[1]

Every good wish,

Anthony

1. Eisenhower underwent surgery for ileitis on June 9 at Walter Reed Hospital in Washington, D.C. He made a full recovery, but he had suffered from chronic stomach problems for years, which together with anxiety over his heart condition meant that Eisenhower's health was a matter of constant concern.

EDEN TO EISENHOWER ─────────────────────

June 13, 1956

Dear Ike,[1]

Thank you so much for your birthday letter. I was touched by your thoughtfulness in writing and even more by the friendship of what you said. You can't imagine how much I value the trust there is between us and how much it helps one to carry on.

I hope that by the time you get this you will be feeling better and more comfortable. Clarissa and I have felt so much for you in all this trying business. We know so well what you and Mamie must have been through.

Greetings and every possible good wish from us both.

Yours ever,

Anthony

1. Unusually, Eden addressed Eisenhower as Ike rather than the normal form of Dear Friend.

EISENHOWER TO EDEN ─────────────────────

June 13, 1956

Dear Anthony,

Many thanks for your note of the twelfth. There is no way to disguise the discomfort of the last few days, as I know you understand all too well, but I am beginning to feel something like myself once again.

Mamie greatly appreciated your earlier message.

With warm regard,

As ever,

DE

EISENHOWER TO EDEN

June 23, 1956

Dear Anthony,

Thank you very much for your letter of June seventh concerning Cyprus. Despite my present physical difficulty, I have studied it with much interest. I know your deep concern with this problem and it is a concern which I, too, share.

Foster has told me of the statement which you propose to make on the Cyprus question. He has, I think, some questions which he has raised with Roger Makins.[1] Is it wise, I wonder, for you to dilute your own authority by giving both Greece and Turkey what amounts to an indefinite veto power over any future change in the international status of Cyprus? Might not that further complicate a problem already complicated enough? Of course, they have legitimate interests which should be taken into account. But it seems to me important that the United Kingdom should retain a sufficient initiative and flexibility in its own hands to meet the changing circumstances which are bound to occur in a situation as complicated and as charged with emotion as is this one. Could you not therefore avoid giving an inflexible veto power to anybody?

I know it is much easier to put questions than to answer them. But I want you to know of my interest and our desire, as far as I properly can, to help at the right moment and in the right way to achieve some acceptable solution which will relieve NATO of the great risks which have developed around the present situation.

At last I can report that I seem steadily to regain my strength.

With warm personal regard,

As ever,

Ike E.

1. Roger Makins, British ambassador to the United States.

EDEN TO EISENHOWER

June 26, 1956

Dear Friend,

Thank you so much for your message about Cyprus. I feel distressed that you should have been inflicted with this at this time.

Harding is making good progress in restoring law and order, but he had told us that if he is to get a constitution working, the issue of self-determination must in some way be put into cold storage. Hence the period of years and a submission to N.A.T.O. on certain conditions at the end of it.

You will have heard that the initial Turkish reaction to our proposals was sharp and tough. Although it was more violent than I expected, I am not entirely surprised. The Greeks are good talkers, the Turks are not. But they have a habit of boiling slowly inside. When the lid of the kettle finally blows off, it can be very unpleasant for anyone nearby. Our Ambassador has warned us of the danger of a serious crisis in Anglo-Turkish relations.

All this is troublesome to us because we certainly need the Turks both for the Bagdad Pact and for N.A.T.O. Indeed I am sure that you will agree that if anyone holds a strategic position it is they.

However we have done all we can to put arguments for our proposals to them and expect to have their considered reply in a day or two. It may be that they will produce some suggestions of their own.

Meanwhile I do not propose to make any kind of public statement, difficult as it will be to refuse our Parliament any information.

It was because I am sure that we will never get this matter solved without agreement on military matters that we introduced the conception of a Tripartite treaty. I do not think that there is anything very new in this.

Our formula has much to recommend it to the Greeks. No doubt they will always ask for more. But, all else apart, I am sure that we cannot go further in placating them without disaster in our relations with the Turks.

The best news of all is of your improving health. It gladdens the hearts of millions here, and especially

Yours ever,
Anthony

EDEN TO EISENHOWER
July 18, 1956
Dear Friend,

I am so happy to hear that you are back at the White House again. This tempts me to send you some thoughts on the future of NATO which have been in my mind for some time.

I am fully in sympathy with the current project for improving the political cohesion of the Organisation, but I am sure that this alone will not suffice. It was on the military aspects of the alliance that the strength of the Organisation was founded; and its military policy must command public confidence if its authority is to be maintained.

As it seems to me the strategic situation has been evolving since the development of the thermo-nuclear weapon. Two new factors have now been introduced. First, both sides now stand possessed of this weapon, and each now realises the devastation which its use would involve. Second, and perhaps as important, public opinion throughout the democracies has begun to realise that the danger of major war has for this reason receded and that the nature of such a war, if it came, would be very different from anything we have known hitherto. As this understanding deepens there is bound to be a growing reluctance, among the peoples of the free world, to accept the social and human sacrifices required for the maintenance of large forces of the conventional pattern.

It can be argued that even the Russians are adjusting the balance of their resources. They are certainly doing everything they can to develop the most up-to-date weapons and the means of delivering them. From this it is pretty clear that they believe in the power of the deterrent. Having taken that decision they have decided, it seems to me, to increase their labour force for industrial expansion and correspondingly to reduce their conventional military forces. They are skilfully making the maximum propaganda use of this decision.

We have surely to take account of these new elements in the situation. Some no doubt will say that these considerations lead to the logical conclusion that you, at any rate, and perhaps we, should fall back on a peripheral defence. This is not my view. I feel sure it would not be yours. The maintenance of independence and freedom in Western Europe is essential to any policy designed to preserve our free way of life in the world. You know, better than anyone, how the increasing military strength of the North Atlantic Alliance helped to build up political stability in Western Europe, for you did it. It was the forces in being under NATO Command, and particularly the presence of United States and British forces in Europe, that gave confidence and courage to those who were ready to resist political encroachment by Communism in Europe. Or to put it another way: the political cohesion of the Western European countries in resisting the internal threat of Communism was inspired by growing confidence in the military side of the alliance. The political need to maintain the solidarity of the European countries is as strong as ever. For this purpose, even if for no other, it would still be important that some United States and British forces should remain on the ground in Europe under NATO Command.

The military purposes for which these forces are now required are, however, different from those on which the military policy of NATO was first framed. It was originally designed to meet the threat of a Soviet land invasion, and its pattern was established before the advent of the nuclear weapon. Today, the situation is changing. It is on the thermo-nuclear bomb and atomic weapons that we now rely, not only to deter aggression, but to deal with aggression if it should be launched. A "shield" of conventional forces is still required; but it is no longer our principal military protection. Need it be capable of fighting a major land battle? Its primary military function seems now to be to deal with any local infiltration, to prevent external intimidation and to enable aggression to be identified as such. It may be that it should also be capable of imposing some delay on the progress of a Soviet land invasion until the full impact is felt of the thermo-nuclear retaliation which would be launched against the Soviet Union.

The application of this concept would, I think, involve significant changes in the shape and size of the NATO forces, and possibly in their deployment. It would certainly have a profound effect on existing plans for reserve forces and for logistic support. I believe that it could lead to a reduction in the numbers of conventional forces stationed in Germany—though I should not wish such a reduction to be carried below the levels necessary to serve the political objectives outlined in paragraph 5 above. A reappraisal of the military policy of NATO along these lines is, I believe, necessary and urgent. It is necessary on its merits. It is urgent because we believe that NATO will not continue to command public confidence unless it shows its ability to adjust its policies to accord with changing circumstances and, as I have said, I doubt whether the peoples of the free world will be willing to go on bearing the heavy burden of defence programmes unless they are satisfied that these are directed realistically towards the new situation.

Much of this, as you know, was put by Roger Makins to Foster last month. His reaction was most helpful. Since then we have had useful and encouraging conversations here in London with Al Gruenther.[1] But above all I have now been greatly heartened to hear that you are yourself proposing to take a hand in all this next month. Big decisions will be called for and maybe we shall have to take some risks if we are to carry our people with us and maintain public confidence in the Alliance. However, I am quite sure that this can be done and that we shall go forward together to shape the future as we have done the past. We have had many more difficult problems than this and as long as we are in step I have no doubt that we can handle this one without causing disarray. It is for this reason that I am writing to you now to let you know how my mind is working. I should be much encouraged if I could hear that you were in general agreement with this broad approach.

I hope that you will enjoy your trip to Panama.[2] Do not let any other kinds of Americans tire you too much.

Yours ever,
Anthony

1. General Albert M. Gruenther, supreme Allied commander of NATO forces.
2. Eisenhower went to Panama for a meeting of Presidents of the Americas, July 21–24, 1956.

EISENHOWER TO EDEN

July 27, 1956

Dear Anthony,

Thank you for your recent message concerning the future of NATO, which reached me as I was about to leave for the meeting in Panama. I greatly appreciate your letting me know your thoughts on this matter. As you know, it is a subject in which I have the deepest personal interest.

I know that you are aware of the profound and far-reaching political and military implications of the question of NATO defense policy, which must be considered most carefully in terms of their effect on the continuing unity and strength of our NATO alliance. We have to think about the effect on Germany and on our friend Adenauer.[1]

As Foster has told Roger Makins, we are giving our urgent attention to these matters and we hope to be ready about the middle of August to give you our views. I am confident that our exchange of views will help us to find the right solution.

With warm regard,

As ever,

DE

1. Konrad Adenauer, chancellor of West Germany.

General Eisenhower warmly greets British Foreign Secretary Anthony Eden on his arrival at Eisenhower's headquarters in Normandy, August 21, 1944. (Signal Corps photograph; courtesy Dwight D. Eisenhower Library)

President-Elect Eisenhower greets British Foreign Secretary Anthony Eden in New York, November 20, 1952. (Associated Press/World Wide Photos)

Chairman of the USSR Council of Ministers Nikolai Bulganin, President Eisenhower, French Prime Minister Edgar Faure, and British Prime Minister Anthony Eden at the summit meeting in Geneva, Switzerland, July 18–23, 1955. (International Newsphoto)

President Eisenhower welcomes Prime Minister Eden to the White House, January 30, 1956. British Foreign Secretary Selwyn Lloyd stands beside Eden, and U.S. Secretary of State John Foster Dulles is between Eden and Eisenhower. (United Press Photos)

Prime Minister Eden leaves 10 Downing Street on his way to the House of Commons, June 12, 1956. (PA Photos)

Eisenhower delivers a radio and television address to the American people from the White House on the Suez crisis, October 31, 1956. (National Park Service photograph; courtesy Dwight D. Eisenhower Library)

Eisenhower acknowledges the acclaim of supporters at the Sheraton Park Hotel in Washington, D.C., after his victory over Adlai Stevenson in the U.S. presidential election, November 6, 1956. (National Park Service photograph; courtesy Dwight D. Eisenhower Library)

Eden leaves 10 Downing Street on his way to Buckingham Palace to tender his resignation as prime minister, January 9, 1957. (PA Photos)

CORRESPONDENCE, PART II

The Suez Crisis and Eden's Resignation, July 1956–January 1957

THE SUEZ CRISIS

On July 26, 1956, in a speech in Alexandria, Nasser announced Egypt's decision to nationalize the Suez Canal. Eden regarded this action as unacceptable and was determined to reverse it, by force if necessary. Eisenhower was opposed to the use of force and sought a means to defuse the crisis peacefully.

To Eden, Nasser's action was not only a threat to Britain's economic interests, but also a provocative repudiation of British power and authority, since the Suez Canal symbolized Britain's worldwide imperial reach. To Eisenhower, Nasser's action was legally justifiable, since compensation would be paid to stockholders and since the canal was due to revert to Egypt in any case in 1968 at the expiration of the ninety-nine-year lease to the Suez Canal Company. Eisenhower was perturbed by Nasser's policies, which had aimed to gain for himself leadership of the Arab radical nationalistic movement, but Eisenhower felt that Suez was not the issue over which to confront Nasser. Eisenhower felt that the use of force over Suez was likely to win increasing support for Nasser and to provide opportunities for a greater degree of Soviet penetration and influence in the Middle East.

Eden, however, made immediate military plans after July 26 for an assault on Egypt. Eisenhower took steps to try to bring about a resolution by diplomatic means, or at the very least to demonstrate that all peaceful avenues had been explored before a recourse to military means was taken. Dulles went to London on August 1. Agreement was reached that a Suez Canal Conference should be held among the representatives of twenty-four nations that were the principal users of the canal and had signed the 1888 Constantinople Convention, which guaranteed unhindered passage through the Suez Canal to all nations. Egypt was also invited. In the cases where nations that had signed the Constantinople Convention no longer existed, their successor nations, as could best be defined, were invited. Egypt refused the invitation, as did Greece, which was in dispute with Britain over Cyprus. The other twenty-two nations—Britain, the United States, Australia, Denmark, Ethiopia, West Germany, France, Holland, Iran, Italy, Japan, New Zealand, Norway, Pakistan, Portugal, Spain, Sweden, Turkey, India, Ceylon, Indonesia, and the Soviet Union—accepted the invitation and each sent a representative, normally the foreign minister, to the Suez Canal Conference, which met in London on August 16–23. Agreement was reached, except by India, Ceylon, Indonesia, and the Soviet Union, on terms which should be offered to Nasser, and a delegation of representatives of five nations among the eighteen who agreed on the terms, led by Robert Menzies, prime minister of Australia, went to Egypt on September 3–9 to present the terms to Nasser. The main features of the terms were arrangements for an international board to have control over the canal, while recognizing Egyptian sovereignty and guaranteeing a fair share of canal tolls to Egypt. Nasser rejected these terms, insisting upon Egyptian control over the canal, while promising unhindered passage to all nations and a reasonable rate of tolls.

In the face of Nasser's response, Britain and France were inclined to resort to force to take control over the canal and to overthrow Nasser. In an attempt to continue attempts to find a peaceful solution, Dulles proposed that, if Nasser would not accept the terms proposed by the eighteen nations, the users of the canal should take the initiative and form a users association, which would collect tolls, appoint pilots, and play a part in the operation of the canal.

A second Suez Canal Conference met in London, September 19–21, attended by the same eighteen nations, and agreement was reached on the establishment of the Suez Canal Users Association (SCUA), though not all of the eighteen nations agreed to join SCUA. SCUA was designed to be an interim measure to demonstrate to Nasser that the users would not accept total Egyptian control over the canal, while it was hoped that a long-term solution could be negotiated in due course.

Before SCUA was firmly established, however, Britain and France decided on September 21 to refer the Suez matter to the United Nations Security Council. The United States was suspicious that Britain and France did not expect a satisfactory resolution of the crisis to emerge from this referral. The Americans suspected that the British and French were going through the motions of taking the matter to the United Nations in the expectation that their proposals would be rejected and that they would then be in a stronger position if they resorted to force after peaceful means had been tried at the UN and had failed. Somewhat surprisingly, however, negotiations at the United Nations showed signs of considerable progress. Egypt appeared to be under pressure from other Arab nations to seek a peaceful solution, and while France remained eager to use military force against Nasser, whom France blamed for stirring up and giving aid to rebels in Algeria, Britain seemed more interested in the possibility of a peaceful solution. By October 10, agreement was reached, not only by Britain, France, the United States, and Egypt, but also by the Soviet Union, on six principles for the settlement of the Suez crisis: unhindered transit through the canal for all nations; respect for Egypt's sovereignty over the territory; operation of the canal to be insulated from the politics of any country; tolls to be decided by agreement between Egypt and users of the canal; a fair proportion of income from tolls to be allocated to the development of the canal; and cases of dispute between the Suez Canal Company and the Egyptian government to be resolved by arbitration. Arrangement of some of the details for the implementation of these principles remained to be resolved, but agreement on the six principles led Eisenhower optimistically to announce at a press conference on October 11 that the Suez crisis was over. On October 13 the UN Security Council passed a resolution accepting the six principles, though the Soviet Union vetoed a further statement on the arrangements for implementation. There seemed room for further negotiation to resolve these differences and to reach a settlement, but Eden decided that, given Soviet obstructiveness and the lack of means to enforce the six principles, a solution by force was necessary.

On October 14, Eden met secretly at Chequers, the prime minister's country residence, with two French envoys, Acting Foreign Minister Albert Gazier and General Maurice Challe, and agreed to a plan of collusion with Israel to provide an excuse for military action against Egypt by Britain and France. The extraordinary plan was that Israel would invade Egypt through the Sinai desert; Britain and France, feigning no foreknowledge of this action, would, under the pretext of protecting the Suez Canal, issue an ultimatum to Israel and Egypt to withdraw to a line ten miles on each side from the Suez Canal; and Israel would accept the ultimatum and withdraw the ten miles. Assuming that Egypt rejected the ultimatum, Britain and France would intervene militarily, supposedly to keep apart the warring parties of Israel and Egypt and to protect the Suez Canal from damage, but in fact in order to gain control over the canal and hopefully to bring about Nasser's downfall. On October 22–24, representatives of Britain, France, and Israel met in a villa in Sèvres on the outskirts of Paris and on October 24 signed the Protocol of Sèvres, which outlined the plan of collusion and set the date of October 29 for the Israeli attack on Egypt.

To complicate matters, on October 23 revolution broke out in Hungary.

Soviet troops and Hungarian secret police killed large numbers of protesters in Budapest and other Hungarian cities, but within a few days the violence receded and the Soviet government seemed to be willing to accept the reform Communist government of Imre Nagy. The Israeli attack on Egypt and the onset of the violent phase of the Suez crisis was one factor that led the Soviet government to its decision to intervene militarily in Hungary with massive brutal force on November 4 to crush the Hungarian revolution. Neither Eden nor the French or Israelis allowed events in Hungary to alter their plans, but in America the Hungarian Revolution had a huge impact.

A further complication was the American presidential election on November 6. An important part of Eisenhower's electoral appeal was that he was a man of peace. It would embarrass him considerably and would seem to be contrary to an unwritten agreement if Britain and France took military action before the election. This did not, however, deter Eden nor the French or Israelis. All details of the plan of collusion were, of course, kept very carefully concealed from the Americans.

On October 29 Israel invaded Egypt through the Sinai desert and advanced rapidly toward the Suez Canal. Britain and France duly issued an ultimatum, with a twelve hour time limit, to Israel and Egypt to withdraw to a line ten miles on either side of the Suez Canal. The Israelis had in fact not yet reached a point within ten miles of the canal, but they accepted the ultimatum. Egypt indignantly rejected the ultimatum, which demanded a withdrawal within their own sovereign territory. On October 30 the United States introduced a resolution in the UN Security Council calling for a ceasefire and withdrawal of Israeli forces from Egypt and calling on all UN members to refrain from the threat or use of force in the area or from providing assistance to Israel. The resolution was supported by the Soviet Union but vetoed by Britain and France. On October 31 British planes bombed Egyptian airfields and effectively destroyed the Egyptian air force. Meantime, British troops sailed from their base in Malta to land in Egypt, along with their French allies.

As the ships conveying the British and French troops made their way along the Mediterranean, a flurry of activity took place. On November 2, the Egyptians sunk a number of ships in the Suez Canal to block passage through the canal, while the oil pipeline that ran from Iraq to Lebanon through Syria was blown up by Syrian engineers. Meanwhile, Saudi Arabia broke off diplomatic relations with Britain and imposed an oil boycott. On November 3 a Canadian resolution was introduced in the United Nations calling for a UN force to intervene in Egypt. On November 4 this resolution was unanimously passed, but Britain and France felt that they should form part of the UN force and that, until the UN force was formed, their independent action was still required. On November 5 the Soviet Union ominously warned Britain that the Suez crisis might lead to a world war and made reference to Soviet rockets. Eden dismissed the Soviet threat, since intelligence sources informed him that the Soviets had no effective missile capability, and regarded the Soviet note as a diversion from Soviet intervention in Hungary. But the dangers of Soviet involvement heightened tensions further. On November 5, British troops landed at Port Said and the French landed at Port Faud. Approximately fifty British and French troops were killed, while about a thousand Egyptians died, many of them civilians. The Americans put severe pressure on Britain and France to call an immediate ceasefire. With the loss of Middle Eastern oil, Britain was dependent on an increase in oil supplies from New World sources, while the financial crisis of massive withdrawals of sterling, as many holders of sterling transferred funds from sterling into dollars, made Britain dependent on an International Monetary Fund loan. The United States used its financial muscle to refuse an increase in New World oil supplies and to withhold support for an IMF loan unless there was an immediate ceasefire. On November 6 Britain and France agreed to a ceasefire.

On November 15 the first troops of the United Nations force, from which Britain and France were excluded, arrived in Egypt. On November 24 the UN General Assembly passed a resolution censuring Britain and France and demanding the immediate withdrawal of their forces from Egypt. On December 3, British troops began to withdraw, and on December 22 the last British troops left Egypt. Oil supplies and financial support began to be provided by the United States.

Meanwhile, Eden's health had suffered under the strain of the crisis. On November 23 he went on holiday to Jamaica. He returned on December 14. His continuing health problems, however, together with his seriously weakened political position as a result of the Suez crisis, resulted in his resignation on January 9, 1957.

EDEN TO EISENHOWER
July 27, 1956
Dear Friend,

You will have had by now a report of the talk which I had last night with your Charge d'Affaires about the Suez Canal.[1] This morning I have reviewed the whole position with my Cabinet colleagues and Chiefs of Staff. We are all agreed that we cannot afford to allow Nasser to seize control of the Canal in this way, in defiance of international agreements. If we take a firm stand over this now, we shall have the support of all the maritime powers. If we do not, our influence and yours throughout the Middle East will, we are convinced, be irretrievably undermined.

The immediate threat is to the oil supplies to Western Europe, a great part of which flows through the Canal. We have reserves in the United Kingdom which would last us for six weeks; and the countries of Western Europe have stocks, rather smaller as we believe, on which they could draw for a time. We are, however, at once considering means of limiting current consumption so as to conserve our supplies; and if the Canal were closed we should have to ask you to help us by reducing the amount which you draw from the pipeline terminals in the Eastern Mediterranean and possibly by sending us supplementary supplies for a time from your side of the world.

It is, however, the outlook for the longer term which is more threatening. The Canal is an international asset and facility, which is vital to the free world. The maritime powers cannot afford to allow Egypt to expropriate it and to exploit it by using the revenues for her own internal purposes irrespective of the interests of the Canal and of the Canal users. Apart from the Egyptians' complete lack of technical qualifications, their past behaviour gives no confidence that they can be trusted to manage it with any sense of international obligation. Nor are they capable of providing the capital which will soon be needed to widen and deepen it so that it may be capable of handling the increased volume of traffic which it must carry in the years to come. We should, I am convinced, take this opportunity to put its management on a firm and lasting basis as an international trust.

We should not allow ourselves to become involved in legal quibbles about the rights of the Egyptian Government to nationalise what is technically an Egyptian company, or in financial arguments about their capacity to pay the compensation which they have offered. I feel sure that we should take issue with Nasser on the broader international grounds summarised in the preceding paragraph.

As we see it we are unlikely to attain our objective by economic pressures alone. I gather that Egypt is not due to receive any further aid from you. No large payments from her sterling balances here are due before January. We ought in the first instance to bring the maximum political pressure to bear on Egypt. For this, apart from our own action, we should invoke the support of all the interested powers. My colleagues and I are convinced that we must be ready, in the last resort, to use force to bring Nasser to his senses. For our part we are prepared to do so. I have this morning instructed our Chiefs of Staff to prepare a military plan accordingly.

However, the first step must be for you and us and France to exchange views, align our policies and concert together how we can best bring the maximum pressure to bear on the Egyptian Government. This we cannot easily do by correspondence. A tripartite meeting will, I am sure, be required at the earliest date. It should be at a high level. So far as we are concerned, it could be held either here or in Washington. But, as it happens, Pineau[2] was due to come over here for talks with Selwyn and will be arriving on Sunday next, July 29. Could you possibly arrange to send someone over at once who could join in discussions, not later than Monday of next week with Selwyn and Pineau. We should, of course, be delighted to see Foster, if that were practicable.

Meanwhile we are in close touch with the French and with the Commonwealth Governments. The High Commissioners here have all expressed their readiness to meet me to discuss the situation this evening. Some or all of them might be glad to join in the tripartite discussions. They are deeply interested, financially and otherwise.

Yours ever,
Anthony

1. Andrew Foster. Ambassador Winthrop Aldrich had left London earlier in the day for a short vacation. After receiving news of Nasser's speech declaring the nationalization of the Suez Canal, Eden held a meeting of his leading advisers on the evening of July 26 and at 11:00 P.M. invited Andrew Foster to join them. Foster cabled a report of this meeting to Washington.
2. Christian Pineau, foreign minister of France.

EISENHOWER TO EDEN
July 27, 1956

Your cable just received. To meet immediate situation we are sending Robert Murphy to London to arrive there Sunday or very early Monday.[1] In view of Foster's long trip, I doubt that he will be able to join in these talks, particularly since he could scarcely reach there Monday in any event.[2]

I shall not take time in this cable to outline for you the trend of our own thinking. While we agree with much that you have to say, we rather think there are one or two additional thoughts that you and we might profitably consider.

We are of the earnest opinion that the maximum number of maritime nations affected by the Nasser action should be consulted quickly in the hope of obtaining an agreed basis of understanding.

D.E.

1. Robert Murphy, deputy under secretary for Political Affairs.
2. Dulles arrived in Lima, Peru, on July 27 to attend the inauguration of President Manuel Prado y Ugarteche on July 28.

EISENHOWER TO EDEN
July 31, 1956
Dear Anthony,

From the moment that Nasser announced nationalization of the Suez Canal Company, my thoughts have been constantly with you. Grave problems are placed before both our governments, although for each of us they naturally differ in type and character. Until this morning, I was happy to feel that we were approaching decisions as to applicable procedures somewhat along parallel lines, even though there were, as would be expected, important differences as to detail. But early this morning I received the messages, communicated to me through Murphy from you and Harold Macmillan, telling me on a most secret basis of your decision to employ force without delay or attempting any intermediate and less drastic steps.[1]

We recognize the transcendent worth of the Canal to the free world and the possibility that eventually the use of force might become necessary in order to protect international rights. But we have been hopeful that through a Conference in which would be represented the signatories to the Convention of 1888, as well as other maritime nations, there would be brought about such pressures on the Egyptian government that the efficient operation of the Canal could be assured for the future.

For my part, I cannot over-emphasize the strength of my conviction that some such method must be attempted before action such as you contemplate should be undertaken. If unfortunately the situation can finally be resolved only by drastic means, there should be no grounds for belief anywhere that corrective measures were undertaken merely to protect national or individual investors, or the legal rights of a sovereign nation were ruthlessly flouted. A conference, at the very least, should have a great educational effect throughout the world. Public opinion here and, I am convinced, in most of the world, would be outraged should there be a failure to make such efforts. Moreover, initial military successes might be easy, but the eventual price might become far too heavy.

I have given you my own personal conviction, as well as that of my associates, as to the unwisdom even of contemplating the use of military force at this moment. Assuming, however, that the whole situation continued to deteriorate to the point where such action would seem the only recourse, there are certain political facts to remember. As you realize, employment of

United States forces is possible only through positive action on the part of the Congress, which is now adjourned but can be reconvened on my call for special reasons.² If those reasons should involve the issue of employing United States military strength abroad there would have to be a showing that every peaceful means of resolving the difficulty had previously been exhausted. Without such a showing, there would be a reaction that could very seriously affect our peoples' feeling towards our Western Allies. I do not want to exaggerate, but I assure you that this could grow to such an intensity as to have the most far reaching consequences.

I realize that the messages from both you and Harold stressed that the decision taken was already approved by the government and was firm and irrevocable. But I personally feel sure that the American reaction would be severe and that the great areas of the world would share that reaction. On the other hand, I believe we can marshal that opinion in support of a reasonable and conciliatory, but absolutely firm, position. So I hope that you will consent to reviewing this matter once more in its broadest aspects. It is for this reason that I have asked Foster to leave this afternoon to meet with your people tomorrow in London.

I have given you here only a few highlights in the chain of reasoning that compels us to conclude that the step you contemplate should not be undertaken until every peaceful means of protecting the rights and the livelihood of great portions of the world had been thoroughly explored and exhausted. Should these means fail, and I think it is erroneous to assume in advance that they needs must fail, then world opinion would understand how earnestly all of us had attempted to be just, fair and considerate, but that we simply could not accept a situation that would in the long run prove disastrous to the prosperity and living standards of every nation whose economy depends directly or indirectly upon East-West shipping.

With warm personal regard—and with earnest assurances of my continuing respect and friendship,

With warm regard,

As ever,

D.E.

1. Robert Murphy arrived in London on July 28. He held meetings with Eden and Macmillan, and on July 31 he reported on the very belligerent attitude of the British government, which was inclined toward an immediate resort to force against Nasser.

2. Under the U.S. Constitution, the power to declare war rests with Congress rather than with the executive branch. In practice, however, presidents throughout American history had used extraordinary powers, such as their power as commander-in-chief, to engage American forces in action without a declaration of war by Con-

gress, from Thomas Jefferson's use of naval forces against the Barbary pirates in the first decade of the nineteenth century to Harry Truman's commitment of American troops in the Korean War in 1950. Since Eisenhower's time, presidential commitment of American forces to military action without a declaration of war by Congress has been even more commonplace, from the Vietnam War to intervention in Kosovo and Afghanistan.

EDEN TO EISENHOWER

August 5, 1956

Dear Friend,

Thank you for the message which you sent me via Foster.[1]

In the light of our long friendship I will not conceal from you that the present situation causes me the deepest concern. I was grateful to you for sending Foster over and for his help. It has enabled us to reach firm and rapid conclusions and to display to Nasser and to the world the spectacle of a United Front between our two countries and the French. We have, however, gone to the very limits of the concessions which we can make.

I do not think that we disagree about our primary objective. As it seems to me, this is to undo what Nasser has done and to set up an International Regime for the Canal. The purpose of this regime will be to ensure the freedom and security of transit through the Canal, without discrimination, and the efficiency and economy of its operation.

But this is not all. Nasser has embarked on a course which is unpleasantly familiar. His seizure of the Canal was undoubtedly designed to impress opinion not only in Egypt but in the Arab world and in all Africa too. By this assertion of his power he seeks to further his ambitions from Morocco to the Persian Gulf. In this connection you have no doubt seen Nasser's own speech at Aboukir on August 1, in which he said "We are very strong because we constitute a limitless strength extending from the Atlantic Ocean to the Arab Gulf."

I know that Nasser is active wherever Muslims can be found, even as far as Nigeria. The Egyptians tried to get one of the Nigerian Amirs who was on his way through Cairo to sign a message endorsing Nasser's deeds. The man tore it up, but, if Nasser keeps his loot, how long can such loyalty last? At the other end of the line, the Sheik of Kuwait has spoken to us stoutly of his views of Nasser. But all these men and millions of others are watching and waiting now.

I have never thought Nasser a Hitler; he has no warlike people behind him. But the parallel with Mussolini is close. Neither of us can forget the lives and treasure he cost us before he was finally dealt with.

The removal of Nasser, and the installation in Egypt of a regime less hostile to the West, must therefore also rank high among our objectives. We must hope, as you say in your message, that the forthcoming conference will bring such pressures upon Nasser that the efficient operation of the Canal can be assured for the future. If so, everyone will be relieved and there will be no need of force. Moreover, if Nasser is compelled to disgorge his spoils, it is improbable that he will be able to maintain his internal position. We should thus have achieved our secondary objective.

Nevertheless I am sure you will agree that we must prepare to meet the eventuality that Nasser will refuse to accept the outcome of the conference; or, no less dangerous, that he, supported by the Russians, will seek by stratagems and wiles to divide us so that the conference produces no clear result in the sense we both seek. We and the French Government could not possibly acquiesce in such a situation. I really believe that the consequences of doing so would be catastrophic, and that the whole position in the Middle East would thereby be lost beyond recall. But by all means let us first see what the conference can do—on the assumption that Nasser commits no further folly meanwhile.

You know us better than anyone, and so I need not tell you that our people here are neither excited nor eager to use force. They are, however, grimly determined that Nasser shall not get away with it this time, because they are convinced that if he does their existence will be at his mercy. So am I.

I am infinitely grateful for your patience and understanding of our feelings. I cannot tell you how much they mean to us in this time of anxiety.

It is splendid news to hear of your growing strength.

We will do our best not to add to the strain.

Yours ever,

Anthony

1. Eisenhower's letter to Eden of July 31 was delivered personally by Dulles to Eden when Dulles arrived in London on August 1.

EISENHOWER TO EDEN
August 9, 1956
Dear Anthony,

I have read very carefully, and with a great deal of sympathy, your response to my message dated July 31, 1956, which Foster left with you in London last week. It was extremely good of you to send me so promptly your thinking on this subject.

What you say is very much in our thoughts and we are devoting the major part of our time to this important problem.

I was glad to hear from Foster that you are looking so well.

With warm personal regard,

Sincerely,

D.E.

EDEN TO EISENHOWER ─────────────────────

August 27, 1956

Dear Friend,

This is a message to thank you for all the help Foster has given. Though I could not be at the Conference myself, I heard praise on all sides for the outstanding quality of his speeches and his constructive leadership. He will tell you how things have gone. It was, I think, a remarkable achievement to unite eighteen nations on an agreed statement of this clarity and force.[1]

Before he left, Foster spoke to me of the destructive efforts of the Russians at the Conference. I have been giving some thought to this and I would like to give you my conclusions.

I have no doubt that the bear is using Nasser, with or without his knowledge, to further his immediate aims. These are, I think, first to dislodge the West from the Middle East, and second to get a foothold in Africa so as to dominate that continent in turn. In this connexion I have seen a reliable report from someone who was present at the lunch which Shepilov gave for the Arab Ambassadors.[2] There the Soviet claim was that they "only wanted to see Arab unity in Asia and Africa and the abolition of all foreign bases and exploitation. An agreed, unified Arab nation must take its rightful place in the world."

This policy is clearly aimed at Wheelus Field and Habbaniya, as well as at our Middle East oil supplies.[3] Meanwhile the Communist bloc continue their economic and political blandishments towards the African countries which are already independent. Soon they will have a wider field for subversion as our colonies, particularly in the West, achieve self-government. All this makes me more than ever sure that Nasser must not be allowed to get away with it this time. We have many friends in the Middle East and in Africa and others who are shrewd enough to know where the plans of a Nasser or a Mossadeq would lead them.[4] But they will not be strong enough to stand against the power of the mobs if Nasser wins again. The firmer the front we show together, the greater the chance that Nasser will give way without the need for any resort to force. That is why we were grateful for your policy and Foster's expression of it at the Conference. It is also one of the reasons why we have to continue our military preparations in conjunction with our French allies.

We have been examining what other action could be taken if Nasser refuses to negotiate on the basis of the London Conference. There is the question of the dues.[5] The Dutch and the Germans have already indicated that they will give support in this respect. The Dutch may even be taking action in the next few days. Then there is the question of currency and economic action. We are studying these with your people and the French in London and will be sending our comments soon. It looks as though we shall have a few days until Nasser gives Menzies his final reply.[6] After that we should be in a position to act swiftly. Selwyn Lloyd is telegraphing to Foster about tactics particularly in relation to the United Nations.

Meanwhile I thought I should set out some of our reflections on the dangerous situation which still confronts us. It is certainly the most hazardous that our country has known since 1940. I was so glad to see such excellent photographic testimony of your growing health and abounding energy. That is the very best news for us all.

With kindest regards,

Yours ever,

Anthony

1. On August 23, 1956, the first Suez Canal Conference ended in London, with agreement on the part of eighteen of the twenty-two participating nations on a position to be presented to Nasser by a delegation of representatives of five of the eighteen nations, led by Robert Menzies, prime minister of Australia.

2. Dimitri T. Shepilov, foreign minister of the Soviet Union.

3. Wheelus Field was an American military base in Libya. Habbaniya was a British military base in Iraq.

4. Mohammed Mossadeq, prime minister of Iran, 1951–53, who nationalized the Anglo-Iranian Oil Company (AIOC) and who was overthrown in 1953 following demonstrations that were organized and financed by the CIA.

5. Britain hoped that as many countries as possible would refuse to pay Suez Canal dues to Egypt and would instead place payments in a special account and take other economic measures against Egypt.

6. Nasser gave his reply to Menzies on September 9.

EISENHOWER TO EDEN

September 2, 1956

Dear Anthony,

I am grateful for your recent letter, and especially for your kind words on the role of the United States during the London Conference on the Suez

Canal. I share your satisfaction at the large number of nations which thought as we do about the future operation of the Canal. In achieving this result we have set in motion a force which I feel will be very useful to us—the united and clearly expressed opinion of the majority users of the Suez waterway and of those nations most dependent upon it. This will exert a pressure which Nasser can scarcely ignore. From Foster I know that this accomplishment is due in no small measure to the expert leadership exhibited by Selwyn Lloyd as Chairman of the Conference, and to the guidance which he received from you.

As for the Russians, it is clear that they sought, at London, to impede the consolidation of a majority point of view, and to generate an atmosphere in the Near East which would make it impossible for Nasser to accept our proposals. I entirely agree with you that the underlying purpose of their policy in this problem is to undermine the Western position in the Near East and Africa, and to weaken the Western nations at home. We must never lose sight of this point.

Now that the London Conference is over, our efforts must be concentrated on the successful outcome of the conversations with Nasser. This delicate situation is going to require the highest skill, not only on the part of the five-nation Committee but also on the part of our Governments. I share your view that it is important that Nasser be under no misapprehension as to the firm interest of the nations primarily concerned with the Canal in safeguarding their rights in that waterway.

As to the possibility of later appeal to the United Nations, we can envisage a situation which would require UN consideration and of course there should be no thought of military action before the influences of the UN are fully explored. However, and most important, we believe that, before going to the UN, the Suez Committee of Five should first be given full opportunity to carry out the course of action agreed upon in London, and to gauge Nasser's intentions.

If the diplomatic front we present is united and is backed by the overwhelming sentiment of our several peoples, the chances should be greater that Nasser will give way without the need for any resort to force. This belief explains our policy at the Conference and also explains the statement which I gave out through Foster after I got back from San Francisco and had a chance to talk fully with him.[1]

I am afraid, Anthony, that from this point onward our views on this situation diverge. As to the use of force or the threat of force at this juncture, I continue to feel as I expressed myself in the letter Foster carried to you some weeks ago. Even now military preparations and civilian evacuation exposed to public view seem to be solidifying support for Nasser which has been shaky in many important quarters. I regard it as indispensable that if we are to proceed solidly together to the solution of this problem, public opinion in our several countries must be overwhelmingly in its support. I must tell you frankly that American public opinion flatly rejects the thought of using force, particularly when it does not seem that every possible peaceful means of protecting our vital interests has been exhausted without result. Moreover, I gravely doubt we could here secure Congressional authority even for the lesser support measures for which you might have to look to us.

I really do not see how a successful result could be achieved by forcible means. The use of force would, it seems to me, vastly increase the area of jeopardy. I do not see how the economy of Western Europe can long survive the burden of prolonged military operations, as well as the denial of Near East oil. Also, the peoples of the Near East and of North Africa and, to some extent, of all of Asia and all of Africa, would be consolidated against the West to a degree which, I fear, could not be overcome in a generation and, perhaps, not even in a century particularly having in mind the capacity of the Russians to make mischief. Before such action were undertaken, all our peoples should unitedly understand that there were no other means available to protect our vital rights and interests.

We have two problems, the first of which is the assurance of permanent and efficient operation of the Suez Canal with justice to all concerned. The second is to see that Nasser shall not grow as a menace to the peace and vital interests of the West. In my view, these two problems need not and possibly cannot be solved simultaneously and by the same methods, although we are exploring further means to this end. The first is the most important for the moment and must be solved in such a way as not to make the second more difficult. Above all, there must be no grounds for our several peoples to believe that anyone is using the Canal difficulty as an excuse to proceed forcibly against Nasser. And we have friends in the Middle East who tell us they would like to see Nasser's deflation brought about. But they seem unanimous in feeling that Suez is not the issue on which to attempt to do this by force. Under those circumstances, because of the temper of their populations, they say they would have to support Nasser even against their better judgment.

Seldom, I think, have we been faced by so grave a problem. For the time being we must, I think, put our faith in the processes already at work to bring Nasser peacefully to accept the solution along the lines of the 18-nation proposal. I believe that even though this procedure may fail to give the setback to Nasser that he so much deserves, we can better retrieve our position subsequently than if military force were hastily invoked.

Of course, our departments are looking into the implications of all future developments. In this they will keep in close touch with appropriate officials of your Government, as is my wish.

With warm regard,

As ever,

D.E.

1. Eisenhower had been in San Francisco for the Republican National Convention, where he was renominated as Republican candidate for president in 1956. On receipt of Dulles's report on the London Suez Conference, Eisenhower issued a statement expressing the hope that this would lead to a peaceful resolution of the crisis.

EDEN TO EISENHOWER
September 6, 1956
Dear Friend,

Thank you for your message and for writing thus frankly. There is no doubt as to where we are agreed and have been agreed from the very beginning, namely, that we should do everything we can to get a peaceful settlement. It is in this spirit that we favoured calling the twenty-two power Conference and that we have worked in the closest cooperation with you about this business ever since. There has never been any question of our suddenly or without further provocation resorting to arms while these processes were at work. In any event as your own wide knowledge would confirm we could not have done this without extensive preparation lasting several weeks.

This question of precautions has troubled me considerably and still does. I have not forgotten the riots and murders in Cairo in 1952, for I was in charge here at the time when Winston was on the high seas on his way back from the United States.

We are both agreed that we must give the Suez Committee every chance to fulfil their mission. This is our firm resolve. If the Committee and subsequent negotiations succeed in getting Nasser's agreement to the London proposals of the Eighteen powers there will be no call for force. But if the Committee fails we must have some immediate alternative which will show that Nasser is not going to get his way. In this connection we are attracted by Foster's suggestion if I understand it rightly for the running of the Canal by the users in virtue of their rights under the 1888 Convention. We heard about this from our Embassy in Washington yesterday. I think that we could go along with this provided that the intention was made clear by both of us immediately the Menzies Mission finishes its work. But unless we can proceed with this or something very like it what should the next step be?

You suggest that this is where we diverge. If that is so I think that the divergence springs from a difference in our assessment of Nasser's plans and intentions. May I set our view of the position. In the 1930s Hitler established his position by a series of carefully planned movements. These began with the occupation of the Rhineland and were followed by successive acts of aggression against Austria, Czechoslovakia, Poland and the West. His actions were tolerated and excused by the majority of the population of Western Europe. It was argued either that Hitler had committed no act of aggression against anyone or that he was entitled to do what he liked in his own territory or that it was impossible to prove that he had any ulterior designs or that the covenant of the League of Nations did not entitle us to use force and that it would be wiser to wait until he did commit an act of aggression.

In more recent years Russia has attempted similar tactics. The blockade of Berlin was to have been the opening move in a campaign designed at least to deprive the Western powers of their whole position in Germany. On this occasion we fortunately reacted at once with the result that the Russian design was never unfolded. But I am sure that you would agree that it would be wrong to infer from this circumstance that no Russian design existed. Similarly the seizure of the Suez Canal is, we are convinced, the opening gambit in a planned campaign designed by Nasser to expel all Western influence and interests from Arab countries. He believes that if he can get away with this and if he can successfully defy eighteen nations his prestige in Arabia will be so great that he will be able to mount revolutions of young officers in Saudi Arabia, Jordan, Syria and Iraq. (We know from our joint sources that he is already preparing a revolution in Iraq which is the most stable and progressive.) These new Governments will in effect be Egyptian satellites if not Russian ones. They will have to place their united oil resources under the control of a united Arabia led by Egypt and under Russian influence. When that moment comes Nasser can deny oil to Western Europe and we here shall all be at his mercy.

There are some who doubt whether Saudi Arabia, Iraq and Kuwait will be prepared even for a time to sacrifice their oil revenues for the sake of Nasser's ambitions. But if we place ourselves in their position I think the dangers are clear. If Nasser says to them, "I have nationalised the Suez Canal. I have successfully defied eighteen powerful nations, including the United States, I have defied the whole of the United Nations in the matter of the

Israel blockade, I have expropriated all Western property. Trust me and withhold oil from Western Europe. Within six months or a year the continent of Europe will be on its knees before you." Will the Arabs not be prepared to follow this lead? Can we rely on them to be more sensible than were the Germans? Even if the Arabs eventually fall apart again as they did after the early Caliphs, the damage will have been done meanwhile.[1]

In short we are convinced that if Nasser is allowed to defy the eighteen nations it will be a matter of months before revolution breaks out in the oil bearing countries and the West is wholly deprived of Middle Eastern oil. In this belief we are fortified by the advice of friendly leaders in the Middle East.

The Iraqis are the most insistent in their warnings, both Nuri and the Crown Prince have spoken to us several times of the consequences of Nasser succeeding in his grab.[2] They would be swept away. Other warnings have been given by the Shah to our Ambassador when he said that he gave getting rid of Nasser a very high priority.[3] The Libyan Ambassador here, who was formerly Prime Minister, said that wise men must see the danger of Nasser succeeding.[4] King Saud of whose advice you will know more than we do also spoke in apprehension to Prince Zaid of Iraq when he was there the other day. He said that it would be bad if Nasser emerged triumphant for he agreed that Nasser's ambition was to become the Napoleon of the Arabs and if he succeeded the regimes in Iraq and Saudi Arabia would be swept away.

The difference which separates us today appears to be a difference of assessment of Nasser's plans and intentions and of the consequences in the Middle East of military action against him.

You may feel that even if we are right it would be better to wait until Nasser has unmistakeably unveiled his intentions. But this was the argument which prevailed in 1936 and which we both rejected in 1948. Admittedly there are risks in the use of force against Egypt now. It is however clear that military intervention designed to reverse Nasser's revolutions in the whole continent would be a much more costly and difficult undertaking. I am very troubled as it is that if we do not reach a conclusion either way about the Canal very soon one or other of these Eastern lands may be toppled at any moment by Nasser's revolutionary movements.

I agree with you that prolonged military operations as well as the denial of Middle East oil would place an immense strain on the economy of Western Europe. I can assure you that we are conscious of the burdens and perils attending military intervention. But if our assessment is correct and if the only alternative is to allow Nasser's plans quietly to develop until this country and all Western Europe are held to ransom by Egypt acting at Russia's behest it seems to us that our duty is plain. We have many times led Europe in the fight for freedom. It would be an ignoble end to our long history if we tamely accepted to perish by degrees.

With kindest regards,
Yours ever,
Anthony

1. The caliphs were the successors of the prophet Mohammed. After Mohammed's death in 632, there was agreement on the choice of the first three caliphs, but in the time of Ali, the fourth caliph, 656–61, there were divisions, rival claimants, and civil war, such that Arab unity was destroyed.
2. Nuri al-Said, prime minister of Iraq; Crown Prince Amir Abdullah of Iraq.
3. Mohammed Reza Pahlavi, the shah of Iran.
4. Mahmud Muntasser.

EISENHOWER TO EDEN
September 8, 1956
Dear Anthony,

Whenever, on any international question, I find myself differing even slightly from you, I feel a deep compulsion to re-examine my position instantly and carefully. But permit me to suggest that when you use phrases in connection with the Suez affair, like "ignoble end to our long history" in describing the possible future of your great country, you are making of Nasser a much more important figure than he is.

We have a grave problem confronting us in Nasser's reckless adventure with the Canal, and I do *not* differ from you in your estimate of his intentions and purposes. The place where we apparently do not agree is on the probable effects in the Arab world of the various possible reactions by the Western world.

You seem to believe that any long, drawn-out controversy either within the 18-nation group or in the United Nations will inevitably make Nasser an Arab hero and seriously damage the prestige of Western Europe, including the United Kingdom, and that of the United States. Further you apparently believe that there would soon result an upheaval in the Arab nations out of which Nasser would emerge as the acknowledged leader of Islam. This, I think, is a picture too dark and is severely distorted.

I shall try to give you a somewhat different appraisal of the situation. First, let me say that my own conclusions are based to some degree upon an understanding of current Arab feeling that differs somewhat from yours. I believe that as this quarrel now stands before the world, we can expect the Arabs to rally firmly to Nasser's support in either of two eventualities.

The first of these is that there should be a resort to force without thoroughly exploring and exhausting every possible peaceful means of settling the issue, regardless of the time consumed, and when there is no evidence before the world that Nasser intends to do more than to nationalize the Canal Company. Unless it can be shown to the world that he is an actual aggressor, then I think all Arabs would be forced to support him, even though some of the ruling monarchs might very much like to see him toppled.

The second would be what seemed like a capitulation to Nasser and complete acceptance of his rule of the Canal traffic.

The use of military force against Egypt under present circumstances might have consequences even more serious than causing the Arabs to support Nasser. It might cause a serious misunderstanding between our two countries because I must say frankly that there is as yet no public opinion in this country which is prepared to support such a move, and the most significant public opinion that there is seems to think that the United Nations was formed to prevent this very thing.

It is for reasons such as these that we have viewed with some misgivings your preparations for mounting a military expedition against Egypt. We believe that Nasser may try to go before the United Nations claiming that these actions imply a rejection of the peaceful machinery of settling the dispute, and therefore may ask the United Nations to brand these operations as aggression.

At the same time, we do not want any capitulation to Nasser. We want to stand firmly with you to deflate the ambitious pretensions of Nasser and to assure permanent free and effective use of the Suez waterway under the terms of the 1888 Treaty.

It seems to Foster and to me that the result that you and I both want can best be assured by slower and less dramatic processes than military force. There are many areas of endeavor which are not yet fully explored because exploration takes time.

We can, for example, promote a semi-permanent organization of the user governments to take over the greatest practical amount of the technical problems of the Canal, such as pilotage, the organization of the traffic pattern, and the collection of dues to cover actual expenses. This organization would be on the spot and in constant contact with Egypt and might work out a *de facto* "coexistence" which would give the users the rights which we want.

There are economic pressures which, if continued, will cause distress in Egypt.

There are Arab rivalries to be exploited and which can be exploited if we do not make Nasser an Arab hero.

There are alternatives to the present dependence upon the Canal and pipelines which should be developed perhaps by more tankers, a possible new pipeline to Turkey and some possible rerouting of oil, including perhaps more from this hemisphere, particularly to European countries which can afford to pay for it in dollars.

Nasser thrives on drama. If we let some of the drama go out of the situation and concentrate upon the task of deflating him through slower but sure processes such as I described, I believe the desired results can more probably be obtained.

Gradually it seems to me we could isolate Nasser and gain a victory which would not only be bloodless, but would be more far-reaching in its ultimate consequences than could be anything brought about by force of arms. In addition, it would be less costly both now and in the future.

Of course, if during this process Nasser himself resorts to violence in clear disregard of the 1888 Treaty, then that would create a new situation and one in which he and not we would be violating the United Nations Charter.

I assure you we are not blind to the fact that eventually there may be no escape from the use of force. Our resolute purpose must be to create conditions of operation in which all users can have confidence. But to resort to military action when the world believes there are other means available for resolving the dispute would set in motion forces that could lead, in the years to come, to the most distressing results.

Obviously there are large areas of agreement between us. But in these exchanges directed toward differing methods I gain some clarification of the confusing and conflicting considerations that apply to this problem.

With warmest regard,
As ever your friend,
Dwight D. Eisenhower

EISENHOWER TO EDEN
September 18, 1956
Dear Anthony,

You may remember raising with me early this year the question of medium tanks for Germany. As you know, our policy was and is to encourage the Germans to satisfy their armament requirements, insofar as possible, from United Kingdom and European sources. Since the time of our discussion, we have continued to stress this policy with the Germans. We have particularly urged upon them the advantages of purchasing tanks in the United Kingdom, making specific reference to your Centurions.

Despite these efforts, we received a short time ago an official request from the Germans that the United States sell them a sufficient number of our M-47 tanks to meet their medium tank needs. The study I mentioned to you in my letter of March sixth has meanwhile been completed and it is clear that we are able to supply M-47s in the number the Germans want.

I believe we will have to accede to the German request as I can see no alternative for us short of refusing to sell them United States tanks, which I do not believe we can do.

We will be informing them of our decision in a few days, but before doing this I did want you to know the background which surrounded it.

I know this creates difficulties for you and I regret that this matter has turned out as it has.

With warm regard,

As ever,

Dwight D. Eisenhower

EDEN TO EISENHOWER
September 20, 1956
Dear Friend,

You may like to see for your own eyes, and those of Foster only, the enclosed copies of the message which Mr. Bulganin sent to me on September 11 and of the reply which I have sent him.[1]

These continue to be anxious days for us all. We are glad to have Foster here, and pray that a firm and united front will result.

Yours ever,

Anthony

1. On September 11, 1956, Nikolai Bulganin, chairman of the Council of Ministers of the Soviet Union, sent a letter to Eden in which he expressed concern over apparent preparations for resort to force in the Suez crisis on the part of Britain and France. Bulganin argued that Egypt had a good case in the dispute and that the issue should be settled by peaceful means within the United Nations and not by means of force, which were similar to the means which had been employed by colonial powers in their acquisition of empire. On September 16 Eden replied that Nasser's actions in nationalizing the Suez Canal had been provocative and unjustifiable and threatened the interests of the nations which used the Suez Canal but that Britain had striven to seek a peaceful solution to the crisis.

This was the first of several letters exchanged between Bulganin and Eden throughout the Suez crisis. The letters were signed by Bulganin although he was in reality the front man for the Soviet government, which was by that time dominated by Khrushchev. As chairman of the Council of Ministers, Bulganin was the official head of government, but Khrushchev, who was first secretary of the Communist Party of the

Soviet Union, was the effective leader in the Soviet Union, though his power was restricted within a collective leadership. In 1957 Khrushchev's power increased further after a failed attempt to depose him, and in 1958 Bulganin was removed, and Khrushchev assumed the post of chairman of the Council of Ministers as well as first secretary of the Communist Party of the Soviet Union, so that his leadership was unquestioned throughout the remainder of his time in office until he was deposed in 1964.

EISENHOWER TO EDEN

September 22, 1956

Dear Anthony,

Thank you very much for sending me the documents that accompanied your recent note. When I see Foster I will go over them with him, but will show them to no one else.

From Foster's report it appears that the going has been far from easy. But I was hopeful that India would begin to see a little bit more eye-to-eye with the West in regard to this matter.

With warm regard,

As ever,

D.E.

EDEN TO EISENHOWER

September 29, 1956

Dear Friend,

Thank you for your letter of September 18 about tanks for Germany. Of course we are disappointed that the Germans have decided not to buy Centurions. This will create difficulties for us, as you know, but we shall surmount these as best we can. I am most grateful to you for going into this matter personally on our behalf.

Yours ever,

Anthony

EDEN TO EISENHOWER

October 1, 1956

Personal message to the President.

Harold has told me of his conversation with you.[1] I was particularly delighted to hear from him that you were in such splendid form.

You can be sure that we are fully alive to the wider dangers of the Middle East situation. They can be summed up in one word—Russia.

I thought that you would like to see this further message from Bulganin to me. I shall not reply for a day or two.[2]

There is no doubt in our minds that Nasser, whether he likes it or not, is now effectively in Russian hands, just as Mussolini was in Hitler's. It would be as ineffective to show weakness to Nasser now in order to placate him as it was to show weakness to Mussolini. The only result was and would be to bring the two together.

No doubt your people will have told you of the accumulating evidence of Egyptian plots in Libya, Saudi Arabia and Iraq. At any moment any of these may be touched off unless we can prove to the Middle East that Nasser is losing. That is why we are so concerned to do everything we can to make the Users' Club an effective instrument. If your ships under the Panamanian and Liberian flags would follow the example of those under your flag that would greatly help.³

I feel sure that anything which you can say or do to show firmness to Nasser at this time will help the peace by giving the Russians pause.

As usual I sent you my thoughts in this frank way.

1. Macmillan came to the United States for a meeting of the International Monetary Fund. He had a meeting with Eisenhower on September 25, 1956. Their conversation was wide-ranging and fairly general, with only a brief discussion of Suez. Macmillan gained the false impression from this conversation that Eisenhower would acquiesce in, if not openly support, the use of force by Britain to resolve the Suez crisis. Macmillan passed on this impression to Eden.

2. On September 28, 1956, Bulganin wrote a further letter to Eden in which he argued that Eden's protestations of peaceful intentions were contradicted by the facts of British and French military preparations and threats to use force. Bulganin also argued that the Suez Canal Users Association (SCUA) was an infringement of Egyptian sovereignty. Eden replied on October 6 that Nasser had used force in taking over the Suez Canal when Egyptian troops had forcefully occupied the offices of the Suez Canal Company; Eden added that Nasser's inflammatory rhetoric created the danger of a violent outburst by the mob, such as had occurred on previous occasions in Egypt, resulting in a loss of British lives, so British military preparations were justifiable and compatible with a quest for a peaceful solution. Eden argued that SCUA was not an infringement of Egyptian sovereignty but a reasonable attempt to find a compromise settlement.

3. American ships that were registered in Panama or Liberia, and used the Panamanian or Liberian flag as a flag of convenience, accepted without protest Nasser's new terms for use of the Suez Canal.

EDEN TO EISENHOWER

October 5, 1956

Dear Friend,

As a result of the understanding we reached with you at the Bermuda Conference in 1953, the United States Air Force has been providing us with technical information to enable us to modify some of our aircraft to carry certain types of U.S. atomic weapons. Work is now so well advanced that we shall shortly be withdrawing aircraft from the front line for modification. As you know, a United States Air Force team is over here training our instructors who will then train our air-crews to operate the weapons in the air.

Hitherto, all this work has been carried out in the strictest secrecy. But the developments I have mentioned above will inevitably widen greatly the circle of those who must know something of what is going on. I feel therefore that some public announcement in very general terms ought to be made soon unless you see serious objection. Moreover such an announcement would at the present time provide helpful evidence of continuing solidarity between our two countries. If you think well of this idea, I would suggest that the announcement might be in the following terms:—

> "The President of the United States of America and the Prime Minister of the United Kingdom announced today that a programme directed towards adapting certain Royal Air Force aircraft to carry U.S. atomic weapons is under way and is nearing completion. The programme has been undertaken under the provisions of the Atomic Energy Act of 1954 and provides for aircraft modifications and the training of loading and delivery crews."

Yours ever,
Anthony

EDEN TO EISENHOWER

October 9, 1956

Dear Ike,[1]

It is always a pleasure to write to you and never more so than to wish you many happy returns of your birthday.[2] Clarissa joins me in sending every good wish, and our fervent hope that you will enjoy the best of health during the coming year, and always.

Our friendship remains one of my greatest rewards. Public life makes one value such a relationship more than ever in these anxious times.

I cannot say that I envy you your campaign.[3] If you feel about those things as I do, it is good to kick off the days on the calendar!

Yours always,
Anthony

1. Unusually, Eden addresses Eisenhower as Ike rather than the usual Dear Friend.
2. On October 14, Eisenhower celebrated his sixty-sixth birthday.
3. The U.S. election was due to be held on November 6.

EISENHOWER TO EDEN

October 11, 1956

Dear Anthony,

Let me acknowledge the note from you which transmitted a copy of Bulganin's letter to you.[1] Truly, this is a rather forbidding letter, and it is scarcely couched in the terms which one would expect in a communication from one Head of Government to another. Also, Foster tells me that Shepilov made a quite nasty speech at the United Nations Council last Monday.[2]

It is clear that the Soviets are playing hard to gain a dominant position in the Near East area, and it is likely they have developed quite a hold on Nasser. This problem will probably remain with us whatever may be the results of the talks in New York. I know that Foster is working there closely with Selwyn Lloyd, and I deeply deplore the suggestions of the press both here and abroad that you and we are at cross purposes.

With warm regard,

As ever,

Ike E.

P.S. I got a chance, at this morning's Press Conference, to say something on how much Britain & the British mean to us.[3]

DE

1. Letter from Bulganin to Eden, September 28, 1956.
2. Dimitri T. Shepilov, foreign minister of the Soviet Union.
3. At a press conference on October 11, Eisenhower stated emphatically how important Britain's friendship was to the United States, not only sentimentally but politically, economically, and militarily.

EISENHOWER TO EDEN

October 12, 1956

Dear Anthony,

I was very much interested in the thoughts expressed in your letter of October 5 and wanted to tell you promptly of my views on the announcement you have proposed.

In the first place I am in hearty agreement on the desirability of keeping before the world the high degree of cooperation and mutual confidence in United States–United Kingdom relations which is typified by our joint efforts in the military atomic field; this is valuable evidence of the continuing strength of a relationship which lies at the heart of the defense efforts of the free world.

On the other hand I am sure that you are aware of a number of sensitive issues, both in our domestic political situation and in our relations with our other allies, which the proposed announcement might raise. In particular I have reservations about the desirability of such an announcement at this moment. It would seem unwise to invite speculation and debate at this time on the delicate matters which are the subject of your letter and risk the freezing of attitudes and positions in a way which might well impede further fruitful progress in this field.[1]

Therefore I wonder whether you would agree to holding in abeyance the proposal which was the subject of your letter with the understanding that we would continue our study of the question and that at a later date we might again examine the advisability of proceeding.

With warm regard,
Dwight D. Eisenhower

1. The domestic political situation to which reference is made was the American elections on November 6, 1956. Relations with allies to which reference is made was the danger of resentment on the part of America's European allies over favored American treatment of Britain as part of a special relationship with the United States in comparison with American treatment of other European allies. Eisenhower also did not wish to make a public statement of solidarity with Britain over nuclear cooperation at a time when there were such serious Anglo-American differences over Suez, whereas such a statement of Anglo-American solidarity would have suited Eden's interests very well.

EISENHOWER TO EDEN

October 14, 1956
Dear Anthony,

I am more than grateful for the good wishes for my birthday that you extend on behalf of Clarissa and yourself. These "milestones" seem to creep up with ever-increasing frequency.

All you say about our friendship is heartily reciprocated by me. I am always grateful for the understanding you have of our problems—and I know that nothing can ever seriously mar either our personal friendship or the respect that our government and peoples have for each other.

With all your knowledge of our American customs, I venture that you are still constantly amazed by some of the activities. I am.[1]

With warm personal regard, and again my thanks,
As ever,
Ike E.

1. The reference is to the American election campaign.

EDEN TO EISENHOWER

October 28, 1956

Message to the President from the Prime Minister.

Thank you for your message of October 12 in reply to mine, in which I proposed an announcement of the programme for adapting certain R.A.F. aircraft.

In view of what you say, I accept that we should leave this in abeyance for the time being.

EISENHOWER TO EDEN

October 30, 1956

Dear Anthony,

I address you in this note not only as head of Her Majesty's Government but as my long time friend who has, with me, believed in and worked for real Anglo-American understanding.

Last night I invited Mr. Coulson, currently your Washington representative, to come to my house to talk over the worsening situation in the Mid East.[1] I have no doubt that the gist of our conversation has already been communicated to you. But it seemed to me desirable that I should give you my impressions concerning certain phases of this whole affair that are disturbing me very much.

Without bothering here to discuss the military movements themselves and their possible grave consequences, I should like to ask your help in clearing up my understanding as to exactly what is happening between us and our European allies—especially between us, the French and yourselves.

We have learned that the French had provided Israel with a considerable amount of equipment, including airplanes, in excess of the amounts of which we were officially informed. This action was, as you know, in violation of agreements now existing between our three countries.[2] We know also that this process has continued in other items of equipment.

Quite naturally we began watching with increased interest the affairs in the Eastern Mediterranean. Late last week we became convinced that the Israel mobilization was proceeding to a point where something more than mere defense was contemplated, and found the situation serious enough to send a precautionary note to Ben Gurion.[3] On Sunday we repeated this note of caution and made a public statement of our actions, informing both you and the French of our concern. On that day we discovered that the volume of communication traffic between Paris and Tel Aviv jumped enormously;

alerting us to the probability that France and Israel were concerting detailed plans of some kind.

When on Monday actual military moves began, we quickly decided that the matter had to go immediately to the United Nations, in view of our Agreement of May, 1950, subscribed to by our three governments.[4]

Last evening our Ambassador to the United Nations met with your Ambassador, Pierson Dixon, to request him to join us in presenting the case to the United Nations this morning. We were astonished to find that he was completely unsympathetic, stating frankly that his government would not agree to any action whatsoever to be taken against Israel. He further argued that the tri-partite statement of May, 1950, was ancient history and without current validity.

Without arguing the point as to whether or not the tri-partite statement is or should be outmoded, I feel very seriously that whenever any agreement or pact of this kind is in spirit renounced by one of its signatories, it is only fair that the other signatories should be notified. Since the United States has continued to look upon that statement as representing the policies and determination of our three governments, I have not only publicly announced several times that it represents our policy, but many of our actions in the Mid East have been based upon it. For example, we have in the past denied arms both to Egypt and to Israel on the ground that the 1950 statement was their surest guarantee of national security. We have had no thought of repudiating that statement and we have none now.

All of this development, with its possible consequences, including the possible involvement of you and the French in a general Arab war, seems to me to leave your government and ours in a very sad state of confusion, so far as any possibility of unified understanding and action are concerned. It is true that Egypt has not yet formally asked this government for aid. But the fact is that if the United Nations finds Israel to be an aggressor, Egypt could very well ask the Soviets for help—and then the Mid East fat would really be in the fire. It is this latter possibility that has led us to insist that the West must ask for a United Nation's examination and possible intervention, for we may shortly find ourselves not only at odds concerning what we should do, but confronted with a de facto situation that would make all our present troubles look puny indeed.

Because of all these possibilities, it seems to me of first importance that the UK and the US quickly and clearly lay out their present views and intentions before each other, and that, come what may, we find some way of concerting our ideas and plans so that we may not, in any real crisis be powerless to act in concert because of misunderstanding of each other. I think it important that our two peoples, as well as the French, have this clear understanding of our common or several viewpoints.

With warm personal regard.

As ever,

Ike E.

1. Roger Makins, British ambassador to the United States, had returned to London to take up a post in the treasury. His successor, Harold Caccia, arrived in Washington, D.C., on November 9. During the critical days of the Suez crisis Britain was not represented in Washington by an ambassador but by the chargé d'affaires, John Coulson.
2. The Tripartite Agreement, May 25, 1950, provided that arms supplies by the three main Western powers should not be of such a quantity as to upset the balance between Israel and the Arab states.
3. David Ben-Gurion, prime minister of Israel.
4. Tripartite Agreement of May 25, 1950.

EDEN TO EISENHOWER
October 30, 1956
Personal Message from the Prime Minister to the President.

I am sending you this hurried message to let you know at once how we regard the Israel-Egypt conflict.

We have never made any secret of our belief that justice entitled us to defend our vital interests against Nasser's designs. But we acted with you in summoning the London Conference, in despatching the abortive Menzies Mission and in seeking to establish S.C.U.A.[1] As you know from our secret sources, the Russians regarded the Security Council proceedings as a victory for themselves and Egypt. Nevertheless we continued through the Secretary General of the United Nations to seek a basis for the continuation of the negotiations.

Now this has happened.[2] When we received news of the Israel mobilisation, we instructed our Ambassador in Tel Aviv to urge restraint. Soon afterwards he sought and obtained an assurance that Israel would not attack Jordan. This seems to me important, since it means that Israel will not enlarge the area of conflict or involve us in virtue of the Anglo-Jordan Treaty. In recent months we have several times warned the Israel Government, both publicly and privately, that if they attacked Jordan we would honour our obligations. But we feel under no obligation to come to the aid of Egypt. Apart from the feelings of public opinion here, Nasser and his press have relieved us of any such obligation by their attitude to the Tripartite Declaration.[3]

Egypt has to a large extent brought this attack on herself by insisting that the state of war persists, by defying the Security Council and by declaring her intention to marshal the Arab States for the destruction of Israel. The latest example of Egyptian intentions is the announcement of a joint command between Egypt, Jordan and Syria.[4]

We have earnestly deliberated what we should do in this serious situation. We cannot afford to see the Canal closed or to lose the shipping which is daily on passage through it. We have a responsibility for the people in these ships. We feel that a decisive action should be taken at once to stop hostilities. We have agreed with you to go to the Security Council and instructions are being sent this moment. Experience shows that its procedure is unlikely to be either rapid or effective.

Selwyn saw Winthrop this morning. We are meeting with the French later. I will send you a further message immediately after that meeting.

1. Suez Canal Users Association. .
2. The reference is to the Israeli attack on Egypt, October 29, 1956.
3. The supply of arms to Egypt by the Soviet Union via Czechoslovakia in September 1955 was regarded by Eden as an action that rendered the Tripartite Declaration obsolete.
4. On October 25, 1956, Egypt, Jordan, and Syria announced the signing of an agreement that they would increase their military cooperation and that in the event of war with Israel they would place their combined armed forces under an Egyptian commander.

EISENHOWER TO EDEN
October 30, 1956
Dear Anthony,

This morning I sent you a long cable to say that we here felt very much in the dark as to your attitude and intentions with respect to the Mid East situation. I have just now received your cable on this subject for which I thank you very much. I shall be waiting the further message to which you refer.

It seems obvious that your Government and ours hold somewhat different attitudes toward the Tripartite Declaration of 1950. Since we have never publicly announced any modification of the Declaration or any limitations upon its interpretation, we find it difficult at this moment to see how we can violate our pledged word.

In any event, I shall earnestly and even anxiously watch the unfolding situation.

With warm regard,
As ever,
Ike E.

EDEN TO EISENHOWER

October 30, 1956

Personal Message from the Prime Minister to the President.

I undertook this morning to send you a further message immediately after we had met Monsieur Mollet and Monsieur Pineau.[1]

It may be that Israel could be accused of a technical aggression. On the other hand, for the reasons set forth in my earlier message, we think that Israel has a case for arguing that she is acting in self-defence under the ever increasing pressure of certain Arab States led by Egypt. Nevertheless we would not wish to support or even condone the action of Israel. We consider that, in view of the massive interests involved, the first thing to do is to take effective and decisive steps to halt the fighting.

We have had to act quickly for time is short, and since there appears to be very little fighting up to now, there is still a chance of preventing serious hostilities. Selwyn is giving a copy of the text of the Declaration to Winthrop. I shall be announcing it this afternoon in the House of Commons at 4.30 P.M. This is absolutely necessary, since Parliament is sitting.

The purpose of the Declaration is to make similar requests upon each Party. First, that all hostilities by land and air should cease. Second, that the Canal Zone should be left free so that no fighting or incidents can take place there. But knowing what these people are, we felt it essential to have some kind of physical guarantees in order to secure the safety of the Canal.

We are asking for Port Said and Ismailia and Suez. As the Israelites appear to be very near to Suez, the requirement affects them as well as the Egyptians.[2] We are emphasizing, of course, that this is to be a temporary measure pending settlement of all these problems.

As I told you in my previous message, we entirely agree that this should go to the Security Council. But, as you know well, the Council cannot move quickly in a critical position and we have felt it right to act, as it were, as trustees to protect the general interest as well as to protect our own interests and nationals. You may say that we should wait until we are asked to move by the Security Council. But, of course, there could never be agreement on such a request.

Either side may refuse; in which case we shall take the necessary measures to enforce the Declaration.

Now you will wonder why apart from the Security Council we have acted so promptly. Of course, my first instinct would have been to ask you to associate yourself and your country with the Declaration. But I know the Constitutional and other difficulties in which you are placed. I think there is a chance that both sides will accept. In any case it would help this result very much if you found it possible to support what we have done, at least in general terms. We are well aware that no real settlement of Middle Eastern problems is possible except through the closest cooperation between our two countries. Our two Governments have tried with the best will in the world all sorts of public and private negotiations through the last two or three years and they have all failed. This seems an opportunity for a fresh start.

I can assure you that any action which we may have to take to follow up the Declaration is not part of a harking back to the old Colonial and occupational concepts. We are most anxious to avoid this impression. Nothing could have prevented this volcano from erupting somewhere. But when the dust settles there may well be a chance for our doing a really constructive piece of work together and thereby strengthening the weakest point in the line against Communism.

1. Guy Mollet, prime minister of France; Christian Pineau, foreign minister of France.
2. Israel, as well as Egypt, was required by the Declaration to withdraw to a line ten miles from the Suez Canal. In fact, Israel had not reached this line.

EISENHOWER TO EDEN

October 30, 1956

Dear Mr. Prime Minister,[1]

I have just learned from the press of the 12-hour ultimatum which you and the French Government have delivered to the Government of Egypt requiring, under threat of forceful intervention, the temporary occupation by Anglo-French forces of key positions at Port Said, Ismailia and Suez in the Suez Canal Zone.[2] I feel I must urgently express to you my deep concern at the prospect of this drastic action even at the very time when the matter is under consideration as it is today by the United Nations Security Council. It is my sincere belief that peaceful processes can and should prevail to secure a solution which will restore the armistice condition as between Israel and Egypt and also justly settle the controversy with Egypt about the Suez Canal.

Sincerely,

Dwight D. Eisenhower

1. Eisenhower uses the formal Mr. Prime Minister rather than the normal Dear Anthony. An identical message was sent to the French prime minister, Guy Mollet.
2. The ultimatum was announced in the media before the arrival of Eden's letter to Eisenhower explaining the matter.

EDEN TO EISENHOWER ──────────────────────────
October 31, 1956
Message for the President from the Prime Minister.

I have received your formal message, and I see that its substance has already been published. I realise that you wrote in this way in order to avoid encroaching upon the confidential nature of personal exchanges. But, in view of the publicity given to it, I shall be obliged in our Parliamentary discussion, which are to be resumed tomorrow, to comment on some of the points made in your letter in order to justify British policy and action. For this purpose, I think I must be free to make public the substance—though not, of course, the full text—of the two messages which I sent to you in the course of today. I am sure you will understand.

EISENHOWER TO EDEN ──────────────────────────
October 31, 1956

By all means feel free to use any part of the exchanges between us that you see fit.

EDEN TO EISENHOWER ──────────────────────────
November 5, 1956
Dear Friend,

I am sending you a personal message to explain why, although we welcome the request to the Secretary-General contained in the Canadian resolution, we find it impossible to accept the Afro-Asian resolution.[1] I sent you this preliminary notice remembering the last occasion, when owing to ciphering delays my message failed to reach you before our announcement was made.[2]

Yours ever,
Anthony

1. The substance of the Canadian and Afro-Asian resolutions were not dissimilar, calling for British and French withdrawal and the dispatch of a United Nations force, but the tone of the Canadian resolution was moderate whereas the Afro-Asian resolution was scathing in its denunciation of Britain and France.
2. Eden to Eisenhower, October 30, 1956.

EDEN TO EISENHOWER ──────────────────────────
November 5, 1956
Dear Friend,

It is a great grief to me that the events of the last few days have placed such a strain on the relations between our two countries. Of course I realise your feelings about the action which we felt compelled to take at such short notice. But if you will refer to my message of September 6, I think you will agree that what I said then has already begun to be confirmed by events.

I have always felt, as I made very clear to Mr. Khrushchev, that the Middle East was an issue over which, in the last resort, we would have to fight.

I know that Foster thought we could have played this longer. But I am convinced that, if we had allowed things to drift, everything would have gone from bad to worse. Nasser would have become a kind of Moslem Mussolini and our friends in Iraq, Jordan, Saudi Arabia and even Iran would gradually have been brought down. His efforts would have spread westwards, and Libya and all North Africa would have been brought under his control. It may be that we might have obtained by negotiation a settlement of the Canal question which gave to us a part of what we needed. But at best it would have taken a long time. Meanwhile Nasser would have been taking the tricks all round the Middle East. His last action in making a military command with Jordan and Syria was bound to provoke the Israelis, and of course it did so. They felt themselves imprisoned and naturally tried to break out. We were of course relieved that they broke in the direction of Egypt rather than of Jordan. But once they had moved, in whatever direction, there was not a moment to be lost. We and the French were convinced that we had to act at once to forestall a general conflagration throughout the Middle East. And now that police action has been started it must be carried through.[1] I am sure that this is the moment to curb Nasser's ambitions. If we let it pass, all of us will bitterly regret it. Here is our opportunity to secure an effective and final settlement of the problems of the Middle East. If we draw back now, chaos will not be avoided. Everything will go up in flames in the Middle East. You will realise, with all your experience, that we cannot have a military vacuum while a United Nations force is being constituted and is being transported to the spot. This is why we feel we must go on to hold the position until we can hand over the responsibility to the United Nations. If a barrier can be established in this way between the Arabs and the Israelis we shall then be strongly placed to call on the Israelis to withdraw. This in its turn will reduce the threat to the Canal and restore it to the general use of the world. By this means, we shall have taken the first step towards re-establishing authority in this area for our generation.

It is no mere form of words to say that we would be happy to hand over to an international organisation as soon as we possibly can. As you can imagine no one feels more strongly about this than Harold, who has to provide the money.[2] We do not want occupation of Egypt, we could not afford it, and that is one of many other reasons why we got out of Suez two years ago.

The Suez Crisis and Eden's Resignation : 183

I know how strongly you feel, as I do, the objections to the use of force, but this is not a situation which can be mended by words or resolutions. It is indeed ironical that at this very moment, when we are being pilloried as aggressors Russia is brutally reoccupying Hungary and threatening the whole of Eastern Europe, and no voice is raised in the United Nations in favour of intervention there.[3] It may be that our two countries can take no practical action to redress that situation. But the Middle East is an area in which we could still take practical and effective action together.

I am sending you this message in the hope that you will at least understand the grievous decisions which we have had to make. I was deeply moved by your last message before our initial action, although I was not able to reply to it as I would have liked at the time.

After a few days you will be in a position to act with renewed authority.[4] I beg you to believe what we are doing now will in our view facilitate your action. I would most earnestly ask you to put the great weight of your authority behind the proposal which we are now making to the United Nations.

I believe as firmly as ever that the future of all of us depends on the closest Anglo-American cooperation. It has of course been a grief to me to have had to make a temporary breach into it which I cannot disguise, but I know that you are a man of big enough heart and vision to take up things again on the basis of fact. If you cannot approve, I would like you at least to understand the terrible decisions that we have had to make. I remember nothing like them since the days when we were comrades together in the war. History alone can judge whether we have made the right decision, but I do want to assure you that we have made it from a genuine sense of responsibility, not only to our country, but to all the world.

Yours ever,
Anthony

1. British and French forces landed in Egypt at dawn on November 5.
2. Harold Macmillan was British chancellor of the exchequer.
3. On November 4, Soviet forces moved into Hungary to crush the Hungarian revolution.
4. The American election was due to be held on November 6.

EISENHOWER TO EDEN
November 6, 1956
Dear Anthony,

I was delighted at the opportunity to talk with you on the telephone and to hear that the U.K. will order a cease-fire this evening. On thinking over our talk I wish to emphasize my urgent view a) that the UN Resolution on cease-fire and entry of a UN force be accepted without condition so as not to give Egypt with Soviet backing an opportunity to quibble or start negotiations; items such as use of technical troops to clear the canal can be handled later; b) that it is vital no excuse be given for Soviet participation in UN force, therefore all big five should be excluded from force as UN proposes. Any attack on UN force would meet immediate reaction from all UN; c) I think immediate consummation UN plan of greatest importance otherwise there might be invitation to developments of greatest gravity.

Sincerely hope you find it possible to agree with these views and can so inform Hammarskjold before tonight's meeting.[1]

Let me say again that I will be delighted to have you call me at any time. The telephone connection seemed very satisfactory.

Warmest regard,
Ike E.

1. Dag Hammarskjöld, secretary-general of the United Nations.

EDEN TO EISENHOWER
November 6, 1956
Dear Friend,

Thank you so much for your message. I am so grateful for the help which you are giving us.

I entirely understand the force of what you say. As regards your point (A) I do not think there need be any difficulty. In our reply to the Secretary General, we did not in fact make it a condition of our acceptance of the cease-fire and entry of a United Nations Force that the obstructions in the Canal should be cleared by our troops. This is, however, something which has got to be done most urgently in the interests of the world. We are on the spot and the only people who can do it quickly. We therefore think it right that we should be allowed to carry it through unhindered. I am personally inclined to agree with your point (B) namely that the Big Five should be excluded from the United Nations Force. This is, however, a matter on which there are very deep feelings here. I could not take a decision of such magnitude without consulting my colleagues and I will do so as soon as possible in the morning. I think that before we can take a decision we may want to know more about what the functions of the United Nations Force are to be.

I am asking our Representative at the United Nations to explain matters to Hammarskjold on the above lines. Do please believe that I am sincerely anxious that we should work together in all this. But these are matters of such importance for our country that I must ask for a little further time to consider them.

I too was delighted to hear your voice this evening. I hope that we can keep in close touch.

Yours ever,
Anthony

EISENHOWER TO EDEN

November 7, 1956

Dear Anthony,

I want you to know that I welcome the suggestion you made in our telephone conversation today regarding early consultation on many of our mutual problems, and that I agree we should meet at an early date.[1] Now that the election is over, I find it most necessary to consult urgently the leaders of both Houses of the Congress. As you can understand, it will take some days to accomplish this. Furthermore, after a thorough study of all the factors and after talking to various branches of the government here, I feel that while such a meeting should take place quickly, we must be sure that its purpose and aims are not misunderstood in other countries. This would be the case if the UN Resolution had not yet been carried out.

I am heartened by the news that there is a cease-fire in Egypt and sincerely hope that the UN Force will promptly begin its work and that the Anglo-French Forces will be withdrawn from Egypt without delay. Once these things are done, the ground will be favorable for our meeting. I would hope that this would permit us to meet here by the end of next week. As I suggested by telephone I would hope that Al Gruenther might meet with you or your people shortly to get your evaluation of the matter you mentioned to me this morning.[2]

With warm regard,
As ever,
Ike

1. Eden suggested in his telephone conversation with Eisenhower that Eden should come to Washington for talks with Eisenhower. Eisenhower responded very favorably, but after consultation with Herbert Hoover Jr., acting secretary of state since Dulles entered the hospital with cancer on November 3, Eisenhower stalled Eden, accepting Hoover's advice that an early visit by Eden to Washington could give the impression to Arab countries that the United States had been in support of British policies.

2. General Albert M. Gruenther, supreme Allied commander of NATO forces.

EDEN TO EISENHOWER

November 7, 1956

Dear Friend,

When you told me of your pre-occupations with Congress during the next two days I did not feel able to press my suggestion for an immediate meeting. I explained the position to Mollet, who readily accepted these reasons for postponement.

I do, however, hope that it will be possible for us to meet in the very near future. I should feel much more confidence about the decisions and actions which we shall have to take in the short term if we had first reached some common understanding about the attitude which we each intended to take towards a long-term settlement of the outstanding issues in the Middle East. I have for a long time felt that some at least of our troubles there derived from the lack of a clear understanding between our two countries, ever since the end of the war, on policy in the Middle East. And I doubt whether we shall ever be able to secure stability there unless we are working towards common objectives.

It may well be that even wider issues are now at stake. If the Soviets intend to seize this opportunity of intervening by giving substantial support to Nasser, they may create a situation which could lead to major war. Hitherto I have not thought it likely that Russia would take this dangerous step. I have believed that it was anxious to avoid world war and that, although it would make all possible minor trouble it would stick to the policy of making mischief by all means short of war. But the new men in the Kremlin may be less coldly calculating than their predecessor and, if so, they may be led into taking a step which may precipitate a really grave situation. The Swiss, as you know, have suggested another "Geneva" Meeting. It may be that this would be worth considering.

On matters such as this it is difficult to come to considered conclusions by correspondence. I would feel much happier if we had been able to meet and talk them over soon. It was with these grave issues in mind that I suggested this morning that I might come out to Washington at once. I still hope that it may be possible for us to meet within the next few days, as soon as your immediate preoccupations are over.

Yours Ever,
Anthony

EDEN TO EISENHOWER

November 7, 1956

Dear Friend,

The letter which you sent me yesterday crossed the one which I sent to you.

I understand your immediate preoccupations, but continue to hope that a meeting between us can take place soon.

I very much welcome your suggestion that Al Gruenther should meet some of our people to make an evaluation. Dixon is going to see him tomorrow.[1] After that, if Al feels that these talks should be pursued further, I hope that he may be able to come here and talk to us all.

Yours ever,

Anthony

1. Pierson Dixon, British permanent representative at the United Nations.

EISENHOWER TO EDEN

November 11, 1956

Dear Anthony,

I am in full agreement with the objectives set forth in your message of November 7 which crossed mine of that same day. We have the problems you describe very much in mind and I, too, hope that we could meet in the near future. Meanwhile, I feel we must continue to push forward on the introduction of the UN Force and the withdrawal of Anglo-French forces, and that these things should be done with the utmost speed. We should then be in a position to consider arranging a meeting. I have sent similar word to Prime Minister Mollet.

My preliminary reports from Al Gruenther indicate that it would not seem necessary for him to come to London to see you.[1]

With warm regard,

As ever,

Ike

1. Gruenther had written to Eisenhower that Gruenther's position as NATO commander put him in a sensitive position which would make a visit to Eden at that time difficult.

EDEN TO EISENHOWER

November 11, 1956

Dear Friend,

M. Guy Mollet has told me of the letter which he has sent to you and asked me to support his views. As you know mine already I will only add that I am sure it would help the free world as a whole if we could meet as early as your plans will allow.

Yours ever,
Anthony

EISENHOWER TO EDEN ———————————————————

November 11, 1956

Dear Anthony,

Your last message of this morning must have crossed mine.

The meeting with you is an important event and I shall communicate with you about its timing just as soon as I can.

Warm regards,
As ever,
Dwight D. Eisenhower

EISENHOWER TO EDEN ———————————————————

November 29, 1956

My dear friend,

I understand you are recuperating in Jamaica.[1] This short note brings you my very best wishes for an enjoyable and restful vacation, and a complete return to health.

As ever,
Ike E.

1. Eden went to Jamaica from November 23 to December 14 to recuperate from illness. He stayed at Goldeneye, the home of Ian Fleming, author of the James Bond novels.

EDEN TO EISENHOWER ———————————————————

November 30, 1956

My dear friend,

Thank you so much for your very kind message. It is very pleasant and peaceful here and I am sure I shall be quite fit in a week or two.

Meanwhile, I am of course available if you should want to call on me at any time.

Every good wish.

Yours ever,
Anthony

EISENHOWER TO EDEN

January 10, 1957

Dear Anthony,

I cannot tell you how deeply I regret that the strains and stresses of these times finally wore you down physically until you felt it necessary to retire.[1] To me it seems only yesterday that you and I and others were meeting with Winston almost daily—or nightly—to discuss the next logical move of our forces in the war.

Now you have retired, I have had a heart attack as well as a major operation, and many others of our colleagues of that era are either gone or no longer active. The only reason for recalling those days is to assure you that my admiration and affection for you have never diminished; I am truly sorry that you had to quit the office of Her Majesty's First Minister.

Yesterday I issued a short public statement expressing my regret and my good wishes for your future. But I wanted to tell you in a personal note how sincerely Mamie and I pray that you and Lady Eden will have a long, busy and happy life ahead.

With personal regard,

As ever,

Ike

1. After his return from Jamaica on December 14, 1956, Eden engaged in discussions with political associates that made evident the weakness of his political position while he also received medical advice that his health could not stand up to the strain of continuing in office. On January 9, 1957, Eden therefore submitted his resignation.

EDEN TO EISENHOWER

January 17, 1957

Dear Friend,

Thank you so much for your letter and the kind thoughts in it.

I confess that it is a wrench to go just now, but the doctors really gave me no choice.

Clarissa joins me in every wish for happiness to you both.

Yours ever,

Anthony

CONCLUSION

This Conclusion offers an evaluation of points which were raised in the Introduction. It assesses what light the evidence from the correspondence sheds on the nature of the Anglo-American relationship, 1955–57, both with regard to the overall relationship and with regard to particular issues, such as intelligence, trade, relations with the Soviet Union, and in a category by itself, the Suez crisis. Also, an evaluation is offered of what the correspondence reveals with regard to Eden and Eisenhower individually, especially regarding Eden's capability as prime minister and Eisenhower's new historical reputation as a more able and effective president than earlier accounts presented.

The overall conclusion, it might be suggested, is that the Eden-Eisenhower correspondence, 1955–57, reveals a tale of two parts: from Eden's accession to the premiership in April 1955 to the beginning of the Suez crisis in July 1956, and from the beginning of the Suez crisis until Eden's resignation in January 1957. In Part I the Anglo-American relationship was strong, with two leaders of similar outlook and objectives and with solid mutual respect. Disagreements were only of a relatively minor nature, which could be reconciled without great damage to the overall relationship. Eden had difficulty in accepting that Britain was increasingly the junior partner in the Anglo-American relationship, but he was better able to come to terms with this than Churchill had been. Moreover, in Part I, Eden's overall conduct of affairs seems quite impressive, noted by an assurance in his handling of matters with an intelligent, experienced approach. Similarly, Eisenhower's record seems impressive, with a demonstration of a clear grasp of the essentials of the issues and with a self-confidence in his leadership combined with an awareness of the grave perils in the international situation. By contrast, in Part II, during the Suez crisis, the correspondence clearly reveals not only a fundamental disagreement over policy but a distrust that culminated in a total breakdown of the Anglo-American relationship at the height of the crisis. At the same time, Eden's conduct of affairs seems seriously flawed and provides abundant evidence in support of the view that Eden lacked the qualities of leadership which were required of an effective prime minister. On the other hand, the correspondence during the Suez crisis provides strong evidence of Eisenhower's impressive capabilities as president, especially in a time of crisis.

On the issue of intelligence, the correspondence contains some fascinating details, which are all the more interesting since many of the letters on this subject have only recently been declassified. These letters deal with a subject that is by its nature dramatic and intriguing, gathering intelligence from balloons floating across the Soviet Union or from the sinister, high-flying U-2. The correspondence illustrates that, with the longstanding Anglo-American intelligence partnership, Eden was willing to cooperate in the somewhat harebrained Genetrix project, allowing balloons to be launched from Scotland. The unsatisfactory results of this first scheme of overflying the Soviet Union did not deter Eden from agreeing to cooperate in the next attempt by means of the U-2. The correspondence reveals that, in line with the traditions of the Anglo-American relationship, Eisenhower's natural inclination on this matter of such delicacy and importance was to turn to his closest ally for the use of a base for the U-2. Eden, though wary, acceded to the request to make Lakenheath the base for U-2 flights over the Soviet Union. Interestingly, the correspondence reveals that one of Eden's concerns was that a U-2 might develop engine trouble while on a flight over the Soviet Union and need to descend to a lower altitude, at which height it would be vulnerable to Soviet antiaircraft defenses. When Francis Gary Powers's U-2 was shot down in May 1960, there was widespread speculation that this was precisely the problem which Powers had encountered. Later information, however, revealed that this was not so but that by 1960 the Soviets had developed surface-to-air missiles which could rise to the maximum height of a U-2 at around 70,000 feet.[1] Following the debacle of the Crabb affair during Bulganin and Khrushchev's visit to Britain in April 1956, Eden's decision not to risk another incident of an intelligence operation going wrong and setting back Anglo-Soviet relations was accepted by Eisenhower as reasonable grounds for Eden's reversal of his decision to permit U-2s to fly from a British base, necessitating the move of the U-2 base to Weisbaden in West Germany. Eden's decision, far from being resented by Eisenhower, added to Eisenhower's growing apprehension over the risks involved in U-2 flights over the Soviet Union. After five flights during July 4–10, 1956, there was a hiatus in U-2 overflights of the Soviet Union until November 20, 1956.[2] Moreover, the focus of interest in gathering intelligence began to center on missile sites in the southern part of the Soviet Union, especially Tyuaratam, near the Aral Sea. The U-2 base was, therefore, moved from Weisbaden to Incirlik in Turkey. It is likely, therefore, that the U-2 base would have been moved from Britain in any event. The United States would nevertheless have wished to have had British involvement in the U-2 program, including overflights of the Soviet Union by British pilots. But Eisenhower accepted that British noninvolvement in the U-2 program was temporary and for good reasons, so that Eden's reversal of his decision to allow the use of Lakenheath as the base for the U-2 did not constitute a breach in the close Anglo-American intelligence relationship.

With regard to trade, the correspondence contains quite a number of references to disputes over various matters, especially relating to trade with Communist countries. Eisenhower's letters on the subject appear to be perfunctory and, although he gives the official American position, there are signs that he was going through the motions and that his heart was not in the matter. The British were able gradually to modify American policy on trade with Communist countries, as Ian Jackson has shown.[3] Eisenhower's personal view on trade in general and trade with Communist countries in particular was much more liberal than those of his American colleagues, so that trade issues did not upset the Anglo-American relationship as far as Eisenhower was concerned.

Some issues on which Eisenhower felt much more strongly, such as European unity or relations with China, were not raised in the correspondence. In the case of China, this was no doubt due to the fact that the issue had quietened down by Eden's time in office. Indeed, the contentious issues on various aspects of policy in the Far East, which caused acute problems in Churchill's time over Korea, Indochina, China, and the offshore islands of Quemoy and Matsu, had settled down by the time of Eden's premiership. Lack of mention of those issues in the correspondence did not indicate that the issues were no longer present but was a sign of their relative decline as divisive issues in Anglo-American relations.

European unity, on the other hand, was a central matter of policy discussion in 1955–56, as negotiations were conducted over the creation of the Common Market. This culminated in the Treaty of Rome in 1957, signed by France, West Germany, Italy, Belgium, Holland, and Luxembourg, but, very significantly, not by Britain. Eisenhower was a very strong advocate of European unity. Moreover, he firmly believed that Britain's future lay in a united Europe rather than in remaining outside of Europe and placing too much weight on ties with the Commonwealth and the United States. It is significant, however, that this extremely important issue was not raised in the correspondence. Perhaps Eisenhower realized that advocacy on his part would have been resented as interference in British affairs on a matter on which constant American hectoring since 1945 had severely irritated the British. In any event, the absence of the issue in the correspondence illustrates that not raising some matters can be as significant in some respects as the raising of some other issues.

Another issue on which Eisenhower tended to tread warily was colonialism. Although Eisenhower was basically anticolonialist, he was a moderate and gradualist in the pursuit of policies designed to persuade the colonial powers to move toward independence for their colonies. On the one occasion in his correspondence with Churchill when he had explicitly put forward his views on colonialism, he had been given short shrift.[4] On a matter such as Cyprus, the correspondence with Eden indicates a fairly sympathetic attitude on Eisenhower's part with an appreciation of the complexities of the situation rather than a simplistic advocacy of immediate end to colonial rule. Similarly, on relations with the Middle East, Eisenhower indicates an awareness of the need to reconcile strategic and idealistic objectives. Eisenhower was well aware of the resentment of Middle Eastern countries over their manipulation by the colonial powers. Moreover, it is clear that Eisenhower feared that this resentment presented an opportunity to the Soviet Union to gain inroads into the Middle East. Eisenhower appreciated that identification of the United States with the European colonial powers was one of the reasons for strong anti-American feelings in the Middle East as in the rest of the Third World. Yet Eisenhower shows awareness of the need to balance the best interests of the countries of the Middle East with the interests of America's close allies, who were the colonial powers. In 1953 enthusiasts in the State Department and CIA had been more inclined to take sides with Arab nationalists, such as Nasser. By 1955, however, the deviousness and unreliability of such figures and their gravitation toward neutrality made the United States more inclined to side with their traditional allies. In the competing pulls toward siding with Arab nationalists who seemed to be the wave of the progressive future in the Middle East and siding with European allies who pursued quasi-colonialist policies to suit their own economic and political interests but who were fairly dependable Cold War partners, the United States ultimately sided with the latter. As Peter Hahn puts it, "American officials were forced to decide whether to bend to the processes of Egyptian nationalism or to endorse British guardianship of Western strategic interests.... The Cold War compelled American officials to align their policy with that of Britain."[5] The Eden-Eisenhower correspondence would tend to show that this was even more so the case by 1955–56 than earlier in the 1950s when, for example, in 1953–54 on such issues as encouraging Britain to withdraw from the Suez base, the United States had taken a less supportive stance than Britain would have wished.

The correspondence produces evidence of clear differences on some substantive issues regarding the Middle East between Britain and America. The evidence does not suggest, however, that there was an overall American objective on the part of the Eisenhower administration to replace Britain in the Middle East. On the contrary, it was Eden who, in several letters to Eisenhower, strongly urged fuller American strategic involvement in the Middle East, particularly by means of American accession to the Baghdad Pact. Eisenhower became irritated by British persistence on this matter since Eisenhower realized that American accession to the Baghdad Pact would alienate both Nasser and the Israelis. Nevertheless, the matter was resolved reasonably satisfactorily by America's declaration of support for the Baghdad Pact without joining and becoming a full member.

On the most important single issue of policy, namely, relations with the Soviet Union, the correspondence suggests that there was a clear meeting of minds between Eden and Eisenhower. Eden's final letter to Eisenhower before the Suez crisis arose was a long, reflective letter on NATO and broad issues of the Cold War that was very much in tune with Eisenhower's thinking. Neither Eden nor Eisenhower was enamored by siren calls for swift solutions to the Cold War conflict, such as by means of a summit meeting. Eisenhower was willing, nevertheless, to go along with Eden's proposal of a summit meeting in 1955. Eisenhower appreciated that there was a groundswell of public opinion in Britain and America for such a meeting and that a response should be made to this popular feeling while keeping public expectations under control. Also, Eisenhower recognized that the Soviets had made some positive gestures, such as the Austrian State Treaty. Moreover, Eisenhower was, significantly, prepared to make a concession to his British ally on this matter in order to assist Eden in winning reelection in 1955. It was in America's interests to try to ensure that the Conservatives won the British general election in 1955 rather than being replaced by the Labour Party in which left-wing elements that inclined toward neutrality, embodied by Aneurin Bevan, were gaining influence. Eisenhower was also supportive of Eden's initiative in personal diplomacy in the invitation to Bulganin and Khrushchev to visit Britain in April 1956. On his side, Eden clearly kept in close contact with Eisenhower in providing full information about the progress of this visit. Eden and Eisenhower appeared to be in accord on the need for some measures of gesture politics and media spectaculars in international relations while retaining a fundamental skepticism over the chances of the success of such initiatives and placing much greater faith in a long-term, patient search for solutions, based on a steady consolidation of Western strength. Britain's partnership with the United States on these basic matters seemed solid in Eden's time. Moreover, fears over details such as the use of British bases for an American nuclear assault against the Soviet Union, which had become acute in 1954 in the wake of Soviet thermonuclear explosions and fears of the effects of hydrogen bombs on Britain, diminished by the mid-1950s.

On the personal level, Eden as prime minister had fewer dealings with John Foster Dulles than when he was foreign secretary. Harold Macmillan succeeded Eden as foreign secretary and proved more adept in dealing with the awkward aspects of Dulles's personality. After Macmillan was moved from the Foreign Office in December 1955 and replaced by Selwyn Lloyd, Eden played a greater part in shaping foreign policy since Lloyd was a weaker presence as foreign secretary than Macmillan. Nevertheless, Eden's dealings were now primarily with Eisenhower and the problems that had arisen from the prickly Eden-Dulles relationship in 1953–55 were greatly reduced.

With regard to Eden's relationship with Eisenhower, there seems no reason to doubt that there was strong mutual high regard and friendliness. In July 1955, Eisenhower's younger brother, Milton, came to London and reported that U.S. Ambassador Winthrop Aldrich "arranged a private dinner at the Embassy, and I spent three delightful hours with Eden. He was engaging and completely candid. . . . Eden and I hit it off together about as well as two folks can."[6] Milton was extremely close to Eisenhower, spending every weekend at the White House even though he was president of Pennsylvania State University.[7] Eisenhower described Milton as "my most intimate general adviser."[8] Milton's view of Eden was bound to resonate with Eisenhower. The evidence of the correspondence, from Eisenhower's initial congratulations to Eden on his appointment as prime minister through Eden's visit to Washington in January 1956 and up to July 1956, would add credence to the view that Eisenhower's relationship with Eden up to the Suez crisis was one of strong respect and solid friendship. On Eden's side, the importance that he attached to his letters to Eisenhower, as well as the details of the letters, suggest that Eden was aware, as Roger Makins frequently reiterated, that Eisenhower was not the weak figurehead portrayed in some segments of the British media and British public life but a well-informed, intelligent, authoritative leader.[9]

Eisenhower's entire career from World War II onward indicates that he was a strong Anglophile. Yet as the Eden-Eisenhower correspondence indicates, he was a hard-headed Anglophile. In World War II, the vital wartime need to work cooperatively with America's most important ally was the mainspring of Eisenhower's Anglophilia. So, in the mid-1950s, America's need of Britain as a crucial ally in the Cold War was at the heart of Eisenhower's attitude toward Britain. Yet Eisenhower's Anglophilia went well beyond a realpolitik consideration of America's interests. Aside from his strong sense of the common values and traditions of the two countries, Eisenhower developed a deep emotional attachment to Britain. On the one occasion during his presidency when he visited Britain, in 1959, he received a very warm welcome not only from the queen and the government but from the thousands of people who lined the streets of London as he drove from the airport to the city center. After a very enjoyable and successful visit, he wrote to Harold Macmillan that "I sometimes feel a right to be an adopted son of Great Britain. Certainly, I feel completely at home here."[10] Yet Eisenhower declined invitations extended to him by Eden to come on a visit to Britain as he had previously declined invitations from Churchill in 1953–55. Partly this was due to pressures of time, but as was illustrated most clearly in his rejection of Eden's invitation to him to come to Britain en route to the Geneva summit in July 1955, it was also because he did not wish to complicate America's relations with other countries by appearing to have too cozy and intimate a relationship with Britain. That these considerations with other countries outweighed his instinctive desire to associate more closely with Britain illustrates Eisenhower's hard-headed Anglophilia.

With regard to Eden's competence as prime minister, the correspondence up to the Suez crisis suggests a very sound, levelheaded command of the issues and effectiveness in leadership. His willingness to hold a summit meeting in 1955 and to gain Eisenhower's support for this, when Eden had strong doubts about the usefulness of a summit for foreign policy reasons but appreciated its value for domestic political reasons, illustrated Eden's maturing political skills as prime minister. On all of the major issues before the Suez crisis, such as relations with the Soviet Union, the Middle East, Cyprus, and other matters, Eden's views indicate not only a manifest mastery of the details of the issues but also in his writing the careful, felicitous expression of a seasoned diplomat.

Eisenhower's letters similarly reveal a very sound grasp of the issues and an intelligent approach to matters along with a pleasing, lucid manner of expression in his writing. Eisenhower's correspondence with Churchill, 1953–55, and his letters to his friend, Swede Hazlett, as well as Eisenhower's voluminous correspondence throughout his career, demonstrates his considerable natural writing skills, which his letters to Eden likewise illustrate. With regard to issues of policy, the evidence of Eisenhower's sound and sensible approach to matters adds a further nail in the coffin of the discredited myth of Eisenhower as a weak, ill-informed figurehead more interested in golf than government.

In Part II, on the Suez crisis, however, the situation on almost all aspects is very different. With regard to Eden's handling of the Suez crisis, the correspondence adds to an understanding of Eden's view but does not seem to produce evidence to make his handling of the crisis more defensible. John Charmley defends Eden, arguing that he "attempted to plough a British furrow."[11] Charmley writes that Eden "wished to maintain as much of Britain's place in the world as could be managed. He was not so much anti-American as pro-British, and when the interests of the two countries clashed, to put his own country first. . . . Where co-operation with America was to be had, he was happy to go along with America. . . . But where it was not possible, or not forthcoming, . . . then he felt free to pursue Britain's interests by his own means."[12] As a general matter of principle, this was quite reasonable. The ground on which he took his main stand on this principle, however, at Suez, appeared to be as unsuitable as could be imagined. Similarly Jonathan Pierce, in defense of Eden, argues that Eden wished for a peaceful solution to the Suez crisis but was reluctantly compelled to resort to force.[13] Yet Eden's terms for a solution to the crisis were manifestly unattainable by peaceful means so that in fact he created a situation where his only alternative to the use of force was a humiliating retreat. Eden was motivated by protection of Britain's interests, especially since a quarter of Britain's imports and two-thirds of Western Europe's oil passed through the Suez Canal. But he was even more strongly motivated by emotional sentiment. As Diane Kunz puts it, "It was intolerable to a man like Eden, born in the last century and come to maturity at the apogee of empire, that an upstart like Nasser could strip Britain of one of its most glorious imperial possessions."[14]

When, in passing over the succession, Churchill had wondered if Anthony Eden "can do it," Churchill had said that "Anthony has courage. He would charge . . . but would he charge at the right time and in the right place?"[15] Eisenhower made the same point, writing that "my conviction was that the Western world had gotten into a lot of difficulties by selecting the wrong issue about which to be tough. To choose a situation in which Nasser had legal and sovereign rights and in which world opinion was on his side, was not in my opinion a good one on which to make a stand."[16] Eden does not offer any convincing points in the correspondence by way of counter-arguments to these accusations. He does not produce a defense which would meet the condemnation of Pierson Dixon, for example, that "we intervened by virtue of no clear and defensible principle, but what was worse, gave a reason which was generally considered at best a lame excuse, or at worst a conspiracy. It is difficult to conceive of any single way in which we could have made matters worse than by appearing to attack an Arab state in collusion with the Israelis. It would have made far more sense to have let the Israelis do the job or to have gone in by ourselves squarely to protect British interests."[17] Eden's feigned surprise over the news of the Israeli attack in his letter to Eisenhower on October 30—"Now this has happened"—was part of a pattern of dishonorable deception on Eden's part which led him to omit any mention of collusion with Israel in his memoirs and to lie to the House of Commons on the matter, stating on December 20, 1956, that "there was not foreknowledge that Israel would attack Egypt."[18] The ultimatum to Egypt and Israel of October 30 appears to be bizarre and bungling incompetence as well as deception, with insult added to injury by its announcement on the radio before Eisenhower received the copy that Eden sent to him. Evelyn Shuckburgh wrote that when he heard of the ultimatum he was "staggered by this. It seems to have *every* fault. It is clearly not genuinely impartial since the Israelis are nowhere near the Canal; it puts us on the side of the Israelis; the Americans were not consulted; the United Nations is flouted; we are about to be at war without the nation or Parliament having been given a hint of it. We think A.E. has gone off his head."[19]

Some critics suggest, however, that Eisenhower was more at fault for failing to send a clear message that the United States would not support the use of force. Eden wrote in his memoirs with respect to Eisenhower's letter to him of July 31, 1956, that "the President did not rule out the use of force."[20] British statesmen such as Harold Macmillan concluded, as Macmillan later wrote, that if Britain used force, "I believed that the Americans would issue a protest, even a violent protest in public; but that they would in their hearts be glad to see the matter brought to a conclusion. They would therefore content themselves with overt disapproval, while feeling covert sympathy."[21] Such feelings led Macmillan to advise Eden with regard to how Eisenhower would act that "Ike will lie doggo."[22] Richard Neustadt suggests that Eisenhower's letters to Eden on Suez were not sufficiently forthright on the point of American opposition to the use of force. Neustadt writes that Eisenhower's letters "state the American logic most completely, although with more courtesy than clarity."[23] Neustadt writes that Eisenhower expressed himself "perhaps overpolitely" in his letters to Eden, such as on September 8, 1956, when "Eisenhower dispatched a long letter conveying strong if generalised distaste for the use of force."[24] From a reading of Eisenhower's letters to Eden on

Suez, however, it is difficult to accept the conclusion that Eden could be left with any misunderstanding of Eisenhower's position, especially on the matter of the use of force. Eisenhower commented with regard to his exchange of letters on Suez with Eden that "this is getting to be a sort of trans-Atlantic essay contest."[25] In such an essay contest Eisenhower would merit high marks, especially for lucidity. As Cole Kingseed argues, "The president's personal messages to Eden left little room for doubt as to Eisenhower's position. Regardless of Eden's and Lloyd's later attempts at self-justification, Eisenhower had made it abundantly clear that the United States preferred a diplomatic, not a military, solution to the crisis."[26] Even Eden's sympathetic official biographer, Robert Rhodes James, writes, with regard to Eden's statement that in his July 31, 1956, letter Eisenhower did not rule out the use of force, that "this is technically true, but the whole tenor of the letter was in the opposite direction."[27] Roger Makins later wrote that "I have always been astonished that, ignoring Eisenhower's specific and repeated rejection of armed action against Egypt, they held to their view that 'old Ike' would, when the moment came, either back them or at worst stand aside."[28] At the end of November 1956, Eisenhower conferred with Dulles about a message which Eisenhower had received from his wartime comrade in arms, Field Marshall Sir Hastings Ismay, complaining that "we deserted our two friends in their hour of trial." In response, "the Secretary said it was they who double-crossed us, and now they are trying to put the blame on us. He said, 'Nothing has been stronger and clearer than your letters to Eden.'"[29]

There is perhaps more substance in the argument that Eisenhower did not clarify the strong steps that he would take if the British, against his wishes, resorted to force. Louise Richardson, for example, writes that "while Eisenhower states clearly that he did not support a policy of force, he never spelled out what his government would do if Britain employed it. The British can, then, be forgiven for assuming that the United States would content itself with a few words of condemnation but remain, in effect, benignly neutral."[30] Even Cole Kingseed, in his sympathetic study of Eisenhower's policy on Suez, suggests that "what the president should have done was . . . reveal the extent to which he would impose economic sanctions, oppose monetary loans from the World Bank and threaten to devalue the British pound sterling unless he (Eden) abandoned his military policy."[31] Against such arguments, however, it might be suggested that, while it is true that such points are indeed absent in Eisenhower's letters to Eden on Suez, such stark specific threats would have been out of place in the context of diplomatic efforts to persuade a close ally.

The suggestion has been made, in Jonathan Aitken's biography of Richard Nixon, for example, that Eisenhower later regretted that he had not supported Britain over Suez. As evidence in support of this view, Aitken cites a letter from Nixon to the Conservative MP, Julian Amery.[32] More reliable testimony, however, is perhaps offered by Stephen Ambrose, who, in a review of Aitken's book, wrote that in his interviews with Eisenhower in the 1960s Eisenhower had always stated that the stance which he had taken over Suez, although painful in its necessity to be at such odds with his British ally, had been the correct policy to pursue. "He was proud of what he had done with regard to Suez," Ambrose writes, "and insisted that he had been right to support Egypt."[33] Robert R. Bowie supports Ambrose on this point, concluding in a discussion about "second thoughts on the crisis" that "Eisenhower . . . apparently had no doubts" and in later life in the 1960s "had no misgivings about the course he had followed."[34]

There is perhaps more validity in the point that, if the British and French had acted more swiftly and efficiently in their military conduct of the Suez operation, Eisenhower would have accepted a fait accompli. Eisenhower pointed out in his letter of July 31, however, that while military operations were easy to begin they did not necessarily end the matter. Eisenhower was clearly incensed at the military incompetence that was displayed in the Suez operation with the British fleet sailing slowly from Malta for a week after the initial Israeli attack. Eisenhower said to his aide, Emmet John Hughes, "Of course there's nobody in a war I'd rather have fighting alongside me than the British. . . . But this thing! My God!"[35] A swift seizure of the Suez Canal by British and French forces would have seemed militarily feasible, and if this had been carried out promptly and efficiently, Eisenhower would have been simply presented with a fait accompli. As he had pointed out, however, this was not the end of the matter but only the beginning. Military occupation forces along the canal would have faced the same problems of sabotage and terrorism that British forces had suffered in the early 1950s. Even more so, Eisenhower had expressed quite eloquently in his letters how an old-style colonial gunboat approach would inflame public opinion in Egypt and throughout the entire Middle East so that military seizure of the canal would result not in Nasser's downfall but in the strengthening of his position in Egypt and throughout the Arab world.

It might be argued that, although Eisenhower made his views clear, Dulles took a more ambiguous position and that Eden thought that Dulles rather than Eisenhower determined the course of American foreign policy. Robin Renwick writes that "Eden had no particularly high regard for Eisenhower.

In that he shared the fashionable prejudices of the time. Most of the foreign press corps in Washington underestimated the president, depicting him as a golf-player figurehead. Eden was not alone in imagining that the president was not the real decision maker in U.S. foreign policy."[36] Chester Cooper, who was CIA liaison in London at the time of the Suez crisis, expresses this commonly held view, writing that "the President seemed to have little talent and little concern for the complexities of foreign affairs. It was Secretary Dulles . . . who, virtually single-handed, managed the foreign policies of the United States."[37] If Chester Cooper, an American in London, held such a view, it is perhaps not surprising that, as Robert Rhodes James writes, "The British in London, in spite of all Makins told them of the reality, genuinely believed that Dulles ran foreign policy, with a somewhat lazy and uninvolved President somewhere in the background, who would, if it came to the crunch, support his old wartime allies and friends. They seriously underestimated Eisenhower's strength and resolution, and also his personal vanity and hot temper."[38] It is conceivable that to some extent Eisenhower's style of "hidden-hand" presidency, as Fred Greenstein phrased it, misled Eden, as many others, into believing that Eisenhower was a well-meaning amateur who left control of policy to others.[39]

But only to a slight degree would it be convincing to suggest that, while Eden was receiving such a clear message in the letters from Eisenhower, Eden felt that Eisenhower was not the real determinant of American foreign policy. Eden had known Eisenhower for a very long time; he had worked with Eisenhower and Dulles over many years; he had learned, partly as a result of his many wrangles with Dulles, that Dulles was not the final determinant of American foreign policy. Furthermore, though Dulles was ambiguous in certain respects, his overall position was fairly clearly discernible. Robin Renwick writes that "the contemporary records belie the myth propagated by Eden and others that Dulles supported the use of force. While Dulles supported the *threat* of force, he never gave any indication that, in his view, the moment for military action had been realised."[40] To a hard-headed diplomat such as Robert Murphy, Dulles's purpose was clear and obvious. Murphy wrote that Dulles "devised various delaying tactics designed to support Eisenhower's policy of avoiding military intervention. It was philosophically assumed the danger of bellicose action would disappear if negotiations were prolonged and that delays would reduce the heat and make possible some kind of non-violent struggle in Egypt."[41] Dulles used phrases which possibly encouraged the belief that he was more inclined toward an ultimate resort to force, such as that Nasser should "disgorge" the canal. This may have inclined some British statesmen to feel that America would eventually support a British use of force since, as Thomas Risse-Kappen wrote, Eden and Lloyd "convinced themselves that Dulles' ambivalent remarks throughout the crisis supported this assessment."[42] Dulles, moreover, as Lloyd put it, gained a reputation of "saying one thing and doing another."[43] There is also the extraordinary piece of evidence of Dulles's question to Lloyd on the crisis when Lloyd visited Dulles in the hospital on November 17, 1956; Dulles asked Lloyd, "Selwyn, why did you stop? Why didn't you go through with it and get Nasser down?"[44] Dulles's questions indicate, it might be argued, that all along Dulles was hinting in his ambiguous fashion that America would turn a blind eye and give at least tacit support if Britain took a forceful lead. In fact, however, Dulles had made the same point to Eisenhower when Eisenhower had visited Dulles in the hospital on November 12, 1956, and it is clear that Dulles's main point was not that he regretted that Britain and France had not pressed forward but that, as he said to Eisenhower, "they now have the worst of both possible worlds. They had received the onus of making the move and at the same time had not accomplished their major purpose."[45] A review of all of the evidence would seem to substantiate Robin Renwick's conclusion that only "on the basis of an extraordinary exercise of self-deception, the prime minister and his colleagues believed that the Americans would acquiesce."[46]

A further piece of compelling evidence that Eden was well aware of Eisenhower's view was the absence of communications on Eden's part from early October 1956. On November 2, 1956, Eisenhower wrote a long letter to his friend Swede Hazlett in which he outlined the arguments that he had put forward throughout the crisis. "All these thoughts I communicated to Eden time and again," Eisenhower wrote. "It was undoubtedly because of his knowledge of our bitter opposition to using force in the matter that when he finally decided to undertake the plan he just went completely silent."[47] Under cover of this silence, Eden was, of course, planning the fateful moves that he would make in late October and early November. One of the few figures who had full knowledge of these planned moves was the minister of state at the Foreign Office, Anthony Nutting, who was aghast by Eden's intentions and who resigned over Suez. Nutting later recorded that on October 25, 1956, after failing to persuade Eden not to go ahead with the proposed plan, "as I wound my way back to the Foreign Office, I was seized with a sudden wild desire to make straight for the American embassy and to tell the Ambassador everything I knew in the hope that this would bring Eisenhower to weigh in and prevent us and the French from going ahead." However, Nutting went on, "As quickly as I thought of it I rejected the idea. I could not take upon myself such a responsibility. However strongly I felt and however much I might be prepared to do to prevent this act of criminal folly I could not betray my Government's plans, even to their closest ally." Nevertheless, Nutting concluded, "Looking back on that fateful October afternoon, I wish in more ways than one I had yielded to that first impulse."[48] It is fascinating to speculate what might have been the result if Nutting had followed his impulse to inform the Americans. One result might have been a letter from Eisenhower to Eden which would claim pride of place as the most significant in the Eden-Eisenhower correspondence; in the trans-Atlantic essay contest to which Eisenhower referred, such a letter may well have taken first prize.

The historian, however, must deal with what happened rather than with what might have happened, however fascinating speculation on the latter may sometimes be. With regard to what happened, Eisenhower was faced with the problems of ending the crisis and restoring good Anglo-American relations. Eisenhower's resolute, sometimes brutal, action brought the crisis to an end promptly. Significantly, however, he paid close attention at the same time to the restoration of the broken Anglo-American relationship. This fits in with other evidence of the same nature on this matter. When preparing a television address on October 31, Eisenhower told his speechwriter, Emmet John Hughes, not to be too critical of Britain and to include clearly "how vital we think our alliances are." "Those British," Eisenhower said to Hughes, "they're still my right arm."[49] On the phone to Eden on November 7, when a ceasefire had been arranged, Eisenhower said that Suez was "like a family spat."[50] The correspondence with Eden provides further evidence along the same lines in Eisenhower's initial willingness to accept Eden's suggestion that when the crisis had been brought to an end by ceasefire Eden should fly over to Washington to meet Eisenhower. Advice from Dulles and under secretary of state Herbert Hoover Jr. led to a swift squashing of this proposal on the grounds that it would have been very badly received in Arab countries and aroused deep suspicions. Hoover said that "we must be very careful not to give the impression that we are teaming with the British and French."[51] Eisenhower prudently accepted the counsel of Hoover on the matter, but his exchange of letters with Eden indicates clearly his eagerness to repair the damage of Suez to the Anglo-American relationship as soon as possible. This was in line with the attitude that Eisenhower demonstrated in an exchange of letters with Churchill in November 1956. Churchill poignantly wrote to Eisenhower that "there is not much left for me to do in this world, and I have neither the wish nor the strength to involve myself in the present political stress and turmoil. But I do believe, with unfaltering conviction, that the theme of Anglo-American alliance is more important today than at any time since the war. You and I had some part in raising it to the plane on which it has stood. Now, whatever the arguments adduced here and in the United States for or against Anthony's action in Egypt, to let events in the Middle East become a gulf between us, would be an act of folly, on which our whole civilisation may founder."[52] In reply, Eisenhower thanked Churchill for "your moving letter" and wrote that "quite naturally I agree unequivocally with your main theme."[53]

Eisenhower is more open to the criticism that his alternative solution to the problems of the Middle East was unconvincing. He suggested in the correspondence with Eden that Nasser should be deflated and undermined whereas other Arab figures should be promoted and efforts should be made to solve underlying problems, especially the Arab-Israeli conflict. Such ideas proved to be wishful thinking. On the other hand, the problems of the area have seemed to be fundamentally intractable. With regard to Eisenhower's handling of the Suez crisis in itself, the Eden-Eisenhower correspondence would seem to support Cole Kingseed's evaluation that Eisenhower "remained unflappable in the face of dissenting allies, contentious military chiefs and political opposition in a presidential election year. Though he failed to keep the crisis from escalating, he, more than any other statesman, restored peace to the troubled region. It was a splendid performance."[54]

With regard to Eden's overall reputation, his name is so linked to the Suez episode that it overshadows other aspects of his premiership, let alone the rest of his long career. A. J. P. Taylor, for example, in his characteristic, acerbic style wrote in a foreword for a biography of Eden that "Eden will be remembered as the prime minister who steered the ship of state onto the rocks."[55] The question had been widely posed whether Eden had the capability to hold the highest office. Many historians conclude that his term of office as prime minister demonstrated that the doubts with regard to his capability were justified. John Young, for instance, writes that "Eden, in sum, was a brittle hero, whose many undoubted gifts were balanced by blind spots which were tragically exposed when he finally reached the premiership."[56] Others suggest, however, that in matters other than Suez Eden was an able leader and prime minister and that Suez was exceptional. Anthony Nutting, in the severely critical account of Eden's policy over Suez, wondered "why Eden should have come to act so completely out of character" and "what had happened to transform Eden so completely."[57]

Some explanations have been offered in terms of Eden's health. Jonathan Pierce, for example, places strong emphasis on this matter as an explanation for Eden's behavior.[58] Yet while Eden clearly had serious health problems, Eisenhower had a heart attack and a bout of ileitis and Dulles suffered from cancer, but it did not affect their judgment on political issues or international affairs too severely. Eden lived for a further twenty years after 1956, so that his health is not a convincing explanation for his misjudgments over Suez. Of more substance is the view that Suez was the breaking point for Britain as the empire receded, making Britain's economic and political weaknesses and American dominance increasingly evident. Eden was, after all, by no means alone in taking the stand which he took over Suez. Not only right-wing elements such as the Suez Group but large segments within the British government and society were behind Eden in a determination not to let Nasser tweak the British lion's tail with impunity and resented that their American ally had let them down. In some ways Anthony Eden might be viewed more sympathetically as the victim of the forces of history that were liable to explode in some manner or another in British society at the time; Eden happened to have the misfortune to hold office at the wrong time. The point can also be made that, though the Suez episode had serious consequences, it hardly compares with a major debacle, such as American involvement in Vietnam. Such points concerning Eden's reputation will continue to be argued by historians and other commentators as they have been already by Robert Rhodes James in his sympathetic, official biography, David Carlton in his highly critical biography, David Dutton in his measured, sophisticated analysis, and D. R. Thorpe in his well-balanced evaluation. With regard to such an evaluation of Eden, the Eden-Eisenhower correspondence would seem to produce evidence in support of the view that Eden was not fundamentally unfit to hold such high office but that a change occurred with the Suez affair that was a catalyst for forces within British society and within Eden's personality, leading him to conduct affairs during the crisis in a manner that ended in disaster.

With regard to Eisenhower's overall reputation, the Eden-Eisenhower correspondence would seem to provide evidence to support the revisionist view of Eisenhower's presidency. Eisenhower comes across in the correspondence as an intelligent, engaged, well-informed chief executive with very reasonable views on world affairs. He was eager to promote stronger Anglo-American ties while appreciating that times had moved on by the mid-1950s from the more exclusive World War II style of Anglo-American relationship that Churchill had wished to maintain. In the time of crisis over Suez, Eisenhower advocated a prudent, cautious course, and when his allies acted with rash imprudence, he took decisive action to bring the conflict to a close and to repair the damage to the alliance as swiftly as possible.

The Eden-Eisenhower correspondence, then, vividly documents the disappointment of a relationship that began with much promise in April 1955, developed quite soundly for fifteen months, and was then blown dangerously off course. Eisenhower was deeply disappointed by this. In a conversation with Dulles on November 17, 1956, "the President made the following comment: He said that one of the most pleasant things in life was to find that one's estimate of a man increased each time one had dealings with him. Conversely he thought one of the most disappointing things was to start with an exceedingly high opinion of a person and then have continually to downgrade this estimate on the basis of succeeding contacts with him. He indicated that Eden fell into the latter category."[59] Perhaps Eisenhower was judging Eden too harshly in an overreaction to the immediate past of the experience of their relationship during the Suez crisis, since the evidence from the whole of the correspondence suggests a good working relationship up to the time of the crisis, when matters changed considerably. On the other hand, Eisenhower's evaluation of Eden perhaps illustrates the point that the correspondence is, of course, only one source of evidence, containing considerable limitations as well as providing insightful revelations, so that judgments and evaluations of personalities and the issues can only be made on the basis of the totality of all sources of evidence and not upon a single source.

Eisenhower continued to send birthday greetings to Eden after Eden's retirement and to exchange occasional brief letters containing some general reflections on international affairs.[60] When Eisenhower went to Britain in 1962, he visited Eden. But in early 1957 Eisenhower's main concern was no longer with Eden but with his successor, and this revived Eisenhower's spirits. As speculation had grown in the autumn of 1956 that Eden would resign, Eisenhower knew that one of the leading contenders as Eden's successor was his old friend from wartime days in North Africa, Harold Macmillan. Eisenhower wrote that he had always thought most highly of Macmillan, whom he described as "a straight, fine man . . . the outstanding one of the British he served with during the war."[61] When Eden resigned on January 9, 1957, and was succeeded by Macmillan, Eisenhower and Macmillan were not only eager to make every effort to repair the damage that the Anglo-American relationship had suffered in general but also in particular to continue the tradition of a personal correspondence between the prime minister of Britain and the president of the United States.

NOTES

1. Curtis Peebles, *Shadow Flights: America's Secret Air War against the Soviet Union* (Novato, Calif.: Presidio Press, 2000), 275.

2. Memo, U-2 Overflights of the Soviet Union, August 18, 1960, White House Office, Office of the Staff Secretary, Subject Series, Alphabetical Subseries, box 15, Intelligence Matters (17), DDEL.

3. Ian Jackson, *The Economic Cold War: America, Britain and East-West Trade, 1948–1963* (London: Palgrave, 2003).

4. Eisenhower to Churchill, July 22, 1954, Churchill to Eisenhower, August 8, 1956, in *The Churchill-Eisenhower Correspondence, 1953–1955*, ed. Peter G. Boyle (Chapel Hill: University of North Carolina Press, 1990), 162–65.

5. Peter L. Hahn, *The United States, Great Britain and Egypt, 1945–1956* (Chapel Hill: University of North Carolina Press, 1991), 38.

6. Milton Eisenhower to Dwight D. Eisenhower, July 7, 1955, AWF, Name Series, box 12, Eisenhower, Milton S. (12).

7. Milton S. Eisenhower, *The President Is Calling* (Garden City, N.Y.: Doubleday, 1974), 309.

8. Diary Entry, May 14, 1953, in *The Eisenhower Diaries*, ed. Robert H. Ferrell (New York: W. W. Norton, 1981), 238.

9. Saul Kelly, "A Very Considerable and Largely Unsung Success: Sir Roger Makins' Washington Embassy, 1953–1956," chapter 8 in *Twentieth Century Anglo-American Relations*, ed. Jonathan Hollowell (London: Palgrave, 2001), 127.

10. Eisenhower to Harold Macmillan, September 1, 1959, AWF, International Series, box 25(a), Macmillan 7/1/59–12/31/59 (6).

11. John R. Charmley, *Churchill's Grand Alliance: The Anglo-American Special Relationship, 1940–1957* (London: Hodder and Stoughton, 1995), 350.

12. Ibid., 294.

13. Jonathan Pierce, *Sir Anthony Eden and the Suez Crisis* (London: Palgrave, 2003).

14. Diane B. Kunz, *The Economic Diplomacy of the Suez Crisis* (Chapel Hill: University of North Carolina Press, 1991), 79.

15. Lord Moran, *Winston Churchill: The Struggle for Survival, 1940–1965* (London: Constable, 1966), 771.

16. Dwight D. Eisenhower, *Waging Peace, 1956–1961* (Garden City, N.Y.: Doubleday, 1965), 50.

17. Piers Dixon, *Double Diploma: The Life of Sir Pierson Dixon, Don and Diplomat* (London: Hutchison, 1968), 278.

18. *Parliamentary Debates*, 5th ser., vol. 562 (1956–57), col. 1518.

19. Evelyn Shuckburgh, *Descent to Suez: Diaries, 1951–1956* (London: Weidenfeld and Nicholson, 1986), 362.

20. Anthony Eden, *Full Circle* (London: Cassell, 1960), 436.

21. Harold Macmillan, *Riding the Storm, 1956–1959* (London: Macmillan, 1971), 157.

22. Alistair Horne, *Macmillan* (London: Macmillan, 1988), 434.

23. Richard Neustadt, *Alliance Politics* (New York: Columbia University Press, 1970), 156.

24. Ibid., 13, 16.

25. Eisenhower to Dulles, telephone conversation, October 30, 1956, in *The Presidency: The Middle Way*, vol. 17 of *The Papers of Dwight David Eisenhower*, ed. Alfred D. Chandler Jr. (Baltimore: Johns Hopkins University Press, 1996), 2345.

26. Cole Kingseed, *Eisenhower and the Suez Crisis of 1956* (Baton Rouge: Louisiana State University Press, 1995), 55.

27. Robert Rhodes James, *Anthony Eden* (London: Weidenfeld and Nicholson, 1986), 473.

28. Lord Sherfield (Roger Makins) to Peter G. Boyle, April 18, 1995, personal correspondence in editor's possession. Roger Makins was elevated to the peerage as Lord Sherfield in 1964.

29. Memorandum of a telephone conversation between the president and the secretary of state, November 27, 1956, AWF, DDE Diary Series, box 19, Nov. '56 Phone Calls.

30. Louise Richardson, *When Allies Differ: Anglo-American Relations during the Suez and Falklands Crises* (New York: St. Martin's Press, 1996), 188.

31. Kingseed, *Eisenhower and the Suez Crisis*, 153.

32. Richard Nixon to Julian Amery, January 21, 1987, quoted in Jonathan Aitken, *Nixon: A Life* (London: Weidenfeld and Nicholson, 1993), 244.

33. Stephen E. Ambrose, review of *Nixon: A Life*, by Jonathan Aitken, *Foreign Affairs* 74 (July/August 1994): 168.

34. Robert R. Bowie, "Eisenhower, Dulles and the Suez Crisis," chapter 10 in *Suez, 1956: The Crisis and Its Consequences*, eds. William Roger Louis and Roger Owen (Oxford: Clarendon Press, 1989), 214.

35. Emmet J. Hughes, *The Ordeal of Power: A Political Memoir of the Eisenhower Years* (New York: Atheneum, 1963), 217.

36. Robin Renwick, *Fighting with Allies: America and Britain in Peace and War* (Basingstoke: Macmillan, 1996), 196–97.

37. Chester L. Cooper, *The Lion's Last Roar: Suez, 1956* (New York: Harper and Row, 1978), 75.

38. James, *Eden*, 476–77.

39. Fred I. Greenstein, *The Hidden-Hand Presidency: Eisenhower as Leader* (New York: Basic Books, 1982).

40. Renwick, *Fighting With Allies*, 163.

41. Robert Murphy, *Diplomat among Warriors* (Garden City, N.Y.: Doubleday, 1964), 384.

42. Thomas Risse-Kappen, *Cooperation among Democracies: The European Influence on U.S. Foreign Policy* (Princeton: Princeton University Press, 1995).

43. Selwyn Lloyd, *Suez: A Personal Account* (London: Jonathan Cape, 1978), 38.

44. Ibid., 219.

45. Memorandum of conversation between the president and secretary of state, Secretary Dulles's Room, Walter Reed Hospital, November 12, 1956, Dulles Papers, White House Memoranda Series, box 4, Meetings with the President through Dec. 1956, DDEL.

46. Renwick, *Fighting with Allies*, 163.

47. Robert Griffith, ed., *Ike's Letters to a Friend, 1941–1958* (Lawrence: University Press of Kansas), 176.

48. Anthony Nutting, *No End of a Lesson: The Study of Suez* (London: Constable, 1967), 107–8.

49. Hughes, *Ordeal of Power*, 220.

50. Memorandum of a telephone conversation between President Eisenhower and Prime Minister Eden, November 7, 1956, AWF, DDE Diary Series, box 19, Nov. '56 Phone Calls.

51. A. J. Goodpaster, Memorandum for the Record, November 7, 1956, AWF, DDE Diary Series, box 19, Nov '56 Diary—Staff Memos.

52. Churchill to Eisenhower, November 23, 1956, AWF, International Series, box 20, Churchill, Winston, April 8, 1955–December 31, 1957, (3).

53. Eisenhower to Churchill, November 25, 1956, AWF, International Series, box 20, Churchill, Winston, April 8, 1955–December 31, 1957, (3).

54. Kingseed, *Eisenhower and the Suez Crisis*, 148.

55. Sidney Aster, *Anthony Eden* (London: Weidenfeld and Nicholson, 1976), ii.

56. John W. Young, *Winston Churchill's Last Campaign: Britain and the Cold War, 1951–1955* (Oxford: Clarendon Press, 1996), 46.

57. Nutting, *No End of a Lesson*, 14, 107.

58. Jonathan Pierce, *Sir Anthony Eden and the Suez Crisis* (London: Palgrave, 2003).

59. Memorandum of a conversation between the president and the secretary of state, November 17, 1956, Dulles Papers, White House Memoranda Series, box 4, Meetings with the President through Dec. 1956, (3), DDEL.

60. AP 23/29/1-39.

61. A. J. Goodpaster, Memorandum of Conference with the President, November 20, 1956, AWF, DDE Diary Series, box 19, Nov. '56 Diary—Staff Memos.

BIBLIOGRAPHICAL ESSAY

This relatively brief bibliographical essay is designed to be a guide to a selection of the most important works on Eden and Eisenhower and the issues of their time. It is not intended to be a comprehensive bibliography.

The papers of Sir Anthony Eden, who became the Earl of Avon in 1961, are located in the library of the University of Birmingham, where Eden was chancellor, a largely honorary post, between 1945 and 1973. His official government papers are located in the Public Record Office, National Archives, Kew, Surrey. The file of his correspondence with Eisenhower during his term of office as prime minister, 1955–1957, containing the original letters from Eisenhower and copies of the letters from Eden to Eisenhower, are in the Public Record Office in PREM 11/1177.

The most important published primary sources on Eden are his memoirs, which he published in three volumes: *Full Circle* (London: Cassell, 1960), *Facing the Dictators* (London: Cassell, 1962), and *The Reckoning* (London: Cassell, 1965). The most important biographies of Eden are D. R. Thorpe, *Eden: The Life and Times of Anthony Eden, First Earl of Avon, 1897–1977* (London: Chatto and Windus, 2003); David Dutton, *Anthony Eden: A Life and Reputation* (London: Arnold, 1997); Victor Rothwell, *Anthony Eden: A Political Biography* (Manchester: Manchester University Press, 1992); Robert Rhodes James, *Anthony Eden* (London: Weidenfeld and Nicolson, 1986); David Carlton, *Anthony Eden: A Biography* (London: Allen Lane, 1981); and Sidney Astor, *Anthony Eden* (London: Weidenfeld and Nicolson, 1976). A useful guide to historiography on Eden is Alan Lawrance and Peter Dodd, eds., *Anthony Eden, 1897–1977: A Bibliography* (Westport, Conn.: Greenwood Press, 1995).

Eisenhower's papers are located in his presidential library, the Dwight D. Eisenhower Library, in Abilene, Kansas. The file of his correspondence with Eden, 1955–1957, containing the original letters from Eden and copies of the letters from Eisenhower to Eden, are in Papers as President of the United States, 1953–1961 (Ann Whitman File), International Series, Boxes 20–22, Dwight D. Eisenhower Library, Abilene, Kansas.

The most important published primary sources on Eisenhower are his published papers, Alfred D. Chandler Jr., ed., *The Papers of Dwight David Eisenhower*, 21 vols. (Baltimore: Johns Hopkins University Press, 1970–2001); his memoirs, which he published under the overall title of *The White House Years* in two volumes, *Mandate for Change, 1953–1956* (New York: Doubleday, 1963) and *Waging Peace, 1956–1961* (New York: Doubleday, 1965); his informal memoirs, *At Ease: Stories I Like to Tell to Friends* (New York: Doubleday, 1967); his public papers as president, *Public Papers of the Presidents: Dwight D. Eisenhower, 1953–1961*, 8 vols. (Washington, D.C.: U.S. Government Printing Office, 1958–1961); and various volumes of *Foreign Relations of the United States*, especially vol. 16, *Suez Crisis, July 26–December 31, 1956* (Washington, D.C.: U.S. Government Printing Office, 1990) and vol. 27, *Western Europe and Canada* (Washington, D.C.: U.S. Government Printing Office, 1992). Also significant are Robert H. Ferrell, ed., *The Eisenhower Diaries* (New York: W. W. Norton, 1981) and Robert Griffith, ed., *Ike's Letters to a Friend, 1941–1958* (Lawrence: University Press of Kansas, 1984).

Among the many biographies of Eisenhower the most important are Stephen E. Ambrose, *Eisenhower*, 2 vols. (New York: Simon and Schuster, 1983–84); Piers Brandon, *Ike: The Life and Times of Dwight D. Eisenhower* (London: Secker and Warburg, 1987); Robert F. Burk, *Dwight D. Eisenhower: Hero and Politician* (Boston: Twayne Publishers, 1986); Douglas Kinnard, *Eisenhower: Soldier Statesman of the Twentieth Century* (Washington, D.C.: Brassey's, 2002); R. Alton Lee, *Dwight D. Eisenhower: Soldier and Statesman* (Chicago: Nelson, Hall, 1981); Peter Lyon, *Eisenhower: Portrait of a Hero* (Boston: Little, Brown, 1974); Herbert S. Parmet, *Eisenhower and the American Crusades* (New York: Macmillan, 1972); Geoffrey Perret, *Eisenhower* (New York: Random House, 1999); William B. Pickett, *Dwight David Eisenhower and American Power* (Wheeling, Ill.: Harlan Davidson, 1995); and Tom Wicker, *Dwight D. Eisenhower* (New York: Henry Holt, 2002). Significant studies of Eisenhower's presidency include Charles C. Alexander, *Holding the Line: The Eisenhower Era, 1952–1961* (Bloomington: Indiana University Press, 1975); Günter Bischof and Stephen E. Ambrose, eds., *Eisenhower: A Centenary Assessment* (Baton Rouge: Louisiana State University Press, 1995); Blanche W. Cook, *The Declassified Eisenhower* (New York: Doubleday, 1981); Richard V. Damms, *The Eisenhower Presidency, 1953–1961* (London: Pearson, 2002); Fred I. Greenstein, *The Hidden-Hand Presidency: Eisenhower as Leader* (New York: Basic Books, 1982); Michael S. Mayer, ed., *The Eisenhower Presidency and the 1950s* (Boston: Houghton Mifflin, 1998); Chester Pach and Elmo Richardson, *The Presidency of Dwight D. Eisenhower*, rev. ed. (Lawrence: University Press of Kansas, 1991); Shirley A. Warshaw, ed., *Re-examining the Eisenhower Presidency* (Westport: Greenwood Press, 1993); and Richard Melanson and David Mayers, eds., *Re-evaluating Eisenhower: American Foreign Policy in the 1950s* (Urbana: University of Illinois Press, 1989).

Among accounts of aspects of Eisenhower's pre-presidential career the most significant include Carlo d'Este, *Eisenhower: A Soldier's Life* (New York: Henry Holt, 2002); Kenneth S. Davis, *Soldier of Democracy, a Biography of Dwight Eisenhower* (Garden City, N.Y.: Doubleday, 1945); Matthew F. Holland, *Eisenhower Between Wars: The Making of a General and a Statesman* (Westport, Conn.: Praeger, 2001); John S. D. Eisenhower, *Allies: Pearl Harbor to D-Day* (Garden City, N.Y.: Doubleday, 1982); Mark A. Stoler, *Allies and Adversaries: The Joint Chiefs of Staff, the Grand Alliance and U.S. Strategy in World War II* (Chapel Hill: University of North Carolina Press, 2000); Rick Atkinson, *An Army at Dawn: The War in North Africa, 1942–43* (New York: Henry Holt, 2002); David Eisenhower, *Eisenhower at War, 1943–1945* (New York: Random House, 1986); Stephen E. Ambrose, *The Supreme Commander* (Garden City, N.Y.: Doubleday,

1970); Travis B. Jacobs, *Eisenhower at Columbia* (New Brunswick, N.J.: Transactions Publishers, 2001); Steve Neal, *Harry and Ike: The Partnership That Remade the Postwar World* (New York: Scribner's, 2000); and William B. Pickett, *Eisenhower Decides to Run: Presidential Politics and Cold War Strategy* (Chicago: Ivan R. Dee, 2000). A useful guide to historiography on Eisenhower is R. Alton Lee, ed., *Dwight D. Eisenhower: A Bibliography of His Times and Presidency* (Wilmington: Scholarly Resources, 1991).

There is a very large number of memoirs by British contemporaries of Eden, including Lord Butler, *The Art of the Possible* (London: Hamish Hamilton, 1971); William Clark, *From Three Worlds: Memoirs* (London: Sidgwick and Jackson, 1986); John Colville, *The Fringes of Power, 1939–1955* (London: Hodder and Stoughton, 1985); Piers Dixon, *Double Diploma: The Life of Sir Pearson Dixon, Don and Diplomat* (London: Hutchinson, 1968); Paul Gore-Booth, *With Great Truth and Respect* (London: Constable, 1974); Nicholas Henderson, *The Private Office: A Personal View of Five Foreign Secretaries and of Government from the Inside* (London: Weidenfeld and Nicolson, 1984); Gladwyn Jebb, *The Memoirs of Lord Gladwyn* (London: Weidenfeld and Nicolson, 1972); Ivone Kirkpatrick, *The Inner Circle* (London: Macmillan, 1959); Harold Macmillan, *Tides of Fortune, 1945–1955* (London: Macmillan, 1969) and *Riding the Storm, 1956–1959* (London: Macmillan, 1971); Peter Caterall, ed., *The Macmillan Diaries, 1950–1957* (London: Macmillan, 2003); Anthony Montague-Browne, *Long Sunset: Memoirs of Churchill's Last Private Secretary* (London: Cassell, 1995); Lord Moran, *Winston Churchill: The Struggle for Survival, 1940–1965* (London: Constable, 1966); and Frank Roberts, *Dealing with Dictators: The Destruction and Revival of Europe, 1931–1970* (London: Weidenfeld and Nicolson, 1991).

There is a smaller number of memoirs by American contemporaries of Eisenhower. The most important are Sherman Adams, *Firsthand Report: The Story of the Eisenhower Administration* (New York: Harper, 1961); Robert Cutler, *No Time for Rest* (Boston: Little, Brown, 1966); Robert H. Ferrell, ed., *The Diary of James C. Hagerty: Eisenhower in Mid-Course, 1954–1955* (Bloomington: Indiana University Press, 1983); Emmet J. Hughes, *The Ordeal of Power: A Political Memoir of the Eisenhower Years* (New York: Atheneum, 1963); Robert Murphy, *Diplomat Among Warriors* (Garden City, N.Y.: Doubleday, 1964); Richard M. Bissell, *Reflections of a Cold Warrior: From Yalta to the Bay of Pigs* (New Haven, Conn.: Yale University Press, 1996); George F. Kennan, *Memoirs, 1950–1963* (Boston: Little, Brown, 1973); Henry Cabot Lodge, *The Storm Has Many Eyes: A Personal Narrative* (New York: Norton, 1973); and Richard M. Nixon, *RN: The Memoirs of Richard Nixon* (New York: Grosset and Dunlap, 1978).

Important studies of contemporary British figures include Anthony Howard, *RAB: The Life of R. A. Butler* (London: Jonathan Cope, 1987); Alistair Horne, *Macmillan*, 2 vols. (London: Macmillan, 1988–89); D. R. Thorpe, *Selwyn Lloyd* (London: Jonathan Cope, 1989); Martin Gilbert, *Never Despair: Winston Churchill, 1945–65* (London: Heinemann, 1988); Roy Jenkins, *Churchill* (London: Macmillan, 2001); John W. Young, *Winston Churchill's Last Campaign: Britain and the Cold War, 1951–55* (Oxford: Clarendon Press, 1996); Klaus Larres, *Churchill's Cold War: The Politics of Personal*

Diplomacy (New Haven, Conn.: Yale University Press, 2002); and Andrew Roberts, *Eminent Churchillians* (London: Weidenfeld and Nicolson, 1994).

Important studies of contemporary American figures include Stephen E. Ambrose, *Nixon*, 3 vols. (New York: Simon and Schuster, 1987–91); Iwan Morgan, *Nixon* (London: Arnold, 2003); Arthur M. Johnson, *Winthrop W. Aldrich: Lawyer, Banker, Diplomat* (Cambridge, Mass.: Harvard University Press, 1968); James Chace, *Acheson: The Secretary of State Who Created the American World* (New York: Simon and Schuster, 1998); and Douglas Brinkley, *Dean Acheson: The Cold War Years, 1953–71* (New Haven, Conn.: Yale University Press, 1992).

On John Foster Dulles, the most important works are Richard H. Immerman, *John Foster Dulles: Piety, Pragmatism and Power in U.S. Foreign Policy* (Wilmington, Del.: Scholarly Resources, 1999); Frederick W. Marks, *Power and Peace: The Diplomacy of John Foster Dulles* (Westport, Conn.: Praeger, 1993); Townsend Hoopes, *The Devil and John Foster Dulles: The Diplomacy of the Eisenhower Era* (Boston: Little, Brown, 1973); Mark G. Toulouse, *The Transformation of John Foster Dulles: From Prophet of Realism to Priest of Nationalism* (Macon, Ga.: Mercer University Press, 1985); Michael A. Guhin, *John Foster Dulles: A Statesman and His Times* (New York: Columbia University Press, 1972); Louis L. Gerson, *John Foster Dulles* (New York: Cooper Square Publishers, 1967); and Richard H. Immerman, ed., *John Foster Dulles and the Diplomacy of the Cold War* (Princeton, N.J.: Princeton University Press, 1990).

Useful works on British history of this period include Kenneth O. Morgan, *The People's Peace: British History since 1945*, 2nd ed. (Oxford: Oxford University Press, 1999); John Ramsden, *The Age of Churchill and Eden, 1940–1957* (London: Longman, 1995); Henry Pelling, *Churchill's Peacetime Ministry, 1951–1955* (London: 1997); Anthony Seldon, *Churchill's Indian Summer: The Conservative Government, 1951–1955* (London: Hodder and Stoughton, 1981); Peter Hennessy, *The Prime Minister: The Office and Its Holders since 1945* (London: Allen Lane, 2000); David Dutton, *British Politics since 1945: The Rise and Fall of Consensus* (Oxford: Blackwell, 1991); John W. Young, ed., *The Foreign Policy of Churchill's Peacetime Administration, 1951–1955* (Leicester: Leicester University Press, 1988); Correlli Barnett, *The Audit of War: The Illusion and Reality of Britain as a Great Nation* (London: Macmillan, 1986); Robert Holland, *The Pursuit of Greatness: Britain and the World Role, 1900–1970* (London: HarperCollins, 1991); John W. Young, *Britain and the World in the Twentieth Century* (London: Arnold, 1997); and Keith Robbins, *The Eclipse of a Great Power: Modern Britain, 1870–1992*, 2nd ed. (London: Longman, 1994).

Useful works in American history of this period include James T. Patterson, *Grand Expectations: The United States, 1945–1974* (New York: Oxford University Press, 1996); Gary A. Donaldson, *Abundance and Anxiety: America, 1945–1960* (Westport, Conn.: Praeger, 1997); John P. Diggins, *The Proud Decades, 1941–1960* (New York: W. W. Norton, 1988); William L. O'Neill, *American High: Years of Confidence, 1945–1960* (New York: Free Press, 1986); and David Halberstam, *The Fifties* (New York: Villard Books, 1993).

Of the extensive historical literature on the American presidency some of the most important works are Robert Dallek, *Hail to the Chief: The Making and Unmaking of American Presidents* (New York: Hyperion, 1996); Ethan M. Fishman, *The Prudential Presidency: An Aristotelian Approach to Presidential Leadership* (Westport, Conn.: Praeger, 2001); Lewis C. Gould, *The Modern American Presidency* (Lawrence: University Press of Kansas, 2002); Erwin C. Hargrove, *The President as Leader* (Lawrence: University Press of Kansas, 1998); John Kentleton, *President and Nation: The Making of Modern America* (London: Palgrave Macmillan, 2002); Marc Landy and Sidney M. Milkens, *Presidential Greatness* (Lawrence: University Press of Kansas, 2000); Richard E. Neustadt, *Presidential Power and Modern Presidents: The Politics of Leadership from Roosevelt to Reagan* (New York: Free Press, 1990); and James P. Pfiffner, *The Modern Presidency* (New York: St. Martin's Press, 1994).

On Anglo-American relations, the most significant works include C. J. Bartlett, *"The Special Relationship": A Political History of Anglo-American Relations since 1945* (London: Longman, 1992); Robin W. Renwick, *Fighting with Allies: America and Britain in Peace and War* (Basingstoke: Macmillan, 1996); David Dimbleby and David Reynolds, *An Ocean Apart: The Relationship between Britain and America in the Twentieth Century* (London: Hodder and Stoughton, 1988); William Roger Louis and Hedley Bull, eds., *The "Special Relationship": Anglo-American Relations since 1945* (Oxford: Clarendon Press, 1984); John Charmley, *Churchill's Grand Alliance: The Anglo-American Special Relationship, 1940–1957* (London: Hodder and Stoughton, 1995); Donald Cameron Watt, *Succeeding John Bull: America in Britain's Place* (Cambridge: Cambridge University Press, 1984); John Dickie, *"Special" No More: Anglo-American Relations: Rhetoric and Reality* (London: Weidenfeld and Nicolson, 1994); Coral Bell, *The Debatable Alliance: An Essay in Anglo-American Relations* (Oxford: Oxford University Press, 1964); Robert M. Hathaway, *Great Britain and the United States: Special Relations since World War II* (Boston: Twayne Publications, 1990); Alan P. Dobson, *Anglo-American Relations in the Twentieth Century* (London: Routledge, 1995); Jonathan Hollowell, ed., *Twentieth-Century Anglo-American Relations* (Basingstoke: Palgrave, 2001); and Michael F. Hopkins, *Oliver Franks and the Truman Administration: Anglo-American Relations, 1948–1952* (London: Frank Cass, 2003).

On relations with the Soviet Union, important works include Robert A. Divine, *Eisenhower and the Cold War* (New York: Oxford University Press, 1981); H. W. Brands, *Cold Warriors: Eisenhower's Generation and American Foreign Policy* (New York: Columbia University Press, 1988); Robert R. Bowie and Richard H. Immerman, *Waging Peace: How Eisenhower Shaped an Enduring Strategy* (New York: Oxford University Press, 1998); Saki Dockrill, *Eisenhower's New Look Security Policy, 1953–1960* (London: Macmillan, 1996); Gerard H. Clarfield, *Security with Solvency: Dwight D. Eisenhower and the Shaping of the American Military Establishment* (Westport, Conn.: Praeger, 1999); Curtis Keeble, *Britain and the Soviet Union, 1917–1989* (London: Macmillan, 1990); Anne Deighton, ed., *Britain and the First Cold War* (Basingstoke: Macmillan, 1990); Günter Bischof and Saki Dockrill, eds., *Cold War Respite: The Geneva Summit of*

1955 (Baton Rouge: Louisiana State University Press, 2000). On Eastern Europe and the Hungarian Revolution, see Gyorgy Litvan, ed., *The Hungarian Revolution of 1956: Reform, Revolt and Repression* (London: Longman, 1996); Daniel F. Calhoun, *Hungary and Suez, 1956* (Lanham, Md.: University Press of America, 1990); Ronald R. Krebs, *Dueling Visions: U.S. Strategy toward Eastern Europe under Eisenhower* (College Station: Texas A&M Press, 2001); Bennett Kovrig, *Of Walls and Bridges: The United States and Eastern Europe* (New York: Oxford University Press, 1991); Peter Grose, *Operation Rollback: America's Secret War Behind the Iron Curtain* (Boston: Houghton Mifflin, 2000); Scott Lucas, *Freedom's War: The U.S. Crusade Against the Soviet Union, 1945–1956* (Manchester: Manchester University Press, 1999); and Gregory Mitrovich, *Undermining the Kremlin: America's Strategy to Subvert the Soviet Bloc, 1947–1956* (Ithaca, N.Y.: Cornell University Press, 2000).

On nuclear issues, important works include Timothy Botti, *The Long Wait: The Forging of the Anglo-American Nuclear Alliance, 1945–1958* (New York: Greenwood Press, 1987); Stephen Twigge and Len Scott, *Planning Armageddon: Britain, the United States and the Command of Western Nuclear Forces, 1945–1964* (Amsterdam: Harwood Academic Publishers, 2000); John Bayliss, *Ambiguity and Deterrence: British Nuclear Strategy, 1945–1964* (Oxford: Clarendon, 1995); Duncan Campbell, *Unsinkable Aircraft Carrier: America Military Power in Britain* (London: Michael Joseph, 1984); and Craig Campbell, *Destroying the Village: Eisenhower and Thermonuclear War* (New York: Columbia University Press, 1998).

On intelligence, significant studies include Richard J. Aldrich, *The Hidden Hand: Britain, America and Cold War Intelligence* (London: John Murray, 2001); Paul Lashmar, *Spy Flights of the Cold War* (Stroud: Sutton Publishing, 1996); William E. Burrows, *By Any Means Necessary: America's Secret Air War in the Cold War* (New York: Farrar, Straus and Giroux, 2001); Curtis Peebles, *Shadow Flights: America's Secret Air War Against the Soviet Union* (Novato, Cal.: Presidio Press, 2000); John Prados, *Presidents' Secret Wars: CIA and Pentagon Covert Operations from World War II through the Persian Gulf* (Chicago: Ivan R. Dee, 1996); Jeffrey T. Richelson, *American Espionage and the Soviet Target* (New York: William Morrow, 1987); Chris Pocock, *The U-2 Spyplane: Toward the Unknown: A New History of the Early Years* (Atglen, Pa.: Schiffer Publications, 2000); Norman Polmar and Mike Haenggi, eds., *Spyplane: The U-2 History Declassified* (Asceola, Wis.: Motorbooks International, 2001); Michael Beschloss, *Mayday: Eisenhower, Khrushchev and the U-2 Affair* (New York: Harper and Row, 1986); Gregory W. Pedlow and Donald E. Welzenbach, *The CIA and the U-2 Program, 1954–1974* (Washington, D.C.: Center for the Study of Intelligence, Central Intelligence Agency, 1998); Jeffrey T. Richelson and Desmond Ball, *The Ties That Bind: Intelligence Co-operation between the UK-USA Countries—the United Kingdom, the United States of America, Canada, Australia and New Zealand* (London: Allen and Unwin, 1985); Bradley Smith, *The Ultra-Magic Deals and the Most Secret Special Relationship* (Shrewsbury: Airlife Publishers, 1993); Stephen Dorril, *M16: Fifty Years of Special Operations* (London: Fourth Estate, 2000); Rhodri Jeffreys-Jones, *The CIA and*

American Democracy, 2nd ed. (New Haven, Conn.: Yale University Press, 1998); John Ranelagh, *The Agency: The Rise and Decline of the CIA* (New York: Simon and Schuster, 1986); Christopher Andrew, *For the President's Eyes Only: Secret Intelligence and the American Presidency from Washington to Bush* (New York: HarperCollins, 1995); and Stephen E. Ambrose, *Ike's Spies: Eisenhower and the Espionage Establishment* (Garden City, N.Y.: Doubleday, 1981).

On economic issues, useful works are Ian Jackson, *The Economic Cold War: America, Britain and East-West Trade, 1948–1963* (London: Palgrave, 2003); Philip J. Funigiello, *American-Soviet Trade in the Cold War* (Chapel Hill: University of North Carolina Press, 1988); and Burton I. Kaufman, *Trade and Aid: Eisenhower's Foreign Economic Policy, 1953–1961* (Baltimore: Johns Hopkins University Press, 1982).

On colonialism, significant studies include William Roger Louis, *Imperialism at Bay: The United States and the Decolonization of the British Empire, 1945–1951* (New York: Oxford University Press, 1978); Anne Orde, *The Eclipse of Great Britain: The United States and British Imperial Decline, 1895–1956* (Basingstoke: Macmillan, 1996); and John T. McNay, *Acheson and Empire: The British Accent in American Foreign Policy* (Columbia: University of Missouri Press, 2001).

On the Far East, important works include Qiang Zhai, *The Dragon, the Lion, and the Eagle: Chinese-British-American Relations, 1949–1958* (Kent, Ohio: Kent State University Press, 1994); Warren I. Cohen and Akira Iriye, eds., *The Great Powers in East Asia, 1953–1960* (New York: Columbia University Press, 1990); Gordon H. Chang, *Friends and Enemies, 1948–1972* (Stanford, Cal.: Stanford University Press, 1990); Shu Guang Zhang, *Economic Cold War: America's Embargo against China and the Sino-Soviet Alliance, 1949–1963* (Washington, D.C.: Woodrow Wilson Center Press, 2001); Robert J. McMahon, *The Limits of Empire: The United States and South-East Asia since World War II* (New York: Columbia University Press, 1999); John P. Bourke and Fred I. Greenstein, *How Presidents Test Reality: Decisions on Vietnam, 1954 and 1965* (New York: Russell Sage Foundation, 1989); and David L. Anderson, *Trapped by Success: The Eisenhower Administration and Vietnam, 1953–1961* (New York: Columbia University Press, 1991).

There is an extensive historiography on both British and American relations with the Middle East. Of particular value are Ritchie Ovendale, *Britain, the United States and the Transfer of Power in the Middle East, 1945–1962* (Leicester: Leicester University Press, 1996); Peter L. Hahn, *The United States, Great Britain and Egypt, 1945–1956* (Chapel Hill: University of North Carolina Press, 1991); Magnus Persson, *Great Britain, the United States and the Security of the Middle East: The Formation of the Baghdad Pact* (Lund: Lund University Press, 1998); Nigel J. Ashton, *Eisenhower, Macmillan and the Problem of Nasser: Anglo-American Relations and Arab Nationalism, 1955–1959* (London: Macmillan, 1997); Ray Takeyh, *The Origins of the Eisenhower Doctrine: The United States, Britain and Nasser's Egypt, 1953–1957* (Basingstoke: Macmillan, 2000); Robert McNamara, *Britain, Nasser and the Balance of Power in the Middle East, 1952–1967* (London: Frank Cass, 2003); Matthew F. Holland, *America and Egypt: From Roosevelt to*

Eisenhower (Westport, Conn.: Praeger, 1996); Douglas Little, *American Orientalism: The United States and the Middle East since 1945* (Chapel Hill: University of North Carolina Press, 2003); H. W. Brands, *Into the Labyrinth: The United States and the Middle East, 1945–1993* (New York: McGraw-Hill, 1994); Steve Marsh, *Anglo-American Relations and Cold War Oil: Crisis in Iran* (London: Palgrave Macmillan, 2003); Stephen Kinzer, *All the Shah's Men: An American Coup and the Roots of Middle Eastern Terror* (New York: Wiley, 2003); Zach Levey, *Israel and the Western Powers, 1952–1960* (Chapel Hill: University of North Carolina Press, 1997); Orna Almorg, *Britain, Israel and the United States, 1955–1958* (London: Frank Cass, 2003); and Peter L. Hahn, *Caught in the Middle East: U.S. Policy Toward the Arab-Israeli Conflict, 1945–1961* (Chapel Hill: University of North Carolina Press, 2004).

The historical literature on the Suez Crisis is very extensive. Important memoirs include Anthony Nutting, *No End of a Lesson: The Story of Suez* (London: Constable, 1967); Selwyn Lloyd, *Suez, 1956: A Personal Account* (London: Jonathan Cope, 1978); and Evelyn Shuckburgh, *Descent to Suez: Diaries, 1951–1956* (London: Weidenfeld and Nicolson, 1986). The most useful secondary accounts include W. Scott Lucas, *Divided We Stand: Britain, the United States and the Suez Crisis* (London: Hodder and Stoughton, 1991); Keith Kyle, *Suez* (London: Weidenfeld and Nicolson, 1991); Jonathan Pierce, *Sir Anthony Eden and the Suez Crisis* (London: Palgrave, 2003); Cole C. Kingseed, *Eisenhower and the Crisis of 1956* (Baton Rouge: Louisiana State University Press, 1995); Derek Varble, *The Suez Crisis* (Oxford: Osprey, 2003); William Roger Louis and Roger Owen, eds., *Suez, 1956: The Crisis and Its Consequences* (Oxford: Clarendon Press, 1989); Louise Richardson, *When Allies Differ: Anglo-American Relations during the Suez and Falklands Conflicts* (Basingstoke: Macmillan, 1996); Chester L. Cooper, *The Lion's Last Roar: Suez, 1956* (New York: Harper and Row, 1978); Diane B. Kunz, *The Economic Diplomacy of the Suez Crisis* (Chapel Hill: University of North Carolina Press, 1991); David Carlton, *Britain and the Suez Crisis* (Oxford: Basil Blackwell, 1988); Saul Kelly and Tony Gorst, eds., *Whitehall and the Suez Crisis* (London: Frank Cass, 2000); Tony Shaw, *Eden, Suez and the Mass Media* (London: I. B. Tauris, 1996); Bertjan Verbelk, *Decision Making in Great Britain during the Suez Crisis: Small Groups and a Persistent Leader* (Aldershot: Ashgate, 2003).

INDEX

Abdullah, Crown Prince Amir, 166, 167n
Acheson, Dean, 16–17, 18, 43
Adenauer, Konrad, 141
Aerial reconnaissance: Eisenhower's open skies proposal, Geneva summit, 92, 96, 97n, 114; Genetrix (balloon operation), 63, 64, 94–97, 98, 108–9, 114, 192; U-2 spy planes, 63–64, 96, 114–18, 120–21, 131–33, 192–93; U.S.–Soviet U-2 spy plane incident, 92, 117, 192. *See also* Central Intelligence Agency (CIA); Intelligence, U.S./British sharing; Secret Intelligence Service (SIS) (British)
Aitken, Jonathan, 201
Aldrich, Winthrop, 100, 122, 127, 155n, 179, 180, 196
Allen, Harry, 75
Alpha Project (1955), 69
Ambrose, Stephen, 201
Amery, Julian, 201
Anglo-Iranian Oil Company (AIOC), 68, 161n
Anglo-Jordan Treaty (1948), 178
Anglo-Soviet Treaty (1942), 12
Aquatone. *See* U-2 spy planes
Arab Caliphs, 166, 167n
Arabian American Oil Company, 68
Aswan Dam, 103–7, 108; removal of historic sites destroyed by, 105–6
Atomic Energy Act (1954), 61, 173
Attlee, Clement, 11, 14, 59
Austrian State Treaty (1955), 57, 58, 83n, 195
Avon Papers, 4–5

B-29 planes, 59
B-47 planes, 59

Baghdad Pact (1955), 70, 124, 125, 129, 138; lack of U.S. involvement in, 71, 119, 120n, 123, 195
Baldwin, Stanley, 8, 9
Balfour, John, 68
Balfour Declaration (1917), 68
Barclay, Roderick, 18
Baruch Plan (1946), 60
Battle, Laurie C., 74
Battle Monuments Commission booklet, 25
Beatty, Countess (Dorothy Rita Furey), 14–15
Beatty, Earl (David Field Beatty, 2nd Earl), 15
Beckett, Beatrice. *See* Eden, Beatrice (first wife)
Ben-Gurion, David, 176, 178n
Beria, Lavrenti, 53
Berlin blockade, 165
Bermuda Conference (1953), 44, 172–73
Bevan, Aneurin, 195
Bevin, Ernest, 15
Bissell, Richard, 114–15
Black, Eugene, 104–5
Blunt, Anthony, 62
Bowie, Robert R., 201
Bradley, Omar, 60
British loan (1946), 73
Brooke, Alan, 28
Brownjohn, Nevil, 90
Bulganin, Nikolai, 53, 110, 111; Geneva summit (1955), 91, 92, 144; Suez crisis, 170–71, 172n, 174; visit to Britain, 101, 109, 115–16, 126, 128–30, 192, 195
Burgess, Guy, 62
Burnham, James, 56
Butler, R. A., 111, 112n
Byrnes, James, 40

C-119 recovery planes, 95
Caccia, Harold, 105, 178n
Cadogan, Alexander, 42
Campbell, Duncan, 58
Canberra bombers, 111, 112
Canton Island, 98–99
Carlton, David, 206
Central Intelligence Agency (CIA), 61–62, 70; U-2 spy planes and, 63–64, 114–18
Centurion tanks, 93, 113–14, 119, 121, 122–23, 169–70, 171
Challe, Maurice, 151
Chamberlain, Austen, 8
Chamberlain, Neville, 10–11, 12
Charmley, John, 198
China: and Fischer group of U.S. airmen, 84–85, 86; Nasser's recognition of Communist government of, 105; Quemoy and Matsu islands (Taiwan Straits crisis, 1954–55), 72, 193; Taiwan (Formosa) and, 72, 89; trade issues, 74, 127–28, 130; U.S.–British differences over, 71–72, 193
China Committee of the Paris Consultative Group of Nations (CHINCOM), 74, 127–28, 130
Churchill, Clarissa. *See* Eden, Clarissa (second wife)
Churchill, Jack, 16
Churchill, Randolph, 11
Churchill, Winston S.: British Empire, feelings about, 64, 66; colonialism and, 65–66, 70; Dulles, relationship with, 42, 44–45; Eden, relationship with, 10–12, 20, 21–22, 198; Eisenhower, relationship with, 1–3, 27, 30–31, 33, 37–38, 44–45, 55–57, 80, 194, 204–5; European unity and, 72; Far East issues and, 72; nuclear weapons and, 57, 59–60, 72; postwar activities of, 15; as postwar prime minister, 1, 16–22, 35, 56–59, 70; Soviet relations and, 17, 21, 56–59; and "special relationship" with U.S., 11–12, 37–38, 191, 204–5, 206; as wartime prime minister, 1, 11–14
Civilian Conservation Corps, 25
Clark, Mark, 27
Cline, Ray, 62
Cold War, 5, 15, 17, 35, 53–54, 56, 104, 194, 195
Colonialism, 64–66, 70, 194
Columbia University, 32–33, 34
Colville, John "Jock," 19, 22, 55
Commission on Foreign Economic Policy. *See* Randall Commission
Common Market, 193
Connor, Fox, 24–25
Conservative party (Great Britain), 58, 82n, 195; postwar elections and, 14, 16
Constantinople Convention (1888), 149, 156, 164, 168, 169
Cooper, Chester, 202
Coordinating Committee of the Paris Consultative Group of Nations (COCOM), 74, 127, 128n
Copper wire export ban to Eastern bloc, 127, 128n, 130n, 131
Coulson, John, 176, 178n
Crabb, Lionel "Buster," 116, 132n, 192
Cranborne, Viscount (Robert Arthur James Gascoyne-Cecil), 12
Crusade in Europe (Eisenhower), 32–33
Cunningham, Andrew, 28
Cyprus, 3, 133–35, 137–38, 149, 194

Darlan, Jean, 27
Dawes Plan (1924), 40
De Gaulle, Charles, 12, 27
Dewey, Thomas, 33–34, 40–41, 44
Disraeli, Benjamin, 67
Dixon, Pierson, 177, 188, 198
Donnelly, John, 55
Doud, Mary Geneva "Mamie." *See* Eisenhower, Mary Geneva "Mamie" (wife)
Dulles, Allen M., 39
Dulles, John Foster: anticommunism of, 43, 56; Aswan Dam and, 104–6; career assessment, 42–43; Churchill

and, 42, 44–45; Cyprus and, 137; diplomatic deficiencies, 41–43; early life, 39–41; Eden, relationship with, 5, 39, 42, 43–46, 103, 196, 202–3; Geneva summit (1955) and, 93n; hospitalization for cancer, 186n, 203, 206; India and, 89, 112; Indochina and, 71–72; Nasser, views on, 202–3; nuclear weapons and, 45–46; Secretary of State appointment, 41, 44; as Secretary of State opposite Lloyd, 119, 120n, 122, 123, 125, 127, 128n, 130–31, 135, 196; as Secretary of State opposite Macmillan, 80–85, 87–88, 100, 196; as Secretary of State to Eisenhower, 2–3, 42–43, 81, 83, 111, 126, 140, 145, 156n, 174, 201–3; Suez crisis and, 149–50, 155, 157, 158, 159–62, 164, 164n, 168, 183, 200, 202–3; Yugoslavia and, 101

Dulles, John W., 39

Dutton, David, 8, 10, 18, 19, 206

Dwight D. Eisenhower Library, 3, 4

Eastern Europe, 56, 87; copper wire export ban to Eastern bloc, 127, 128n, 130n, 131; trade with, U.S.–British differences, 73–74, 127–31, 193

Eden, Anthony: Acheson, relationship with, 16–17, 18; Avon Papers and, 4–5; Baghdad Pact and, 119, 120n, 123, 124, 125, 129, 138, 195; British Empire, feelings about, 12, 64, 149, 198; Chamberlain, relationship with, 10–11; Churchill, relationship with, 10–12, 20, 21–22, 198; Cyprus and, 133–35, 137–38; Dulles, relationship with, 5, 39, 42, 43–46, 103, 196, 202–3; early life, 7–10; Eisenhower, meeting with (Jan.-Feb. 1956), 102–3, 110, 112–13, 145; Eisenhower, relationship with, 38–39, 79–81, 112–13, 144–45, 196, 207; Eisenhower, wartime relationship with, 13, 143; Eisenhower correspondence, summary, 1–5, 191–97, 205, 206–7; European unity and, 13, 17–18, 45, 72, 193–94; Far East issues and, 71; foreign policy issues of prime ministership, 46–47, 53; foreign policy successes, 17–18, 45; Genetrix (aerial reconnaissance balloon operation), 94, 96–97, 108–9, 192; Geneva summit preparations (1955), 81–82, 85–86, 88, 90, 195; Geneva summit (1955) and, 91–92, 93n, 94, 96–97, 100–101, 144; Germany, Centurion tank trade to, 113–14, 122–23, 169–70, 171; health problems, after Suez crisis, 189–90, 206; health problems, postwar, 14, 20–21; and intelligence incident, frogman spying on Soviet cruiser, 115–16, 131, 132n, 192; Iraq, Centurion tank trade to, 93, 113, 119, 121, 122–23; Khrushchev, meeting in Britain, 101, 109, 115–16, 126, 128–30, 192, 195; Macmillan's views on, 18–19, 21; Middle East concerns, 109–10, 119, 123–25, 126–27, 194–95; military, lack of sympathy with, 13; NATO, interest in, 14, 15, 17–18; NATO, views on future of, 138–41, 195; nuclear weapons and, 98–99, 138–40, 172–73, 176; personal life difficulties, 9–10, 13, 14–15; as postwar foreign minister, 16–22; postwar political life, 15; as prewar foreign minister, 10; as prewar secretary of state for Dominions, 11; as prime minister, 145; as prime minister, competence, 197–98, 205–6; as prime minister, expecting to become, 1, 22, 35, 45, 79; as prime minister, reelection, 82n, 84, 195; as prime minister, resignation (1957), 1, 45, 148, 153, 207; Roosevelt, feelings about, 12–13; Soviet relations, general attitudes toward, 12, 17, 46–47, 58, 195–96; and "special relationship" with U.S., 11–13, 15, 16–17, 18, 38–39, 45–46, 184, 191; temperament, 18–20; trade issues and, 90–91, 129, 130,

131, 193; United Nations, interest in, 13–14, 44; U-2 spy planes and, 115, 116–18, 120, 121, 131–32, 133, 192–93; wartime political service, 11–14
—and Suez crisis: canal nationalization, 149, 153–55, 158–59; ceasefire, 182, 185–86; correspondence with Eisenhower about, overall picture, 3–4, 191, 205, 207; correspondence with Soviet Union, 170–72, 174; deception over Israeli attack, 151–52, 176–81, 199, 201; economic measures, hoping for against Egypt, 154, 160–61; Eisenhower, proposed meeting with, 186, 187, 188–89, 204; inability to deal with, 191, 198, 205–6; military force, justifying, 154, 164–67, 172n, 180–81, 182–84; military force, use of British/French troops, 150–53, 159, 170–71n, 183–84, 201, 203; Nasser, views on, 101, 119, 158–59, 160–61, 165–66, 171–72, 178, 183, 187, 198, 206; Suez Canal Conferences, 159, 160–61, 164

Eden, Beatrice (first wife), 8, 9, 13, 14
Eden, Clarissa (second wife), 16, 21, 81
Eden, John (brother), 8
Eden, Marjorie (sister), 7
Eden, Nicholas (son), 9, 14
Eden, Robert (father), 7
Eden, Simon (son), 9, 14
Eden, Timothy (brother), 7, 8
Eden, William (brother), 8
Egypt: Aswan Dam, 103–7; British influence on, pre–Suez crisis, 67–68, 70, 103–7, 109–10, 119, 120n; military trade with, 70, 104, 106, 107n, 178, 179n; Suez Canal history, 66–68; Treaty of 1936, 70; United Arab States plan, 123–24, 125; U.S.–British disagreements, pre–Suez crisis, 18, 70–71; U.S. influence on, 103–7; Young Officers Movement, 70, 107n. *See also* Suez crisis of 1956
Egyptology, 67
Eisenhower, Arthur (brother), 22

Eisenhower, David (father), 22–23
Eisenhower, David (grandson), 32
Eisenhower, Doud Dwight "Icky" (son), 24
Eisenhower, Dwight D.: Aswan Dam and, 105; Churchill, relationship with, 1–3, 27, 30–31, 33, 37–38, 44–45, 55–57, 80, 194, 204–5; colonialism and, 65–66, 194; Cyprus and, 137, 194; Dulles, as Secretary of State advising, 2–3, 42–43, 81, 83, 111, 126, 140, 145, 156n, 174, 201–3; Dwight D. Eisenhower Library, 3, 4; early life, 22–25; early military career, 24–25; Eden, meeting with (Jan.-Feb. 1956), 110, 112–13, 145; Eden, relationship with, 38–39, 79–81, 112–13, 133, 144–45, 196, 207; Eden, wartime relationship with, 13, 143; Eden correspondence, summary, 1–5, 191–97, 205, 206–7; European unity and, 72, 193–94; family home at Gettysburg, Pa., 24, 33, 100n; Far East issues and, 72; foreign policy issues of presidency, 53; foreign policy stance, 35, 36–37, 38, 39, 42, 47; Genetrix (aerial reconnaissance balloon operation) and, 94–97, 114, 192; Geneva summit open skies proposal and, 92, 96, 97n, 114; Geneva summit preparations (1955), 82–83, 86–87, 88, 90, 195; Geneva summit (1955) and, 91–92, 93n, 94, 96–97, 114, 144; health problems, 135–36, 138, 206; heart attack (1955), 99, 100, 118, 206; Israel and, 102, 122–23; letter-writing ability, 2, 23; Macmillan, meetings with, 90, 117; Macmillan, relationship with, 28, 207; Middle East concerns, 122–23, 125–26, 194–95; military trade to Germany and, 121–22, 169–70; NATO, views on future of, 141; nickname "Ike," origins of, 23; nuclear weapons and, 47, 59, 60, 61, 83, 174–75; Panama, meeting of Presidents of the Americas and, 140, 141;

222 : INDEX

postwar activities, 32–34; as president, goals and issues, 35–36; as president, revised assessment, 35–36, 42, 76, 191, 196, 197–98, 202, 205, 206–7; as president, travel restrictions, 86, 87n, 88; as president, view of as incompetent, 35, 42, 196, 198, 202; presidential aspirations, 33–34; presidential win, 34, 38, 41, 44, 55–56, 69; reelection, 147, 186; reelection bid, 58, 118–19, 152, 162, 164n, 173, 175n, 184; Soviet relations, general attitudes toward, 35–37, 46–47, 57–59, 110, 195–96; "special relationship" with Britain and, 26–28, 30–31, 37–39, 47, 174–75, 196–97, 204–5, 206–7; Summersby, Kay, relationship with, 28–29, 31–32; as supreme Allied commander (1951), 34, 37, 44, 47, 80, 81n, 90n; trade issues and, 74, 127–28, 131, 193; U-2 spy planes and, 114–18, 120, 131–33, 192–93; West Point, time at, 23–24; as World War II American forces commander, 25–30; as World War II supreme Allied commander, 30–31, 47, 90n
—and Suez crisis, 146; ceasefire, 184–85, 186, 204; correspondence with Eden about, overall picture, 3–4, 191, 205, 207; Eden's proposed meeting with, 186, 204; Macmillan, meeting with, 171, 172n; military force, against use of, 149, 152, 155–57, 157–58n, 162–64, 168–69, 172n, 176–78, 181, 199–201, 203, 205; Nasser, views on, 122, 162, 163–64, 167–69, 198, 201, 205; Suez Canal Conferences, 161–62, 164n; United Nations involvement and, 151, 162, 177

Eisenhower, Earl (brother), 22
Eisenhower, Edgar (brother), 22, 23
Eisenhower, Ida (mother), 22–23
Eisenhower, Jacob (grandfather), 22
Eisenhower, John S. D. (son), 2, 24, 26, 27, 30, 32

Eisenhower, Mary Geneva "Mamie" (wife), 24, 29, 32
Eisenhower, Milton (brother), 22, 196
Eisenhower, Roy (brother), 22
Elizabeth II, Queen, 21
European Advisory Commission, 13
European Defense Community (EDC), 17–18, 45
European unity, 13, 17–18, 45, 72, 193–94

Farouk, King (Egypt), 70
Faure, Edgar, 85, 86n, 88, 91, 144
Fischer, Harold, 84, 85n
Flooding, in Northeast U.S. (1955), 97–98
Flooding, in Western U.S. (1955), 109
Foreign Relations of the United States (U.S. Government Printing Office), 4, 5
Formosa. *See* Taiwan
Foster, John W., 39
Four Power Declaration (1943), 13
Four-Power talks. *See* Geneva summit (1955)
France: and arms to Israel, 176–78; Suez Canal construction/ownership, 66–67; Suez crisis, and military force, 150–53, 159, 170–71n, 183–84, 201, 203; U.S.–British postwar ideas for, 11–13
Franks, Oliver, 16, 54–55, 60

Gage, Bernard, 55
Gathering Storm, The (Churchill), 10
Gault, James, 28, 90, 91
Gazier, Albert, 151
Genetrix (aerial reconnaissance balloon operation), 95, 97n, 98, 108–9, 114, 192
Geneva Conference (1954), 18, 41–42, 44, 45, 71, 110–11
Geneva summit (1955), 91–92, 93n, 94, 97n, 102, 114, 144; Eisenhower's open skies proposal, 92, 96, 97n, 114; for-

INDEX : 223

eign ministers' follow up (Oct.-Nov. 1955), 96–97, 100–101; preparations, 81–83, 85–88, 90, 195
George VI, King, 11, 21
Germany, 141; and intelligence on Soviet Union, 62; military trade to, 113–14, 121–22, 169–70, 171; NATO admission of, 17–18, 45; rearmament, 17–18; reunification, 83, 91, 101, 102
Gibb, Alexander, 106
Giraud, Henri, 27
Goodpaster, Andrew, 2–3
Grayback. *See* Genetrix
Greece, 134–35, 137–38, 149. *See also* Cyprus
Greenstein, Fred, 36, 42, 202
Groves, Leslie, 60
Gruenther, Albert M., 140, 141n, 186, 188
Guatemala, 38

Hahn, Peter, 194
Halifax, 1st Earl of (Edward Frederick Lindley Wood), 11
Hammarskjöld, Dag, 185
Hanes, John W., Jr., 4
Harding, John, 133–35, 137
Harriman, Averell, 54
Harrison, Benjamin, 39
Hathaway, Robert, 75
Hazlett, Everett "Swede," 2, 23, 197, 203
Henderson, Nicholas, 20
al-Hilmi, Salmir, 106, 107n, 108
Hitler, Adolf, 9, 10, 27, 54, 165
Hoare, Samuel, 9
Hoare-Laval Plan, 9
Hodgson, P. A., 23
Hoffman, Paul, 33
Holland, Matthew F., 25
Holland, Robert, 13
Hoopes, Townsend, 42
Hoover, Herbert, 35
Hoover, Herbert, Jr., 186n, 204

Hopkins, Harry, 13
House Appropriations Subcommittee on Foreign Aid, 104
Hughes, Emmet John, 201, 204
Hull, Cordell, 13, 93
Humphrey, Hubert, 33, 104
Hungary, 151–52, 153, 184

IL G bombers (Russian), 111, 112n
Immerman, Richard, 41, 42, 43
India, 171; China, negotiations with, 84, 89; military trade with, Britain vs. Soviet Union, 107, 111, 112
Indochina, 18, 41, 44, 71–72, 111n
Intelligence, U.S./British sharing: Genetrix (aerial reconnaissance balloon operation), 63, 64, 94–97, 108–9; nuclear technology, 59, 60–62, 172–73, 174–75, 176; U-2 spy planes, 63–64, 114–18, 120–21, 131–33, 192–93. *See also* Central Intelligence Agency (CIA); Secret Intelligence Service (SIS) (British)
International Monetary Fund (IMF), 153
Iran, 68, 123, 161n, 166, 167n
Iraq, 167n; Baghdad Pact (1955), 70, 71, 119, 120n, 123, 124; British influence, fears of erosion in, 101, 124, 165–66; British influence in, 68, 70, 71; Centurion tanks from Britain for, 93, 113, 119, 121, 122–23
Ismail Pasha, 67
Ismay, Hastings, 20, 28, 200
Isolationism, 35, 41, 46, 54–55
Israel: attack on Egypt, 151–52, 176–81, 199, 201; creation of, 68–69; military arms trade to, 127, 176–78; Tripartite Declaration (1950), 69, 124–25, 176, 177, 178, 179, 180–81; United Nations involvement with, 69, 126–27, 177, 178–79, 180; U.S. involvement with, 69, 71, 101, 102, 104, 120n, 122–23, 195
Italy, 9, 29–30; Trieste dispute and, 17, 101, 101–2n

224 : INDEX

Jackson, C. D., 13, 14
Jackson, Ian, 193
James, Robert Rhodes, 7, 200, 202, 206
Japan, 41, 43–44
Jebb, Gladwyn, 18
Johnson, Lyndon B., 104
Jordan, 109–10, 119, 120n, 123, 165, 178

Kardelj, Eduard, 101
Kassouni, Adb al-Moneim, 106, 107n
Kefauver, Estes, 104
Kennan, George, 56
Khrushchev, Nikita: Dulles, views on, 42; Geneva summit (1955) and, 91–92, 114; Soviet internal power struggles and, 53, 170–71n; U-2 spy plane incident (1960) and, 92, 117; visit to Britain, 101, 109, 115–16, 126, 128–30, 192, 195; Yugoslavia, 130
Kingseed, Cole, 200, 205
Kipling, Rudyard, 64
Kirkpatrick, Ivone, 3
Knowland, William F., 104
Korean War, 35, 57, 58, 113, 157–58n; British involvement in, 15, 54–55, 59, 71; Fischer group of U.S. airmen and, 84–85, 86
Kunz, Diane, 198
Kuwait, 68, 134, 165

Labour party (Great Britain), 128, 129n, 195; postwar government, 14–16
Lansing, Robert, 39
Laval, Pierre, 9
Lawrence of Arabia, 67
League of Nations, 9, 28, 165
Lesseps, Ferdinand de, 66
Life magazine, 94
Lloyd, Selwyn, 145; Aswan Dam, 105; foreign secretary appointment, 110–11; as foreign secretary to Eden, 120n, 128n, 130–31, 135, 196; Middle East concerns, 119, 122, 123, 125, 127; Suez crisis and, 155, 161, 162, 174, 179, 180, 200, 203

Lockhart, Robert Bruce, 21
Lodge, Henry Cabot, 34
Lothian, Lord (Philip Henry Kerr, 11th Marquess of Lothian), 11
Louis, William Roger, 75

M-47 tanks, 113–14, 170
MacArthur, Douglas, 25, 26
MacDonald, Ramsay, 8–9
MacLean, Donald, 62
Macmillan, Harold: as chancellor of exchequer to Eden, 111n, 183, 184n; Dulles, views on, 42; Eden, views on, 18–19, 21; Eisenhower, meetings with, 90, 117, 171, 172n; Eisenhower, relationship with, 28, 207; as foreign secretary to Eden, 80–85, 87–88, 100, 103, 106, 196; Geneva summit (1955) and, 93n; as prime minister, 117, 197, 207; "special relationship" with U.S. and, 12; Suez crisis and, 156, 157, 183, 199
Mahan, Alfred T., 64
Makarios III, Archbishop, 134, 135n
Makins, Roger: as British Ambassador to U.S., 3, 28, 105, 108, 111, 178n; Dulles, relationship with, 42, 43, 137, 140; Eisenhower, views on, 42, 196, 200, 202
Malenkov, Georgi, 53, 57
Manhattan Project, 60
Marks, Frederick, 43, 45
Marshall, George, 25, 30, 31–32
Marshall Plan, 15, 54, 55, 73
McCarthy, Joseph, 36, 58
McCarthyism, 36, 43, 57, 58
McCormack, John, 104
McMahon Act (1946), 60–61
Menon, Krishna, 84, 85n, 89
Menzies, Robert: Nasser mission, 150, 161, 165, 178
Middle East: Cyprus situation, impact on, 134, 138; Eden/Eisenhower differences on, 194–95; Eden to Eisenhower, concern over, 109–10, 119,

123–25, 126–27; Eisenhower to Eden, views on, 122–23, 125–26; Jordan, 109–10, 119, 120n, 123, 165, 178; Kuwait, 68, 134, 165; Palestine, 68–69, 126–27; Saudi Arabia, 68, 109–10, 124, 152, 165–66; Soviet influence on, 69–70, 109–10, 119, 120n, 122, 124, 125–27, 129, 149, 194; and "special relationship" between U.S. and Britain, 68–71; Suez Canal, history of, 66–68; Syria, 109–10, 152, 165; Tripartite Declaration (1950) and, 69, 124–25, 176, 177, 178, 179, 180–81. *See also* Egypt; Israel; Oil; Suez crisis of 1956

MIG-15 fighter planes, 95–96

Military arms trade: of Canberra bombers, 111, 112; of Centurion tanks, 93, 113–14, 119, 121, 122–23, 169–70, 171; to Egypt, from Soviet Union, 104, 106, 107n, 178, 179n; to Egypt, from U.S., 70; to Germany, of Centurion tanks, 113–14, 121–22, 169–70, 171; to Holland, 113, 121; to India, Britain vs. Soviet Union, 107, 111, 112; to Iraq, of Centurion tanks, 93, 113, 119, 121, 122–23; to Israel, 127, 176–78; Tripartite Declaration (1950) and, 176, 177, 178. *See also* Trade issues

Mohammed Ali Pasha, 66
Mohammed Said Pasha, 66–67
Mollet, Guy, 180, 181n, 187, 188
Molotov, Viacheslav I., 13, 53
Monnet, Jean, 72
Montague-Browne, Anthony, 19, 21, 42
Montgomery, Bernard, 30, 67–68
Morrison, Herbert, 44
Morse, Wayne, 104
Mossadeq, Mohammed, 68, 160, 161n
Murphy, Robert, 28, 45, 155, 156, 157n, 202
Mussolini, Benito, 9
Mutual Defense Control Act (Battle Act) (1951), 74
Mutual Security Program, 37, 121

Nagy, Imre, 152
Nasser, Gamal Abdel, 194; Aswan Dam and, 103–7, 108; Baghdad Pact, dislike of, 71, 119, 120n, 195; China, recognition of Communist government by, 105; Dulles, views on, 202–3; Eden, views on, 101, 119, 158–59, 160–61, 165–66, 171–72, 178, 183, 187, 198, 206; Eisenhower, views on, 122, 162, 163–64, 167–69, 198, 201, 205; Menzies, mission to, 150, 161, 165, 178; rise to power, 70; Suez Canal nationalization and, 105, 149, 153–54, 155n, 156, 158, 165–66, 170–71n, 172; Suez crisis, military force threat/consequences, 158–59, 160–61, 162, 172n, 201; United Arab States plan, 123–24

National Archives, Prime Minister's Papers, Public Record Office, 3, 4

National Security Council, 35, 36, 37, 99n

Neguib, Mohammed, 70
Nehru, Jawaharlal, 84–85
Neustadt, Richard, 199
Nicholas, Herbert, 75
Nixon, Richard M., 36, 43, 99n, 201
North Atlantic Treaty Organization (NATO), 57, 105, 113, 130n; British/American roles within, 47, 55; Cyprus and, 134, 137–38; Eden's interest in, 14, 15, 17–18; Eden's views on future of, 138–41, 195; Eisenhower's views on future of, 141; formation of, 34, 37, 54; Germany, admission of to, 17–18, 45; nuclear weapons and, 138–40

Nuclear weapons: aircraft carrying, 59, 172–73, 176; Britain's Suez base and, 70; British nuclear tests, 61, 98–99; British/U.S. cooperation over, 58–61, 174–75; British/U.S. intelligence sharing and, 59, 60–62; Churchill and, 57, 59–60, 72; Dulles and, 45–46; Eden and, 98–99, 138–40, 172–73, 176; Eisenhower and, 47, 59, 60, 61, 83, 174–75; Far East and, 72; Gen-

etrix (aerial reconnaissance balloon operation) and, 96; NATO, role of with, 138–40; Roosevelt and, 59–60; Soviet development of, 35, 53, 70, 138–40, 196; United Nations involvement with, 60
Nuri al-Said, 101, 119, 120n, 124, 166, 167n
Nutting, Anthony, 18, 203–4, 205

Oil, 66, 68, 126–27, 129, 134–35, 161n; Suez crisis and, 152–53, 154, 160, 165–66, 169, 198
Operation Overlord, 30
Ordzhonikidze cruiser spying incident, 115–16, 131, 132n, 192

Pakistan, 70, 120n, 123
Palestine, 68–69, 126–27. See also Israel
Pan American Airways, 98, 98–99n
Paris summit (1960), 92, 117
Parmet, Herbert, 41
Passman, Otto, 104
Patton, George, 24, 30
Peace Conference, First (1899), 39
Peace Conference, Second (1907), 39
Pearson, Lester, 16
Pétain, Henri, 27
Philby, Kim, 62
Philippines, Republic of the, 25, 64–65
Pierce, Jonathan, 198, 206
Pineau, Christian, 155, 180, 181n
Places in the Sun (Eden), 8
Powers, Francis Gary, 117, 192
Protocol of Sèvres (1956), 151. See also Suez crisis of 1956

Quebec Agreement (1948), 59
Quemoy and Matsu islands, 72, 193. See also China; Taiwan

Radford, Arthur W., 98, 99
Randall, Clarence, 91n
Randall Commission, 90, 91n

Ranelagh, John, 62
Reciprocal Trades Agreement Act (1955), 90, 91n
Renwick, Robin, 37, 42, 75, 201–2, 203
Reynolds, David, 75
Reza Shah Pahlavi, 68, 166, 167n
Richardson, Louise, 200
Risse-Kappen, Thomas, 203
Roberts, Frank, 19
Rommel, Erwin, 67–68
Roosevelt, Franklin D., 31, 35, 40; Canton Island and, 98–99n; colonialism and, 65; correspondence with Churchill, 1; Eden, relationship with, 12–13; nuclear weapons and, 59–60; World War II and, 10, 28, 30
Roosevelt, Theodore, 64, 65

Sadat, Anwar, 106
Saud, King (Saudi Arabia), 166
Saudi Arabia, 109–10, 124; Suez crisis and, 152, 165–66; U.S. influence in, 68
Schlesinger, Arthur, Jr., 33
Secret Intelligence Service (SIS) (British), 62; attempt to spy on Soviet cruiser, 115–16, 131, 132n, 192. See also Intelligence, U.S./British sharing
Shah of Iran. See Reza Shah Pahlavi
Shepilov, Dimitri T., 160, 161n, 174
Shuckburgh, Evelyn, 13, 16, 20, 44, 199
Signal Intelligence, 62
Smith, Bradley, 61
Soviet Union: Aswan Dam, 104, 105–7; Austrian State Treaty (1955), 57, 58, 83n, 195; Churchill and, 17, 21, 56–59; Eden, correspondence with during Suez crisis, 170–72; Eden, general attitudes toward, 12, 17, 46–47, 58, 195–96; Eisenhower, general attitudes toward, 35–37, 46–47, 57–59, 110, 195–96; Genetrix (U.S. aerial reconnaissance balloon operation) and, 63, 64, 94–97, 108–9, 114, 192; Geneva summit (1955) and, 83, 85–86, 88,

INDEX : 227

91–92, 97, 100–101, 195; Hungary and, 151–52, 153, 184; frogman spying on Soviet cruiser and, 115–16, 131, 132n, 192; intelligence strategy against, 62–63; Khrushchev, power struggles, 53, 170–71n; Khrushchev/Bulganin visit to Britain, 101, 109, 115–16, 126, 128–30, 192, 195; Middle East influence of, 69–70, 109–10, 119, 120n, 122, 124, 125–27, 129, 149, 194; military trade with Egypt, 104, 106, 107n, 178, 179n; military trade with India, 107, 111, 112; nuclear weapons and, 35, 46–47, 53, 70, 138–40, 196; Paris summit (1960) and, 92, 117; relations with in mid-1950s, 36–37, 46–47, 53–54, 56–59, 81–82, 85–86, 101, 102, 107, 110; Suez crisis and, 151, 153, 159, 160, 162, 163, 170–72, 174, 187

Spaatz, Carl, 58–59

Spaatz-Tedder agreement, 59

"Special relationship" between U.S. and Britain: Churchill and, 11–12, 37–38, 191, 204–5, 206; colonialism and, 64–66, 70; economic issues and, 73–75; Eden and, 11–13, 15, 16–17, 18, 38–39, 45–46, 184, 191; Eisenhower and, 26–28, 30–31, 37–39, 47, 174–75, 196–97, 204–5, 206–7; European unity and, 72; Far East and, 65, 71–72; Middle East and, 68–71; NATO and, 47, 55; nuclear weapons, cooperation over, 58–61, 174–75; nuclear weapons, sharing information, 59, 60–62, 172–73, 174–75, 176; qualities of, 54–55, 74–76; World War II, forged during, 11–13, 26–28, 30–31, 54, 196–97; World War II, weakening of Britain after, 15, 16–17, 18, 37–38, 45–46, 54, 73, 191

Stalin, Joseph, 9, 17, 21, 53, 56, 129

Standard Oil of California, 68

Stevenson, Adlai, 34

Stoler, Mark, 26

Storer, Ida. *See* Eisenhower, Ida (mother)

Strategic Air Command (SAC), 58–59

Strauss, Lewis L., 98, 99

Suez Canal: construction of, 66–67; during World War II, 67–68

Suez Canal Company, 66–67, 151; expiration of 99-year lease, 149

Suez Canal Conferences, 149–50, 159–62, 164

Suez Canal Users Association (SCUA), 150, 164, 172n, 178, 179n, 206

Suez crisis of 1956, 1, 146, 149–53; background, 66–70; ceasefire, 182, 184–86, 204; economic measures against Egypt over, 154, 160–61; Eden, correspondence with Soviet Union, 170–72, 174; Eden, justifying military force, 154, 164–67, 172n, 180–81, 182–84; Eden, use of British/French troops, 150–53, 159, 170–71n, 183–84, 201, 203; Eden/Eisenhower correspondence, overall picture, 3–4, 191, 205, 207; Eden's inability to deal with, 191, 198, 205–6; Eden's proposed meeting with Eisenhower after, 186, 187, 188–89, 204; Eisenhower, against military force, 149, 152, 155–57, 157–58n, 162–64, 168–69, 172n, 176–78, 181, 199–201, 203, 205; Israeli attack on Egypt, 151–52, 176–81, 199, 201; Nasser, military force threat and consequences, 158–59, 160–61, 162, 172n, 201; Nasser's nationalization of Suez Canal, 105, 149, 153–54, 155n, 156, 158, 165–66, 170–71n, 172; oil and, 152–53, 154, 160, 165–66, 169, 198; Soviet Union and, 151, 153, 159, 160, 162, 163, 170–72, 174, 187; Suez Canal Conferences, 149–50, 159–62, 164; UN involvement, Canadian resolution for, 152–53, 182, 183, 185–86, 188; UN involvement, initial negotiations, 150–51, 161, 162, 170–71n, 178; UN involvement,

response to military force used in, 177, 179, 180, 181
Summersby, Gordon, 28
Summersby, Kay, 28–29, 31–32
Syria, 109–10, 152, 165

Taft, Robert, 34, 35, 41, 54
Taiwan, 72, 89
Taiwan Straits crisis (1954–55), 72, 193
Taylor, A. J. P., 205
Tedder, Arthur William (Lord), 59
Thorpe, D. R., 17, 20, 206
Thurmond, Strom, 33
Trade issues, 3, 73–74, 90–91, 127–31, 193. *See also* Military arms trade
Treaty of Rome (1957), 193
Treaty of Versailles (1919), 40, 68, 75, 87n
Trieste dispute, 17, 101, 101–2n
Tripartite Declaration (1950), 69, 124–25, 176, 177, 178, 179, 180–81
Truman, Harry S., 16, 31–32, 35, 41, 59, 74; Israel and, 69; Korean War and, 157–58n; reelection, 33–34, 69
Truman Doctrine, 54
Turkey, 70, 120n, 134–35, 137–38. *See also* Cyprus

U-2 spy planes: development of, 63–64, 96, 120–21; Eden and, 115, 116–18, 120, 121, 131–32, 133, 192–93; Eisenhower and, 114–18, 120, 131–33, 192–93; U.S.–Soviet incident (1960), 92, 117, 192
United Nations, 90n, 174; Eden's interest in, 13–14, 44; Fischer group of U.S. airmen and, 85n; formation of, 13, 40, 65; Israel and, 69, 126–27, 177, 178–79, 180; Khrushchev visit (1960), 117; nuclear weapons and, 60; Suez crisis, Canadian resolution for UN force, 152–53, 182, 183, 185–86, 188; Suez crisis, initial negotiations, 150–51, 161, 162, 170–71n, 178; Suez crisis,

response to military force used, 177, 179, 180, 181
U.S. Air Force: Genetrix (aerial reconnaissance balloon operation), 63, 64, 94–97, 108–9, 114, 192; postwar return to British bases, 58–59; U-2 spy planes, 63–64, 96, 114–18, 120–21, 131–33, 192–93; U.S.–Soviet U-2 spy plane incident (1960), 92, 117, 192

V bomber, 61
Versailles Peace Conference (1919). *See* Treaty of Versailles (1919)
Vietnam. *See* Indochina
VT (variable time) fuze, 107, 108n

Wagner, Robert, 41
Waldegrave, William, 4
Waldegrave initiative, 4
Wallace, Henry, 33
War, Peace and Change (Dulles), 40
War Plans Division, U.S. Army, 25
Watson, Thomas, 33
West Point Military Academy, 23–24
Wheeler-Bennett, John, 44
Whiteley, John, 111, 112n
Whitman, Ann, 2, 3–4
Wilson, Charles, 73
Wilson, Woodrow, 39, 87n
World Bank, 104–5, 200
World War I, 8, 24, 25
World War II, 1, 165; Churchill and Eden during, 11–14; Eisenhower as American forces commander in, 25–30; Eisenhower as supreme Allied commander in, 30–31, 47, 90n; in Far East, 65, 71; Holocaust and, 69; North African campaign, 28–29, 67–68; Roosevelt and, 1, 10, 28, 30; "special relationship" between U.S. and Britain during, 11–13, 26–28, 30–31, 54, 196–97; "special relationship," weakening of Britain after, 15, 16–17, 18, 37–38, 45–46, 54, 73, 191

Yorkshire Post, 8
Young, John, 17, 19, 43
Young Officers Movement (Egypt), 70, 107n
Young Plan (1929), 40

Yugoslavia, 58, 101, 130; Trieste dispute and, 17, 101, 101–2n

Zhou En-lai, 41–42, 84, 85n, 89, 110, 111n